FINANCIAL REPORT FOUND ON	CATEGORY	PERMANENT OR TEMPORARY
Balance Sheet	Current Liability	Permanent
Balance Sheet	Current Asset	Permanent
Balance Sheet	Contra Plant & Equipment	Permanent
Income Statement	Operating Expense	Temporary
Balance Sheet	Contra Current Asset	Permanent
Income Statement	Other Income	Temporary
Income Statement	Operating Expense	Temporary
Statement of Owner's Equity; Balance Sheet	Owner's Equity	Permanent
Balance Sheet	Current Asset	Permanent
Income Statement	Miscellaneous Expense	Temporary
Income Statement	Other Income	Temporary
Balance Sheet	Current Asset	Permanent
Income Statement	Revenue	Temporary
Balance Sheet	Current Liability	Permanent
Income Statement	Other Expense	Temporary
Income Statement	Operating Expense	Temporary
Balance Sheet	Contra Current Liability	Permanent
Balance Sheet	Plant & Equipment	Permanent
Income Statement	Cost of Goods Sold	Temporary
—	Owner's Equity	Temporary
Balance Sheet	Current Liability	Permanent
Income Statement	Operating Expense	Temporary
Income Statement	Other Income	Temporary
Income Statement	Other Expense	Temporary
Balance Sheet	Current Liability	Permanent
Balance Sheet; Income Statement	Current Asset: Cost of Goods Sold	Permanent
Balance Sheet	Long-Term Liability	Permanent
Balance Sheet	Current Liability	Permanent
Balance Sheet	Current Asset	Permanent
Income Statement	Operating Expense	Temporary
Balance Sheet	Current Asset	Permanent
Balance Sheet	Current Asset	Permanent
Balance Sheet	Current Asset	Permanent
Income Statement	Cost of Goods Sold	Temporary
Income Statement	Contra Cost of Goods Sold	Temporary
Income Statement	Contra Cost of Goods Sold	Temporary
Income Statement	Operating Expense	Temporary
Balance Sheet	Current Liability	Permanent
Income Statement	Revenue	Temporary
Income Statement	Contra Revenue	Temporary
Income Statement	Contra Revenue	Temporary
Balance Sheet	Current Liability	Permanent
Balance Sheet	Current Asset	Permanent
Balance Sheet	Current Liability	Permanent
Balance Sheet	Current Liability	Permanent
Statement of Owner's Equity; Balance Sheet	Owner's Equity	Temporary

COLLEGE

ACCOUNTING
A PRACTICAL APPROACH

CANADIAN
FOURTH
EDITION

COLLEGE ACCOUNTING

A PRACTICAL APPROACH

CANADIAN FOURTH EDITION

JEFFREY SLATER
North Shore Community College
Beverly, Massachusetts

BRIAN ZWICKER
Grant MacEwan Community College
Edmonton, Alberta

PRENTICE HALL CANADA CAREER AND TECHNOLOGY
Scarborough, Ontario

Canadian Cataloguing in Publication Data

Slater, Jeffrey, 1947-
    College accounting

Canadian 4th ed.
ISBN 0-13-120817-9

1. Accounting.   I. Zwicker, Brian, 1944-   .
II. Title.

HF5635.S53 1994   657'.044   C93-094700-2

Prentice-Hall, Inc., Englewood Cliffs, New Jersey
Prentice-Hall International (UK) Limited, London
Prentice-Hall of Australia, Pty. Limited, Sydney
Prentice-Hall Hispanoamericana, S.A., Mexico City
Prentice-Hall of India Private Limited, New Delhi
Prentice-Hall of Japan, Inc., Tokyo
Simon and Schuster Asia Private Ltd., Singapore
Editora Prentice-Hall do Brasil, Ltda., Rio de Janeiro

ISBN: 0-13-120817-9

Acquisitions Editor: Clifford J. Newman
Developmental Editor: Lisa Penttilä
Production Editor: Dawn du Quesnay
Production Coordinator: Deborah Starks
Design: Carole Giguère
Cover Image: Ed Honowitz/Tony Stone Images
Page Layout: Heather Brunton/ArtPlus Limited

2 3 4 5   98 97 96 95

Printed and bound in the U.S.A.

To Shelley, my best friend. Love, Jeff.

To the Memory of Alma Loraine Zwicker.

TABLE OF CONTENTS

9   PAYROLL CONCEPTS AND PROCEDURES: EMPLOYEE TAXES / 308

PREFACE

TO THE STUDENT

College Accounting, Canadian Fourth Edition, was written to introduce you to accounting, a dynamic tool of business. What is accounting, and why will you find it useful? Accounting is a planned and orderly way of keeping records for the purpose of seeing how a business is performing. It answers such questions as: Is the business profitable, or is it losing money? Which business activities are contributing most to profits, and which to losses? Which resources are well employed, and which are being wasted? Who owes the business money, and how much? What does the business owe? Accounting is also important for regulatory and tax purposes. You will be surprised at how often your understanding of accounting will work for you on the job.

Learning accounting means familiarizing yourself with many new terms and concepts. Don't be tempted to cut corners and take shortcuts; you will get the most out of your study of accounting if you follow the detailed, step-by-step directions provided in this text. Once you have learned the basic terms and concepts, the rest will quickly fall into place. Be sure to review Appendix A, *Accounting Forms Sampler*. It will be a great help to you during the course.

We have set up each chapter according to a special format that we believe makes it easier to learn and remember the material in the chapter. Let's look at each component of a chapter and see why it was set up that way:

- *Broad objectives to introduce the chapter.* These objectives allow you to see where you're headed; they set the stage for the more specific objectives to be found later in the chapter. Page references are given where the material for each objective can be found.
- *Chapter broken down into learning units.* Students continually tell us that they learn best when material is broken into small, manageable units. This way, if a question comes up it can be identified and solved immediately without waiting until the whole chapter is read. And in this way you can test yourself on smaller amounts of material to be sure that you've mastered each bit before going on to the next.
- *Objectives follow each unit with page references.* After you have read the unit, the objectives give you a change to recap what you've read. Stop to see if you can answer the objective—if not, go back to the page referred to and review the material.
- *Self-review quiz follows each unit.* This is a chance to test yourself on what you've just learned and try some hands-on applications of the theory just covered. The forms for the quizzes are in your *Study Guide/Working Papers*. The solution to the quiz follows right after the quiz in the text. Don't worry if you get something wrong in the quiz—these quizzes are for you, not for your professor. If you do have trouble with the quiz, go back to the problem area in the unit and review before going on to the next unit.
- *Discussion questions at the end of the chapter.* These questions cover the theory covered in the chapter. It is important to make sure you can answer them before going on to the next chapter.

- *Exercises at the end of the chapter.* Exercises review specific topics covered in the chapter. Notes in the margin identify the topic covered by each exercise—if you know you need more work on a certain topic that you feel uncertain about, seek out those exercises that deal with that topic.
- *Problems at the end of the chapter.* There are A, B, and C problems in the text; forms for the problems are provided in your *Study Guide/Working Papers*. As with the exercises, notes in the margin identify the topic covered by each problem.
- *Practical accounting applications at the end of the chapter.* These give you a way to test your accounting knowledge in a situation that might occur on the job. They're challenging and fun.
- *Comprehensive review problems follow certain chapters.* These problems give a list of transactions and information needed to perform certain tasks in accounting covered by a set of chapters. At the end of Chapter 5 is a problem that reviews the accounting cycle; in this problem you go through the accounting cycle twice to give you a more complete idea of the procedures involved at the end of each month. At the end of Chapter 10 there is a summary of payroll procedures. After Chapter 13 there is a problem that deals with transactions of a sole proprietorship merchandise company. These problems help put all the theory together in a practical way. Forms for completing the problems are provided in your *Study Guide/Working Papers*.
- *Accounting Recall: A Cumulative Approach* Since accounting builds from one chapter to another, it is important to review vocabulary and accounting applications. At the end of each chapter you will find a cumulative review quiz. Each quiz, with page references, will have three parts: vocabulary review, accounting theory, and application problems. The forms for these quizzes, along with the worked out solutions, will be found in your *Study Guide/Working Papers*.

Some chapters also contain career boxes highlighting individuals who have used their college accounting course work to help them attain a rewarding career. Their advice and experiences are informative, interesting, and inspiring.

If you follow this chapter layout carefully you will find that you learn the basic terms and concepts easily and remember them better, and that the many chances to apply them in a practical way help you to remember them.

TO THE INSTRUCTOR

GENESIS

College Accounting: A Practical Approach, Canadian Fourth Edition, is the result of years of teaching and writing experience in accounting. Our intention in writing this book was to create a vehicle to help maximize student mastery of accounting concepts and procedures.

The needs of students who are not, at this time, considering a career in accounting are unique. It has been our goal in the Canadianization of this text to preserve all of the quality features of the US edition and to insert high-quality Canadian material in order to present the best possible resource for students.

Our approach is based on tried and proven learning techniques, and these techniques have, in turn, been reinforced and shaped by in-class experience with students. We have also listened to a number of concerns from instructors, and this edition has been changed to incorporate several of your ideas. Principal among these is the "Type C" problems. This new material should greatly benefit the many institutions that have multiple sections and will provide increased choices for all adopters. We have chosen to increase the length and complexity of the Type C problems slightly, but have also tried to be faithful to the text's original purpose— to present accounting for students who are not currently planning a career in the area. A number of other significant changes are also incorporated into the new edition, including integrating GST into chapters 6, 7, and 11. Most of those reviewers who were approached found this preferable to adding another appendix. We have, however, tried to intelligently compartmentalize the presentation so as not to get in the way of any instructor who may choose to de-emphasize the topic of GST. The end result is, we believe, a clear, accurate, pedagogically effective text, accompanied by a fully articulated package. The text and its ancillaries offer a full range of teaching and learning tools from which the instructor can choose. It's our hope that the Canadian Fourth Edition will continue to be a positive experience for students and instructors alike.

ABOUT THE BOOK

College Accounting: A Practical Approach, Canadian Fourth Edition, is set up so that students have small, manageable units of material to learn followed by immediate feedback through the self-review quizzes at the end of each unit. Each chapter is divided into learning units, and is organized in the following way.

Broad Objectives to Introduce the Chapter
These objectives allow students to see where they're headed; they set the stage for the more specific objectives to be found later in the chapter. Page references are given so that the material for each objective can be found easily.

Chapter Broken Down into Learning Units
Students continually tell us that they learn best when material is broken into small, manageable

units. This way, if a question comes up it can be identified and solved immediately without waiting until the whole chapter is read. And in this way students can test themselves on smaller amounts of material, to be sure that they've mastered each bit before going on.

Objectives Follow Each Unit with Page References

At the end of each unit, the objectives give students a chance to recap what they've read. If they can't answer the objective, they can go back to the page referred to and review the material.

Self-Review Quiz Follows Each Unit

This is a chance for students to test themselves on what they've just learned and try some hands-on applications of the theory just covered. The forms for the quiz are in the *Study Guide/Working Papers*. The solution to the quiz follows right after the quiz in the text. If students have trouble with the quiz, they can go back to the problem area in the unit and review before going on to the next unit.

Career Box Profile

Integrated into the text are profiles of people working in the fields of bookkeeping and accounting, which show what their jobs involve and how they used their education to obtain their jobs.

Summary of Key Points and Key Terms at the End of the Chapter

The material covered in the chapter is reviewed by unit at the end of the chapter. The key points of the summary provide one more chance to review and to point up any weak spots in the chapter. Accounting as a discipline is full of new vocabulary. The trick to learning this new vocabulary is to take it slowly and review it often. The terms introduced in the chapter are listed and defined at the end of the chapter by unit so that students can review them and make sure they know what they mean and how they are used in the chapter.

Blueprint at the End of the Chapter

Some people learn better by seeing something in chart or diagram form rather than reading about it. And we all remember things better if we learn them several different ways. The goal of the blueprint is to review visually the key concepts or procedures in the chapter. It is like a roadmap, showing you in simple steps what you have just been through in the chapter.

Discussion Questions at the End of the Chapter

These questions cover the theory covered in the chapter. Students should make sure they can answer them before going on to the next chapter.

Exercises at the End of the Chapter

Exercises review specific topics covered in the chapter. Notes in the margin identify the topic covered by each exercise—students who know they need more work on a certain topic can seek out those exercises that deal with the topic.

Problems at the End of the Chapter

There are A, B and C problems in the test; forms to be used to answer them are provided in your *Study Guide/Working Papers*. As with the exercises, notes in the margin identify the topic covered by each problem.

Practical Accounting Applications at the End of the Chapter   These are a way to test accounting knowledge in a situation that might occur on the job. They're fun and challenging.

Comprehensive Review Problems Follow Certain Chapters   These problems give a list of transactions and information needed to perform certain tasks in accounting covered by a set of chapters. At the end of Chapter 5 is a problem that reviews the accounting cycle; in this problem you go through the accounting cycle twice to give you a more complete idea of the procedures involved at the end of each month. At the end of Chapter 10 there is a summary of payroll procedures. After Chapter 13 there is a problem that deals with transactions of a sole proprietorship merchandise company. This project covers a three-month period. These problems help put all the theory together in a practical way. Forms for completing the problems are provided in your *Study Guide/Working Papers*. The comprehensive problems after Chapters 10 and 13 have been fully revised, and include GST where appropriate.

CANADIAN FOURTH EDITION HIGHLIGHTS AND CHANGES

There have been numerous changes and improvements to the text and its ancillary package. The following are some key changes that make the text and its supplements more current and supportive of classroom and homework activities.

Payroll Updated   Chapters 9 and 10 have been substantially rewritten to reflect the latest laws in effect in Canada. Up-to-date tables are also included in Chapter 9.

GST Accounting   This new tax is a reality in Canada. The essential details of how to account for GST are covered beginning in Chapter 6. Chapters 6 and 7 have been designed to accommodate instructors who choose either to emphasize or to de-emphasize this topic.

Comprehensive Problems   The comprehensive review problems at the end of Chapters 10 and 13 have been rewritten and expanded. GST is covered appropriately.

New Material on Inventory   In Chapter 16, students are provided with theory, practice, and applications regarding inventory costing methods and practices.

Accounting Recall: A Cumulative Approach   At the end of each chapter students get a chance to cumulatively recall what they've learned in past chapters. The recall is broken into 3 parts: Vocabulary, Theory, and Practical Applications (page references are provided for each question). The *Study Guide/Working Papers* contains the forms as well as solutions for the Accounting Recall materials. It's a great review before beginning the next chapter.

Problem Material Expanded   As in previous editions, the A and B sets of problems are designed to reinforce concepts introduced in the chapters. Now, however, instructors may also choose from a C set of problems, newly created for this edition. These C problems are more rigorous than the A and B sets, and will require students to stretch a bit.

Study Guide/Working Papers   New to this edition are fold-out forms for all worksheets. Forms for all the exercises are also provided. The forms you need for the Accounting Recall, as well as the solutions, have been added to this expanded *Study Guide/Working Papers*. Note that the *Study Guide/Working Papers* are now all-Canadian, customized for Canadian students' needs.

THE SLATER/ZWICKER PACKAGE

The text is just the starting point. Because the needs of Canadian instructors are very high on our priority list, we have taken certain other steps designed to maximize instructor effectiveness and efficiency. These steps include the provision of an *Instructor's Resource Manual* (new for this edition), a test item bank (expanded from the previous edition) and the availability of all questions in the published text in Word Perfect format. Another significant change is the complete Canadianization of the *Study Guide/Working Papers*, *Solutions Manual*, and *Transparency Masters*. We have invested a great many hours to ensure the highest quality possible and we hope it shows up in increased clarity, accuracy, and consistency. Let's look at some of the support systems that are included in the Slater/Zwicker package.

Learning Aids to Support the Slater/Zwicker System

Instructor's Resource Manual   New for this edition is the *Instructor's Resource Manual*. It is intended to bring together between two covers all of the materials that act to facilitate and augment each instructor's own special skills, strengths, and experience. The *Instructor's Resource Manual* includes:

- **Class Quizzes**   Short exercise or review questions designed to reinforce aspects of the chapter coverage.
- **Class Activities**   Something the whole class can take part in. Reviews and reinforces key points.
- **Lesson Outlines**   Chapter material is allocated to a variety of classroom situations. There is probably a design that closely fits most educational institutions' scheduling preferences.
- **Typical Student Misconceptions**   Gathered from more than 35 years of combined accounting teaching experience, these common errors may be invaluable—especially to those instructors who are just beginning their careers.
- **Teaching Tips**   Valuable suggestions that help students remember and assimilate the material.
- **Business World Notes**   What actually happens in accounting in the real world. Takes students beyond the textbook.
- **Lecture Notes**   While not intended to replace an appropriate lesson plan, these notes may be very useful as a check that nothing critical is overlooked.

Study Guide/Working Papers   This has undergone substantial revision and enhancement. It now contains forms for the quizzes at the end of each learning unit in the chapter, for all exercises, for the problems (A, B, or C) at the end of each chapter, and for the comprehensive review problems that follow Chapters 5, 10, and 13. In addition, all work sheets are now treated as foldouts—a significant enhancement over prior editions. At the end of each chapter of the *Study Guide/Working Papers*, there is a summary practice test designed to prepare students for in-class exams. It consists of fill-in-the-blank questions, a matching question, and true/false questions. In addition, the forms and solutions to the end-of-chapter Accounting Recalls in the text help students review the concepts covered in each chapter before going on to the next. The answers to the tests are at the end of each chapter of the *Study Guide/Working Papers*. For the first time, the *Study Guide/Working Papers* is a completely Canadian publication. Many changes have been made to help ensure that the student's experience is as smooth as possible.

Solutions Manual   Provides answers to discussion questions and solutions to exercises, problems, comprehensive review problems, and practical accounting applications.

In the front of the manual there is a grid of all problems showing level of difficulty and estimated time needed to complete.

The Solutions Manual now contains a section of 24 key forms that can be reproduced.

Transparency Masters   Since the *Solutions Manual* was created using fonts appropriate for use in projection equipment, no transparencies are available. Instructors may wish to copy certain answers from the *Solutions Manual* to plastic transparencies for classroom use. Certain other useful figures, blueprints and blank forms are included in this supplement in an attempt to enhance each student's learning experience.

Test Item File   The test item file has been substantially revised and expanded. Each volume contains true/false, multiple choice, problem, and essay-type questions. Adopters may request that this supplement be supplied to them on diskette in a suitable word processing format.

ACKNOWLEDGMENTS

The task of publishing a Canadian edition of any textbook is a challenging venture. In this case it helped to be working from an outstanding original and with an outstanding team.

Thanks are certainly due to the many helpful folks at Prentice Hall Canada Inc., including Acquisitions Editor Cliff Newman, Developmental Editor Lisa Penttilä, and Production Editor, Dawn du Quesnay.

Thanks are due to the reviewers of the Canadian Third Edition for their valuable feedback. Special recognition is due to Larry Knechtel, Nancy Samuell, and Doug Ringrose from Grant MacEwan Community College, who have used portions of the text in their classes. Thanks are also due to Eric Saemisch at Revenue Canada for his able assistance in obtaining most of the government forms.

Finally, closer to home I would be very remiss if I failed to reflect upon the hours of support and encouragement provided by my wife, Carol, and daughters, Heather and Shannon. All three are very gifted with words and their efforts were always appreciated and often incorporated.

CHAPTER ONE

INTRODUCTION TO ACCOUNTING CONCEPTS AND PROCEDURES

IN THIS CHAPTER WE WILL COVER THE FOLLOWING TOPICS:

Accounting is the language of business; it provides information to managers, own-ers, customers, investors, and other decision makers inside and outside an organiza-tion. Accounting provides answers and insights to questions like these:

- Is Canadian Tire's cash balance sufficient?
- Should Burger King expand its product line?
- Can Canadian Airlines pay its debt obligations?
- What percentage of Northern Telecom's marketing budget is for magazine advertisement? How does this compare with the competition? What is the overall financial condition of this company?

Smaller businesses also need answers to their financial questions:

- Did business increase enough over the last year to warrant hiring a new assistant?
- Should we spend money to design, produce, and send out new brochures in an effort to create more business?

Accounting is as important to individuals as it is to business; it answers ques-tions such as:

- Should I take out a loan to buy a car or wait until I can afford to pay cash for it?
- Would my money work better in a savings bank or in a credit union savings plan?

Think of accounting as a process that analyzes, records, classifies, summarizes, and reports financial information. The purpose of the accounting process is to pro-vide this information to decision makers—whether individuals, small businesses, large corporations, or governmental agencies—in a timely fashion.

BOOKKEEPING, ACCOUNTING, AND THE COMPUTER

Confusion often arises concerning the difference between bookkeeping and accounting. **Bookkeeping** is the recording (record-keeping) function of the accounting process; a bookkeeper enters accounting information in the company's books. An accountant takes that information and prepares the financial reports that are used to analyze the company's financial position. **Accounting** involves many complex activities and often includes the preparation of tax and financial reports, budgeting, and analyses of financial information.

People sometimes wonder if the computer is taking over the accountant's job of completing financial reports. It is important to understand that *the computer is only a tool* that is helping to do the routine bookkeeping operations that previously took days or months to complete. To date, the computer has not caused fewer jobs but has, in fact, created more jobs because businesses are getting more information than they could previously get by manual record keeping.

It is important that students studying accounting understand the "whys" rather than the mere mechanics of the accounting process. For this reason the text illus-trates manual accounting and also explains how you can apply the advantages of the computer to your manual accounting system by using your hands-on knowledge of how accounting works.

Let's begin our study of accounting concepts and procedures by looking at a small business: Sylvia Mosco's law practice.

LEARNING UNIT 1-1
The Accounting Equation

ASSETS AND EQUITIES

At the end of August, Sylvia Mosco decided to open her own law practice. Her accountant told her that, first of all, a law practice (or any company) is considered a **business entity**, a separate unit, and its finances have to be kept distinct from Sylvia's personal finances. The accountant went on to say that all business transactions can be analyzed by something called the basic accounting equation. Sylvia had never heard of the basic accounting equation. She listened carefully as the accountant explained it:

1. Cash, land, supplies, office equipment, buildings, and other properties of value *owned* by a firm are called **assets**.

2. The rights or financial claims to the assets are called **equities** and they belong to those who supply the assets. If you are the only person to supply assets to the firm, you have the sole rights, or financial claims, to them. For example, if you supply the law firm with $3,000 in cash and $2,000 in office equipment, your equity in the firm is $5,000.

3. The relationship between assets and equities is:

    Assets = Equities

    The total dollar value of the assets of the law firm will be equal to the total dollar value of the financial claims to those assets—that is, equal to the total dollar value of the equities.

    The total dollar value is broken down on the left-hand side of the equation to show the specific items of value owned by the business and on the right-hand side to show the types of claims against the assets owned.

4. A firm may have to borrow money to buy more assets. When this occurs it means the firm is buying assets *on account* (buy now, pay later). Suppose the law firm purchases a desk for $200 on account from Joe's Stationery, and the store is willing to wait ten days for payment. The law firm has created a **liability**: an obligation to pay that comes due in the future. Joe's Stationery is called the *creditor*. This liability—the amount owed to Joe's Stationery—gives the store the right, or the financial claim, to $200 of the law firm's assets. When Joe's Stationery is paid, the store's rights to the assets of the law firm will end, since the obligation has been paid off.

To best understand the various claims to a business's assets, accountants divide equities into two parts. The claims of creditors—parties from outside the business—are labelled **liabilities**. The claims of the business's owner are labelled **owner's equity**. Let's see how the accounting equation looks now.

Assets =   **Equities**

     1. Liabilities: rights of creditors
     2. Owner's equity: rights of owner

Assets = Liabilities + Owner's Equity

Elements of the basic accounting equation.

The total value of all the assets of a firm equals the combined total value of the financial claims of the creditors (liabilities) and the claims of the owners (owner's equity). This is known as the **basic accounting equation**. The basic accounting equation provides a basis for understanding the conventional accounting system of a business. The equation organizes business transactions in a logical and orderly way that shows their impact on the company's assets, liabilities, and owner's equity.

The purpose of the accounting equation.

Another way of presenting the basic accounting equation is:

Assets – Liabilities = Owner's Equity

Assets
– Liabilities
‾‾‾‾‾‾‾‾‾‾
= Owner's Equity

This form of the equation stresses the importance of creditors. The owner's rights to the assets of a business are determined by first subtracting the rights of the creditor(s). Creditors have first claim to assets. If a firm has no liabilities—and therefore no creditors—the owner has the total rights to the assets. Another term we will be using in this text is **capital**—the owner's current investment, or equity, in the assets of a business. For now, think of capital as one subdivision of owner's equity; we will look at other subdivisions later in the chapter.

In accounting, capital does not mean cash. Capital is the owner's current investment, or equity, in the assets of the business.

As Sylvia Mosco's law firm engages in business transactions (paying bills, serving customers, and so on), changes will take place in the firm's assets, liabilities, and owner's equity (capital). Let's analyze some of these transactions.

> *(A) Aug. 28: Mosco invests $8,000 in cash and $100 of office equipment into the business.*

On August 28 Sylvia Mosco withdraws $8,000 from her personal bank account and deposits the money in the newly opened bank account of the law firm. She also invests $100 of office equipment in the business. She plans to open the law office on September 1, 19XX. With the help of her accountant, Sylvia begins to prepare her accounting records. Remember, we are analyzing the assets of the law firm, not the personal assets of Sylvia Mosco.

Using accounting terminology, we say that (1) the law practice owns $8,100 worth of assets, in the form of cash and office equipment, and (2) Mosco has the rights to the full $8,100 in assets, since no liabilities exist. (Remember, assets minus liabilities equals owner's equity.) We put this information into the basic accounting equation as follows:

Sylvia Mosco
Barrister and Solicitor

Assets			= Liabilities	+	Owner's Equity
Cash	+	Office Equip.	=		S. Mosco, Capital
$8,000	+	$100	=		$8,100
		$8,100	= $8,100		

Note: Capital is part of owner's equity; it is not an asset.

Note that the total value of the assets, cash, and office equipment—$8,100—is equal to the combined total value of liabilities (none, so far) and owner's equity ($8,100). Remember, Mosco has supplied all the cash and office equipment, so she has the sole financial claim to the assets. Note how the heading "Sylvia Mosco, Capital" is written under the Owner's Equity heading. The $8,100 is Mosco's investment, or equity, in the assets of the law firm.

(B) Aug. 29: Law practice buys office equipment for cash, $300.

From the initial investment of $8,000 cash, the law firm buys $300 worth of office equipment for cash from Brooks Company. Keep in mind that equipment (such as a desk) lasts a long time, while **supplies** (such as pens) tend to be used up relatively quickly.

In our analyses, assume that any number without a sign in front of it is a +.

Sylvia Mosco
Barrister and Solicitor

	Assets		=	Liabilities	+	Owner's Equity
	Cash	+ *Office Equip.*	=			*S. Mosco, Capital*
Bal. For.	$8,000	+ $100	=			$8,100
Trans.	−300	+ 300	=			
End. Bal.	$7,700	+ $400				$8,100
		$8,100	=	$8,100		

Shift in Assets

As a result of the last transaction, the law office has less cash but has increased its amount of office equipment. This is called a **shift in assets**—the makeup of the assets has changed, but the total of the assets remains the same.

Suppose you go food shopping at the supermarket with $100 and spend $60. Now you have two assets, food and money. The composition of the assets has been *shifted*—you have more food and less money than you did—but the *total* of the assets has not increased or decreased. The total value of the food, $60, plus the cash, $40, is still $100. When you borrow money from the bank, on the other hand, you have an increase in cash (an asset) and an increase in liabilities; overall there is an increase in assets, not just a shift.

An accounting equation can remain in balance even if only one side is updated. The key point to remember is that the left-side total of assets must always equal the right-side total of liabilities and owner's equity.

(C) Aug. 30: Buys additional office equipment on account, $400.

The law firm purchases an additional $400 worth of chairs and desks from Brooks Company. Instead of demanding cash right away, Brooks Company agrees to deliver the equipment and to allow up to sixty days for the law practice to pay the invoice (bill).

This liability, or obligation to pay in the future, has some interesting effects on the basic accounting equation. Brooks Company has accepted as payment a partial claim against the assets of the law practice. This claim exists until the law firm pays the bill. This promise to pay the creditor is a liability called **accounts payable**.

Sylvia Mosco
Barrister and Solicitor

	Assets			=	Liabilities	+	Owner's Equity
	Cash	+	*Office Equip.*	=	*Accts. Pay.*		*S. Mosco, Capital*
Bal. For.	$7,700	+	$400			+	$8,100
Trans.			+400		+ $400		
End. Bal.	$7,700	+	$800	=	$400	+	$8,100
			$8,500	=	$8,500		

In analyzing this information, notice that the law practice has increased what it owes (accounts payable) as well as increased an asset (office equipment) by $400. The law practice gains $400 in an asset but has an obligation to pay Brooks Company at a future date.

Note that the owner's equity remains unchanged. This transaction results in an increase of total assets from $8,100 to $8,500.

Finally, note that after each transaction the basic accounting equation remains in balance.

Let us review the objectives of this unit. At this time, in your own words, you should be able to

1. List the functions of accounting. (p. 2)
2. Compare and contrast bookkeeping and accounting. (p. 2)
3. Explain the role of the computer as an accounting tool. (p. 2)
4. State the purpose of the accounting equation. (p. 3)
5. Explain the difference between liabilities and owner's equity. (p. 3)
6. Define capital. (p. 4)
7. Explain the difference between a shift in assets and an increase in assets. (p. 5)

To test your understanding of this material, complete Self-Review Quiz 1-1. The blank forms you need are in the *Study Guide and Working Papers* for Chapter 1. The solution to the quiz immediately follows here in the text. If you have difficulty doing the problems, review Learning Unit 1-1 and the solution to the quiz.

Keep in mind that learning accounting is like learning to type—the more you practice, the better you become. You will not be an expert in one day. Be patient. It will all come together.

☐ SELF-REVIEW QUIZ 1-1

Record the following transactions in the basic accounting equation:

1. John Sullivan invests $12,000 to begin a real estate office.
2. The real estate office buys computer equipment for cash, $400.
3. Buys additional computer equipment on account, $800.

■ SOLUTION TO SELF-REVIEW QUIZ 1-1

John Sullivan Real Estate

	Assets		=	Liabilities	+	Owner's Equity
	Cash	+ Computer Equipment	=	Accounts Payable	+	John Sullivan, Capital
1.	+$12,000				+	$12,000
Balance	12,000		=			12,000
2.	−400	+$400				
Balance	11,600	+ 400	=			12,000
3.		+$800		+$800		
Ending Balance	$11,600	+ $1,200	=	$800	+	$12,000
		$12,800	=	$12,800		

LEARNING UNIT 1-2

The Balance Sheet

Since Sylvia Mosco's law firm plans to begin formal operations in September, there is a need to develop a report that will show, as of August 31, the following:

1. The amount of assets owned by the law practice.
2. The amount of claims (liabilities and owner's equity) against these assets.

This report is called a **balance sheet** or statement of financial position. The balance sheet presents the information from the ending balances of both sides of the accounting equation. Think of a balance sheet as a snapshot of the business's financial position taken on a particular date.

Let's look at the balance sheet of Sylvia Mosco's law practice for August 31, 19XX, shown in Figure 1-1 (p. 8). The figures in the balance sheet come from the ending balances of the accounting equation for Mosco's law practice as shown in Learning Unit 1-1.

Note that in Figure 1-1 the assets owned by Mosco's practice appear on the left side and that liabilities and owner's equity appear on the right side. Both sides equal

> The balance sheet shows *where we are now* (in our example, at the end of August). This report shows us the financial position of the company as of a particular date.

$8,500. This *balance* between left and right gives the balance sheet its name. In later chapters we will be looking at other ways to set up a balance sheet.

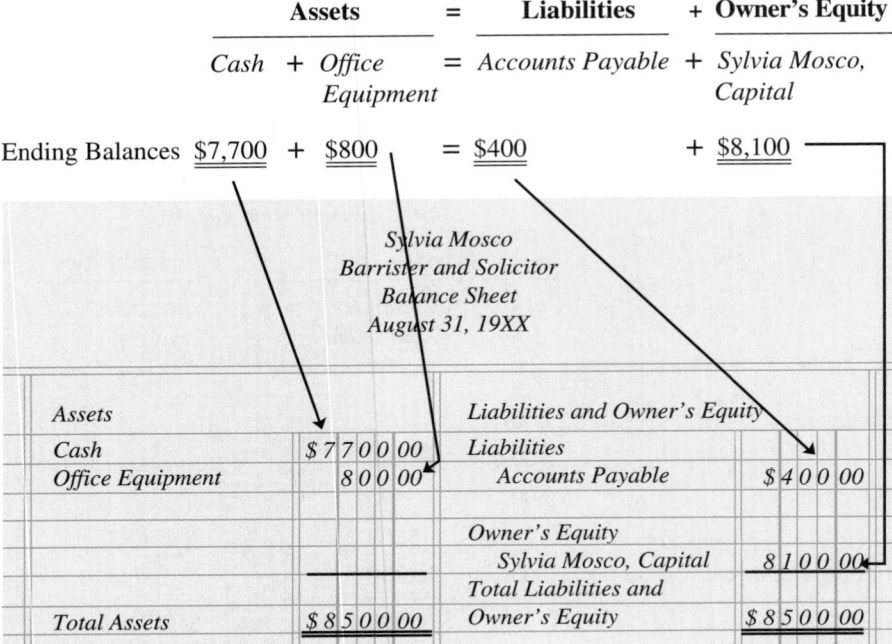

	Assets	=	Liabilities	+	Owner's Equity
	Cash + Office Equipment	=	Accounts Payable	+	Sylvia Mosco, Capital
Ending Balances	$7,700 + $800	=	$400	+	$8,100

Sylvia Mosco
Barrister and Solicitor
Balance Sheet
August 31, 19XX

Assets		Liabilities and Owner's Equity	
Cash	$ 7 700 00	Liabilities	
Office Equipment	800 00	Accounts Payable	$ 400 00
		Owner's Equity	
		Sylvia Mosco, Capital	8 100 00
		Total Liabilities and	
Total Assets	$ 8 500 00	Owner's Equity	$ 8 500 00

FIGURE 1-1
The Balance Sheet

Points to Remember in Preparing a Balance Sheet

Point 1:   Note that the heading of the balance sheet answers the following three questions:

1. Who? The company's name: Sylvia Mosco, Barrister and Solicitor.
2. What? The name of the report: Balance Sheet.
3. When? As of a specific date, the date for which the report is prepared: August 31, 19XX.

Remember:
The balance sheet is a formal report.

Point 2:   In the balance sheet of Mosco's law practice the dollar sign is not repeated each time a figure appears. Usually it is placed to the left of each column's top figure and to the left of the column's total.

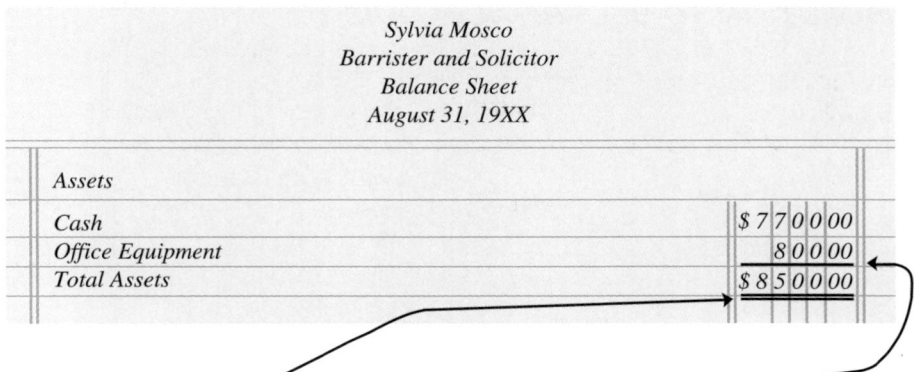

Point 3: When adding numbers down a column, use a single line before the total and a double line beneath it. Also be careful to line the numbers up in the column; many errors occur because these figures are not lined up. The *Study Guide and Working Papers* has been designed in part to make it easy to control this process.

The balance sheet gives Sylvia Mosco the information she needs to see the law firm's financial position before it opens for business. This information does not tell her, however, whether or not the firm will make a profit.

Do you remember the three elements that make up a balance sheet? Assets, liabilities, and owner's equity.

Let us review the objectives of Learning Unit 1-2. At this time you should be able to

1. Define and state the purpose of a balance sheet. (p. 7)
2. Identify and define the elements making up a balance sheet. (p. 8)
3. Show the relationship between the accounting equation and the balance sheet. (p. 7)
4. Prepare a balance sheet in proper form from information provided. (p. 8)

Now complete Self-Review Quiz 1-2. The solution follows. Remember that the *Study Guide and Working Papers* contains the forms needed to complete the quiz.

☐ **SELF-REVIEW QUIZ 1-2**

The date is November 30, 19XX. Prepare in proper form a balance sheet for Downtown Electronics Company using the following information:

Accounts Payable	$25,000
Cash	3,000
A. Boone, Capital	8,000
Office Equipment	30,000

■ SOLUTION TO SELF-REVIEW QUIZ 1-2

Downtown Electronics Company
Balance Sheet
November 30, 19XX

Assets		Liabilities and Owner's Equity	
Cash	$ 3 000 00	Liabilities	
Office Equipment	30 000 00	Accounts Payable	$25 000 00
		Owner's Equity	
		A. Boone, Capital	8 000 00
		Total Liabilities and	
Total Assets	$33 000 00	Owner's Equity	$33 000 00

NOTE:　Capital does not mean cash. The capital amount is the owner's current investment of assets in the business. So Boone's $8,000 in capital means the owner may have supplied some cash and some equipment to the business.

LEARNING UNIT 1-3

The Accounting Equation Expanded: Revenue, Expenses, and Withdrawals

As soon as she opened her office, Mosco began performing legal services for clients and earning revenue for her business. At the same time, as a part of doing business, she incurred various expenses, such as rent and utilities. Mosco asked her accountant to find out how to fit these transactions into the accounting equation. Her accountant began by defining some terms.

> Accounts *receivable* is an asset. The law firm expects to be *able* to *receive* amounts owed from customers at a later date.

1. When the law firm provides legal services to clients for legal fees, the business earns **revenue**. Revenue is a subdivision of owner's equity, so when revenue is earned, owner's equity is increased. Assets are also increased, either in the form of cash, if the client pays right away, or in the promise to pay in the future, which is called **accounts receivable**. When revenue is earned, the transaction is recorded as an increase in revenue and an increase in assets (either as cash or as accounts receivable, depending on whether it was paid right away or will be paid in the future).

2. In business there are also **expenses**, which are the costs the company incurs in carrying on operations in its effort to create revenue. Expenses are also a subdivision of owner's equity; when expenses are incurred, they *decrease* owner's equity. We can pay for expenses in cash or charge them.

3. When revenue totals more than expenses, **net income** is the result; when expenses total more than revenue, **net loss** is the result.

Before looking at the September transactions of Mosco's law firm, we must explain one more element in the accounting equation. At some point Sylvia Mosco may need to withdraw cash or other assets from the business to pay living or other personal expenses that do not relate to the business. The account title we will use to record these transactions is called **withdrawals**. Withdrawals is a subdivision of owner's equity that records personal expenses paid for by the business, but not related to the business. Withdrawals decrease owner's equity. Think of withdrawals as the opposite of a contribution by an owner.

It is important to remember the difference between expenses and withdrawals. Expenses relate to business operations; withdrawals are the result of personal needs outside the normal operations of the business.

Let us now analyze the September transactions for Sylvia Mosco's law firm, noting how we are using an **expanded accounting equation** to include withdrawals, revenue, and expenses.

(D) *Sept. 1-30: Provided legal services for cash, $3,000.*

Transactions A, B, and C were discussed earlier, when the law office was being formed in August. See Learning Unit 1-1.

Sylvia Mosco
Barrister and Solicitor

	Cash	+	Accts. Rec.	+	Office Equip.	=	Accts. Pay.	+	S. Mosco, Capital	−	S. Mosco, Withdr.	+	Revenue	−	Expenses
Bal. For.	$7,700			+	$800	=	$400	+	$8,100						
Trans.	+ 3,000		____								_____	+ 3,000			_____
End. Bal.	$10,700			+	$800	=	$400	+	$8,100			+	$ 3,000		
					$11,500	=	$11,500								

(Assets = Liabilities + Owner's Equity)

In the law firm's first month of operation a total of $3,000 in cash was received for legal services performed. In the accounting equation the asset Cash is increased by $3,000. Revenue is also increased by $3,000, resulting in a corresponding increase in owner's equity. Notice the addition of a revenue column to the basic accounting equation. This new column will help the accountant in preparing financial reports.

Amounts are recorded in the revenue column when they are earned. They are also recorded in the assets column, under Cash and/or under Accounts Receivable. Do not think of revenue as an asset. It is part of owner's equity. It is the revenue that creates an inward flow of cash and accounts receivable.

> When revenue is earned, it is recorded as an increase in owner's equity and an increase in assets.

(E) *Sept. 1-30: Provided legal services on account, $1,500.*

Sylvia Mosco
Barrister and Solicitor

	Assets			= Liabilities	+		Owner's Equity			
	Cash	+ Accts. Rec.	+ Office Equip.	= Accts. Pay.	+	S. Mosco, Capital	− S. Mosco, Withdr.	+ Revenue	− Expenses
Bal. For.	$10,700		+ $800	= $400	+	$8,100		+ $ 3,000	
Trans.		+ $ 1,500						+ 1,500	
End. Bal.	$10,700	+ $ 1,500	+ $800	= $400	+	$8,100		+ $ 4,500	
			$13,000	= $13,000					

Remember:
Accounts receivable results from earning revenue even when cash is not yet received.

Sylvia Mosco's law practice performed legal work on account for $1,500. The firm did not receive the cash for these earned legal fees; it accepted an unwritten promise from these clients that payment would be received in the future.

> *(F) Sept. 1-30: Received $700 cash as partial payment from previous services performed on account.*

Sylvia Mosco
Barrister and Solicitor

	Assets			= Liabilities	+		Owner's Equity			
	Cash	+ Accts. Rec.	+ Office Equip.	= Accts. Pay.	+	S. Mosco, Capital	− S. Mosco, Withdr.	+ Revenue	− Expenses
Bal. For.	$10,700	+ $1,500	+ $800	= $400	+	$8,100		+ $ 4,500	
Trans.	+ 700	− 700							
End. Bal.	$11,400	+ $ 800	+ $800	= $400	+	$8,100		+ $ 4,500	
			$13,000	= $13,000					

Revenue is recorded *once*—when it is earned. In this situation no new revenue has been earned.

During September some of Mosco's clients who had received services and promised to pay in the future reduced what they owed the practice by $700 by paying promptly when their bills came due.

Note in the columns of the accounting equation that the law firm increased the asset Cash by $700 and reduced another asset, Accounts Receivable, by $700. The *total* of assets does not change. Also notice that the right-hand side of the expanded accounting equation has not been touched. The revenue was recorded when it was earned. *Do not record the same revenue twice.* This transaction is analyzing the situation *after* the revenue has been previously earned and recorded. What is really happening is a shifting of the composition of the assets—more cash and less accounts receivable.

Since one asset (Cash) went up by $700 and another (Accounts Receivable) went down by $700, the total of the left side of the accounting equation has not changed at all. Therefore, the right side of the equation does not need to change.

(G) Paid salaries expense, $800.

Sylvia Mosco
Barrister and Solicitor

	Assets			=	Liabilities	+		Owner's Equity			
Cash	+ *Accts. Rec.*	+ *Office Equip.*		= *Accts. Pay.*		+	*S. Mosco, Capital*	− *S. Mosco, Withdr.*	+ *Revenue*	− *Expenses*
Bal. For. $11,400	+ $800	+ $800		= $400		+ $8,100			+ $ 4,500	
Trans. − 800										+ $800
End. Bal. $10,600	+ $800	+ $800		= $400		+ $8,100			+ $ 4,500	− $800
			$12,200	= $12,200						

Because expenses are opposite to revenues, as expenses increase, they decrease owner's equity. This salaries expense of $800 reduces the cash by $800. Although the expense was paid, the total of our expenses to date has *increased* by $800.

(H) Paid rent expense, $200.

Sylvia Mosco
Barrister and Solicitor

	Assets			=	Liabilities	+		Owner's Equity			
Cash	+ *Accts. Rec.*	+ *Office Equip.*		= *Accts. Pay.*		+	*S. Mosco, Capital*	− *S. Mosco, Withdr.*	+ *Revenue*	− *Expenses*
Bal. For. $10,600	+ $800	+ $800		= $400		+ $8,100			+ $ 4,500	− $800
Trans. − 200										+ 200
End. Bal. $10,400	+ $800	+ $800		= $400		+ $8,100			+ $ 4,500	− $1,000
			$12,000	= $12,000						

During September the practice incurred rent expenses of $200. This rent was not paid in advance; it was paid when it came due. The payment of rent reduces the asset Cash by $200 and increases the expenses of the firm, resulting in a decrease in owner's equity. The firm's total expenses are now $1,000.

(I) Incurred advertising expenses of $150, to be paid next month.

Sylvia Mosco
Barrister and Solicitor

	Assets			= Liabilities	+	Owner's Equity				
	Cash +	Accts. Rec. +	Office Equip.	= Accts. Pay.	+	S. Mosco, Capital	− S. Mosco, Withdr.	+ Revenue	− Expenses
Bal. For.	$10,400 +	$800 +	$800	= $400	+	$8,100		+ $ 4,500	− $1,000
Trans.				+ 150					+ 150
End. Bal.	$10,400 +	$800 +	$800	= $550	+	$8,100		+ $ 4,500	− $1,150
				$12,000	= $12,000				

Record an expense when it is incurred, whether it is paid then or is to be paid later.

Sylvia's firm ran an ad in the local newspaper and incurred an expense of $150. The firm's expenses are thus increased by $150, which causes owner's equity to decrease. Since the business has not paid the newspaper for the advertising yet, it *owes* them the $150 and, thus, liabilities (Accounts Payable) increase by $150. Eventually, when the bill comes in and is paid, both Cash and Accounts Payable will be decreased.

(J) Mosco withdrew $40 for personal use.

Sylvia Mosco
Barrister and Solicitor

	Assets			= Liabilities	+	Owner's Equity				
	Cash +	Accts. Rec. +	Office Equip.	= Accts. Pay.	+	S. Mosco, Capital	− S. Mosco, Withdr.	+ Revenue	− Expenses
Bal. For.	$10,400 +	$800 +	$800	= $550	+	$8,100		+ $ 4,500	− $1,150
Trans.	− 40						+ $40		
End. Bal.	$10,360 +	$800 +	$800	= $550	+	$8,100	− $40	+ $ 4,500	− $1,150
				$11,960	= $11,960				

Withdrawal decreases owner's equity.

By taking $40 for personal use, Sylvia has *increased* her withdrawals from the business by $40 and the asset Cash in the business has been decreased by $40. Note that as withdrawals increase, they will *decrease* the owner's equity. Keep in mind that a withdrawal is *not* a business expense. It is a subdivision of owner's equity that records money or other assets an owner withdraws from the business for *personal* use.

Take a moment to review the subdivisions of owner's equity:

As capital increases, owner's equity increases

As withdrawals increase, owner's equity decreases

As revenue increases, owner's equity increases

As expenses increase, owner's equity decreases

Let us review the objectives of Learning Unit 1-3. At this time you should be able to

1. Define and explain the difference between revenue and expenses. (p. 10)
2. Define and explain the difference between net income and net loss. (p. 10)
3. Explain the subdivisions of owner's equity. (pp. 11-13)
4. Explain the effects of withdrawals, revenue, and expenses on owner's equity. (p. 14)
5. Record transactions in an expanded accounting equation and balance the basic accounting equation as a means of checking the accuracy of your calculations. (pp. 11-13)

Now complete Self-Review Quiz 1-3.

☐ SELF-REVIEW QUIZ 1-3

Record the following transactions into the expanded accounting equation. Note that all titles have a beginning balance.

1. Received cash revenue, $2,000.
2. Billed customers for services rendered, $6,000.
3. Received a bill for telephone expenses (to be paid next month), $125.
4. Abby Ellen withdrew cash for personal use, $500.
5. Received $1,000 from customers in partial payment for services performed in transaction 2.

◼ *SOLUTION TO SELF-REVIEW QUIZ 1-3*

Abby Ellen Co.

	Cash	+	Accts. Rec.	+	Clean. Equip.	=	Accts. Pay.	+	A. Ellen, Capital	−	A. Ellen, Withdr.	+	Revenue	−	Expenses
Beg. Bal.	$10,000	+	$2,500	+	$6,500	=	$1,000	+	$11,800	−	$800	+	$9,000	−	$2,000
1.	+ 2,000												+2,000		
Balance	12,000	+	2,500	+	6,500	=	1,000	+	11,800	−	800	+	11,000	−	2,000
2.			+6,000										+6,000		
Balance	12,000	+	8,500	+	6,500	=	1,000	+	11,800	−	800	+	17,000	−	2,000
3.							+125								+125
Balance	12,000	+	8,500	+	6,500	=	1,125	+	11,800	−	800	+	17,000	−	2,125
4.	−500										+500				
Balance	11,500	+	8,500	+	6,500	=	1,125	+	11,800	−	1,300	+	17,000	−	2,125
5.	+1,000		−1,000												
End. Bal.	$12,500	+	$7,500	+	$6,500	=	$1,125	+	$11,800	−	$1,300	+	$17,000	−	$2,125

$26,500 $26,500

LEARNING UNIT 1-4

Preparing Financial Reports

Sylvia Mosco is in business to make money. To find out if the operation is making a profit, Mosco asks her accountant how she can measure the financial performance of the law practice on a monthly basis. Her accountant replies that there are a number of financial reports that she can prepare for Sylvia, one of which is the income statement, which shows how well the law firm has performed in a specific period of time. From the income statement, the accountant will get the information needed to prepare other reports.

THE INCOME STATEMENT

The income statement is prepared from data found in the revenue and expense columns of the expanded accounting equation.

The **income statement** is an accounting report that shows business results in terms of revenue and expenses. If revenues are greater than expenses, the result is net income. If expenses are greater than revenues, the result is net loss. An income statement can cover one, three, six, or twelve months, but almost never more than one year. The income statement is shown in Figure 1-2.

The inside column of numbers ($800, $200, $150) is used to subtotal all expenses ($1,150) before subtracting from revenue.

Sylvia Mosco
Barrister and Solicitor
Income Statement
For month ended September 30, 19XX

Revenue:		
Legal Fees		$ 4 5 0 0 00
Operating Expenses:		
Salaries Expense	$ 8 0 0 00	
Rent Expense	2 0 0 00	
Advertising Expense	1 5 0 00	
Total Operating Expenses		1 1 5 0 00
Net Income		$ 3 3 5 0 00

FIGURE 1-2
The Income Statement

Points to Remember in Preparing an Income Statement

POINT 1:   Note that the heading of the income statement answers the following three questions:

1. Who? The company's name: Sylvia Mosco, Barrister and Solicitor
2. What? The name of the report: Income Statement
3. When? The period of time covered by the report: month of September. (Can be one, three, six, or twelve months; almost never more than a year. The report shows the results of all revenue and expenses throughout the entire period and not just as of a specific date.)

POINT 2: As you can see on the income statement, the inside column of numbers ($800, $200, and $150) is used to subtotal all expenses ($1,150) before subtracting them from revenue ($4,500 – $1,150 = $3,350).

POINT 3: Operating expenses may be listed in several ways: in alphabetical order, in order of largest amounts to smallest, or in another sensible order established by the accountant.

POINT 4: Finally, as we noted with the balance sheet earlier, the dollar signs are not repeated for every number, but only for the first number in a column and the final total. A single line is used when adding numbers before the total and a double line beneath the total. As before, be careful to line the numbers up properly in the column to avoid errors in adding.

As we said, the income statement is a business report that shows business results in terms of revenue and expenses. But how does net income or net loss affect owner's equity? To find that out we have to look at a second type of report, the **statement of owner's equity**.

THE STATEMENT OF OWNER'S EQUITY

The statement of owner's equity shows for a certain period of time what changes occurred in Sylvia Mosco, Capital. The statement of owner's equity is shown in Figure 1-3.

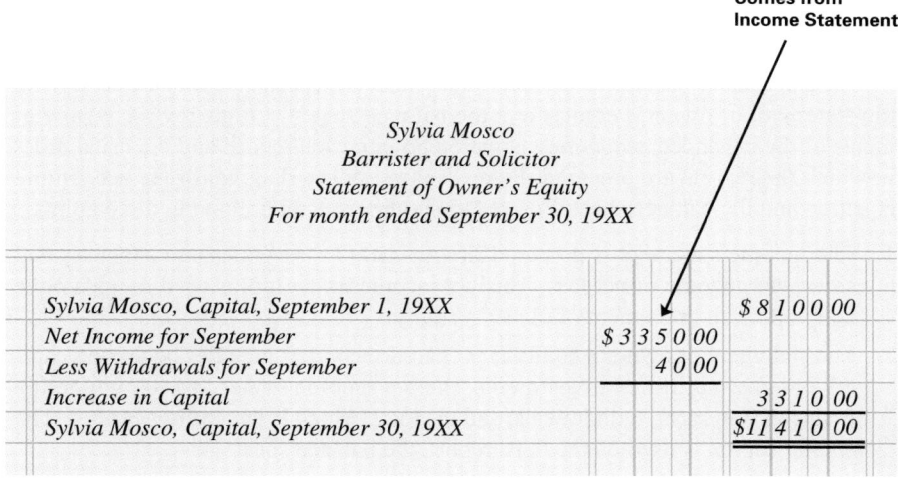

Comes from Income Statement

	Sylvia Mosco Barrister and Solicitor Statement of Owner's Equity For month ended September 30, 19XX		
Sylvia Mosco, Capital, September 1, 19XX			*$ 8 1 0 0 00*
Net Income for September	*$ 3 3 5 0 00*		
Less Withdrawals for September	*4 0 00*		
Increase in Capital			*3 3 1 0 00*
Sylvia Mosco, Capital, September 30, 19XX			*$11 4 1 0 00*

FIGURE 1-3

Statement of Owner's Equity

The capital of Sylvia Mosco can be

Increased by: Owner Investments
*   Net Income (Revenue – Expenses)*

- -

Decreased by: Owner Withdrawals
*   Net Loss*

Keep in mind that a withdrawal is *not* a business expense and thus is not involved in the calculation of net income or net loss on the income statement. It appears on the statement of owner's equity. The statement of owner's equity summarizes the effects of all the subdivisions of owner's equity (revenue, expenses, withdrawals) on beginning capital. The ending capital figure of $11,410 will be the beginning figure in the next statement of owner's equity.

Suppose that Sylvia Mosco's law firm had operated at a loss in the month of September. Suppose that instead of net income there was a net loss, and Sylvia also made an additional investment of $600 on September 15. This is how the statement would look if this had happened.

Sylvia Mosco
Barrister and Solicitor
Statement of Owner's Equity
For month ended September 30, 19XX

Sylvia Mosco, Capital, September 1, 19XX		$ 8 1 0 0 00
Additional Investment, September 15, 19XX		6 0 0 00
Total Investment for September		$ 8 7 0 0 00
Less: Net Loss for September	$ 3 5 0 00	
Withdrawals for September	4 0 00	
Decrease in Capital		3 9 0 00
Sylvia Mosco, Capital, September 30, 19XX		$ 8 3 1 0 00

In this chapter we have discussed three financial reports: the income statement, the statement of owner's equity, and the balance sheet.[*] Let us review what elements of the expanded accounting equation go into each report, and the usual order in which the reports are prepared. Figure 1-4 presents a diagram of the accounting equation and the balance sheet. Figure 1-5 summarizes the following three points:

1. The income statement is prepared first; it includes revenues and expenses and shows net income or net loss. This net income or net loss is used to update the next report, the statement of owner's equity.

If this statement of owner's equity is omitted, the information will be included in the owner's equity section of the balance sheet.

2. The statement of owner's equity is prepared second; it includes beginning capital and any additional investments, the net income or net loss shown on the financial statement, withdrawals, and the total, which is the **ending capital**. The ending capital is used on the third report, the balance sheet.

3. The balance sheet is prepared last; it includes the final balances of each of the elements listed in the accounting equation under Assets and Liabilities. The balance in Capital comes from the statement of owner's equity.

* There is a fourth report called the Statement of Changes in Financial Position that will not be covered at this time.

FIGURE 1-4

The Accounting Equation and the Balance Sheet

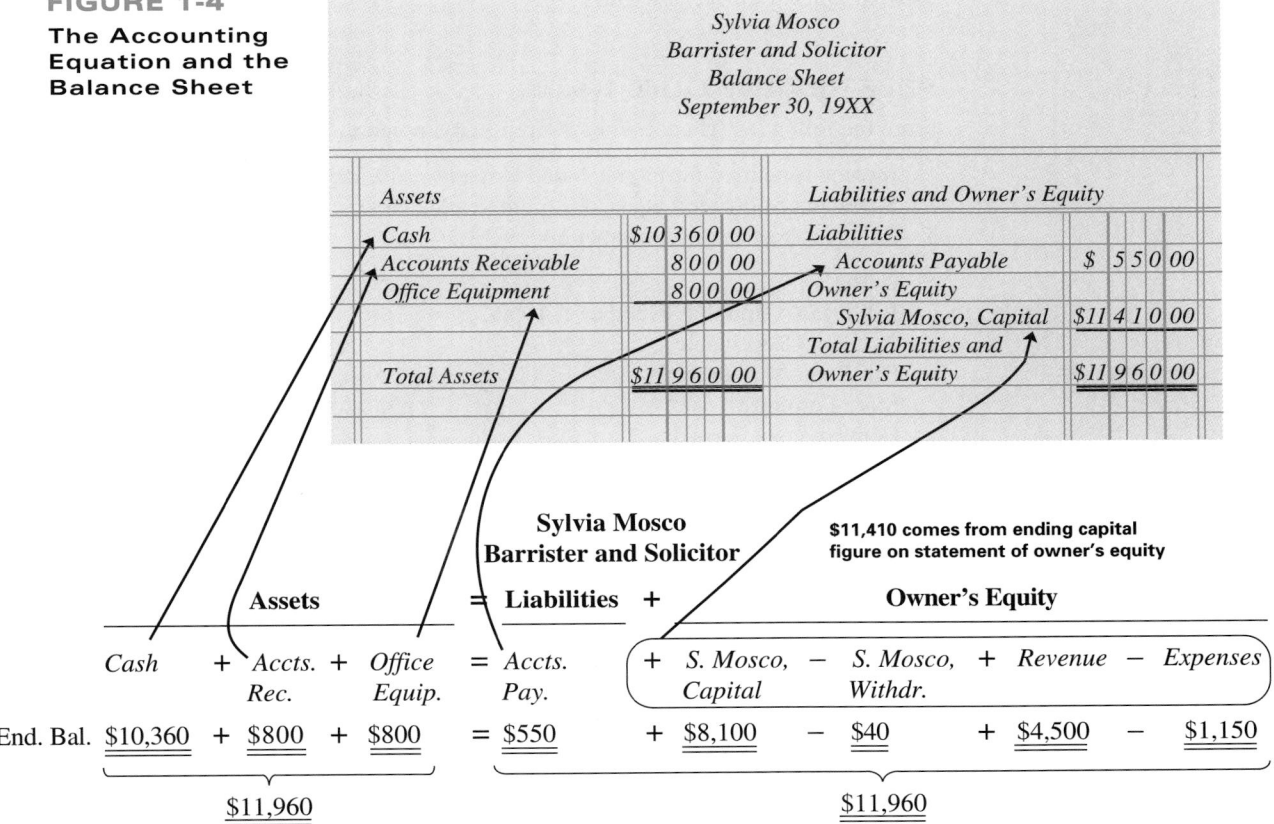

Assets		Liabilities and Owner's Equity	
Cash	$10 3 6 0 00	Liabilities	
Accounts Receivable	8 0 0 00	Accounts Payable	$ 5 5 0 00
Office Equipment	8 0 0 00	Owner's Equity	
		Sylvia Mosco, Capital	$11 4 1 0 00
		Total Liabilities and	
Total Assets	$11 9 6 0 00	Owner's Equity	$11 9 6 0 00

Sylvia Mosco
Barrister and Solicitor
Balance Sheet
September 30, 19XX

Sylvia Mosco Barrister and Solicitor

$11,410 comes from ending capital figure on statement of owner's equity

Assets			=	**Liabilities**	+	**Owner's Equity**				
Cash	+ Accts. Rec.	+ Office Equip.	= Accts. Pay.		+	S. Mosco, Capital	− S. Mosco, Withdr.	+ Revenue	− Expenses
End. Bal. $10,360	+ $800	+ $800	= $550		+	$8,100	− $40	+ $4,500	− $1,150
$11,960						$11,960			

	Income Statement 1	Statement of Owner's Equity 2	Balance Sheet 3
Assets			X
Liabilities			X
Capital† (beg)		X	
Capital (end)		X	X
Withdrawals		X	
Revenues	X		
Expenses	X		

FIGURE 1-5

What Goes On Each Financial Report

† Note additional investments go on the Statement of Owner's Equity

Let us review the objectives of Learning Unit 1-4. At this time you should be able to

1. Define and state the purpose of the income statement, the statement of owner's equity, and the balance sheet. (pp. 16-17)
2. Discuss why the income statement should be prepared first. (p. 18)
3. Compare and contrast these three financial reports. (p. 18)
4. Calculate a new figure for capital on the statement of owner's equity. (p. 17)
5. Prepare an income statement, statement of owner's equity, and balance sheet. (pp. 16-17)
6. Show what happens on a statement of owner's equity if there is a net loss. (p. 18)

Now complete Self-Review Quiz 1-4.

☐ **SELF-REVIEW QUIZ 1-4**

From the following balances for Assure Realty, prepare:

1. Income statement for month ended November 30, 19XX.
2. Statement of owner's equity for month ended November 30, 19XX.
3. Balance sheet as of November 30, 19XX.

Cash	$4,730
Bill Ryan, Capital, November 1, 19XX	5,000
Accounts Receivable	640
Bill Ryan, Withdrawals	100
Store Furniture	1,350
Commissions Earned	1,360
Accounts Payable	900
Rent Expense	200
Advertising Expense	150
Salaries Expense	90

■ **SOLUTION TO SELF-REVIEW QUIZ 1-4**

1.

Assure Realty
Income Statement
For month ended November 30, 19XX

Revenue:		
Commissions Earned		$ 1 3 6 0 00
Operating Expenses:		
Rent Expense	$ 2 0 0 00	
Advertising Expense	1 5 0 00	
Salaries Expense	9 0 00	
Total Operating Expenses		4 4 0 00
Net Income		$ 9 2 0 00

2.

Assure Realty
Statement of Owner's Equity
For month ended November 30, 19XX

Bill Ryan, Capital, November 1, 19XX		$ 5 0 0 0 00
Net Income for November	$ 9 2 0 00	
Less Withdrawals for November	1 0 0 00	
Increase in Capital		8 2 0 00
Bill Ryan, Capital, November 30, 19XX		$ 5 8 2 0 00

3.

Assure Realty
Balance Sheet
November 30, 19XX

Assets		Liabilities and Owner's Equity	
Cash	$ 4 7 3 0 00	Liabilities	
Accounts Receivable	6 4 0 00	Accounts Payable	$ 9 0 0 00
Store Furniture	1 3 5 0 00		
		Owner's Equity	
		Bill Ryan, Capital	5 8 2 0 00
		Total Liabilities and	
Total Assets	$ 6 7 2 0 00	Owner's Equity	$ 6 7 2 0 00

SUMMARY OF KEY POINTS AND KEY TERMS

LEARNING UNIT 1-1

1. The functions of accounting involve analyzing, recording, classifying, summarizing, and reporting financial information.

2. Bookkeeping is the recording part of accounting.

3. The computer is a tool to use in the accounting process.

4. Assets = Liabilities + Owner's Equity is the basic accounting equation that aids in analyzing business transactions.

5. Liabilities represent amounts owed to creditors while capital represents what is invested by the owner.

6. Capital does not mean cash. Capital is the owner's current investment. The owner could have invested equipment that was purchased before the new business was started.

7. In a shift of assets, the composition of assets changes, but the total of assets does not change. For example, if a bill is paid by a customer, the firm increases cash (an asset) but decreases accounts receivable (an asset), so there is no overall increase in assets; total assets remain the same. When you borrow money from the bank, on the other hand, you have an increase in cash (an asset) and an increase in liabilities; overall there is an increase in assets, not just a shift.

Accounts payable: Amounts owed creditors that result from the purchase of goods or services on account; a liability.

Assets: Properties (resources) of value owned by a business (cash, supplies, equipment, land).

Basic accounting equation: Assets = Liabilities + Owner's Equity.

Bookkeeping: The recording function of the accounting process.

Business entity: In *accounting* it is assumed that a business is separate and distinct from the personal assets of the owner. Each unit or entity requires separate accounting functions.

Capital: The owner's investment or equity in the company.

Equities: The interest or financial claim of creditors (liabilities) and owners (owner's equity) who supply the assets to a firm.

Liabilities: Obligations that come due in the future. Liabilities result in increasing the financial rights or claims of creditors to assets.

Owner's equity: Rights or financial claims to the assets of a business (in the accounting equation, assets minus liabilities).

Shift in assets: A shift that occurs when the composition of the assets has changed, but the total of the assets remains the same.

Supplies: One type of asset acquired by a firm; has much shorter life than equipment.

LEARNING UNIT 1-2

1. The balance sheet is a report written as of a particular date. It lists the assets, liabilities, and owner's equity of a business. The heading of the balance sheet answers the questions Who, What, and When (as of a specific date).
2. The balance sheet is a formal report of a financial position.

Balance sheet: A report, as of a particular date, that shows the amount of assets owned by a business as well as the amount of claims (liabilities and owner's equity) against these assets.

LEARNING UNIT 1-3

1. Revenue generates an inward flow of assets. Expenses generate an outward flow of assets or a potential outward flow. Revenue and expenses are subdivisions of owner's equity. Revenue is not an asset.
2. When revenue totals more than expenses, net income is the result; when expenses total more than revenue, net loss is the result.
3. Owner's equity can be subdivided into four elements: capital, withdrawals, revenue, and expenses.
4. Withdrawals decrease owner's equity; revenue increases owner's equity; expenses decrease owner's equity. A withdrawal is *not* a business expense; it is for personal use.

Accounts receivable: An asset that indicates amounts owed by customers.

Expanded accounting equation: Assets = Liabilities + Capital – Withdrawals + Revenue – Expenses.

Expense: A cost incurred in running a business by consuming goods or services in producing revenue; a subdivision of owner's equity. When expenses *increase,* there is a *decrease* in owner's equity.

Net income: When revenue totals more than expenses, the result is net income.

Net loss: When expenses total more than revenue, the result is net loss.

Revenue: An amount earned by performing services for customers or selling goods to customers; can be in the form of cash and/or accounts receivable; a subdivision of owner's equity—as revenue increases, owner's equity increases.

Withdrawals: A subdivision of owner's equity that records money or other assets an owner withdraws from a business for personal use.

LEARNING UNIT 1-4

1. The income statement is a report written for a specific period of time that lists earned revenue and expenses incurred to produce the earned revenue. The net income or net loss will be used in the statement of owner's equity.

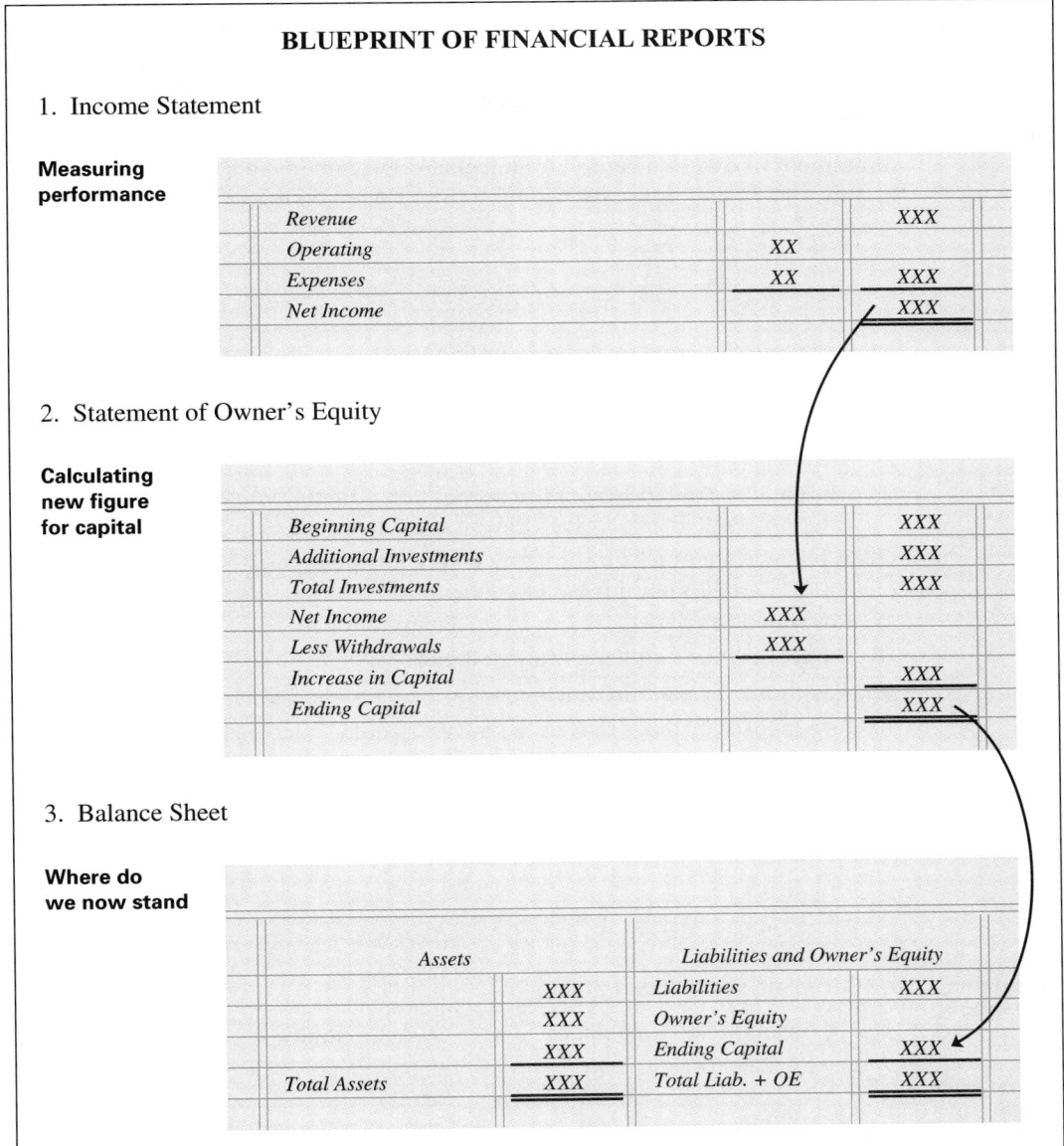

BLUEPRINT OF FINANCIAL REPORTS

1. Income Statement

Measuring performance

Revenue		XXX
Operating	XX	
Expenses	XX	XXX
Net Income		XXX

2. Statement of Owner's Equity

Calculating new figure for capital

Beginning Capital		XXX
Additional Investments		XXX
Total Investments		XXX
Net Income	XXX	
Less Withdrawals	XXX	
Increase in Capital		XXX
Ending Capital		XXX

3. Balance Sheet

Where do we now stand

Assets		Liabilities and Owner's Equity	
	XXX	Liabilities	XXX
	XXX	Owner's Equity	
	XXX	Ending Capital	XXX
Total Assets	XXX	Total Liab. + OE	XXX

2. The statement of owner's equity reveals the causes of a change in capital. This report lists any investments, net income (or net loss), and withdrawals. The ending figure for capital will be used on the balance sheet.

3. The balance sheet uses some of the ending balances of assets and liabilities from the accounting equation and the capital from the statement of owner's equity.

4. The income statement should be prepared first because the information on it as to net income or net loss is used to prepare the statement of owner's equity, which in turn provides information about capital for the balance sheet. One statement builds upon the next, and the process begins with the income statement.

Ending capital: Beginning Capital + Additional Investments + Net Income – Withdrawals = Ending Capital. Or: Beginning Capital + Additional Investments – Net Loss – Withdrawals = Ending Capital.

Income statement: An accounting report that details the performance of a firm (revenue minus expenses) for a specific period of time.

Statement of owner's equity: A financial report that reveals the change in capital. The ending figure for capital is then placed on the balance sheet.

DISCUSSION QUESTIONS

1. What are the functions of accounting?
2. What is the relationship of bookkeeping to accounting?
3. List the three elements of the basic accounting equation.
4. Define capital.
5. The total of the left side of the accounting equation must equal the total of the right side. True or false? Please explain.
6. A balance sheet tells a company where it is going and how well it will perform. True or false? Please explain.
7. Revenue is an asset. True or false? Please explain.
8. What is owner's equity subdivided into?
9. A withdrawal is a business expense. True or false? Please explain.
10. As expenses increase they cause owner's equity to increase. Defend or reject.
11. What does an income statement show?
12. The statement of owner's equity only calculates ending withdrawals. Defend or reject.

EXERCISES

The accounting equation.

1. Complete the following table:

	Assets	=	Liabilities	+	Owner's Equity
A.	$ 9,000	=	?	+	$2,000
B.	?	=	$2,000	+	$8,000
C.	$14,000	=	$4,000	+	?

2. Record the following transactions in the basic accounting equation. Treat each one separately.

   Assets = Liabilities + Owner's Equity

Recording transactions into the accounting equation.

A. Al invests $30,000 in company
B. Bought equipment for cash, $400
C. Bought equipment on account, $600

Preparing a balance sheet.

3. From the following, prepare a balance sheet for Ralph's Cleaners at the end of November 19XX: Cash, $19,000; Cleaning Equipment, $8,000; Accounts Payable, $7,000; A. Ralph, Capital,??

4. Record the following transactions of Roe's Computer Company into the expanding accounting equation. (A running balance may be omitted for simplicity.)

Recording transactions into the expanded accounting equation.

Assets	=	Liabilities	+		Owner's Equity		
Cash + Account + Computer Receivable Equipment	=	Accounts Payable	+	Al Roe, − Capital	Al Roe, Withdrawals	+ Revenue −	Expenses

- A. Al Roe invested $30,000 in the computer company.
- B. Bought computer equipment on account, $8,000.
- C. Al Roe paid personal telephone bill from company chequebook, $100.
- D. Received fees for services rendered, $11,000.
- E. Billed customers for services rendered for month, $40,000.
- F. Paid current rent expense, $2,800.
- G. Paid supplies expense, $1,400.

5. From the following account balances, prepare in proper form (a) an income statement for June, (b) a statement of owner's equity, and (c) a balance sheet for Katz Realty.

Preparing the income statement, statement of owner's equity, and balance sheet.

Cash	$2,000
Accounts Receivable	1,290
Office Equipment	6,700
Accounts Payable	2,000
Abby Katz, Capital, June 1	7,700
Abby Katz, Withdrawals	50
Professional Fees	1,700
Salaries Expense	500
Utilities Expense	360
Rent Expense	500

GROUP A PROBLEMS

1A-1. Jane Rang decided to open Jane's Realty. The following transactions resulted:

The accounting equation.

- A. Jane invested $14,000 cash from her personal bank account into the business.
- B. Bought equipment for cash, $1,500.
- C. Bought additional equipment on account, $900.
- D. Paid $500 cash to partially reduce what was owed from transaction C.

Based on the above information, record these transactions into the basic accounting equation.

1A-2. Ronda French is the accountant for Wells' Advertising Service. From the following information, her task is to construct a balance sheet as of September 30, 19XX, in proper form. Could you help her?

Preparing a balance sheet.

Cash	$16,000
Equipment	12,000
Building	18,000
Accounts Payable	25,000
Melissa Wells, Capital	21,000

Recording transactions in the expanded accounting equation.

1A-3. At the end of November, Alvin Hass decided to open his own typing service. Analyze the following transactions by recording their effects on the expanded accounting equation.

A. Alvin Hass invested $15,000 in his typing service.
B. Bought new office equipment on account, $6,000.
C. Received cash for typing services rendered, $250.
D. Performed typing services on account, $1,800.
E. Paid secretary's salary, $450.
F. Paid office supplies expense for the month, $190.
G. Rent expense for office due but unpaid, $700.
H. Alvin Hass withdrew cash for personal use, $300.

Preparing an income statement, statement of owner's equity, and balance sheet.

1A-4. Amy Peel, owner of Peel's Stenciling Service, has requested that you prepare from the following balances: (a) an income statement for June 19XX, (b) a statement of owner's equity for June, and (c) a balance sheet as of June 30, 19XX.

Cash	$1,115
Accounts Receivable	280
Equipment	290
Accounts Payable	310
Amy Peel, Capital, June 1, 19XX	950
Amy Peel, Withdrawals	200
Stenciling Fees	1,550
Advertising Expense	110
Repair Expense	25
Travel Expense	350
Supplies Expense	190
Rent Expense	250

Comprehensive Problem

1A-5. Bob Fran, a retired army officer, opened Fran's Catering Service. As his accountant, analyze the transactions listed below and present to Mr. Fran the following information, in proper form:

1. The analysis of the transactions by utilizing the expanded accounting equation.
2. A balance sheet showing the position of the firm before opening on November 1, 19XX.
3. An income statement for the month of November.
4. A statement of owner's equity for November.
5. A balance sheet as of November 30, 19XX.

Oct. 25   Bob Fran invested $15,000 in the catering business from his personal savings account.
      27   Bought equipment for cash from Munroe Co., $800.
      28   Bought additional equipment on account from Ryan Co., $700.
      29   Paid $400 to Ryan Co. as partial payment of the October 28 transaction.

(You should now prepare your balance sheet as of October 31, 19XX.)

Nov.   1   Catered a graduation and immediately collected cash, $1,800.
       5   Paid salaries of employees, $650.
       8   Prepared desserts for customers on account, $180.
      10   Received $60 cash as partial payment of November 8 transaction.

15   Paid telephone bill, $39.
17   Fran paid his home electric bill from the company's chequebook, $69.
20   Catered a wedding and received cash, $1,600.
25   Bought additional equipment on account, $150.
28   Rent expense due but unpaid, $500.
30   Paid supplies expense, $280.

GROUP B PROBLEMS

1B-1. Jane Rang began a new business called Jane's Realty. The following transactions resulted: *The accounting equation.*

   A. Jane invested $17,000 cash from her personal bank account into the realty company.
   B. Bought equipment on account, $1,800.
   C. Paid $800 cash to partially reduce what was owed from transaction B.
   D. Purchased additional equipment for cash, $3,000.

Record these transactions into the basic accounting equation.

1B-2. Ronda French has asked you to prepare a balance sheet as of September 30, 19XX, for Wells' Advertising Service. Could you assist Ronda?   *Preparing a balance sheet.*

Melissa Wells, Capital	$19,000
Accounts Payable	70,000
Equipment	41,000
Building	16,000
Cash	32,000

1B-3. Alvin Hass decided to open his own typing service company at the end of November. Analyze the following transactions by recording their effects on the expanded accounting equation.   *Recording transactions in the expanded accounting equation.*

   A. Alvin Hass invested $9,000 in the typing service.
   B. Purchased new office equipment on account, $3,000.
   C. Received cash for typing services rendered, $1,290.
   D. Paid secretary's salary, $310.
   E. Billed customers for typing services rendered, $2,690.
   F. Paid rent expense for the month, $500.
   G. Alvin Hass withdrew cash for personal use, $350.
   H. Advertising expense due but unpaid, $100.

1B-4. Amy Peel, owner of Peel's Stenciling Service, has requested that you prepare from the following balances: (a) an income statement for June 19XX, (b) a statement of owner's equity for June, and (c) a balance sheet as of June 30, 19XX.   *Preparing an income statement, statement of owner's equity, and balance sheet.*

Cash	$2,043
Accounts Receivable	1,140
Equipment	540
Accounts Payable	45
Amy Peel, Capital, June 1, 19XX	3,720
Amy Peel, Withdrawals	360
Stenciling Fees	1,098
Advertising Expense	135

Repair Expense	$ 45
Travel Expense	90
Supplies Expense	270
Rent Expense	240

Comprehensive Problem

1B-5. Bob Fran, a retired army officer, opened Fran's Catering Service. As his accountant, analyze the transactions and present to Mr. Fran the following information, in proper form:

1. The analysis of the transactions by utilizing the expanded accounting equation.
2. A balance sheet showing the financial position of the firm before opening on November 1, 19XX.
3. An income statement for the month of November.
4. A statement of owner's equity for November.
5. A balance sheet as of November 30, 19XX.

Oct.	25	Bob Fran invested $17,500 in the catering business.
	27	Bought equipment on account from Munroe Co., $900.
	28	Bought equipment for cash from Ryan Co., $1,500.
	29	Paid $300 to Munroe Co. as partial payment of the October 27 transaction.

Nov.	1	Catered a business luncheon and immediately collected cash, $2,000.
	5	Paid salaries of employees, $350.
	8	Provided catering services to North West Community College on account, $4,500.
	10	Received from North West Community College $1,000 cash as partial payment of November 8 transaction.
	15	Paid telephone bill, $95.
	17	Fran paid his home mortgage from the company's chequebook, $650.
	20	Provided catering services and received cash, $1,800.
	25	Bought additional equipment on account, $300.
	28	Rent expense due but unpaid, $750.
	30	Paid supplies expense, $600.

GROUP C PROBLEMS

The accounting equation.

1C-1. Fred Payne began a new business called Payne's Realty. The following transactions resulted:

A. Fred invested $24,000 cash from his personal bank account into the realty company.
B. Bought equipment on account, $3,500.
C. Paid $1,200 cash to partially reduce what was owed from transaction B.
D. Purchased additional equipment for cash, $5,000.

Record these transactions into the basic accounting equation.

Preparing a balance sheet.

1C-2. Gabriella Fortunata has asked you to prepare a balance sheet as of April 30, 19XX, for Fortune Graphics Service. Could you assist her?

Gabriella Fortunata, Capital	$37,000
Accounts Payable	21,000
Equipment	18,000

Building	31,000
Cash	9,000

1C-3. Kevin Merkowicz decided to open his own data base consulting service company at the end of October. Analyze the following transactions by recording their effects on the expanded accounting equation.

Recording transactions into the expanded accounting equation.

A. Kevin invested $10,000 in the consulting service.
B. Purchased new office equipment on account, $4,500.
C. Received cash for services rendered, $1,870.
D. Paid secretary's salary, $450.
E. Billed customers for data services rendered, $2,875.
F. Paid rent expense for the month, $600.
G. Kevin withdrew cash for personal use, $750.
H. Advertising expense due but unpaid, $250.
I. Repair to office equipment paid, $168.

1C-4. Jennifer Cheung, owner of Jennifer's Fashion Service, has requested that you prepare from the following balances: (a) an income statement for July 19XX, (b) a statement of owner's equity for July, and (c) a balance sheet as of July 31, 19XX.

Preparing the income statement, statement of owner's equity, and balance sheet.

Cash	$2,746
Accounts Receivable	3,450
Equipment	2,580
Accounts Payable	1,830
Jennifer Cheung, Capital, July 1, 19XX	6,430
Jennifer Cheung, Withdrawals	610
Consulting Fees Earned	3,785
Advertising Expense	435
Repair Expense	135
Travel Expense	1,290
Supplies Expense	284
Rent Expense	340
Office Expenses	175

1C-5. Wilma Starko opened First City Surveying Service. As her accountant, analyze the transactions and present to Ms. Starko the following information, in proper form:

Comprehensive Problem

1. The analysis of the transactions by utilizing the expanded accounting equation.
2. A balance sheet showing the financial position of the firm before opening on May 1, 19XX.
3. An income statement for the month of May.
4. A statement of owner's equity for May.
5. A balance sheet as of May 31, 19XX.

April	25	Wilma invested $14,000 in the surveying business.
	27	Bought equipment on account from Chapman & Co., $1,600.
	28	Bought equipment for cash from Majestic Co., $2,045.
	29	Paid $500 to Chapman & Co. as partial payment of the April 27 transaction.
May	1	Surveyed a new business location and immediately collected cash, $1,800.

5   Paid salaries of employees, $650.
8   Provided surveying services to City Community College on account, $5,800.
10   Received from City Community College $2,000 cash as partial payment of May 8 transaction.
15   Paid telephone bill, $105.
17   Wilma paid her home mortgage from the company's chequebook, $718.
20   Provided surveying services and received cash, $1,475.
25   Bought additional equipment on account from Jensen Bros, $800.
28   Paid rent expense for the month, $680.
30   Paid supplies expense, $330.
31   Advertising bill received but not paid, $245.

PRACTICAL ACCOUNTING APPLICATION #1

You have just been hired to prepare, if possible, an income statement for the year ended December 31, 19XX, for Logan's Window Washing Company. The problem is that Bill Logan kept only the following records (on the back of a piece of cardboard).

Money in:

Window cleaning	$ 11,376
My investment	1,200
Loan from brother in law	4,000

Money out:

Salaries	$ 5,080
Withdrawals	6,200
Supplies expense	1,400

What I owe or they owe me

A. People that worked for me but I still owe salaries to $1,800
B. Owe bank interest of $300
C. Work done but clients still owe me $2,900
D. Advertising bill due but not paid $95

Assume that Logan's Window Washing Company records all revenues when earned and all expenses when incurred.

PRACTICAL ACCOUNTING APPLICATION #2

While Jon Lune was on a business trip, he asked Abby Slowe, the bookkeeper for Lune Co., to try to complete a balance sheet for the year ended December 31, 19XX. Abby, who had been on the job only two months, submitted the following.

Lune Co.
For year ended December 31, 19XX

Building	$44 6 0 0 00	Accounts Payable	$127 6 0 4 00
Land	72 9 3 5 00	Accounts Receivable	104 3 3 7 00
Notes Payable	75 3 2 8 00	Auto	14 2 6 8 00
Cash	10 0 1 6 00	Desks	6 8 2 5 00
J. Lune, Capital	?	Total Equity	$250 0 3 4 00

1. Could you help Abby correct and complete the balance sheet?
2. What recommendations would you make about the bookkeeper? Should she be retained?
3. Suppose that (a) Jon Lune invested an additional $20,000 in cash as well as additional desks with a value of $8,000, and (b) Lune Co. bought an auto for $6,000 that was originally marked $8,000, paying $2,000 down and issuing a note for the balance. Could you prepare an updated balance sheet? Assume that these two transactions occurred on January 4.

ACCOUNTING RECALL
A Cumulative Approach

THIS EXAM REVIEWS CHAPTER 1.

Your *Study Guide and Working Papers* have forms to complete this exam, as well as worked-out solutions. The page references next to each question identify what page to turn back to if you answer the question incorrectly.

PART I Vocabulary Review

Match the terms to the appropriate definition or phrase.

Page

(4)	1. Capital	A. Prepared as of a particular date
(10)	2. Accounts receivable	B. A liability
(5)	3. Supplies	C. For personal use
(10)	4. Expense	D. Provides an inward flow of assets
(7)	5. Balance sheet	E. An asset
(10)	6. Revenue	F. Amount owed by customers
(11)	7. Withdrawals	G. Owner's investment
(16)	8. Income statement	H. A cost of running a business
(6)	9. Accounts payable	I. Broken into four subdivisions
(4)	10. Owner's equity	J. Prepared for specific period of time

PART II True or False (Accounting Theory)

(11) 11. Revenue is an asset.

(10) 12. The four subdivisions of owner's equity are capital, withdrawals, revenue, and expenses.

(11) 13. As expenses increase, owner's equity increases.

(16) 14. Accounts receivable goes on the income statement.

(17) 15. The statement of owner's equity calculates a new figure for capital.

PART III Applications Problem (18)

From the following, prepare the Income Statement, Statement of Owner's Equity, and Balance Sheet for Rowe Company.

Cash	$2,000	Jay Rowe, Withdrawals	$ 100
Accounts receivable	1,000	Fees earned	5,000
Office furniture	1,500	Salaries expense	700
Accounts payable	500	Advertising expense	200
		Rent expense	600
Jay Rowe, Capital June 1, 19XX	600		

C H A P T E R   T W O

DEBITS
AND CREDITS:
Analyzing and Recording
Business Transactions

**IN THIS CHAPTER WE WILL COVER THE
FOLLOWING TOPICS:**

1. SETTING UP AND ORGANIZING A CHART OF ACCOUNTS.
    (P. 34)

2. RECORDING TRANSACTIONS IN T ACCOUNTS ACCORDING
    TO THE RULES OF DEBIT AND CREDIT. (P. 35)

3. PREPARING A TRIAL BALANCE. (P. 48)

4. PREPARING FINANCIAL REPORTS FROM A TRIAL
    BALANCE. (P. 50)

Can you imagine the problems IBM Canada or Northern Telecom would have keeping track of their accounting records if they used the expanded accounting equation? Even though we used it in the last chapter with only a few transactions, the cash column quickly developed into a long list of pluses and minuses. There was no quick system of recording and summarizing the increases and decreases of cash or other items. Imagine how inefficient this accounting equation would become, and how much space it would require, as hundreds and thousands of transactions occurred. Luckily, there is a better way, as we will see in this next section.

Let's look at the problem a little more closely. Each business transaction is recorded in the accounting equation under a specific **account**. There are different accounts for each of the subdivisions of the accounting equation—there are asset accounts, liability accounts, expense accounts, revenue accounts, and so on. What is needed is a way to record the increases and decreases in specific account *categories* and yet keep them together in one place. And that is the subject of Learning Unit 2-1, The T Account.

LEARNING UNIT 2-1

The T Account

What we need is a way to record the increases and decreases of business transactions in specific account categories (such as cash, salaries expense, and rent expense) and yet keep them together in one place. The answer is the **standard account** form (see Figure 2-1). In this system, each account has a separate form. All transactions affecting that account are recorded on the form. All the account forms are then placed in a **ledger**, which may be in the form of a bound or a loose-leaf book.

Account Title							Account No.	
Date	Item	PR	Debit	Date	Item	PR	Credit	

FIGURE 2-1

The Standard Account Form

Each page of the ledger contains one account, along with an assigned account number. Where computers are used, the ledger may be part of a computer printout.

We will talk more about account forms and ledgers in the next chapter. Here, for simplicity's sake, we will use the **T account** form, so called because it looks like the letter T.

Each T account contains three basic parts:

1
Title of Account
―――――――――――――――――――――
2 Left side | Right side 3

All T accounts have this structure. In accounting, the left side of any T account is called the **debit** side.

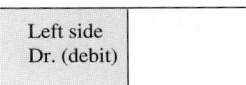

Just as the word *left* has many meanings, the word *debit* for now in accounting means a position, the left side of an account. Don't think of it as good (+) or bad (−).

Amounts entered on the left side of any account are said to be *debited* to an account. The abbreviation for debit (Dr.) is from the Latin *debere*.

The right side of any T account is called the **credit** side.

Amounts entered on the right side of an account are said to be *credited* to an account. Be very sure you do not associate the word *credit* with either good or bad. The abbreviation for credit (Cr.) is from the Latin *credere*.

NOTE: At this point do not associate the definition of debit and credit with the words *increase* or *decrease*. Think of debit or credit as only indicating a *position* (left side or right side) of a T account.

BALANCING AN ACCOUNT

A T account with no heading follows. The heading is omitted to emphasize that, no matter which individual account is being balanced, the procedure used to balance it will be the same.

Dr.		Cr.	
4/2	2,000	4/3	200
4/20	300	4/25	300
	2,300		500
Bal. 1,800			

Notice that on the debit (left) side the numbers add up to $2,300. On the credit (right) side the numbers add up to $500. The numbers 4/2, 4/20, 4/3, and 4/25 are the *dates* when the amounts were debited or credited.

The $2,300 and the $500 written in small type are called **footings**. These figures help us calculate the new balance of $1,800. This is called the ending balance. Notice that the ending balance, $1,800, is placed on the debit or left side, since the balance of the debit side is greater than that of the credit side.

Remember, the ending balance of $1,800 does not tell us anything about increase or decrease. What it does tell us is that we have an ending balance of $1,800 on the debit side.

Debit defined:
1. The left side of any account.
2. A number entered on the left side of any account is said to be debited to an account.

Credit defined:
1. The right side of any account.
2. A number entered on the right side of an account is said to be credited to an account.

Footings aid in balancing an account. The ending balance is the difference between the footings.

Let us review the objectives of Learning Unit 2-1. At this time you should be able to

1. Define ledger. (p. 34)
2. State the purpose of a T account. (p. 34)
3. Identify the three parts of a T account. (p. 34)
4. Define debit. (p. 35)
5. Define credit. (p. 35)
6. Explain footings and calculate the balance of an account. (pp. 35-36)

Now Complete Self-Review Quiz 2-1.

□ SELF-REVIEW QUIZ 2-1

Respond True or False to the following:

1.

Dr.	Cr.
2,000	100
50	50

The balance of the account is $1,900 Cr.
2. A credit always means increase.
3. A debit is the left side of any account.
4. A ledger can be prepared manually or by computer.
5. Footings replace the need for debits and credits.

▦ *SOLUTIONS TO SELF-REVIEW QUIZ 2-1*

1. False   2. False   3. True   4. True   5. False

LEARNING UNIT 2-2

Recording Business Transactions: Debit and Credits

Do you drive your car on the left-hand side of the road? Do you drive through red lights? Can you get a queen in checkers? In a baseball game does a runner rounding first base skip second base and run over the pitcher's mound to get to third? No—most of us don't do such things because we follow the rules. Usually we learn the rules first and reflect on the reasons for them afterward. Think back on how you first learned to play the game of Monopoly.

Instead of first trying to understand all the rules of debit and credit and how they were developed in accounting, it will be easier to "play the game" first and then reflect on the whys.

Have patience. Learning the rules of debit and credit is like learning to play any game—the more you play, the easier it will become. Figure 2-2 shows the rules for

Account Category	Increase	Decrease	Normal Balance
Assets	Debit	Credit	Debit
Liabilities	Credit	Debit	Credit
Owner's Equity			
Capital	Credit	Debit	Credit
Withdrawals	Debit	Credit	Debit
Revenue	Credit	Debit	Credit
Expenses	Debit	Credit	Debit

FIGURE 2-2

Rules of Debit and Credit

the side on which you enter an increase or a decrease for each of the separate accounts in the accounting equation. For example, an increase is entered on the debit side in the asset account, but on the credit side for a liability account.

A **normal balance of an account** is the side that increases by the rules of debit and credit. For example, the normal balance of cash is a debit balance, because an asset is increased by a debit. In Chapter 3 we will discuss normal balance further.

It might be easier to visualize these rules of debit and credit if we show them in the T account form, using + to show increase and – to show decrease.

Assets	=	Liabilities	+	Owner's Equity								
Dr. | Cr.		Dr. | Cr.	+	**Capital** –		**Withdrawals** +		**Revenue** –		**Expenses**	
+ | –		– | +		Dr. | Cr.		Dr. | Cr.		Dr. | Cr.		Dr. | Cr.	
				– | +		+ | –		– | +		+ | –	

Insight to the rules: First of all, note that the rules for assets work in the opposite direction to those for liabilities. As for owner's equity, the rules for withdrawals and expenses, which decrease owner's equity, work in the opposite direction to the rules for capital and revenue, which increase owner's equity.

Second, it is important to remember that any amount(s) entered on the debit side of a T account or accounts must also be entered on the credit side of another T account or accounts. This will make certain that the total amount added to the debit side will equal the total amount added to the credit side, thereby keeping the accounting equation in balance.

Our job now is to analyze Sylvia Mosco's business transactions—the transactions we looked at in Chapter 1—using a system of accounts guided by the rules of debits and credits that will summarize increases and decreases of individual accounts in the ledger. The goal is to prepare an income statement, statement of owner's equity, and balance sheet for Sylvia Mosco. Sound familiar? If this system works, the rules of debits and credits and the use of accounts will provide us with the same answers as in Chapter 1, but with greater ease and accuracy.

The accountant for Mosco developed what is called a **chart of accounts** (see Figure 2-3). The chart of accounts is a numbering system for all Mosco's accounts. It allows Mosco to locate and identify accounts quickly; for example, 100s are assets, 200s are liabilities, and so on. As companies grow or as changes occur, the chart may be expanded as needed.

The rules of debit and credit are arbitrary. The rules will aid us in recording information in the ledger.

The chart of accounts aids in locating and identifying accounts quickly.

Large companies may have up to four digits assigned to each title.

BALANCE SHEET ACCOUNTS

1. Assets

111   Cash
112   Accounts Receivable
121   Office Equipment

2. Liabilities

211   Accounts Payable

3. Owner's Equity

311   Sylvia Mosco, Capital
312   Sylvia Mosco, Withdrawals

INCOME STATEMENT ACCOUNTS

4. Revenue

411   Legal Fees

5. Expenses

511   Salaries Expense
512   Rent Expense
513   Advertising Expense

FIGURE 2-3

Chart of Accounts for Sylvia Mosco, Barrister and Solicitor

In the next section we will present a handy chart to use for analyzing these transactions more easily.

THE TRANSACTION ANALYSIS: FIVE STEPS

There are five steps to analyzing each business transaction of Sylvia Mosco's law practice. We will use a device called a *transaction analysis chart* to record these five steps. (Please keep in mind that the transaction analysis chart is a *teaching device,* not part of any formal accounting system.) The five steps include determining the following:

Steps to analyze and record transactions. *Note*: Steps 1 and 2 will come from the chart of accounts.

1. Which accounts are affected? Example: cash, accounts payable, rent expense. A transaction always has at least two accounts affected, but may have more.
2. Which categories do the accounts belong to? You have six choices: assets, liabilities, capital, withdrawals, revenue, and expenses. Example: cash is an asset.
3. Are the accounts increasing or decreasing? Example: If you receive cash, that account is increasing.
4. What is the rule? Go to rule chart. (p. 37)

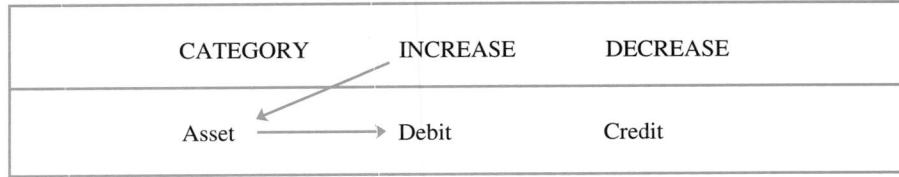

CATEGORY	INCREASE	DECREASE
Asset ⟶	Debit	Credit

5. Where do the amounts belong? Place amounts into accounts (in our case, T accounts) either on the left or right side depending on the rules from the rule chart.

Note again that every transaction affects at least two T accounts, and that the total amount added to the debit side(s) must equal the total amount added to the credit side(s) of the T accounts of each transaction.

ANALYSIS OF TRANSACTIONS OF SYLVIA MOSCO'S LAW PRACTICE

> (A) *August 28: Sylvia Mosco invests $8,000 cash and $100 of office equipment in the business.*

1	2	3*	4	5
Accounts Affected	**Category**	↓ ↑	**Rules**	**Appearance of T Accounts**
Cash	**Asset**	↑	**Dr.**	**Cash 111** (A) 8,000
Office Equipment	**Asset**	↑	**Dr.**	**Office Equipment 121** (A) 100
Sylvia Mosco, Capital	**Capital**	↑	**Cr.**	**Sylvia Mosco, Capital 311** 8,100 (A)

* *Note*: ↑ **means increase**, ↓ **means decrease**.

The transaction analysis chart is a teaching technique to aid you in learning how to record debits and credits.

Let us go through the transaction analysis for this transaction step by step:

1. Which accounts are affected? The law firm receives cash and office equipment. Are other accounts involved in this transaction? The law firm receives cash and office equipment through Sylvia Mosco's investment, so a third account is involved— Sylvia Mosco, Capital. Note these titles come from the chart of accounts.
2. Which categories do these accounts belong to? (The categories are assets, liabilities, capital, withdrawals, revenue, or expenses.) Cash and office equipment are assets and Sylvia Mosco, Capital, is capital.
3. Are the accounts increasing or decreasing? The cash and office equipment, both assets, are increasing in the business. The rights or claims of Sylvia Mosco, Capital, are also increasing, since she invested money and office equipment in the business.
4. What do the rules say? According to the rules of debit and credit, an increase in assets (cash and office equipment) is a debit. An increase in capital is a credit. Note that the total dollar amount of debits will equal the total dollar amount of credits when T accounts are updated in column 5.

Note in column 3 of the chart: It doesn't matter if both arrows go up, as long as the sum of the debits equals the sum of the credits in the T accounts in column 5.

5. Where do the amounts belong? Place the amounts into the T accounts. Enter the amount for cash and office equipment on the debit side and the amount for Sylvia Mosco, Capital, on the credit side.

If a transaction involves more than one credit or more than one debit we call it a **compound entry**. This first transaction of Sylvia Mosco's law firm is a compound entry; it involves a debit of $8,000 to Cash and a debit of $100 to Office Equipment (as well as a credit of $8,100 to Sylvia Mosco, Capital).

Let us now emphasize a major point: *Do not try to debit or credit an account until you have gone through the first three steps of the transaction analysis:*

The rules of debit and credit only tell us on which side to place information. Whether the debit or credit represents increases or decreases depends on the account category—assets, liabilities, capital, etc. Think of a business transaction as an exchange—you get something and you give or part with something.

1. Which accounts are affected (from the chart of accounts)?
2. Which categories do the accounts belong to (Assets, Liabilities, Capital, Withdrawals, Revenue, Expenses)?
3. Are the accounts increasing or decreasing?

Having completed these steps, go to the rules of debit and credit before updating the individual accounts.

As we continue, the explanations will be brief, but do not forget to apply the five steps in analyzing and recording each business transaction.

(B) August 29: Law practice bought office equipment for cash, $300.

1	2	3	4	5
Accounts Affected	Category	↑ ↓	Rules	T Account Update
Office Equipment	Asset	↑	Dr.	**Office Equipment 121**
				(A) 100 / (B) 300
Cash	Asset	↓	Cr.	**Cash 111**
				(A) 8,000 | 300 (B)

Analysis of Transaction B

1. What did the law firm receive? Office equipment. How did the firm get it? It paid cash. These are the accounts involved in the transaction.
2. Which categories do the accounts belong to? Office Equipment is an asset. Cash is an asset.
3. Are the accounts increasing or decreasing? The asset Office Equipment is increasing. The asset Cash is decreasing—it is being reduced in order to buy the office equipment.
4. What is the rule? An increase in the asset Office Equipment is a debit; a decrease in the asset Cash is a credit.

5. Where do the amounts belong? Place the amounts into the T accounts. Enter the amount for office equipment on the debit side and the amount for cash on the credit side.

(C) August 30: Bought more office equipment on account, $400.

1	2	3	4	5
Accounts Affected	**Category**	**↑ ↓**	**Rules**	**T Account Update**
Office Equipment	**Asset**	↑	**Dr.**	**Office Equipment 121** (A) 100 (B) 300 (C) 400
Accounts Payable	**Liability**	↑	**Cr.**	**Accounts Payable 211** 400 (C)

Analysis of Transaction C

1. The law firm receives office equipment by promising to pay in the future. An obligation or liability, Accounts Payable, is created.
2. Office Equipment is an asset. Accounts Payable is a liability.
3. The asset Office Equipment is increasing; the liability Accounts Payable is increasing because the law firm is increasing what it owes.
4. An increase in the asset Office Equipment is a debit. An increase in the liability Accounts Payable is a credit.
5. Enter the amount for office equipment on the debit side and the amount for the accounts payable on the credit side.

(D) September 1-30: Provided legal services for cash, $3,000.

1	2	3	4	5
Accounts Affected	**Category**	**↑ ↓**	**Rules**	**T Account Update**
Cash	**Asset**	↑	**Dr.**	**Cash 111** (A) 8,000 300 (B) (D) 3,000
Legal Fees	**Revenue**	↑	**Cr.**	**Legal Fees 411** 3,000 (D)

Analysis of Transaction D

1. The firm has earned revenue from legal services and receives $3,000 in cash.
2. Cash is an asset. Legal Fees are revenue.
3. Cash, an asset, is increasing. Legal Fees, or revenue, are also increasing.
4. An increase in Cash, an asset, is debited. An increase in Legal Fees, or revenue, is credited.

(E) September 1-30: Provided legal services on account, $1,500.

1	2	3	4	5
Accounts Affected	**Category**	↑ ↓	**Rules**	**T Account Update**
Accounts Receivable	**Asset**	↑	**Dr.**	**Accounts Receivable 112** **(E) 1,500**
Legal Fees	**Revenue**	↑	**Cr.**	**Legal Fees 411** **3,000 (D)** **1,500 (E)**

Analysis of Transaction E

1. The law practice has earned revenue but has not yet received payment (cash). The amounts owed by these clients are called accounts receivable. Revenue is earned at the time the legal services are provided, whether payment is received then or will be received sometime in the future.
2. Accounts Receivable is an asset. Legal Fees are revenue.
3. Accounts Receivable is increasing because the law practice has increased the amount owed to it for legal fees that have been earned but not paid. Legal Fees or revenue are increasing.
4. An increase in the asset Accounts Receivable is a debit. An increase in revenue is a credit.

(F) September 1-30: Received $700 cash from clients for services rendered previously on account.

1	2	3	4	5
Accounts Affected	**Category**	↓ ↑	**Rules**	**T Account Update**
Cash	**Asset**	↑	**Dr.**	**Cash 111**
				(A) 8,000 300 (B) (D) 3,000 (F) 700
Accounts Receivable	**Asset**	↓	**Cr.**	**Accounts Receivable 112**
				(E) 1,500 700 (F)

Analysis of Transaction F

1. The law firm collects $700 in cash from previous revenue earned. Since the revenue is recorded at the time it is earned, and not when the payment is made, in this transaction we are concerned only with the payment, which affects the Cash and Accounts Receivable accounts.
2. Cash is an asset. Accounts Receivable is an asset.
3. Since clients are paying what is owed, cash (asset) is increasing and the amount owed (accounts receivable) is decreasing (the total amount owed by clients to Mosco is going down). This transaction results in a shift in assets, more cash for less accounts receivable.
4. An increase in Cash, an asset, is a debit. A decrease in Accounts Receivable, an asset, is a credit.

(G) September 1-30: Paid salaries expense, $800.

1	2	3	4	5
Accounts Affected	**Category**	↑ ↓	**Rules**	**T Account Update**
Salaries Expense	**Expense**	↑	**Dr.**	**Salaries Expense 511**
				(G) 800
Cash	**Asset**	↓	**Cr.**	**Cash 111**
				(A) 8,000 300 (B) (D) 3,000 800 (G) (F) 700

Analysis of Transaction G

1. The law firm pays $800 worth of salaries expense by cash.
2. Salaries Expense is an expense. Cash is an asset.
3. The salaries expense of the law firm is increasing, which results in a decrease in cash.
4. An increase in Salaries Expense, an expense, is a debit. A decrease in Cash, an asset, is a credit.

(H) September 1-30: Paid rent expense, $200.

1	2	3	4	5
Accounts Affected	**Category**	↑ ↓	**Rules**	**T Account Update**
Rent Expense	**Expense**	↑	**Dr.**	**Rent Expense 512** **(H) 200**
Cash	**Asset**	↓	**Cr.**	**Cash 111** (A) 8,000 300 (B) (D) 3,000 800 (G) (F) 700 200 (H)

Analysis of Transaction H

1. The law firm rent expenses are paid in cash.
2. Rent is an expense. Cash is an asset.
3. The rent expense increases the expenses, and the payment for the rent expense decreases the cash.
4. An increase in Rent Expense, an expense, is a debit. A decrease in Cash, an asset, is a credit.

(I) September 1-30: Received a bill for Advertising Expense
(to be paid next month), $150.

1	2	3	4	5
Accounts Affected	Category	↑ ↓	Rules	T Account Update
Advertising Expense	Expense	↑	Dr.	**Advertising Expense 513** (I) 150
Accounts Payable	Liability	↑	Cr.	**Accounts Payable 211** 400 (C) 150 (I)

Analysis of Transaction I

1. The advertising bill has come in and payment is due but has not yet been made. Therefore the accounts involved here are Advertising Expense and Accounts Payable; the expense has created a liability.
2. Advertising Expense is an expense. Accounts Payable is a liability.
3. Both the expense and the liability are increasing.
4. An increase in an expense is a debit. An increase in a liability is a credit.

> (J) Mosco withdrew cash for personal use, $40.

1	2	3	4	5
Accounts Affected	Category	↑ ↓	Rules	T Account Update
Sylvia Mosco, Withdrawals	Withdrawals	↑	Dr.	**Sylvia Mosco, Withdrawals 312** (J) 40
Cash	Asset	↓	Cr.	**Cash 111** (A) 8,000 300 (B) (D) 3,000 800 (G) (F) 700 200 (H) 40 (J)

Analysis of Transaction J

Withdrawals are always increased by debits.

1. Mosco withdraws cash from business for *personal* use. This withdrawal is not a business expense.
2. This transaction affects Withdrawal and Cash accounts.
3. Mosco has increased what she has withdrawn from the business for personal use. The business cash has been decreased.
4. An increase in withdrawals is a debit. A decrease in cash is a credit. (*Remember*: Withdrawals go on the statement of owner's equity; expenses go on the income statement.)

Let us review the objectives of Learning Unit 2-2. At this time you should be able to

1. State the rules of debit and credit. (p. 37)
2. Explain the difference between an expense and a withdrawal. (p. 37)
3. List the five steps of a transaction analysis. (p. 38-39)
4. Show how to fill out a transaction analysis chart. (p. 39)

Now complete Self-Review Quiz 2-2.

☐ SELF-REVIEW QUIZ 2-2

Revon Company uses the following accounts from its chart of accounts:
Cash (111), Accounts Receivable (112), Equipment (121), Accounts Payable (211), Ann Roe, Capital (311), Ann Roe, Withdrawals (312), Professional Fees (411), Utilities Expense (511), and Salaries Expense (512).
    Record the following transactions into transaction analysis charts.

A. Ann Roe invested in the business $400 cash and equipment worth $500 from her personal assets.
B. Billed clients for services rendered, $8,000.
C. Utilities bill due but unpaid, $90.
D. Ann Roe withdrew cash for personal use, $50.
E. Paid salaries expense, $100.

■ *SOLUTION TO SELF-REVIEW QUIZ 2-2*

A.

1 Accounts Affected	2 Category	3 ↑ ↓	4 Rules	5 T Account Update
Cash	Asset	↑	Dr.	Cash 111 (A) 400
Equipment	Asset	↑	Dr.	Equipment 121 (A) 500
Ann Roe, Capital	Capital	↑	Cr.	Ann Roe, Capital 311 (A) 900

B.

1 Accounts Affected	2 Category	3 ↑ ↓	4 Rules	5 T Account Update
Accounts Receivable	Asset	↑	Dr.	Acc. Rec. 112
				(B) 8,000
Professional Fees	Revenue	↑	Cr.	Prof. Fees 411
				(B) 8,000

C.

1 Accounts Affected	2 Category	3 ↑ ↓	4 Rules	5 T Account Update
Utilities Expense	Expense	↑	Dr.	Utilities Exp. 511
				(C) 90
Accounts Payable	Liability	↑	Cr.	Acct. Pay. 211
				(C) 90

D.

1 Accounts Affected	2 Category	3 ↑ ↓	4 Rules	5 T Account Update
Ann Roe, Withdrawals	Withdrawals	↑	Dr.	Ann Roe, Withd. 312
				(D) 50
Cash	Asset	↓	Cr.	Cash 111
				(A) 400 (D) 50

E.

1 Accounts Affected	2 Category	3 ↑ ↓	4 Rules	5 T Account Update
Salaries Expense	Expense	↑	Dr.	Salaries Expense 512
				(E) 100
Cash	Asset	↓	Cr.	Cash 111
				(A) 400 (D) 50
				(E) 100

LEARNING UNIT 2-3

The Trial Balance and Preparation of Financial Reports

Let us now look at all the transactions we have discussed, arranged by T accounts and recorded using the rules of debit and credit.

Cash 111		Accounts Receivable 112		Office Equipment 121	
(A) 8,000	300 (B)	(E) 1,500	700 (F)	(A) 100	
(D) 3,000	800 (G)	800		(B) 300	
(F) 700	200 (H)			(C) 400	
11,700	40 (J)			800	
10,360	1,340				

Accounts Payable 211		Sylvia Mosco, Capital 311		Sylvia Mosco, Withdrawals 312	
	400 (C)		8,100 (A)	(J) 40	
	150 (I)				
	550				

Legal Fees 411		Salaries Expense 511		Rent Expense 512	
	3,000 (D)	(G) 800		(H) 200	
	1,500 (E)				
	4,500				

Advertising Expense 513	
(I) 150	

Notice how this grouping of accounts gives a much better organization than the expanded accounting equation. As previously mentioned, and as shown in each of the transactions analyzed in the past unit, the total of all the debits must be equal to the total of all the credits (columns 4 and 5 of the transaction analysis chart). For example, when Mosco invested $8,100 in the business, the debits ($8,000 to Cash and $100 to Office Equipment) were equal to the credit ($8,100 to Sylvia Mosco, Capital). This double-entry analysis of transactions, where two or more accounts are affected and the total of debits and credits is equal, is called **double-entry bookkeeping**. This double-entry system helps in checking the recording of business transactions.

Double-entry book-keeping system: the total of all debits is equal to the total of all credits.

When all the transactions are recorded in the accounts, the total of all the debits should be equal to the total of all the credits.

THE TRIAL BALANCE

As discussed earlier, *footings* are used to obtain the balance of each side of each T account (unless there is only one entry in the account, and then there is no need for a footing). Then the *ending balance* is found. For example, in the Cash account, the footing for the debit side is $11,700 and the footing for the credit side is $1,340. Since the debit side is larger, we subtract $1,340 from $11,700 to arrive at an ending balance of $10,360. When this has been done for all the accounts, we should be able to show that the total of all debits equals the total of all credits. To do this we prepare a **trial balance**, which is a listing of all the accounts in the ledger with their ending balances.

As mentioned earlier, the ending balance of cash, $10,360, is a normal balance because it is on the side that increases the asset account.

LORI LIEVRE:
FULL-CHARGE BOOKKEEPER

Lori Lievre started out to be a secretary, but, she says, "I really didn't like the work at all. When I was working for a major supermarket chain, I was put in charge of the books. Even though I didn't know much about bookkeeping, I learned that I loved to work with numbers. But I was very slow because I didn't have the background. So I decided to get a background in the field."

At her Community College, Lori found a 1-year certificate program in accounting that had evening classes. She studied bookkeeping, college accounting, business writing, economics, and other subjects. "The certificate program helped me enormously," she says. "It gave me the theoretical background I needed. I was working by intuition before. The courses taught me to think things through and follow correct procedures. They also built up my confidence. I know what I'm talking about, and I use the right terminology."

Now working as a full-charge bookkeeper for a paper-converting company, Lori goes through all journals, including cash receipts, disbursements, sales, receivables, payables, and expenses. "I love this job," Lori says. "I got it through an employment agency, and one of the best things about it is that I get to do so many different things."

What advice does Lori offer to people starting out in a college accounting course? "If you're working in bookkeeping already, a course like this can be a lifesaver. It fills in the gaps in your knowledge. If you don't have a job in the field yet, the course gives you a combination of practical skills and a strong theoretical foundation. It gives you a sense of what you will be doing in the future. It really does prepare you for the workplace."

A trial balance of Sylvia Mosco's accounts is shown in Figure 2-4. Keep in mind that the trial balance is *not* a formal report. It is used as an aid in preparing the financial statement and in proving the accuracy of the recording of transactions into accounts. The trial balance lists all the accounts with their balances in the same order as they appear in the chart of accounts. Keep in mind that the figure for capital might

Only the ending balance of each account is listed.

Sylvia Mosco
Barrister and Solicitor
Trial Balance
September 30, 19XX

	Dr.	Cr.
Cash	1 0 3 6 0 00	
Accounts Receivable	8 0 0 00	
Office Equipment	8 0 0 00	
Accounts Payable		5 5 0 00
Sylvia Mosco, Capital		8 1 0 0 00
Sylvia Mosco, Withdrawals	4 0 00	
Legal Fees		4 5 0 0 00
Salaries Expense	8 0 0 00	
Rent Expense	2 0 0 00	
Advertising Expense	1 5 0 00	
Totals	1 3 1 5 0 00	1 3 1 5 0 00

FIGURE 2-4

A Trial Balance

not be the beginning figure if any additional investment has taken place during the period. You can tell this by looking at the capital account in the ledger.

A more detailed discussion of the trial balance will be provided in the next chapter. For now, notice the heading, how the accounts are listed, the debits in the left column, the credits in the right, and the fact that the total of debits is equal to the total of credits. Note also that since this is not a formal report, there is no need to use dollar signs; however, the single and double lines under subtotals and final totals are still used for clarity.

From the trial balance we can now go on to prepare the financial reports.

PREPARING FINANCIAL REPORTS

In Chapter 1 we prepared financial reports using the expanded accounting equation. Now look at the diagram in Figure 2-5 carefully. It shows how financial reports can be prepared from a trial balance. A key point to remember is that *there are no debit or credit columns on financial reports.* The information is entered in the ledger by debits and credits to eventually supply the amounts (ending balances) needed to prepare financial reports, but the financial reports themselves do not use debit or credit columns. The left columns are used only to subtotal numbers.

Let us review the objectives of learning Unit 2-3. At this point you should be able to

1. Explain double-entry bookkeeping. (p. 48)
2. Explain the role of footings. (p. 48)
3. Prepare a trial balance from a set of accounts. (p. 49)
4. Prepare financial reports from a trial balance. (p. 50)

Now complete Self-Review Quiz 2-3.

☐ **SELF-REVIEW QUIZ 2-3**

As the bookkeeper of Mel's Hair Salon you are to prepare from the following accounts on June 30, 19XX (1) a trial balance as of June 30, (2) an income statement for June, (3) a statement of owner's equity for the month ended June 30, and (4) a balance sheet as of June 30, 19XX.

Cash 111		Accounts Payable 211		Salon Fees 411
4,000	300	300	700	3,000
2,000	100			1,000
1,000	1,200			
300	1,300			
	2,600			

Accounts Receivable 121 — 1,000 | 300

Mel Harris, Capital 311 — | 4,000*

Rent Expense 511 — 1,200 |

Salon Equipment 131 — 700 |

Mel Harris, Withdrawals 321 — 100 |

Salon Supplies Expense 521 — 1,300 |

Salon Expense 531 — 2,600 |

* No additional investment.

FIGURE 2-5

Steps in Preparing Financial Reports from a Trial Balance

Sylvia Mosco
Barrister and Solicitor
Trial Balance
September 30, 19XX

	Dr.	Cr.
Cash	10 3 6 0 00	
Accounts Receivable	8 0 0 00	
Office Equipment	8 0 0 00	
Accounts Payable		5 5 0 00
Sylvia Mosco, Capital		8 1 0 0 00
Sylvia Mosco, Withdrawals	4 0 00	
Legal Fees		4 5 0 0 00
Salaries Expense	8 0 0 00	
Rent Expense	2 0 0 00	
Advertising Expense	1 5 0 00	
Totals	$13 1 5 0 00	$13 1 5 0 00

Assets and Liabilities

Capital Withdrawals

Revenue and Expenses

Sylvia Mosco
Barrister and Solicitor
Balance Sheet
September 30, 19XX

Assets			Liabilities and Owner's Equity		
Cash		$10 3 6 0 00	Liabilities		
Accounts Receivable	8 0 0 00		Accounts Payable		$ 5 5 0 00
Office Equipment	8 0 0 00		Owner's Equity		
			Sylvia Mosco, Capital		11 4 1 0 00
Total Assets		$11 9 6 0 00	Total Liab. and Owner's Eq.		$11 9 6 0 00

Sylvia Mosco
Barrister and Solicitor
Statement of Owner's Equity
For month ended September 30, 19XX

Sylvia Mosco, Capital September 1, 19XX		$3 3 5 0 00
Net Income for September	$8 1 0 0 00	
Less Withdrawals for September	4 0 00	
Increase in Capital		3 3 1 0 00
Sylvia Mosco, Capital September 30, 19XX		$11 4 1 0 00

Sylvia Mosco
Barrister and Solicitor
Income Statement
For month ended September 30, 19XX

Revenue:		
Legal Fees		$4 5 0 0 00
Operating Expenses:		
Salaries Expense	$8 0 0 00	
Rent Expense	2 0 0 00	
Advertising Expense	1 5 0 00	
Total Operating Expenses		1 1 5 0 00
Net income		$3 3 5 0 00

■ *SOLUTION TO SELF-REVIEW QUIZ 2-3*

1.

Mel's Hair Salon
Trial Balance
June 30, 19XX

	Dr.	Cr.
Cash	$ 1 800 00	
Accounts Receivable	700 00	
Salon Equipment	700 00	
Accounts Payable		400 00
Mel Harris, Capital		4 000 00
Mel Harris, Withdrawals	100 00	
Salon Fees		4 000 00
Rent Expense	1 200 00	
Salon Supplies Expense	1 300 00	
Salaries Expense	2 600 00	
Totals	8 400 00	8 400 00

2.

Mel's Hair Salon
Income Statement
For month ended June 30, 19XX

Revenue:		
Salon Fees		$ 4 000 00
Operating Expenses:		
Rent Expense	$ 1 200 00	
Salon Supplies Expense	1 300 00	
Salaries Expense	2 600 00	
Total Operating Expenses		5 100 00
Net Loss		$ 1 100 00

3.

Mel's Hair Salon
Statement of Owner's Equity
For month ended June 30, 19XX

Mel Harris, Capital		
June 1, 19XX		$ 4 000 00
Less: Net Loss for June	$ 1 100 00	
Withdrawals for June	100 00	
Decrease in Capital		1 200 00
Mel Harris, Capital,		
June 30, 19XX		$ 2 800 00

4.

Mel's Hair Salon
Balance Sheet
June 30, 19XX

Assets			Liabilities and Owner's Equity	
Cash		$1 800 00	Liabilities	
Accounts Receivable		700 00	Accounts Payable	$ 400 00
Salon Equipment		700 00		
			Owner's Equity	
			Mel Harris, Capital	2 800 00
			Total Liabilities and	
Total Assets		$3 200 00	Owner's Equity	$3 200 00

SUMMARY OF KEY POINTS AND KEY TERMS

LEARNING UNIT 2-1

1. A T account is a simplified version of a standard account.
2. A ledger is a group of accounts.
3. A debit is the left position (side) of an account and a credit is the right position (side) of an account.
4. A footing is the total of one side of an account; the ending balance is the difference between the footings.

Account: An accounting device used in bookkeeping to record increases and decreases of business transactions relating to individual assets, liabilities, capital, withdrawals, revenue, expenses, and so on.

Credit: The right side of any account. A number entered on the right side of any account is said to be credited to an account.

Debit: The left side of any account. A number entered on the left side of any account is said to be debited to an account.

Ending balance: The difference between footings in a T account.

Footings: The totals of each side of a T account.

Ledger: A group of accounts that records data from business transactions.

Standard account: A formal account that includes columns for date, explanation, posting reference, debit and credit.

T account: A skeleton version of a standard account, used for demonstration purposes.

LEARNING UNIT 2-2

1. A chart of accounts lists the account titles and their numbers for a company.
2. The transaction analysis chart is a teaching device, not to be confused with standard accounting procedures.
3. A compound entry is a transaction involving more than one debit or credit.

Chart of accounts: A numbering system of accounts that lists the account titles and account numbers to be used by a company.

Compound entry: A transaction involving more than one debit or credit.

Normal balance of an account: The side of an account that increases by the rules of debit and credit.

LEARNING UNIT 2-3

1. In double-entry bookkeeping, the recording of each business transaction affects two or more accounts, and the total of debits equals the total of credits.
2. A trial balance is a list of the ending balances of all accounts, listed in the same order as on the chart of accounts.
3. Any additional investments during the period result in capital on the trial balance not being the beginning figure for capital.
4. There are *no* debit or credit columns on the three financial reports.

BLUEPRINT FOR PREPARING FINANCIAL REPORTS FROM A TRIAL BALANCE

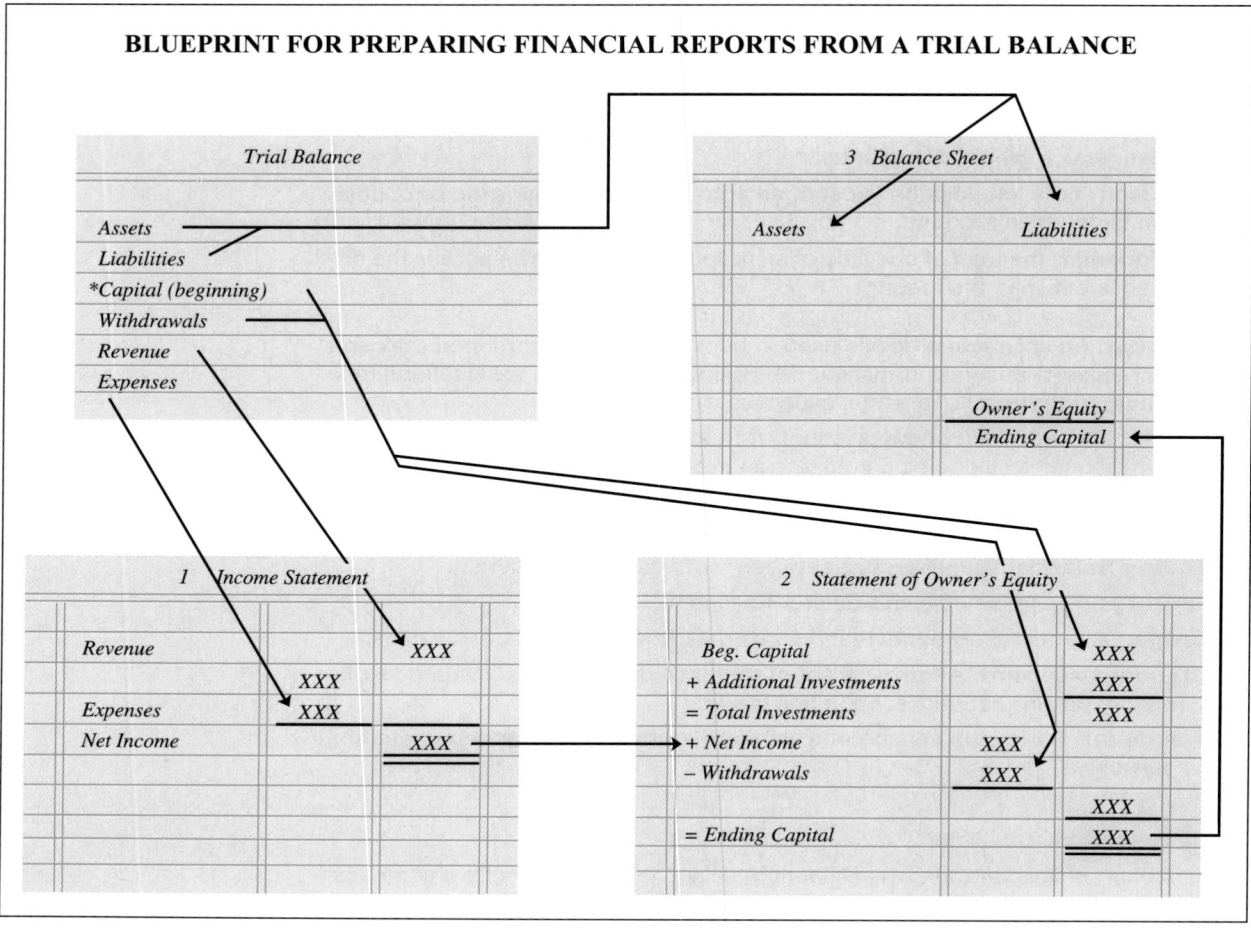

Double-entry bookkeeping: An accounting system in which the recording of each transaction affects two or more accounts, and the total of the debits is equal to the total of the credits.

Trial balance: A list of the ending balances of all the accounts in a ledger. The total of the debits should equal the total of the credits.

DISCUSSION QUESTIONS

1. Define a ledger.
2. Why is the left side of an account called a debit?
3. Footings are used in balancing all accounts. True or false? Please explain.
4. What is the end product of the accounting process?
5. What do we mean when we say that a transaction analysis chart is a teaching device?
6. What are the five steps of the transaction analysis chart?
7. Explain the concept of double-entry bookkeeping.

8. A trial balance is a formal report. True or false? Please explain.

9. Why are there no debit or credit columns on financial reports?

10. Compare the financial statements prepared from the expanded accounting equation with those prepared from a trial balance.

EXERCISES

1. From the following, prepare a chart of accounts, using the same numbering system used in this chapter.

Office Equipment   Professional Fees
Rent Expense   J. Deen, Capital
Accounts Payable   Cash
Accounts Receivable   Salaries Expense
Repair Expense   J. Deen, Withdrawals

Preparing a chart of accounts.

2. Record the following transaction into the transaction analysis chart: Alice Flynn bought a new piece of office equipment for $7,000, paying $500 down and charging the rest.

Preparing a transaction analysis chart.

3. Complete the table: For each account listed on the left, fill in what category it belongs to, whether increases and decreases in the account are marked on the debit or credit sides, and which financial report the account appears on. A sample is provided.

Accounts: categorizing, rules, and which reports they appear on.

Account	Category	↑	↓	Appears on which Financial Report
Cash	Asset	Dr.	Cr.	Balance Sheet
Professional Fees Earned				
B. Blank, Withdrawals				
Accounts Payable				
Rent Expense				
Truck				

4. Given the following accounts, complete the table at the top of p. 56 by inserting appropriate numbers next to the individual transaction to indicate which account is debited and which account is credited.

(1) Cash   (6) K. Ray, Withdrawals
(2) Accounts Receivable   (7) Plumbing Fees Earned
(3) Equipment   (8) Salaries Expense
(4) Accounts Payable   (9) Advertising Expense
(5) K. Ray, Capital   (10) Supplies Expense

Rules of debits and credits.

5. From the following trial balance of Lee Cleaners, prepare the following:

1. Income Statement
2. Statement of Owner's Equity
3. Balance Sheet

Preparing financial reports.

TRANSACTION	RULES	
	Dr.	Cr.
Example: A. Paid salaries expense.	8	1
B. Ray paid personal utilities bill from company chequebook.		
C. Advertising bill received but unpaid.		
D. Received cash from plumbing fees.		
E. Paid supplies expense.		
F. Ray invested additional equipment into the business.		
G. Billed customers for plumbing services rendered.		
H. Received one-half the balance from transaction G.		
I. Bought equipment on account.		

Lee Cleaners
Trial Balance
July 31, 19XX

	Dr.	Cr.
Cash	3 3 7 00	
Equipment	6 9 2 00	
Accounts Payable		2 4 2 00
B. Lee, Capital		8 0 0 00
B. Lee, Withdrawals	1 9 8 00	
Cleaning Fees		4 5 8 00
Salaries Expense	1 6 0 00	
Utilities Expense	1 1 3 00	
Totals	1 5 0 0 00	1 5 0 0 00

GROUP A PROBLEMS

Use of a transaction analysis chart.

2A-1. The following transactions occurred in the opening and operation of Amy's Bookkeeping Service.

A. Amy opened the bookkeeping service by investing $3,000 from her personal savings account.
B. Purchased office equipment on account, $2,000.
C. Rent expense due but unpaid, $300.
D. Received cash for bookkeeping services rendered, $550.
E. Billed a client on account, $600.
F. Amy Rice withdrew cash for personal use, $100.

Complete the transaction analysis chart in the *Study Guide and Working Papers.* The chart of accounts includes Cash; Accounts Receivable; Office Equipment; Accounts Payable; Amy Rice, Capital; Amy Rice, Withdrawals; Bookkeeping Fees Earned; and Rent Expense.

2A-2. Rick Cerone opened a travel agency, and the following transactions resulted:

Recording transactions into ledger accounts.

- A. Rick Cerone invested $20,000 in the travel agency.
- B. Bought office equipment on account, $4,000.
- C. Agency received cash for travel arrangements that it completed for a client, $2,500.
- D. Rick Cerone paid a personal bill from the company chequebook, $50.
- E. Paid advertising expense for the month, $700.
- F. Rent expense for the month due but unpaid, $500.
- G. Paid $800 as partial payment of what was owed from transaction B.

As Rick Cerone's accountant, analyze and record the transactions in T-account form. Set up the T accounts and label each entry with the letter of the transaction.

CHART OF ACCOUNTS	
Assets Cash 111 Office Equipment 121	**Revenue** Travel Fees Earned 411
Liabilities Accounts Payable 211	**Expenses** Advertising Expense 511 Rent Expense 512
Owner's Equity R. Cerone, Capital 311 R. Cerone, Withdrawals 312	

2A-3. From the following T accounts of Al's Window Washing Service, (a) record and foot the balances in the *Study Guide and Working Papers* where appropriate, and (b) prepare a trial balance in proper form for May 31, 19XX.

Preparing a trial balance from the T accounts.

Cash 111

5,000 (A)	100 (D)
3,000 (G)	200 (E)
	400 (F)
	200 (H)
	900 (I)

Accounts Payable 211

100 (D)	300 (C)

Fees Earned 411

	6,000 (B)

Accounts Receivable 112

6,000 (B)	3,000 (G)

Al Hart, Capital 311

	5,000 (A)

Rent Expense 511

400 (F)	

Office Equipment 121

300 (C)	
200 (H)	

Al Hart, Withdrawals 312

900 (I)	

Utilities Expense 512

200 (E)	

Preparing financial reports from the trial balance.

2A-4. From the trial balance of Janet Foss, Barrister and Solicitor, prepare (a) an income statement for the month of May, (b) a statement of owner's equity for the month ended May 31, and (c) a balance sheet as of May 31, 19XX.

	Dr.	Cr.
Janet Foss *Barrister and Solicitor* *Trial Balance* *May 31, 19XX*		
Cash	1 8 0 0 00	
Accounts Receivable	7 5 0 00	
Office Equipment	7 5 0 00	
Accounts Payable		1 2 0 0 00
Salaries Payable		6 7 5 00
Janet Foss, Capital		1 2 7 5 00
Janet Foss, Withdrawals	3 0 0 00	
Revenue from Legal Fees		1 3 5 0 00
Utilities Expense	3 0 0 00	
Rent Expense	4 5 0 00	
Salaries Expense	1 5 0 00	
Totals	4 5 0 0 00	4 5 0 0 00

Comprehensive Problem

2A-5. The chart of accounts for Pete's Delivery Service is as follows:

CHART OF ACCOUNTS

Assets
Cash 111
Accounts Receivable 112
Office Equipment 121
Delivery Trucks 122

Liabilities
Accounts Payable 211

Owner's Equity
Pete Jean, Capital 311
Pete Jean, Withdrawals 312

Revenue
Delivery Fees Earned 411

Expenses
Advertising Expense 511
Gas Expense 512
Salaries Expense 513
Telephone Expense 514

The following transactions resulted for Pete's Delivery Service during the month of March:

A. Pete Jean invested $25,000 in the delivery service from his personal savings account.
B. Bought delivery trucks on account, $20,000.
C. Bought office equipment for cash, $400.
D. Paid advertising expense, $250.
E. Collected cash for delivery services rendered, $2,600.

F. Paid drivers' salaries, $900.

G. Paid gas expense for trucks, $1,200.

H. Performed delivery services for a customer on account, $800.

I. Telephone expense due but unpaid, $700.

J. Received $300 as partial payment of transaction H.

K. Pete Jean withdrew cash for personal use, $300.

As Pete's newly employed accountant, your task is to

1. Set up T accounts in a ledger.
2. Record transactions in the T accounts. (Place the letter of the transaction next to the entry.)
3. Foot the T accounts where appropriate.
4. Prepare a trial balance at the end of March.
5. Prepare from the trial balance, in proper form, (a) an income statement for the month of March, (b) a statement of owner's equity, and (c) a balance sheet as of March 31, 19XX.

GROUP B PROBLEMS

2B-1. Amy Rice decided to open a bookkeeping service. Record each of the following transactions in a transaction analysis chart:

Use of a transaction analysis chart.

A. Amy invested $1,500 in the bookkeeping service from her personal savings account.
B. Purchased office equipment on account, $900.
C. Rent expense due but unpaid, $250.
D. Performed bookkeeping services for cash, $1,200.
E. Billed clients for bookkeeping services rendered, $700.
F. Amy paid her home heating bill from the company chequebook, $275.

The chart of accounts for the shop includes Cash; Accounts Receivable; Office Equipment; Accounts Payable; Amy Rice, Capital; Amy Rice, Withdrawals; Bookkeeping Fees Earned; and Rent Expense.

2B-2. Rick Cerone established a new travel agency. Record the following transactions for Rick in T-account form. Label each entry with the letter of the transaction.

Recording transactions into ledger accounts.

A. Rick Cerone invested $18,000 in the travel agency from his personal bank account.
B. Bought office equipment on account, $6,000.
C. Travel agency rendered service to Jensen Corp. and received cash, $1,200.
D. Rick Cerone withdrew cash for personal use, $200.
E. Paid advertising expense, $600.
F. Rent expense due but unpaid, $500.
G. Paid $400 in partial payment of transaction B.

The chart of accounts includes Cash, 111; Office Equipment, 121; Accounts Payable, 211; R. Cerone, Capital, 311; R. Cerone, Withdrawals, 312; Travel Fees Earned, 411; Advertising Expense, 511; and Rent Expense, 512.

Preparing a trial balance from the T accounts.

2B-3. From the following T accounts of Al's Window Washing Service, (1) record and foot the balances in the *Study Guide and Working Papers* where appropriate, and (2) prepare a trial balance for May 31, 19XX.

Cash 111	
10,000 (A)	4,000 (C)
4,000 (F)	310 (D)
2,000 (G)	50 (E)
	600 (I)

Accounts Receivable 112	
2,000 (G)	

Office Equipment 121	
2,000 (B)	
4,000 (C)	

Accounts Payable 211	
	2,000 (B)

Al Hart, Capital 311	
	10,000 (A)

Al Hart, Withdrawals 312	
600 (I)	

Fees Earned 411	
	4,000 (F)
	4,000 (G)

Rent Expense 511	
310 (D)	

Utilities Expense 512	
50 (E)	

Preparing financial reports from the trial balance.

2B-4. From the trial balance of Janet Foss, Barrister and Solicitor, prepare (1) an income statement for the month of May, (2) a statement of owner's equity for the month ended May 31, and (3) a balance sheet as of May 31, 19XX.

Janet Foss
Barrister and Solicitor
Trial Balance
May 31, 19XX

	Debit	Credit
Cash	6 0 0 0 00	
Accounts Receivable	2 4 0 0 00	
Office Equipment	2 4 0 0 00	
Accounts Payable		2 0 0 00
Salaries Payable		6 0 0 00
Janet Foss, Capital		4 0 0 0 00
Janet Foss, Withdrawals	2 0 0 0 00	
Revenue from Legal Fees		8 8 0 0 00
Utilities Expense	1 0 0 00	
Rent Expense	3 0 0 00	
Salaries Expense	4 0 0 00	
Totals	13 6 0 0 00	13 6 0 0 00

Comprehensive Problem

2B-5. The chart of accounts of Pete's Delivery Service includes the following: Cash, 111; Accounts Receivable, 112; Office Equipment, 121; Delivery Trucks, 122; Accounts Payable, 211; Pete Jean, Capital, 311; Pete Jean, Withdrawals, 312; Delivery Fees Earned, 411; Advertising Expense, 511; Gas Expense, 512; Salaries Expense, 513; and Telephone Expense, 514. The following transactions resulted for Pete's Delivery Service during the month of March:

A. Pete invested $40,000 in the business from his personal savings account.
B. Bought delivery trucks on account, $25,000.

C. Advertising bill received but unpaid, $800.
D. Bought office equipment for cash, $2,500.
E. Received cash for delivery services rendered, $13,000.
F. Paid salaries expense, $1,850.
G. Paid gas expense for company trucks, $750.
H. Billed customers for delivery services rendered, $5,500.
I. Paid telephone bill, $400.
J. Received $1,600 as partial payment of transaction H.
K. Pete paid home telephone bill from company chequebook, $88.

As Pete's newly employed accountant, your task is to

1. Set up T accounts in a ledger.
2. Record transactions in the T accounts. (Place the letter of the transaction next to the entry.)
3. Foot the T accounts where appropriate.
4. Prepare a trial balance at the end of March.
5. Prepare from the trial balance, in proper form, (a) an income statement for the month of March, (b) a statement of owner's equity, and (c) a balance sheet as of March 31, 19XX.

GROUP C PROBLEMS

2C-1. Kerri Ford decided to open a bookkeeping service. Record the following transactions into the transaction analysis charts:

Use of a transaction analysis chart.

A. Kerri invested $1,800 in the bookkeeping service from her personal savings account.
B. Purchased office equipment on account, $1,400.
C. Rent expense due but unpaid, $350.
D. Performed bookkeeping services for cash, $1,700.
E. Billed clients for bookkeeping services rendered, $1,100.
F. Kerri paid a home repair bill from the company chequebook, $165.

The chart of accounts for the shop includes Cash; Accounts Receivable; Office Equipment; Accounts Payable; Kerri Ford, Capital; Kerri Ford, Withdrawals; Bookkeeping Fees Earned; and Rent Expense.

2C-2. Robert Chang established a new travel agency. Record the following transactions for Robert in T-account form. Label each entry with the letter of the transaction.

Recording transactions into ledger accounts.

A. Robert Chang invested $22,000 in the travel agency from his personal bank account.
B. Bought office equipment on account, $7,500.
C. Travel agency rendered service to Portias Corp. and received cash, $1,800.
D. Robert Chang withdrew cash for personal use, $500.
E. Paid advertising expense, $450.
F. Rent expense due but unpaid, $640.
G. Paid $2,500 in partial payment of transaction B.

The chart of accounts includes Cash, 111; Office Equipment, 121; Accounts Payable, 211; R. Chang, Capital, 311; R. Chang, Withdrawals, 312; Travel Fees Earned, 411; Advertising Expense, 511; and Rent Expense, 512.

Preparing a trial balance from the T accounts.

2C-3. From the following T accounts of Tim's Small Engine Repair Service, (1) record and foot the balances in the *Study Guide and Working Papers* where appropriate, and (2) prepare a trial balance for October 31, 19XX.

Cash 111	
10,000 (A)	4,000 (C)
4,000 (F)	310 (D)
2,000 (G)	50 (E)
	600 (I)

Accounts Receivable 112	
2,000 (G)	

Office Equipment 121	
2,000 (B)	
4,000 (C)	

Accounts Payable 211	
	2,000 (B)

Tim Tobias, Capital 311	
	10,000 (A)

Tim Tobias, Withdrawals 312	
600 (I)	

Fees Earned 411	
	4,000 (F)
	4,000 (G)

Rent Expense 511	
310 (D)	

Utilities Expense 512	
50 (E)	

Preparing financial reports from the trial balance.

2C-4. From the trial balance of Annette Gold, Architect, prepare (1) an income statement for the month of June, (2) a statement of owner's equity for the month ended June 30, and (3) a balance sheet as of June 30, 19XX.

Annette Gold, Architect
Trial Balance
June 30, 19XX

	Dr.	Cr.
Cash in Bank	1 6 0 0 00	
Accounts Receivable	7 0 0 00	
Supplies	1 4 0 00	
Equipment	4 7 0 0 00	
Accounts Payable		4 0 0 00
Annette Gold, Capital		6 0 0 0 00
Annette Gold, Withdrawals	1 0 0 0 00	
Fees Earned		4 0 0 0 00
Rent Expense	1 2 0 0 00	
Advertising Expense	4 6 0 00	
Utilities Expense	6 0 0 00	
Totals	10 4 0 0 00	10 4 0 0 00

Comprehensive Problem

2C-5. The chart of accounts of Dave's Design Service includes the following: Cash, 111; Accounts Receivable, 112; Office Equipment, 121; Design Equipment, 122; Accounts Payable, 211; Dave Sieg, Capital, 311; Dave Sieg, Withdrawals, 312; Design Fees Earned, 411; Advertising Expense, 511; Repair Expense, 512; Salaries Expense, 513; and Telephone Expense, 514. The following transactions resulted for Dave's Design Service during the month of March:

A. Dave invested $38,000 in the business from his personal savings account.
B. Bought design equipment on account, $17,000.
C. Advertising bill received but unpaid, $450.
D. Bought office equipment for cash, $2,800.

E. Received cash for design services rendered, $6,000.
F. Paid salaries expense, $1,340.
G. Paid repair expense for design equipment, $280.
H. Billed customers for design services rendered, $3,500.
I. Paid telephone bill, $180.
J. Received $1,750 as partial payment of transaction H.
K. Dave paid home telephone bill from company chequebook, $54.
L. Paid $225 on the bill received in transaction C.

As Dave's newly employed accountant, your task is to

1. Set up T accounts in a ledger.
2. Record transactions in the T accounts. (Place the letter of the transaction next to the entry.)
3. Foot the T accounts where appropriate.
4. Prepare a trial balance at the end of March.
5. Prepare from the trial balance, in proper form, (a) an income statement for the month of March, (b) a statement of owner's equity, and (c) a balance sheet as of March 31, 19XX.

PRACTICAL ACCOUNTING APPLICATION #1

Andy Leaf is a careless bookkeeper. He is having a terrible time getting his trial balance to balance. Andy has asked for your assistance in preparing a correct trial balance. The following is the incorrect trial balance.

Ranch Company
Trial Balance
June 30, 19XX

	Dr.	Cr.
Cash	5 1 0 00	
Accounts Receivable		6 3 5 00
Office Equipment	3 6 0 00	
Accounts Payable	1 1 0 00	
Wages Payable	1 0 00	
H. Clo, Capital	6 3 5 00	
H. Clo, Withdrawals	1 4 4 0 00	
Professional Fees		2 2 4 0 00
Rent Expense		2 4 0 00
Advertising Expense	2 5 00	
Totals	3 0 9 0 00	3 1 1 5 00

Facts you have discovered:

1. Debits to the Cash account were $2,640; credits to the Cash account were $2,150.
2. Amy Hall paid $15 but was not updated in Accounts Receivable.
3. A purchase of office equipment for $5 on account was never recorded in the ledger.
4. Revenue was understated in the ledger by $180.

Show how these errors would have affected the ending balances for the accounts involved, and show how once they are corrected the trial balance will indeed balance.

PRACTICAL ACCOUNTING APPLICATION #2

Given the following six independent situations, Alice Groove, owner of Lonton Company, has asked her bookkeeper how each situation would have affected the totals of the trial balance as well as individual ledger accounts. As the bookkeeper, could you respond to Alice's concerns? Be specific in telling whether accounts are overstated, understated, or correctly stated.

1. An $850 payment for a desk was recorded as a debit to Office Equipment, $85, and a credit to Cash, $85.
2. A payment of $300 to a creditor was recorded as a debit to Accounts Payable, $300, and a credit to Cash, $100.
3. The collection of an Accounts Receivable for $400 was recorded as a debit to Cash, $400, and a credit to J. Ray, Capital, $400.
4. The payment of a liability for $400 was recorded as a debit to Accounts Payable, $40, and a credit to Supplies, $40.
5. A purchase of equipment of $800 was recorded as a debit to Supplies, $800, and a credit to Cash, $800.
6. A payment of $95 to a creditor was recorded as a debit to Accounts Payable, $95, and a credit to Cash, $59.

ACCOUNTING RECALL
A Cumulative Approach

THIS EXAM REVIEWS CHAPTERS 1 AND 2.

Your *Study Guide and Working Papers* have forms to complete this exam, as well as worked-out solutions. The page references next to each question identify what page to turn back to if you answer the question incorrectly.

PART I Vocabulary Review

Match the terms to the appropriate definition or phrase.

Page Ref.

(48)	1. Trial balance	A.	Total remains the same
(35)	2. Debit	B.	Entering numbers on right side
(37)	3. Normal balance	C.	Subdivisions of owner's equity
(10)	4. Revenue	D.	Group of accounts
(35)	5. Crediting	E.	Numbering system
(51)	6. Balance sheet	F.	Left side of an account
(5)	7. Shift in assets	G.	Prepared as of a particular date
(37)	8. Chart of accounts	H.	Not an asset
(34)	9. Ledger	I.	Side of account that increases it
(10)	10. Capital, withdrawals, revenue, expenses	J.	List of the ledger

PART II True or False (Accounting Theory)

(35) 11. A debit always means increase.

(45) 12. There are no debit or credit columns on financial reports.

(48) 13. The trial balance lists only the ending figure for capital that goes on the balance sheet.

(36) 14. An increase in a withdrawal is a credit.

(48) 15. The trial balance is not a formal report.

PART III Applications Problem (50)

(1) Record the following transaction into the ledger; (2) prepare a trial balance for July; and (3) prepare the three Financial Reports for Alice Wong's Bookstore.

A. On July 1, Alice Wong invested $6,000 in a bookstore.

B. Completed a sale of books to a school for $3,000. School paid $1,000 down and promised to pay balance in 30 days.

C. Bought store equipment on account, $500.
D. Paid utilities bill, $100.
E. Paid rent, $1,400.
F. Alice withdrew $500 for personal use.
G. Paid salaries, $600.
H. Paid $300 on balance owed in (C).

BEGINNING THE ACCOUNTING CYCLE:
Journalizing, Posting, and the Trial Balance

IN THIS CHAPTER WE WILL COVER THE FOLLOWING TOPICS:

1. JOURNALIZING—ANALYZING AND RECORDING BUSINESS TRANSACTIONS INTO A JOURNAL. (P. 69)

2. POSTING—TRANSFERRING INFORMATION FROM A JOURNAL TO A LEDGER. (P. 79)

3. PREPARING A TRIAL BALANCE. (P. 86)

The example of Sylvia Mosco, Barrister and Solicitor, gave you some insights into accounting terms and basic procedures as well as the preparation of the three financial reports. Now our attention will shift to Brenda Clark, who is planning to open a word processing business. In this chapter, and in Chapters 4 and 5, we will follow step by step the normal accounting procedures that her business, Clark's Word Processing Services, performs over a period of time.

FIGURE 3-1

Steps of the Accounting Cycle

Use this as a reference table in your study of Chapters 3, 4, and 5.

STEPS	EXPLANATION
1. Business transactions occur and generate source documents.	Source documents are cash register tapes, sales tickets, bills, cheques, payroll cards.
2. Analyze and record business transactions into a journal.	Called journalizing.
3. Post or transfer information from journal to ledger.	Copying the debits and credits of the journal entries, placing them into the ledger accounts.
4. Prepare a trial balance.	Summarizing each individual ledger account and listing these accounts and their balances to test for accurancy in recording transactions.
5. Prepare a work sheet.	A multicolumn form that summarizes accounting information to complete the accounting cycle.
6. Prepare financial statements.	Income statement, statement of owner's equity, balance sheet.
7. Journalize and post adjusting entries.	Refers to adjustment columns of work sheet.
8. Journalize and post closing entries.	Refers to income statement columns to work sheet.
9. Prepare a post-closing trial balance.	Prove the equality of debits and credits after adjusting and closing entries are posted.

The normal accounting procedures that are performed over a period of time are called the **accounting cycle**. The accounting cycle takes place in a period of time called an **accounting period**—it can be a month, three months, one year, and so on. An accounting period is the period of time covered by the income statement. The norm for accounting periods is one year.

A **fiscal year** is an accounting period that runs for any 12 consecutive months. Clark has chosen to use a fiscal year of January 1 to December 31, which also is the **calendar year**. A fiscal year can be a calendar year but does not have to be; a business can choose any fiscal year that is convenient. For example, some companies, such as retail furniture companies, may decide to end their fiscal year when inventories and business activity are at a low point (in this case, Feb. 28). This is called a natural business year. It allows the business to count year-end inventory at the time when it is easiest to do so.

Whether we are talking about a calendar year or a fiscal year, financial reports can be prepared monthly, quarterly, or every six months. These reports are called **interim reports**.

To keep things simple, we will look at an accounting cycle for one month for Clark's Word Processing Services. Please keep in mind that her actual accounting cycle is 12 months.

The blueprint shown in Figure 3-1 on page 68 is a list of the steps of the accounting cycle for Clark's Word Processing Services. Please do not try to memorize this blueprint. It will be repeated frequently in the next three chapters. Simply use it as a reference table. By the end of Chapter 5 all the steps and the notes of the blueprint will have been explained and illustrated.

This chapter covers Steps 1 to 4 of the accounting cycle.

LEARNING UNIT 3-1

Analyzing and Recording Business Transactions into a Journal: Steps 1 and 2 of the Accounting Cycle

THE GENERAL JOURNAL

In the last chapter we analyzed and recorded business transactions of Sylvia Mosco's law practice into T accounts, or ledger accounts. Dealing only with accounts, however, makes it difficult to locate errors (because a debit may be in one account—on one page of the ledger—and a credit in another account—on another page of the ledger). We need a place where the entire transaction (debit and credit) can be found. For this reason we record business transactions in a **journal**. The simplest form of journal is the **general journal**. Transactions are entered in the journal in chronological order (January 1, 8, 15, etc.), and then this recorded information is used to update the ledger accounts. In computerized accounting, a journal may be recorded on disk or tape.

The general journal, the simplest form of a journal, will be used to record the transactions of Clark's Word Processing Services (see Figure 3-2). A transaction (debit(s) + credit(s)) that has been analyzed and recorded in a journal is called a **journal entry**. The process of recording the journal entry into the journal is called **journalizing**.

A business uses a journal to record transactions in chronological order. A ledger accumulates information from a journal. The journal and the ledger are in two different books.

FIGURE 3-2
**The General
Journal**

Clark's Word Processing Serivces
General Journal

Page 1

Date	Account Titles and Description	PR	Dr.*	Cr.

**Journal—book of
original entry.**

**Ledger—book of
final entry.**

The journal is called the **book of original entry**, since it will contain the first formal information about the business transactions. The ledger, a group of accounts, will be known as the **book of final entry**, since the information in the journal will eventually be transferred to the ledger. Like the ledger, the journal is a bound or loose-leaf book. The journal pages are each like the one illustrated in Figure 3-2. The journal is numbered by page (1, 2, 3, and so on), while the ledger is set up with one or more pages for each account, and each account in order according to the account number assigned. Keep in mind that the journal and the ledger are separate books.

**Relationship of
journal to chart
of accounts.**

Before the accountant can journalize the business transactions of Clark's Word Processing Services, a chart of accounts is needed to identify what account name to use for each debit and each credit. Most companies have their own "unique" chart of accounts. Seldom do two companies have exactly the same chart. Don't worry about accounts in the chart we haven't talked about or seen—you will learn about them by the end of the accounting cycle. The chart of accounts of Clark's Word Processing Services is presented below.

CLARK'S WORD PROCESSING SERVICES
CHART OF ACCOUNTS

Assets (100-199)
111 Cash
112 Accounts Receivable
114 Office Supplies
115 Prepaid Rent
121 Word Processing Equipment
122 Accumulated Depreciation,
      Word Processing Equipment

Liabilities (200-299)
211 Accounts Payable

Owner's Equity (300-399)
311 Brenda Clark, Capital
312 Brenda Clark, Withdrawals
313 Income Summary

Revenue (400-499)
411 Word Processing Fees

Expenses (500-599)
511 Office Salaries Expense
512 Advertising Expense
513 Telephone Expense
514 Office Supplies Expense
515 Rent Expense
516 Depreciation Expense,
      Word Processing Equipment

Journalizing the Transactions of Clark's Word Processing Services

With a chart of accounts available, we can proceed to record business transactions in chronological order in the general journal. (Note that we are still using the transaction analysis charts as a teaching aid in the journalizing process.)

May 1, 19XX: Brenda Clark began the business by investing $7,000 in cash.

---

1 Accounts Affected	2 Category	3 ↑ ↓	4 Rules
Cash	Asset	↑	Dr.
Brenda Clark, Capital	Capital	↑	Cr.

Clark's Word Processing Services
General Journal

Page 1

Date	Account Titles and Description	PR	Dr.*	Cr.
19XX May 1	Cash		7 0 0 0 00	
	Brenda Clark, Capital			7 0 0 0 00
	Initial investment of cash by owner			

* You may, if you prefer, use dashes instead of zeros (for example, 7,000.00 or 7,000--). Be sure to check with your instructor.

Let's now look at the structure of this journal entry. The entry contains the following information:

1. Year of the journal entry   19XX
2. Month of journal entry   May
3. Day of journal entry   1
4. Name(s) of accounts debited   Cash
5. Name(s) of accounts credited   Brenda Clark, Capital
6. Explanation of transaction   Investment of cash
7. Amount of debit(s) $7,000
8. Amount of credit(s) $7,000

For now the PR (posting reference) column is blank; we will discuss it later. Notice the following in this journal entry:

1. The location of the year, month, and day.

Debit is listed *first*, next to date column.

2. The account name Cash is written on the first line next to the date column in the account titles and description section. The amount of the account is entered in the debit column. *Note*: The debit portion of the transaction is usually recorded in the journal first.

Credit is listed second and is indented 1 cm to right of date column.

3. The account B. Clark, Capital, is written on the second line, indented one cm from the left side of the account titles and description (or date column). The credit portion of a transaction is placed below the debit portion.

4. The explanation of the journal entry follows immediately after the debit and credit account titles, indented two cm from the date column.

5. Following each transaction and explanation leave a one line space. This makes the journal easier to read, and there is less chance of mixing transactions.

6. The total amount of debits ($7,000) is equal to the total amount of credits ($7,000).

> *May 1: Purchased word processing equipment from Ben Co. for $8,000, paying $2,000 and promising to pay the balance within 30 days.*

1 Accounts Affected	2 Category	3 ↑ ↓	4 Rules
Word Processing Equipment	Asset	↑	Dr.
Cash	Asset	↓	Cr.
Accounts Payable	Liability	↑	Cr.

Note that there are three accounts affected here.

Note that in this compound entry we have one debit and two credits—but the total amount of debits equals the total amount of credits.

	1	Word Processing Equipment		8 0 0 0 00		
		Cash			2 0 0 0 00
		Accounts Payable			6 0 0 0 00
		Purchase of equipment from Ben Co.			

Notice that only the day is entered in the date column. Since the year and month are entered at the top of the page from the first transaction, there is no need to repeat the month until a new page is needed or a change of month occurs. Note again that the debit is listed first, and then the two credits are indented and listed below the debit. When a journal entry has more than two accounts, it is called a **compound journal entry**. We introduced this idea in Chapter 1.

A journal entry that requires three or more accounts is called a compound journal entry.

> *May 1: Rented office space, paying $900 in advance for the first three months.*

1 Accounts Affected	2 Category	3 ↑ ↓	4 Rules
Prepaid Rent	Asset	↑	Dr.
Cash	Asset	↓	Cr.

In this transaction Clark gains an asset called prepaid rent but gives up an asset, cash. When the rent *expires*, it will become an expense. In the last chapter the rent for Sylvia Mosco had expired; thus we recorded it as an expense. However, for now prepaid rent is an asset.

Rent paid in advance is an asset.

	1	Prepaid Rent		9 0 0 00	
		Cash			9 0 0 00
		Rent paid in advance-3 mo.			

> *May 3: Purchased office supplies from Norris Co. on account, $400.*

1 Accounts Affected	2 Category	3 ↑ ↓	4 Rules
Office Supplies	Asset	↑	Dr.
Accounts Payable	Liability	↑	Cr.

Remember the following guidelines:

1. When we purchase supplies, they are an *asset* that has not been used up.
2. When the supplies are used up or consumed in the operation of the business, they become an expense.

Supplies become an *expense* when used up.

	3	Office Supplies		4 0 0 00	
		Accounts Payable			4 0 0 00
		Purchase of supplies on account			
		from Norris			

May 7: Completed sales promotion pieces for a client and immediately collected $2,500.

1 Accounts Affected	2 Category	3 ↑ ↓	4 Rules
Cash	Asset	↑	Dr.
Word Processing Fees	Revenue	↑	Cr.

7	Cash		2 500 00	
	Word Processing Fees			2 500 00
	Cash received for services rendered			

May 15: Paid office salaries, $450.

1 Accounts Affected	2 Category	3 ↑ ↓	4 Rules
Office Salaries Expense	Expense	↑	Dr.
Cash	Asset	↓	Cr.

15	Office Salaries Expense		450 00	
	Cash			450 00
	Payment of office salaries			

May 18: Advertising bill from Al's News Co. comes in but is not paid, $175.

1 Accounts Affected	2 Category	3 ↑ ↓	4 Rules
Advertising Expense	Expense	↑	Dr.
Accounts Payable	Liability	↑	Cr.

As we noted in Chapter 1, we record an expense when it is incurred, no matter when it is paid.

	18	Advertising Expense		1 7 5 00		
		Accounts Payable			1 7 5 00	
		Bill in but not paid from Al's News				

> *May 20: Brenda Clark wrote a cheque on the bank account of the business to pay her home mortgage payment of $430.*

1 Accounts Affected	2 Category	3 ↑ ↓	4 Rules
Brenda Clark, Withdrawals	Withdrawals	↑	Dr.
Cash	Asset	↓	Cr.

Keep in mind that as withdrawals *increase*, the end result is to *reduce* owner's equity.

	20	Brenda Clark, Withdrawals		4 3 0 00		
		Cash			4 3 0 00	
		Personal withdrawal of cash				

> *May 22: Billed Morris Company for a sophisticated word processing job, $4,100.*

1 Accounts Affected	2 Category	3 ↑ ↓	4 Rules
Accounts Receivable	Asset	↑	Dr.
Word Processing Fees	Revenue	↑	Cr.

As we discussed in Chapter 1, revenue is recorded when earned, no matter when the actual cash is received.

	22	Accounts Receivable		4 1 0 0 00		
		Word Processing Fee			4 1 0 0 00	
		Billed Morris Co. for fees earned				

May 27: Paid office salaries, $450.

1 Accounts Affected	2 Category	3 ↑ ↓	4 Rules
Office Salaries Expense	Expense	↑	Dr.
Cash	Asset	↓	Cr.

Clark's Word Processing Services
General Journal

Page 2

Date	Account Titles and Description	PR	Dr.	Cr.
19XX May 27	Office Salaries Expense		450 00	
	Cash			450 00
	Payment of office salaries			

Note that, since we are on page 2 of the journal, the year and month are repeated.

May 28: Paid half the amount owed for word processing equipment purchased May 1 from Ben Co., $3,000.

1 Accounts Affected	2 Category	3 ↑ ↓	4 Rules
Accounts Payable	Liability	↓	Dr.
Cash	Asset	↓	Cr.

28	Accounts Payable		3000 00	
	Cash			3000 00
	Paid half the amount owed Ben Co.			

> *May 29: Paid telephone bill, $180.*

1 Accounts Affected	2 Category	3 ↑ ↓	4 Rules
Telephone Expense	Expense	↑	Dr.
Cash	Asset	↓	Cr.

	29	*Telephone Expense*			1 8 0 00	
		Cash				1 8 0 00
		Paid telephone bill				

This concludes the journal transactions of Clark's Word Processing Services.

At this point, you should be able to

1. Explain the purpose of the accounting cycle. (p. 69)
2. Define and explain the relationship of the accounting period to the income statement. (p. 69)
3. Compare and contrast a calendar year to a fiscal year. (p. 69)
4. Explain the term natural business year. (p. 69)
5. Explain the function of interim reports. (p. 69)
6. Define and state the purpose of a journal. (p. 69)
7. Compare and contrast a book of original entry to a book of final entry. (p. 70)
8. Differentiate between a chart of accounts and a journal. (p. 70)
9. Explain a compound entry. (p. 72)
10. Journalize business transactions. (pp. 71-77)

☐ SELF-REVIEW QUIZ 3-1

The following are the transactions of Pete's Repair Service. Journalize the transactions in proper form. The chart of accounts includes Cash; Accounts Receivable; Prepaid Rent; Repair Supplies; Repair Equipment; Accounts Payable; P. Quick, Capital; P. Quick, Withdrawals; Repair Fees Earned; Salaries Expense; Advertising Expense; and Supplies Expense.

19XX
June 1   Pete invested $5,000 cash and $2,000 of repair equipment in the business.
      1   Paid two months' rent in advance, $900.
      4   Bought repair supplies from Melvin Co. on account, $500. (These supplies have not yet been consumed or used up.)
     15   Performed repair work, received $600 cash, and had to bill Doe Co. for remaining balance of $300.

18   Pete paid his home telephone bill, $50, with a cheque from the company.
20   Advertising bill for $400 from Jones Co. received but payment not due yet.
      (Advertising has already appeared in the newspaper.)
24   Paid salaries, $1,400.

■ *SOLUTION TO SELF-REVIEW QUIZ 3-1*

Pete's Repair
General Journal

Page 1

Date			Account Titles and Description	PR*	Dr.	Cr.
19XX						
June	1		Cash		5 0 0 0 00	
			Repair Equipment		2 0 0 0 00	
			P. Quick, Capital			7 0 0 0 00
			Owner investment			
	1		Prepaid Rent		9 0 0 00	
			Cash			9 0 0 00
			Rent paid in advance			
	4		Repair Supplies		5 0 0 00	
			Accounts Payable			5 0 0 00
			Purchase of supplies on account			
	15		Cash		6 0 0 00	
			Accounts Receivable		3 0 0 00	
			Repair Fees Earned			9 0 0 00
			Performed repairs			
	18		P. Quick, Withdrawals		5 0 00	
			Cash			5 0 00
			Personal withdrawal			
	20		Advertising Expense		4 0 0 00	
			Accounts Payable			4 0 0 00
			Advertising bill			
	24		Salaries Expense		1 4 0 0 00	
			Cash			1 4 0 0 00
			Paid salaries			

Posting to the Ledger:
Step 3 of the Accounting Cycle

If you were asked to find the balance of the cash account from the general journal, you would not be able to find it in one place. You would have to go through the journal, look for only the cash entries, add up the debits and credits, and take the difference between the two. Thus, what we really need to do to find *balances of accounts* is to transfer, copy, or record the information from the journal to the ledger. This is called **posting**. In the ledger we will *accumulate* an ending balance for each account so that we can prepare financial statements.

> The ledger accumulates information from the journal.

Before looking at how to post, let's first introduce a **three-column account** that we will be using instead of the standard two-column account. This three-column account will be used throughout the rest of the text and will make accumulating items in the ledger a bit easier.

The two-column account was valuable for learning debits and credits. It forced you to think of lefts and rights. In actual practice there has been a shift to forms that use a three-column account. A sample of a standard three-column account is shown in Figure 3-3. (We will explain the Post. Ref. column in a moment.) Keep in mind: in balancing two debits would be added. Similarly, two credits would be added. If you have a debit and credit, the difference would be taken with the balance placed in the appropriate column. A Dr. in the Dr./Cr. column identifies a debit balance and a Cr., a credit balance.

General Ledger

Accounts Payable   Acct. No. 211

Date 19XX	Explanation	Post Ref.	Debit	Credit	DR or CR	Balance
May 1		GJ1		6 0 0 0 00	CR	6 0 0 0 00
3		GJ1		4 0 0 00	CR	6 4 0 0 00
18		GJ1		1 7 5 00	CR	6 5 7 5 00
28		GJ2	3 0 0 0 00		CR	3 5 7 5 00

FIGURE 3-3

Three-Column Account

Advantages of the three-column account:

1. You will need only one date column.
2. It is very easy to see whether the balance is a debit or credit.
3. Footings will *not* be needed.

When using this account, we need to be very familiar with the type of balance each account usually has. As stated in the last chapter, the **normal balance** of an account is the side of the account where we record increases. Figure 3-4 (p. 80) reviews the rules of normal balances.

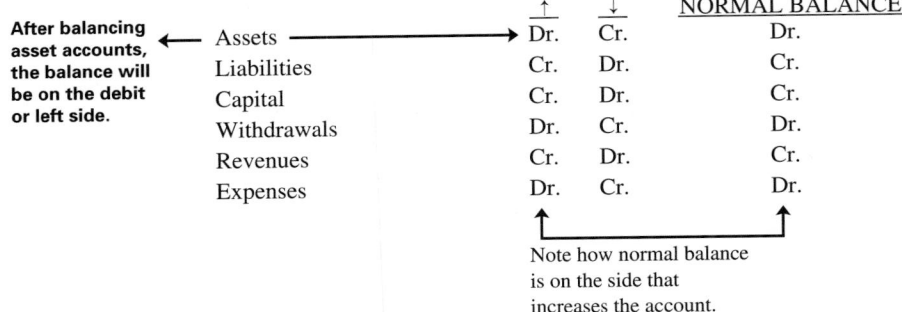

		↑	↓	NORMAL BALANCE
After balancing ←	Assets ——————→	Dr.	Cr.	Dr.
asset accounts,	Liabilities	Cr.	Dr.	Cr.
the balance will	Capital	Cr.	Dr.	Cr.
be on the debit	Withdrawals	Dr.	Cr.	Dr.
or left side.	Revenues	Cr.	Dr.	Cr.
	Expenses	Dr.	Cr.	Dr.

Note how normal balance
is on the side that
increases the account.

FIGURE 3-4

Normal Balances

If, after an account is totalled, the ending balance is not the same as is normal for that account, it is said to have an *unusual balance.* If we were using a single balance column (discussed in Chapters 6 and 7), brackets [ ] would be placed around the number to indicate that it is opposite to the usual balance.

Now let's look at how to post the transactions of Clark's Word Processing Service from its journal.

POSTING

The diagram in Figure 3-5 (p. 81) shows how to post the cash line from the journal to the ledger. Again, *posting* is the transferring, copying, or recording of information to the ledger from the journal.

Note the following key points:

- Journal and ledger are in separate books.
- PR column of general journal will be the last to be filled in.
- No new analysis is taking place in the ledger. We are just copying transactions from the journal into the ledger.

Steps to Post

These steps are numbered and illustrated in Figure 3-5.

1. In the Cash account in the ledger, record the date (May 1, 19XX) and the amount of the entry ($7,000).

2. Record the page number of the journal "GJ1" in the posting reference (Post. Ref.) column of the Cash account.

3. Record the account number of Cash (111) in the posting reference (PR) column of the journal. This is called **cross-referencing**.

4. Calculate the new balance of the account. You keep a running balance in each account as you would in your chequebook. To do this you take the present balance in the account on the previous line and add or subtract the transaction as necessary to arrive at your new balance. Be sure to identify the balance as debit (Dr.) or credit (Cr.).

The same sequence of steps occurs for each line in the journal. In a manual system like Clark's, the debits and credits in the journal may be posted in the order they were recorded, or all the debits may be posted first and then all the credits. It is

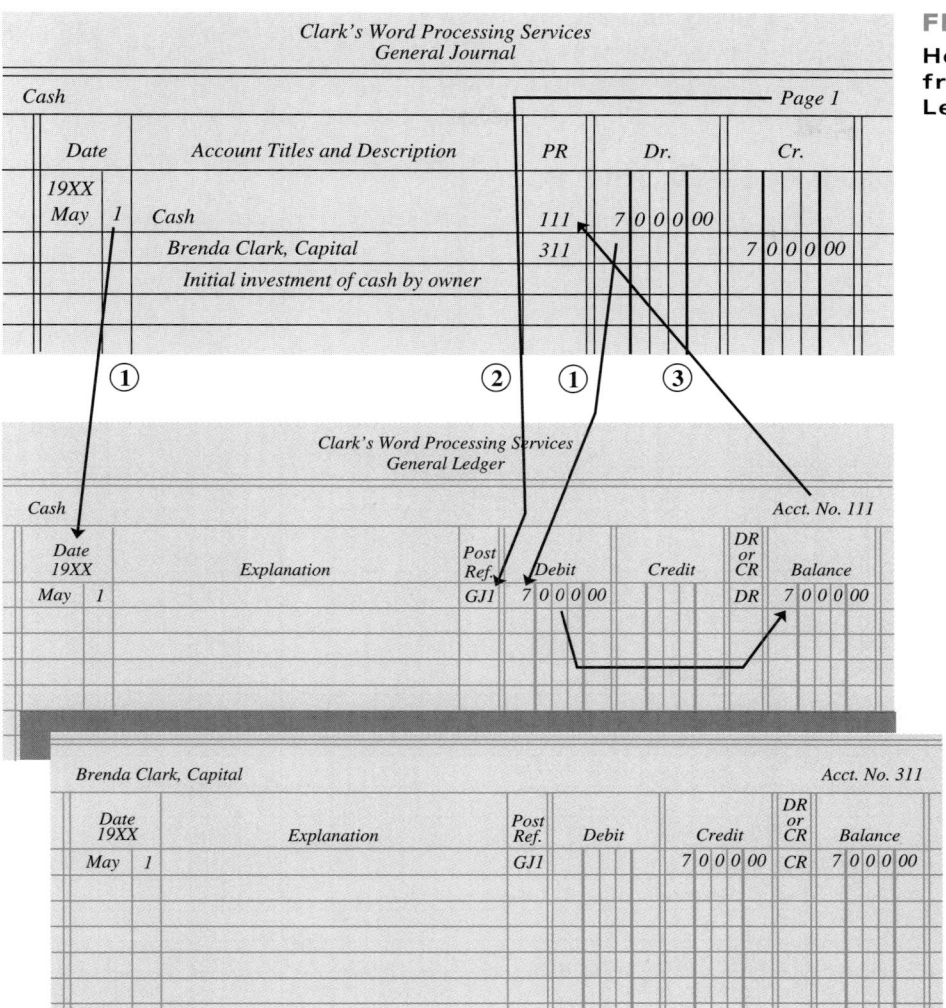

FIGURE 3-5

How to Post from Journal to Ledger

also acceptable to record all the postings to a single ledger account (Cash, for example) before going on to another account. However, students should develop a bit of experience in posting before attempting this.

Using Posting References

The posting references are very helpful. In the journal, the PR column tells us which transactions have or have not been posted and also to which accounts they were posted. In the ledger, the posting reference leads us back to the original transaction in its entirety, so that we can see why the debit or credit was recorded and what other accounts were affected. (It leads us back to the original transaction by identifying the journal and the page in the journal the information came from.)

At this point you should be able to

1. State the purpose of posting. (p. 80)
2. Discuss the advantages of the three-column account. (p. 80)

3. Define a normal balance. (p. 79-80)
4. Identify the elements to be posted. (p. 81)
5. From journalized transactions, post to the general ledger. (p. 80)

☐ **SELF-REVIEW QUIZ 3-2**

The following are the journalized transactions of Clark's Word Processing Services. Your task is to post information to the ledger. The ledger in your workbook has all the account titles and numbers that were used from the chart of accounts on p. 70. *To keep things simple, assume in the quiz that all journal entries are "p. 1."*

Clark's Word Processing Services
General Journal

Page 1

Date		Account Titles and Description	PR*	Dr.	Cr.
19XX					
May	1	Cash		7 000 00	
		Brenda Clark, Capital			7 000 00
		Initial investment of cash by owner			
	1	Word Processing Equipment		8 000 00	
		Cash			2 000 00
		Accounts Payable			6 000 00
		Purchase of equip. from Ben Co.			
	1	Prepaid Rent		9 00 00	
		Cash			9 00 00
		Rent paid in advance (3 months)			
	3	Office Supplies		4 00 00	
		Accounts Payable			4 00 00
		Purchase of supplies on acct. from Norris			
	7	Cash		2 500 00	
		Word Processing Fees			2 500 00
		Cash received from services rendered			
	15	Office Salaries Expense		4 50 00	
		Cash			4 50 00
		Payment of office salaries			
	18	Advertising Expense		1 75 00	
		Accounts Payable			1 75 00
		Bill received but not paid from Al's News			
	20	Brenda Clark, Withdrawals		4 30 00	
		Cash			4 30 00
		Personal withdrawal of cash			

					Dr.		Cr.	
	22	Accounts Receivable			4 1 0 0 00			
		Word Processing Fees					4 1 0 0 00	
		Billed Morris Co. for fees earned						
	27	Office Salaries Expense			4 5 0 00			
		Cash					4 5 0 00	
		Payment of office salaries						
	28	Accounts Payable			3 0 0 0 00			
		Cash					3 0 0 0 00	
		Paid half the amount owed Ben Co.						
	29	Telephone Expense			1 8 0 00			
		Cash					1 8 0 00	
		Paid telephone bill						

* Note that the PR column is empty–this is because these entries have not been posted yet.

SOLUTION TO SELF-REVIEW QUIZ 3-2

Clark's Word Processing Services
General Journal

Page 1

Date		Account Titles and Description	PR	Dr.	Cr.
19XX					
May	1	Cash	111	7 0 0 0 00	
		Brenda Clark, Capital	311		7 0 0 0 00
		Initial investment of cash by owner			
	1	Word Processing Equipment	121	8 0 0 0 00	
		Cash	111		2 0 0 0 00
		Accounts Payable	211		6 0 0 0 00
		Purchase of equip. from Ben Co.			
	1	Prepaid Rent	115	9 0 0 00	
		Cash	111		9 0 0 00
		Rent paid in advance (3 months)			
	3	Office Supplies	114	4 0 0 00	
		Accounts Payable	211		4 0 0 00
		Purchase of supplies on acct. from Norris			
	7	Cash	111	2 5 0 0 00	
		Word Processing Fees	411		2 5 0 0 00
		Cash received for services rendered			
	15	Office Salaries Expense	511	4 5 0 00	
		Cash	111		4 5 0 00
		Payment of office salaries			

Clark's Word Processing Services
General Journal

Page 1

Date			Account Titles and Description	PR	Dr.	Cr.
19XX May	18		Advertising Expense	512	175 00	
			Accounts Payable	211		175 00
			Bill received but not paid from Al's News			
	20		Brenda Clark, Withdrawals	312	430 00	
			Cash	111		430 00
			Personal withdrawal of cash			
	22		Accounts Receivable	112	4 100 00	
			Word Processing Fees	411		4 100 00
			Billed Morris Co. for fees earned			
	27		Office Salaries Expense	511	450 00	
			Cash	111		450 00
			Payment of office salaries			
	28		Accounts Payable	211	3 000 00	
			Cash	111		3 000 00
			Paid half the amount owed Ben Co.			
	29		Telephone Expense	513	180 00	
			Cash	111		180 00
			Paid telephone bill			

Clark's Word Processing Services
Partial General Ledger

Cash   Acct. No. 111

Date 19XX	Explanation	Post Ref.	Debit	Credit	DR or CR	Balance
May 1		GJ1	7 000 00		DR	7 000 00
1		GJ1		2 000 00	DR	5 000 00
1		GJ1		900 00	DR	4 100 00
7		GJ1	2 500 00		DR	6 600 00
15		GJ1		450 00	DR	6 150 00
20		GJ1		430 00	DR	5 720 00
27		GJ1		450 00	DR	5 270 00
28		GJ1		3 000 00	DR	2 270 00
29		GJ1		180 00	DR	2 090 00

Accounts Receivable   Acct. No. 112

Date 19XX	Explanation	Post Ref.	Debit	Credit	DR or CR	Balance
May 22		GJ1	4 1 0 0 00		DR	4 1 0 0 00

Office Supplies   Acct. No. 114

Date 19XX	Explanation	Post Ref.	Debit	Credit	DR or CR	Balance
May 3		GJ1	4 0 0 00		DR	4 0 0 00

Prepaid Rent   Acct. No. 115

Date 19XX	Explanation	Post Ref.	Debit	Credit	DR or CR	Balance
May 1		GJ1	9 0 0 00		DR	9 0 0 00

Word Processing Equipment   Acct. No. 121

Date 19XX	Explanation	Post Ref.	Debit	Credit	DR or CR	Balance
May 1		GJ1	8 0 0 0 00		DR	8 0 0 0 00

Accounts Payable   Acct. No. 211

Date 19XX	Explanation	Post Ref.	Debit	Credit	DR or CR	Balance
May 1		GJ1		6 0 0 0 00	CR	6 0 0 0 00
3		GJ1		4 0 0 00	CR	6 4 0 0 00
18		GJ1		1 7 5 00	CR	6 5 7 5 00
28		GJ1	3 0 0 0 00		CR	3 5 7 5 00

Brenda Clark, Capital   Acct. No. 311

Date 19XX	Explanation	Post Ref.	Debit	Credit	DR or CR	Balance
May 1		GJ1		7 0 0 0 00	CR	7 0 0 0 00

Brenda Clark, Withdrawals   Acct. No. 312

Date 19XX	Explanation	Post Ref.	Debit	Credit	DR or CR	Balance
May 20		GJ1	4 3 0 00		DR	4 3 0 00

Word Processing Fees   Acct. No. 411

Date 19XX	Explanation	Post Ref.	Debit	Credit	DR or CR	Balance
May 7		GJ1		2 5 0 0 00	CR	2 5 0 0 00
22		GJ1		4 1 0 0 00	CR	6 6 0 0 00

Office Salaries Expense   Acct. No. 511

Date 19XX	Explanation	Post Ref.	Debit	Credit	DR or CR	Balance
May 15		GJ1	4 5 0 00		DR	4 5 0 00
27		GJ1	4 5 0 00		DR	9 0 0 00

Advertising Expense   Acct. No. 512

Date 19XX	Explanation	Post Ref.	Debit	Credit	DR or CR	Balance
May 18		GJ1	1 7 5 00		DR	1 7 5 00

Telephone Expense   Acct. No. 513

Date 19XX	Explanation	Post Ref.	Debit	Credit	DR or CR	Balance
May 29		GJ1	1 8 0 00		DR	1 8 0 00

LEARNING UNIT 3-3

Preparing the Trial Balance: Step 4 of the Accounting Cycle

Did you note in Quiz 3-2 how each account had a running balance figure? Did you know the normal balance of each account in Clark's ledger? As we discussed in Chapter 2, the list of the individual accounts with their balances taken from the ledger is called a **trial balance**.

The trial balance shown in Figure 3-6 was developed from the ledger accounts of Clark's Word Processing Services that were posted and balanced in Quiz 3-2. If information is journalized or posted incorrectly, you can be sure your trial balance will not be correct.

It is important to remember that the capital figure on the trial balance might not be the beginning capital figure. This could happen if Brenda Clark had made additional investments during the period. This additional investment would be journalized and posted to the capital account. The only way to tell if the capital balance on the trial balance is the original balance is to check the ledger capital account to see if any additional investments have taken place. This will be important when we make financial reports.

The trial balance of Clark's Word Processing Services shows that the total of debits is equal to the total of credits. This does *not*, however, guarantee that transactions have been properly recorded. For example, the following errors would remain undetected: (1) a transaction that may have been omitted in the journalizing process; (2) a transaction incorrectly analyzed and recorded in the journal; (3) a journal entry journalized or posted twice.

Let's look at an instance of how a trial balance can be in balance, debits equalling credits, but the correct amount is not recorded in each ledger account. If a journal entry should have been a debit to cash and credit to salaries payable, but was instead recorded as a credit to accounts payable, the entry will balance, but the analysis of the transaction is incorrect. Accounts payable is thus too high and salaries payable is too low, but total liabilities are correct.

The totals of a trial balance can balance and yet be incorrect.

Clark's Word Processing Services
Trial Balance
May 31, 19XX

	Dr.	Cr.
Cash	(2 090 00)	
Accounts Receivable	4 100 00	
Office Supplies	400 00	
Prepaid Rent	900 00	
Word Processing Equipment	8 000 00	
Accounts Payable		3 575 00
B. Clark, Capital		7 000 00
B. Clark, Withdrawals	430 00	
Word Processing Fees		6 600 00
Office Salaries Expense	900 00	
Advertising Expense	175 00	
Telephone Expense	180 00	
Totals	17 175 00	17 175 00

The trial balance lists the accounts in the same order as in the ledger. The $2,090 figure of cash came from the ledger, p. 74.

FIGURE 3-6
Trial Balance

Obviously, it is of crucial importance to be accurate in the journalizing and posting process. We will look at how to specifically correct entries in a moment.

WHAT TO DO IF A TRIAL BALANCE DOESN'T BALANCE

If the total amounts of debits and credits are not equal, the following should be considered:

Correcting the trial balance: What to do if your trial balance doesn't balance.

Did you clear your adding machine?

1. If the difference is 10, 100, 1,000, etc., you have probably made a mathematical error in addition.
2. If the difference is equal to one individual account balance in the ledger, see if you omitted one by error. Possibly the figure was not posted from the general journal.
3. Divide the difference (the amount you are off) by 2; then check to see if a debit should have been a credit and vice versa in the ledger or trial balance. Example: $150 difference ÷ 2 = $75. This means you may have placed $75 as a debit to an account instead of a credit or vice versa.
4. Divide the difference by 9. If it is evenly divisible by 9, a **slide** or transposition may have occurred. A slide is an error resulting from adding or deleting zeros in writing numbers. For example, $4,175.00 may have been copied as $41.75. A **transposition** is the accidental rearrangement of digits of a number. For example, $4,175 might have been accidentally written as $4,157.
5. Compare the balances in the trial balance with the ledger accounts to check for copying errors.
6. Recompute balances in each ledger account.
7. Trace all postings from journal to ledger.
8. Take a coffee break before beginning again.

CORRECTING ERRORS IN JOURNALIZING AND POSTING

What should you do if you find an error? First, don't panic. Everyone makes mistakes, and there are accepted ways of correcting them. Only pencilled-in data can be erased. Once an entry has been made in ink, correcting an error in it must always show that the entry has been changed and who changed it. Sometimes, you must also explain why a change has been made.

Making a Correction before Posting

Before posting, error correction is straightforward. Simply draw a line through the incorrect entry, write the correct information above the line, and write your initials near the change. The following illustration shows an error and its correction in an account title:

	1	Word Processing Equipment		8 0 0 0 00			
		Cash				2 0 0 0 00	
		Accounts Payable *amp*				6 0 0 0 00	
		~~Accounts Receivable~~					
		Purchase of equipment from Ben Co.					

Numbers are handled the same way as account titles, as the next change from 571 to 175 shows:

	18	Advertising Expense		1 7 5 00	
		Accounts Payable			amp ~~1 7 5 00~~ ~~5 7 1 00~~
		Bill from Al's News			

If a number has been entered in the wrong column, a straight line is drawn through it, and the number is then written in the correct column:

	1	Word Processing Equipment		8 0 0 0 00	
		Cash			2 0 0 0 00
		Accounts Payable		amp ~~6 0 0 0 00~~	6 0 0 0 00
		Purchase of equipment from Ben Co.			

Making a Correction after Posting

What if an amount is correctly entered in the journal but posted incorrectly to the ledger of the proper account? The first step is to draw a line through the error and write the correct figure above it. Then, the running balance must be changed to reflect the corrected posting. Here too a line is drawn through the balance and the corrected balance is written above it. Both changes are initialed.

Word Processing Fees   Account No. 411

Date 19XX	Explanation	Post Ref.	Debit	Credit	DR or CR	Balance
May 7		GJ1		2 5 0 0 00	CR	2 5 0 0 00
22		GJ1		amp ~~4 1 0 0 00~~ ~~1 0 0 00~~	CR	~~6 6 0 0 00~~ ~~2 6 0 0 00~~ amp

Correcting an Entry
Posted to the Wrong Account

Drawing a line through an error and writing the correction above it is possible when a mistake has occurred within the proper account. But when an error involves posting to the wrong account, then a correction accompanied by an explanation must be made in the journal. The correct information is then posted to the appropriate ledgers.

Suppose, for example, that as a result of tracing postings from journal entries to ledgers you find that a $180 telephone bill has been incorrectly debited as an advertising expense. First, the journal entry should be corrected and the correction explained, like this:

	Date	Account Titles and Description	PR	Dr.		Cr.	
	19XX						
	May 29	Telephone Expense	513	1 8 0 00			
		Advertising Expense	112			1 8 0 00	
		To correct error in which					
		Advertising Exp. was debited					
		for charges to Telephone Exp.					

General Journal — *Page 3*

This is what the corrected ledger account would look like:

Advertising Expense — Acct. No. 512

Date 19XX	Explanation	Post Ref.	Debit	Credit	DR or CR	Balance
May 18		GJ1	1 7 5 00		DR	1 7 5 00
23		GJ1	1 8 0 00		DR	3 5 5 00
29		GJ3		1 8 0 00	DR	1 7 5 00

and the Telephone Expense account would look like this:

Telephone Expense — Acct. No. 513

Date 19XX	Explanation	Post Ref.	Debit	Credit	DR or CR	Balance
May 29		GJ3	1 8 0 00		DR	1 8 0 00

At this point you should be able to

1. Prepare a trial balance with a ledger, using three-column accounts. (p. 86)
2. Analyze and correct a trial balance that doesn't balance. (p. 87)
3. Correct journal and posting errors. (p. 88)

☐ ## SELF-REVIEW QUIZ 3-3

1.

Interoffice Memo

TO: Al Vincent

FROM: Professor Jones

RE: Trial Balance

You have submitted to me an incorrect trial balance. Could you please rework and turn in to me before next Friday?
Note: Individual amounts look OK.

J. Flynn
Trial Balance
October 31, 19XX

	Dr.	Cr.
Cash		7 6 6 0 00
Operating Expenses		1 6 0 0 00
J. Flynn, Withdrawals		8 0 0 00
Service Revenue		5 3 0 0 00
Equipment	6 0 0 0 00	
Accounts Receivable	2 5 4 0 00	
Accounts Payable	2 0 0 0 00	
Supplies	3 0 0 00	
J. Flynn, Capital		11 6 0 0 00

2. A $4,000 debit to office equipment was mistakenly posted on June 9, 19XX to office supplies. Prepare the appropriate journal entry to correct this error.

SOLUTION TO SELF-REVIEW QUIZ 3-3

1.

J. Flynn
Trial Balance
October 31, 19XX

	Dr.	Cr.
Cash	7 6 6 0 00	
Accounts Receivable	2 5 4 0 00	
Supplies	3 0 0 00	
Equipment	6 0 0 0 00	
Accounts Payable		2 0 0 0 00
J. Flynn, Capital		11 6 0 0 00
J. Flynn, Withdrawals	8 0 0 00	
Service Revenue		5 3 0 0 00
Operating Expenses	1 6 0 0 00	
Totals	18 9 0 0 00	18 9 0 0 00

2.

	General Journal				Page 4	
Date	Account Titles and Description	PR	Dr.		Cr.	
19XX						
June 9	Office Equipment		4 0 0 0 00			
	Office Supplies				4 0 0 0 00	
	To correct error in which office					
	supplies had been debited for					
	purchase of office equipment					

SUMMARY OF KEY POINTS AND KEY TERMS

LEARNING UNIT 3-1

1. The accounting cycle is a sequence of accounting procedures that are usually performed during an accounting period.

2. An accounting period is the time period for which the income statement is prepared.

3. A calendar year is from January 1 to December 31. The fiscal year is any twelve-month period. A fiscal year could be a calendar year but does not have to be.

4. Interim reports are statements that are usually prepared for a month or a quarter (a portion of the fiscal year).

5. A general journal is a book where transactions are recorded in chronological order. Here debits and credits are shown together on one page. This is the book of original entry.

6. The ledger is a collection of accounts where information is accumulated from the postings of the journal. The ledger is the book of final entry.

7. Journalizing is the process of recording journal entries.

8. The chart of accounts provides the specific titles of accounts to be entered in the journal.

9. When journalizing, the post reference column is left blank.

10. A compound journal entry occurs when more than two accounts are affected in the journalizing process of a business transaction.

Accounting cycle: For each accounting period, the process that begins with the recording of business transactions or procedures into a journal and ends with the completion of a post-closing trial balance.

Accounting period: The period of time for which an income statement is prepared.

Book of final entry: Book that receives information about business transactions from a book of original entry (a journal). Example: a ledger.

Book of original entry: Book that records the first formal information about business transactions. Example: a journal.

Calendar year: January 1 to December 31.

Compound journal entry: A journal entry that affects more than two accounts.

Fiscal year: The twelve-month period a business chooses for its accounting year.

General journal: The simplest form of a journal, which records information from transactions in chronological order as they occur. This journal links the debit and credit parts of transactions together.

Interim reports: Financial reports that are prepared for a month, quarter, or some other portion of the fiscal year.

Journal: A listing of business transactions in chronological order. The journal links on one page the debit and credit parts of transactions.

Journal entry: The transaction (debits and credits) that is recorded into a journal once it is analyzed.

Journalizing: The process of recording a transaction entry into the journal.

Natural business year: A business's fiscal year that ends at the same time as a slow seasonal period begins.

LEARNING UNIT 3-2

1. Posting is the process of transferring information from the journal to the ledger.
2. The journal and ledger contain the same information but in a different form.
3. The three-column account aids in keeping a running balance of an account.
4. The normal balance of an account will be located on the side that increases it according to the rules of debits and credits. For example, the normal balances of liabilities occur on the credit side.
5. The mechanical process of posting requires care in transferring appropriate dates, post references, titles, and amounts.

Cross-referencing: Adding to the PR column of the journal the account number of the ledger account that was updated from the journal.

Three-column account: A running balance account that records debits and credits and has a column for an ending balance (debit or credit). Replaces the standard two-column account we used earlier.

Normal balance: The side of an account that is increasing according to the rules of debit and credit. For example, the normal balance of assets is on the debit side; the normal balance of liabilities is on the credit side.

Posting: The transferring, copying, or recording of information from a journal to a ledger.

LEARNING UNIT 3-3

1. A trial balance can balance but be incorrect. For example, an entire journal entry may not have been posted.
2. If a trial balance doesn't balance, check for errors in addition, omission of postings, slides, transpositions, copying errors, and so on.
3. Specific procedures should be followed in making corrections in journals and ledgers.

Slide: The error that results in adding or deleting zeros in the writing of a number. Example: 79,200 → 79,20.

Transposition: The accidental rearrangement of digits of a number. Example: 152 → 125.

Trial balance: An informal listing of the ledger accounts and their balances in the ledger that aids in proving the equality of debits and credits.

DISCUSSION QUESTIONS

1. Explain the concept of the accounting cycle.
2. An accounting period is based on the balance sheet. Agree or disagree.
3. Compare and contrast a calendar year versus a fiscal year.
4. What are interim reports?
5. Why is the ledger called the book of final entry?
6. How do transactions get "linked" in a general journal?
7. What is the relationship of the chart of accounts to the general journal?
8. What is a compound journal entry?

BLUEPRINT OF FIRST FOUR STEPS OF ACCOUNTING CYCLE

Business Transactions
(in monetary terms)

Step 1: Business transactions occur and generate source documents.

Moore Company
General Journal

p. 2

Date			PR	Dr.	Cr.
19XX Jan.	10	Supplies	114	5	
		Cash	111		5

Book of original entry — records in chronological order

Step 2: Analyze and record business transactions in a journal.

Step 3: Post information from journal to ledger.

POST

Book of final entry accumulates information from journal

Ledger

Cash   Acct. No. 111

Date 19XX	Explanation	Post Ref.	Debit	Credit	DR or CR	Balance
Jan 1	Bal.	✔			DR	2 0 0 00
10		GJ2		5 00	DR	1 9 5 00

Step 4: Prepare a trial balance.

Moore Company
Trial Balance
January 31, 19XX

	Dr.	Cr.
Assets	X	
Liabilities		X
Capital		X
Withdrawals	X	
Revenues		X
Expenses	X	
Totals	XXX	XXX

List of balances from each of the ledger accounts

Ledger

Supplies   Acct. No. 114

Date 19XX	Explanation	Post Ref.	Debit	Credit	DR or CR	Balance
Jan 10		GJ2	5 00		DR	5 00

9. Posting means updating the journal. Agree or disagree. Please comment.

10. The side that decreases an account is the normal balance. True or false?

11. The PR column of a general journal is the last item to be filled in during the posting process. Agree or disagree.

12. Discuss the concept of cross-referencing.

13. What is the difference between a transposition and a slide?

EXERCISES

1. Prepare journal entries for the following transactions that occurred during October:

Preparing journal entries.

19XX
Oct. 1   M. Slade invested $600 cash and $200 of equipment into his new business.
      3   Purchased building for $25,000 on account.
      12   Purchased from Long Co. a truck for $6,000 cash.
      18   Bought supplies from Rolo Co. on account, $400.

2. Record the following into the general journal of Paul's Repair Shop:

Preparing journal entries.

19XX
Jan. 1   Paul Keen invested $15,000 cash in the repair shop.
      5   Paid $6,000 for shop equipment.
      8   Bought from Hal Co. shop equipment for $8,000 on account.
      14   Received $500 for repair fees earned.
      18   Billed Rusty David $400 for services rendered.
      20   Paul withdrew $100 for personal use.

3. Post the following transactions to the ledger of Hester Company. The partial ledger of Hester is Cash, 111; Equipment, 121; Accounts Payable, 211; and J. Hester, Capital, 311. Please use three-column accounts in the posting process.

Posting.

																						Page 4
Date 19XX			PR	Dr.	Cr.	
Mar.	4	Cash		2 0 0 0 00		
		J. Hester, Capital			2 0 0 0 00	
		Cash investment				
	9	Equipment		6 0 0 0 00		
		Cash			1 0 0 0 00	
		Accounts Payable			5 0 0 0 00	
		Purchase of equipment				

4. From the following transactions for Veel Company for the month of July, (a) prepare journal entries (assume that it is p. 1 of the journal), (b) post to the ledger (use three-column account), and (c) prepare a trial balance.

Journalizing, posting, and preparing a trial balance.

July 1   Nancy Veel invested $4,000 in the business.
      4   Bought from Jee Co. equipment on account, $600.
      15   Billed Langley Co. for services rendered, $3,000.

18   Received $2,000 cash for services rendered.

24   Paid salaries expense, $1,600.

28   Nancy withdrew $200 for personal use.

Partial chart of accounts includes: Cash, 111; Accounts Receivable, 112; Equipment, 121; Accounts Payable, 211; N. Veel, Capital, 311; N. Veel, Withdrawals, 312; Fees Earned, 411; Salaries Expense, 511.

Correcting a trial balance.

5. You have been hired to correct the following trial balance that has been recorded improperly from the ledger to the trial balance.

Potter Co.
Trial Balance
March 31, 19XX

	Dr.	Cr.
Cash	9 8 0 0 00	
Accounts Receivable		1 2 0 0 00
Accounts Payable	1 8 0 0 00	
A. Potter, Capital		6 5 0 0 00
A. Potter, Withdrawals		3 0 0 00
Services Earned		4 7 0 0 00
Concessions Earned	2 5 0 0 00	
Rent Expense	4 0 0 00	
Salaries Expense	2 5 0 0 00	
Miscellaneous Expense		1 3 0 0 00
Totals	17 0 0 0 00	14 0 0 0 00

6. On February 6, 19XX, Bob Allen made the following journal entry to record the purchase on account of office equipment priced at $1,200. This transaction had not yet been posted when the error was discovered. Make the appropriate correction.

General Journal

Date		Account Titles and Description	PR	Dr.	Cr.
19XX					
Feb.	6	Office Equipment		9 0 0 00	
		Accounts Payable			9 0 0 00
		Purchase of office equip. on account			

GROUP A PROBLEMS

3A-1. Jessie Roy has decided to open Roy's Dog Grooming Center. As the bookkeeper, you have been requested to journalize the following transactions:

Journalizing.

19XX
April   1   Paid rent for two months in advance, $1,600.
       3   Purchased grooming equipment on account from Rick's Supply House, $2,200.
     10   Purchased grooming supplies from Pete's Wholesale for $300 cash.
     12   Received $900 cash from grooming fees earned.
     20   Jessie withdrew $200 for her personal use.
     21   Advertising bill received from *Daily Sun* but unpaid, $75.
     25   Paid cleaning expense, $70.
     28   Paid salaries expense, $300.
     29   Performed grooming work for $1,200; however, payment will not be received from Jay's Kennel until May.
     30   Paid Rick's Supply House half the amount owed from April 3 transaction.

Your task is to journalize the above transactions. The chart of accounts for Roy's Dog Grooming Center is as follows:

Assets	**Owner's Equity**
111 Cash	311 Jessie Roy, Capital
112 Accounts Receivable	312 Jessie Roy, Withdrawals
114 Prepaid Rent	
116 Grooming Supplies	**Revenue**
121 Grooming Equipment	411 Grooming Fees Earned
Liabilities	**Expenses**
211 Accounts Payable	511 Advertising Expense
	512 Salaries Expense
	514 Cleaning Expense

3A-2. On June 1, 19XX, Mike Wallace opened Mike's Dance Studio. The following transactions occurred in June:

Comprehensive Problem: Journalizing, posting, and preparing a trial balance.

19XX
June   1   Mike Wallace invested $5,000 in the dance studio.
      1   Paid three months' rent in advance, $900.
      3   Purchased $600 of equipment from Moore Co. on account.
      5   Received $700 cash for fitness-training workshop for dancers.
      8   Purchased $400 of supplies for cash.
      9   Billed Ranger Co. $1,800 for group dance lesson for its employees.
     10   Paid salaries of assistants, $600.
     15   Mike Wallace withdrew $200 from the business for his personal use.
     28   Paid electrical expense, $150.
     29   Paid telephone bill for June, $220.

Your task is to
    A. Set up the ledger based on the chart of accounts below.
    B. Journalize (journal is Page 1) and post the June transactions.
    C. Prepare a trial balance as of June 30, 19XX.

The chart of accounts for Mike's Dance Studio is as follows:

Assets
111 Cash
112 Accounts Receivable
114 Prepaid Rent
121 Supplies
131 Equipment

Liabilities
211 Accounts Payable

Owner's Equity
311 Mike Wallace, Capital
321 Mike Wallace, Withdrawals

Revenue
411 Fees Earned

Expenses
511 Electrical Expense
521 Salaries Expense
531 Telephone Expense

Comprehensive Problem: Journalizing, posting, and preparing a trial balance.

3A-3. The following transactions occurred in June 19XX for R. Black's Placement Agency:

19XX
June 1   R. Black invested $8,000 cash in the placement agency.
      1   Bought equipment on account from Rolo Co., $1,000.
      3   Earned placement fees of $1,400, but payment will not be received until July.
      5   R. Black withdrew $200 for his personal use.
      7   Paid wage expense, $400.
      9   Placed a client on a local TV show, receiving $500 cash.
     15   Bought supplies on account from Roger Co., $300.
     28   Paid telephone bill for June, $280.
     29   Advertising bill from Globe Co. received but not paid, $600.

The chart of accounts for R. Black's Placement Agency is as follows:

Assets
111 Cash
112 Accounts Receivable
131 Supplies
141 Equipment

Liabilities
211 Accounts Payable

Owner's Equity
311 R. Black, Capital
321 R. Black, Withdrawals

Revenue
411 Placement Fees Earned

Expenses
511 Wage Expense
521 Telephone Expense
531 Advertising Expense

Your task is to
   A. Set up the ledger based on the chart of accounts.
   B. Journalize (P. 1) and post the June transactions.
   C. Prepare a trial balance as of June 30, 19XX.

GROUP B PROBLEMS

3B-1. In April Jessie Roy opened a new dog grooming center. Please assist her by journalizing the following business transactions:

Journalizing.

19XX

April	1	Jessie Roy invested $4,000 of grooming equipment as well as $6,000 cash in the new business.
	3	Purchased grooming supplies on account from Rex Co., $500.
	10	Purchased office equipment on account from Ross Stationery, $400.
	12	Jessie paid her home telephone bill from the company chequebook, $60.
	20	Received $600 cash for grooming services performed.
	21	Advertising bill received but not paid, $75.
	25	Cleaning bill received but not paid, $90.
	28	Performed grooming work for Jay Kennels, $700; however, payment will not be received until May.
	29	Paid salaries expense, $400.
	30	Paid Ross Stationery half the amount owed from April 10 transaction.

The chart of accounts for Roy includes: Cash, 111; Accounts Receivable, 112; Prepaid Rent, 114; Grooming Supplies, 116; Office Equipment, 120; Grooming Equipment, 121; Accounts Payable, 211; Jessie Roy, Capital, 311; Jessie Roy, Withdrawals, 312; Grooming Fees Earned, 411; Advertising Expense, 511; Salaries Expense, 512; and Cleaning Expense, 514.

3B-2. In June the following transactions occurred for Mike's Dance Studio.

Comprehensive Problem: Journalizing, posting, and preparing a trial balance.

19XX

June	1	Mike Wallace invested $6,000 in the dance studio.
	1	Paid four months' rent in advance, $1,200.
	3	Purchased supplies on account from A.J.K., $700.
	5	Purchased equipment on account from Reese Company, $900.
	8	Received $1,300 cash for dance-training program provided to Northwest Jr. College.
	9	Billed Long Co. for dance lessons provided, $600.
	10	Mike withdrew $400 from the dance studio to buy a new chain saw for his home.
	15	Paid salaries expense, $400.
	28	Paid telephone bill, $118.
	28	Electric bill received but unpaid, $120.

Your task is to
   A. Set up a ledger.
   B. Journalize (all P. 1) and post the June transactions.
   C. Prepare a trial balance as of June 30, 19XX.

Chart of accounts includes: Cash, 111; Accounts Receivable, 112; Prepaid Rent, 114; Supplies, 121; Equipment, 131; Accounts Payable, 211; Mike Wallace, Capital, 311; Mike Wallace, Withdrawals, 321; Fees Earned, 411; Electrical Expense, 511; Salaries Expense, 521; Telephone Expense, 531.

Comprehensive Problem: Journalizing, posting, and preparing a trial balance.

3B-3. In June, R. Black's Placement Agency had the following transactions:

19XX
June 1   R. Black invested $6,000 in the new placement agency.
      2   Bought equipment for cash, $350.
      3   Earned placement fee commission, $2,100, but payment from Avon Co. will not be received until July.
      5   Paid wages expense, $400.
      7   R. Black paid his home utility bill from the company chequebook, $69.
      9   Placed Jay Diamond on a national TV show, receiving $900 cash.
     15   Paid cash for supplies, $350.
     28   Telephone bill received but not paid, $185.
     29   Advertising bill received but not paid, $200.

The chart of accounts includes: Cash, 111; Accounts Receivable, 112; Supplies, 131; Equipment, 141; Accounts Payable, 211; R. Black, Capital, 311; R. Black, Withdrawals, 321; Placement Fees Earned, 411; Wage Expense, 511; Telephone Expense, 521; Advertising Expense, 531.

Your task is to
   A. Set up a ledger based on the chart of accounts.
   B. Journalize (all P. 1) and post transactions.
   C. Prepare a trial balance for June 30, 19XX.

GROUP C PROBLEMS

Journalizing.

3C-1. In August, Brian Korg opened a personal financial planning center. Please assist him by journalizing the following business transactions:

19XX
Aug. 1   Brian Korg invested $4,000 of computer equipment as well as $6,000 cash in the new business.
      3   Purchased computer supplies on account from Kent Co., $360.
     10   Purchased office equipment on account from Apex Stationery, $940.
     12   Brian paid his home telephone bill from the company chequebook, $30.
     20   Received $700 cash for planning services performed.
     21   Advertising bill received but not paid, $125.
     25   Cleaning bill received but not paid, $75.
     28   Performed planning services for Franklin Corp., $2,100; however, payment will not be received until September.
     29   Paid salaries expense, $700.
     30   Paid Apex Stationery half the amount owed from August 10 transaction, $470.
     31   Received bill for Repairs on equipment, $235. Not yet paid.

The chart of accounts for the company includes: Cash, 111; Accounts Receivable, 112; Prepaid Rent, 114; Computer Supplies, 116; Office Equipment, 120; Computer Equipment, 121; Accounts Payable, 211; Brian Korg, Capital, 311; Brian Korg, Withdrawals, 312; Planning Fees Earned, 411; Advertising Expense, 511; Salaries Expense, 512; Repairs Expense, 513 and Cleaning Expense, 514.

3C-2. In July the following transactions occurred for Joan's Aerobic Studio.

19XX

July 1   Joan Clements invested $8,400 in the studio.
      1   Paid three months' rent in advance, $1,800.
      3   Purchased supplies on account from Marlin Supplies, $470.
      5   Purchased equipment on account from Brinkley Company, $2,500.
      8   Received $1,750 cash for aerobic training program provided to Anne Webber Dance Group.
      9   Billed Short Co. for aerobic lessons provided, $1,600.
      10 Joan withdrew $800 from the dance studio to buy a new sofa for her apartment.
      15 Paid salaries expense, $1,100.
      28 Paid telephone bill, $88.
      28 Electric bill received but unpaid, $155.
      31 Advertising bill received from City Newspaper, $350.

Comprehensive Problem: Journalizing, posting, and preparing a trial balance.

Your task is to
   A. Set up a ledger.
   B. Journalize (all P. 1) and post the July transactions.
   C. Prepare a trial balance as of July 31, 19XX.

Chart of accounts includes: Cash, 111; Accounts Receivable, 112; Prepaid Rent, 114; Supplies, 121; Equipment, 131; Accounts Payable, 211; Joan Clements, Capital, 311; Joan Clements, Withdrawals, 321; Fees Earned, 411; Advertising Expense, 511; Electrical Expense, 515; Salaries Expense, 521; Telephone Expense, 531.

3C-3. In June, Ernie Jacobson's Investigative Agency had the following transactions:

19XX

June 1   Ernie Jacobson invested $12,000 in the new agency.
      2   Bought equipment for cash, $2,200.
      3   Earned investigative fee, $2,600, but payment from client will not be received until later.
      5   Paid wages expense, $750.
      7   E. Jacobson paid his home water and gas bill from the company chequebook, $99.
      9   Located missing spouse, receiving $700 cash.
      15 Paid cash for supplies, $200.
      25 Received half of the fee earned on June 3, $1,300.
      28 Telephone bill received but not paid, $125.
      29 Advertising bill received but not paid, $380.

Comprehensive Problem: Journalizing, posting, and preparing a trial balance.

The chart of accounts includes: Cash, 111; Accounts Receivable, 112; Supplies, 131; Equipment, 141; Accounts Payable, 211; E. Jacobson, Capital, 311; E. Jacobson, Withdrawals, 321; Investigative Fees Earned, 411; Wage Expense, 511; Telephone Expense, 521; Advertising Expense, 531.

Your task is to
   A. Set up a ledger based on the chart of accounts.
   B. Journalize (all P. 1) and post transactions.
   C. Prepare a trial balance for June 30, 19XX.

PRACTICAL ACCOUNTING APPLICATION #1

Paul Regan, bookkeeper of Hampton Co., has been up half the night trying to get his trial balance to balance. Here are his results:

Hampton Co.
Trial Balance
June 30, 19XX

	Dr.	Cr.
Office Sales		5 7 2 0 00
Cash in Bank	3 2 6 0 00	
Accounts Receivable	5 6 6 0 00	
Office Equipment	8 4 0 0 00	
Accounts Payable		4 1 6 0 00
D. Hole, Capital		11 5 6 0 00
D. Hole, Withdrawals		7 0 0 00
Wage Expense	2 6 0 0 00	
Rent Expense	9 4 0 00	
Utilities Expense	2 6 00	
Office Supplies	1 2 0 00	
Prepaid Rent	1 8 0 00	

Ken Small, the accountant, compared Paul's amounts in the trial balance with those in the ledger, recomputed each account balance, and compared postings. Ken found the following errors:

1. A $200 debit to D. Hole, Withdrawals, was posted as a credit.
2. D. Hole, Withdrawals, was listed on the trial balance as a credit.
3. A Note Payable account with a credit balance of $2,400 was not listed on the trial balance.
4. The pencil footings for Accounts Payable were debits of $5,320 and credits of $8,800.
5. A debit of $180 to Prepaid Rent was not posted.
6. Office Supplies bought for $60 was posted as a credit to Supplies.
7. A debit of $120 to Accounts Receivable was not posted.
8. A cash payment of $420 was credited to Cash for $240.
9. The pencil footing of the credits to Cash was overstated by $400.
10. The Utilities Expense of $260 was listed in the trial balance as $26.

Assist Paul Regan by preparing a correct trial balance. What advice could you give Ken about Paul? Can you explain the situation to Paul?

PRACTICAL ACCOUNTING APPLICATION #2

Lauren Oliver, an accounting lab tutor, is having a debate with some of her assistants. They are trying to find out how each of the following five unrelated situations would affect the trial balance:

1. A $5 debit to Cash in the ledger was not posted.
2. A $10 debit to Computer Supplies was debited to Computer Equipment.

3. An $8 debit to Wage Expense was debited twice to the account.
4. A $4 debit to Computer Supplies was debited to Computer Sales.
5. A $35 credit to Accounts Payable was posted as a $53 credit.

Could you indicate to Lauren the effect that each situation will have on the trial balance? If a situation will have no effect, indicate that fact.

ACCOUNTING RECALL
A Cumulative Approach

THIS EXAM REVIEWS CHAPTERS 1 THROUGH 3.

Your *Study Guide and Working Papers* have forms to complete this exam, as well as worked-out solutions. The page references next to each question identify what page to turn back to if you answer the question incorrectly.

PART I Vocabulary Review

Match the terms to the appropriate definition or phrase.

Page

(70)	1. Chart of Accounts	A. Process of recording transactions
(70)	2. Ledger	B. Rearrangement of digits
(88)	3. Slide	C. Book of original entry
(69)	4. Calendar year	D. Running balance
(88)	5. Transposition	E. Transferring information
(79)	6. Three-column account	F. January 1 to December 31
(69)	7. Journalizing	G. Adding or deleting numbers
(72)	8. Compound entry	H. Numbering system
(79)	9. Posting	I. More than two accounts
(69)	10. Journal	J. Book of final entry

PART II True or False (Accounting Theory)

(70) 11. The Ledger is located in same book as a Journal.

(80) 12. The PR column of a General Journal is completed after the posting to the ledger is complete.

(88) 13. Correcting errors in journalizing can only be done before posting.

(69) 14. A calendar year could be a fiscal year.

(87) 15. A trial balance could balance but be incorrect.

PART III Applications Problem (69-85)

From the following transactions of Jesse Company (a) journalize, (b) post, and (c) prepare a trial balance.

May	1	Ray Jesse invests $5,000 in the business.
	4	Bought from Lowe Co., office equipment on account, $700.
	18	Billed Smith for fees earned, $4,000.
	24	Ray Jesse withdrew $600 for personal use.
	28	Paid salaries, $1,400.

Partial chart of accounts includes: Cash 111; Accounts Receivable 112; Office Equipment 121; Accounts Payable 211; R. Jesse, Capital 311; R. Jesse, Withdrawals 312; Fees Earned 411; Salaries Expense 511.

THE ACCOUNTING CYCLE CONTINUED:
Preparing Work Sheets and Financial Reports

IN THIS CHAPTER WE WILL COVER THE FOLLOWING TOPICS:

1. ADJUSTMENTS: PREPAID RENT, OFFICE SUPPLIES, DEPRECIATION ON EQUIPMENT, AND ACCRUED SALARIES. (PP. 107-115)

2. PREPARATION OF ADJUSTED TRIAL BALANCE ON THE WORK SHEET. (P. 116-118)

3. THE INCOME STATEMENT AND BALANCE SHEET SECTIONS OF THE WORK SHEET. (PP. 118-120)

4. PREPARING FINANCIAL REPORTS FROM THE WORK SHEET. (PP. 123-126)

The accompanying diagram shows the steps of the accounting cycle that were completed for Clark's Word Processing Services in the last chapter. This chapter continues the cycle with the preparation of a work sheet and then three financial reports.

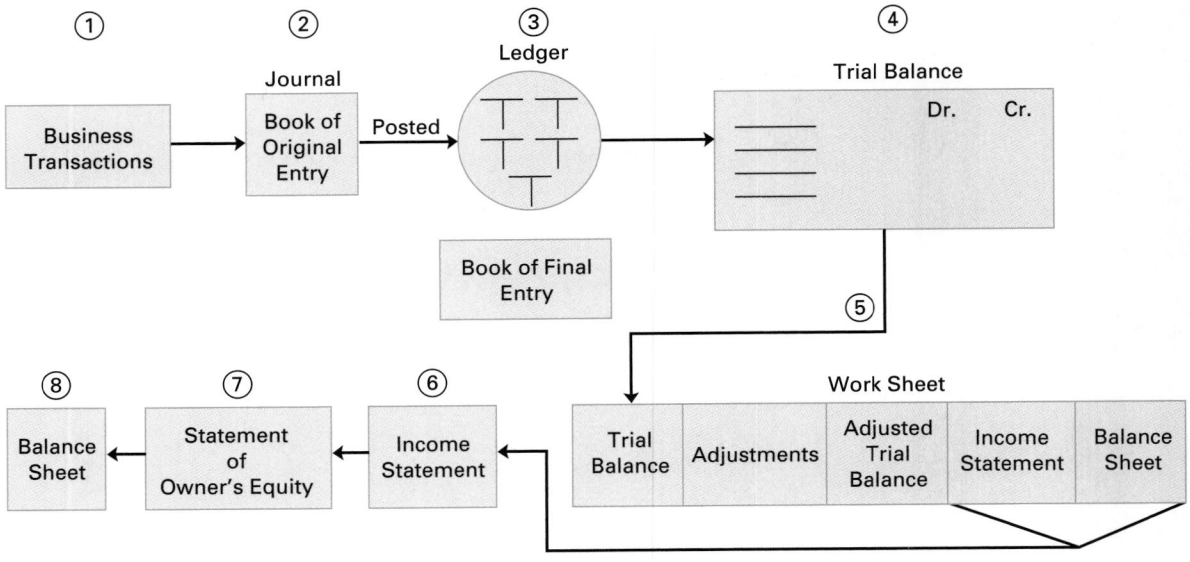

LEARNING UNIT 4-1

Step 5 of the Accounting Cycle: Preparing a Work Sheet

The work sheet helps to organize the data needed to prepare financial reports.

An accountant uses a **work sheet** like a scratch pad, in order to organize and check data before preparing the financial reports necessary to complete the accounting cycle. A sample work sheet is shown in Figure 4-1. The work sheet is not a formal report, and no dollar signs appear on it. You could compare it with the rough draft of a research paper that you prepare for a course. When the research paper is complete, in proper form, no one sees the scratch paper that made the final report possible. The most important function of the work sheet is to allow the accountant to find and correct errors before financial statements are prepared.

Notice the heading on the work sheet for Clark's Word Processing Services shown here:

Clark's Word Processing Services	(Name of company)
Work Sheet	(Name of the working paper)
For Month Ended May 31, 19XX	(Date and the length of the accounting period represented by the work sheet)

The accounts listed on the far left of the work sheet are the only ones in the ledger with balances. The rest of the work sheet is made up of five sections, each divided into debit and credit columns. These five sections are the trial balance, adjustments, adjusted trial balance, income statement, and balance sheet sections. We will discuss each in turn.

FIGURE 4-1   **The Work Sheet**

Clark's Word Processing Services
Work Sheet
For month ended May 31, 19XX

Account Titles	Trial Balance		Adjustments		Adjusted Trial Balance		Income Statement	
	Dr.	Cr.	Dr.	Cr.	Dr.	Cr.	Dr.	Cr.
Cash	2 0 9 0 00							
Accounts Receivable	4 1 0 0 00							
Office Supplies	4 0 0 00							
Prepaid Rent	9 0 0 00							
Word Processing Equipment	8 0 0 0 00							
Accounts Payable		3 5 7 5 00						
B. Clark, Capital		7 0 0 0 00						
B. Clark, Withdrawals	4 3 0 00							
Word Processing Fees		6 6 0 0 00						
Office Salaries Expense	9 0 0 00							
Advertising Expense	1 7 5 00							
Telephone Expense	1 8 0 00							
	17 1 7 5 00	17 1 7 5 00						

THE TRIAL BALANCE SECTION

We discussed how to prepare a trial balance in Chapter 2. Some companies prepare a separate trial balance; others, such as Clark's Word Processing Services, place the trial balance directly on the work sheet. In any case, the trial balance consists of the list of the individual accounts taken from the ledger with their balances. Note that the accountant has listed only those titles in the ledger that have a balance. New titles from the ledger will be added as needed (we will be doing this in a moment).

THE ADJUSTMENTS SECTION

Before the financial reports are prepared, the accountant wants to calculate the *latest* up-to-date balances of each account. In the last few chapters we have been discussing transactions that occur with outside suppliers and companies. But there are also inside transactions that occur during the accounting cycle that must be recorded. By analyzing each of Clark's accounts, the accountant is able to identify specific accounts that must be **adjusted**, or brought up to date. The following accounts are of concern to the accountant for Clark's Word Processing Services:

Adjusting is like fine-tuning your TV set.

Office Supplies
Prepaid Rent
Word Processing Equipment
Office Salaries Expense

} Need to be adjusted so as to bring their balances up to date before financial reports are prepared.

Let's look at each account separately. After each one is analyzed, the work sheet will be reproduced to show how the adjustments columns will help to update the trial balance. And, after adjustments are completed, a new adjusted trial balance will be prepared.

Adjustment A: Office Supplies

At the end of May the accountant received information that of the $400 worth of purchased office supplies, only $80 worth were left (or on hand) as of May 31.

Remember, when the supplies were purchased they were considered an asset. But as supplies get used in the operation of the word processing firm, they become expenses. Let's look at office supplies:

1. Office supplies available, $400.
2. Office supplies left or on hand as of May 31, $80.

The adjustment for supplies deals with the amount of supplies *used up*.

3. Office supplies used up or consumed in the operation of the business for the month of May, $320 ($400 − $80 = $320).

Therefore, the asset Office Supplies is really too high on the trial balance (it should be $80, not $400). At the same time, if we don't show the additional expense of supplies used, the *net income* of Clark's Word Processing Services will be too high.

To summarize, if the adjustment to Office Supplies does *not* take place:

1. Expenses for May will be too low.
2. The asset Office Supplies will be too high.

Adjustments affect both the income statement and balance sheet.

As a consequence:

1. On the income statement, net income will be too high.
2. On the balance sheet, both sides (assets and owner's equity) will be too high.

Now let's look at the adjustment for office supplies in terms of the transaction analysis chart.

Office Supplies Expense 514

320	

This is supplies used up.

Will go on income statement

Accounts Affected	Category	↑ ↓	Rules
Office Supplies Expense	Expense	↑	Dr. ←
Office Supplies	Asset	↓	Cr. ←

Will go on balance sheet

Office Supplies 114

400	320
	80

This is supplies on hand.

Office Supplies Expense comes from the chart of accounts, p. 70. Remember Office Supplies Expense records amount of supplies used up.

The account Office Supplies is called a **mixed account** because the amount entered on the trial balance is partly a balance sheet amount and partly an income statement amount. On the balance sheet, Office Supplies will be an unexpired cost. On the income statement, Office Supplies Expense will be an expired cost.

Let's see how we enter this adjustment on the work sheet (note how the letter A is used to code the adjustment):

(A) 1. An increase in Office Supplies Expense, $320.
     2. A decrease in Office Supplies, $320.

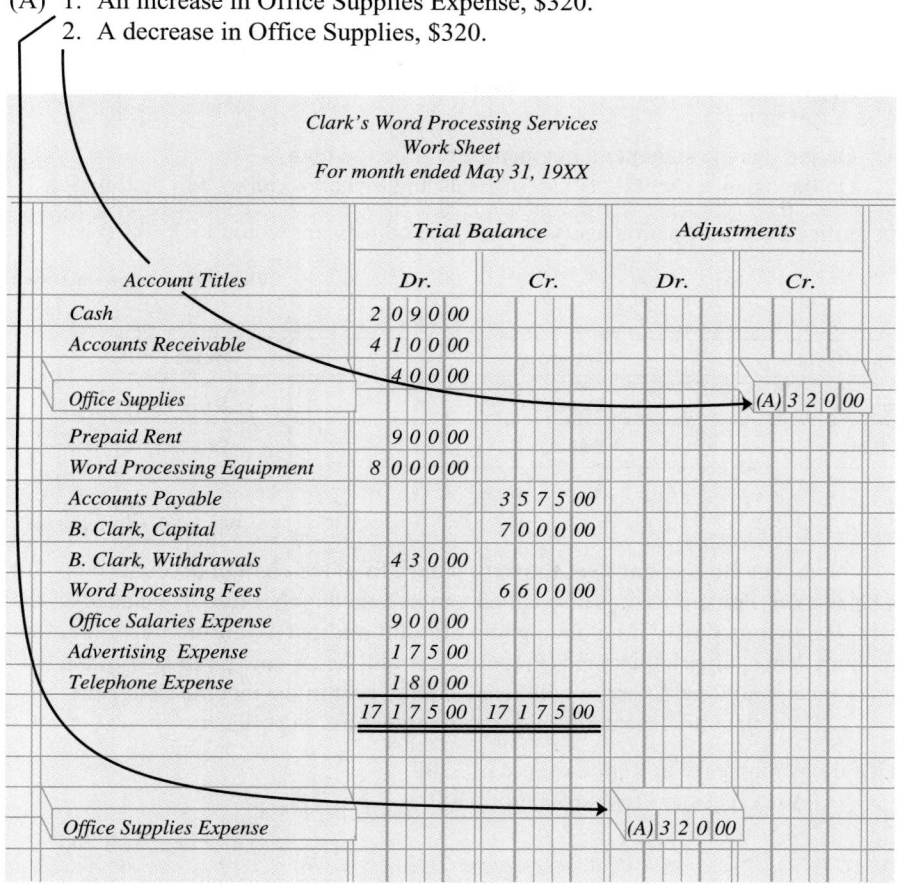

Clark's Word Processing Services
Work Sheet
For month ended May 31, 19XX

Account Titles	Trial Balance		Adjustments	
	Dr.	Cr.	Dr.	Cr.
Cash	2 0 9 0 00			
Accounts Receivable	4 1 0 0 00			
	4 0 0 00			
Office Supplies				(A) 3 2 0 00
Prepaid Rent	9 0 0 00			
Word Processing Equipment	8 0 0 0 00			
Accounts Payable		3 5 7 5 00		
B. Clark, Capital		7 0 0 0 00		
B. Clark, Withdrawals	4 3 0 00			
Word Processing Fees		6 6 0 0 00		
Office Salaries Expense	9 0 0 00			
Advertising Expense	1 7 5 00			
Telephone Expense	1 8 0 00			
	17 1 7 5 00	17 1 7 5 00		
Office Supplies Expense			(A) 3 2 0 00	

Note: All accounts added below the trial balance are increasing.

Since the account Office Supplies Expense is not listed in the account titles, we must list it below the trial balance. Place $320 in the debit column of the adjustments section on the same line as Office Supplies Expense. Place $320 in the credit column of the adjustments section on the same line as Office Supplies. These numbers in the adjustment column show what is used, *not* what is on hand.

Adjustment B: Prepaid Rent

Back on May 1, Clark's Word Processing Services paid three months' rent in advance. The accountant realized that the rent expense would be $300 per month ($900 ÷ 3 months = $300).

Remember, when rent is paid in advance, it is considered an asset called *prepaid rent*. When the asset, prepaid rent, begins to expire or be used up, it becomes an expense. Now it is May 31, and one month's rent, which was paid in advance, has expired and thus becomes an expense.

Should the account be $900, or is there really only $600 of prepaid rent left as of May 31? What do we need to do to bring prepaid rent to the "true" or up-to-date balance? We need to increase Rent Expense by $300 and decrease Prepaid Rent by $300.

The Office Supplies Expense account indicates the amount of supplies used up. It is listed below other trial balance accounts, since it was not on the original trial balance. Think of the Office Supplies Expense account as office supplies used.

A debit will increase the account Office Supplies Expense; a credit will reduce the account Office Supplies.

Adjusting Prepaid Rent.

On p. 107 the trial balance showed a figure for Prepaid Rent of $900.

The amount of rent *expired* is the adjustment figure used to update Prepaid Rent and Rent Expense.

To summarize, if we don't adjust or bring our rent expense up to its proper amount:

1. Expenses for Clark's Word Processing Services for May will be too low.
2. The asset Prepaid Rent will be too high.

The result of this is:

1. On the income statement, net income will be too high.
2. On the balance sheet, both sides (assets and owner's equity) will be too high.

In terms of our transaction analysis chart, the adjustment would look like this:

Will go on income statement

Accounts Affected	Category	↑ ↓	Rules
Rent Expense	Expense	↑	Dr. ←
Prepaid Rent	Asset	↓	Cr. ←

Will go on balance sheet

Rent Expense 515

300	

Prepaid Rent 115

900	300 Adj.
600	

Note that the account Rent Expense comes from the chart of accounts on p. 70. The account Prepaid Rent is also called a mixed account because its balance on the trial balance is partly a balance sheet amount and partly an income statement amount. Thus, after adjustment, Prepaid Rent will be an unexpired cost in the balance sheet, and Rent Expense will be an expired cost in the income statement.

Let's look at how we enter this adjustment on the work sheet:

Rent expense is listed below other trial balance accounts, since it was not on the original balance.

(B) 1. An increase in Rent Expense of $300.
    2. A decrease in Prepaid Rent of $300.

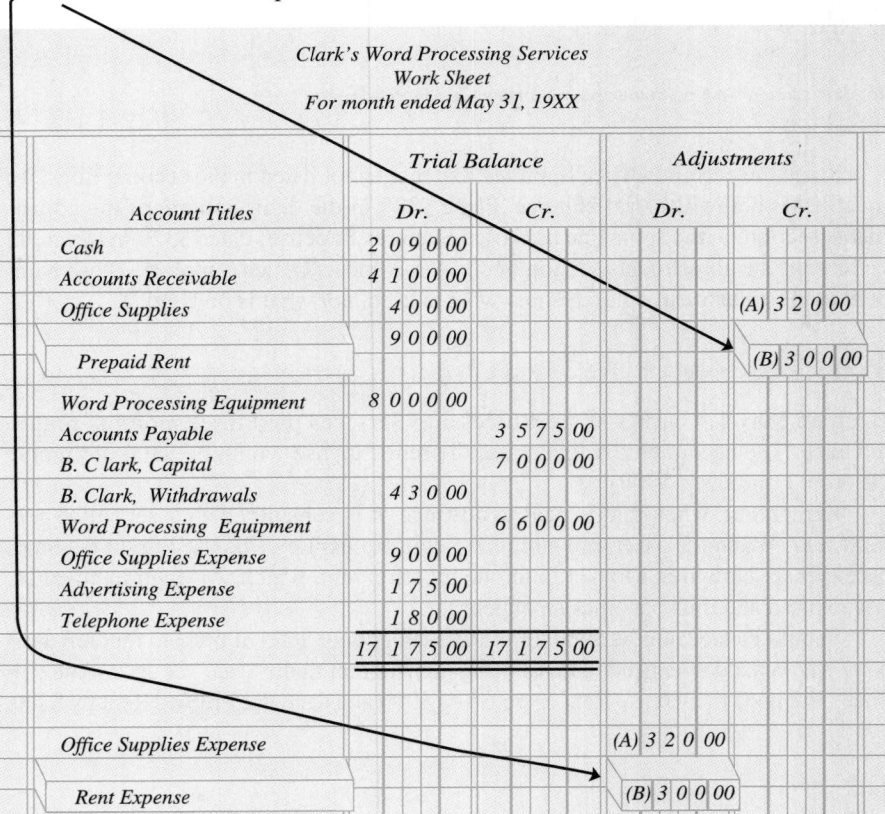

Clark's Word Processing Services
Work Sheet
For month ended May 31, 19XX

Account Titles	Trial Balance Dr.	Trial Balance Cr.	Adjustments Dr.	Adjustments Cr.
Cash	2 0 9 0 00			
Accounts Receivable	4 1 0 0 00			
Office Supplies	4 0 0 00			(A) 3 2 0 00
	9 0 0 00			
Prepaid Rent				(B) 3 0 0 00
Word Processing Equipment	8 0 0 0 00			
Accounts Payable		3 5 7 5 00		
B. C lark, Capital		7 0 0 0 00		
B. Clark, Withdrawals	4 3 0 00			
Word Processing Equipment		6 6 0 0 00		
Office Supplies Expense	9 0 0 00			
Advertising Expense	1 7 5 00			
Telephone Expense	1 8 0 00			
	17 1 7 5 00	17 1 7 5 00		
Office Supplies Expense			(A) 3 2 0 00	
Rent Expense			(B) 3 0 0 00	

Since the account Rent Expense is not listed in the account titles, we must list it below the trial balance (and below Office Supplies Expense). Place $300 in the debit column of the adjustments section, on the same line as Rent Expense. Place $300 in the credit column of the adjustments section, on the same line as Prepaid Rent.

Adjustment C: Word Processing Equipment

Did you note in the first two adjustments how the asset office supplies and the asset prepaid rent were reduced? Our next adjustment, for word processing equipment, will not be handled in quite the same way. Why not? Supplies and prepaid rent tend to be used up in a relatively *short* period of time, but equipment is assumed to have a long life and thus helps to produce revenue over a longer period. Thus accountants choose to keep a record on the balance sheet of the **historical cost**, or original amount of cost, of the equipment. This means that when the adjustment for the word processing equipment is complete, the original cost of $8,000 will still be shown on the balance sheet, as well as reflected in the ledger.

Our goal in making this adjustment is to allocate or spread the cost of the equipment over its expected useful life while still maintaining a record of the full original cost. This spreading is called **depreciation**. To reach this goal we must be able to figure out how much the equipment depreciates per month, and then keep a running total of how that depreciation mounts up over the years.

Our first step is to calculate the amount of depreciation that will be taken for May. (The Income Tax Department has a particular method called **Capital Cost Allowance**, which all businesses in Canada must use to calculate the amount of depreciation. For the moment, we will use the straight-line method of depreciation—so called because equal amounts are taken over successive periods of time.) The calculation of depreciation for the year for Clark's Word Processing Services is as follows (see the Appendix at end of text for more details on calculating depreciation):

$$\frac{\text{cost of equipment} - \text{residual value}}{\text{estimated years of usefulness}}$$

Think of **residual value** as the estimated value of the equipment at end of the fifth year. For Clark, the equipment has an estimated residual value of $2,000.

$$\frac{\$8,000 - \$2,000}{5 \text{ years}} = \frac{\$6,000}{5} = \$1,200 \text{ per year}$$

Since the adjustment for May is only for *one* month, we further calculate the depreciation as follows:

$$\frac{\$1,200}{12 \text{ months}} = \$100 \text{ depreciation per month}$$

This $100 is known as **Depreciation Expense** and will be shown on the income statement.

The question now is, how can we keep this running total of the depreciation amount and yet still keep a record of the full original cost of the equipment? To do this we have to create a new account, called **Accumulated Depreciation**. This is a **contra asset** account; it has the opposite balance of an asset such as equipment. Accumulated Depreciation will summarize, accumulate, or build up the amount of depreciation that is taken on the word processing equipment over its estimated useful life.

Debit increases rent expense and credit reduces amount of rent paid in advance.

Take this one slowly.

Original cost of $8,000 for word processing equipment remains *unchanged* after adjustments.

Assume equipment has a 5-year life.

Clark will record $1,200 of depreciation each year.

Depreciation is an expense reported on the income statement.

The purposes of Accumulated Depreciation are to

1. Let the amount listed on Clark's books for word processing equipment remain at the original cost of $8,000.

Accumulated Depreciation

Dr.	Cr.
–	+

is a contra asset account found on the balance sheet.

2. As of May 31, summarize or accumulate the amount of depreciation taken on the equipment to that date.

Let's see how this would look on a partial balance sheet of Clark's Word Processing Services.

At end of June the accumulated depreciation will be $200, but historical cost will stay at $8,000.

1. Historical cost of $8,000 of equipment is not changed.

2. Amount of accumulated depreciation is $100.

3. This shows the unused amount of the equipment that may be depreciated in future periods of time. This figure, the cost of the asset less its accumulated depreciation, is often termed **net book value** or carrying value.

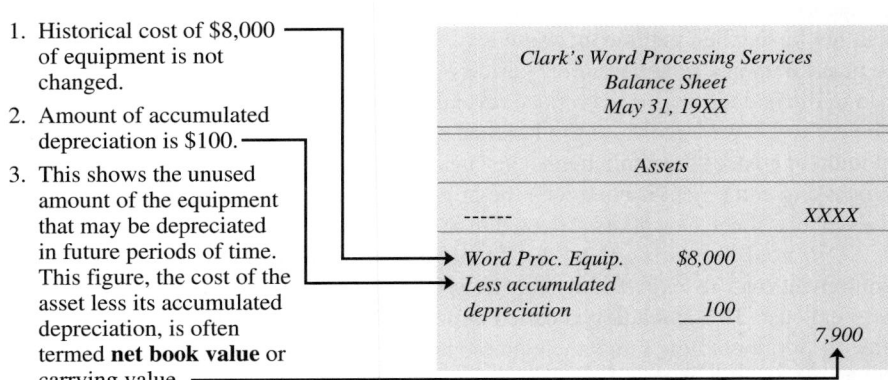

We need an Accumulated Depreciation account to see the relationship of the original or historical cost of the equipment and the amount of depreciation that has been taken or accumulated over a period of time. Remember, Accumulated Depreciation is a contra asset account found on the balance sheet.

Taking depreciation does not result in any new payment of cash. The result of depreciation provides some tax savings.

Let's summarize the key points before going on to mark the adjustment on the work sheet:

1. Depreciation Expense goes on the income statement, which results in
   (a) An increase in total expenses.
   (b) A decrease in net income.
   (c) Therefore, less to be paid in taxes.

Dep. Expense, W.P. 516

100	

Accum. Dep., W.P. 122

	100

2. Accumulated depreciation is a contra asset account found on the balance sheet next to its related equipment account.

3. The original cost of equipment is not reduced; it stays the same until the equipment is sold or removed.

4. Each month the amount in the Accumulated Depreciation account grows larger while the cost of the equipment remains the same.

Now let's analyze the adjustment on the transaction analysis chart:

Accounts Affected	Category	↑ ↓	Rules	
Depreciation Expense, Word Processing Equipment	**Expense**	↑	Dr.	⟵ Will go on income statement
Accumulated Depreciation, Word Processing Equipment	**Contra asset**	↑	Cr.	⟵ Will go on balance sheet

Note that the accounts affected do not include the equipment account, because we leave the original cost of the equipment as is. Note also that as the Accumulated Depreciation increases (as a credit), the end result will be to lower the equipment's net book value, but the original cost of the equipment is not changed.

We enter the adjustment for depreciation of word processing equipment on the work sheet in the following way:

Note that the original cost of the equipment on the work sheet has *not* been changed ($8,000).

(C) 1. An increase in Depreciation Expense, W. P. Equipment.
  2. An increase in Accumulated Depreciation, W. P. Equipment.

Clark's Word Processing Services
Work Sheet
For month ended May 31, 19XX

Account Titles	Trial Balance Dr.	Trial Balance Cr.	Adjustments Dr.	Adjustments Cr.
Cash	2 0 9 0 00			
Accounts Receivable	4 1 0 0 00			
Office Supplies	4 0 0 00			(A) 3 2 0 00
Prepaid Rent	9 0 0 00			(B) 3 0 0 00
Word Processing Equipment	8 0 0 0 00			
Accounts Payable		3 5 7 5 00		
B. Clark, Capital		7 0 0 0 00		
B. Clark, Withdrawals	4 3 0 00			
Word Processing Fees		6 6 0 0 00		
Office Salaries Expense	9 0 0 00			
Advertising Expense	1 7 5 00			
Telephone Expense	1 8 0 00			
	17 1 7 5 00	17 1 7 5 00		
Office Supplies Expense			(A) 3 2 0 00	
Rent Expense			(B) 3 0 0 00	
Depreciation Expense, W.P. Equip.			(C) 1 0 0 00	
Accum. Depreciation, W.P. Equip.				(C) 1 0 0 00

Since this is a new business, neither account that we are adjusting is listed in the account titles. We need to list both accounts below Rent Expense in the account titles section. Next month accumulated depreciation will be listed in the original trial balance. On the work sheet, place $100 in the debit column of the adjustments section, on the same line as Depreciation Expense, W. P. Equipment. Place $100 in the credit column of the adjustments section, on the same line as Accumulated Depreciation, W. P. Equipment.

In the next month, on June 30, you would enter $100 under Depreciation Expense, and Accumulated Depreciation would show a balance of $200. Remember in May, Clark was a new company, with no previous depreciation having been taken.

Now let's look at the last adjustment for Clark's Word Processing Services.

Accumulated Depreciation

Dr.	Cr.
	History of amount of depreciation taken to date

Adjustment D: Salaries Accrued

Adjusting Salaries

Clark's Word Processing Services paid $900 in Office Salaries Expense (see the trial balance of any previous work sheet in this chapter).

On May 27 the last salary cheques were paid for the month. Since we are concerned with information as of May 31, our goal is to update the Office Salaries Expense. What is the true figure for May? Is it $900?

During the days of May 28, 29, 30, 31, John Murray worked for Clark, but his next paycheque is not due until June. For these four days he earned $250. The question is whether this $250 is an expense to Clark in May, before it is actually paid. Or should it be shown as an expense to Clark in June when it is due and is paid?

May						
S	M	T	W	T	F	S
						1
2	3	4	5	6	7	8
9	10	11	12	13	14	15
16	17	18	19	20	21	22
23	24	25	26	27	28	29
30	31					

An expense can be incurred without being paid as long as it has helped in creating earned revenue for a period of time.

Think back to Chapter 1, when we first discussed revenue and expenses. We noted then that revenue is recorded when it is earned, not when the money actually comes in, and expenses are recorded when they are incurred, not when they are actually paid off. This is a principle that we will be discussing in a later chapter; for now it is enough to remember that we record revenue and expenses when they occur, because we want to match earned revenue with the expenses that resulted in earning those revenues. In this case, by working those four days, John Murray was able to create some revenues for Clark in May. Although John will not be paid until June, it is important to show his office salaries expense in May when the revenue was earned.

The results are:

1. Office Salaries Expense is increased by $250. This unpaid and unrecorded expense for salaries for which payment is not due is called **accrued salaries**. In effect, we now show the true expense for salaries ($1,150 instead of $900):

Office Salaries Expense

900	
250	

2. The second result is that salaries payable is increased by $250. Clark's has created a liability called Salaries Payable, meaning that the firm owes money for salaries. Next month, when the firm pays John Murray, it will reduce its liability, Salaries Payable, as well as decrease its cash.

In terms of the transaction analysis chart, the following would be done:

Office Salaries Exp. 511

900	
250	

Salaries Payable 212

	250

Accounts Affected	Category	↑ ↓	Rules
Office Salaries Expense	Expense	↑	Dr.
Salaries Payable	Liability	↑	Cr.

We enter the adjustment for accrued salaries in the following way:

(D) 1. An increase in Office Salaries Expense, $250.
     2. An increase in Salaries Payable, $250.

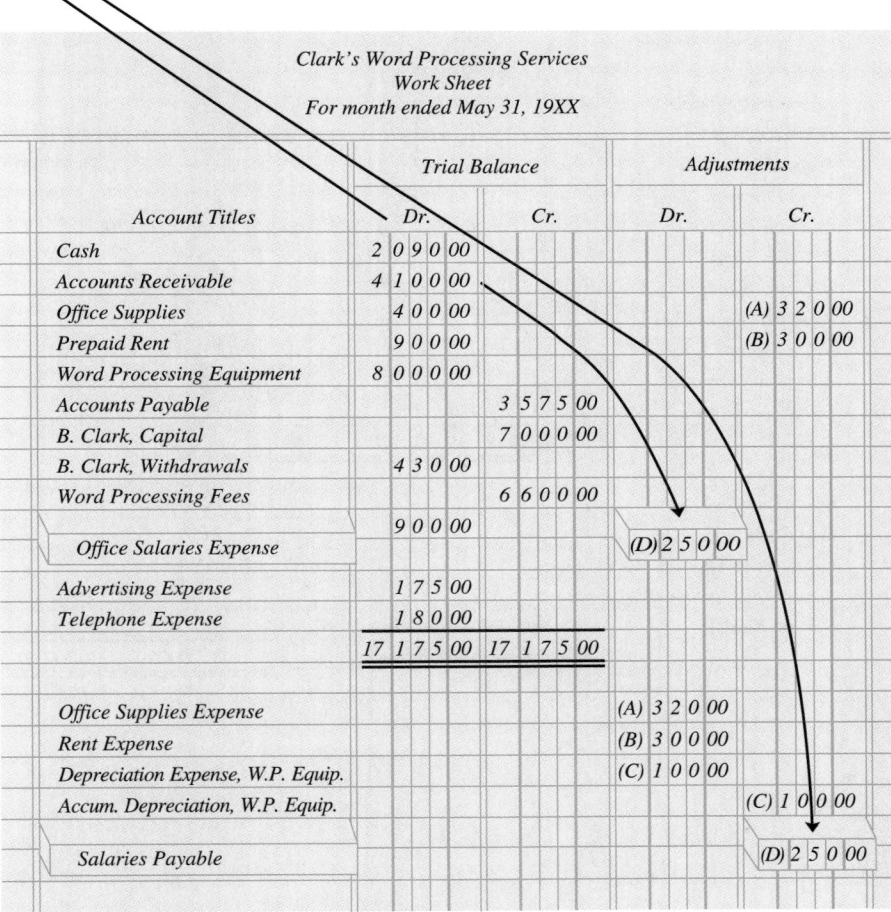

Account Titles	Trial Balance Dr.	Cr.	Adjustments Dr.	Cr.
Cash	2 0 9 0 00			
Accounts Receivable	4 1 0 0 00			
Office Supplies	4 0 0 00			(A) 3 2 0 00
Prepaid Rent	9 0 0 00			(B) 3 0 0 00
Word Processing Equipment	8 0 0 0 00			
Accounts Payable		3 5 7 5 00		
B. Clark, Capital		7 0 0 0 00		
B. Clark, Withdrawals	4 3 0 00			
Word Processing Fees		6 6 0 0 00		
	9 0 0 00			
Office Salaries Expense			(D) 2 5 0 00	
Advertising Expense	1 7 5 00			
Telephone Expense	1 8 0 00			
	17 1 7 5 00	17 1 7 5 00		
Office Supplies Expense			(A) 3 2 0 00	
Rent Expense			(B) 3 0 0 00	
Depreciation Expense, W.P. Equip.			(C) 1 0 0 00	
Accum. Depreciation, W.P. Equip.				(C) 1 0 0 00
Salaries Payable				(D) 2 5 0 00

Clark's Word Processing Services — Work Sheet — For month ended May 31, 19XX

Note again that all accounts added below the trial balance are *increasing.*

Since the account Office Salaries Expense is already listed in the account titles, place $250 in the debit column of the adjustments section on the same line as Office Salaries Expense. Since Salaries Payable is not listed in the account titles, add the account title Salaries Payable below the trial balance, below Accumulated Depreciation, W. P. Equipment. Place $250 in the credit column of the adjustments section on the same line as Salaries Payable.

Now that we have finished all the adjustments that we intended to make, we total the adjustments section, as shown in Figure 4-2.

FIGURE 4-2

**The Adjustments
Section of the
Work Sheet**

Clark's Word Processing Services
Work Sheet
For month ended May 31, 19XX

Account Titles	Trial Balance Dr.	Trial Balance Cr.	Adjustments Dr.	Adjustments Cr.
Cash	2 0 9 0 00			
Accounts Receivable	4 1 0 0 00			
Office Supplies	4 0 0 00			(A) 3 2 0 00
Prepaid Rent	9 0 0 00			(B) 3 0 0 00
Word Processing Equipment	8 0 0 0 00			
Accounts Payable		3 5 7 5 00		
B. Clark, Capital		7 0 0 0 00		
B. Clark, Withdrawals	4 3 0 00			
Word Processing Fees		6 6 0 0 00		
Office Salaries Expense	9 0 0 00		(D) 2 5 0 00	
Advertising Expense	1 7 5 00			
Telephone Expense	1 8 0 00			
	17 1 7 5 00	17 1 7 5 00		
Office Supplies Expense			(A) 3 2 0 00	
Rent Expense			(B) 3 0 0 00	
Depreciation Expense, W.P. Equip.			(C) 1 0 0 00	
Accum. Depreciation, W.P. Equip.				(C) 1 0 0 00
Salaries Payable				(D) 2 5 0 00
			9 7 0 00	9 7 0 00

THE ADJUSTED TRIAL
BALANCE SECTION

Next on the work sheet is the adjusted trial balance section. In order to fill it out, we summarize the information that has been placed in the trial balance and adjustments sections, as shown in Figure 4-3.

It is important to note carefully that, when bringing numbers across from the trial balance to the adjusted trial balance, two debits will be added together and two credits will be added together. If you have a debit and a credit, take the difference and place it on the side that is larger.

FIGURE 4-3   The Adjusted Trial Balance Section of the Work Sheet

Clark's Word Processing Services
Work Sheet
For month ended May 31, 19XX

Account Titles	Trial Balance Dr.	Trial Balance Cr.	Adjustments Dr.	Adjustments Cr.	Adjusted Trial Balance Dr.	Adjusted Trial Balance Cr.
Cash	2 0 9 0 00				2 0 9 0 00	
Accounts Receivable	4 1 0 0 00				4 1 0 0 00	
Office Supplies	4 0 0 00			(A) 3 2 0 00	8 0 00	
Prepaid Rent	9 0 0 00			(B) 3 0 0 00	6 0 0 00	
Word Processing Equipment	8 0 0 0 00				8 0 0 0 00	
Accounts Payable		3 5 7 5 00				3 5 7 5 00
B. Clark, Capital		7 0 0 0 00				7 0 0 0 00
B. Clark, Withdrawals	4 3 0 00				4 3 0 00	
Word Processing Fees		6 6 0 0 00				6 6 0 0 00
Office Salaries Expense	9 0 0 00		(D) 2 5 0 00		1 1 5 0 00	
Advertising	1 7 5 00				1 7 5 00	
Telephone Expense	1 8 0 00				1 8 0 00	
	17 1 7 5 00	17 1 7 5 00				
Office Supplies Expense			(A) 3 2 0 00		3 2 0 00	
Rent Expense			(B) 3 0 0 00		3 0 0 00	
Depreciation Expense, W.P. Equip.			(C) 1 0 0 00		1 0 0 00	
Accum. Depreciation, W.P. Equip.				(C) 1 0 0 00		1 0 0 00
Salaries Payable				(D) 2 5 0 00		2 5 0 00
			9 7 0 00	9 7 0 00	17 5 2 5 00	17 5 2 5 00

Side annotations:

If no adjustment is made, just carry over amount from trial balance on same side.

Supplies were $400 but we used up $320, leaving us with an $80 balance in supplies. **Note**: If there are a debit and a credit, take the *difference* between the two and place it on the side that is larger.

Note: Equipment is not adjusted here.

Two debits are added together. If two credits, they also would have been added together.

Carry these amounts over to adjusted trial balance in the same positions.

Note: The total of the left (debit) must equal the total of the right (credit) ($17,525).

TABLE 4-1   **Normal Balances and Account Categories**

ACCOUNT TITLES	CATEGORY	NORMAL BALANCE ON ADJUSTED TRIAL BALANCE	INCOME STATEMENT		BALANCE SHEET	
			Dr.	Cr.	Dr.	Cr.
Cash	Asset	Dr.			X	
Accounts Receivable	Asset	Dr.			X	
Office Supplies	Asset	Dr.			X	
Prepaid Rent	Asset	Dr.			X	
Word Proc. Equip.	Asset	Dr.			X	
Accounts Payable	Liability	Cr.				X
B. Clark, Capital	Capital	Cr.				X
B. Clark, Withdrawals	Withdrawal	Dr.			X	
Word Proc. Fees	Revenue	Cr.		X		
Office Salaries Exp.	Expense	Dr.	X			
Advertising Expense	Expense	Dr.	X			
Telephone Expense	Expense	Dr.	X			
Office Supplies Exp.	Expense	Dr.	X			
Rent Expense	Expense	Dr.	X			
Dep. Exp., W. P. Equip.	Expense	Dr.	X			
Acc. Dep., W. P. Equip.	Contra Asset	Cr.				X
Salaries Payable	Liability	Cr.				X

Now that we have completed the adjustments and adjusted trial balance sections of the work sheet, it is time to move on to the income statement section and the balance sheet section. But before we do that, take a look at the chart shown in Table 4-1. Do not try to memorize this aid, just use it as a reference to help you in filling out the next two sections of the work sheet. Keep in mind that we first carry over the numbers from the adjusted trial balance to one of the last four columns of the work sheet and then we complete the bottom section.

THE INCOME STATEMENT SECTION

The income statement section lists only revenue and expenses from the adjusted trial balance. Note how this is accomplished in Figure 4-4, p. 119.

Did you notice that accumulated depreciation and salaries payable do not go on the income statement? Accumulated depreciation is a contra asset found on the balance sheet. Salaries payable is a liability found on the balance sheet.

The revenue of $6,600 and all the individual expenses are listed in the income statement section. The revenue, since it has a credit balance, is placed in the credit column of the income statement section. The expenses, since they have debit balances, are placed in the debit column of the income statement section. Once the debits and credits are placed in the columns, you should

1. Total the debits and credits.
2. Calculate the balance between the debit and credit columns and place the difference on the smaller side.
3. Total the columns.

The difference between $2,225 Dr. and $6,600 Cr. indicates a net income of $4,375. Notice on the work sheet in Figure 4-4 that the label Net Income is added in the account title column on the same line as $4,375. When there is a net income, it

FIGURE 4-4   The Income Statement Section of the Work Sheet

Clark's Word Processing Services
Work Sheet
For month ended May 31, 19XX

Account Titles	Adjusted Trial Balance Dr.	Adjusted Trial Balance Cr.	Income Statement Dr.	Income Statement Cr.
Cash	2 0 9 0 00			
Accounts Receivable	4 1 0 0 00			
Office Supplies	8 0 00			
Prepaid Rent	6 0 0 00			
Word Processing Equipment	8 0 0 0 00			
Accounts Payable		3 5 7 5 00		
B. Clark, Capital		7 0 0 0 00		
B. Clark, Withdrawals	4 3 0 00			
Word Processing Fees		6 6 0 0 00		6 6 0 0 00
Office Salaries Expense	1 1 5 0 00		1 1 5 0 00	
Advertising Expense	1 7 5 00		1 7 5 00	
Telephone Expense	1 8 0 00		1 8 0 00	
Office Supplies Expense	3 2 0 00		3 2 0 00	
Rent Expense	3 0 0 00		3 0 0 00	
Depreciation Expense, W.P. Equip.	1 0 0 00		1 0 0 00	
Accum. Depreciation, W.P. Equip.		1 0 0 00		
Salaries Payable		2 5 0 00		
	17 5 2 5 00	17 5 2 5 00	2 2 2 5 00	6 6 0 0 00
Net Income			4 3 7 5 00	
			6 6 0 0 00	6 6 0 0 00

will be placed in the debit column of the income statement section of the work sheet. If you have a net loss, it will be placed in the credit column. The $6,600 total indicates that the two columns are in balance.

> Do not think of Net Income as a Dr. or Cr. The $4,375 is placed in the debit column to balance both columns to $6,600. In actuality the credit side is larger by $4,375.

THE BALANCE SHEET SECTION

In order to fill out the balance sheet section of the work sheet, we carry over the following from the adjusted trial balance section: assets, contra assets, liabilities, capital, and withdrawals. Because the beginning figure for capital* is used on the work sheet, we have to bring over net income to the credit column of the balance sheet in order to have both columns balance *Remember: The ending figure for capital is not on the work sheet.*

Let's now look at the completed work sheet in Figure 4-5 (p. 120) to see how the balance sheet section is completed. Note how the net income of $4,375 is

> The amounts come from the adjusted trial balance, except the $4,375, which was carried over from the income statement section.

---

* Remember, to see if additional investments occurred for period you will have to check the capital account in the ledger.

FIGURE 4-5　The Completed Work Sheet

Clark's Word Processing Services
Work Sheet
For month ended May 31, 19XX

Account Titles	Trial Balance Dr.	Trial Balance Cr.	Adjustments Dr.	Adjustments Cr.	Adjusted Trial Balance Dr.	Adjusted Trial Balance Cr.	Income Statement Dr.	Income Statement Cr.	Balance Sheet Dr.	Balance Sheet Cr.
Cash	2 0 9 0 00				2 0 9 0 00				2 0 9 0 00	
Accounts Receivable	4 1 0 0 00				4 1 0 0 00				4 1 0 0 00	
Office Supplies	4 0 0 00			(A) 3 2 0 00	8 0 00				8 0 00	
Prepaid Rent	9 0 0 00			(B) 3 0 0 00	6 0 0 00				6 0 0 00	
Word Processing Equipment	8 0 0 0 00				8 0 0 0 00				8 0 0 0 00	
Accounts Payable		3 5 7 5 00				3 5 7 5 00				3 5 7 5 00
B. Clark, Capital		7 0 0 0 00				7 0 0 0 00				7 0 0 0 00
B. Clark, Withdrawals	4 3 0 00				4 3 0 00				4 3 0 00	
Word Processing Fees		6 6 0 0 00				6 6 0 0 00		6 6 0 0 00		
Office Salaries Expense	9 0 0 00		(D) 2 5 0 00		1 1 5 0 00		1 1 5 0 00			
Advertising Expense	1 7 5 00				1 7 5 00		1 7 5 00			
Telephone Expense	1 8 0 00				1 8 0 00		1 8 0 00			
	17 1 7 5 00	17 1 7 5 00								
Office Supplies Expense			(A) 3 2 0 00		3 2 0 00		3 2 0 00			
Rent Expense			(B) 3 0 0 00		3 0 0 00		3 0 0 00			
Depreciation Expense W. P. Equip.			(C) 1 0 0 00		1 0 0 00		1 0 0 00			
Accum. Depreciation, W. P. Equip.				(C) 1 0 0 00		1 0 0 00				1 0 0 00
Salaries Payable				(D) 2 5 0 00		2 5 0 00				2 5 0 00
			9 7 0 00	9 7 0 00	17 5 2 5 00	17 5 2 5 00	2 2 2 5 00	6 6 0 0 00	15 3 0 0 00	10 9 2 5 00
Net Income							4 3 7 5 00			4 3 7 5 00
							6 6 0 0 00	6 6 0 0 00	15 3 0 0 00	15 3 0 0 00

brought over to the credit column of the work sheet. The figure for capital is also on the credit column while the figure for withdrawals is on the debit column. By placing the net income in the credit column both sides total $15,300. If a net loss were to occur it would be placed in the debit column of the balance sheet column.

Now that we have completed the work sheet, our next goal is to complete the three financial reports. But first let's summarize our progress.

At this point you should be able to

1. Define and explain the purpose of a work sheet. (p. 106)
2. Explain the need as well as the process for adjustments. (p. 107)
3. Define and give an example of a mixed account. (p. 108)
4. Explain the concept of depreciation. (p. 111)
5. Explain the difference between depreciation expense and accumulated depreciation. (p. 111)
6. Prepare a work sheet from a trial balance and adjustment data. (p. 120)

☐ **SELF-REVIEW QUIZ 4-1**

From the accompanying trial balance and adjustment data, complete a work sheet for B. Bass Co. for the month ended Dec. 31, 19XX.

NOTE: The numbers used on this quiz may seem impossibly small. We have done that on purpose, so that at this point you don't have to worry about arithmetic, just about preparing the work sheet correctly.

B. Bass Co.
Trial Balance
December 31, 19XX

	Dr.	Cr.
Cash	16 00	
Accounts Receivable	2 00	
Prepaid Insurance	3 00	
Store Supplies	5 00	
Store Equipment	6 00	
Accumulated Depreciation, Store Equipment		4 00
Accounts Payable		2 00
B. Bass, Capital		14 00
B. Bass, Withdrawals	3 00	
Revenue from Clients		25 00
Rent Expense	2 00	
Salaries Expense	8 00	
	45 00	45 00

Adjustment data:
 (A) Depreciation Expense, Store Equipment, $1.
 (B) Insurance Expired, $2.
 (C) Supplies on hand, $1.
 (D) Salaries owed but not paid to employees, $3.

■ SOLUTION TO SELF-REVIEW QUIZ 4-1

B. Bass Company
Work Sheet
For month ended December 31, 19XX

Account Titles	Trial Balance Dr.	Trial Balance Cr.	Adjustments Dr.	Adjustments Cr.	Adjusted Trial Balance Dr.	Adjusted Trial Balance Cr.	Income Statement Dr.	Income Statement Cr.	Balance Sheet Dr.	Balance Sheet Cr.
Cash	16 00				16 00				16 00	
Accounts Receivable	2 00				2 00				2 00	
Prepaid Insurance	3 00			(B) 2 00	1 00				1 00	
Store Supplies	5 00			(C) 4 00	1 00				1 00	
Store Equipment	6 00				6 00				6 00	
Accum. Dep., Store Equipment		4 00		(A) 1 00		5 00				5 00
Accounts Payable		2 00				2 00				2 00
B. Bass, Capital		14 00				14 00				14 00
B. Bass, Withdrawals	3 00				3 00				3 00	
Revenue from Clients		25 00				25 00		25 00		
Rent Expense	2 00				2 00		2 00			
Salaries Expense	8 00		(D) 3 00		11 00		11 00			
	45 00	45 00								
Dep. Exp., Store Equipment			(A) 1 00		1 00		1 00			
Insurance Expense			(B) 2 00		2 00		2 00			
Supplies Expense			(C) 4 00		4 00		4 00			
Salaries Payable				(D) 3 00		3 00				3 00
			10 00	10 00	49 00	49 00	20 00	25 00	29 00	24 00
Net Income							5 00			5 00
							25 00	25 00	29 00	29 00

Don't adjust this line! Store Equipment always contains the historical cost.

Note that Accumulated Depreciation is listed in trial balance, since this is not a new company. Store Equipment has already been depreciated $4.00 from an earlier period.

LEARNING UNIT 4-2

Step 6 of the Accounting Cycle: Preparing the Financial Statements from the Work Sheet

From the work sheet completed in Unit 4-1 we will now be able to prepare the *formal* financial reports. Let's first prepare the income statement for Clark for the month of May.

PREPARING THE INCOME STATEMENT

There are several points to remember when preparing the income statement:

1. Every figure on the formal report is on the work sheet. The diagram below shows where each of these figures goes on the income statement.
2. There are no debit or credit columns on the formal report.
3. The inside column on financial reports is used for subtotaling.
4. Withdrawals do not go on the income statement; they go on the statement of owner's equity.

Take a moment to look at the income statement in the diagram in Figure 4-6). Note which items go where from the income statement section of the work sheet onto the formal report.

FIGURE 4-6   **From Work Sheet to Income Statement**

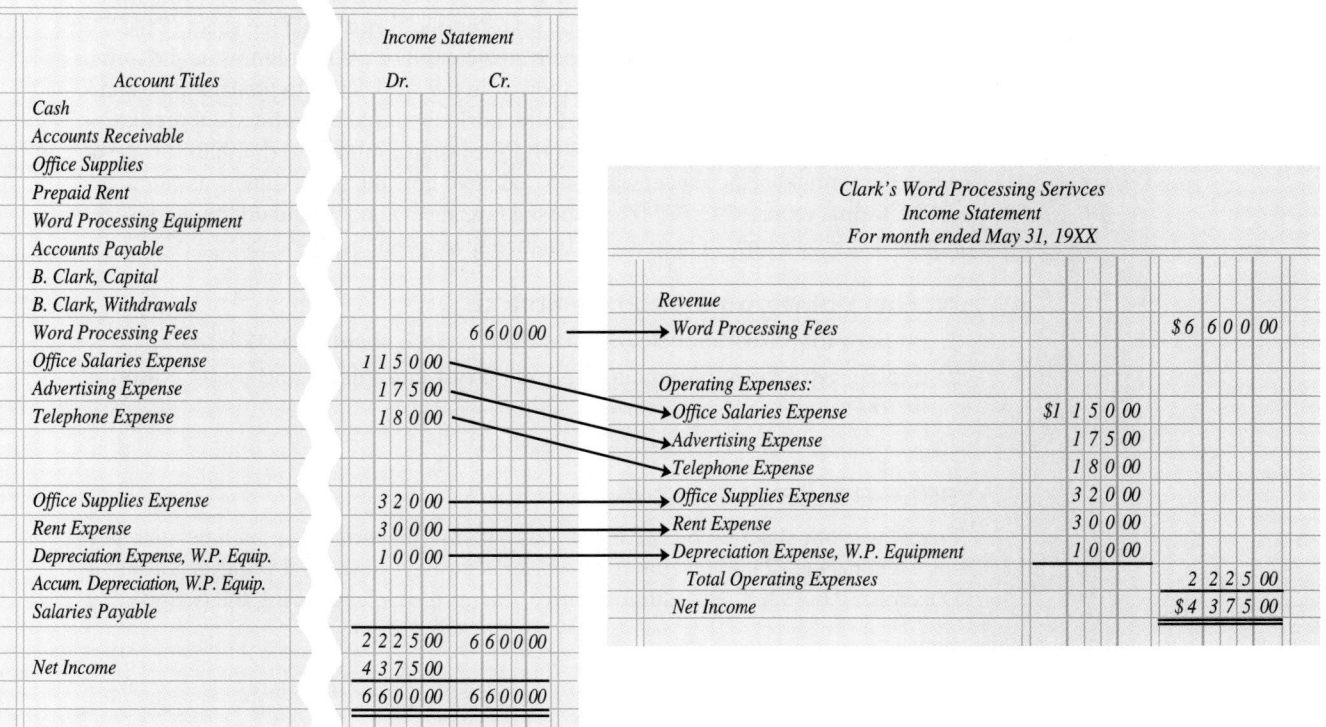

PREPARING THE STATEMENT OF OWNER'S EQUITY

Figure 4-7 is the statement of owner's equity for Clark showing where the information comes from on the work sheet. When the statement of owner's equity is prepared from the work sheet, recall that the figure on the work sheet for capital might not be the beginning figure for capital if any additional investments have taken place. You can find this out by checking the ledger account for capital. Note how net income and withdrawals aid in calculating the new figure for capital.

FIGURE 4-7   Completing a Statement of Owner's Equity

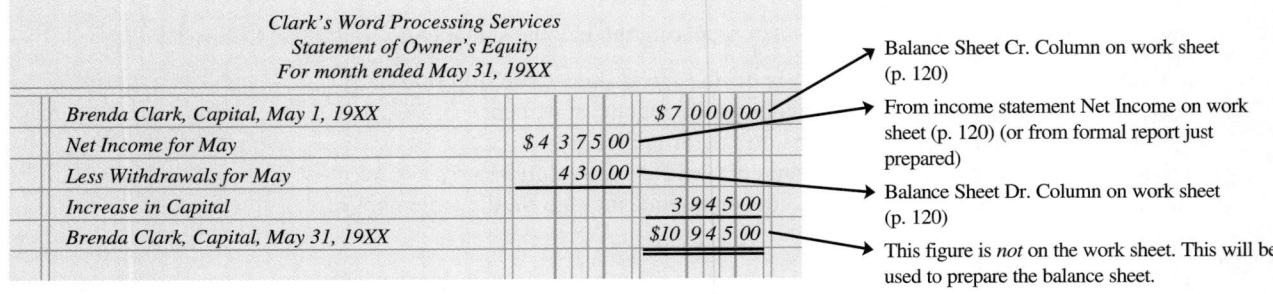

Clark's Word Processing Services
Statement of Owner's Equity
For month ended May 31, 19XX

Brenda Clark, Capital, May 1, 19XX		$7 000 00
Net Income for May	$4 375 00	
Less Withdrawals for May	430 00	
Increase in Capital		3 945 00
Brenda Clark, Capital, May 31, 19XX		$10 945 00

Balance Sheet Cr. Column on work sheet (p. 120)

From income statement Net Income on work sheet (p. 120) (or from formal report just prepared)

Balance Sheet Dr. Column on work sheet (p. 120)

This figure is *not* on the work sheet. This will be used to prepare the balance sheet.

PREPARING THE BALANCE SHEET

In preparing the balance sheet, remember that the balance sheet section totals on the work sheet ($15,300) do *not* match the totals on the formal balance sheet ($14,770) (Figure 4-8, p. 125). This is because there are no debit or credit columns on the formal report. We must rearrange the information from the work sheet to prepare the balance sheet. For example, at the bottom of the work sheet, Accumulated Depreciation ($100) was in the column opposite Word Processing Equipment ($8,000); however, when the formal balance sheet was prepared, note how the book value was calculated on the formal report. The $7,900 on the balance sheet is not found on the work sheet. Figure 4-8 shows how to prepare the balance sheet from the work sheet.

At this point you should be able to

1. Prepare the three financial reports from a work sheet. (pp. 123-124)
2. Explain why formal financial reports do not have debit and credit columns. (p. 124)

☐ SELF-REVIEW QUIZ 4-2

From the work sheet on p. 122 for B. Bass, please prepare (1) an income statement for December; (2) a statement of owner's equity; and (3) a balance sheet for December 31, 19XX. No additional investments took place during the period.

FIGURE 4-8   **From Work Sheet to Balance Sheet**

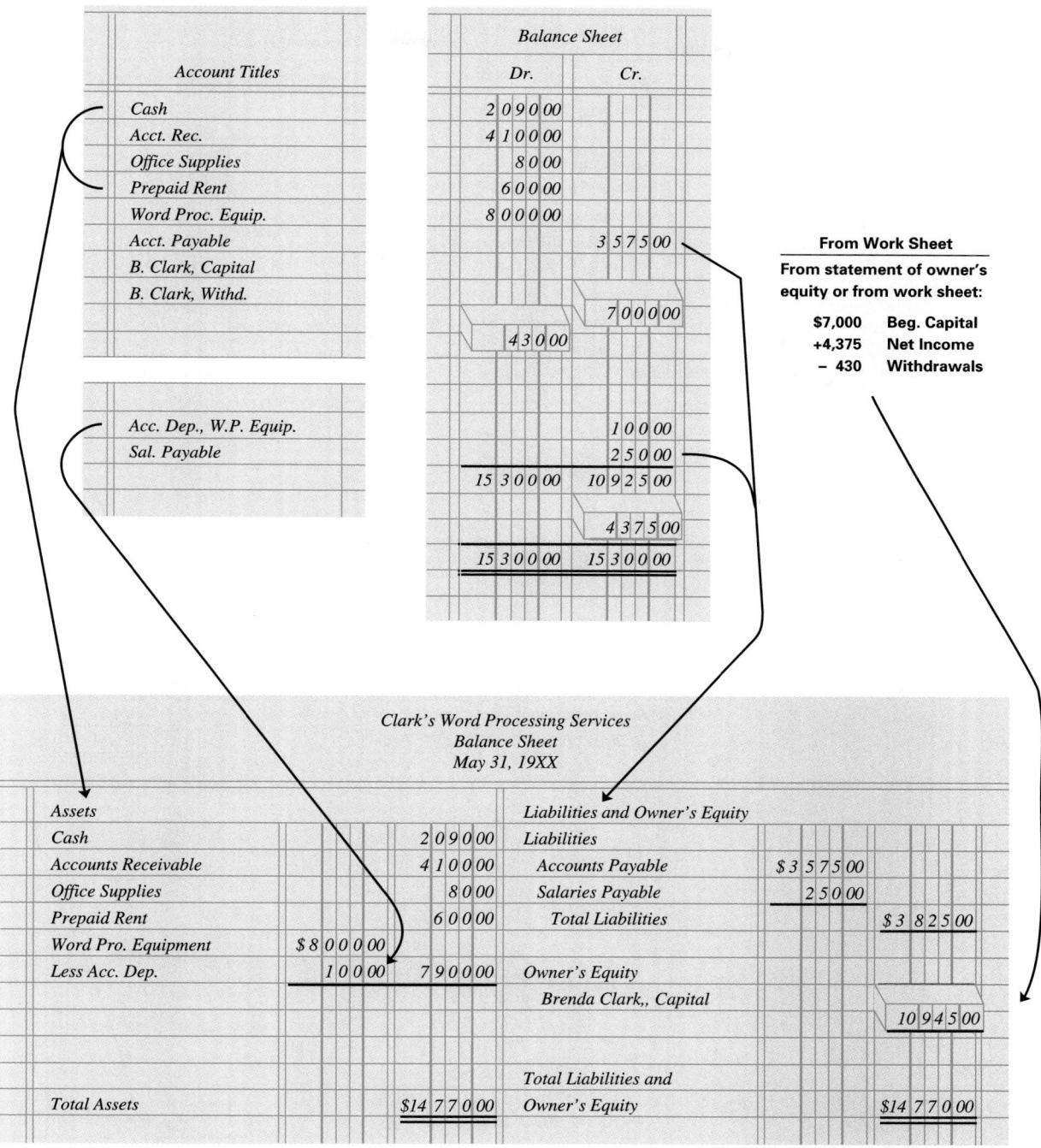

Account Titles	Balance Sheet Dr.	Cr.
Cash	2 0 9 0 00	
Acct. Rec.	4 1 0 0 00	
Office Supplies	8 0 00	
Prepaid Rent	6 0 0 00	
Word Proc. Equip.	8 0 0 0 00	
Acct. Payable		3 5 7 5 00
B. Clark, Capital		7 0 0 0 00
B. Clark, Withd.	4 3 0 00	
Acc. Dep., W.P. Equip.		1 0 0 00
Sal. Payable		2 5 0 00
	15 3 0 0 00	10 9 2 5 00
		4 3 7 5 00
	15 3 0 0 00	15 3 0 0 00

From Work Sheet

From statement of owner's equity or from work sheet:

$7,000	Beg. Capital
+4,375	Net Income
− 430	Withdrawals

Clark's Word Processing Services
Balance Sheet
May 31, 19XX

Assets			Liabilities and Owner's Equity		
Cash		2 0 9 0 00	Liabilities		
Accounts Receivable		4 1 0 0 00	Accounts Payable	$ 3 5 7 5 00	
Office Supplies		8 0 00	Salaries Payable	2 5 0 00	
Prepaid Rent		6 0 0 00	Total Liabilities		$ 3 8 2 5 00
Word Pro. Equipment	$ 8 0 0 0 00				
Less Acc. Dep.	1 0 0 00	7 9 0 0 00	Owner's Equity		
			Brenda Clark,, Capital		10 9 4 5 00
			Total Liabilities and		
Total Assets		$14 7 7 0 00	Owner's Equity		$14 7 7 0 00

■ *SOLUTION TO SELF-REVIEW QUIZ 4-2*

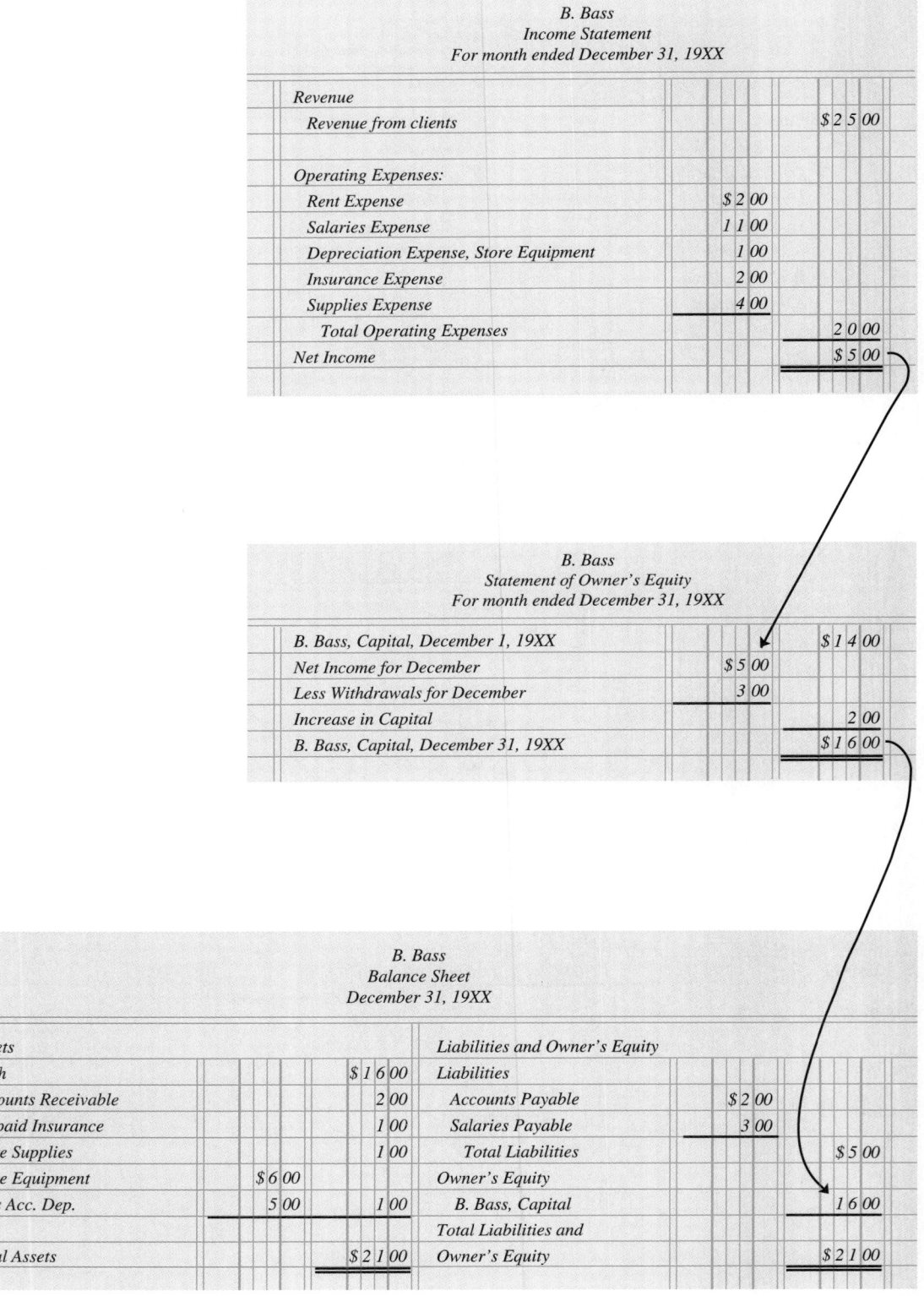

B. Bass
Income Statement
For month ended December 31, 19XX

Revenue			
Revenue from clients			$2 5 00
Operating Expenses:			
Rent Expense	$2 00		
Salaries Expense	1 1 00		
Depreciation Expense, Store Equipment	1 00		
Insurance Expense	2 00		
Supplies Expense	4 00		
Total Operating Expenses		2 0 00	
Net Income		$5 00	

B. Bass
Statement of Owner's Equity
For month ended December 31, 19XX

B. Bass, Capital, December 1, 19XX		$1 4 00
Net Income for December	$5 00	
Less Withdrawals for December	3 00	
Increase in Capital		2 00
B. Bass, Capital, December 31, 19XX		$1 6 00

B. Bass
Balance Sheet
December 31, 19XX

Assets			Liabilities and Owner's Equity		
Cash		$1 6 00	Liabilities		
Accounts Receivable		2 00	Accounts Payable	$2 00	
Prepaid Insurance		1 00	Salaries Payable	3 00	
Store Supplies		1 00	Total Liabilities		$5 00
Store Equipment	$6 00		Owner's Equity		
Less Acc. Dep.	5 00	1 00	B. Bass, Capital		1 6 00
			Total Liabilities and		
Total Assets		$2 1 00	Owner's Equity		$2 1 00

SUMMARY OF KEY POINTS AND KEY TERMS

LEARNING UNIT 4-1

1. The work sheet is not a formal report.
2. Adjustments update certain accounts so that they will be up to their latest balance before financial reports are prepared. Adjustments are the result of internal transactions.
3. Adjustments will affect both the income statement and the balance sheet.
4. A mixed account results in balances partly on the balance sheet and partly on the income statement.
5. Accounts listed *below* the account titles on the trial balance of the work sheet are *increasing*.
6. The original cost of a piece of equipment is not adjusted; historical cost is not lost.
7. Depreciation is the process of spreading the original cost of the asset over its expected useful life.
8. Accumulated depreciation is a contra asset on the balance sheet that summarizes, accumulates, or builds up the amount of depreciation that an asset has accumulated.
9. Book value is the original cost less accumulated depreciation.
10. Accrued salaries are unpaid and unrecorded expenses that are accumulating but for which payment is not yet due.
11. Revenue and expenses go on income statement sections of the work sheet. Assets, contra assets, liabilities, capital, and withdrawals go on balance sheet sections of the work sheet.

Accrued salaries: Salaries that are earned but unpaid and unrecorded during the period (and thus need to be recorded by an adjustment) and will not come due for payment until the next accounting period.

Accumulated Depreciation: A contra asset account that summarizes or accumulates the amount of depreciation that has been taken on an asset.

Adjusting: The process of calculating the latest up-to-date balance of each account at the end of an accounting period.

Net book value: Cost of equipment less accumulated depreciation.

Capital Cost Allowance: Income Tax Department method of calculating depreciation.

Depreciation: The allocation (spreading) of the cost of an asset (such as an auto or equipment) over its expected useful life.

Historical cost: The actual cost of an asset at time of purchase.

Mixed account: An account whose balance is partly an income statement amount and partly a balance sheet amount on the trial balance. Examples: Prepaid Rent, Supplies.

Residual value: Estimated value of an asset after all the allowable depreciation has been taken.

Work sheet: A columnar device used by accountants to aid them in completing the accounting cycle. It is not a formal report. Often called a spreadsheet, especially when a computer is involved.

BLUEPRINT OF STEPS 5 AND 6 OF THE ACCOUNTING CYCLE

Prepare Work Sheet

	Trial Balance		Adjustments		Adjusted Trial Balance		Income Statement		Balance Sheet	
	Dr.	Cr.	Dr.	Cr.	Dr.	Cr.	Dr.	Cr.	Dr.	Cr.
	Assets Withd. Exp.	Liab. Capital (beg.) Contra Assets Revenue			Assets Withd. Exp.	Liab. Capital (beg.)* Contra Assets Revenue	Exp.	Rev.	Assets Withd.	Liab. Contra Assets Capital (beg.)*

Net Income   **Net Income**

A
List of ledger before adjustments

B
Updating internal transactions

C
Accounts brought up to latest balance

E

Statement of Owner's Equity

Beg. Cap.*		XX
+ Net Income	XX	
– Withd.	XX	
= End. Cap.		XX

D

Income Statement

Rev.		XX
Exp.	XX	
	XX	XX
Net Income		XXX

Prepare Financial Reports

E

Balance Sheet

Assets	Liabilities Capital (end)

* No additional investment during the period.

LEARNING UNIT 4-2

1. The formal reports prepared from a work sheet do not have debit or credit columns.
2. Revenue and expenses go on the income statement. Beginning capital plus net income less withdrawals (or: beginning capital minus net loss, less withdrawals) go on the statement of owner's equity. Be sure to check the capital account in the ledger to see if any additional investments took place. Assets, liabilities, and the new figure for capital go on the balance sheet.

DISCUSSION QUESTIONS

1. Work sheets are required in every company's accounting cycle. Please agree or disagree and explain why.
2. What is the purpose of adjusting accounts?
3. What is the relationship of internal transactions to the adjusting process?
4. Explain how an adjustment can affect both the income statement and balance sheet. Please give an example.
5. What is a mixed account?
6. Why do we need the accumulated depreciation account?
7. Depreciation expense goes on the balance sheet. True or false. Why?
8. Each month the cost of accumulated depreciation grows while the cost of equipment goes up. Agree or disagree. Defend your position.
9. Define accrued salaries.
10. Why don't the formal financial reports contain debit or credit columns?
11. Explain how the financial reports are prepared from the work sheet.

EXERCISES

1. Complete the following table.

Categorizing accounts.

ACCOUNT	CATEGORY	NORMAL BALANCE	WHICH FINANCIAL REPORT(S) FOUND ON
Accounts Payable			
Prepaid Insurance			
Equipment			
Accumulated Dep.			
B. Avery, Capital			
B. Avery, Withd.			
Salaries Payable			
Advertising Expense			

2. Use transaction analysis charts to analyze the following adjustments:

    A. Depreciation on equipment, $400.
    B. Rent expired, $200.

Reviewing adjustments and the transaction analysis charts.

Recording adjusting entries.

3. From the following adjustment data, calculate the adjustment amount and record appropriate debits or credits:

  A. Supplies available beginning of month, $700.
      Supplies on hand end of month, $100.
  B. Store equipment, $9,000.
      Accumulated depreciation before adjustment, $700.
      Depreciation expense, $100.

Preparing a work sheet.

4. From the following trial balance and adjustment data, complete a work sheet for B. Jay as of December 31, 19XX:

  A. Depreciation expense, equipment $1.00
  B. Insurance Expired   3.00
  C. Supplies on hand   2.00
  D. Wages owed, but not paid
      (they are an expense in the old year) 3.00

B. Jay
Trial Balance
December 31, 19XX

	Dr.	Cr.
Cash	8 00	
Accounts Receivable	3 00	
Prepaid Insurance	5 00	
Store Supplies	6 00	
Store Equipment	7 00	
Accumulated Depreciation, Equipment		2 00
Accounts Payable		2 00
B. Jay, Capital		1 7 00
B. Jay, Withdrawals	4 00	
Revenue from Clients		2 0 00
Rent Expense	4 00	
Wages Expense	4 00	
	4 1 00	4 1 00

Preparing financial reports from a work sheet.

5. From the completed work sheet in Exercise 4, prepare

  A. An income statement for December.
  B. A statement of owner's equity for December.
  C. A balance sheet as of December 31, 19XX.

GROUP A PROBLEMS

4A-1.

Completing a partial work sheet up to the adjusted trial balance.

Viki's Gym
Trial Balance
December 31, 19XX

	Dr.	Cr.
Cash in Bank	2 4 0 0 00	
Accounts Receivable	3 0 0 0 00	
Gym Supplies	5 4 0 0 00	
Gym Equipment	7 2 0 0 00	
Accumulated Depreciation, Gym Equipment		2 2 5 0 00
Viki Kahn, Capital		9 0 0 0 00
Viki Kahn, Withdrawals	3 0 0 0 00	
Gym Fees		10 8 0 0 00
Rent Expense	9 0 0 00	
Advertising Expense	1 5 0 00	
	22 0 5 0 00	22 0 5 0 00

Given the following adjustment data on December 31:

- A. Gym supplies on hand, $900.
- B. Depreciation taken on gym equipment, $600.

Complete a partial work sheet up to the adjusted trial balance.

4A-2. Below is the trial balance for Al's Plumbing Service for December 31, 19XX.

Completing a work sheet.

Al's Plumbing Service
Trial Balance
December 31, 19XX

	Dr.	Cr.
Cash in Bank	2 1 5 6 00	
Accounts Receivable	5 8 4 00	
Prepaid Rent	7 4 4 00	
Plumbing Supplies	7 4 2 00	
Plumbing Equipment	1 2 0 0 00	
Accumulated Depreciation, Plumbing Equipment		5 6 0 00
Accounts Payable		4 6 00
Al Sullivan, Capital		2 2 0 0 00
Plumbing Revenue		4 4 8 0 00
Heat Expense	4 0 0 00	
Advertising Expense	2 0 0 00	
Wages Expense	1 2 6 0 00	
	7 2 8 6 00	7 2 8 6 00

Adjustment data to update the trial balance:

    A. Rent expired, $250.
    B. Plumbing supplies on hand (left), $290.
    C. Depreciation expense, plumbing equipment, $150.
    D. Wages earned by workers but not paid or due until January, $100.

Your task is to prepare a work sheet for Al's Plumbing Service for the month of December.

Comprehensive Problem

4A-3. The following is the trial balance for Bert's Moving Co.

Bert's Moving Co. Trial Balance October 31, 19XX	Dr.	Cr.
Cash	5 3 7 0 00	
Prepaid Insurance	2 2 8 8 00	
Moving Supplies	1 5 1 0 00	
Moving Truck	10 6 5 8 00	
Accumulated Depreciation, Moving Truck		7 2 6 0 00
Accounts Payable		3 1 2 00
Bert Jess, Capital		5 4 4 2 00
Bert Jess, Withdrawals	2 2 4 0 00	
Revenue from Moving		14 1 6 2 00
Wages Expense	3 7 1 2 00	
Rent Expense	1 0 8 0 00	
Advertising Expense	3 1 8 00	
	27 1 7 6 00	27 1 7 6 00

Adjustment data to update trial balance:

    A. Insurance expired, $350.
    B. Moving supplies on hand, $300.
    C. Depreciation on moving truck, $450.
    D. Wages earned but unpaid, $525.

Your task is to
    1. Complete a work sheet for Bert's Moving Co. for the month of October.
    2. Prepare an income statement for October, a statement of owner's equity for October, and a balance sheet as of October 31, 19XX.

Comprehensive Problem

4A-4.

Adjustment data to update trial balance:

    A. Insurance expired, $500.
    B. Repair supplies on hand, $260.
    C. Depreciation on repair equipment, $410.
    D. Wages earned but unpaid, $350.

Ed's Repair Service
Trial Balance
November 30, 19XX

	Dr.	Cr.
Cash	2 7 6 6 00	
Prepaid Insurance	2 0 0 0 00	
Repair Supplies	5 7 0 00	
Repair Equipment	2 8 8 6 00	
Accumulated Depreciation, Repair Equipment		6 3 4 00
Accounts Payable		1 6 2 00
Ed Clean, Capital		3 8 0 0 00
Revenue from Repairs		6 0 0 0 00
Wages Expense	1 9 0 4 00	
Rent Expense	3 6 0 00	
Advertising Expense	1 1 0 00	
	10 5 9 6 00	10 5 9 6 00

Your task is to
1. Complete a work sheet for Ed's Repair Service for the month of November.
2. Prepare an income statement for November, a statement of owner's equity for November, and a balance sheet as of November 30, 19XX.

GROUP B PROBLEMS

4B-1.

Completing a partial work sheet up to adjusted trial balance.

Viki's Gym
Trial Balance
December 31, 19XX

	Dr.	Cr.
Cash in Bank	2 0 0 0 00	
Accounts Receivable	2 0 0 0 00	
Gym Supplies	4 2 0 0 00	
Gym Equipment	8 0 0 0 00	
Accumulated Depreciation, Gym Equipment		5 7 0 0 00
Viki Kahn, Capital		11 0 0 0 00
Viki Kahn, Withdrawals	1 0 0 0 00	
Gym Fees		1 4 0 0 00
Rent Expense	8 0 0 00	
Advertising Expense	1 0 0 00	
	18 1 0 0 00	18 1 0 0 00

Please complete a partial work sheet up to the adjusted trial balance using the following adjustment data:

A. Gym supplies on hand, $2,600.
B. Depreciation taken on gym equipment, $500.

Completing a work sheet.

4B-2. Given the following trial balance and adjustment data of Al's Plumbing Service, your task is to prepare a work sheet for the month of December.

Al's Plumbing Service
Trial Balance
December 31, 19XX

	Dr.	Cr.
Cash in Bank	396 00	
Accounts Receivable	284 00	
Prepaid Rent	400 00	
Plumbing Supplies	310 00	
Plumbing Equipment	1000 00	
Accumulated Depreciation, Plumbing Equipment		200 00
Accounts Payable		346 00
Al Sullivan, Capital		456 00
Plumbing Revenue		4680 00
Heat Expense	632 00	
Advertising Expense	1200 00	
Wages Expense	1460 00	
Total	5682 00	5682 00

Adjustment data:
A. Plumbing supplies on hand, $60.
B. Rent expired, $150.
C. Depreciation on plumbing equipment, $200.
D. Wages earned but unpaid, $115.

Comprehensive Problem

4B-3. Using the following trial balance and adjustment data of Bert's Moving Co., prepare:

Bert's Moving Co.
Trial Balance
October 31, 19XX

	Dr.	Cr.
Cash	3920 00	
Prepaid Insurance	3288 00	
Moving Supplies	1400 00	
Moving Truck	10658 00	
Accumulated Depreciation, Moving Truck		3660 00
Accounts Payable		1312 00
Bert Jess, Capital		17482 00
Bert Jess, Withdrawals	4240 00	
Revenue from Moving		8162 00
Wages Expense	5712 00	
Rent Expense	1080 00	
Advertising Expense	318 00	
	30616 00	30616 00

1. A work sheet for the month of October.
2. An income statement for October, a statement of owner's equity for October, and a balance sheet as of October 31, 19XX.

Adjustment data:
  A. Insurance expired, $600.
  B. Moving supplies on hand, $310.
  C. Depreciation on moving truck, $580.
  D. Wages earned but unpaid, $410.

4B-4. As the bookkeeper of Ed's Repair Service, use the information that follows to prepare

Comprehensive Problem

1. A work sheet for the month of November.
2. An income statement for November, a statement of owner's equity for November, and a balance sheet as of November 30, 19XX.

Ed's Repair Service
Trial Balance
November 30, 19XX

	Dr.	Cr.
Cash	3 2 0 4 00	
Prepaid Insurance	4 0 0 0 00	
Repair Supplies	7 7 0 00	
Repair Equipment	3 1 0 6 00	
Accumulated Depreciation, Repair Equipment		6 5 0 00
Accounts Payable		1 9 0 4 00
Ed Clean, Capital		6 2 5 8 00
Revenue from Repairs		5 6 3 4 00
Wages Expense	1 6 0 0 00	
Rent Expense	1 5 6 0 00	
Advertising Expense	2 0 6 00	
	14 4 4 6 00	14 4 4 6 00

Adjustment data:
  A. Insurance expired, $300.
  B. Repair supplies on hand, $170.
  C. Depreciation on repair equipment, $250.
  D. Wages earned but unpaid, $106.

GROUP C PROBLEMS

4C-1.

Please complete a partial work sheet up to the adjusted trial balance for Allen's Art Studio using the following adjustment data:

Completing a partial work sheet up to adjusted trial balance.

  A. Art supplies on hand, $1,620.
  B. Depreciation taken on equipment, $425.

Allen's Art Studio
Trial Balance
December 31, 19XX

	Dr.	Cr.
Cash in Bank	1 6 5 0 00	
Accounts Receivable	8 9 0 00	
Art Supplies	2 1 4 0 00	
Equipment	4 7 2 5 00	
Accumulated Depreciation, Equipment		2 8 7 5 00
Allen Day, Capital		6 0 3 0 00
Allen Day, Withdrawals	1 0 5 0 00	
Fees Earned		3 8 7 0 00
Rent Expense	1 2 0 0 00	
Advertising Expense	4 8 0 00	
Utilities Expense	6 4 0 00	
Totals	12 7 7 5 00	12 7 7 5 00

Completing a work sheet. **4C-2.** Given the following trial balance and adjustment data of Wong's Heating Service, your task is to prepare a work sheet for the month of November.

Wong's Heating Service
Trial Balance
November 30, 19XX

	Dr.	Cr.
Cash in Bank	7 1 8 00	
Accounts Receivable	6 4 0 00	
Prepaid Rent	8 0 0 00	
Heating Supplies	5 6 0 00	
Heating Equipment	2 6 0 0 00	
Accumulated Depreciation, Heating Equipment		6 2 0 00
Accounts Payable		4 7 5 00
Bob Wong, Capital		1 6 9 1 00
Heating Service Revenue		5 6 6 0 00
Advertising Expense	4 6 8 00	
Utilities Expense	8 2 0 00	
Wages Expense	1 8 4 0 00	
Totals	8 4 4 6 00	8 4 4 6 00

Adjustment data:
A. Heating supplies on hand, $240.
B. Rent expired, $400.
C. Depreciation on heating equipment, $475.
D. Wages earned but unpaid, $175.

4C-3. Using the following trial balance and adjustment data of Freeman's Storage Co., prepare

Comprehensive Problem

1. A work sheet for the month of October.
2. An income statement for October, a statement of owner's equity for October, and a balance sheet as of October 31, 19XX.

Freeman's Storage Co.
Trial Balance
October 31, 19XX

	Dr.	Cr.
Cash in Bank	1 6 4 2 00	
Prepaid Insurance	8 7 0 00	
Storage Supplies	1 2 6 0 00	
Storage Equipment	9 4 7 0 00	
Building	40 0 0 0 00	
Accumulated Depreciation, Storage Equipment		4 2 6 0 00
Accumulated Depreciation, Building		12 8 0 0 00
Accounts Payable		9 2 0 00
Vivian Freeman, Capital		35 4 2 9 00
Vivian Freeman, Withdrawals	6 8 2 0 00	
Storage Fees Revenue		12 6 5 0 00
Wages Expense	4 8 2 5 00	
Utilities Expense	7 5 6 00	
Advertising Expense	4 1 6 00	
Totals	66 0 5 9 00	66 0 5 9 00

Adjustment data:
   A. Insurance expired, $320.
   B. Storage supplies on hand, $630.
   C. Depreciation on Storage Equipment, $720.
   D. Depreciation on Building, $460.
   E. Wages earned but unpaid, $310.

4C-4. As the bookkeeper of Vanessa's Computer Dating Service, use the information that follows to prepare

Comprehensive Problem

1. A work sheet for the month of August.
2. An income statement for August, a statement of owner's equity for August, and a balance sheet as of August 31, 19XX.

Adjustment data:
   A. Insurance expired, $205.
   B. Computer supplies on hand, $190.
   C. Depreciation on computer equipment, $320.
   D. Wages earned but unpaid, $216.
   E. Advertising bill received, not paid, $112.

Vanessa's Computer Dating Service
Trial Balance
August 31, 19XX

	Dr.	Cr.
Cash in Bank	9 2 6 00	
Prepaid Insurance	8 2 0 00	
Computer Supplies	4 6 0 00	
Computer Equipment	8 1 7 0 00	
Accumulated Depreciation, Computer Equipment		1 6 8 0 00
Accounts Payable		1 2 6 0 00
Vanessa Roberts, Capital		4 3 6 7 00
Vanessa Roberts, Withdrawals	5 0 0 00	
Revenue from Services Provided		7 4 9 0 00
Wages Expense	1 9 2 0 00	
Rent Expense	1 2 7 5 00	
Advertising Expense	7 2 6 00	
Totals	14 7 9 7 00	14 7 9 7 00

PRACTICAL ACCOUNTING APPLICATION #1

TO: Hal Hogan, Bookkeeper

FROM: Petra Tennant, V. P.

RE: Adjustments for year ended December 31, 19XX

Hal, here is the information you requested. Please supply me with the adjustments needed ASAP.

Thanks

Attached to memo:

(a) Insurance data:

POLICY NO.	DATE OF POLICY PURCHASE	POLICY LENGTH	COST
100	November 1 of previous year	4 years	$480
200	May 1 of current year	2 years	600
300	September 1 of current year	1 year	240

(b) Rent data: Prepaid rent had a $500 balance at beginning of year. An additional $400 of rent was paid in advance in June. At year end, $200 of rent had expired.

(c) Revenue data: Accrued storage fees of $500 were earned but uncollected and unrecorded at year end.

PRACTICAL ACCOUNTING APPLICATION #2

Hint: Unearned Rent is a liability on the balance sheet.

On Friday, Harry Swag's boss asks him to prepare a special report, due on Monday at 8:00 A.M. Harry gathers the following material in his briefcase:

	DEC. 31	
	19X1	19X2
Prepaid Advertising	$300	$600
Interest Payable	150	350
Unearned Rent	500	300

Cash paid for:	Advertising	$1,900
	Interest	1,500
Cash received for:	Rent	2,300

As his best friend, could you help Harry show the amounts that are to be reported on the 19X2 income statement for (a) Advertising Expense, (b) Interest Expense, and (c) Rent Fees Earned.

ACCOUNTING RECALL
A Cumulative Approach

THIS EXAM REVIEWS CHAPTERS 1 THROUGH 4.

Your *Study Guide and Working Papers* have forms to complete this exam, as well as worked-out solutions. The page references next to each question identify what page to turn back to if you answer the question incorrectly.

PART I Vocabulary Review

Match the terms to the appropriate definition or phrase.

Page Ref.

(109)	1. Prepaid rent	A. Estimated value of an asset after all depreciation taken
(114)	2. Accrued salaries	B. Earned but unpaid
(111)	3. Depreciation expense	C. Actual cost at time of purchase
(111)	4. Accumulated depreciation	D. Columnar device
(37)	5. Normal balance	E. Rent paid in advance
(111)	6. Residual value	F. Cost—accumulated depreciation
(108)	7. Mixed account	G. Supplies
(106)	8. Work sheet	H. Shown on the income statement
(112)	9. Net book value	I. Side that increases it
(111)	10. Historical cost	J. Contra asset

PART II True or False (Accounting Theory)

(107) 11. Adjustments are the result of external transactions.

(108) 12. Adjustments affect only the balance sheet

(111) 13. Accumulated depreciation and equipment will both go on the balance sheet.

(112) 14. The normal balance of accumulated depreciation is a debit.

(123) 15. All financial reports could be prepared from a work sheet.

PART III Applications Problem (112, 126)

From the following prepare a work sheet and the three financial reports.

Pete Sove
Trial Balance
December 31, 19XX

Cash	20	
Accounts receivable	25	
Prepaid insurance	19	
Store supplies	18	
Store equipment	40	
Accumulated depreciation, Equipment		10
Accounts payable		30
Pete Sove, Capital		52
Pete Sove, Withdrawals	2	
Fees earned		49
Rent expense	10	
Wage expense	7	
	141	141

Adjustment Data

A.	Insurance expired	$4
B.	Supplies on hand	4
C.	Depreciation expense	5
D.	Wages owed, but not paid yet	6

C H A P T E R   F I V E

THE ACCOUNTING CYCLE COMPLETED:
Adjusting, Closing, and Post-Closing Trial Balance

IN THIS CHAPTER WE WILL COVER THE FOLLOWING TOPICS:

In Chapters 3 and 4 we completed the following steps of the accounting cycle for Clark's Word Processing Services:

1. Business transactions occurred and generated source documents.
2. Business transactions were analyzed and recorded into a journal.
3. Information was posted or transferred from journal to ledger.
4. A trial balance was prepared.
5. A work sheet was completed.
6. Financial statements were prepared.

> Remember, for ease of presentation we are using a month as the accounting cycle for Clark's business.

This chapter completes the accounting cycle for Clark for the month of May by taking the following steps:

7. Journalizing and posting adjusting entries.
8. Journalizing and posting closing entries.
9. Preparing a post-closing trial balance.

LEARNING UNIT 5-1

Journalizing and Posting Adjusting Entries: Step 7 of the Accounting Cycle

RECORDING JOURNAL ENTRIES FROM THE WORK SHEET

Many students have asked the purpose of journalizing adjusting entries. They claim that the information is already on the work sheet—why do it again? They forget that the work sheet is an *informal* report. The information concerning the adjustments has not been (a) placed into the journal, or (b) posted to the ledger accounts. We may have made the financial reports, but the ledger is not up-to-date. It was management that needed the reports quickly. Now we need to get the books ready for the upcoming accounting period. For example, at this point the ledger shows prepaid rent for Clark at $900 (p. 83), when in reality the balance sheet we prepared in Chapter 4 revealed a $600 balance. The work sheet is a tool in preparing financial reports *before* updating the ledger. Now we must use the adjustment columns of the work sheet as a basis for **adjusting journal entries** to bring certain amounts up-to-date in the ledger before beginning the next accounting period (see Figure 5-1).

> Purpose of adjusting entries.

> At this point, many ledger accounts are *not up to date.*

Figure 5-2 shows the adjusting journal entries for Clark taken from the adjustments section of the work sheet.

Once these adjusting journal entries are posted to the ledger, the accounts making up the financial statements that were prepared from the work sheet will equal the updated ledger. (Keep in mind that this is the same journal we have been using, but now we are on page 2.) Let's look at some simplified T accounts to show the ledger of Clark before and after posting the adjustments (see p. 145).

Account Titles	Trial Balance Dr.	Trial Balance Cr.	Adjustments Dr.	Adjustments Cr.
Cash	2 0 9 0 00			
Accounts Receivable	4 1 0 0 00			
Office Supplies	4 0 0 00			(A) 3 2 0 00
Prepaid Rent	9 0 0 00			(B) 3 0 0 00
Word Processing Equipment	8 0 0 0 00			
Accounts Payable		3 5 7 5 00		
B. Clark, Capital		7 0 0 0 00		
B. Clark, Withdrawals	4 3 0 00			
Word Processing Fees		6 6 0 0 00		
Office Salaries Expense	9 0 0 00		(D) 2 5 0 00	
Advertising Expense	1 7 5 00			
Telephone Expense	1 8 0 00			
	17 1 7 5 00	17 1 7 5 00		
Office Supplies Expense			(A) 3 2 0 00	
Rent Expense			(B) 3 0 0 00	
Depreciation Exp., W.P. Equip.			(C) 1 0 0 00	
Accum. Depreciation, W.P. Equip.				(C) 1 0 0 00
Salaries Payable				(D) 2 5 0 00
			9 7 0 00	9 7 0 00

FIGURE 5-1

Journalizing and Posting Adjustments Section of the Work Sheet

Clark's Word Processing Services
General Journal

Page 2

Date	Account Titles and Description	PR	Dr.	Cr.
	Adjusting Entries			
May 31	Office Supplies Expense	514	3 2 0 00	
	Office Supplies	114		3 2 0 00
31	Rent Expense	515	3 0 0 00	
	Prepaid Rent	115		3 0 0 00
31	Depreciation Expense, W.P. Equip.	516	1 0 0 00	
	Accumulated Depreciation, W.P. Equip.	122		1 0 0 00
31	Office Salaries Expense	511	2 5 0 00	
	Salaries Payable	212		2 5 0 00

FIGURE 5-2

Adjusting Journal Entries

Only the first adjustment in (C) will result in balances of Depreciation Expense and Accumulated Depreciation being the same. In subsequent adjustments the Accumulated Depreciation *balance* will be larger and larger, but the debit to Depreciation Expense and the credit to Accumulated Depreciation will be the same. We will see why in a moment.

Accounts Before Adjustment Posted: Adjustment (A):

Office Supplies 114	Office Supplies Expense 514
400	

Accounts After Adjustment Posted:

Office Supplies 114		Office Supplies Expense 514	
400	320	320	

Accounts Before Adjustment Posted: Adjustment (B):

Prepaid Rent 115	Rent Expense 515
900	

Accounts After Adjustment Posted:

Prepaid Rent 115		Rent Expense 515	
900	300	300	

Accounts Before Adjustment Posted: Adjustment (C):

Word Processing Equipment 121	Depreciation Expense, W. P. Equipment 516	Accumulated Depreciation, W. P. Equipment 122
8,000		

Accounts After Adjustment Posted:

Word Processing Equipment 121	Depreciation Expense, W. P. Equipment 516	Accumulated Depreciation, W. P. Equipment 122
8,000	100	100

Accounts Before Adjustment Posted: Adjustment (D):

Office Salaries Expense 511	Salaries Payable 212
450	
450	

Accounts After Adjustment Posted:

Office Salaries Expense 511	Salaries Payable 212
450	250
450	
250	

TIMOTHY WALKES:
WORK-STUDY PROGRAM PARTICIPANT

When he entered University, Timothy Walkes knew he wouldn't be a traditional full-time student as he worked to fulfil his educational goals. "Luckily," he says, "I was able to enter a program in which I studied one semester and worked one semester. I was very fortunate to work at General Motors, where I started as a payroll clerk and worked my way up."

Timothy liked being in the business world while he was in school. "I was able to apply what I learned in school right away. The college accounting course reinforced what I learned on the job, and for the most part the job reinforced what I learned in the course. The best part was being able to go back to the classroom and relate my work experiences to the class. In some cases, I had the opportunity to tell the professor that General Motors handled some things—straight-line depreciation,

for instance—differently from the way they were taught in class. I got to explain General Motors' policy, and that was an eye-opener for the professor.

"I felt that I was a role model," he says. "The other students looked to my real-world experience, and I especially enjoyed helping the ones who wanted to work and take classes at the same time. But there's a very practical payoff, too. I've moved and as I look for a new job, I'm finding would-be employers are impressed with my combination of business experience and academic background."

What advice does Timothy have for college accounting students? "Learn all you can about computers. Computer literacy is important in your field, whether you become a bookkeeper or are doing general-ledger accounting."

The main point to remember is that the adjusting entries are not journalized and posted until *after* the financial reports are prepared.

At this point you should be able to

1. Define and state the purpose of adjusting entries. (p. 143)
2. Journalize adjusting entries from the work sheet. (p. 144)
3. Post journalized adjusting entries to the ledger. (p. 145)
4. Compare specific ledger accounts before and after posting of the journalized adjusting entries. (p. 145)

☐ **SELF-REVIEW QUIZ 5-1**

Turn to the work sheet of B. Bass (p. 122) and (1) journalize and post the adjusting entries and (2) compare the adjusted ledger accounts before and after the adjustments are posted. T accounts are provided in your study guide with beginning balances.

■ SOLUTION TO SELF-REVIEW QUIZ 5-1

Page 2

Date			Account Titles and Description	PR	Dr.		Cr.	
			Adjusting Entries					
Dec.	31		Depreciation Expense, Store Equip.	511	1	00		
			Accumulated Depreciation, Store Equip.	122			1	00
	31		Insurance Expense	516	2	00		
			Prepaid Insurance	116			2	00
	31		Supplies Expense	514	4	00		
			Store Supplies	114			4	00
	31		Salaries Expense	512	3	00		
			Salaries Payable	212			3	00

PARTIAL LEDGER

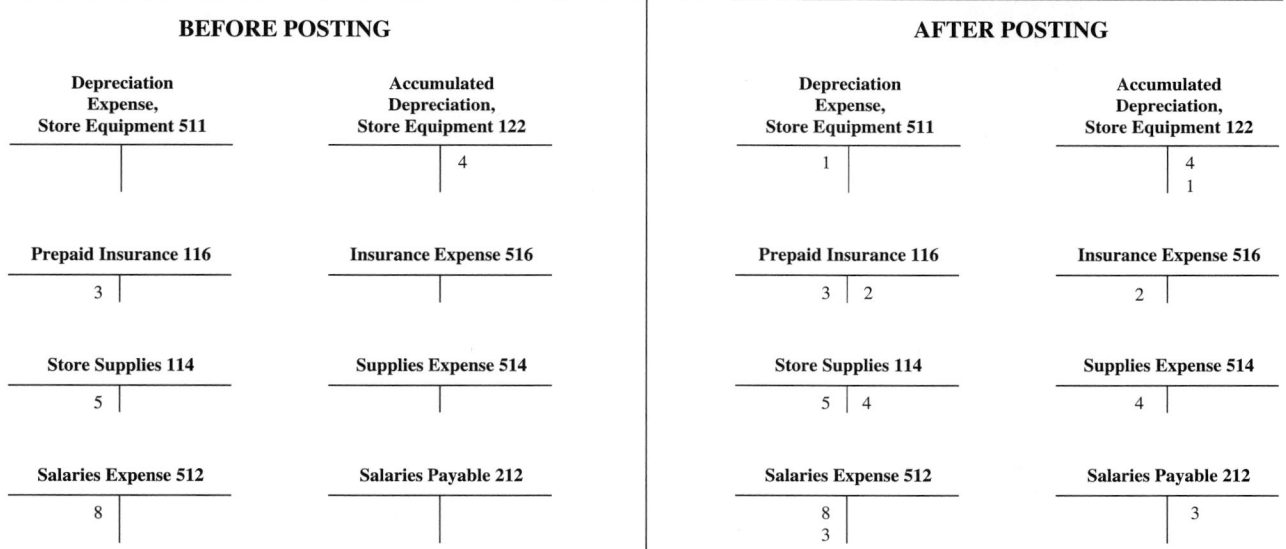

BEFORE POSTING		AFTER POSTING	
Depreciation Expense, Store Equipment 511	Accumulated Depreciation, Store Equipment 122	Depreciation Expense, Store Equipment 511	Accumulated Depreciation, Store Equipment 122

LEARNING UNIT 5-2

Journalizing and Posting Closing Entries: Step 8 of the Accounting Cycle

In order to make the recording of the next period's transactions easier, a mechanical step, called closing, is taken by Clark's accountant. Before we discuss closing, however, let's look carefully at the difference between temporary (nominal) accounts and permanent (real) accounts.

TEMPORARY AND PERMANENT ACCOUNTS

First recall the expanded accounting equation:

Assets = Liabilities + Capital – Withdrawals + Revenues – Expenses

Permanent accounts are found on the balance sheet.

Assets, liabilities, and capital are known as **real** or **permanent accounts**, because their balances are carried over from one accounting period to another.

Withdrawals, revenue, and expenses are called **nominal** or **temporary accounts**, because their balances are not carried over from one accounting period to another. Why not? By setting their "balances" back to zero, we will be able to accumulate new data about revenue, expenses, etc., in the new accounting period.

Goals of closing.

Thus in the process called *closing*, accomplished by means of journalizing and posting **closing journal entries**, we will summarize the effects of the temporary accounts on capital for that period. When the closing process is complete, the accounting equation will be reduced to:

Assets = Liabilities + Ending Capital

All closing entries are journalized and posted to the ledger; all temporary accounts will have a zero balance in the ledger.

All revenue, expenses, and withdrawals will have a zero balance in the ledger at the end of the closing process. These balances, which are cleared to zero, are used to calculate the new or ending figure for capital at the end of the accounting period. In the next period we can gather new information about revenue, expenses, and withdrawal transactions.

Remember, closing requires mechanical steps. If you look back to p. 125 in Chapter 4 you will see that we have already calculated the new capital on the balance sheet to be $10,945 for Clark's Word Processing Services. But before the mechanical closing procedures are journalized and posted, the capital account of Clark in the ledger is only $7,000 (Chapter 3, p. 84). Let's look now at how to journalize and post closing entries.

HOW TO JOURNALIZE CLOSING ENTRIES

For our present purpose, the information needed to complete closing entries will be found in *the income statement and balance sheet sections of the work sheet*.

There are four steps to be performed in journalizing closing entries:

On p. 70 Income Summary is a temporary account located in the chart of accounts under owner's equity. It does not have a normal balance of debit or credit.

1. *Clear the revenue balance and transfer it to Income Summary.*
   Income Summary is a temporary account in the ledger needed for closing. At the end of the closing process there will be no balance in Income Summary.
   Revenue → Income Summary
2. *Clear the individual expense balances and transfer them to Income Summary.*
   Expenses → Income Summary
3. *Clear the balance in Income Summary and transfer it to Capital.*
   Income Summary → Capital
4. *Clear the balance in Withdrawals and transfer it to Capital.*
   Withdrawals → Capital

Remember, Income Summary is a temporary account in the ledger used to summarize revenue and expenses. After steps 1 and 2 are journalized and posted, the Income Summary account in the ledger will contain:

Income Summary

Exp.	Rev.

Figure 5-3 summarizes these four steps in a visual form.

Keep in mind that this information must first be journalized and then posted to the appropriate ledger accounts. To do this, use the work sheet presented in Figure 5-4, in which all the figures we will need for the closing process will be found.

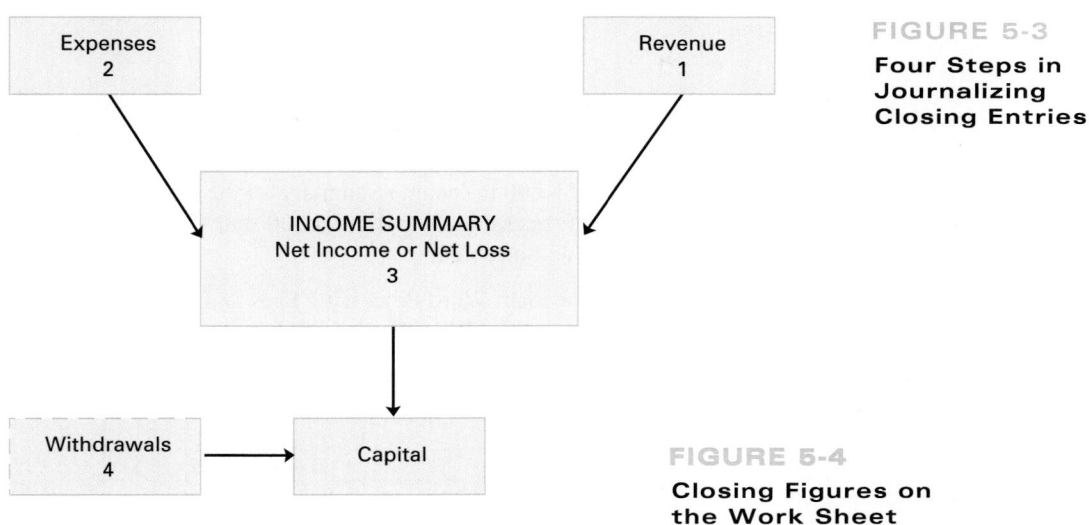

FIGURE 5-3

Four Steps in Journalizing Closing Entries

FIGURE 5-4

Closing Figures on the Work Sheet

Account Titles	Income Statement		Balance Sheet	
	Dr.	Cr.	Dr.	Cr.
Cash			2 0 9 0 00	
Accounts Receivable			4 1 0 0 00	
Office Supplies			8 0 00	
Prepaid Rent			6 0 0 00	
Word Processing Equipment			8 0 0 0 00	
Accounts Payable				3 5 7 5 00
B. Clark, Capital				7 0 0 0 00
B. Clark, Withdrawals			4 3 0 00	
Word Processing Fees		6 6 0 0 00		
Office Salaries Expense	1 1 5 0 00			
Advertising Expense	1 7 5 00			
Telephone Expense	1 8 0 00			
Offie Supplies Expense	3 2 0 00			
Rent Expense	3 0 0 00			
Depreciation Expense, W.P. Equip.	1 0 0 00			
Accum. Depreciation, W.P. Equip.				1 0 0 00
Salaries Payable				2 5 0 00
	2 2 2 5 00	6 6 0 0 00	1 5 3 0 0 00	1 0 9 2 5 00
Net Income	4 3 7 5 00			4 3 7 5 00
	6 6 0 0 00	6 6 0 0 00	1 5 3 0 0 00	1 5 3 0 0 00

Step 1, Step 2, Step 3, Step 4

Step 1: Clear Revenue Balance and Transfer to Income Summary

Here is what is in the ledger before closing entries are journalized and posted:

Word Processing Fees 411	Income Summary 313
6,600	

Notice by looking at the income statement section on the work sheet on p. 149 that the Word Processing Fees have a credit balance. To close or clear this to zero, a debit of $6,600 is needed. But if we add an amount to the debit side, we must also add a credit—so we add $6,600 to Income Summary on the credit side.

By debiting Word Processing Fees for $6,600 and then crediting Income Summary for $6,600 we will be able to

1. Bring the temporary account Word Processing Fees to a zero balance.
2. Transfer the information from Word Processing Fees to Income Summary.

The following is the journalized closing entry for step 1:

May	31	Word Processing Fees	411	6 6 0 0 00	
		Income Summary	313		6 6 0 0 00

Don't forget two goals of closing:
1. Clear all temporary accounts in the ledger.
2. Update capital to a new balance that reflects a summary of all the temporary accounts.

All numbers used in the closing process can be found on the work sheet. Note that the *account* Income Summary is *not* on the work sheet.

This is what Word Processing Fees and Income Summary should look like in the ledger after the first step of closing entries is journalized and posted:

Word Processing Fees 411		Income Summary 313	
6,600	6,600		6,600
Closing	Revenue		Revenue

Note that the revenue balance is cleared to 0 and transferred to Income Summary, a temporary account also located in the ledger.

Step 2: Clear Individual Expense Balances and Transfer the Total to Income Summary

Here is what is in the ledger for each expense before step 2 of closing entries is journalized and posted. Each expense is listed on the work sheet in the debit column of the income statement section on p. 149.

Office Salaries Expense 511	Advertising Expense 512
1,150	175

Telephone Expense 513	Office Supplies Expense 514
180	320

Rent Expense 515	Depreciation Expense, W. P. Equipment 516
300	100

In order to reach our goal, what must be done with these expenses before closing?

In the income statement section of the work sheet, all the expenses were listed as debits. If we want to reduce each expense to zero and they are all debits, we will have to credit each one.

The work sheet, once again, doesn't tell you where the total of the expenses is to be brought in the closing process, but it does give you the amount of $2,225. Remember, the work sheet is a tool. The accountant realizes that the information about the total of the expenses will be transferred to Income Summary.

By crediting each individual expense and debiting Income Summary for the total of all the expenses we will be able to

1. Bring all expenses to a zero balance.
2. Transfer the information about the expenses to Income Summary.

The following is the journalized closing entry for step 2:

31	Income Summary	313	2 2 2 5 00	
	Office Salaries Expense	511		1 1 5 0 00
	Advertising Expense	512		1 7 5 00
	Telephone Expense	513		1 8 0 00
	Office Supplies Expense	514		3 2 0 00
	Rent Expense	515		3 0 0 00
	Depreciation Expense, W.P. Equipment	516		1 0 0 00

This is what individual expenses and Income Summary should look like in the ledger after step 2 of closing entries is journalized and posted:

Office Salaries Expense 511
1,150 | Closing 1,150

Advertising Expense 512
175 | Closing 175

Telephone Expense 513
180 | Closing 180

Office Supplies Expense 514
320 | Closing 320

Rent Expense 515
300 | Closing 300

Depreciation Expense 516
100 | Closing 100

Income Summary 313
expenses | revenue
Step 2 2,225 | 6,600 Step 1

Step 3: Clear Balance in Income Summary (Net Income) and Transfer It to Capital

This is how the Income Summary and B. Clark, Capital, accounts look before step 3:

Income Summary 313
2,225 | 6,600
| 4,375

B. Clark, Capital 311
| 7,000

What do we have to do in order to accomplish step 3? First, note that the *balance* of Income Summary (revenue minus expenses or $6,600 – $2,225) is $4,375. It is this amount that we must clear from the income summary account and transfer to the B. Clark Capital, account.

In order to transfer the balance of $4,375 from income summary (check the bottom debit column of the income statement section on work sheet) to capital it will be necessary to debit Income Summary for $4,375 (the difference between the revenue and expenses) and credit or increase capital of B. Clark.* The results will be to:

1. Clear Income Summary (a temporary account) to zero.
2. Summarize the effects on capital of revenue and expenses, which have been accumulated in Income Summary from steps 1 and 2 of the closing process.

The journalized closing entry for step 3 is:

31	Income Summary	313	4 3 7 5 00	
	B. Clark, Capital	311		4 3 7 5 00

This is what the Income Summary and B. Clark, Capital, accounts will look like in the ledger after step 3 of closing entries is journalized and posted:

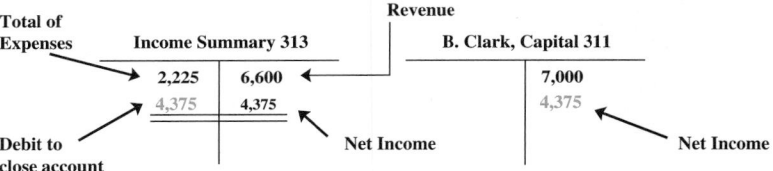

To this point the three closing journal entries when posted will have (1) cleared all revenue and expense accounts to arrive at a zero balance, and (2) summarized the effect of the revenue and expense accounts on capital.

Now let's look at how to close the withdrawals account.

Income Summary now has a zero balance. If we had a net loss the end result would be to decrease capital. The entry would be to debit capital and credit income summary for the loss.

Step 4: Clear the Withdrawals Balance and Transfer it to Capital

The B. Clark, Withdrawals, and B. Clark, Capital, accounts now look like this:

B. Clark, Withdrawals 312		B. Clark, Capital 311	
430			7,000
			4,375

In order to reach the goal of bringing the Withdrawals account to a zero balance, as well as summarizing its effect on Capital, the following must be done:

1. Credit Withdrawals.
2. Debit Capital.

Remember, withdrawals are a non-business expense and thus not transferred to Income Summary.

* For a net loss, the opposite process would take place.

The closing entry would be journalized as follows:

	31	B. Clark, Capital	311	4 3 0 00	
		B. Clark, Withdrawals	312		4 3 0 00

At this point the B. Clark, Withdrawals, and B. Clark, Capital, accounts would look like this in the ledger.

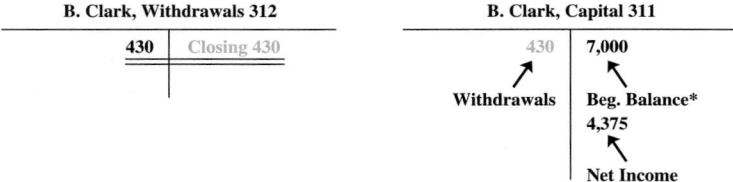

* It is beginning balance since no additional investments took place during the period.

Now let's look at the complete ledger for Clark Word Processing Services (see Figure 5-5). Note how the word "adjusting" or "closing" is written in the explanation column of individual ledgers, as for example in the one for Office Supplies. If the goals of closing have been achieved, only permanent accounts will have balances carried to the next accounting period. All temporary accounts should have zero balances.

FIGURE 5-5
Complete Ledger

Brenda Clark's Word Processing Services
General Ledger

Cash   Acct. No. 111

Date 19XX	Explanation	Post Ref.	Debit	Credit	DR or CR	Balance
May 1		GJ1	7 0 0 0 00		DR	7 0 0 0 00
1		GJ1		2 0 0 0 00	DR	5 0 0 0 00
1		GJ1		9 0 0 00	DR	4 1 0 0 00
7		GJ1	2 5 0 0 00		DR	6 6 0 0 00
15		GJ1		4 5 0 00	DR	6 1 5 0 00
20		GJ1		4 3 0 00	DR	5 7 2 0 00
27		GJ2		4 5 0 00	DR	5 2 7 0 00
28		GJ2		3 0 0 0 00	DR	2 2 7 0 00
29		GJ2		1 8 0 00	DR	2 0 9 0 00

Accounts Receivable   Acct. No. 112

Date 19XX	Explanation	Post Ref.	Debit	Credit	DR or CR	Balance
May 22		GJ1	4 1 0 0 00		DR	4 1 0 0 00

Office Supplies   Acct. No. 114

Date 19XX		Explanation	Post Ref.	Debit	Credit	DR or CR	Balance
May	3		GJ1	4 0 0 00		DR	4 0 0 00
	31	Adjusting	GJ2		3 2 0 00	DR	8 0 00

Prepaid Rent   Acct. No. 115

Date 19XX		Explanation	Post Ref.	Debit	Credit	DR or CR	Balance
May	1		GJ1	9 0 0 00		DR	9 0 0 00
	31	Adjusting	GJ2		3 0 0 00	DR	6 0 0 00

Word Processing Equipment   Acct. No. 121

Date 19XX		Explanation	Post Ref.	Debit	Credit	DR or CR	Balance
May	1		GJ1	8 0 0 0 00		DR	8 0 0 0 00

Accumulated Depreciation, Word Processing Equipment   Acct. No. 122

Date 19XX		Explanation	Post Ref.	Debit	Credit	DR or CR	Balance
May	31	Adjusting	GJ2		1 0 0 00	CR	1 0 0 00

Accounts Payable   Acct. No. 211

Date 19XX		Explanation	Post Ref.	Debit	Credit	DR or CR	Balance
May	1		GJ1		6 0 0 0 00	CR	6 0 0 0 00
	3		GJ1		4 0 0 00	CR	6 4 0 0 00
	18		GJ1		1 7 5 00	CR	6 5 7 5 00
	28		GJ2	3 0 0 0 00		CR	3 5 7 5 00

Salaries Payable   Acct. No. 212

Date 19XX		Explanation	Post Ref.	Debit	Credit	DR or CR	Balance
May	31	Adjusting	GJ2		2 5 0 00	CR	2 5 0 00

Brenda Clark, Capital   Acct. No. 311

Date 19XX		Explanation	Post Ref.	Debit	Credit	DR or CR	Balance
May	1		GJ1		7 0 0 0 00	CR	7 0 0 0 00
	31	Closing (Net Income)	GJ3		4 3 7 5 00	CR	11 3 7 5 00
	31	Closing (Withdrawals)	GJ3	4 3 0 00		CR	10 9 4 5 00

Note how this is the same ending balance as p. 125.

Brenda Clark, Withdrawals   Acct. No. 312

Date 19XX		Explanation	Post Ref.	Debit	Credit	DR or CR	Balance
May	20		GJ1	4 3 0 00		DR	4 3 0 00
	31	Closing	GJ3		4 3 0 00		– 0 –

Income Summary   Acct. No. 313

Date 19XX		Explanation	Post Ref.	Debit	Credit	DR or CR	Balance
May	31	Closing (Revenue)	GJ2		6 6 0 0 00	CR	6 6 0 0 00
	31	Closing (Expense)	GJ2	2 2 2 5 00		CR	4 3 7 5 00
	31	Closing (Net Income)	GJ2	4 3 7 5 00			– 0 –

Word Processing Fees   Acct. No. 411

Date 19XX		Explanation	Post Ref.	Debit	Credit	DR or CR	Balance
May	7		GJ1		2 5 0 0 00	CR	2 5 0 0 00
	22		GJ1		4 1 0 0 00	CR	6 6 0 0 00
	31	Closing	GJ2	6 6 0 0 00			– 0 –

Office Salaries Expense Acct. No. 511

Date 19XX		Explanation	Post Ref.	Debit	Credit	DR or CR	Balance
May	15		GJ1	4 5 0 00		DR	4 5 0 00
	27		GJ2	4 5 0 00		DR	9 0 0 00
	31	Adjusting	GJ2	2 5 0 00		DR	1 1 5 0 00
	31	Closing	GJ2		1 1 5 0 00		– 0 –

Advertising Expense Acct. No. 512

Date 19XX		Explanation	Post Ref.	Debit	Credit	DR or CR	Balance
May	18		GJ1	1 7 5 00		DR	1 7 5 00
	31	Closing	GJ2		1 7 5 00		– 0 –

Telephone Expense Acct. No. 513

Date 19XX		Explanation	Post Ref.	Debit	Credit	DR or CR	Balance
May	29		GJ2	1 8 0 00		DR	1 8 0 00
	31	Closing	GJ2		1 8 0 00		– 0 –

Office Supplies Expense Acct. No. 514

Date 19XX		Explanation	Post Ref.	Debit	Credit	DR or CR	Balance
May	31	Adjusting	GJ2	3 2 0 00		DR	3 2 0 00
	31	Closing	GJ2		3 2 0 00		– 0 –

Rent Expense Acct. No. 515

Date 19XX		Explanation	Post Ref.	Debit	Credit	DR or CR	Balance
May	31	Adjusting	GJ2	3 0 0 00		DR	3 0 0 00
	31	Closing	GJ2		3 0 0 00		– 0 –

Depreciation Expense, Word Processing Equipment Acct. No. 516

Date 19XX		Explanation	Post Ref.	Debit	Credit	DR or CR	Balance
May	31	Adjusting	GJ2	1 0 0 00		DR	1 0 0 00
		Closing	GJ2		1 0 0 00		– 0 –

At this point you should be able to

1. Define closing. (p. 148)
2. Differentiate between temporary (nominal) and permanent (real) accounts. (p. 148)
3. List the four mechanical steps of closing. (p. 148)
4. Explain the role of the Income Summary account. (p. 149)
5. Explain the role of the work sheet in the closing process. (p. 150)

☐ SELF-REVIEW QUIZ 5-2

Go to the work sheet of B. Bass on p. 122 and (1) journalize and post the closing entries and (2) calculate the new balance for B. Bass, Capital.

■ *SOLUTION TO SELF-REVIEW QUIZ 5-2*

		Closing				
Dec.	31	Revenue from Clients	410	2 5 00		
		Income Summary	312		2 5 00	
	31	Income Summary	312	2 0 00		
		Rent Expense	518		2 00	
		Salaries Expense	512		1 1 00	
		Depreciation Expense, Store Equip.	510		1 00	
		Insurance Expense	516		2 00	
		Supplies Expense	514		4 00	
	31	Income Summary	312	5 00		
		B. Bass, Capital	310		5 00	
	31	B. Bass, Capital	310	3 00		
		B. Bass, Withdrawals	311		3 00	

PARTIAL LEDGER

B. Bass, Capital 310

3	14
	5
	16

B. Bass, Withdrawals 311

3	3

Income Summary 312

20	25
5	5

Revenue from Clients 410

25	25

Dep. Exp., Store Equip 510

1	1

Salaries Expense 512

11	11

Supplies Expense 514

4	4

Insurance Expense 516

2	2

Rent Expense 518

2	2

B. Bass, Capital		$14
Net Income	$5	
Less Withdrawals	_3_	
Increase in Capital		2
B. Bass, Capital (ending)		$16

LEARNING UNIT 5-3

The Post-Closing Trial Balance: Step 9 of the Accounting Cycle and the Cycle Reviewed

PREPARING A POST-CLOSING TRIAL BALANCE

The post-closing trial balance helps prove the accuracy of the adjusting and closing process. It contains the true ending balance for capital.

The last step in the accounting cycle is the preparation of a **post-closing trial balance**, which lists only permanent accounts in the ledger and their balances after adjusting and closing entries have been posted. This post-closing trial balance aids in checking whether the ledger is in balance. This checking is important to do because so many new postings go to the ledger from the adjusting and closing process.

The procedure for taking a post-closing trial balance is the same as for a trial balance, except that, since closing entries have closed all temporary accounts, the post-closing trial balance will contain only permanent accounts (balance sheet). Keep in mind, however, that adjustments have occurred.

THE ACCOUNTING CYCLE REVIEWED

Figure 5-6 is the list of the steps we completed in the accounting cycle for Clark for the month of May:

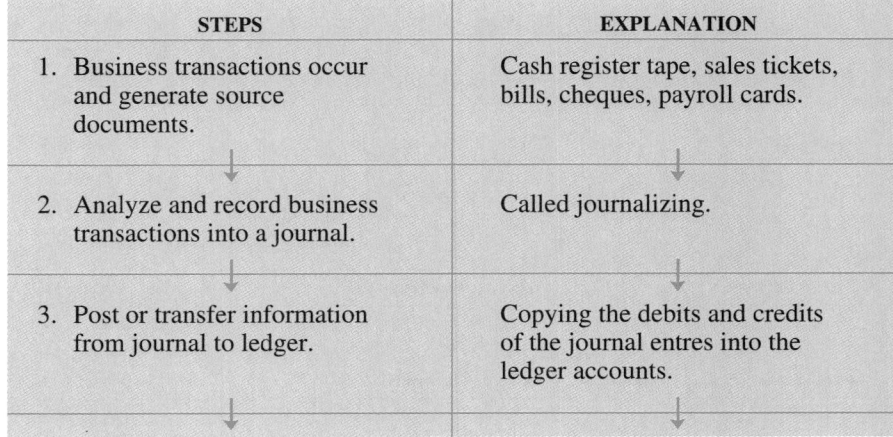

FIGURE 5-6

Steps of the Accounting Cycle

STEPS	EXPLANATION
1. Business transactions occur and generate source documents.	Cash register tape, sales tickets, bills, cheques, payroll cards.
2. Analyze and record business transactions into a journal.	Called journalizing.
3. Post or transfer information from journal to ledger.	Copying the debits and credits of the journal entres into the ledger accounts.

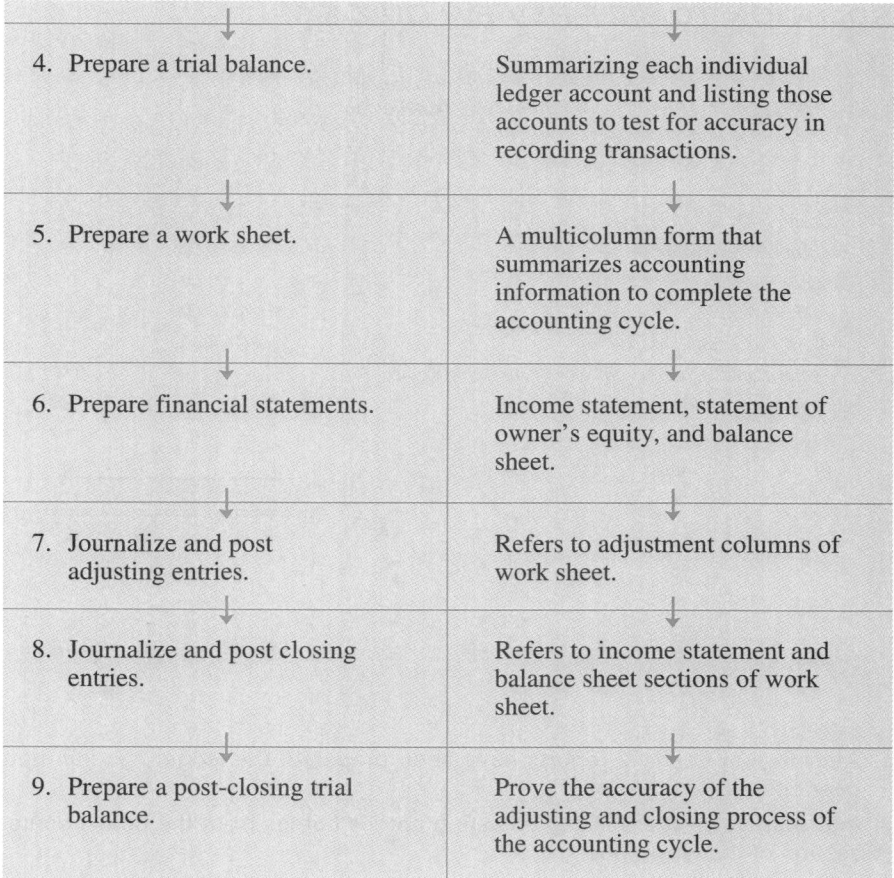

FIGURE 5-6

**Steps of the
Accounting Cycle**

4. Prepare a trial balance.	Summarizing each individual ledger account and listing those accounts to test for accuracy in recording transactions.
5. Prepare a work sheet.	A multicolumn form that summarizes accounting information to complete the accounting cycle.
6. Prepare financial statements.	Income statement, statement of owner's equity, and balance sheet.
7. Journalize and post adjusting entries.	Refers to adjustment columns of work sheet.
8. Journalize and post closing entries.	Refers to income statement and balance sheet sections of work sheet.
9. Prepare a post-closing trial balance.	Prove the accuracy of the adjusting and closing process of the accounting cycle.

NOTE: Most companies journalize and post adjusting and closing entries only at the end of their fiscal year. When a company prepares interim reports, it may be that only the first six steps of the cycle are completed. Work sheets allow the preparation of interim reports without the formal adjusting and closing of the books. If this happens, footnotes on the interim report will indicate the extent to which adjusting and closing were completed or not.

For example, to prepare a financial report for March, the data needed can be obtained by subtracting the work sheet accumulated totals from the end of March from the work sheet prepared at the end of February. In the situation we have described in this chapter, with Clark's Word Processing Service, we chose a month that would show the completion of an entire cycle.

At this point you should be able to

1. Prepare a post-closing trial balance. (p. 158)
2. Explain the relationship of interim reports to the accounting cycle. (above)

☐ **SELF-REVIEW QUIZ 5-3**

From the ledger of Clark, p. 153, prepare a post-closing trial balance.

SOLUTION TO SELF-REVIEW QUIZ 5-3

Clark's Word Processing Service
Post-Closing Trial Balance
May 31, 19XX

	Dr.	Cr.
Cash	2 0 9 0 00	
Accounts Receivable	4 1 0 0 00	
Office Supplies	8 0 00	
Prepaid Rent	6 0 0 00	
Word Processing Equipment	8 0 0 0 00	
Accumulated Depreciation, Word Processing Equip.		1 0 0 00
Accounts Payable		3 5 7 5 00
Salaries Payable		2 5 0 00
Brenda Clark, Capital		10 9 4 5 00
Totals	14 8 7 0 00	14 8 7 0 00

NOTE: No revenue, expense or withdrawals accounts are found on the post-closing trial balance.

SUMMARY OF KEY POINTS AND KEY TERMS

LEARNING UNIT 5-1

1. After formal financial reports have been prepared, the ledger has still not been brought up-to-date.

2. Information for journalizing adjusting entries comes from the adjustments section of the work sheet.

Adjusting journal entries: Journal entries that are needed in order to update specific ledger accounts to reflect correct balances at the end of an accounting period.

LEARNING UNIT 5-2

1. Closing is a mechanical process that aids the accountant in recording transactions for the next period.

2. Assets, liabilities, and capital are permanent (real) accounts; their balances are carried over from one accounting period to another. Withdrawals, revenue, and expenses are nominal (temporary) accounts; their balances are *not* carried over from one accounting period to another.

3. Income Summary is a temporary account in the general ledger and does not have a normal balance. It will summarize revenue and expenses and transfer the balance to capital. Withdrawals do not go into Income Summary, because they are *not* business expenses.

4. All information for closing can be obtained from the work sheet or ledger.

5. When closing is complete, all temporary accounts in the ledger will have a zero balance (to get ready to accumulate the next period's data), and all this information will be updated in the capital account.

6. Closing entries are usually done only at year end. Interim reports can be prepared from work sheets which are prepared monthly, quarterly, and so on.

Closing journal entries: Journal entries that are prepared to (a) reduce or clear all temporary accounts to a zero balance, or (b) update capital to a new balance.

Income Summary: A temporary account in the ledger that summarizes revenue and expenses and transfers its balance (net income or net loss) to capital. Does not have a normal balance.

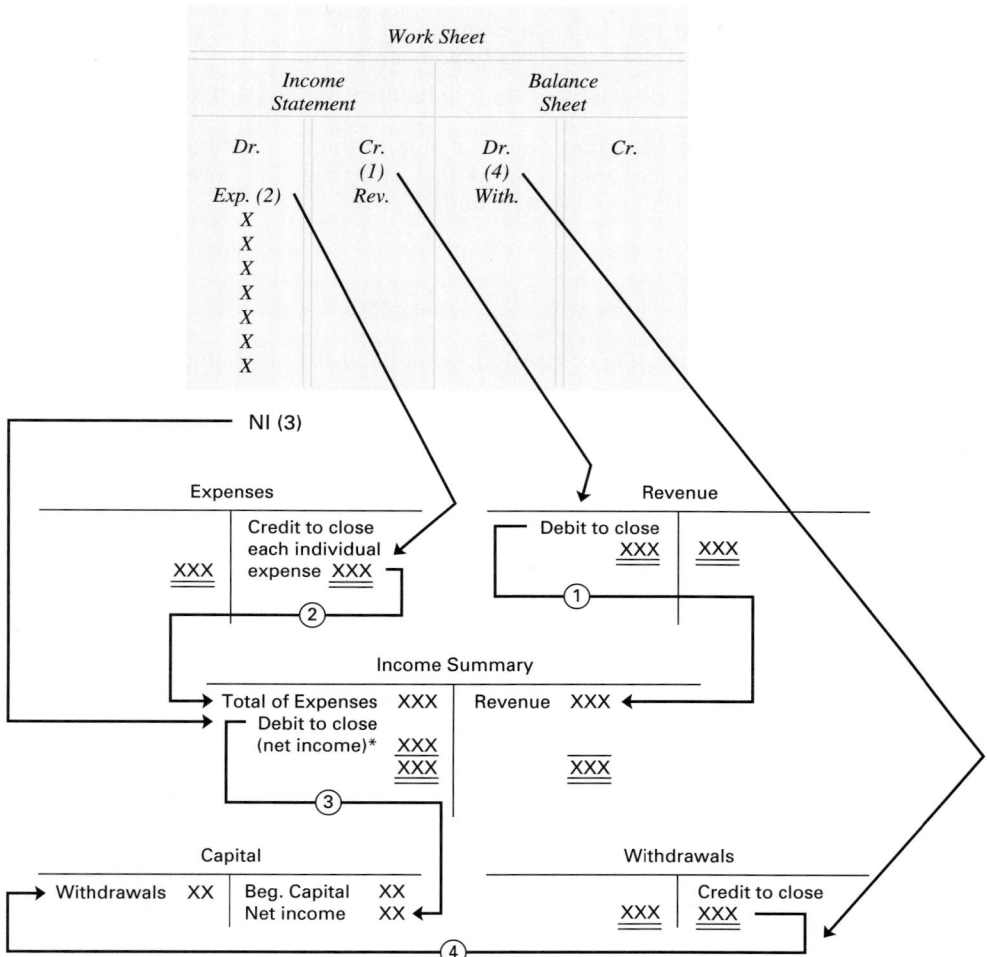

* If a net loss, it would be a credit to close.

THE CLOSING STEPS

1. Close revenue balance to Income Summary.
2. Close each *individual* expense and transfer *total* of all expenses to Income Summary.
3. Transfer balance in Income Summary (Net Income or Net Loss) to Capital.
4. Close Withdrawals to Capital.

Permanent accounts (real): Accounts whose balances are carried over to the next accounting period. Examples: assets, liabilities, capital.

Temporary accounts (nominal): Accounts whose balances at end of an accounting period are not carried over to the next accounting period. These accounts—revenue, expenses, withdrawals—help summarize a new or ending figure for capital to begin the next accounting period. Keep in mind that Income Summary is also a temporary account.

LEARNING UNIT 5-3

1. The post-closing trial balance is prepared from the ledger accounts after the adjusting and closing entries have been posted.
2. The accounts on the post-closing trial balance are all permanent titles.

Post-closing trial balance: The final step in the accounting cycle that lists only permanent accounts in the ledger and their balances after adjusting and closing entries have been posted.

DISCUSSION QUESTIONS

1. When a work sheet is completed, what balances are found in the general ledger?
2. Why must adjusting entries be journalized even though the formal reports have already been prepared?
3. "Closing slows down the recording of next year's transactions." Defend or reject this statement with supporting evidence.
4. What is the difference between temporary and permanent accounts?
5. What are the two major goals of the closing process?
6. List the four mechanical steps of closing.
7. What is the purpose of Income Summary and where is it located?
8. How can a work sheet aid the closing process?
9. What accounts are usually listed on a post-closing trial balance?
10. Closing entries are always prepared once a month. Agree or disagree. Why?

EXERCISES

Journalize adjusting entries.

1. From the adjustments section of a work sheet at top of page 163, prepare adjusting journal entries for end of December.

Temporary vs. permanent accounts.

2. Complete the following table by placing an X in the correct column.

	TEMPORARY	PERMANENT	WILL BE CLOSED
Ex. Accounts Receivable		X	
1. Withdrawals			
2. Al Jones, Capital			
3. Salary Expense			
4. Income Summary			
5. Fees Earned			
6. Accounts Payable			
7. Cash			

	Adjustments	
	Dr.	*Cr.*

Prepaid Insurance		(A) 6 0 0 00
Office Supplies		(B) 1 0 0 00
Accumulated Depreciation, Equipment		(C) 4 0 0 00
Salaries Payable		(D) 1 0 0 00

Insurance Expense	(A) 6 0 0 00	
Office Supplies Expense	(B) 1 0 0 00	
Depreciation Expense, Equipment	(C) 4 0 0 00	
Salaries Expense	(D) 1 0 0 00	
	1 2 0 0 00	1 2 0 0 00

3. From the following T accounts, journalize the four closing entries on December 31, 19XX.   **Closing entries.**

Bobbie Burn, Capital	
	7,000

Rent Expense	
4,100	

Bobbie Burn, Withdrawals	
5,200	

Wage Expense	
3,000	

Income Summary	

Insurance Expense	
1,400	

Fees Earned	
	40,500

Dep. Expense, Office Equipment	
800	

4. From the following posted T accounts, reconstruct the closing journal entries for December 31, 19XX.   **Reconstructing closing entries.**

B. Boe, Capital	
Withdrawals 75	2,000 (Dec. 1)
	700 Net Income

Insurance Expense	
50	Closing 50

B. Boe, Withdrawals	
75	Closing 75

Wage Expense	
100	Closing 100

Income Summary		**Rent Expense**	
Expenses 600	Revenue 1,300	200	Closing 200
700	Net Income 700		

Salon Fees		**Depreciation Expense, Equipment**	
Closing 1,300	1,300	250	Closing 250

Post-closing trial balance.

5. From the following accounts (not in order), prepare a post-closing trial balance for Lowe Co. on December 31, 19XX. **NOTE:** These balances are **before** closing.

Legal Fees Earned	$12,000
Accounts Payable	45,000
Cash	22,125
Accounts Receivable	18,750
Legal Supplies	14,250
Office Equipment	59,700
Repair Expense	2,850
Salaries Expense	1,275
A. Lowe, Capital	63,450
A. Lowe, Withdrawals	1,500

GROUP A PROBLEMS

5A-1. Given the following data for Sue's Consulting Service:

Review in preparing a work sheet and journalizing adjusting and closing entries.

Sue's Consulting Service
Trial Balance
June 30, 19XX

	Dr.	Cr.
Cash	17 1 5 0 00	
Accounts Receivable	4 0 0 0 00	
Prepaid Insurance	3 5 0 00	
Supplies	1 2 0 0 00	
Equipment	2 0 0 0 00	
Accumulated Depreciation, Equipment		7 5 0 00
Accounts Payable		6 0 0 0 00
Sue French, Capital		12 7 5 0 00
Sue French, Withdrawals	2 5 0 00	
Consulting Fees Earned		8 2 0 0 00
Salaries Expense	1 2 0 0 00	
Telephone Expense	1 0 3 0 00	
Advertising Expense	5 2 0 00	
	27 7 0 0 00	27 7 0 0 00

Adjustment data:
   A. Insurance expired, $100.
   B. Supplies on hand, $415.
   C. Depreciation on equipment, $150.
   D. Salaries earned by employees but not to be paid till July, $150.

Your task is to
1. Prepare a work sheet.
2. Journalize adjusting and closing entries.

5A-2. Enter beginning balance in each account in your working papers from the trial balance columns of the work sheet. From the work sheet on p. 166, (1) journalize and post adjusting and closing entries after entering beginning balance in each account in the ledger, and (2) prepare from the ledger a post-closing trial balance for the month of March.

Journalizing and posting adjusting and closing entries. Preparing a post-closing trial balance.

5A-3. As the bookkeeper of Dorin's Plowing, you have been asked to complete the entire accounting cycle for Tom from the following information:

Comprehensive review of the entire accounting cycle, Chapters 1-5.

Jan.	1	Tom invested $9,000 cash and $6,000 worth of snow equipment into the plowing company.
	1	Paid rent for three months in advance for garage space, $1,500.
	4	Purchased office equipment on account from Regan Corp., $7,200.
	6	Purchased snow supplies for $600 cash.
	8	Collected $12,000 from plowing local shopping centres.
	12	Tom Dorin withdrew $800 from the business for his own personal use.
	20	Plowed North East Co. parking lots, payment not to be received until March, $4,000.
	26	Paid salaries to employees, $1,300.
	28	Paid Regan Corp. one-half amount owed for office equipment.
	29	Advertising bill received from Joyce Co. but will not be paid until March, $700.
	30	Paid telephone bill, $150.

Adjustment data:
A. Snow supplies on hand, $250.
B. Rent expired, $500.
C. Depreciation on office equip., $120. ($7,200 ÷ 5 yr. = $1,440/12 = $120)
D. Depreciation on snow equip., $100. ($6,000 ÷ 5 = $1,200/12 mo. = $100)
E. Accrued salaries, $260.

CHART OF ACCOUNTS

Assets
111 Cash
112 Accounts Receivable
114 Prepaid Rent
115 Snow Supplies
121 Office Equipment
122 Accumulated Depreciation, Office Equipment
123 Snow Equipment
124 Accumulated Depreciation, Snow Equipment

Liabilities
211 Accounts Payable
212 Salaries Payable

Owner's Equity
311 Tom Dorin, Capital
312 Tom Dorin, Withdrawals
313 Income Summary

Revenue
411 Plowing Fees

Expenses
511 Salaries Expense
512 Advertising Expense
513 Telephone Expense
514 Rent Expense
515 Snow Supplies Expense
516 Depreciation Expense, Office Equipment
517 Depreciation Expense, Snow Equipment

Larson Cleaning Service
Work Sheet
For month ended March 31, 19XX

Account Titles	Trial Balance Dr.	Trial Balance Cr.	Adjustments Dr.	Adjustments Cr.	Adjusted Trial Balance Dr.	Adjusted Trial Balance Cr.	Income Statement Dr.	Income Statement Cr.	Balance Sheet Dr.	Balance Sheet Cr.
Cash	5 0 0 00				5 0 0 00				5 0 0 00	
Prepaid Ins.	4 2 0 00			(A) 1 8 0 00	2 4 0 00				2 4 0 00	
Cleaning Supp.	1 4 4 00			(B) 1 0 0 00	4 4 00				4 4 00	
Auto	2 7 2 0 00				2 7 2 0 00				2 7 2 0 00	
Accumulated Depreciation, Auto		8 6 0 00		(C) 1 5 0 00		1 0 1 0 00				1 0 1 0 00
Accounts Payable		2 2 4 00				2 2 4 00				2 2 4 00
T. Larson, Capital		5 4 0 00				5 4 0 00				5 4 0 00
T. Larson, Withdrawals	4 6 0 00				4 6 0 00				4 6 0 00	
Cleaning Fees		4 6 8 0 00				4 6 8 0 00		4 6 8 0 00		
Salaries Expense	1 4 4 0 00		(D) 1 6 0 00		1 6 0 0 00		1 6 0 0 00			
Telephone Expense	2 6 4 00				2 6 4 00		2 6 4 00			
Advertising Expense	1 9 6 00				1 9 6 00		1 9 6 00			
Gas Expense	1 6 0 00				1 6 0 00		1 6 0 00			
	6 3 0 4 00	6 3 0 4 00								
Insurance Expense			(A) 1 8 0 00		1 8 0 00		1 8 0 00			
Cleaning Supplies Expense			(B) 1 0 0 00		1 0 0 00		1 0 0 00			
Depreciation Expense, Auto			(C) 1 5 0 00		1 5 0 00		1 5 0 00			
Salaries Payable				(D) 1 6 0 00		1 6 0 00				1 6 0 00
			5 9 0 00	5 9 0 00	6 6 1 4 00	6 6 1 4 00	2 6 5 0 00	4 6 8 0 00	3 9 6 4 00	1 9 3 4 00
Net Income							2 0 3 0 00			2 0 3 0 00
							4 6 8 0 00	4 6 8 0 00	3 9 6 4 00	3 9 6 4 00

GROUP B PROBLEMS

5B-1.

> TO: Ron Ear
>
> FROM: Sue French
>
> RE: Accounting Needs
>
> *Please prepare ASAP from the following information (attached) (1) a work sheet along with (2) journalized adjusting and closing entries.*

Review in preparing a work sheet and journalizing adjusting and closing entries.

Sue's Consulting Service
Trial Balance
June 30, 19XX

	Dr.	Cr.
Cash	10 1 5 0 00	
Accounts Receivable	5 0 0 0 00	
Prepaid Insurance	7 0 0 00	
Supplies	3 0 0 00	
Equipment	12 9 5 0 00	
Accumulated Depreciation, Equipment		4 0 0 0 00
Accounts Payable		5 7 5 0 00
Sue French, Capital		15 1 5 0 00
Sue French, Withdrawals	4 0 0 00	
Consulting Fees Earned		5 2 0 0 00
Salaries Expense	4 5 0 00	
Telephone Expense	7 0 00	
Advertising Expense	8 0 00	
	30 1 0 0 00	30 1 0 0 00

Adjustment data:
   A. Insurance expired, $100.
   B. Supplies on hand, $20.
   C. Depreciation on equipment, $200.
   D. Salaries earned by employees but not due to be paid till July, $490.

5B-2. Enter beginning balance in each account in your working papers from the trial balance columns of the work sheet. From the work sheet on p. 168, (1) journalize and post adjusting and closing entries after entering beginning balances in each account in the ledger, and (2) prepare from the ledger a post-closing trial balance at end of March.

Journalizing and posting adjusting and closing entries. Preparing a post-closing trial balance.

Larson Cleaning Service
Work Sheet
For month ended March 31, 19XX

Account Titles	Trial Balance Dr.	Trial Balance Cr.	Adjustments Dr.	Adjustments Cr.	Adjusted Trial Balance Dr.	Adjusted Trial Balance Cr.	Income Statement Dr.	Income Statement Cr.	Balance Sheet Dr.	Balance Sheet Cr.
Cash	1 7 2 4 00				1 7 2 4 00				1 7 2 4 00	
Prepaid Insurance	3 5 0 00			(A) 2 0 0 00	1 5 0 00				1 5 0 00	
Cleaning Supplies	8 0 0 00			(B) 6 0 0 00	2 0 0 00				2 0 0 00	
Auto	1 2 2 0 00				1 2 2 0 00				1 2 2 0 00	
Accumulated Depreciation, Auto		6 6 0 00		(C) 1 5 0 00		8 1 0 00				8 1 0 00
Accounts Payable		6 7 4 00				6 7 4 00				6 7 4 00
T. Larson, Capital		2 4 8 0 00				2 4 8 0 00				2 4 8 0 00
T. Larson, Withdrawals	6 0 0 00				6 0 0 00				6 0 0 00	
Cleaning Fees		3 7 0 0 00				3 7 0 0 00		3 7 0 0 00		
Salaries Expense	2 0 0 0 00		(D) 1 7 5 00		2 1 7 5 00		2 1 7 5 00			
Telephone Expense	2 8 4 00				2 8 4 00		2 8 4 00			
Advertising Expense	2 7 6 00				2 7 6 00		2 7 6 00			
Gas Expense	2 6 0 00				2 6 0 00		2 6 0 00			
	7 5 1 4 00	7 5 1 4 00								
Insurance Expense			(A) 2 0 0 00		2 0 0 00		2 0 0 00			
Cleaning Supplies Expense			(B) 6 0 0 00		6 0 0 00		6 0 0 00			
Depreciation Expense, Auto			(C) 1 5 0 00		1 5 0 00		1 5 0 00			
Salaries Payable				(D) 1 7 5 00		1 7 5 00				1 7 5 00
			1 1 2 5 00	1 1 2 5 00	7 8 3 9 00	7 8 3 9 00	3 9 4 5 00	3 7 0 0 00	3 8 9 4 00	4 1 3 9 00
Net Loss								2 4 5 00	2 4 5 00	
							3 9 4 5 00	3 9 4 5 00	4 1 3 9 00	4 1 3 9 00

5B-3. From the following transactions as well as additional data, please complete the entire accounting cycle for Dorin's Plowing (use the chart of accounts on p. 165).

Comprehensive review of the entire accounting cycle, Chapters 1-5.

Jan. 1   To open the business, Tom invested $8,000 cash and $9,600 worth of snow equipment.
      1   Paid rent for 5 months in advance, $3,000.
      4   Purchased office equipment on account from Russell Co., $6,000.
      6   Bought snow supplies, $350.
      8   Collected $7,000 for plowing during winter storm emergency.
      12   Tom paid his home telephone bill from the company chequebook, $70.
      20   Billed Eastern Freight Co. for plowing fees earned but not to be received until March, $6,500.
      24   Advertising bill received from Jones Co. but will not be paid until next month, $350.
      26   Paid salaries to employees, $1,800.
      28   Paid Russell Co. one-half of amount owed for office equipment.
      29   Paid telephone bill of company, $165.

Adjusting data:
   A. Snow supplies on hand, $200.
   B. Rent expired, $600.
   C. Depreciation on office equipment, $125.
      ($6,000/4 yrs = $1,500 ÷ 12 = $125)
   D. Depreciation on snow equipment, $400.
      ($9,600 ÷ 2 = $4,800 ÷ 12 = $400)
   E. Salaries accrued, $300.

GROUP C PROBLEMS

5C-1.

> TO: Joan Bishop
>
> FROM: Jason Stockwell
>
> RE: Accounting Procedures
>
> Please prepare from the following information (attached) (1) a work sheet along with (2) journalized adjusting and closing entries for the period ending May 31, 19XX.

Review in preparing a work sheet and journalizing adjusting and closing entries.

Adjustment data:
   A. Insurance expired, $230.
   B. Supplies on hand, $770.
   C. Depreciation on storage equipment, $490.
   D. Depreciation on building, $870.
   E. Wages earned by employees but not due to be paid till June, $1,140.

Stockwell Storage Co.
Trial Balance
May 31, 19XX

	Dr.	Cr.
Cash in Bank	2 5 6 2 00	
Prepaid Insurance	5 7 0 00	
Storage Supplies	1 5 8 0 00	
Storage Equipment	8 4 3 0 00	
Building	53 0 0 0 00	
Accumulated Depreciation, Storage Equipment		3 9 1 0 00
Accumulated Depreciation, Building		18 5 0 0 00
Accounts Payable		2 4 6 0 00
Jason Stockwell, Capital		37 8 9 7 00
Jason Stockwell, Withdrawals	4 6 2 0 00	
Storage Fees Revenue		15 4 9 0 00
Wages Expense	5 6 7 5 00	
Utilities Expense	8 9 6 00	
Advertising Expense	9 2 4 00	
Totals	78 2 5 7 00	78 2 5 7 00

Journalizing and posting adjusting and closing entries. Preparing a post-closing trial balance.

5C-2. Refer to the work sheet for Vandersteen Computer Repair Service on p. 171. The balances (from the trial balance column) in each account are already entered in your working papers. (1) Journalize and post adjusting and closing entries to each account in the ledger, and (2) prepare from the ledger a post-closing trial balance at the end of November.

Comprehensive review of the entire accounting cycle, Chapters 1-5.

5C-3. From the following transactions as well as additional data, please complete the entire accounting cycle for Dora's Plumbing (use a chart of accounts similar to the one on p. 165).

May	1	To open the business, Dora Fowkes invested $10,000 cash and $4,600 worth of snow equipment.
	1	Paid rent for 4 months in advance, $2,000.
	4	Purchased office equipment on account from MacKenzie Co., $3,800.
	6	Bought plumbing supplies, $640.
	8	Collected $3,000 for plumbing services provided
	9	Dora paid her home utility bill from the company chequebook, $110.
	10	Billed Western Construction Co. for plumbing fees earned but not to be received until later, $8,400.
	14	Advertising bill received from ABCD Radio Co. but not to be paid until next month, $455.
	21	Received cheque from Western Construction Co. re partial payment on transaction dated May 10. $4,200.
	26	Paid salaries to employees, $2,300.
	28	Paid MacKenzie Co. one-half of amount owed for office equipment, $1,900.
	29	Paid telephone bill of company, $134.
	31	Received bill from George's Cleaning to be paid in June, $185.

Vandersteen Computer Repair Service
Work Sheet
For month ended November 30, 19XX

Account Titles	Trial Balance Dr.	Trial Balance Cr.	Adjustments Dr.	Adjustments Cr.	Adjusted Trial Balance Dr.	Adjusted Trial Balance Cr.	Income Statement Dr.	Income Statement Cr.	Balance Sheet Dr.	Balance Sheet Cr.
Cash in Bank	2356.48			(A) 38.20	2318.28				2318.28	
Prepaid Insurance	682.34			(C) 206.14	476.20				476.20	
Accounts Receivable	4784.53				4784.53				4784.53	
Repair Parts and Supplies	2743.65			(D) 1178.82	1564.83				1564.83	
Van	21475.00				21475.00				21475.00	
Accumulated Depreciation, Van		7827.00		(B) 1591.70		9418.70				9418.70
Accounts Payable		3442.76		(F) 140.00		3582.76				3582.76
Ted Vandersteen, Capital		16636.53				16636.53				16636.53
Ted Vandersteen, Withdrawals	2800.00				2800.00				2800.00	
Computer Repair Fee Revenue		14457.25				14457.25		14457.25		
Advertising Expense	652.50		(F) 140.00		792.50		792.50			
Automobile Expenses	2645.84				2645.84		2645.84			
Cleaning Expense	350.00				350.00		350.00			
Miscellaneous Expenses	165.45				165.45		165.45			
Postage and Office Expenses	247.75				247.75		247.75			
Salaries Expense	3460.00		(E) 385.00		3845.00		3845.00			
	42363.54	42363.54								
Insurance Expense			(C) 206.14		206.14		206.14			
Bank Charges Expense			(A) 38.20		38.20		38.20			
Depreciation Expense, Van			(B) 1591.70		1591.70		1591.70			
Salaries Payable				(E) 385.00		385.00				385.00
Supplies Expense			(D) 1178.82		1178.82		1178.82			
			3539.86	3539.86	44480.24	44480.24	11061.40	14457.25	33418.84	30022.99
Net Income							3395.85			3395.85
							14457.25	14457.25	33418.84	33418.84

Adjusting data:
- A. Snow supplies on hand, $200.
- B. Rent expired, $600.
- C. Depreciation on office equipment, $125.
  ($6,000/4 yrs = $1,500 ÷ 12 = $125)
- D. Depreciation on plumbing equipment, $400.
  ($9,600 ÷ 2 = $4,800 ÷ 12 = $400)
- E. Salaries accrued, $300.

PRACTICAL ACCOUNTING APPLICATION #1

Ann Humphrey needs a loan from the Charles Bank to help finance her business. She has submitted to the Charles Bank the following unadjusted trial balance. As the loan officer, you will be meeting with Ann tomorrow. Could you make some specific suggestions to Ann as regards her loan request?

Cash in Bank	770	
Accounts Receivable	1,480	
Office Supplies	8,310	
Equipment	7,606	
Accounts Payable		684
A. Humphrey, Capital		8,000
Service Fees		17,350
Salaries	11,240	
Utilities Expense	842	
Rent Expense	360	
Insurance Expense	280	
Advertising Expense	146	
Totals	26,034	26,034

PRACTICAL ACCOUNTING APPLICATION #2

Janet Smother is the new bookkeeper who replaced Dick Burns, owing to his sudden illness. Janet finds on her desk a note requesting that she close the books and supply the ending capital figure. Janet is concerned, since she can only find the following:

- A. Revenue and expense accounts all were zero balance.
- B.   **Income Summary**

14,360	19,300

- C. Owner withdrew $8,000.
- D. Owner beginning capital was $34,400.

Could you help Janet accomplish her assignment?

COMPREHENSIVE REVIEW PROBLEM
Valdez Realty

Reviewing the Accounting Cycle Twice

This comprehensive review problem requires you to complete the accounting cycle for Valdez Realty twice. This will allow you to review Chapters 1-5, at the same time reinforcing the relationships among all parts of the accounting cycle. By completing two cycles, you will see how the ending June balances in the ledger are used to accumulate data in July.

In case you want a quick review of the accounting cycle before you start the problem, or if you need to check back when you are in the middle of the problem, the following chart shows the steps of the accounting cycle and the pages in the text where each step is covered:

STEPS IN THE ACCOUNTING CYCLE	PAGE IN TEXT WHERE COVERED
1. Business transactions occur and generate source documents.	1. p. 69
2. Analyze and record business transactions into a journal.	2. p. 69
3. Post or transfer information from journal to ledger.	3. p. 70
4. Prepare a trial balance.	4. p. 86
5. Prepare a work sheet.	5. p. 106
6. Prepare financial statements.	6. p. 123
7. Journalize and post adjusting entries.	7. p. 143
8. Journalize and post closing entries.	8. p. 147
9. Prepare a post-closing trial balance.	9. p. 158

First let's look at the chart of accounts for Valdez Realty.

VALDEZ REALTY
CHART OF ACCOUNTS

Assets
111 Cash
112 Accounts Receivable
114 Prepaid Rent
115 Office Supplies
121 Office Equipment
122 Accumulated Depreciation,
    Office Equipment
123 Automobile
124 Accumulated Depreciation, Automobile

Liabilities
211 Accounts Payable
212 Salaries Payable

Owner's Equity
311 Juan Valdez, Capital
312 Juan Valdez, Withdrawals
313 Income Summary

Revenue
411 Commissions Earned

Expenses
511 Rent Expense
512 Salaries Expense
513 Gas Expense
514 Repairs Expense
515 Telephone Expense
516 Advertising Expense
517 Office Supplies Expense
518 Depreciation Expense,
    Office Equipment
519 Depreciation Expense, Automobile
524 Miscellaneous Expense

On June 1 Juan Valdez opened a real estate office called Valdez Realty. The following transactions were completed for the month of June:

19XX

June	1	Juan Valdez invested $6,000 cash in the real estate agency along with $3,000 of office equipment.
	1	Rented office space and paid three months rent in advance, $2,100.
	1	Bought an automobile on account, $12,000.
	4	Purchased office supplies for cash, $300.
	5	Purchased additional office supplies on account, $150.
	6	Sold a house and collected a $6,000 commission.
	8	Paid gas bill, $22.
	15	Paid the salary of the office secretary, $350.
	17	Sold a building lot and earned a commission, $6,500. Payment is to be received on July 8.
	20	Juan Valdez withdrew $1,000 from the business to pay personal expenses.
	21	Sold a house and collected a $3,500 commission.
	22	Paid gas bill, $25.
	24	Paid $600 to repair automobile.
	30	Paid the salary of the office secretary, $350.
	30	Paid the June telephone bill $510.
	30	Received advertising bill for June, $1,200. The bill is to be paid on July 2.

Required Work for June:
1. Journalize transactions and post to ledger accounts.
2. Prepare a trial balance in the first two columns of the work sheet and complete the work sheet using the following adjustment data:
   A. One month's rent had expired.
   B. An inventory shows $50 of office supplies remaining.

      C. Depreciation on office equipment, $100.

      D. Depreciation on automobile, $200.

3. Prepare a June income statement, statement of owner's equity, and balance sheet.
4. From the work sheet, journalize and post adjusting and closing entries (p. 3 of journal).
5. Prepare a post-closing trial balance.

During July, Valdez Realty completed these transactions:

July	1	Purchased additional office supplies on account, $700.
	2	Paid advertising bill for June.
	3	Sold a house and collected a commission, $6,600.
	6	Paid for gas expense, $29.
	8	Collected commission from sale of building lot on June 17.
	12	Paid $300 to send employees to realtor's workshop.
	15	Paid the salary of the office secretary, $350.
	17	Sold a house and earned a commission of $2,400. Commission to be received on August 10.
	18	Sold a building lot and collected a commission of $7,000.
	22	Sent a cheque for $40 to help sponsor a local road race to aid the poor. (This is not to be considered an advertising expense, but it is a business expense.)
	24	Paid for repairs to automobile, $590.
	28	Juan Valdez withdrew $1,800 from the business to pay personal expenses.
	30	Paid the salary of the office secretary, $350.
	30	Paid the July telephone bill, $590.
	30	Advertising bill for July, $1,400. The bill is to be paid on August 2.

Required Work for July:

1. Journalize transactions in a general journal (p. 4) and post to ledger accounts.
2. Prepare a trial balance in the first two columns of the work sheet and complete the work sheet using the following adjustment data:

      A. One month's rent had expired.

      B. An inventory shows $90 of office supplies remaining.

      C. Depreciation on office equipment, $100.

      D. Depreciation on automobile, $200.

3. Prepare a July income statement, statement of owner's equity, and balance sheet.
4. From the work sheet, journalize and post adjusting and closing entries (p. 6 of journal).
5. Prepare a post-closing trial balance.

ACCOUNTING RECALL
A Cumulative Approach

THIS EXAM REVIEWS CHAPTERS 1 THROUGH 5.

Your *Study Guide and Working Papers* have forms to complete this exam, as well as worked-out solutions. The page references next to each question identify what page to turn back to if you answer the question incorrectly.

PART I Vocabulary Review

Match the terms to the appropriate definition or phrase.
Page Ref.

(148)	1. Closing entries	A.	Updates specific ledger accounts
(112)	2. Book Value	B.	A temporary account usually with debit balance
(149)	3. Income summary	C.	A permanent account
(111)	4. Contra asset	D.	Lists only permanent account
(73)	5. Supplies	E.	Clears all temporary accounts
(69)	6. Journal	F.	Book of original entry
(158)	7. Post-closing trial balance	G.	A temporary account in the ledger
(143)	8. Adjusting journal entries	H.	Cost—accumulated depreciation
(70)	9. Ledger	I.	Book of final entry
(11)	10. Withdrawals	J.	Accumulated depreciation

PART II True or False (Accounting Theory)

(148) 11. Income summary has a normal balance of a debit.

(148) 12. After closing, all temporary accounts will be cleared to a zero balance.

(149) 13. Closing entries cannot be made from a work sheet.

(124) 14. The work sheet shows the beginning figure for capital.

(68) 15. Financial reports are prepared after journalizing and posting adjusting and closing entries.

PART III Applications Problem (150)

From the following work sheet journalize the adjusting and closing entries for Dec. 31.

Work Sheet

Account Titles	Trial Balance Dr.	Trial Balance Cr.	Adjustments Dr.	Adjustments Cr.	Adjusted Trial Balance Dr.	Adjusted Trial Balance Cr.	Income Statement Dr.	Income Statement Cr.	Balance Sheet Dr.	Balance Sheet Cr.
Cash	2000				2000				2000	
Accounts Receivable	2500				2500				2500	
Prepaid Insurance	1900			(A) 400	1500				1500	
Store Supplies	1800			(B) 1400	400				400	
Store Equipment	4000				4000				4000	
Accum. Depr., Equipment		1000		(C) 500		1500				1500
Accounts Payable		3000				3000				3000
P. Sove, Capital		5200				5200				5200
P. Sove, Withdrawals	200				200				200	
Fees Earned		4900				4900		4900		
Rent Expense	1000				1000		1000			
Wage Expense	700		(D) 600		1300		1300			
	14100	14100								
Insurance Expense			(A) 400		400		400			
Supplies Expense			(B) 1400		1400		1400			
Depreciation Expense			(C) 500		500		500			
Wages Payable				(D) 600		600				600
			2900	2900	15200	15200	4600	4900	10600	10300
Net Income							300			300
							4900	4900	10600	10600

SPECIAL JOURNALS:
Sales and Cash Receipts

IN THIS CHAPTER WE WILL COVER THE FOLLOWING TOPICS:

1. JOURNALIZING SALES ON ACCOUNT IN A SALES JOURNAL. (P. 184)

2. POSTING FROM A SALES JOURNAL TO THE GENERAL LEDGER. (P. 185)

3. RECORDING TO THE ACCOUNTS RECEIVABLE LEDGER FROM A SALES JOURNAL. (P. 185)

4. PREPARING, JOURNALIZING, RECORDING AND POSTING A CREDIT MEMORANDUM. (P. 187)

5. RECORDING PST AND GST IN THE SALES JOURNAL AS WELL AS WITH A CREDIT MEMORANDUM. (PP. 188-189, 192-193)

6. JOURNALIZING AND POSTING TRANSACTIONS USING A CASH RECEIPTS JOURNAL, AS WELL AS RECORDING TO THE ACCOUNTS RECEIVABLE LEDGER. (P. 182)

7. PREPARING A SCHEDULE OF ACCOUNTS RECEIVABLE. (P. 203)

In the first five chapters of this book we have analyzed the accounting cycle for businesses that perform personal services for customers, such as word processing or legal services. In this chapter we turn our attention to Art's Wholesale Clothing Company, a merchandise company, which earns revenue by selling goods or merchandise to customers. This will call for some new concepts and procedures. To understand why we need these new concepts and procedures, let's look at some key terms relating to merchandise companies in general.

LEARNING UNIT 6-1
Merchandise Companies: An Overview

Merchandise is the goods purchased by a business for resale to customers. Merchandise companies may be either **wholesalers** (which buy goods from importers or manufacturers for resale) or **retailers** (which buy goods from wholesalers or distributors for resale to customers). For a service company, net income equals revenue from services minus operating expenses. For a merchandise company more is involved in figuring net income. One way to see the special concerns of a merchandise company is to look at its income statement:

Wholesaler buys goods from suppliers and manufacturers for sale to retailers. Retailer buys goods from wholesalers for resale to customers.

Merchandise Company	
(1) Gross Sales	$7,000
(2) – Sales Returns and Allowances	1,860
(3) – Sales Discounts	140
(4) = Net Sales	5,000
(5) – Cost of Goods Sold	3,000
(6) = Gross Profit	2,000
(7) – Operating Expenses	600
(8) = Net Income	$1,400

As you can see, there is a lot more going on here than we had looked at in a service company. To begin with we should introduce and define some of the new accounts and concepts we will be dealing with for a merchandise company. We'll take them one by one, as numbered in the chart above.

1. **Gross sales.** Think of gross sales as the total of all the cash and credit sales made by a business over a specific period of time. This is a revenue account with a credit balance.

2. **Sales returns and allowances.** This is a contra revenue account with a debit balance; it shows the effect of customers returning merchandise or of being given price adjustments. This account will help management keep track of customer dissatisfaction. If the balance in this account is higher one month than another, it may mean that customers have been returning goods at a higher rate than usual, or that they have been given price reductions for damaged goods.

3. **Sales discount.** This is also a contra revenue account with a debit balance; it accumulates the amount of cash discounts that customers are granted for mak-

Sales (gross)

Dr.	Cr.
	7,000

Sales Returns and Allowances

Dr.	Cr.
1,860	

Sales Discount

Dr.	Cr.
140	

ing early payment. Many companies allow a cash discount to encourage early payment of bills. If customers pay within a certain period of time (called the **discount period**), they are granted a discount. Note that a discount period is shorter than the **credit period**, which is the total length of time allowed to pay the amount owed on the bill. We will give two examples of discounts and credit periods here:

2/10, n/30 (Two Ten, Net Thirty). This means that the discount period is the first 10 days, and the credit period is 30 days. In this example, a 2% discount is allowed off the price of the bill if the bill is paid within 10 days. The full amount of the bill is due anywhere from days 11 to 30 with *no* discount.

> *Example:* Total bill, $8,000; terms 2/10, n/30
> Date of sale, August 3, 19XX
> Bill paid on August 7, 19XX
> Sales discount = .02 × $8,000 = $160

n/10, EOM. This means that the full amount of the bill is due within 10 days after the end of the month (EOM), and there is no discount.

> *Example:* Total bill, $6,000; terms n/10, EOM
> Date of bill, July 16, 19XX
> Final date to pay bill is August 10, 19XX

Credit terms will vary from company to company, and cash discounts are not usually taken on Provincial Sales Tax (PST), Goods and Services Tax (GST), freight, or goods returned. For now, the key point is that sales discounts provide an incentive to the customer to pay early.

4. **Net sales.** This is the total reached after subtracting sales returns and allowances and sales discounts from gross sales.

5. **Cost of goods sold (COGS).** This means the total cost of the goods that are sold to customers (but is *not* the same thing as the selling price). Note in Figure 6-1 (p. 181) how the cost of goods sold is arrived at. Thus cost of goods sold = $3,000 ($200 + $4,000 − $1,200). It costs this company $3,000 to buy merchandise that sells for $5,000.

6. **Gross profit.** This figure represents the amount of revenue from sales that remains after deducting COGS to cover the operating expenses and profit of the company. Net Sales − Cost of Goods Sold = Gross Profit. $5,000 − $3,000 = $2,000.

7. **Operating expenses.** These are expenses such as heat, postage, telephone, and all other *expired costs* of operating the company. They are subtracted from gross profit to arrive at net income.

8. **Net income.** Gross Profit − Operating Expenses = Net Income; or, in our example here, $2,000 − $600 = $1,400.

There are, of course, many more terms and concepts involved, but this overview should give you the background you need to look at accounting for a merchandise company. For information on how inventory is calculated see Chapter 16.

FIGURE 6-1

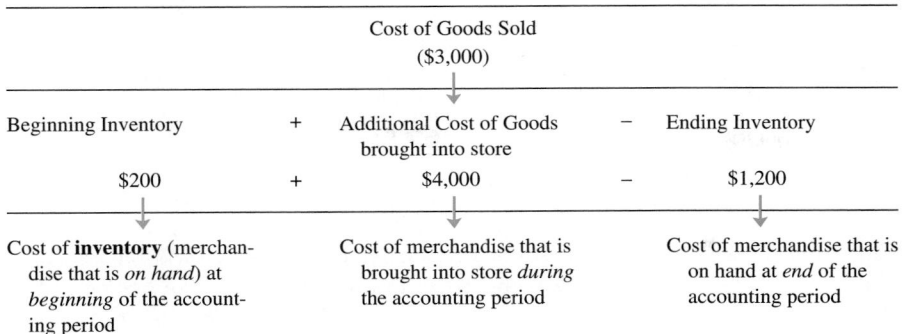

Cost of Goods Sold ($3,000)		
Beginning Inventory	+ Additional Cost of Goods brought into store	− Ending Inventory
$200	+ $4,000	− $1,200
Cost of **inventory** (merchandise that is *on hand*) at *beginning* of the accounting period	Cost of merchandise that is brought into store *during* the accounting period	Cost of merchandise that is on hand at *end* of the accounting period

At this point you should be able to

1. Explain the difference between a service company and a merchandise company. (p. 179)
2. Define and explain gross sales, sales returns and allowances, sales discounts, cost of goods sold, and gross profit. (pp. 179-180)
3. Explain the difference between a discount period and a credit period. (p. 180)
4. Calculate sales discounts. (pp. 179-180)
5. Prepare a simplified income statement for a merchandise company. (p. 179)

☐ **SELF-REVIEW QUIZ 6-1**

Indicate which of the following are false:

1. Sales Returns and Allowances is a contra asset account.
2. Sales Discount has a normal balance of a debit.
3. Net Sales – Cost of Goods Sold = Gross Profit.
4. Ending inventory is added to cost of goods sold.
5. Credit terms are standard in all industries.

▪ *SOLUTION TO SELF-REVIEW QUIZ 6-1*

1, 4, 5

LEARNING UNIT 6-2
Sales Journal and Accounts Receivable Ledger

Art's Wholesale Clothing Company cannot operate its merchandise business efficiently with just the general journal and general ledger that we discussed in Chapters 1-5. To understand why, let's look first at the purpose of special journals and then at the purpose of subsidiary ledgers.

SPECIAL JOURNALS

Need division of labour and flexibility to reduce journalizing effort.

Need to reduce posting time.

Why does Art think that his business needs more than just a general journal?

1. Using just a general journal means that fewer transactions can be recorded in a work day, since only *one* person can work on a general journal at a time.
2. Using just a general journal means that there will be a large number of postings, since each line must be posted individually.

Art thus feels the company needs a set of journals, each of which will record a specific type of transaction. This has the effect of allowing more than one person to work on the journals at the same time, as well as reducing the number of postings that have to be completed. These journals are called **special journals**. Art's Wholesale Clothing Company will use the following special journals:

SPECIAL JOURNAL TYPE	WHAT IT RECORDS
Sales journal	Sale of merchandise on account
Cash receipts journal	Receiving cash from any source
Purchases journal	Buying merchandise or other items on account
Cash payments journal (cash disbursement journal)	Paying of cash for any purpose

Covered in this chapter — { Sales journal, Cash receipts journal }

Covered in next chapter — { Purchases journal, Cash payments journal (cash disbursement journal) }

For a discussion of recording of credit cards in special journals see appendix.

Later in this chapter we will discuss the sales journal and the cash receipts journal, but first let's look at subsidiary ledgers.

SUBSIDIARY LEDGERS

In the same way that he needs more than just a general journal to keep track of his merchandise company, Art needs more than just a general ledger. So far in this text, for example, the only title we have used for recording amounts owed to the seller has been Accounts Receivable. Art could conceivably replace the Accounts Receivable title in the general ledger with the following list of customers who owe him money:

> Accounts Receivable, Bevans Company
> Accounts Receivable, Hal's Clothing
> Accounts Receivable, Mel's Department Store
> Accounts Receivable, Roe Company

As you can see, however, this would not work if Art had 1,000 credit customers —the general ledger would not be a manageable size. To solve this problem, Art sets up in alphabetical order an account for each customer in a separate ledger, an **accounts receivable ledger**. Such a special ledger, often called a **subsidiary ledger**, is one that contains accounts of a single type, such as for customers.

The diagram in Figure 6-2 (p. 183) shows how the accounts receivable ledger fits in with the general ledger. To clarify the difference in updating the general ledger versus the subsidiary ledger we will *post* to the general ledger and *record* to the subsidiary ledger.

The accounts receivable ledger, or any other subsidiary ledger, can be in the form of a card file, a binder notebook, or computer disks. It will not have page numbers. The accounts receivable ledger is organized alphabetically based on customers' names and addresses; new customers can be added and inactive customers deleted.

The general ledger is not in the same book as the accounts receivable ledger.

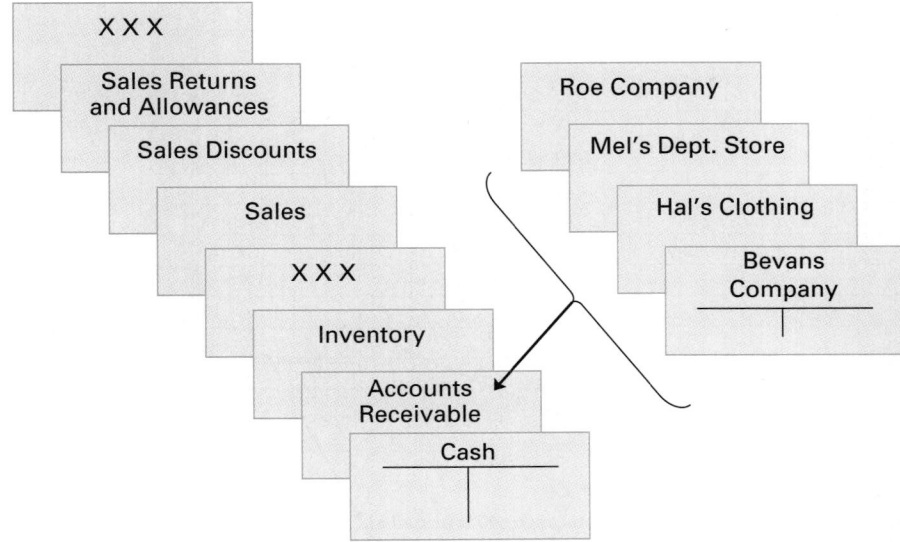

FIGURE 6-2

Partial General Ledger of Art's Wholesale Clothing Company and Accounts Receivable Subsidiary Ledger

When using an accounts receivable ledger, the title **Accounts Receivable** in the general ledger is called the *controlling account*, since it summarizes or controls the accounts receivable ledger. At the end of the month the total of the individual accounts in the accounts receivable ledger will equal the ending balance in Accounts Receivable in the general ledger.

Art's Wholesale Clothing Company will use the following subsidiary ledgers:

Accounts receivable ledger   Records money owed by credit customers   } Covered in this chapter

Accounts payable ledger   Records money owed to creditors   } Covered in next chapter

Let's now look closer at the sales journal, general ledger, and subsidiary ledger for Art's company to see how transactions are updated in the special journal as well as posted and recorded to specific titles.

THE SALES JOURNAL

The **sales journal** for Art's Clothing records all sales made on account to customers. Figure 6-3 shows the sales journal at the end of the first month in operation, along with the recordings to the accounts receivable ledger and posting to the general ledger. Keep in mind that the reason the balances in the accounts receivable ledger are *debit* balances is that the customers listed *owe* Art's Clothing the money. First study the diagram, and then we'll explain when you post or record and where the information comes from.

FIGURE 6-3   **Sales Journal Recording and Postings**

Art's Wholesale Clothing Company
Sales Journal

Page 1

Date		Account Debited	Terms	Invoice Number	Post Ref.	Dr. Acct. Rec. Cr. Sales				
19XX April	3	Hal's Clothing	2/10, n/30	1	✓		8	0	0	00
	6	Bevans Company	2/10, n/30	2	✓	1	6	0	0	00
	18	Roe Company	2/10, n/30	3	✓	2	0	0	0	00
	24	Roe Company	2/10, n/30	4	✓		5	0	0	00
	28	Mel's Dept. Store	2/10, n/30	5	✓		9	0	0	00
	29	Mel's Dept. Store	2/10, n/30	6	✓		7	0	0	00
	30					6	5	0	0	00
						(113)		(411)		

The (✓) in the sales journal PR column indicated that the accounts receivable ledger has been updated *during* the month by posting debits to the individual customers.

The total of $6,500 is posted at the *end of the month* Accounts Receivable (Dr.) and Sales (Cr.) in the general ledger. Note that the heading in the journal tells you whether it is a debit or credit.

References of ledger accounts mean totals were posted at end of month to these accounts.

Accounts Receivable Ledger

Tells us what page of sales journal information comes from

Bevans Company

Dr.	Cr.
4/6 SJ1 1,600	

Hal's Clothing

Dr.	Cr.
4/3 SJ1 800	

Mel's Dept. Store

Dr.	Cr.
4/28 SJ1 900	
4/28 SJ1 700	

Roe Company

Dr.	Cr.
4/18 SJ1 2,000	
4/24 SJ1 500	

Partial General Ledger

Accounts Receivable 113

Dr.	Cr.
4/30 SJ1 6,500	

Sales 411

Dr.	Cr.
	6,500 SJ1 4/30

Let's take the first transaction listed in the sales journal as our example, the one involving Hal's Clothing. On April 3 Art's Wholesale Clothing Company sold merchandise on account to Hal's Clothing for $800. The bill or **sales invoice** for this sale is shown in Figure 6-4.

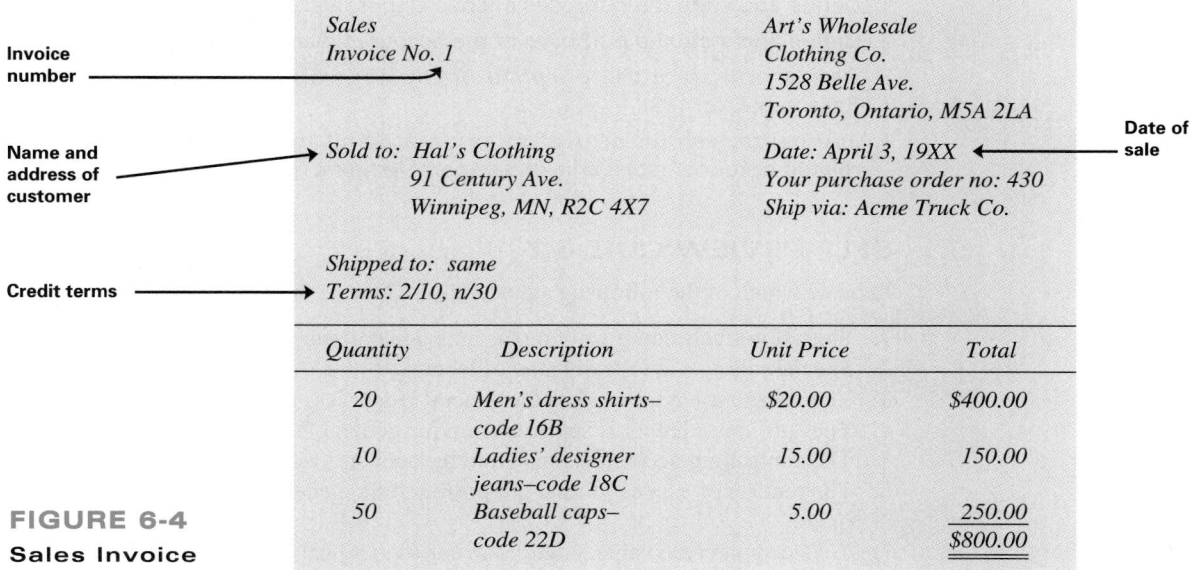

FIGURE 6-4
Sales Invoice

Recording from the Sales Journal to the Accounts Receivable Ledger

From this invoice we record in the *sales journal* the date (April 3), account debited (Hal's Clothing), invoice number (1), and amount ($800). *The PR column is left blank.* As soon as possible we now update the accounts receivable ledger. We go to the Hal's Clothing account and update on the debit side the $800 owed along with the date (April 3) and page of the sales journal (P. 1). When the account of Hal's Clothing is up-to-date, we go back to the sales journal and place a √ in the post reference column of the sales journal. During the month this process continues, and thus at any moment in time we can easily tell Hal his company's balance outstanding without having to go through all the invoices. Note how the sales journal needs only one line instead of the three lines that would have been required in a general journal.

Recording to the accounts receivable ledger occurs daily.

Hal's Clothing

Dr.	Cr.
4/3 SJ1	
800	

√ means accounts receivable ledger has been updated.

Posting at End of Month from the Sales Journal to the General Ledger

At the end of the month the sales journal is totalled ($6,500). If you look back to p. 184, you will see that the heading of Art's sales journal is a debit to accounts receivable and a credit to sales. Therefore, at the end of the month the $6,500 total is posted to Accounts Receivable (debit) *and* to Sales (credit) in the general ledger. In the general ledger we record the date (April 30), the initials of the journal (SJ), the page of the sales journal (1), and appropriate debit or credit ($6,500). Once the

Recording to the general ledger occurs at end of month.

Acc. Rec. 113

Dr.	Cr.
4/30 SJ1	
6,500	

Sales 411

Dr.	Cr.
	6,500 SJ1
	4/30

account in the general ledger is updated, we place below the totals in the sales journal the account numbers to which the information was posted (in this case accounts 113 and 411).

At this point you should be able to

1. Define and state the purposes of special journals. (p. 182)
2. Define and state the purposes of the accounts receivable ledger. (p. 182)
3. Define and state the purpose of the controlling account, Accounts Receivable. (p. 183)
4. Journalize, record, or post sales on account to a sales journal and its related accounts receivable and general ledgers. (p. 184)

□ **SELF-REVIEW QUIZ 6-2**

Indicate which of the following statements are false:

1. Special journals completely replace the general journal.
2. Special journals aid the division of labour.
3. The subsidiary ledger makes the general ledger less manageable.
4. The subsidiary ledger is separate from the general ledger.
5. The controlling account is located in the accounts receivable ledger.
6. The total(s) of a sales journal are posted to the general ledger at the end of the month.
7. The accounts receivable ledger is arranged in alphabetical order.
8. Transactions recorded into a sales journal are recorded weekly to the accounts receivable ledger.

■ *SOLUTION TO SELF-REVIEW QUIZ 6-2*

1, 3, 5, 8

LEARNING UNIT 6-3

Provincial Sales Tax and the Credit Memorandum

The company we have been using as an example in this chapter, Art's Wholesale Clothing Company, sells goods wholesale and thus does not have to deal with a provincial sales tax. Let's look for a moment at a retail company in order to see how sales taxes affect the sales journal and posting. The company is Munroe Menswear Company; the customer is Jones Company; and the PST is illustrated at 5% (although it varies from province to province). Figure 6-5 (p. 187) shows Munroe's Sales Journal.

The existence of provincial sales tax means creating a new account, **Sales Tax Payable**, which is a liability account in the general ledger with a credit balance. The customer owes Munroe the sale amount plus the tax.

Keep in mind that if sales discounts are available, they are not normally calculated on the sales tax. The discount is on the selling price less any returns before the tax. For example, if Jones receives a 2% discount, he pays the following:

Sales Tax Payable

	XXX

A liability in general ledger.

$5,000 \times .02 = \$100$ savings $\rightarrow$

$5,250	Total owed (tax is $250)
−100	Deduction (discount)
$5,150	Amount paid

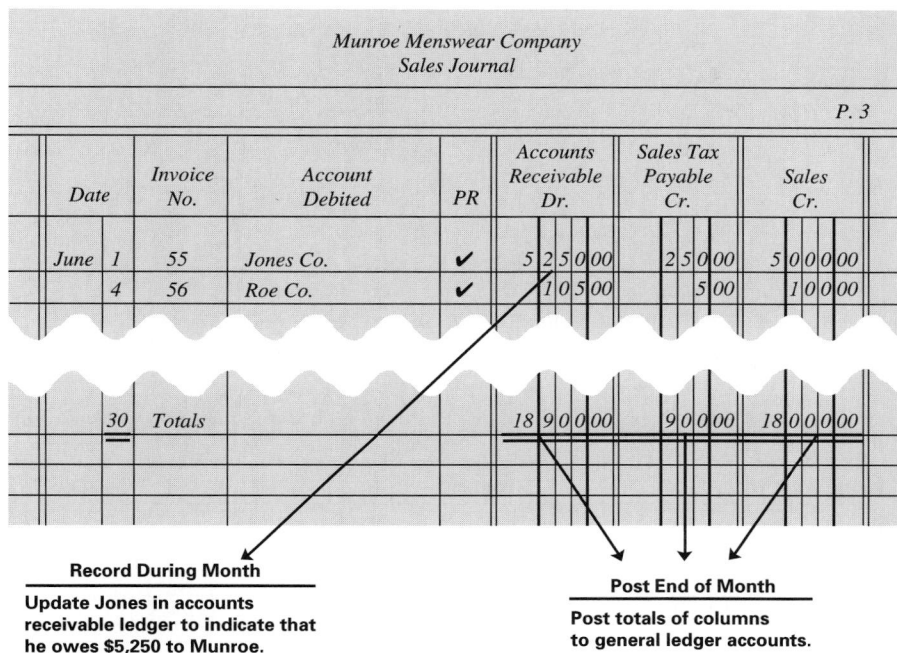

FIGURE 6-5
**Munroe Sales
Journal**

Record During Month

Update Jones in accounts
receivable ledger to indicate that
he owes $5,250 to Munroe.

Post End of Month

Post totals of columns
to general ledger accounts.

THE CREDIT MEMORANDUM

At the beginning of the chapter we introduced several new accounts that are used in the merchandising business. One of these was Sales Returns and Allowances, a contra revenue account with a debit balance. This account handles transactions involving goods that have already been sold. In one transaction the goods are returned, and the money owed for them is credited to the customer. In another type of transaction a customer is given an allowance for damaged goods in the form of a reduction from the original price.

Sales Returns and Allowances is called a contra revenue account because both these transactions *decrease* net sales revenue for the company involved in selling the goods, and thus the normal balance is a debit.

Such sales returns and allowances are usually handled by the company by means of a **credit memorandum**, which informs the customer that the amount of the goods returned or the amount allowed for damaged goods has been subtracted (credited) from the customer's ongoing account with the company. A sample credit memorandum from Art's Wholesale Clothing Company is shown in Figure 6-6.

On April 12 credit memo No. 1 (Figure 6-6) was issued to Bevans Company for defective merchandise that had been returned.

Let's assume that Art's Clothing has high-quality goods and does not expect many sales returns and allowances. Based on this assumption, no special journal for sales returns and allowances will be needed, although one could be used if necessary.

A credit memorandum
reduces accounts
receivable.

**Sales Returns and
Allowances**

Dr.	Cr.
+	−

A contra revenue account.

Thus all returns and allowances will be recorded in the general journal, and all postings and recordings will be done when journalized.

End result is that Bevan Company owes Art's Wholesale less money.

> *Art's Wholesale Clothing Co.*
> *1528 Belle Ave.*
> *Toronto, ON, M5A 2L4*
>
> *Credit*
> *Memorandum No. 1*
> *Date: April 12*
>
> *Credit to Bevans Company*
> *110 Aster Rd.*
> *Amherst, NS, B4H 3A5*
>
> *We credit your account as follows:*
> *Merchandise returned 60 model 8B men's dress gloves—$600*

FIGURE 6-6

Credit Memorandum

Let's look at a transaction analysis chart before we record and post this transaction.

Note that the Sales Returns and Allowances account is increasing, which in turn reduces sales revenue and reduces amount owed by customer (accounts receivable).

Accounts Affected	Category	↑ ↓	Rules
Sales Returns and Allowances	Contra revenue account	↑	Dr.
Accounts Receivable, Bevans Co.	Asset	↓	Cr.

JOURNALIZING, RECORDING, AND POSTING THE CREDIT MEMORANDUM

The credit memorandum results in two postings and one recording—two postings to the general ledger and one recording to the accounts receivable ledger. This can be seen in Figure 6-7 p. 189.

Note in the PR column next to Accounts Receivable, Bevans Co., that there is a diagonal line with the account number 113 above and a √ below. This is to show that the amount of $600 has been credited to Accounts Receivable in the controlling account in the general ledger *and* credited to the account of Bevans Company in the accounts receivable ledger.

Remember, sales discounts are *not* taken on returns.

PROVINCIAL SALES TAX AND THE CREDIT MEMORANDUM

Using the same example as above, if a sales tax had been involved, there would have been three postings from the general journal and one recording to the account receivable ledger. (After all, the seller no longer owes as much sales tax, since the customer has returned merchandise.)

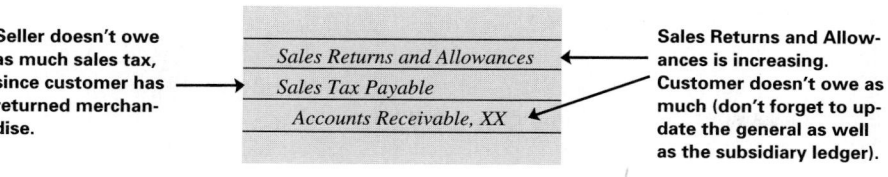

FIGURE 6-7

Postings and Recordings for the Credit Memorandum

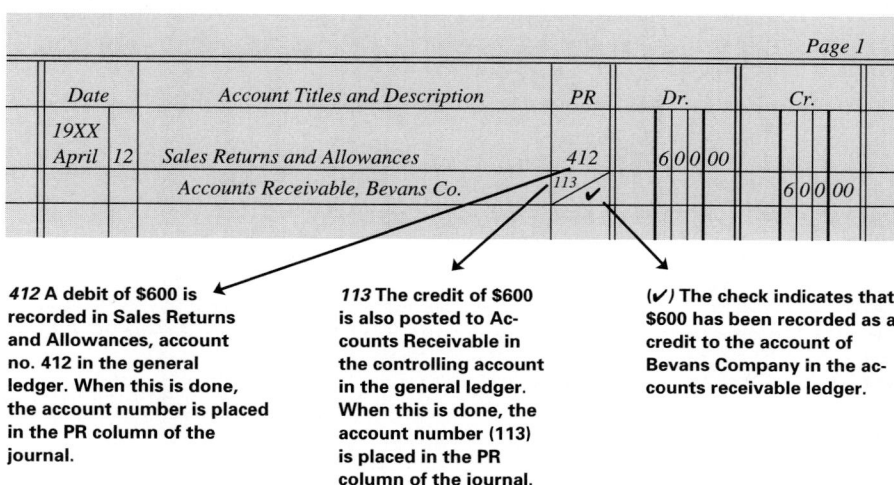

If the accountant for Art's Wholesale Clothing Company at some point decided to develop a special journal for sales allowances and returns, the entry for a credit memorandum such as the one we've been discussing would look like this:

					Sales Ret. and Allow.—Dr. Accts. Rec. — Cr.	
Date		*Credit Memo No.*	*Account Credited*	*PR*		
19XX						
April	12	1	*Bevans Company*	✔	600 00	

Sales Returns and Allowances Journal

At this point you should be able to

1. Explain Provincial Sales Tax Payable in relation to Sales Discount. (p. 186)
2. Explain, journalize, post, and record a credit memorandum with or without sales tax (pp. 187-188)

☐ **SELF-REVIEW QUIZ 6-3**

Journalize the following transactions into the sales journal or general journal for Moss Co. Record to the accounts receivable ledger and post to general ledger accounts as appropriate. Use the same journal headings that we used for Art's Wholesale Clothing Company. (All sales carry credit terms of 2/10, n/30.) There is no tax.

19XX

May 1   Sold merchandise on account to Jane Company, invoice No. 1, $600.

5   Sold merchandise on account to Ralph Company, invoice No. 2, $2,500.

20   Issued credit memo #1 to Jane Company for $200 due to defective merchandise returned.

■ *SOLUTION TO SELF-REVIEW QUIZ 6-3*

Moss Company
Sales Journal

Page 1

Date		Account Debited	Terms	Invoice Number	Post Ref.	Dr. Accts. Rec. Cr. Sales
19XX May	1	Jane Company	2/10, n/30	1	✔	600 00
	5	Ralph Company	2/10, n/30	2	✔	2500 00
	31					3100 00
						(112) (411)

NOTE: Total of accounts receivable ledger $400 + $2,500 does indeed equal the balance in the controlling account, accounts receivable $2,900 at end of month, in the general ledger.

Moss Company
General Journal

Page 1

Date		Account Titles and Description	PR	Dr.	Cr.
19XX May	20	Sales Ret. and Allowances	412	200 00	
		Acct. Rec., Jane Company	112 ✔		200 00
		Issued credit memo #1			

Partial General Ledger

Accounts Receivable   Acct. No. 112

Date 19XX		Explanation	Post Ref.	Debit	Credit	DR or CR	Balance
May	20		GJ1		2 0 0 00	CR	2 0 0 00
	31		SJ1	3 1 0 0 00		DR	2 9 0 0 00

Sales   Acct. No. 411

Date 19XX		Explanation	Post Ref.	Debit	Credit	DR or CR	Balance
May	31		SJ1		3 1 0 0 00	CR	3 1 0 0 00

Sales Returns and Allowances   Acct. No. 412

Date 19XX		Explanation	Post Ref.	Debit	Credit	DR or CR	Balance
May	20		GJ1	2 0 0 00		DR	2 0 0 00

Note the unusual balance of $200 because of the return. Why? Because total of sales journal is not posted till end of month.

Accounts Receivable Ledger

NAME   Jane Company
ADDRESS   118 Broadview Ave., Toronto, ON

Date		Explanation	Post Ref.	Debit	Credit	Dr. Balance
19XX						
May	1		SJ1	6 0 0 00		6 0 0 00
	20		GJ1		2 0 0 00	4 0 0 00

Customers owe Moss money and thus have a debit balance.

NAME   Ralph Company
ADDRESS   1300 Marine Drive, West Vancouver, BC.

Date		Explanation	Post Ref.	Debit	Credit	Dr. Balance
19XX						
May	5		SJ1	2 5 0 0 00		2 5 0 0 00

LEARNING UNIT 6-4

How Companies Record the Goods and Services Tax

INTRODUCTION

On January 1, 1991, Canadians faced a new tax on the majority of the goods and services they purchased—the **Goods and Services Tax (GST)**. This new tax is calculated at 7% on almost every item purchased or service consumed. There are a few exceptions, for example, food and financial services. This learning unit is not intended to provide a complete discussion of the details of the GST. Rather it will illustrate the basics of accounting for the tax, which will apply to most businesses in Canada.

Similarities and differences between PST and GST.

Before illustrating the normal accounting treatment of the GST, notice that there are both similarities and differences between the GST and provincial sales taxes (covered in Learning Unit 6-3). Like the Provincial Sales Tax (PST), the GST is added to the total of each invoice prepared for a customer. And like the PST, the GST must be remitted to the appropriate taxing authority periodically.

However, there are also a few notable differences:

1. GST applies to services as well as goods (for example, a lawyer will add 7% to each invoice for professional services).
2. GST applies at all levels in the economy—not just the retail level as in the case of PST.
3. GST is paid by businesses to their suppliers as well as collected by them from their customers. The *difference* between the tax collected and tax paid is the amount sent to the federal government each period.
4. GST might result in a business receiving a refund in some periods. Since GST is payable on large asset purchases (a delivery van, for example), a business may claim this amount against the GST they owe. In the long run if a business is successful, it should remit more GST than it receives as a refund; however *in a particular period* it may be eligible to receive a refund.

GST COLLECTED ON SALES

To illustrate the basic accounting treatment for **GST collected**, we will refer to an example you have already seen. Figure 6-4 (Sales Invoice) on p. 185 showed what an invoice would look like before GST. Figure 6-8 (p. 193) shows the same invoice with GST added.

You should notice two things about this invoice. First, the GST is added at 7% of the total price of the goods. Second, the invoice shows a GST registration number. Each business in Canada (except very small ones) must obtain a number from the federal government and show it on their invoices.

NOTE: There are more similarities than differences with the bookkeeping procedures described previously.

This invoice is recorded in the sales journal of Art's Wholesale Clothing Company. The main difference is that now the bookkeeping task is made slightly longer because of the need to keep track of the GST. On p. 184, Figure 6-3 showed the sales journal before GST. Figure 6-9 (p. 194) shows how this new invoice (and some others not illustrated individually) are recorded with GST. Posting to the various ledger accounts is also illustrated.

Sales
Invoice No.

Art's Wholesale
Clothing Co.
1528 Belle Ave.
Toronto, Ontario, M5A 2LA

Sold to: *Hal's Clothing*
          91 Century Ave.
          Winnipeg, MN, R2C 4X7

Date: *April 3, 19XX*
Your purchase order no: 430
Ship via: *Acme Truck Co.*

Shipped to: *same*
Terms: *2/10, n/30*

Quantity	Description	Unit Price	Total
20	Men's dress shirts– code 16B	$20.00	$400.00
10	Ladies' designer jeans–code 18C	15.00	150.00
50	Baseball caps–	5.00	250.00
	Sub total		$800.00
Add:	GST		56.00
	TOTAL		$856.00

GST reg # 109309799

FIGURE 6-8
Sales Invoice with GST

The total invoice amounts are posted during the month to the individual customers' accounts in the accounts receivable ledger. This process is identical to the pre-GST method except that the totals are 7% higher.

At the end of the month instead of posting a single amount as *both* a credit (to Sales) and a debit (to Accounts Receivable), there are three totals to post. A new account is now required—GST collected—#212. This is a liability account in the general ledger with a credit balance. Notice that the totals of the two credits (Sales and GST) equal the single debit (Accounts Receivable).

GST AND THE CREDIT MEMORANDUM

As you already know, occasionally a business finds it necessary to issue to a customer a credit memorandum (often called a credit note). The pre-GST form of a credit memorandum is shown on p. 188 (see Figure 6-6). The new form of credit memorandum is shown in Figure 6-10 (p. 195).

As before, we will assume that the volume of credit notes is low and that Art's Clothing uses the general journal to record these. The journal entry will appear as shown in Figure 6-11, p. 195.

Remember that the $42 debit posting will reduce the amount of GST owing to the federal government and must be taken into account when preparing a cheque for the amount owing at period-end. The customer, Bevans Company, now receives a credit totalling $642. This includes the extra 7% for GST. Since the original invoice included this 7% tax as an addition, it is proper that any refund for returned or damaged goods also include the 7% tax. The amount owing to Art's clothing by Bevans Company is reduced by $642.

The credit memorandum with GST is very similar to an invoice with GST except that the amounts are opposite in meaning and effect, and often smaller.

FIGURE 6-9   Sales Journal and Postings with GST

Art's Wholesale Clothing Company
Sales Journal

Page 1

Date	Account Debited	Terms	Invoice Number	Post Ref.	Cr. Sales	CR GST Collected	DR Acct. Rec.
19XX April 3	Hal's Clothing	2/10, n/30	1	✓	8 0 0 00	5 6 00	8 5 6 00
6	Bevans Company	2/10, n/30	2	✓	1 6 0 0 00	1 1 2 00	1 7 1 2 00
18	Roe Company	2/10, n/30	3	✓	2 0 0 0 00	1 4 0 00	2 1 4 0 00
24	Roe Company	2/10, n/30	4	✓	5 0 0 00	3 5 00	5 3 5 00
28	Mel's Dept. Store	2/10, n/30	5	✓	9 0 0 00	6 3 00	9 6 3 00
29	Mel's Dept. Store	2/10, n/30	6	✓	7 0 0 00	4 9 00	7 4 9 00
30					6 5 0 0 00	4 5 5 00	6 9 5 5 00
					(411)	(212)	(113)

The (✓) in the sales journal PR column indicated that the accounts receivable ledger has been updated *during* the month by posting debits to the individual customers.

The total of $6,500.00 is posted at the end of the month to Sales (Cr.) in the general ledger.

References of ledger accounts mean totals were posted at end of month to these accounts.

Accounts Receivable Ledger

Bevans Company

Dr.	Cr.
4/6 SJ1 1,712	

Hal's Clothing

Dr.	Cr.
4/3 SJ1 856	

Mel's Dept. Store

Dr.	Cr.
4/28 SJ1 963	
4/29 SJ1 749	

Roe Company

Dr.	Cr.
4/18 SJ1 2,140	
4/24 SJ1 535	

Partial General Ledger

Accounts Reveivable 113

Dr.	Cr.
4/30 SJ1 6,955	

Sales 411

Dr.	Cr.
	6,500 SJ1 4/30

GST Collected 212

Dr.	Cr.
	455 SJ1 4/30

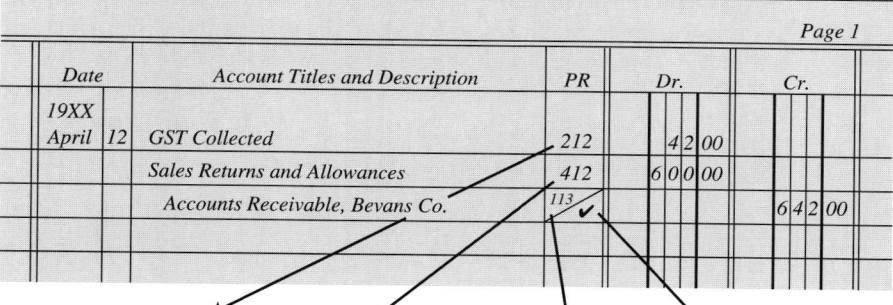

FIGURE 6-10

Credit Memorandum with GST

Art's Wholesale
Clothing Co.
1528 Belle Ave.
Toronto, ON, M5A 2L4

Credit
Memorandum No. 1
Date: April 12

Credit to Bevans Company
110 Aster Rd.
Amherst, NS, B4H 3A5

We credit your account as follows:
Merchandise returned 60 model 8B men's dress gloves—

Plus GST	$600.00
Total Credit	42.00
	$642.00

GST reg. no. 109309799

FIGURE 6-11

Postings for the Credit Memorandum with GST

Art's Wholesale Clothing Co.
General Journal

Page 1

Date	Account Titles and Description	PR	Dr.	Cr.
19XX				
April 12	GST Collected	212	42 00	
	Sales Returns and Allowances	412	600 00	
	Accounts Receivable, Bevans Co.	113 ✔		642 00

212 A debit of $42 is recorded in the GST Collected account 212 in the general ledger. When this is done, the account number is placed in the PR column of the journal.

412 A debit of $600 is recorded in Sales Returns and Allowances, account no. 412 in the general ledger. When this is done, the account number is placed in the PR column of the journal.

113 The credit of $642 is also posted to Accounts Receivable in the controlling account in the general ledger. When this is done, the account number (113) is placed in the PR column of the journal, above the /.

(✔) The check indicates that $642 has been posted as a credit to the account of Bevans Company in the accounts receivable ledger.

PROVINCIAL SALES TAX WITH GST

When a sale is made to a customer at the retail level, Provincial Sales Tax is often added to the invoice (there are exceptions which vary somewhat from province to province). Since January 1, 1991, it is also necessary to add GST to these invoices. A typical invoice in a province with a 9% Provincial Sales Tax might look like the following:

FIGURE 6-12

**Sales Invoice
with PST
and GST**

Munroe Menswear Company
147 Main Street
Saskatoon, Saskatchewan
S8A 2G7

To: Jones Company   Invoice # 1420
      228 Market Street   June 01, 19XX
      Saskatoon, Saskatchewan
      S8J 2P2

10 Company Blazers with logo @ $150.00 each $1,500.00
                                        PST @ 9%   135.00
                                                      1,635.00
                                        GST @ 7%   105.00
                                        Total $1,740.00

GST reg. no. 142716491

SALES INVOICE WITH PST AND GST

The Munroe Menswear Company would record this invoice along with other invoices for June, 19XX in their Sales Journal. This recording and posting process is illustrated below in Figure 6-13. Note that, apart from the addition of one more column (for the GST), this is identical to the illustration shown in Figure 6-9, on p. 194.

FIGURE 6-13

**Munroe's Sales
Journal with GST**

Be aware that in some provinces, the PST is added after the GST. Although the math is changed a bit, the rest of the process remains as shown in Figure 6-13.

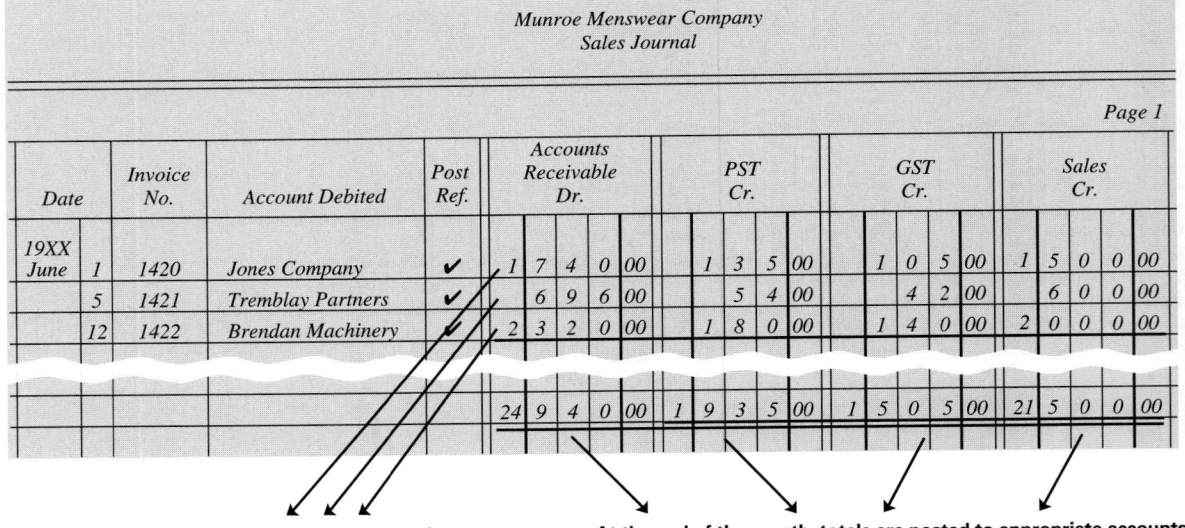

Munroe Menswear Company
Sales Journal

Page 1

Date	Invoice No.	Account Debited	Post Ref.	Accounts Receivable Dr.	PST Cr.	GST Cr.	Sales Cr.
19XX June 1	1420	Jones Company	✔	1 7 4 0 00	1 3 5 00	1 0 5 00	1 5 0 0 00
5	1421	Tremblay Partners	✔	6 9 6 00	5 4 00	4 2 00	6 0 0 00
12	1422	Brendan Machinery	✔	2 3 2 0 00	1 8 0 00	1 4 0 00	2 0 0 0 00
				24 9 4 0 00	1 9 3 5 00	1 5 0 5 00	21 5 0 0 00

During the month, each customer's account in the Accounts Receivable ledger is posted to update the amount they owe. Note that these figures include the PST and GST.

At the end of the month, totals are posted to appropriate accounts in the general ledger. Note that Dr. Total to Accounts Receivable ($24,940.00 equals 3 Cr. postings to PST, GST and Sales (1935.00 + 1505.00 + 21,500.00 = $24,940.00)

Also worthy of repetition is the point that if sales discounts are available, they are usually taken on the *sales amount only*, not the GST or PST. If Jones Co. receives a 2% discount on invoice No. 1420 (see Figure 6-12), they would pay the following amount:

Original Sales Amount of Invoice No. 1420	$1,500.00
Less 2% Discount	30.00
	1,470.00
Plus PST as originally computed	135.00
Plus GST as originally computed	105.00
Amount Paid	$1,710.00

CREDIT MEMORANDUM WITH GST AND PST

Let us assume that Jones Co. receives permission to return part of the goods billed on invoice #1420 (Figure 6-12). This results in a credit memo (or credit note) being prepared by Munroe Menswear Company. This credit memo would appear as shown in Figure 6-14.

FIGURE 6-14

Credit Memo with PST and GST

> **Munroe Menswear Company**
> **147 Main Street**
> **Saskatoon, Saskatchewan**
> **S8A 2G7**
>
> To: Jones Company   Credit Memo # 104
>   228 Market Street   July 15, 19XX
>   Saskatoon, Saskatchewan
>   L8J 2P2
>
> _____
>
> Returned 2 Blazers - Ref Invoice 1420, June 1, 19XX @ $150.00 each
>
> $300.00
>   PST @ 9%   27.00
>   327.00
>   GST @ 7%   21.00
>   Total Credit $348.00
>
> GST reg. no. 142716491

CREDIT MEMO WITH PST AND GST

This credit memo would be recorded by Munroe Company in their general journal (unless there was a large number of returns in which case a special journal could be used). The entry to record credit note No. 104 is as shown in Figure 6-15.

This entry is posted in a similar fashion to the entry in Figure 6-11 (see p. 195). The only change is that there is also a posting of a debit to PST payable (account number 210) as well as to GST collected (account number 212).

FIGURE 6-15

Recording Credit Memo with PST and GST

Munroe Menswear Company
General Journal

Page 1

Date	Account Titles and Description	PR	Dr.	Cr.
19XX July 15	Sales Returns and Allowances	412	3 0 0 00	
	GST Collected	212	2 1 00	
	PST Payable	210	2 7 00	
	Accounts Receivable, Jones Co.	113 ✔		3 4 8 00
	To record credit memo number 104			

At this point you should be able to

1. Explain the basics of GST added to sales invoices in Canada. (p. 192-193)
2. Explain, journalize, and post an invoice which includes both GST and PST. (p. 196)
3. Explain, journalize, and post a credit memorandum which includes both GST and PST. (p. 197)

☐ **SELF-REVIEW QUIZ 6-4**

Journalize the following transactions into the sales journal or the general journal for Moss Company. Post to the accounts receivable and general ledger accounts as appropriate. Use the same journal headings and general ledger account numbers that were used in Figures 6-13 and 6-15.

19XX

May	1	Sold merchandise to Jane Company, invoice No. 101—$400 plus PST $36 plus GST $28—Total $464.00. Terms 2/10, N/30.
May	5	Sold merchandise to Ralph Company, invoice No. 102—$3000 plus PST $270 plus GST $210—Total $3480.00. Terms 2/10, N/30.
May	21	Issued credit memorandum to Ralph Company, CM #4—$500 plus PST $45 plus GST $35—Total $580.00. Reason—defective goods.

■ **SOLUTION TO SELF-REVIEW QUIZ 6-4**

Moss Company
Sales Journal

Page 1

Date	Account Debited	Inv. No.	Post Ref.	Dr. Acct. Rec.	Cr. PST	Cr. GST Collected	Cr. Sales
19XX May 1	Jane Company	101	✔	4 6 4 00	3 6 00	2 8 00	4 0 0 00
5	Ralph Company	102	✔	3 4 8 0 00	2 7 0 00	2 1 0 00	3 0 0 0 00
				3 9 4 4 00	3 0 6 00	2 3 8 00	3 4 0 0 00

Moss Company
General Journal

Date		Account Titles and Description	PR	Dr.	Cr.
19XX					
May	21	Sales Returns and Allowances	412	5 0 0 00	
		GST Collected	212	3 5 00	
		PST Payable	210	4 5 00	
		Accounts Receivable, Ralph Co.	112 ✔		5 8 0 00
		To record credit Memo No. 4			

LEARNING UNIT 6-5
Cash Receipts Journal and Schedule of Accounts Receivable

Besides the sales journal, another special journal often used in a merchandising operation is the cash receipts journal. The **cash receipts journal** records the receipt of cash (or cheques) from any source. The number of columns a cash receipts journal will have depends on how frequently certain types of transactions occur. For example, in the cash receipts journal for Art's Wholesale the accountant has developed the headings shown in Figure 6-16. Note that a column for GST (on cash sales only) has been included. GST on credit sales is recorded in the sales journal as already described. Below each heading is a description of the purpose of each column and when to update the accounts receivable ledger as well as general ledger.

The following transactions occurred in April for Art's Clothing and affected the cash receipts journal:

19XX
April 1 Art Newner invested $8,000 in the business.
4 Received cheque from Hal's Clothing for payment of invoice No. 1 less discount.
15 Cash sales for first half of April, $900 plus GST.
16 Received cheque from Bevans Company in settlement of invoice No. 2 less returns and discount.
22 Received cheque from Roe Company for payment of invoice No. 3 less discount.
27 Sold store equipment, $500.
30 Cash sales for second half of April, $1,200 plus GST.

The diagram in Figure 6-17 p. 201 shows the cash receipts journal for the end of April along with the recordings to the accounts receivable ledger and posting to the general ledger. Study the diagram; we will review it in a moment.

FIGURE 6-16

Cash Receipts Journal with GST

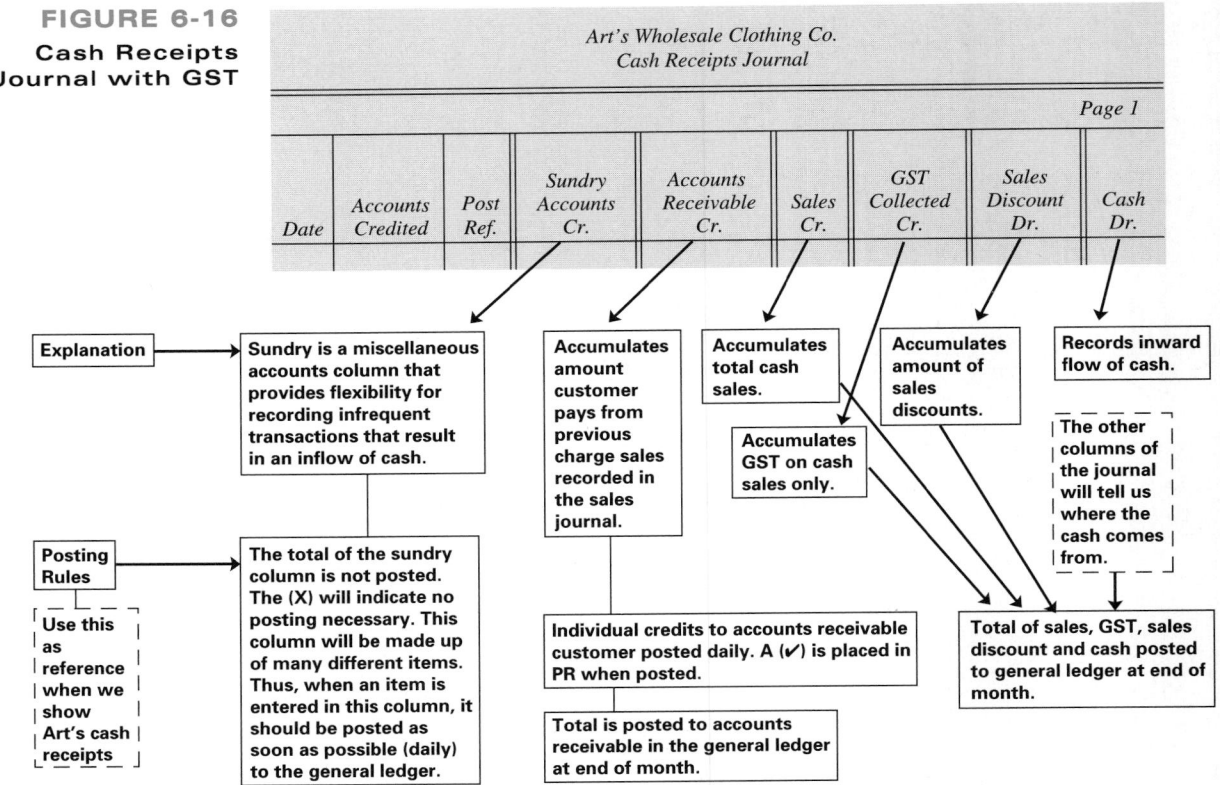

JOURNALIZING, RECORDING, AND POSTING FROM THE CASH RECEIPTS JOURNAL

On April 4 Art's Wholesale received a cheque from Hal's Clothing for payment of invoice No. 1 less discount. Remember, it was in the sales journal that this transaction was first recorded (p. 194). At that time we updated the accounts receivable ledger, indicating that Hal's Clothing owed Art $856. Since Hal's Clothing is paying within the 10-day discount period, Art's Wholesale offers a $16 sales discount ($800 × .02). (Remember, all credit sales carried terms of 2/10, n/30.)

Now, when payment is received, Art's Wholesale updates the cash receipts journal (see pp. 201-202) by entering the date (April 4), cash debit of $840, sales discount debit of $16, credit to accounts receivable of $856, and which account name (Hal's clothing) is to be credited. The terms of sale indicate that Hal's Clothing is entitled to the discount and no longer owes Art's Wholesale the $856 balance. *As soon as this line is entered into the cash receipts journal, Art's Wholesale will update the ledger account of Hal's Clothing.* Note in the accounts receivable ledger of Hal's Clothing how the date (April 4), post reference (CRJ1), and credit amount ($856) are recorded. The balance in the accounts receivable ledger is zero. The last step of this transaction is to go back to the cash receipts journal and put a √ in the post reference column.

In studying this cash receipts journal, note that:

1. All totals of cash receipts journal *except* sundry were posted to the general ledger at the end of the month.
2. Art Newner, Capital, and Store Equipment were posted to the general ledger when entered in the sundry column. For now in the general ledger it was assumed that the equipment account had a beginning balance of $4,000. There is no GST on these two items.
3. The cash sales were not posted when entered (thus the X to show no posting is needed). The sales and cash totals are posted at the *end* of the month.
4. A (√) means information was recorded daily to the accounts receivable ledger.
5. The Account Name column describes each transaction.

We can prove the accuracy of recording transactions of the cash receipts journal by totalling the column with debit balances and the column with credit balances. This process, called **crossfooting**, is done before the totals are posted. Also, if a bookkeeper were using more than one page for the cash receipts journal, the balances on the bottom of one page would be brought forward to the next page. This verifying of totals would result in less work when trying to find journalizing or posting errors at a later date. Let's see how to crossfoot the cash receipts journal of Art's Wholesale (Figure 6-17, p. 202).

> The last step is to put a check mark in the PR of the cash receipts journal to show the accounts receivable ledger is up-to-date.

DEBIT COLUMNS	=	CREDIT COLUMNS
Cash + Sales Discount	=	Accounts Receivable + Sales + Sundry + GST
$14,737 + $76	=	$4,066 + $2,100 + $8,500 + 147
$14,813	=	$14,813

> Proving the cash receipts journal.

Now let's take a moment to see what PST would look like in the cash receipts journal of a business that would need to record sales tax as well as GST. A typical cash receipts journal might look as follows:

Cash Receipts Journal

Date	Accounts Credited	PR	Sundry Cr.	Sales Tax Payable Cr.	GST Cr.	Sales Cr.	Accounts Receivable Cr.	Sales Discount Dr.	Cash Dr.

The total of the sales tax as a result of cash sales would be posted to Sales Tax Payable in the general ledger at the end of the month. It represents a liability of the merchant to forward the tax to the provincial government. Remember, no cash discounts are taken on the sales tax (or GST).

Now let's prove the accounts receivable ledger to the controlling account—Accounts Receivable—at the end of April for Art's Wholesale Clothing Company.

> The total of sales tax payable would be posted to Sales Tax Payable in the general ledger at the end of the month.

SCHEDULE OF ACCOUNTS RECEIVABLE

From Figure 6-17 (pp. 202-203) let's list the customers that have an ending balance in the accounts receivable ledger of Art's Clothing Company. This listing is called a **schedule of accounts receivable**.

FIGURE 6-17

Cash Receipts Journal and Posting with GST

Cash Receipts Journal

Page 1

Date		Account Debited	PR	Sundry Accounts Cr.	Accounts Receivable Cr.	Sales Cr.	GST Collected Cr.	Sales Discount Dr.	Cash Dr.
19XX									
April	1	Art Newner, Capital	311	8000 00					8000 00
	4	Hal's Clothing	✗		856 00			16 00	840 00
	15	Cash Sales	✗			900 00	63 00		963 00
	16	Bevans Company	✓		1070 00			20 00	1050 00
	22	Roe Company	✓		214 00			4 00	2100 00
	27	Store Equipment	121	500 00					500 00
	30	Cash Sales	✗			1200 00	84 00		1284 00
	30			8500 00	4066 00	2100 00	147 00	76 00	14737 00
				(X)	(113)	(411)	(212)	(413)	(111)

Total not posted →

Totals posted to general ledger at end of month

Partial General Ledger

Cash   Acct. No. 111

Date 19XX		Explanation	Post Ref.	Debit	Credit	DR or CR	Balance
April	3		CRJ1	14737 00		DR	14737 00

Accounts Receivable   Acct. No. 113

Date 19XX		Explanation	Post Ref.	Debit	Credit	DR or CR	Balance
April	3		GJ1		642 00	CR	642 00
	30		SJ1	6955 00		DR	6313 00
	30		CRJ1		4066 00	DR	2247 00

Accounts Receivable Ledger

NAME Bevans Company
ADDRESS 101 Aster Rd. Amherst, NS, B4H 3A5

Date		Explanation	Post Ref.	Debit	Credit	Dr. Balance
19XX						
April	6		SJ1	1712 00		1712 00
	12		GJ1		642 00	
	16		CRJ1		1070 00	

NAME Hal's Clothing
ADDRESS 191 Century Ave. Winnipeg, MN, R2C 4X7

Date		Explanation	Post Ref.	Debit	Credit	Dr. Balance
19XX						
April	3		SJ1	856 00		856 00
	4		CRJ1		856 00	– 0 –

FIGURE 6-17 (cont'd.)   Cash Receipts Journal and Posting with GST

Store Equipment   Acct. No. 121

Date 19XX	Explanation	Post Ref.	Debit	Credit	DR or CR	Balance
April 1	Balance				DR	4 0 0 0 00
27		CRJ1		5 0 0 00	DR	3 5 0 0 00

GST Collected   Acct. No. 212

Date 19XX	Explanation	Post Ref.	Debit	Credit	DR or CR	Balance
April 30		SJ1		4 5 5 00	CR	4 5 5 00
30		CRJ1		1 4 7	CR	6 0 2 00

Art Newmer, Capital   Acct. No. 311

Date 19XX	Explanation	Post Ref.	Debit	Credit	DR or CR	Balance
April 30		CRJ1		8 0 0 0 00	CR	8 0 0 0 00

Sales   Acct. No. 411

Date 19XX	Explanation	Post Ref.	Debit	Credit	DR or CR	Balance
April 30		SJ1		6 5 0 0 00	CR	6 5 0 0 00
30		CRJ1		2 1 0 0 00	CR	8 6 0 0 00

Sales Discount   Acct. No. 413

Date 19XX	Explanation	Post Ref.	Debit	Credit	DR or CR	Balance
April 30		CRJ1	7 6 00		DR	7 6 00

NAME Mel's Dept. Store
ADDRESS 181 Foss Rd. Fredericton, NB, E3A 2N8

Date	Explanation	Post Ref.	Debit	Credit	Dr. Balance
19XX April 28		SJ1	9 6 3 00		9 6 3 00
29		SJ1	7 4 9 00		1 7 1 2 00

NAME Roe Company
ADDRESS 18 Rantool St. Regina, SK, S4P 3J7

Date	Explanation	Post Ref.	Debit	Credit	Dr. Balance
19XX April 18		SJ1	2 1 4 0 00		2 1 4 0 00
22		CRJ1		2 1 4 0 00	- 0 -
24		CJ1	5 3 5 00		5 3 5 00

Note on accounts receivable: Very occasionally (due to an error, such as when a customer pays twice for the same invoice) a credit balance may be called for. Credit balances are opposite to the normal debit balance and are signified by placing the balance in brackets. For example, suppose that Hal's Clothing (see above) mistakenly paid its invoice twice. Their account would then appear as follows:

NAME Hal's Clothing
ADDRESS 191 Century Ave. Winnipeg, MN, R2C 4X7

Date	Explanation	Post Ref.	Debit	Credit	Dr. Balance
19XX April 3		SJ1	8 5 6 00		8 5 6 00
4		CRJ1		8 5 6 00	- 0 -
10		CRJ1		8 5 6 00	(8 5 6 00)

Art's Wholesale Clothing Company
Schedule of Accounts Receivable
April 30, 19XX

Schedule is listed in alphabetical order.

Mel's Dept. Store	*$1,712.00*
Roe Company	*535.00*
Total Accounts Receivable	*$2,247.00*

The balance of the controlling account, Accounts Receivable ($2,247), in the general ledger (p. 201) does indeed equal the sum of the individual customer balances in the accounts receivable ledger ($2,247). The schedule of accounts receivable can help forecast potential cash inflows as well as possible credit and collection decisions.

At this point you should be able to

1. Journalize, record, and post transactions with or without sales tax using a cash receipts journal. (pp. 201-202)
2. Prepare a schedule of accounts receivable. (p. 203)

☐ SELF-REVIEW QUIZ 6-5

Journalize, crossfoot, record, and post when appropriate the following transactions into the cash receipts journal of Moore Co. Use the same headings as for Art's Clothing.

ACCOUNTS RECEIVABLE LEDGER

NAME	BALANCE	INVOICE NO.
Irene Welch	$500	1
Chantel Simard	200	2

PARTIAL GENERAL LEDGER

ACCOUNT	ACCT. NO.	BALANCE
Cash	110	$600
Accounts Receivable	120	749
Store Equipment	130	600
GST collected	212	49
Sales	410	700
Sales Discount	420	—

19XX
May 1   Received cheque from Irene Welch for invoice No. 1 less 2% discount.
      8   Cash sales collected, $400 plus GST of $28.
     15   Received cheque from Janis Fross for invoice No. 2 less 2% discount.
     19   Sold store equipment at cost, $300 (no GST).

■ SOLUTION TO SELF-REVIEW QUIZ 6-5

Moore Company
Cash Receipts Journal

Page 1

Date	Accounts Credited	Post. Ref.	Sundry Accounts Cr.	Accounts Receivable Cr.	Sales Cr.	GST Collected Cr.	Sales Discount Dr.	Cash Dr.
19XX May 1	Irene Welch	✔		5 3 5 00			1 0 00	5 2 5 00
8	Cash Sales	✗			4 0 0 00	2 8 00		4 2 8 00
15	Chantel Simard	✔		2 1 4 00			4 00	2 1 0 00
19	Store Equipment	130	3 0 0 00					3 0 0 00
31			3 0 0 00	7 4 9 00	4 0 0 00	2 8 00	1 4 00	1 4 6 3 00
			(X)	(120)	(410)	(212)	(420)	(110)

Crossfooting: $1,477.00 = $1,477.00

Partial General Ledger

Cash   Acct. No. 110

Date 19XX	Explanation	Post Ref.	Debit	Credit	DR or CR	Balance
May 1	Balance	✔			DR	6 0 0 00
31		CRJ2	1 4 6 3 00		DR	2 0 6 3 00

Accounts Receivable   Acct. No. 120

Date 19XX	Explanation	Post Ref.	Debit	Credit	DR or CR	Balance
May 1	Balance	✔			DR	7 4 9 00
31		CRJ2		7 4 9 00		Ø

Store Equipment   Acct. No. 130

Date 19XX	Explanation	Post Ref.	Debit	Credit	DR or CR	Balance
May 1	Balance	✔			DR	6 0 0 00
31		CRJ2		3 0 0 00	DR	3 0 0 00

GST Collected   Acct. No. 212

Date 19XX		Explanation	Post Ref.	Debit	Credit	DR or CR	Balance
May	1		✔			CR	4 9 00
	31		CRJ2		1 4 00	CR	6 3 00

Sales   Acct. No. 410

Date 19XX		Explanation	Post Ref.	Debit	Credit	DR or CR	Balance
May	1	Balance	✔			CR	7 0 0 00
	31		CRJ2		2 0 0 00	CR	9 0 0 00

Sales Discount   Acct. No. 420

Date 19XX		Explanation	Post Ref.	Debit	Credit	DR or CR	Balance
May	31		CRJ2	1 4 00		DR	1 4 00

Accounts Receivable Ledger

NAME   Irene Welch
ADDRESS   10 Rong Rd., Timmins, ON, P4N 4M3

Date		Explanation	Post Ref.	Debit	Credit	Dr. Balance
19XX May	1	Balance	✔			5 3 5 00
	1		CRJ2		5 3 5 00	– 0 –

NAME   Chantal Simard
ADDRESS   9017 Robitaille Rd., Montreal, PQ, H1K 4R3

Date		Explanation	Post Ref.	Debit	Credit	Dr. Balance
19XX May	1	Balance	✔			2 1 4 00
	15		CRJ2		2 1 4 00	– 0 –

SUMMARY OF KEY POINTS AND KEY TERMS

LEARNING UNIT 6-1

1. Sales Returns and Allowances and Sales Discount are contra revenue accounts.
2. Net Sales = Gross Sales – Sales Returns and Allowances – Sales Discounts.
3. Discounts are not taken on sales tax, freight, or goods returned. The discount period is shorter than the credit period.
4. Cost of Goods Sold = Beginning Inventory + Additional Cost of Goods brought into store – Ending Inventory
5. Gross Profit = Net Sales – Cost of Goods Sold
6. Net Income = Gross Profit – Operating Expenses

Cost of goods sold: Total cost of the goods that are sold to customers.

Credit period: Length of time allowed for payment of goods sold on account.

Discount period: Period that is shorter than credit period to encourage early payment of bills.

Gross profit: Net sales less cost of goods sold.

Gross sales: The revenue earned from sale of merchandise to customers.

Inventory: Goods or merchandise for resale to customers.

Merchandise: Goods brought into a business for resale to customers.

Net income: Gross profit less operating expenses.

Net sales: Gross sales less sales returns and allowances less sales discounts.

Operating expenses: Expired costs of earning revenue.

Retailers: Buy goods from wholesalers for resale to customers.

Sales discount: Contra revenue account that records cash discounts granted to customers for payments made within a specific period of time.

Sales Returns and Allowances: Contra revenue account that records price adjustments and allowances granted on merchandise that is defective and has been returned.

Wholesalers: Buy goods from suppliers and manufacturers for sale to retailers.

LEARNING UNIT 6-2

1. A general journal is still used with special journals.
2. A sales journal records sales on account.
3. The accounts receivable ledger, organized in alphabetical order, is not in the same book as Accounts Receivable, the controlling account in the general ledger.
4. At the end of the month the total of all customers' ending balances in the accounts receivable ledger must be equal to the ending balance in Accounts Receivable, the controlling account in the general ledger.

Accounts receivable ledger: A book or file that contains in alphabetical order the individual records of amounts owed by various credit customers.

Controlling account—Accounts Receivable: The Accounts Receivable account in the general ledger, after postings are complete, shows a firm the total amount of money owed to it. This figure is broken down in the accounts receivable ledger, where it indicates specifically who owes the money.

Sales invoice: A bill reflecting a sale on credit.

Sales journal: A special journal used to record only sales made on account.

Special journal: A journal used to record similar groups of transactions. Example: The sales journal records all sales on account.

Subsidiary ledger: A ledger that contains accounts of a single type. Example: The accounts receivable ledger records transactions for all credit customers.

LEARNING UNIT 6-3

1. The √ in the post reference column of the sales journal means a customer's account in the accounts receivable ledger (on the debit side) has been updated (or recorded) during the month.

2. At the end of the month the total(s) of the sales journal is posted to general ledger accounts.

3. Sales Tax Payable is a liability found in the general ledger.

4. When a credit memorandum is issued, the result is that Sales Returns and Allowances increases, and Accounts Receivable decreases. When we record this into a general journal we assume that all parts of the transaction will be posted to the general ledger and recorded in the subsidiary ledger when the entry is journalized.

Credit memorandum: A piece of paper sent by the seller to a customer who has returned merchandise previously purchased on credit. The credit memorandum indicates to the customer that the seller is reducing the amount owed by the customer.

Sales Tax Payable account: An account in the general ledger that accumulates the amount of sales tax owed. It has a credit balance.

LEARNING UNIT 6-4

1. Recording GST in the sales journal requires the addition of one new column. Other procedures are not changed

2. Often both PST and GST will appear on the same invoice. Recording this in the sales journal requires the use of two extra columns but again the basic procedures are little changed.

3. When a sales discount is allowed, it is taken on the pre-PST and pre-GST amount only, not on the total invoice.

4. Recording a credit memorandum with PST and GST requires an extra line in the general journal for each. The credit to the customer's account includes the invoice amount plus PST and GST.

Goods and Services Tax (GST): A new "value added" tax introduced in Canada in 1991. It is added to most sales of goods and services. Currently calculated at 7%.

GST Collected account: The amount collected from customers and due to be sent to the Federal Government. It is a liability account with a credit balance. See also the next chapter for a fuller explanation of the net amount payable.

LEARNING UNIT 6-5

1. The cash receipts journal records receipt of cash from any source.

2. The sundry column records the credit part of a transaction that does not occur frequently. Never post the *total* of sundry. Post items in sundry column to the general ledger when entered.

3. A √ in the post reference column of the cash receipts journal means that the accounts receivable ledger has been updated (recorded) with a credit.

4. An X in the cash receipts journal post reference column means no posting was necessary, since the totals of these columns will be posted at the end of the month.

5. Crossfooting means proving that the total of debits and the total of credits are equal in the special journal, thus verifying the accuracy of recording.

6. A schedule of accounts receivable is a listing of the ending balances of customers' accounts in the accounts receivable ledger. This total should be the same balance as found in the controlling account, Accounts Receivable, in the general ledger.

Cash receipts journal: A special journal that records all transactions involving the receipt of cash from any source.

Crossfooting: The process of proving that the total debit columns of a special journal are equal to the total credit columns of a special journal.

Schedule of accounts receivable: A list of the customers, in alphabetical order, that have an outstanding balance in the accounts receivable ledger. This total should be equal to the balance of the Accounts Receivable controlling account in the general ledger at the end of the month.

Sundry: Miscellaneous accounts column(s) in a special journal, which records parts of transactions that do not occur too often.

BLUEPRINT OF SALES AND CASH RECEIPTS JOURNALS

Summary of How to Post and Record Single-Column Sales Journal

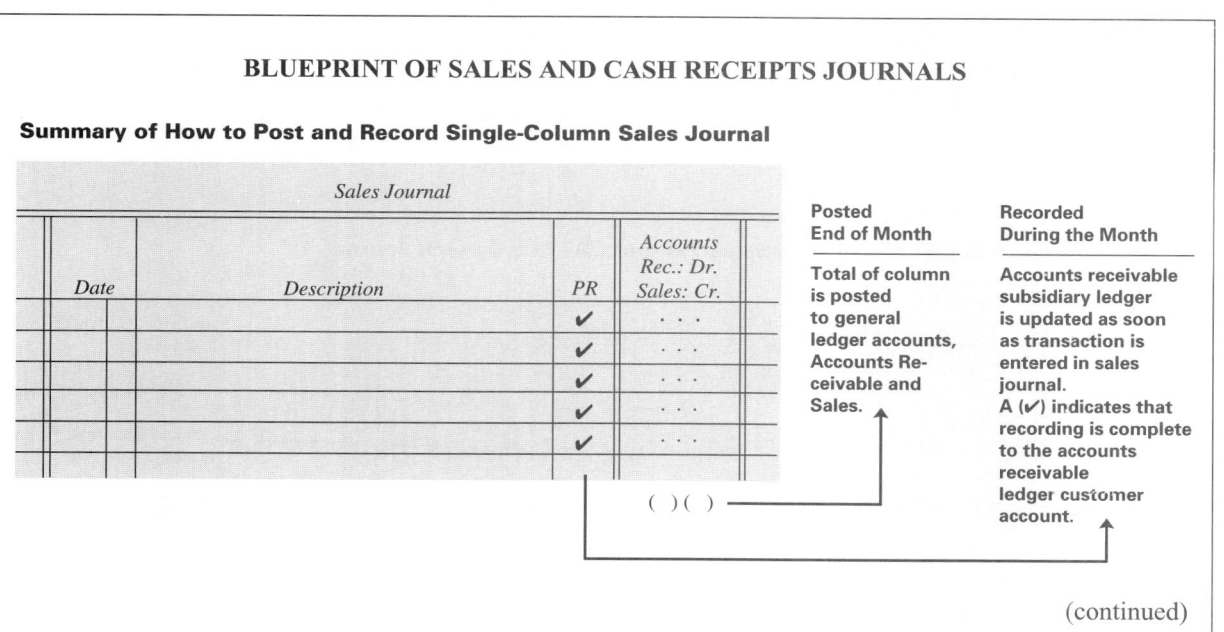

(continued)

Multicolumn Sales Journal

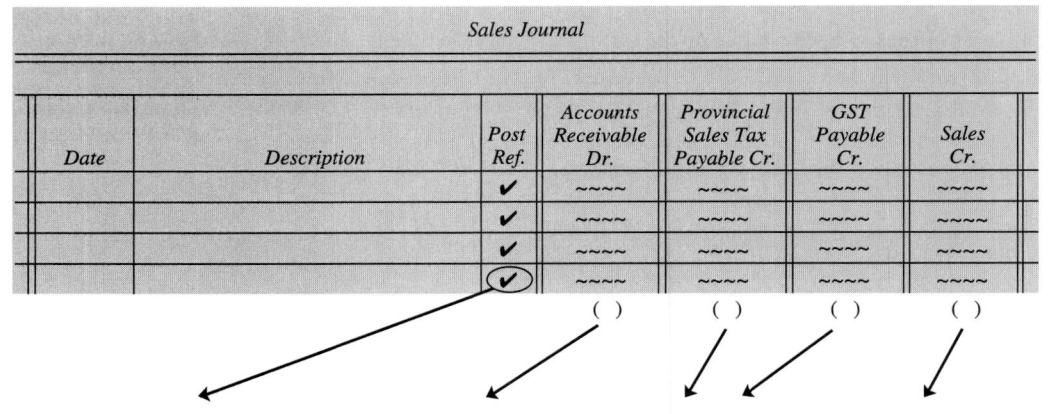

During the month the accounts receivable ledger is updated as soon as transactions are entered in the journal. A check mark indicates that posting is completed to the customer's account in the accounts receivable sub-ledger.

End of month total is posted to Accounts Receivable control account in the general ledger.

End of month totals of both taxes payable accounts are posted to their respective accounts in the general ledger.

End of month total of sales is posted to the general ledger.

Recording a Credit Memo without Sales Tax or GST in a General Journal

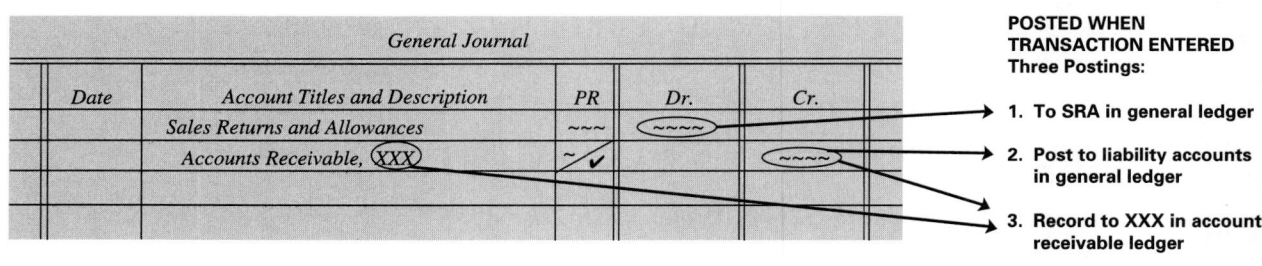

POSTED WHEN TRANSACTION ENTERED
Three Postings:

1. To SRA in general ledger

2. Post to liability accounts in general ledger

3. Record to XXX in accounts receivable ledger

Recording a Credit Memo with Sales Tax and GST in a General Journal

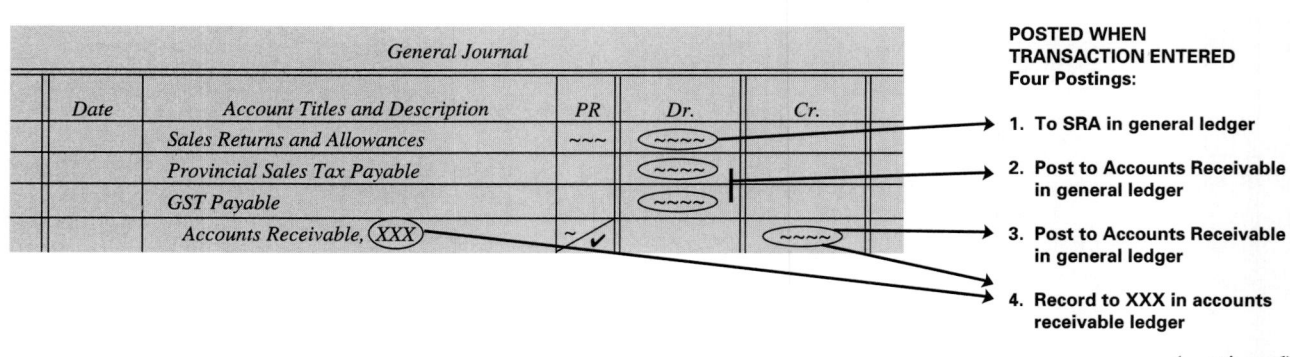

POSTED WHEN TRANSACTION ENTERED
Four Postings:

1. To SRA in general ledger

2. Post to Accounts Receivable in general ledger

3. Post to Accounts Receivable in general ledger

4. Record to XXX in accounts receivable ledger

(continued)

The Cash Receipts Journal with PST and GST

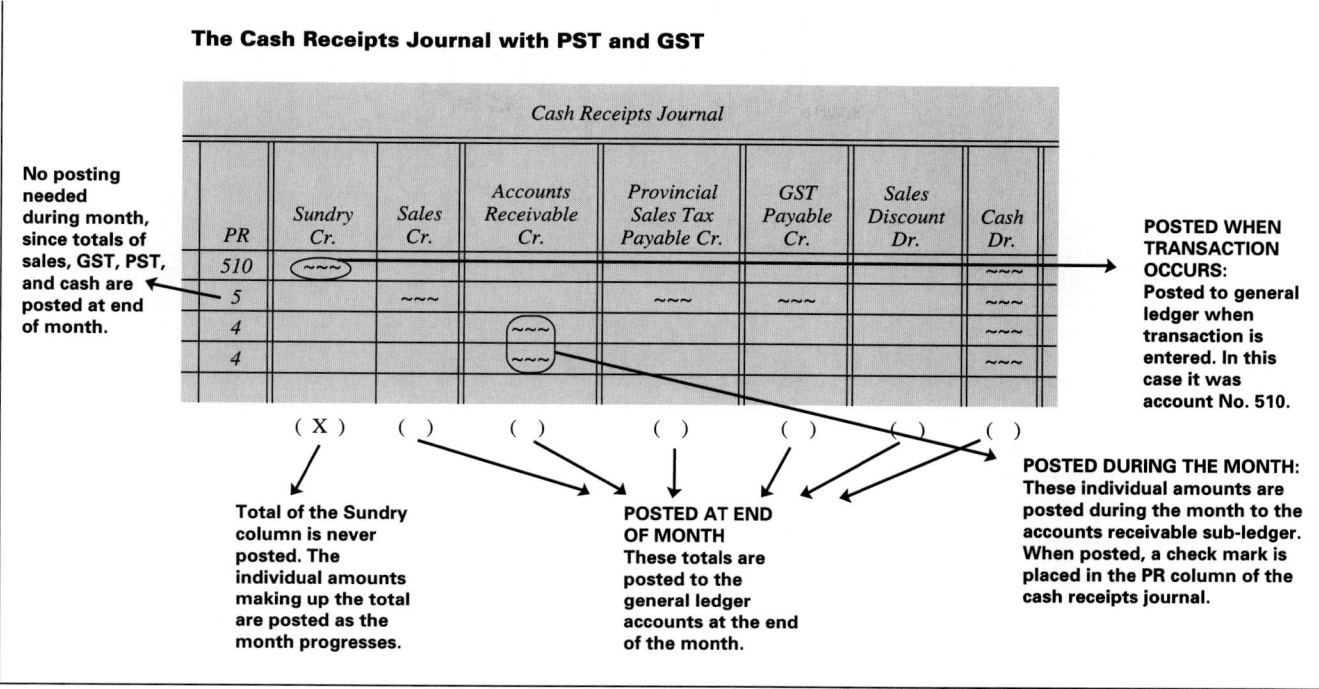

No posting needed during month, since totals of sales, GST, PST, and cash are posted at end of month.

POSTED WHEN TRANSACTION OCCURS: Posted to general ledger when transaction is entered. In this case it was account No. 510.

Total of the Sundry column is never posted. The individual amounts making up the total are posted as the month progresses.

POSTED AT END OF MONTH These totals are posted to the general ledger accounts at the end of the month.

POSTED DURING THE MONTH: These individual amounts are posted during the month to the accounts receivable sub-ledger. When posted, a check mark is placed in the PR column of the cash receipts journal.

DISCUSSION QUESTIONS

1. Explain the difference between retailers and wholesalers.
2. Show how you would calculate net sales, cost of goods sold, gross profit, and net income.
3. Give two examples of contra revenue accounts.
4. What is the difference between a discount period and a credit period?
5. Explain the terms A. 2/10, n/30; B. n/10, EOM.
6. If special journals are used, what purpose will a general journal serve?
7. Compare and contrast the controlling account Accounts Receivable to the accounts receivable ledger.
8. Why is the accounts receivable ledger organized in alphabetical order?
9. When is a sales journal used?
10. What is an invoice? What purpose does it serve?
11. Why is sales tax a liability to the business?
12. Sales discounts are taken on sales tax. Agree or disagree and tell why.
13. When a seller issues a credit memorandum (assume no sales tax), what accounts will be affected?
14. Explain the function of a cash receipts journal.
15. When is the sundry column of the cash receipts journal posted?
16. Explain the purpose of a schedule of accounts receivable.

EXERCISES

1. From the following sales journal, record to the accounts receivable ledger and post to the general ledger accounts as appropriate.

Recording to accounts receivable ledger and posting to general ledger.

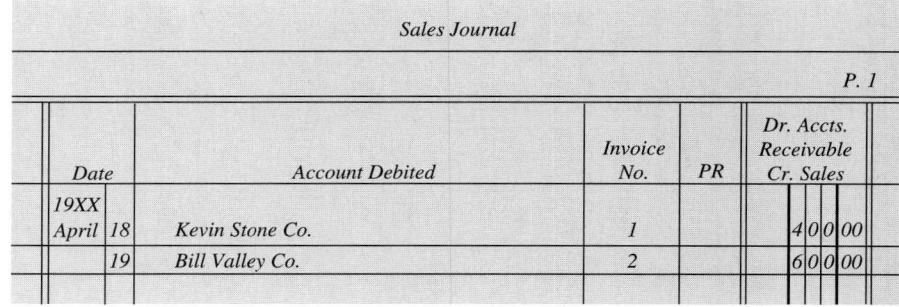

		Sales Journal				
						P. 1
Date		Account Debited	Invoice No.	PR	Dr. Accts. Receivable Cr. Sales	
19XX April 18		Kevin Stone Co.	1		400 00	
	19	Bill Valley Co.	2		600 00	

ACCOUNTS RECEIVABLE LEDGER	PARTIAL GENERAL LEDGER
Kevin Stone Co.	Accounts Receivable 112
Bill Valley Co.	Sales 412

2. Journalize, record, and post when appropriate the following transactions into the sales journal (same heading as Exercise 1) and general journal (P. 1) (All sales carry terms of 2/10, n/30.):

Journalizing, recording, and posting that includes credit memorandum.

19XX
May 16   Sold merchandise on account to Ronald Co., invoice No. 1, $1,000.
     18   Sold merchandise on account to Bass Co., invoice No. 2, $1,700.
     20   Issued credit memorandum No. 1 to Bass Co. for defective merchandise, $700.

Use the following account numbers: Accounts Receivable, 112; Sales, 411; Sales Returns and Allowances, 412.

Journalizing transaction into cash receipts journal with returns and discounts.

3. From Exercise 2, journalize in the cash receipts journal the receipt of a cheque from Ronald Co. for payment of invoice No. 1 on May 24. Use the same headings as for Art's Wholesale Clothing on p. 183.

Journalizing, recording, and posting sales and cash receipts journal; schedule of accounts receivable.

4. From the following transactions for Edna Co., when appropriate, journalize, record, post, and prepare a schedule of accounts receivable. Use the same journal headings (all page 1) and chart of accounts (use Edna Cares, Capital) that Art's Wholesale Clothing used in the text. You will have to set up your own accounts receivable ledger and partial general ledger as needed. All sales terms are 2/10, n/30.

19XX
June 1   Edna Cares invested $3,000 in the business.
      1   Sold merchandise on account to Boston Co., invoice No. 1, $700.
      2   Sold merchandise on account to Gary Co., invoice No. 2, $900.

3   Cash sale, $200.
8   Issued credit memorandum No. 1 to Boston for defective merchandise, $200.
10   Received cheque from Boston for invoice No. 1 less returns and discount.
15   Cash sale, $400.
18   Sold merchandise on account to Boston Co., invoice No. 3, $600.

5. From the following facts calculate what Ann Frost must pay Blue Co. for the purchase of a dining room set. Sale terms are 2/10, n/30.

    A. Sales ticket price before tax, $4,000—dated April 5.
    B. Sales tax, 7%.
    C. Returned one defective chair, for credit of $400 on April 8.
    D. Paid bill on April 13.

Sales tax and cash discount calculation.

6. Peter Rockford purchased eight stereo speakers from Waverly Electronics for his restaurant. The price before any taxes was $400.00 each. Terms were 2/10, n/30 and PST of 10% was added to the total before GST of 7% was included. What amount will Rockford pay, given the following:

    A. Sale was dated June 11, 19XX.
    B. Returned two speakers due to defective sound on June 15, 19XX.
    C. Credit of $400 each plus all applicable taxes was received on June 15.
    D. Full payment was made on June 20, 19XX.

GROUP A PROBLEMS

6A-1. Edna Karras opened Max Co., a wholesale grocery and pizza company. The following transactions occurred in June:

19XX
June   1   Sold grocery merchandise to Joe Kase Co. on account, $400, invoice No. 1.
      4   Sold pizza ingredients to Sue Moore Co. on account, $600, invoice No. 2.
      8   Sold grocery merchandise to Long Co. on account, $700, invoice No. 3.
   10   Issued credit memorandum No. 1 to Joe Kase for $150 of grocery merchandise returned due to spoilage.
   15   Sold pizza ingredients to Sue Moore Co. on account, $160, invoice No. 4.
   19   Sold grocery merchandise to Long Co. on account, $300, invoice No. 5.
   25   Sold pizza ingredients to Joe Kase Co. on account, $1,200, invoice No. 6.

Multicolumn sales journal: Journalizing and posting to general ledger and recording to accounts receivable ledger; and preparing a schedule of accounts receivable.

Required:
1. Journalize the transactions in the appropriate journals.
2. Record to the accounts receivable ledger and post to general ledger as appropriate.
3. Prepare a schedule of accounts receivable.

Multicolumn sales journal: Use of sales tax; journalizing and posting to general ledger and recording to accounts receivable ledger; and preparing a schedule of accounts receivable.

6A-2. The following transactions of Ted's Auto Supply occurred in November (your working papers have balances as of Nov. 1 for certain general ledger and accounts receivable ledger accounts):

19XX

Nov.	1	Sold auto parts merchandise to R. Volan on account, $1,000, invoice No. 60, plus 5% sales tax.
	5	Sold auto parts merchandise to J. Seth on account, $800, invoice No. 61, plus 5% sales tax.
	8	Sold auto parts merchandise to Lance Corner on account, $9,000, invoice No. 62, plus 5% sales tax.
	10	Issued credit memorandum No. 12 to R. Volan for $500 for defective auto parts merchandise returned from Nov. 1 transaction. (Be careful to record the reduction in sales tax payable as well.)
	12	Sold auto parts merchandise to J. Seth on account, $600, invoice No. 63, plus 5% sales tax.

Required:
1. Journalize the transactions in the appropriate journals.
2. Record to the accounts receivable ledger and post to general ledger as appropriate.
3. Prepare a schedule of accounts receivable.

Comprehensive Problem: Recording transactions into sales, cash receipts, and general journals. Recording to accounts receivable and posting to general ledger. Preparing a schedule of accounts receivable.

6A-3. Mark Peaker owns Peaker's Sneaker Shop. (In your working papers balances as of May 1 are provided for the accounts receivable and general ledger accounts.) The following transactions occurred in May:

19XX

May	1	Mark Peaker invested an additional $12,000 in the sneaker store.
	3	Sold $700 of merchandise on account to B. Dale, sales ticket No. 60, terms 1/10, n/30.
	4	Sold $500 of merchandise on account to Ron Lester, sales ticket No. 61, terms 1/10, n/30.
	9	Sold $200 of merchandise on account to Jim Zon, sales ticket No. 62, terms 1/10, n/30.
	10	Received cash from B. Dale in payment of May 3 transaction, sales ticket No. 60, less discount.
	20	Sold $3,000 of merchandise on account to Pam Pry, sales ticket No. 63, terms 1/10, n/30.
	22	Received cash payment from Ron Lester in payment of May 4 transaction, sales ticket No. 61.
	23	Collected cash sales, $3,000.
	24	Issued credit memorandum No. 1 to Pam Pry for $2,000 of merchandise returned from May 20 sales on account.
	26	Received cash from Pam Pry in payment of May 20 sales ticket No. 63. (Don't forget about the credit memo and discount.)
	28	Collected cash sales, $7,000.
	30	Sold sneaker rack equipment for $300 cash. (Beware.)
	30	Sold merchandise priced at $4,000, on account to Ron Lester, sales ticket No. 64, terms 1/10, n/30.
	31	Issued credit memorandum No. 2 to Ron Lester for $700 of merchandise returned from May 30 transaction, sales ticket No. 64.

Required:
1. Journalize the transactions in the appropriate journals.
2. Record to the accounts receivable ledger and post to general ledger as needed.
3. Prepare a schedule of accounts receivable.

6A-4. Bill Murray opened Bill's Cosmetic Market on April 1. There is a 6% provincial sales tax on all cosmetic sales. Bill offers no sales discounts. The following transactions occurred in April:

19XX

April	1	Bill Murray invested $8,000 in the Cosmetic Market from his personal savings account.
	5	From the cash register tapes, lipstick cash sales were $5,000 plus sales tax.
	5	From the cash register tapes, eye shadow cash sales were $2,000 plus sales tax.
	8	Sold lipstick on account to Alice Koy Co., $300, sales ticket No. 1, plus sales tax.
	9	Sold eye shadow on account to Marika Sanchez Co., $1,000, sales ticket No. 2, plus sales tax.
	15	Issued credit memorandum No. 1 to Alice Koy Co. for $150 for lipstick returned. (Be sure to reduce sales tax payable for Bill.)
	19	Marika Sanchez Co. paid half the amount owed from sales ticket No. 2, dated April 9.
	21	Sold lipstick on account to Jeff Tong Co., $300, sales ticket No. 3, plus sales tax.
	24	Sold eye shadow on account to Rusty Neal Co., $800, sales ticket No. 4, plus sales tax.
	25	Issued credit memorandum No. 2 to Jeff Tong Co. for $200 for lipstick returned from sales ticket No. 3, dated April 21.
	29	Cash sales taken from the cash register tape showed: (1) Lipstick—$1,000 + $60 sales tax collected. (2) Eye shadow—$3,000 + $180 sales tax collected.
	29	Sold lipstick on account to Marika Sanchez Co., $400, sales ticket No. 5, plus sales tax.
	30	Received payment from Marika Sanchez Co. of sales ticket No. 5, dated April 29.

Comprehensive problem: Using provincial sales tax in recording transactions into sales, cash receipts, and general journals. Recording to accounts receivable and posting to general ledger. Crossfooting and preparing a schedule of accounts receivable.

Required:
1. Journalize the above in the sales journal, cash receipts journal, or general journal.
2. Record to the accounts receivable ledger and post to general ledger when appropriate.
3. Prepare a schedule of accounts receivable for the end of April.

6A-5. Mary Parker owns Parker's SCUBA Shop. (In your working papers balances as of April 1 are provided for the accounts receivable and general ledger accounts.) In Mary's province it is necessary to add PST of 8% to each invoice, then add GST of 7% to arrive at the final invoice amount. The following transactions occurred in April:

Comprehensive problem: Using PST and GST in recording transactions into sales, cash receipts, and general journals. Recording to accounts receivable and posting to general ledger. Crossfooting and preparing a schedule of accounts receivable.

19XX
April   1   Mary Parker invested an additional $17,000 in the business.
         3   Sold $500 of merchandise on account to J. Simpson, sales ticket No. 614, terms 2/10, n/30.
         4   Sold $1,200 of merchandise on account to R. Langley, sales ticket No. 615, terms 2/10, n/30.
         9   Sold $300 of merchandise on account to J. Fellowes, sales ticket No. 616, terms 2/10, n/30.
        10   Received cash from J. Simpson in payment of April 3 transaction, sales ticket No. 614, less discount.
        20   Sold $2,000 of merchandise on account to Phyllis Leung, sales ticket No. 617, terms 2/10, n/30.
        22   Received cash payment from R. Langley in payment of April 4 transaction, sales ticket No. 615.
        23   Collected cash sales, $1,600 plus necessary taxes.
        24   Issued credit memorandum No. 101 to Phyllis Leung for $500 of merchandise returned from April 20 sales on account.
        26   Received cash from Phyllis Leung in payment of April 20 sales ticket No. 617. (Don't forget about the credit memo, all taxes and discount.)
        28   Collected cash sales, $4,000 plus necessary taxes.
        29   Sold merchandise priced at $3,000, on account to Roland Doncaster, sales ticket No. 618, terms 2/10, n/30.
        30   Issued credit memorandum No. 102 to Roland Doncaster for $800 of merchandise returned from April 29 transaction, sales ticket No. 618.

Required:
1. Journalize the transactions.
2. Record to the accounts receivable ledger and post to general ledger as needed.
3. Prepare a schedule of accounts receivable.

GROUP B PROBLEMS

6B-1. The following transactions occurred for Max Co. for the month of June:

19XX

Multicolumn column journal: Journalizing and posting to general ledger and recording to accounts receivable ledger and preparing a schedule of accounts receivable.

June   1   Sold grocery merchandise to Joe Kase Co. on account, $800, invoice No. 1.
         4   Sold pizza merchandise to Sue Moore Co. on account, $550, invoice No. 2.
         8   Sold grocery merchandise to Long Co. on account, $900, invoice No. 3.
        10   Issued credit memorandum No. 1 to Joe Kase for $160 of grocery merchandise returned due to spoilage.
        15   Sold pizza merchandise to Sue Moore Co. on account, $700, invoice No. 4.
        19   Sold grocery merchandise to Long Co. on account, $250, invoice No. 5.

Required:
1. Journalize the transactions in the appropriate journals.
2. Record to the accounts receivable ledger and post to general ledger as appropriate.
3. Prepare a schedule of accounts receivable.

6B-2. In November the following transactions occurred for Ted's Auto Supply (your working papers have balances as of Nov. 1 for certain general ledger and accounts receivable ledger accounts):

19XX

Nov. 1   Sold merchandise to R. Volan on account, $4,000, invoice No. 70, plus 5% sales tax.

  5   Sold merchandise to J. Seth on account, $1,600, invoice No. 71, plus 5% sales tax.

  8   Sold merchandise to Lance Corner on account, $15,000, invoice No. 72, plus 5% sales tax.

  10   Issued credit memorandum No. 14 to R. Volan for $2,000 for defective merchandise returned from Nov. 1 transaction. (Be careful to record the reduction in sales tax payable as well.)

  12   Sold merchandise to J. Seth on account, $1,400, invoice No. 73, plus 5% sales tax.

Multicolumn sales journal: Use of sales tax; journalizing and posting to general ledger and recording to accounts receivable ledger; and preparing a schedule of accounts receivable.

Required:
1. Journalize the transactions in the appropriate journals.
2. Record to the accounts receivable ledger and post to general ledger as appropriate.
3. Prepare a schedule of accounts receivable.

6B-3. (In your working papers all the beginning balances needed are provided for the accounts receivable and general ledger.) The following transactions occurred for Peaker's Sneaker Shop:

19XX

May 1   Mark Peaker invested an additional $14,000 in the sneaker store.

  3   Sold $2,000 of merchandise on account to B. Dale, sales ticket No. 60, terms 1/10, n/30.

  4   Sold $900 of merchandise on account to Ron Lester, sales ticket No. 61, terms 1/10, n/30.

  9   Sold $600 of merchandise on account to Jim Zon, sales ticket No. 62, terms 1/10, n/30.

  10   Received cash from B. Dale in payment of May 3 transaction, sales ticket No. 60, less discount.

  20   Sold $4,000 of merchandise on account to Pam Pry, sales ticket No. 63, terms 1/10, n/30.

  22   Received cash payment from Ron Lester in payment of May 4 transaction, sales ticket No. 61.

  23   Collected cash sales, $6,000.

  24   Issued credit memorandum No. 1 to Pam Pry for $500 of merchandise returned from May 20 sales on account.

  26   Received cash from Pam Pry in payment of May 20 sales ticket No. 63. (Don't forget about the credit memo and discount.)

  28   Collected cash sales, $12,000.

  30   Sold sneaker rack equipment for $200 cash. (Beware.)

  30   Sold $6,000 of merchandise on account to Ron Lester, sales ticket No. 64, terms 1/10, n/30.

  31   Issued credit memorandum No. 2 to Ron Lester for $800 of merchandise returned from May 30 transaction, sales ticket No. 64.

Comprehensive Problem: Recording transactions into sales, cash receipts, and general journals. Recording to accounts receivable and posting to general ledger. Preparing a schedule of accounts receivable.

Required:
1. Journalize the transactions in the appropriate journals.

2. Record and post as appropriate.
3. Prepare a schedule of accounts receivable.

6B-4. Bill's Cosmetic Market began operating in April. There is a 6% sales tax on all cosmetic sales. Bill offers no discounts. The following transactions occurred in April:

Comprehensive Problem: Using sales tax in recording transactions into sales, cash receipts, and general journals. Recording to accounts receivable and posting to general ledger, and preparing a schedule of accounts receivable.

19XX
April 1 Bill Murray invested $10,000 in the Cosmetic Market from his personal account.
       5 From the cash register tapes, lipstick cash sales were $5,000 plus sales tax.
       5 From the cash register tapes, eye shadow cash sales were $3,000 plus sales tax.
       8 Sold lipstick on account to Alice Koy Co., $400, sales ticket No. 1, plus sales tax.
       9 Sold eye shadow on account to Marika Sanchez Co., $900, sales ticket No. 2, plus sales tax.
      15 Issued credit memorandum No. 1 to Alice Koy Co. for lipstick returned, $200. (Be sure to reduce sales tax payable for Bill.)
      19 Marika Sanchez Co. paid half the amount owed from sales ticket No. 2, dated April 9.
      21 Sold lipstick on account to Jeff Tong Co., $600 sales ticket No. 3, plus sales tax.
      24 Sold eye shadow on account to Rusty Neal Co., $1,000 sales ticket No. 4, plus sales tax.
      25 Issued credit memorandum No. 2 to Jeff Tong Co. for $300, for lipstick returned from sales ticket No. 3, dated April 21.
      29 Cash sales taken from the cash register tape showed:
          (1) Lipstick—$4,000 + $240 sales tax collected.
          (2) Eye shadow—$2,000 + $120 sales tax collected.
      29 Sold lipstick on account to Marika Sanchez Co., $700, sales ticket No. 5, plus sales tax.
      30 Received payment from Marika Sanchez Co. of sales ticket No. 5, dated April 29.

Required:
1. Journalize, record, and post as appropriate.
2. Prepare a schedule of accounts receivable for the end of April.

6B-5. Mary Parker owns Parker's SCUBA Shop. (In your working papers, balances as of April 1 are provided for the accounts receivable and general ledger accounts.) In Mary's province it is necessary to add PST of 9% and GST of 7% to the sales total to arrive at the final invoice amount. This means that PST of $90 and GST of $70 would be added to an invoice for $1,000.00. The following transactions occurred in April:

Comprehensive Problem: Using PST and GST in recording transactions into sales, cash receipts, and general journals. Recording to accounts receivable and posting to general ledger, and preparing a schedule of accounts receivable.

19XX
April 1 Mary Parker invested an additional $13,000 in the business.
       3 Sold $800 of merchandise on account to J. Simpson, sales ticket No. 614, terms 2/10, n/30.
       4 Sold $1,600 of merchandise on account to R. Langley, sales ticket No. 615, terms 2/10, n/30.
       9 Sold $600 of merchandise on account to J. Fellowes, sales ticket No. 616, terms 2/10, n/30.

10   Received cash from J. Simpson in payment of April 3 transaction, sales ticket No. 614, less discount.

20   Sold $3,000 of merchandise on account to Phyllis Leung, sales ticket No. 617, terms 2/10, n/30.

22   Received cash payment from R. Langley in payment of April 4 transaction, sales ticket No. 615.

23   Collected cash sales, $2,500 plus necessary taxes.

24   Issued credit memorandum No. 101 to Phyllis Leung for $900 of merchandise returned from April 20 sales on account.

26   Received cash from Phyllis Leung in payment of April 20 sales ticket No. 617. (Don't forget the credit memo, all taxes and discount.)

28   Collected cash sales, $3,200 plus necessary taxes.

29   Sold merchandise priced at $4,000, on account to Roland Doncaster, sales ticket No. 618, terms 2/10, n/30.

30   Issued credit memorandum No. 102 to Roland Doncaster for $1,000 of merchandise returned from April 29 transaction, sales ticket No. 618.

Required:
1. Journalize the transactions.
2. Record to the accounts receivable ledger and post to general ledger as needed.
3. Prepare a schedule of accounts receivable.

GROUP C PROBLEMS

6C-1. The following transactions occurred for Apex Co. for the month of July:

19XX

July 1   Sold upholstery merchandise to Joan Timkins Co. on account, $1,300, invoice No. 115. Terms net 30 days.

    4   Sold carpet merchandise to Chris Cowan Co. on account, $750, invoice No. 116. Terms net 30 days.

    8   Sold upholstery merchandise to Cross & Co. on account, $1,800, invoice No. 117. Terms net 30 days.

  10   Issued credit memorandum No. 1 to Joan Timkins Co. for $240 of merchandise returned due to faulty coloring match.

  15   Sold carpet merchandise to Chris Cowan Co. on account, $800, invoice No. 118. Terms net 30 days.

  19   Sold upholstery merchandise to Cross & Co. on account, $650, invoice No. 119. Terms net 30 days.

  24   Sold carpet merchandise to Joan Timkins Co. on account, $2,100, invoice No. 120. Terms net 30 days.

Multicolumn column journal: Journalizing and posting to general ledger and recording to accounts receivable ledger and preparing a schedule of accounts receivable.

Required:
1. Journalize the transactions in the appropriate journals.
2. Record to the accounts receivable ledger and post to general ledger as appropriate.
3. Prepare a schedule of accounts receivable.

Multicolumn sales journal: Use of sales tax; journalizing and posting to general ledger and recording to accounts receivable ledger; and preparing a schedule of accounts receivable.

6C-2. In September the following transactions occurred for Kowalsky's Farm Equipment Supply (your working papers have balances as of Sept. 1 for certain general ledger and accounts receivable ledger accounts):

19XX

Sept. 1 Sold merchandise to Ray Fortuna on account, $8,500, invoice No. 703, plus 9% provincial sales tax.

5 Sold merchandise to Wilma Jorge on account, $2,600, invoice No. 704, plus 9% sales tax.

8 Sold merchandise to Cassie Ho on account, $14,600, invoice No. 705, plus 9% sales tax.

10 Issued credit memorandum No. 14 to Ray Fortuna for $1,000 for defective merchandise returned from Sept. 1 transaction. (Be careful to record the reduction in sales tax payable as well.)

12 Sold merchandise to Wilma Jorge on account, $3,400, invoice No. 706, plus 9% sales tax.

Required:
1. Journalize the transactions in the appropriate journals.
2. Record to the accounts receivable ledger and post to general ledger as appropriate.
3. Prepare a schedule of accounts receivable.

Comprehensive Problem: Recording transactions into sales, cash receipts, and general journals. Recording to accounts receivable and posting to general ledger. Preparing a schedule of accounts receivable.

6C-3. (In your working papers all the beginning balances needed are provided for the accounts receivable and general ledger.) The following transactions occurred for First City Sausage Supply Co.:

19XX

Sept. 1 Jack Owens, owner invested an additional $21,000 in the business.

3 Sold $1,700 of merchandise on account to Petra's Meat Market, sales ticket No. 460, terms 1/10, n/30.

4 Sold $765 of merchandise on account to Chapman's Deli, sales ticket No. 461, terms 1/10, n/30.

8 Sold $820 of merchandise on account to Valemont Variety Meats Co, sales ticket No. 462, terms 1/10, n/30.

12 Received cash from Petra's Meat Market in payment of Sept. 3 transaction, sales ticket No. 460, less discount.

21 Sold $1,400 of merchandise on account to Discount Meats, sales ticket No. 463, terms 1/10, n/30.

22 Received cash payment from Chapman's Deli in payment of Sept. 4 transaction, sales ticket No. 461.

23 Collected cash sale, $547.

24 Issued credit memorandum No. 101 to Discount Meats for $400 of merchandise returned from Sept. 21 sales on account.

26 Received cash from Discount Meats in payment of Sept. 21 sales ticket No. 463. (Don't forget about the credit memo and discount.)

27 Collected cash sales, $782.

28 Sold meat cooling equipment for $800 cash. (Beware.)

29 Sold $1,300 of merchandise on account to Chapman's Deli, sales ticket No. 464, terms 1/10, n/30.

30 Issued credit memorandum No. 102 to Chapman's Deli for $500 of merchandise returned from Sept. 29 transaction, sales ticket No. 464.

Required:
1. Journalize the transactions in the appropriate journals.
2. Record and post as appropriate.
3. Prepare a schedule of accounts receivable.

6C-4. Hedy's Communication Sales Co. began operating in August. There is an 8% provincial sales tax on all sales. Hedy offers no discounts (all terms are net 30 days). The following transactions occurred in August:

Comprehensive Problem: Using sales tax in recording transactions into sales, cash receipts, and general journals. Recording to accounts receivable and posting to general ledger, and preparing a schedule of accounts receivable.

19XX

August 1	Hedy Lamoureux invested $25,000 in Communication Sales Co. from her personal account.
5	From the cash register tapes, cellular cash sales were $4,800 plus provincial sales tax.
5	From the cash register tapes, radio cash sales were $7,350 plus sales tax.
8	Sold cellular equipment on account to Kelly's Real Estate Co., $3,700, sales ticket No. 201, plus sales tax.
9	Sold radio equipment on account to Well's Hotshot Service Co., $2,900, sales ticket No. 202, plus sales tax.
15	Issued credit memorandum No. 1 to Kelly's Real Estate Co. for cellular equipment returned, $900. (Be sure to reduce sales tax payable.)
19	Well's Hotshot Service Co. paid half the amount owed from sales ticket No. 202, dated August 9.
20	Sold cellular equipment on account to Mountain Explorations Co., $6,200 sales ticket No. 203, plus sales tax.
21	Received proceeds of loan from the Small Business Development Bank $40,000.
24	Sold radio equipment on account to Walkin's Safety Supply Co., $5,000. Sales ticket No. 204, plus sales tax.
25	Issued credit memorandum No. 2 to Mountain Explorations Co. for $1,600, for equipment returned from sales ticket No. 203, dated August 20.
27	Received payment of net amount due from Kelly's Real Estate Co. as per sales ticket No. 201 less the credit allowed.
29	Cash sales taken from the cash register tape showed: (1) Cellular—$4,750 + $380 sales tax collected. (2) Radio—$6,600 + $528 sales tax collected.
29	Sold cellular equipment on account to Well's Hotshot Service Co., $3,700 sales ticket No. 205, plus sales tax.
30	Received balance from Well's Hotshot Service Co. of sales ticket No. 202, dated August 9.

Required:
1. Journalize, record, and post as appropriate.
2. Prepare a schedule of accounts receivable for the end of August.

6C-5. Charles Silverstien owns Rarity Collectibles Shop. (In your working papers balances as of January 1 are provided for the accounts receivable and general ledger accounts.) In this province it is necessary to add PST of 6% and GST of 7% to the sales total to arrive at the final invoice amount. This means that PST of $6 and GST of $7 would be added to each invoice for $100. The following transactions occurred in January:

Comprehensive Problem: Using PST and GST in recording transactions into sales, cash receipts, and general journals. Recording to accounts receivable and posting to general ledger, and preparing a schedule of accounts receivable.

19XX

January 1	Charles Silverstien invested $38,000 in the business.
3	Sold $2,200 of merchandise on account to Starcraft Reproductions, sales ticket No. 344, terms 2/10, n/30.
4	Sold $2,800 of merchandise on account to Burgess Fancys, sales ticket No. 345, terms 2/10, n/30.

9 Sold $3,400 of merchandise on account to Hard-To-Find Co., sales ticket No. 346, terms 2/10, n/30.
10 Received cash from Starcraft Reproductions in payment of January 3 transaction, sales ticket No. 344, less discount.
20 Sold $2,360 of merchandise on account to Georgina's Collections, sales ticket No. 347, terms 2/10, n/30.
22 Received cash payment from Burgess Fancys in payment of January 4 transaction, sales ticket No. 345.
23 Collected cash sales, $3,810 plus necessary taxes.
24 Issued credit memorandum No. 10 to Georgina's Collections for $600 of merchandise returned from January 20 sales on account.
26 Received cash from Georgina's Collections in payment of January 20 sales ticket No. 347. (Don't forget about the credit memo, all taxes and discount.)
28 Collected cash sales, $4,450 plus necessary taxes.
29 Sold merchandise priced at $4,000, on account to Perfect Sales Co., sales ticket No. 348, terms 2/10, n/30.
30 Issued credit memorandum No. 11 to Perfect Sales Co. for $1,000 of merchandise returned from January 29 transaction, sales ticket No. 348.

Required:
1. Journalize the transactions.
2. Record to the accounts receivable ledger and post to general ledger as needed.
3. Prepare a schedule of accounts receivable.

PRACTICAL ACCOUNTING APPLICATION #1

Ronald Howard has been hired by Green Company to help reconstruct the sales journal, general journal, and cash receipts journal, which were recently destroyed in a fire. The owner of Green has supplied him with the following data. Please ignore dates, invoice numbers, etc., and enter the entries into the reconstructed sales journal, general journal, and cash receipts journal.

Accounts Receivable Ledger

P. Bond		M. Raff	
Bal. 100	150 CRJ	Bal. 200	
SJ 150	(Entitled to 2% discount)	SJ 100	

J. Smooth		R. Venner	
Bal. 300	1,000 GJ	Bal. 200	400 CRJ
SJ 2,000	1,000 CRJ ←	SJ 400	
SJ 1,000	500 GJ (Entitled to 1% discount)		

Partial General Ledger

Cash			Accounts Receivable			Shelving Equipment	
12,737			Bal. 800	1,000 GJ		Bal. 200	200 CRJ
			SJ 3,650	500 GJ			
				1,550 CRJ			

M. Rang, Capital			Sales			Sales Discount	
	1,000 Bal.			800		CRJ 13	
	5,000 (Additional			6,000 ←(5,000			
	investment			3,650 and			
	this month)			1,000)			

Sales Returns and Allowances	
GJ 1,000	
GJ 500	

PRACTICAL ACCOUNTING APPLICATION #2

The bookkeeper of Floore Company records credit sales in a sales journal and returns in a general journal. The bookkeeper did the following:

1. Recorded an $18 credit sales as $180 in the sales journal.

2. Correctly recorded a $40 sale in the sales journal but posted it to B. Blue's account as $400 in the accounts receivable ledger.

3. Made an additional error in determining the balance of J. B. Window Co. in the accounts receivable ledger.

4. Posted a sales return that was recorded in the general journal to the Sales Returns and Allowance account and the Accounts Receivable account but forgot to record to the B. Katz Co.

5. Added the total of the sales column incorrectly.

6. Posted a sales return to the Accounts Receivable account but not to the Sales Returns and Allowances account. Accounts Receivable ledger was recorded correctly.

Could you inform the bookkeeper as to when each error will be discovered?

ACCOUNTING RECALL
A Cumulative Approach

THIS EXAM REVIEWS CHAPTERS 1 THROUGH 6.

Your *Study Guide and Working Papers* have forms to complete this exam, as well as worked-out solutions. The page references next to each question identify what page to turn back to if you answer the question incorrectly.

PART I Vocabulary Review

Match the terms to the appropriate definition or phrase.

Page Ref.

(182)	1. Accounts receivable ledger	A.	Net sales—cost of goods sold
(192)	2. Goods and services tax	B.	Records sales on accounts
(180)	3. Net sales	C.	A contra revenue account
(147)	4. Closing	D.	Clears temporary accounts
(185)	5. Sales invoice	E.	In alphabetical order
(179)	6. Sales returns and allowances	F.	A value-added levy
(183)	7. Controlling account	G.	Records receipt of cash
(184)	8. Sales journal	H.	Gross sales less SRA less sales discount
(199)	9. Cash receipts journal	I.	A bill
(180)	10. Gross profit	J.	Accounts receivable

PART II True or False (Accounting Theory)

(181) 11. Cost of goods sold equals beginning inventory plus additional cost of goods brought into store plus ending inventory.

(203) 12. The controlling account balance at end of month will equal the sum of the subsidiary ledger.

(186) 13. Issuing a credit memo results in sales returns and allowances decreasing.

(203) 14. An (X) means no posting is necessary.

(203) 15. A (√) means the controlling account has been updated.

PART III Applications Problem (199-200)

Record the following transactions into the Cash Receipts Journal for Lang Co. Record and post as appropriate.

19XX

June 1 Received cheque from Al Aoy for invoice #1 less 5% discount.
    7 Cash sales collected $400.
   17 Received cheque from Alice Barr for invoice #2 less 5% discount.
   21 Sold store equipment at cost, $400.

Given: **Account Receivable Ledger**

Al Aoy	$ 600	Invoice #1
Alice Barr	1,000	Invoice #2

Partial General Ledger

	Account #	Balance
Cash	110	$ 500
Acc. receivable	120	1,600
Store equipment	130	1,400
Sales	410	900
Sales discount	420	—

CHAPTER SEVEN

SPECIAL JOURNALS:
Purchases and
Cash Payments

**IN THIS CHAPTER WE WILL COVER THE
FOLLOWING TOPICS:**

In the last chapter we looked at Art's Wholesale Clothing Company as the *seller* of merchandise. In this chapter we will focus on Art's Wholesale as the *buyer* of merchandise and other items. Many of the concepts and rules related to special journals and subsidiary ledgers in Chapter 6 will carry over to this chapter. This chapter continues the illustration of accounting for GST and shows how a business entity keeps track of the GST it pays. Before looking at two new special journals that Art's will use, let's introduce some key concepts and terms relating to cost of goods sold that will be helpful in dealing with the content of this chapter.

LEARNING UNIT 7-1

Cost of Goods Sold

We saw in Chapter 6 that net sales less cost of goods sold equalled gross profit. Up to this point we have defined cost of goods sold as follows:

Cost of Goods Sold
↓

Beginning Inventory	+	Additional cost of goods brought into store	–	Ending Inventory
↓		↓		↓
Cost of merchandise on hand to start accounting period		Cost of merchandise that is brought into store *during* the accounting period		Cost of merchandise that is on hand at end of accounting period

The following is a more detailed example of how cost of goods sold is calculated. Let's say that the cost of goods sold is $3,000, as it was in Chapter 6 (p. 179). Note that the bottom line in the accompanying diagram has the same $3,000 total as in Chapter 6 but is arrived at in a more detailed manner.

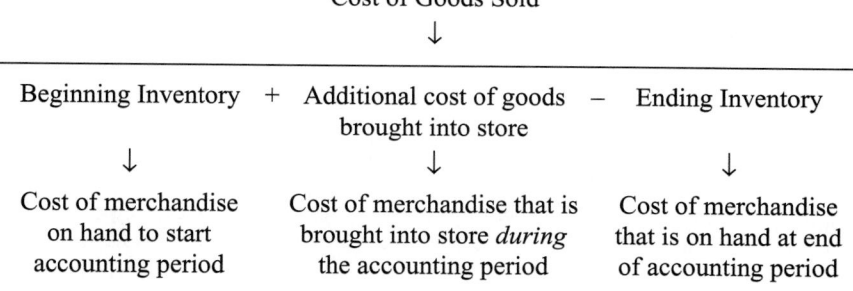

	COST OF GOODS SOLD		
(1) Beginning Inventory	$ 200	→	**Purchases, less**
(2) + Net Purchases	3,900		**Purchases Returns and Allowances, less**
(3) + Freight-In	100		**Purchases Discount**
(4) – Ending Inventory	–1,200	→	**F.O.B. Shipping Point—**
(5) = Cost of Goods Sold	$3,000		**Purchaser pays shipping cost**

1. Beginning Inventory

At the beginning of the accounting period, the cost of merchandise on hand is $200. (NOTE: Cost of merchandise is *not* the same thing as the selling price of merchandise.)

2. Net Purchases

The **Purchases** account accumulates the cost of additional merchandise *bought for resale*. (Anything else purchased, such as supplies or equipment, goes in its own

Purchases	
Dr.	Cr.
4,200	

**Purchases Returns
and Allowances**

Dr.	Cr.
	50

Purchases Discount

Dr.	Cr.
	250

**Net purchases is the
actual cost of bring-
ing additional mer-
chandise for resale
into the store before
considering freight.**

Freight-in

Dr.	Cr.
100	

**Cost of goods sold
account; buyer
responsible for
shipping costs.**

**F.O.B. is an abbrevia-
tion for Free on Board
the carrier.**

**Seller pays freight to
point of destination.**

account—the Purchases account is only for goods that will be resold. It represents a cost to the purchaser, and its usual balance is a debit.)

Purchases Returns and Allowances is an account that accumulates the amount the buyer returns for credit, or the amount of price reductions given the buyer for defective merchandise. (This corresponds to the Sales Returns and Allowances account we discussed in the last chapter, but looked at now from the purchaser's point of view rather than the seller's.) Think of the Purchases Returns and Allowances account as a *contra cost*-of-goods-sold account. It represents a savings to the purchaser, and its normal balance is a credit.

Purchases Discount is an account that accumulates the amount of cash discounts the purchaser receives for making payment within the discount period. (This corresponds to the Sales Discount account we mentioned in the last chapter, but looked at now from the purchaser's point of view.) It can represent a substantial savings to the buyer. Think of this account as a *contra cost*-of-goods-sold account.

Thus, net purchases consists of these accounts, as shown here:

Net purchases = Purchases − Purchases Returns and Allowances − Purchases Discount

$3,900   = $4,200   − $50   − $250

Now we have to look at who pays the shipping costs.

3. Freight-In

The account **Freight-In** accumulates the shipping costs of the *buyer*. Freight-In is added to the net cost of purchases and thus gives us the true cost of buying merchandise for resale. If the *seller* of the goods is responsible for paying the freight, it may be listed as a delivery expense (an operating expense) on the income statement. Let's look at some specific shipping terms that will help us determine who is responsible for the shipping costs.

F.O.B. Shipping Point

F.O.B. shipping point means that from the point goods are shipped it is the responsibility of the *purchaser* to cover the shipping costs. Seller pays *only* the freight to the shipping point. For example, if a Quebec City company buys goods from a Montreal company and shipping terms are F.O.B. Montreal, it is the responsibility of the Quebec City company (the buyer) to pay shipping costs from Montreal to Quebec City.

F.O.B. Destination

F.O.B. destination means the *seller* is responsible for covering the shipping cost till the goods reach their destination. For instance, if the previous example were F.O.B. Quebec City, the Montreal company (the seller) would cover the cost of shipping from Montreal to Quebec City.

Sometimes when the shipping terms are F.O.B. shipping point the seller will prepay the freight costs as a matter of convenience and will add it to the invoice of the purchaser.

Example:

Bill amount ($800 + $80 prepaid freight)	$880
Less 5% cash discount (.05 × $800)	40
Amount to be paid by buyer	$840

(NOTE: The discount is not taken on the $80 freight.)

If the seller ships goods F.O.B. shipping point, legal ownership (title) passes to the buyer *when the goods are shipped*. If goods are shipped by the seller F.O.B. destination, title will change *when goods have reached their destination*.

When does title change to goods shipped?

At this point you should be able to

1. Explain how cost of goods sold is calculated. (p. 227)
2. Explain why Purchases is part of cost of goods sold, while Purchases Returns and Allowances and Purchases Discounts are contra cost-of-goods-sold accounts. (p. 228)
3. Explain the difference between Freight-In and Delivery Expense. (p. 228)
4. Define, compare, and contrast F.O.B. shipping point versus F.O.B. destination. (p. 228)
5. Explain why purchases discounts are not taken on freight. (pp. 228-229)
6. Explain when title passes to the buyer if goods are shipped F.O.B. destination. (p. 229)

☐ SELF-REVIEW QUIZ 7-1

Which of the following statements are false?

1. Net purchases = Purchases – Purchases Returns and Allowances – Purchases Discount.
2. Freight-In is part of Purchases Discount
3. F.O.B. destination means the seller covers shipping cost and retains title till goods reach their destination.
4. Purchases discounts are not taken on freight.
5. Purchases Discount is a contra cost-of-goods-sold account.

■ *SOLUTION TO SELF-REVIEW QUIZ 7-1*

Number 2 is false.

LEARNING UNIT 7-2
Steps Taken in Purchasing Merchandise and Recording Purchases

Specific steps are taken by any merchandising company when purchasing goods for resale. Let's look at the steps taken by Art's Wholesale Clothing Company in ordering goods from Abby Blake Company on April 3.

Step 1: Prepare a Purchase Requisition at Art's Wholesale

Authorized personnel initiate purchase requisition.

When a low inventory level of ladies' jackets for resale is noted, a request to purchase more jackets is sent to the purchasing department. This internal document, called a **purchase requisition**, is sent to the purchasing department along with a duplicate copy for the accounting department. The third copy of this requisition remains with the department that initiated the request, to be used as a check on the purchasing department.

Step 2: Purchasing Department of Art's Wholesale Prepares a Purchase Order

Four copies of purchase order: (1) (original) to supplier, (2) to accounting department, (3) remains with department that initiated purchase requisition, (4) to file of purchasing department.

After a check of various price lists, as well as suppliers' catalogues, a business form called a **purchase order** is prepared by the purchasing department of Art's Wholesale, giving Abby Blake Company the authority to ship ladies' jackets ordered (see Figure 7-1).

Step 3: Sales Invoice Prepared by Abby Blake Company

Abby Blake Company receives the purchase order and prepares a *sales invoice*, as we showed in Chapter 6. The sales invoice for the seller is the **purchase invoice** for the buyer. A sales invoice is shown in Figure 7-2.

Purchase Order No. 1
Art's Wholesale Clothing Co.
1528 Belle Ave.
Toronto, Ontario, M5A 2LA

Purchased From: Abby Blake Company
12 Foster Road
Quebec City, PQ, G1M 4H3

Date: April 1, 19XX
Shipped VIA: Freight truck
Terms: 2/10, n/60
FOB: Quebec City

Quantity	Description	Unit Price	Total
100	Ladies' Jackets Code 14-0	$50	$5,000

Art's Wholesale
By: Bill Joy

Purchase order number must appear on all invoices.

FIGURE 7-1
Purchase Order

NOTE: F.O.B. is Quebec City. This means Art's Clothing will cover shipping costs.

FIGURE 7-2
Sales Invoice

Sales Invoice No. 228
Abby Blake Company
12 Foster Road
Quebec City, PQ, G1M 4H3

Sold to: Art's Wholesale
Clothing Co.
1528 Belle Ave.
Toronto, ON
M5A 2L4

Date: April 3, 19XX
Shipped VIA: Freight truck
Terms: 2/10, n/60
Your order No: 1
FOB: Quebec City

Quantity	Description	Unit Price	Total
100	Ladies' Jackets Code 14-0	$50	$5,000
	Freight		50
			$5,050

Note that the shipping costs are *prepaid* by Abby Blake and thus freight is added to the invoice. Remember, terms are shipping point Quebec City, and it is Art's responsibility to cover the shipping costs to Toronto from Quebec City. Abby pays the cost of shipping as a matter of convenience.

Step 4: Receiving the Jackets

When goods are received, Art's Wholesale inspects the shipment and completes a **receiving report**.

Step 5: Verifying the Numbers

The accounting department checks the purchase order, invoice, and receiving report to make sure all is in agreement and that no steps have been omitted before the invoice is approved for recording and payment. The form used for checking and approval is an **invoice approval form** (see Figure 7-3).

Invoice Approval Form

Purchase Order #
Requisition
check   _____

Purchase Order
check   _____

Receiving Report
check   _____

Invoice
check   _____

Approved for Payment   _____

FIGURE 7-3
Invoice Approval Form

An important point to keep in mind that Art's Wholesale records this purchase when the *invoice is approved for recording and payment*. Why? The purchase requisition, purchase order, and receiving report are supporting documents. On the other hand, Abby Blake Company records this transaction in its records when the sales invoice is prepared.

THE PURCHASES JOURNAL AND ACCOUNTS PAYABLE LEDGER

As we discussed in the last chapter, Art's Wholesale Clothing Company finds it helpful to use special journals as well as the general journal, and subsidiary ledgers as well as the general ledger. Let's look at the purchases journal and show how to journalize and post to the general ledger and record to the accounts payable ledger. The **purchases journal** is a multicolumn special journal that records the buying of merchandise or other items on account. The **accounts payable ledger** is a book or file that lists alphabetically the amounts owed to creditors from purchases on account.

For example, on April 3 Art's Wholesale Clothing Company records in its purchases journal the following:

Date:	April 3, 19XX
Account Credited:	Abby Blake Company
Date of Invoice:	April 3
Invoice Number:	228
Terms:	2/10, n/60
Accounts Payable:	$5,050; Purchases: $5,000; Freight-In, $50

As soon as the information is journalized in the purchases journal (see Fig. 7-4), you should:

See Fig. 7-4 for complete purchases journal.

1. Record to Abby Blake Co. in the accounts payable ledger to indicate that the amount owed is now $5,050. When this is complete, place a √ in the PR column of the purchases journal.

Note that the normal balance in the accounts payable ledger is a credit.

2. Post to Freight-in, account number 514, in the ledger right away. When this is complete, record the 514 in the PR column under sundry in the purchases journal.

The posting and recording rules are quite similar to those in the previous chapter, but here we are looking at the buyer rather than at the seller.

Let's look now at how Art's Wholesale handles returns as a buyer, not a seller.

THE DEBIT MEMORANDUM

A **debit memorandum** is a piece of paper issued by a customer to a seller, indicating that purchases returns and allowances have occurred. On April 6 Art's Wholesale had purchased men's hats for $800 from Thorpe Company (Figure 7-4, p. 233). On April 9, 20 hats with a value of $200 were found to have defective brims. Art issued a debit memorandum to Thorpe Company, as shown in Figure 7-5, p. 234. At some point in the future Thorpe will issue Art a credit memorandum, which we discussed in the last chapter. But right now we are concerned about the accounting records of Art's Wholesale Clothing Company.

FIGURE 7-4 Purchases Journal

Art's Wholesale Clothing Company
Purchases Journal

Page 1

Date	Account Credited	Date of Invoice	Inv. No.	Terms	PR	Accounts Payable Credit	Purchases Debit	Sundry-Dr. Account	PR	Amount
19XX April 3	Abby Blake Company	April 3	228	2/10, n/60	✔	5 050 00	5 000 00	Freight-In	514	50 00
4	Joe Francis Company	April 5	388		✔	4 000 00		Equip.	121	4 000 00
6	Thorpe Company	April 6	415	1/10, n/30	✔	800 00	800 00			
7	John Sullivan Company	April 6	516	n/10, EOM	✔	980 00	980 00			
12	Abby Blake Company	April 13	242	1/10, n/30	✔	600 00	600 00			
25	John Sullivan Company	April 26	612		✔	500 00		Supplies	115	500 00
30						11 930 00	7 380 00			4 550 00
						(211)	(511)			(X)

The (✔) in the purchases journal indicates the accounts payable ledger has been recorded *during* the month.

Total of Accounts Payable and Purchases posted to general ledger accounts at *end of month.*

Posted when transaction is entered:
Posted to general ledger account when transaction is entered

Total of sundry *not* posted

ACCOUNTS PAYABLE LEDGER

Abby Blake Co.

Dr.	Cr.
	5,050 PJ1 4/3
	600 PJ1 4/12

Joe Francis Co.

Dr.	Cr.
	4,000 PJ1 4/4

John Sullivan Co.

Dr.	Cr.
	980 PJ1 4/7
	500 PJ1 4/25

Thorpe Co.

Dr.	Cr.
	800 PJ1 4/6

PARTIAL GENERAL LEDGER

Supplies 115

4/25 PJ1 500	

Equipment 121

4/4 PJ1 4,000	

Tells us what page of journal information came from

Purchases 511

4/30 PJ1 7,380	

Freight-In 514

4/3 PJ1 50	

Accounts Payable 211

	11,930 PJ1 4/30

FIGURE 7-5
Debit Memorandum

Debit Memorandum	No. 1

Art's Wholesale
Clothing Company
1528 Belle Ave.
Toronto, ON, M5A 2L4

To: Thorpe Company   April 9, 19XX
      3 Access Road
      Fredericton, NB, E3B 4T3

WE DEBIT your account as follows:

Quantity		Unit Cost	Total
20	Men's Hats Code 827—defective brims	$10	$200

A debit memo shows that Art's does not owe as much money as was indicated in his purchases journal.

Let's look at a transaction analysis chart first.

Result of debit memo: "debits" or reduces Accounts Payable. On seller's books, accounts affected would include Sales Returns and Allowances and Accounts Receivable.

1 Accounts Affected	2 Category	3 ↑ ↓	4 Rules
Accounts Payable	Liability	↓	Dr.
Purchases Returns and Allowances	Contra cost-of-goods-sold	↑	Cr.

Purchases Returns and Allowances, a credit balance, causes a decrease to the cost of goods for resale.

Journalizing and Posting the Debit Memo

The following is the journal entry for the debit memorandum:

Purchases Returns and Allowances

Dr.	Cr.
–	+

A contra cost-of-goods-sold account

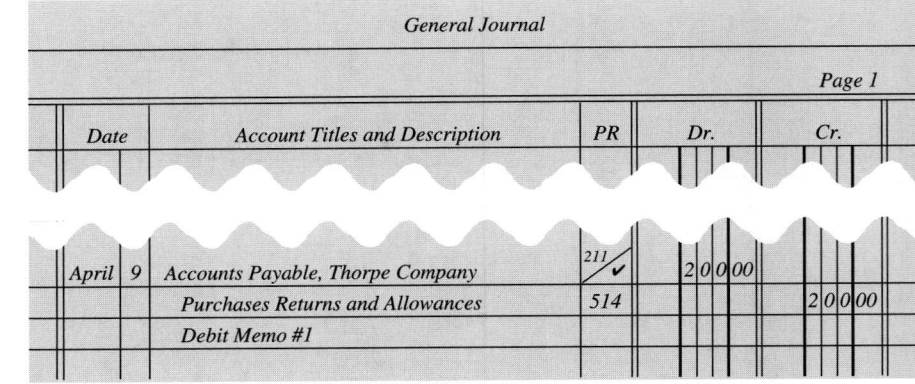

		General Journal				Page 1
Date		Account Titles and Description	PR	Dr.	Cr.	
April	9	Accounts Payable, Thorpe Company	211 ✔	2 0 0 00		
		Purchases Returns and Allowances	514		2 0 0 00	
		Debit Memo #1				

The two postings and one recording are:

1. 211—Post to Accounts Payable as a debit in the general ledger account no. 211. When this is done, place in the PR column the account number, 211, above the diagonal on the same line as Accounts Payable.
2. √—Record to Thorpe Co. in the accounts payable ledger to show we don't owe Thorpe as much money. When this is done, place a (√) in the journal in the PR column below the diagonal line on the same line as Accounts Payable.
3. 513—Post to Purchases Returns and Allowances as a credit in the general ledger (account no. 513). When this is done, place the account number, 513, in the posting reference column of the journal on the same line as Purchases Returns and Allowances. (If equipment was returned that was not merchandise for resale, we would credit Equipment and not Purchase Returns and Allowances.)

At this point you should be able to

1. Explain the relationship between a purchase requisition, a purchase order, and a purchase invoice. (p. 230)
2. Explain why a typical invoice approval form may be used. (p. 231)
3. Journalize transactions into a purchases journal. (p. 233)
4. Explain how to record to the accounts payable ledger and post to the general ledger from a purchases journal. (pp. 231-234)
5. Explain a debit memorandum and be able to journalize an entry resulting from its issuance. (p. 232)

☐ SELF-REVIEW QUIZ 7-2

Journalize the following transactions into the purchases journal or general journal for Munroe Co. Record to accounts payable ledger and post to general ledger accounts as appropriate. Use the same journal headings we used for Art's Wholesale Clothing Company.

19XX

May   5   Bought merchandise on account from Flynn Co., invoice No. 512, dated May 6, terms 1/10, n/30, $900.

       7   Bought merchandise from Marilyn Butler Company, invoice No. 403, dated May 7, terms n/10 EOM, $1,000.

    13   Issued debit memo no. 1 to Flynn Co. for merchandise returned, $300, from invoice No. 512.

    17   Purchased $400 of equipment on account from Marilyn Butler Company, invoice No. 413, dated May 18.

■ SOLUTION TO SELF-REVIEW QUIZ 7-2

Munroe Co.
Purchases Journal

Page 2

Date	Account Credited	Date of Invoice	Inv. No.	Terms	PR	Accounts Payable Credit	Purchases Debit	Sundry-Dr. Account	PR	Amount
19XX May 5	Flynn Co.	May 6	512	1/10, n/30	✔	900 00	900 00			
7	John Butler	May 7	403	n/10, EOM	✔	1 000 00	1 000 00			
17	John Butler	May 18	413		✔	400 00		Equip.	121	400 00
31						2 300 00	1 900 00			400 00
						(212)	(512)			(X)

Munroe Company
General Journal

Page 1

Date	Account Titles and Description	PR	Dr.	Cr.
19XX May 13	Account Payable, Flynn Co.	212 ✔	300 00	
	Purchases Returns and Allowances	513		300 00

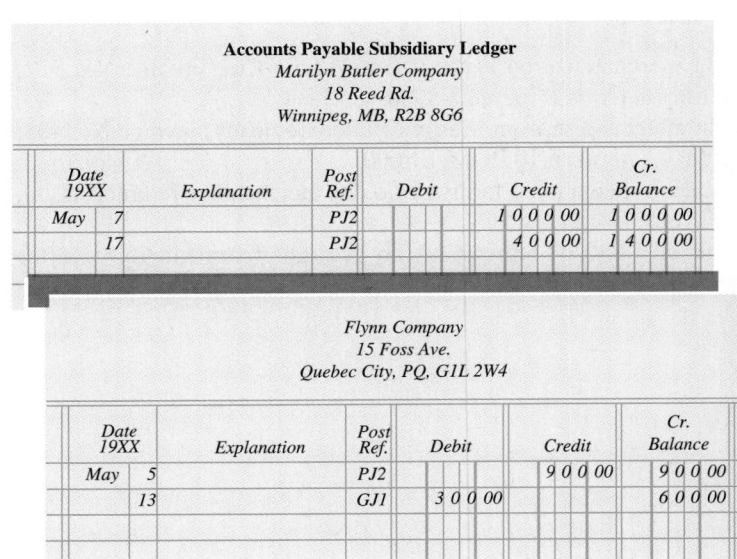

Accounts Payable Subsidiary Ledger
Marilyn Butler Company
18 Reed Rd.
Winnipeg, MB, R2B 8G6

Date 19XX	Explanation	Post Ref.	Debit	Credit	Cr. Balance
May 7		PJ2		1 000 00	1 000 00
17		PJ2		400 00	1 400 00

Flynn Company
15 Foss Ave.
Quebec City, PQ, G1L 2W4

Date 19XX	Explanation	Post Ref.	Debit	Credit	Cr. Balance
May 5		PJ2		900 00	900 00
13		GJ1	300 00		600 00

Partial General Ledger

Equipment   Acct. No. 121

Date 19XX	Explanation	Post Ref.	Debit	Credit	DR or CR	Balance
May 17		PJ2	4 0 0 0 00		DR	4 0 0 0 00

Accounts Payable   Acct. No. 212

Date 19XX	Explanation	Post Ref.	Debit	Credit	DR or CR	Balance
May 13		GJ2	3 0 0 00		DR	3 0 0 00
31		PJ2		2 3 0 0 00	CR	2 0 0 0 00

Purchases   Acct. No. 512

Date 19XX	Explanation	Post Ref.	Debit	Credit	DR or CR	Balance
May 31		PJ2	1 9 0 0 00		DR	1 9 0 0 00

Purchases, Returns and Allowances   Acct. No. 513

Date 19XX	Explanation	Post Ref.	Debit	Credit	DR or CR	Balance
May 13		GJ1		3 0 0 00	CR	3 0 0 00

LEARNING UNIT 7-3

The Cash Payments Journal and Schedule of Accounts Payable

Art's Clothing will record all payments made in cash (or by cheque) in a **cash payments journal** (which is also called a *cash disbursements journal*). The structure of the cash payments journal in many ways resembles that of the cash receipts journal we discussed in Chapter 6, but now we are looking at the outward flow of cash instead of the inward flow (which means that the debits and credits are reversed). The following transactions occurred in April and affected the cash payments journal:

April   2   Issued cheque no. 1 to Pete Blum for insurance paid in advance, $900.
        7   Issued cheque no. 2 to Joe Francis Company in payment of its April 5 invoice No. 388.

> 9   Issued cheque no. 3 to Rick Flo Co. for merchandise purchased for cash, $800.
>
> 12 Issued cheque no. 4 to Thorpe Company in payment of its April 6 invoice No. 414 less the return and discount.
>
> 28 Issued cheque no. 5, $700, for salaries paid.

Posting and recording rules for this journal are similar to those for the cash receipts journal in Chapter 6.

The diagram in Figure 7-6 shows the cash payments journal for the end of April along with the recordings to the accounts payable ledger and postings to the general ledger. Study the diagram; we will review it in a moment.

JOURNALIZING, RECORDING, AND POSTING FROM THE CASH PAYMENTS JOURNAL TO THE ACCOUNTS PAYABLE LEDGER AND THE GENERAL LEDGER

Let's look at the diagram in Figure 7-6 (pp. 239-240) to see how Art's Wholesale recorded the payment of cash on April 12 to Thorpe Company. Back in the purchases journal on April 6, Art had purchased from Thorpe merchandise on account for $800. Now on April 12 Art is paying the amount owed less a purchases discount of 1 percent. As soon as the entry is made into the cash payments journal, the amount owed Thorpe ($800 – $200 returns) is *immediately recorded* in the accounts payable ledger. Note that the payment reduces the balance to Thorpe to zero. Art's Wholesale receives a $6 purchases discount. Be careful not to take a discount on sales tax or freight.

Now let's review some of the end-of-month posting rules, as well as sundry columns. At the end of the month the totals of the Cash, Purchases Discount, and Accounts Payable accounts are posted to the general ledger. The total of sundry is *not* posted. The accounts Prepaid Insurance, Purchases, and Salaries are posted to the general ledger at the time the entry is put in the journal.

The cash payments journal of Art's Wholesale can be crossfooted as follows:

Debit Columns		=	Credit Columns		
Sundry	+ Accounts Payable	=	Purchases Discounts	+	Cash
$2,400	+ $4,600	=	$6	+	$6,994
$7,000		=	$7,000		

Now let's prove that the sum of the accounts payable ledger at the end of the month is equal to the controlling account, Accounts Payable, at the end of April for Art's Wholesale Clothing Company.

Schedule of Accounts Payable

From Figure 7-6 (pp. 239-240) let's list the creditors that have an ending balance in the accounts payable ledger of Art's. This listing of amounts owed is called a **schedule of accounts payable**, which is shown in Figure 7-7 (p. 241).

At the end of the month the total owed ($7,130) in Accounts Payable, the controlling account in the general ledger, does indeed equal the sum owed the individual creditors that are listed on the schedule of accounts payable.

If the schedule doesn't agree with the controlling account, (1) check that the journalizing, recording, and posting are completed and (2) double-check the balances of each title.

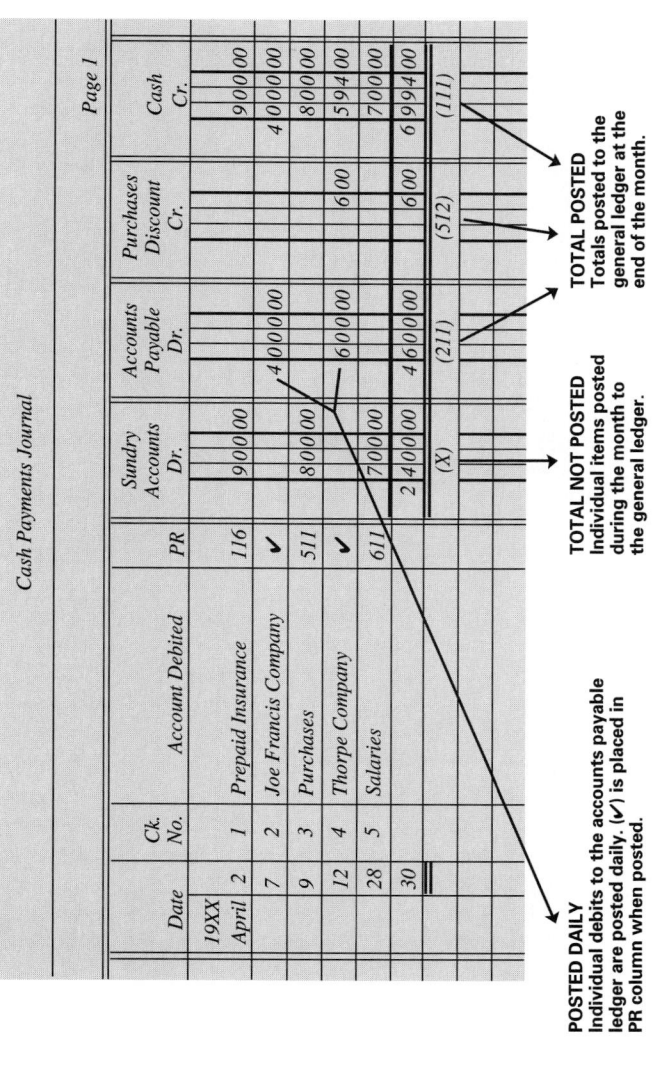

FIGURE 7-6

Cash Payments Journal and Posting

Cash Payments Journal — Page 1

Date	Ck. No.	Account Debited	PR	Sundry Accounts Dr.	Accounts Payable Dr.	Purchases Discount Cr.	Cash Cr.
19XX							
April 2	1	Prepaid Insurance	116	900 00			900 00
7	2	Joe Francis Company	✔		4000 00		4000 00
9	3	Purchases	511	800 00			800 00
12	4	Thorpe Company	✔		600 00	6 00	594 00
28	5	Salaries	611	700 00			700 00
30				2400 00	4600 00	6 00	6994 00
				(X)	(211)	(512)	(111)

POSTED DAILY
Individual debits to the accounts payable ledger are posted daily. (✔) is placed in PR column when posted.

TOTAL NOT POSTED
Individual items posted during the month to the general ledger.

TOTAL POSTED
Totals posted to the general ledger at the end of the month.

Partial General Ledger

Cash — Acct. No. 111

Date 19XX	Explanation	Post Ref.	Debit	Credit	DR or CR	Balance
April 30		CRJ1	1432 4 00		DR	1432 4 00
30		CPJ1		699 4 00	DR	733 0 00

Prepaid Insurance — Acct. No. 116

Date 19XX	Explanation	Post Ref.	Debit	Credit	DR or CR	Balance
April 2		CPJ1	900 00		DR	900 00

Accounts Payable Ledger

NAME Abby Blake Co.
ADDRESS 12 Foster Rd., Quebec City, PQ, GIM 4H3

Date	Explanation	Post Ref.	Debit	Credit	Cr. Balance
19XX					
April 3		PJ1		505 00	505 00
12		PJ1		60 00	565 00

NAME Joe Francis Co.
ADDRESS 2 Roundy Rd., Edmonton, AB, T5H 2E7

Date	Explanation	Post Ref.	Debit	Credit	Cr. Balance
19XX					
April 4		PJ1		4000 00	4000 00
7		CPJ1	4000 00		– 0 –

FIGURE 7-6 (cont'd)   **Cash Payments Journal and Posting**

Accounts Payable   Acct. No. 211

Date 19XX	Explanation	Post Ref.	Debit	Credit	DR or CR	Balance
April 9		GJ1	2 0 00		DR	2 0 0 00
30		PJ1		1 1 9 3 0 00	CR	1 1 7 3 0 00
30		CPJ1	4 6 0 0 00		CR	7 1 3 0 00

Purchases   Acct. No. 511

Date 19XX	Explanation	Post Ref.	Debit	Credit	DR or CR	Balance
April 9		CPJ1	8 0 0 00		DR	8 0 0 00
30		PJ1	7 3 8 0 00		DR	8 1 8 0 00

Purchases Discount   Acct. No. 512

Date 19XX	Explanation	Post Ref.	Debit	Credit	DR or CR	Balance
April 30		CPJ1		6 00	CR	6 00

Salaries Expense   Acct. No. 611

Date 19XX	Explanation	Post Ref.	Debit	Credit	DR or CR	Balance
April 28		CPJ1	7 0 0 00		DR	7 0 0 00

NAME *Joan Sullivan Co.*
ADDRESS *18 Print St., Regina, SA, S4P 2A6*

Date	Explanation	Post Ref.	Debit	Credit	Cr. Balance
19XX April 7		PJ1		9 8 0 00	9 8 0 00
25		PJ1		5 0 0 00	1 4 8 0 00

NAME *Thorpe Co.*
ADDRESS *3 Access Rd., Fredericton, NB, E3B 4T3*

Date	Explanation	Post Ref.	Debit	Credit	Cr. Balance
19XX April 6		PJ1		8 0 00	8 0 00
9		GJ1	2 0 00		6 0 00
12		CPJ1	6 0 00		– 0 –

NAME *Joe Francis Co.*
ADDRESS *2 Roundy Rd., Edmonton, AB, T5H 2E7*

Date	Explanation	Post Ref.	Debit	Credit	Cr. Balance
19XX April 4		PJ1		4 0 0 00	4 0 0 00
7		CPJ1	4 0 0 00		– 0 –
14		GJ4	4 0 0 00		(4 0 0 00)

Note on accounts payable balance: Very occasionally (perhaps due to the return of defective goods after they have been paid for) a debit balance may be called for in accounts payable. Debit balances are opposite to the normal credit balance and are signified by placing the balance in brackets. For example, suppose we get a credit note from Joe Francis Co. for $400.00 after we have paid off their account completely. Their account would then appear as follows:

FIGURE 7-7

**Schedule of
Accounts
Payable**

Art's Wholesale Clothing Company *Schedule of Accounts Payable* *April 30, 19XX*	
Abby Blake Co.	$ 5 6 5 0 00
John Sullivan Co.	1 4 8 0 00
Total Accounts Payable	$ 7 1 3 0 00

Trade Discounts

Trade discounts are reductions from the purchase price to customers who buy items to resell or who will use the items to produce other saleable goods.

Amount of Trade Discount = List Price – Net Price

Different trade discounts are available to different classes of customers. These trade discounts are often listed in catalogues that contain the list price as well as the amount of trade discount available. To allow for flexibility, the catalogue is usually updated by discount sheets rather than the printing of a new catalogue each time a price changes on a certain item.

A key point is that the trade discount has *no relationship* to whether a customer is paying a bill early. Trade discounts and list prices are not going to be shown in the accounts of either the purchaser or the seller of merchandise. Cash discounts are not taken on the amount of trade discount.

For example, let's look at the following:

List price, $800
30% Trade discount
5% Cash discount
Thus: Invoice cost of $560 ($800 – $240) less the cash discount of $28
        ($560 × .05) results in a final cost of $532 if the cash discount is taken.

The purchaser as well as the seller would record the invoice amount at $560.

At this point you should be able to

1. Journalize, record, and post transactions utilizing a cash payments journal. (pp. 238-240)

2. Prepare a schedule of accounts payable. (p. 238)

3. Compare and contrast a cash discount to a trade discount. (p. 241)

□ **SELF-REVIEW QUIZ 7-3**

Given the following information, journalize, crossfoot, and when appropriate, record and post the transactions of Melissa Company. Use the same headings as used for Art's Clothing. All purchases discounts are 2/12, n/30. The cash payments journal is page 2.

ACCOUNTS PAYABLE LEDGER

NAME	BALANCE	INVOICE NO.
Bob Finkelstein	$300	488
Al Jeep	200	410

PARTIAL GENERAL LEDGER

ACCOUNT	NO.	BALANCE
Cash	110	$700
Accounts Payable	210	500
Purchases Discount	511	—
Advertising Expense	610	—

19XX

June 1 Issued cheque no. 15 to Al Jeep in payment of its May 25 invoice No. 410 less purchases discount.

8 Issued cheque no. 16 to Moss Advertising Co. to pay advertising bill due, $75, no discount.

9 Issued cheque no. 17 to Bob Finkelstein in payment of its May 28 Invoice No. 488 less purchases discount.

■ *SOLUTION TO SELF-REVIEW QUIZ 7-3*

Melissa Company
Cash Payments Journal

Page 2

Date		Chq. No.	Account Debited	PR	Sundry Accounts Dr.	Accounts Payable Dr.	Purchases Discount Cr.	Cash Cr.
19XX June	1	15	Al Jeep	✔		200 00	4 00	196 00
	8	16	Advertising Expense	610	75 00			75 00
	9	17	Bob Finkelstein	✔		300 00	6 00	294 00
	30				75 00	500 00	10 00	565 00
					(X)	(210)	(511)	(110)

$75 + $500 = $10 + $565
$575 = $575

Accounts Payable Ledger

NAME Bob Finkelstein
ADDRESS 112 Flying Highway, Montreal, PQ, H1K 2H7

Date 19XX		Explanation	Post Ref.	Debit	Credit	Cr. Balance
June	1	Balance	✔			300 00
	15		CPJ2	300 00		– 0 –

NAME   Al Jeep
ADDRESS   118 Wang Rd., London, ON, N5X 2Y3

Date 19XX		Explanation	Post Ref.	Debit	Credit	Cr. Balance
June	1	Balance	✔			2 0 0 00
	1		CPJ	2 0 0 00		– 0 –

Partial General Ledger

Cash   Acct. No. 110

Date 19XX		Explanation	Post Ref.	Debit	Credit	DR or CR	Balance
June	1	Balance	✔			DR	7 0 0 00
	30		CPJ2		5 6 5 00	DR	1 3 5 00

Accounts Payable   Acct. No. 210

Date 19XX		Explanation	Post Ref.	Debit	Credit	DR or CR	Balance
June	1	Balance	✔			CR	5 0 0 00
	30		CPJ2	5 0 0 00			– 0 –

Purchases Discount   Acct. No. 511

Date 19XX		Explanation	Post Ref.	Debit	Credit	DR or CR	Balance
June	30		CPJ2		1 0 00	CR	1 0 00

Advertising Expense   Acct. No. 610

Date 19XX		Explanation	Post Ref.	Debit	Credit	DR or CR	Balance
June	8		CPJ2	7 5 00		DR	7 5 00

LEARNING UNIT 7-4
GST Paid on Purchases

OVERVIEW

In the previous chapter we learned that GST collected on sales needs to be sent to the government periodically. No surprises here—this is very similar to PST. However, the GST is what we refer to as a *value-added tax*. Without getting overly technical, each business in effect adds a *net* tax to the "improvement" in value it adds to the goods and/or services it provides or sells. If a company buys some merchandise (to resell) for $1,000 and actually sells it for $1,500, then the GST is applicable only to the $500 difference.

Companies remit the net difference between the GST they collect on sales and the GST they pay on purchases.

While that is true, the tax works in the following manner:

First, the business charges the 7% on the selling price of $1,500. This would amount to $105 (7% × $1,500) (covered in chapter 6).

Second, the business pays the 7% tax on the $1,000 merchandise purchased. This amounts to $70 (7% × $1,000) (covered in this chapter).

Finally, the tax sent to the federal government is only $35 (7% × $500) because the business gets a refund for the tax it paid on the purchase.

Summary:

Tax collected on sale of merchandise 7% × $1,500.00 =	105.00
Tax paid on purchase of merchandise 7% × $1,000.00 =	$70.00
Net tax to be remitted	$35.00

Businesses do not keep separate track of GST on each item of inventory they sell, of course. However the above example makes it plain that companies must keep track of the total GST they pay so they can claim a refund when they calculate the GST they must periodically send to the federal government.

This learning unit details the accounting tasks which must be handled properly to accurately record GST.

RECORDING PURCHASES WITH GST

In the above learning units we discussed purchases and cash payments without GST. On p. 230 in Figure 7-1 a typical purchase order is illustrated. Many companies have not changed their purchase orders to include GST since it is now the law for GST to be included even if the purchase order says nothing. Other companies may refer to the fact that the specified price does not include GST. They expect that 7% GST will be added. Still other companies specify and calculate the GST. These companies would produce a purchase order which would look like the one shown below in Figure 7-8.

When the supplier fills the purchase order, an invoice will be prepared which includes GST. On p. 231 in Figure 7-2 a sales invoice before GST was illustrated. The same sales invoice incorporating GST is shown below in Figure 7-9. Note that GST is charged on the shipping charges as well as the amount charged for the goods.

FIGURE 7-8

**Purchase Order
with GST**

Purchase Order No. 1
Art's Wholesale Clothing Co.
1528 Belle Ave.
Toronto, Ontario, M5A 2LA

Purchased From:	*Abby Blake Company*	*Date: April 1, 19XX*
	12 Foster Road	*Shipped VIA: Freight truck*
	Quebec City, PQ, G1M 4H3	*Terms: 2/10, n/60*
		FOB: Quebec City

Quantity	*Description*	*Unit Price*	*Total*
100	*Ladies' Jackets Code 14-0*	*$50*	*$5,000.00*
	Add GST		*350.00*
	Total Price Before Shipping		*$5,350.00*

Art's Wholesale
By: Bill Joy

Purchase order number must appear on all invoices.

FIGURE 7-9

**Sales Invoice
with GST**

Sales Invoice No. 228
Abby Blake Company
12 Foster Road
Quebec City, PQ, G1M 4H3

Sold From:	*Art's Wholesale*	*Date: April 3, 19XX*
	Clothing Co.	*Shipped VIA: Freight truck*
	1528 Belle Ave.	*Terms: 2/10, n/60*
	Toronto, ON	*Your order No: 1*
	M5A 2L4	*FOB: Quebec City*

Quantity	*Description*	*Unit Price*	*Total*
100	*Ladies' Jackets Code 14-0*	*$50*	*$5,000.00*
	Freight		*50.00*
	Sub-total		*$5,050.00*
	GST		*353.50*
	Total		*$5,403.50*
	GST Reg. No. 142714982		

This invoice (and others) is recorded by the purchaser in a manner similar to the original example shown earlier in this chapter (see Figure 7-4, p. 233). The major change is that now the purchases journal has one additional column — **prepaid GST**. Figure 7-10 shows how the purchases journal would appear with GST included.

NOTE: Recording purchases with GST is very similar to recording purchases with no GST—just one extra column is needed.

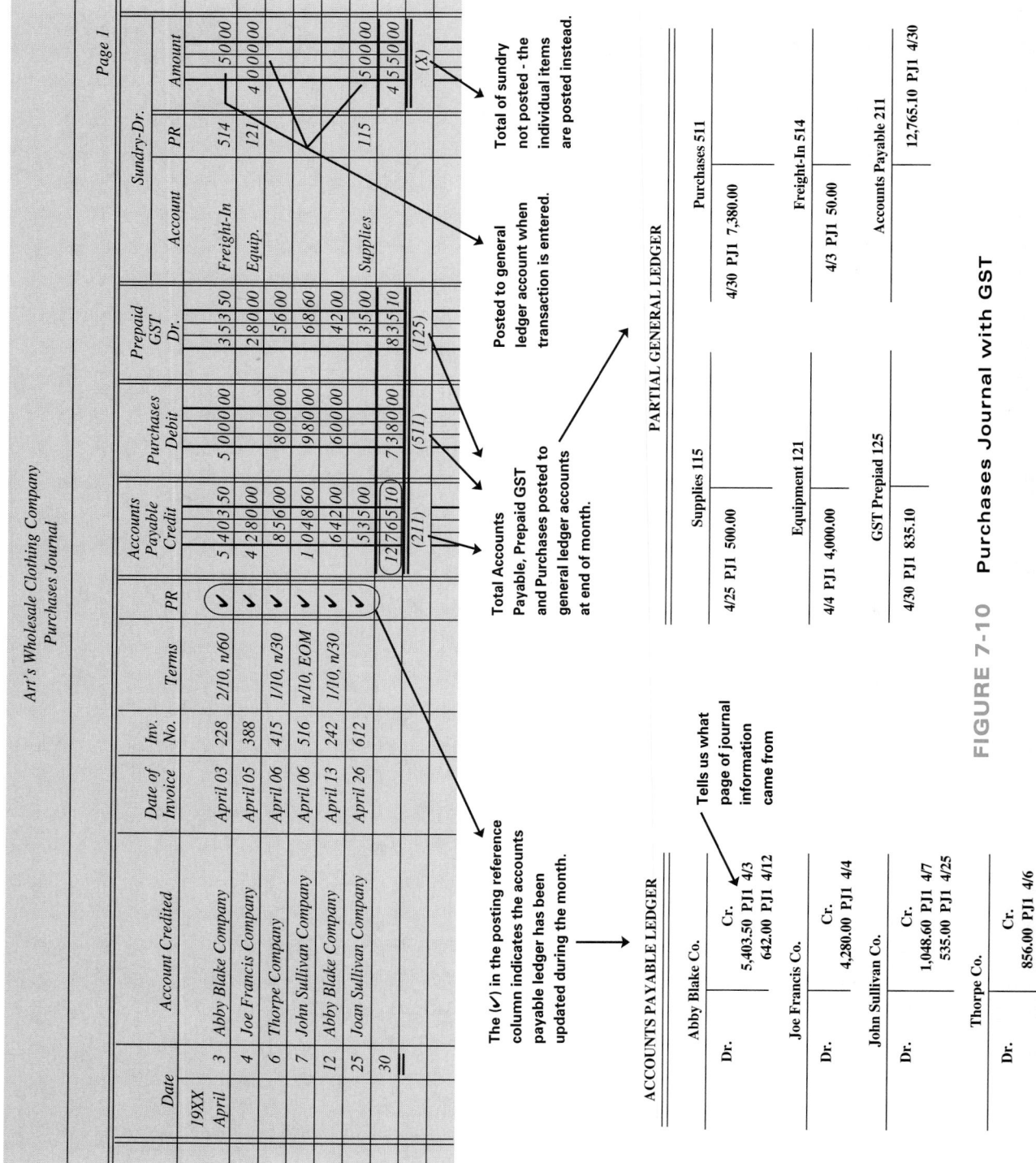

FIGURE 7-10   Purchases Journal with GST

Note the following while you review Figure 7-10:

1. GST is paid on equipment purchases as well as on purchases of goods for resale.
2. A different account (number 125) is used to record GST on purchases than was used to record sales (recall account number 212 was used in chapter 6 for recording GST on sales). While not absolutely required, this procedure can make the preparation of the periodic governmental returns less of a burden.
3. The basic operation of the purchases journal is much the same as before. Crossfooting reveals that the addition of a GST column has not disturbed the equality of debits (7,380 + 4,550 + 835.10 = 12,765.10) and credits (12,765.10).
4. The amounts posted to the accounts payable ledger are posted at the same time and in the same way as previously. The amounts are now higher, of course, as they include GST at 7%.

THE DEBIT MEMORANDUM

As already discussed, from time to time purchased goods are returned to suppliers due to insufficient quality, defective manufacturing and the like. We have seen an example of a debit memorandum which is prepared when goods are returned (refer to p. 234, Figure 7-5). When GST is charged on the original purchase, it must also be added to the debit memorandum as shown in Figure 7-11 below.

A debit memorandum with GST is very similar to a supplier's invoice with GST except that the amounts are opposite in meaning and effect, and often smaller.

	Debit Memorandum		*No. 1*

Art's Wholesale
Clothing Company
1528 Belle Ave.
Toronto, ON, M5A 2L4

To: Thorpe Company
3 Access Road
Fredericton, NB, E3B 4T3

WE DEBIT your account as follows:

Quantity		*Unit Cost*	*Total*
20	*Men's Hats Code 827—defective brims*	*$10.00*	*$200.00*
	Add., GST @ 7%		*14.00*
	Total Adjustment		*$214.00*

FIGURE 7-11

Debit Memorandum with GST

Recording this debit memorandum is usually done in the general journal, although a specialized journal could be used if a large number of debit memos were common in a given business. Art's Wholesale Clothing Company would record the debit memorandum (illustrated in Figure 7-11) in their general journal (see Figure 7-12, p. 248):

FIGURE 7-12

**Posting the Debit
Memo with GST**

General Journal

					Page 1	
Date	Account Titles and Description	PR	Dr.		Cr.	
19XX		211				
April 9	Account Payable, Thorpe Company	✔	2 1 4 00			
	Purchases Returns and Allowances	513			2 0 0 00	
	GST Prepaid	125			1 4 00	
	To record Debit Memo #1					

The four postings are:

1. 211 – Post to Accounts Payable as a debit in the general ledger account No. 211. When this is done, place in the PR column the account number, 211, above the diagonal on the same line as Accounts Payable.
2. √ – Post to Thorpe Co. in the accounts payable ledger to show we don't owe Thorpe as much money. When this is done place a (√) in the journal in the PR column below the diagonal line on the same line as Accounts Payable.
3. 513 – Post to Purchases Returns and Allowances as a credit in the general ledger (account No. 513). When this is done, place the account number, 513, in the posting reference column of the journal on the same line as Purchases Returns and Allowances (if equipment was returned that was not merchandise for resale, we would credit Equipment and not Purchases Returns and Allowances).
4. 125 – Post to GST Prepaid as a credit. This acts to increase the amount of GST owed to the federal government because it decreases the amount which is claimable to offset the liability recorded in account 212 (see Chapter 6 for details of this account).

□ **SELF-REVIEW QUIZ 7-4**

Journalize the following transactions into the purchases journal (page 2) or general journal (page 1) for Munroe Co. Post to accounts payable ledger and general ledger accounts as appropriate. Use the same journal headings we used for Art's Wholesale Clothing Company.

19XX

May 5   Bought merchandise on account from Flynn Co., invoice No. 5121, dated May 6, terms 1/10,n/30 plus GST $63. Total $963.

7   Bought merchandise from Marilyn Butler Company, invoice No. 403, dated May 7, terms n/10 EOM, $1,000 plus GST $70. Total $1,070.

13   Issued debit memo No. 1 to Flynn Co. for merchandise returned, $300, from invoice No. 512, plus GST $21. Total $321.

17   Purchased $400 of equipment on account from Marilyn Butler Company, invoice No. 413, dated May 18, plus GST $28. Total $428.

■ SOLUTION TO SELF-REVIEW QUIZ 7-4

Munroe Co.
Purchases Journal

Page 2

Date	Account Credited	Date of Invoice	Inv. No.	Terms	PR	Accounts Payable Credit	Purchases Debit	GST Prepaid Debit	Sundry-Dr. Account	PR	Amount
19XX May 5	Flynn Co.	May 6	5121	1/10, n/30	✔	963 00	900 00	63 00			
7	Marilyn Butler Co.	May 7	403	n/10, EOM	✔	1070 00	1000 00	70 00			
17	Marilyn Butler Co.	May 18	413		✔	428 00		28 00	Equip.	121	400 00
31						2461 00	1900 00	161 00			400 00
						(212)	(512)	(125)			(X)

Munroe Co.
General Journal

Page 1

Date	Account Titles and Description	PR	Dr.	Cr.
19XX May 13	Account Payable, Flynn Co.	212 ✔	321 00	
	Purchases Returns and Allowances	513		300 00
	GST Prepaid	125		21 00

THE CASH PAYMENTS JOURNAL

The addition of GST does not alter the fact that Art's Clothing will record all payments made by cash (or most likely by cheque) in a cash payments journal. However, as you probably suspect, this journal now has one column more than the original illustration which is shown in Figure 7-6.

Please trace the following cash disbursements through the revised Figure 7-13 shown below. The following (revised) transactions affected the cash disbursements journal:

April 2   Issued cheque no. 1 to Pete Blum for insurance paid in advance, $900.
       7   Issued cheque no. 2 to Joe Francis Company in payment of its April 5 invoice No. 388.
       9   Issued cheque no. 3 to Flo Co. for merchandise purchased for cash $800 plus GST $56. Total $856.
       12 Issued cheque no. 4 to Thorpe Company in payment of its April 6 invoice No. 414 less the return and discount.
       28 Issued cheque no. 5, $700 salaries paid.

In tracing the cash payments to the payments journal, a few points may be of interest:

1. There is no GST on the insurance payment of $900. Insurance premiums are classed as financial services and no GST is paid on these.
2. Similarly, no GST is paid on salaries of $700 on April 28.
3. GST does not affect the $6 purchase discount allowed when payment is made to the Thorpe Company on April 12. This discount is calculated only on the $600 (net) purchase, not on the $642 which is the total amount payable due to the extra 7% GST. The actual amount paid is $636 because the $642 is reduced by $6 due to the allowed purchase discount.

SCHEDULE OF ACCOUNTS PAYABLE

Notice that from Figure 7-13 (p. 249) it is not difficult to prepare a schedule of accounts payable at month end. This schedule would look like:

Art's Wholesale Clothing Company
Schedule of Accounts Payable
April 30, 19XX

Abby Blake Co.	$6,045.50
Joan Sullivan Co.	1,583.60
Total Accounts Payable	$7,629.10

If you refer again to Figure 7-13 you can see that $7,629.10 is exactly the balance in account 211—Accounts Payable. Hence, the subsidiary ledger accounts are in agreement with the controlling account in the general ledger. As always, if the total of the individual accounts in the accounts payable ledger does not agree with the control account, it will be necessary to double check all postings and the mathematical computations of balances in each supplier's account. Also, be sure that any entries made in the general journal are posted to the general ledger accounts.

FIGURE 7-13   Cash Payments Journal and Posting with GST

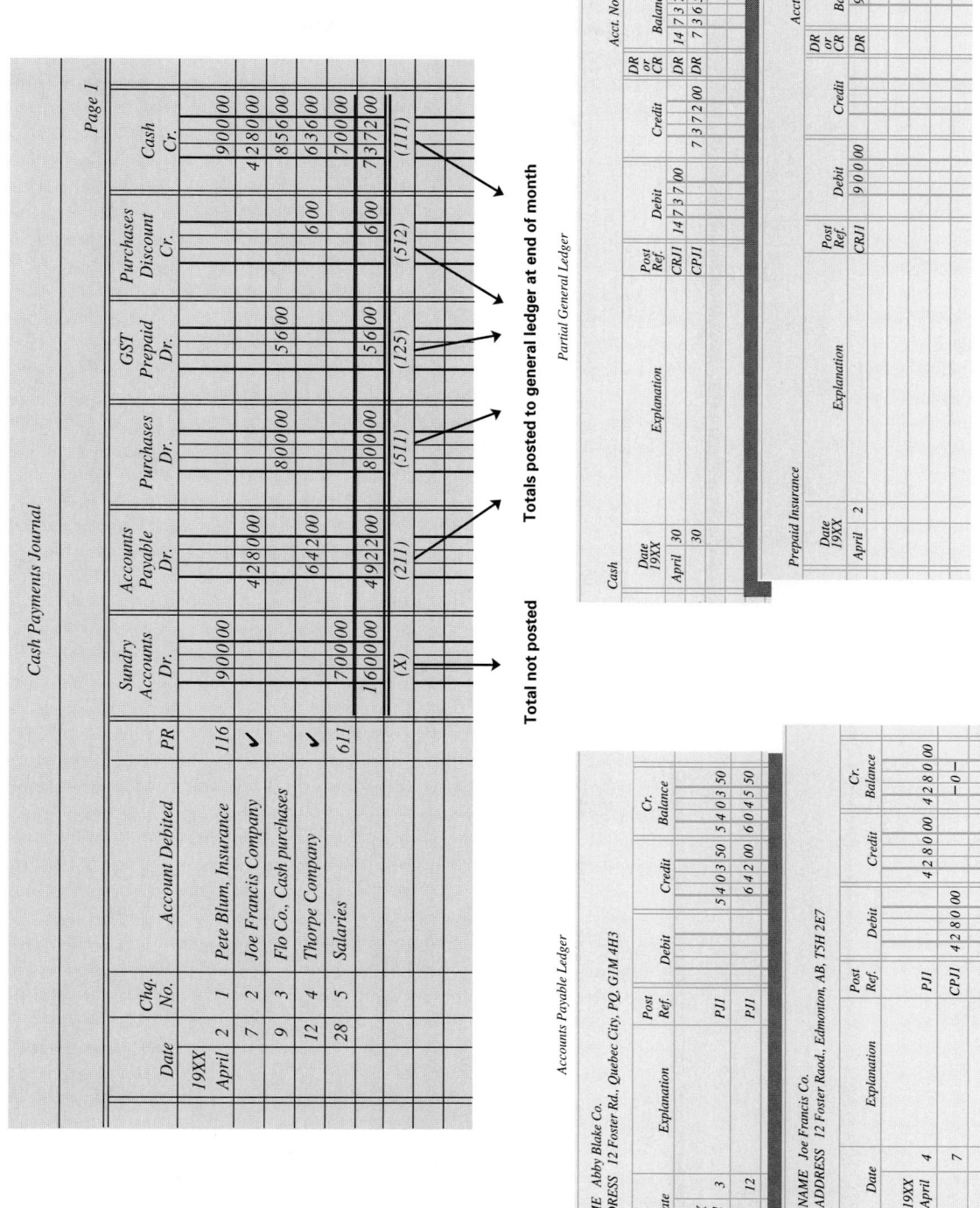

FIGURE 7-13 (cont'd)   Cash Payments Journal and Posting with GST

GST Prepaid — Acct. No. 125

Date 19XX	Explanation	Post Ref.	Debit	Credit	DR or CR	Balance
April 9		GJI		14 00	CR	14 00
30		PJI	8 35 10		DR	8 21 10
30		CPJI	5 60		DR	8 77 10

Accounts Payable — Acct. No. 211

Date 19XX	Explanation	Post Ref.	Debit	Credit	DR or CR	Balance
April 9		GJI	2 1 4 00		DR	2 1 4 00
30		PJI		12 7 65 00	CR	12 5 51 10
30		CPJI	4 9 22 00		CR	7 6 29 10

Purchases — Acct. No. 511

Date 19XX	Explanation	Post Ref.	Debit	Credit	DR or CR	Balance
April 30		PJI	7 3 8 00		DR	7 3 8 00
30		CPJI	8 0 00		DR	8 1 8 00

Purchase Discount — Acct. No. 512

Date 19XX	Explanation	Post Ref.	Debit	Credit	DR or CR	Balance
April 30		CPJI		6 00	CR	6 00

Salaries — Acct. No. 611

Date 19XX	Explanation	Post Ref.	Debit	Credit	DR or CR	Balance
April 30		CPJI	7 0 0 00		DR	7 0 0 00

NAME Joan Sullivan Co.
ADDRESS 18 Print St., Regina, SA, S4P 2A6

Date	Explanation	Post Ref.	Debit	Credit	Cr. Balance
19XX April 7		PJI		10 4 8 60	10 4 8 60
25		PJI		5 3 5 00	15 8 3 60

NAME Thorpe Company
ADDRESS 3 Access Rd., Fredericton, NB, E3B 4T3

Date	Explanation	Post Ref.	Debit	Credit	Cr. Balance
19XX April 6		PJI		8 5 6 00	8 5 6 00
9		GJI	2 1 4 00		6 4 2 00
12		CPJI	6 4 2 00		– 0 –

Note on accounts payable balance: Very occasionally (due, perhaps to the return of defective goods after they have been paid for) a debit balance may be called for on accounts payable. Debit balances are opposite to the normal credit balance and are signified by placing the balance in brackets. For example, suppose we get a credit note from Joe Francis Co. for $428.00 after we have paid off their account completely. Their account would then appear as follows:

NAME Joe Francis Co.
ADDRESS 2 Roundy Rd., Edmonton, AB, T5H 2E7

Date	Explanation	Post Ref.	Debit	Credit	Cr. Balance
19XX April 4		PJI		4 2 8 00	4 2 8 00
7		CPJI	4 2 8 00		– 0 –
14		GJ4	4 2 8 00		(4 2 8 00)

SUMMARY OF KEY POINTS AND KEY TERMS

LEARNING UNIT 7-1

1. Purchases is a cost-of-goods-sold account.
2. Purchases Returns and Allowances and Purchases Discount are contra cost-of-goods-sold accounts.
3. Freight-In is a cost-of-goods-sold account that accumulates the amount of shipping costs the buyer is responsible for.
4. *F.O.B. shipping point* means that the purchaser of the goods is responsible for covering the shipping costs. If the terms were *F.O.B. destination*, the seller would be responsible for covering the shipping costs until the goods reached their destination.
5. Purchases discounts are not taken on freight.

F.O.B.: Free on Board, which means without shipping charge either to the buyer or seller up to or from a specified location. In the view of one or the other, the shipment is *free* on board the carrier.

F.O.B. destination: *Seller* pays or is responsible for the cost of freight to purchaser's location or destination.

F.O.B. shipping point: *Purchaser* pays or is responsible for the shipping costs from seller's shipping point to purchaser's location.

Freight-In: Cost-of-goods-sold account that records for buyer amount of shipping costs incurred in bringing merchandise into store.

Purchases: Merchandise for resale. It is a cost-of-goods-sold account.

Purchases Discount: A contra cost-of-goods-sold account in the general ledger that records discounts offered by suppliers of merchandise for prompt payment of purchases by buyers.

Purchases Returns and Allowances: A contra cost-of-goods-sold account in the ledger that records the amount of defective or unacceptable merchandise returned to suppliers and/or price reductions given for defective items.

LEARNING UNIT 7-2

1. The steps for buying merchandise from a company may include:
   (a) The requesting department prepares a purchase requisition.
   (b) The purchasing department prepares a purchase order.
   (c) Seller receives the order and prepares a sales invoice (a purchase invoice for the buyer).
   (d) Buyer receives the goods and prepares a receiving report.
   (e) Accounting department verifies and approves the invoice for payment.
2. The accounts payable ledger, organized in alphabetical order, is not in the same book as Accounts Payable, the controlling account in the general ledger.
3. At the end of the month the total of all creditors' ending balances in the accounts payable ledger should equal the ending balance in Accounts Payable, the controlling account in the general ledger.
4. The purchases journal records the buying of merchandise or other items on account.
5. A debit memorandum (issued by the buyer) indicates that the amount owed from a previous purchase is being reduced because some goods were defective or not up to a specific standard and thus were returned or an allowance requested. On receiving the debit memorandum, the seller will issue a credit memorandum.

Accounts payable ledger: A book or file that contains in alphabetical order the specific amounts owed companies (creditors) from purchases on account.

Debit memorandum: A memo issued by a purchaser to a seller, indicating that some purchase returns and allowances have occurred and therefore the purchaser now owes less money on account.

Invoice approval form: The accounting department uses this form in checking the invoice and finally approving it for recording and payment.

Purchase invoice: The seller's sales invoice, which is sent to the purchaser.

Purchases journal: A multicolumn special journal that records the buying of merchandise or other items on account.

Purchase order: A form used in business to place an order for the buying of goods from a seller.

Purchase requisition: A form used within a business by the requesting department asking the purchasing department of the business to buy specific goods.

Receiving report: A business form used to notify the appropriate people of the ordered goods received along with the quantities and specific condition of the goods.

LEARNING UNIT 7-3

1. All payments of cash (cheque) are recorded in the cash payments journal.

2. At the end of the month, the schedule of accounts payable, a list of ending amounts owed individual creditors, should equal the ending balance in Accounts Payable, the controlling account in the general ledger.

3. Trade discounts are deductions off the list price that have nothing to do with early payments (cash discounts). Invoice amounts are recorded *after* the trade discount is deducted. Cash discounts are not taken on trade discounts.

Cash payments journal: A special journal that records all transactions involving the payment of cash.

Controlling account: The account in the general ledger that summarizes or controls a subsidiary ledger. Example: The Accounts Payable account in the general ledger is the controlling account for the accounts payable ledger. After postings are complete, it shows the total amount owed from purchases made on account.

Schedule of accounts payable: An alphabetical list of creditors from the accounts payable ledger who have an outstanding balance.

Trade discount: A reduction from the list price; it is the basis for computing and recording the invoice price. Trade discounts have no relationship to cash discounts, which result from early payment.

LEARNING UNIT 7-4

1. GST is paid on most purchases of goods and services in Canada. It is very important for businesses to keep proper track of the GST they pay because they get to deduct this from the GST otherwise payable on their own sales.

2. A separate column is added to the purchases journal and to the cash payments journal to record the GST on things purchased either on account or for cash.

3. When a debit note is received for a purchase return or allowance, the GST is always added to the total. When the debit note is recorded in the general journal, the GST amount is credited to the same account used to track the GST amounts paid for the period. This operates to increase the amount owed to the federal government. Other postings are done in the same way as described earlier.

Prepaid GST: An asset account used to accumulate the GST paid (or payable) to suppliers on goods or services purchased. It is an asset because it can be deducted from the amount otherwise payable to the federal government.

DISCUSSION QUESTIONS

1. Explain how net purchases is calculated.
2. What is a contra cost-of-goods-sold account? Please give an example.
3. What is the purpose of the Freight-In account?
4. Explain the difference between F.O.B. shipping point and F.O.B. destination.
5. F.O.B. destination means that title to the goods will switch to the buyer when goods are shipped. Agree or disagree. Why?
6. What is the normal balance of each creditor in the accounts payable ledger?
7. Why doesn't the balance of the controlling account, Accounts Payable, equal the sum of the accounts payable ledger during the month?
8. What is the relationship between a purchase requisition and a purchase order?
9. What purpose could a typical invoice approval form serve?
10. Explain the difference between merchandise and equipment.
11. Why would the purchaser issue a debit memorandum?
12. Explain the relationship between a purchases journal and a cash payments journal.
13. Explain why a trade discount is not a cash discount.
14. State why it is so important for firms to keep track of the GST they pay each period.
15. Why does GST on a debit note act to increase the net amount of GST payable.

BLUEPRINT OF PURCHASES AND CASH PAYMENTS JOURNALS

Multicolumn Purchases Journal

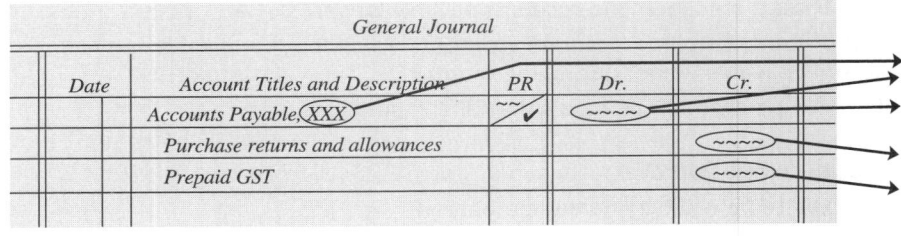

Purchases Jouranl

Page 7

Date	Account Credited	Invoice No.	Terms	PR	Accounts Payable Cr.	Purchases Dr.	Prepaid GST Dr.	Details	Sundry Dr.
				✔					
				⁷/✔					
				✔					
				✔					
				( )		( )	( )		(X)

During the month the accounts payable ledger is updated, as soon as transactions are entered in the journal. A indicates that posting is completed to the supplier's account in the accounts payable sub-ledger. The number above the slash is the GL account number for the sundry posting.

End of month total is posted to Accounts Payable control account in the general ledger.

End of month totals of both GST and purchses accounts are posted to their respective accounts in the general ledger.

End of month total is not posted to the general ledger. Individual amounts are posted as the month progresses.

Recording a Debit Memo with GST in the General Journal

General Journal

Date	Account Titles and Description	PR	Dr.	Cr.
	Accounts Payable, XXX	~~ ✔	~~~~	
	Purchase returns and allowances			~~~~
	Prepaid GST			~~~~

POSTED WHEN TRANSACTION ENTERED
Four Postings:

1. **Record to XXX in accounts payable ledger**
2. **Post to Accounts Payable in general ledger**
3. **To PRA in general ledger**
4. **Post to asset account in general ledger**

Cash Payments Journal with GST

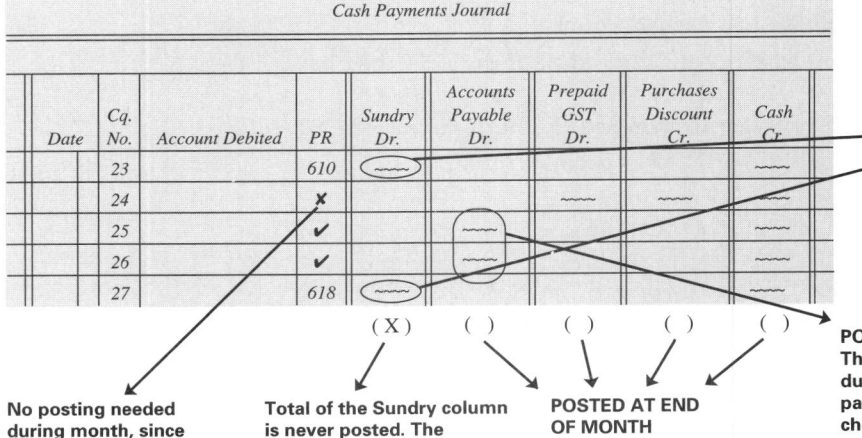

Cash Payments Journal

Date	Cq. No.	Account Debited	PR	Sundry Dr.	Accounts Payable Dr.	Prepaid GST Dr.	Purchases Discount Cr.	Cash Cr
	23		610	~~~				~~
	24		✘		~~~	~~~		~~
	25		✔		~~~			~~
	26		✔		~~~			~~
	27		618	~~~				~~
				(X)	( )	( )	( )	( )

POSTED WHEN TRANSACTION OCCURS: Posted to general ledger when transactions are entered. In this case it was accounts 610, and 618.

POSTED DURING THE MONTH: These individual amounts are posted during the month to the accounts payable sub-ledger. When posted, a check mark is placed in the PR column of the cash payments journal.

No posting needed during month, since totals of sales, GST, PST, and cash are posted at end of month.

Total of the Sundry column is never posted. The individual amounts making up the total are posted as the month progresses.

POSTED AT END OF MONTH These totals are posted to the general ledger accounts at the end of the month.

EXERCISES

1. From the accompanying purchases journal, please record to the accounts payable ledger and post to general ledger accounts as appropriate.

Page 1

Date		Account Credited	Date of Invoice	Terms	Post Ref.	Accounts Payable Credit	Purchases Debit	Sundry-Dr.		
								Account	PR	Amount
19XX										
June	3	Barr Co.	May 6	1/10, n/30		600 00	600 00			
	4	Jess Co.	May 4	n/10, EOM		900 00	900 00			
	8	Rey Co.	May 8			400 00		Equipment		400 00

PARTIAL ACCOUNTS PAYABLE LEDGER   **PARTIAL GENERAL LEDGER**

Recording to the accounts payable ledger and posting to the general ledger from a purchases journal.

Barr Co.

Equipment 120

Jess Co.

Account Payable 210

Rey Co.

Purchases 510

2. On July 10, 19XX, Aster Co. issued debit memorandum No. 1 for $400 to Reel Co. for merchandise returned from invoice No. 312. Your task is to journalize, record, and post this transaction as appropriate. Use the same account numbers as found in the text for Art's Wholesale Clothing Company. The general journal is page 1.

Journalizing, recording, and posting a debit memorandum.

3. Journalize, record, and post when appropriate the following transactions into the cash payments journal (p. 2) for Morgan's Clothing. Use the same headings as found in the text (p. 239). All purchases discounts are 2/10, n/30.

Journalizing, recording, and posting a cash payments journal.

ACCOUNTS PAYABLE LEDGER

NAME	BALANCE	INVOICE NO.
A. James	$1,000	522
B. Foss	400	488
J. Ranch	900	562
B. Swanson	100	821

PARTIAL GENERAL LEDGER

ACCOUNT	BALANCE
Cash 110	$3,000
Accounts Payable 210	2,400
Purchases Discount 511	—
Advertising Expense 610	—

19XX

April 1 Issued cheque no. 20 to A. James Company in payment of its March 28 invoice No. 522.

     8 Issued cheque no. 21 to Flott Advertising in payment of its advertising bill, $100, no discount.

    15 Issued cheque no. 22 to B. Foss in payment of its March 25 invoice No. 488.

Schedule of accounts payable.

4. From Exercise 3, prepare a schedule of accounts payable and verify that the total of the schedule equals the amount in the controlling account.

F.O.B. shipping point.

5. Record the following transaction in a transaction analysis chart for the buyer:

Bought merchandise for $9,000 on account. Shipping terms were F.O.B. shipping point. The cost of shipping was $500.

Trade and cash discounts.

6. Angie Rase bought merchandise with a list price of $4,000. Angie was entitled to a 30% trade discount, as well as a 3% cash discount. What was Angie's actual cost of buying this merchandise after the cash discount?

GROUP A PROBLEMS

Journalizing, recording, and posting a purchases journal.

7A-1. (GST not involved in this problem.) Judy Clark recently opened a sporting goods shop. As the bookkeeper of her shop, please journalize, record, and post when appropriate the following transactions (account numbers are: Store Supplies, 115; Store Equipment, 121; Accounts Payable, 210; Purchases, 510):

19XX

June 4 Bought merchandise on account from Aster Co., invoice #442, dated June 5, terms 2/10, n/30; $900.

     5 Bought store equipment from Norton Co., invoice #502, dated June 6; $4,000.

     8 Bought merchandise on account from Rolo Co., invoice #401, dated June 9; terms 2/10, n/30; $1,400.

    14 Bought store supplies on account from Aster Co., invoice #419, dated June 14; $900.

7A-2. Mabel's Natural Food Store uses a purchases journal (p. 10) and a general journal (p. 2) to record the following transactions (continued from April) the GST rate is 7%:

Journalizing, recording, and posting a purchases journal as well as recording debit memorandum and preparing a schedule of accounts payable.

19XX

May 8 Purchased merchandise on account from Aton Co., invoice #400, dated May 9, terms 2/10, n/60; $600 plus GST.

    10 Purchased merchandise on account from Broward Co., invoice #120, dated May 11, terms 2/10, n/60; $1,200 plus GST

    12 Purchased store supplies on account from Midden Co., invoice #510, dated May 13, $500 plus GST

    14 Issued debit memo #8 to Aton Co. for merchandise returned, $400 (plus GST) from invoice #400.

    17 Purchased office equipment on account from Relar Co., invoice #810, dated May 18, $560 plus GST.

    24 Purchased additional store supplies on account from Midden Co., invoice #516, dated May 25, terms 2/10, n/30; $650 plus GST.

The food store has decided to keep a separate column for the purchases of supplies in the purchases journal which also has a separate column for GST. Your task is to:

1. Journalize the transactions.
2. Post and record as appropriate.
3. Prepare a schedule of accounts payable.

ACCOUNTS PAYABLE LEDGER

NAME	BALANCE
Aton Co.	$ 428
Broward Co.	642
Midden Co.	1,284
Relar Co.	535

PARTIAL GENERAL LEDGER

ACCOUNT	NUMBER	BALANCE
Store Supplies	110	$ —
Prepaid GST	112	498
Office Equipment	120	—
Accounts Payable	210	2,889
Purchases	510	16,000
Purchases Returns and Allowances	512	—

7A-3. Wendy Jones operates a wholesale computer centre. All transactions requiring the payment of cash are recorded in the cash payments journal (p. 5). The account balances as of May 1, 19XX, are as follows:

Journalizing, recording, and posting a cash payments journal with GST. Preparing a schedule of accounts payable.

ACCOUNTS PAYABLE LEDGER

NAME	BALANCE	GST Included
Alvin Co.	$1,284	$84
Henry Co.	642	42
Soy Co.	856	56
Xon Co.	1,498	98

PARTIAL GENERAL LEDGER

ACCOUNT	NUMBER	BALANCE
Cash	110	$17,000
Prepaid GST	132	965
Delivery Truck	150	—
Accounts Payable	210	4,280
Computer Purchases	510	—
Computer Purchases Discount	511	—
Rent Expense	610	—
Utilities Expense	620	—

Your task is to

1. Journalize the following transactions.
2. Record to the accounts payable ledger and post to general ledger as appropriate.
3. Prepare a schedule of accounts payable.

19XX
May 1 Paid half the amount owed Henry Co. from previous purchases of appliances on account, less a 2% purchases discount, cheque no. 21.
     3 Bought a delivery truck for $8,000 cash plus GST of $560, cheque no. 22, payable to Bill Ring Co.
     6 Bought computer merchandise from Lectro Co., cheque no. 23, $2,900, plus GST.
    18 Bought additional computer merchandise from Pulse Co., cheque no. 24, $800, plus GST.
    24 Paid Xon Co. the amount owed less a 2% purchases discount, cheque no. 25.
    28 Paid rent expense to King's Realty Trust, cheque no. 26, $2,000, plus GST.
    29 Paid utilities expense to Stone Utility Co., cheque no. 27, $300, plus GST.
    30 Paid half the amount owed Soy Co., no discount, cheque no. 28.

Comprehensive Review Problem with GST. All special journals and the general journal. Schedule of accounts payable and accounts receivable.

7A-4. Abby Ellen opened Abby's Toy House. As her newly hired accountant, your task is to

1. Journalize the transactions for the month of March.
2. Record to subsidiary ledgers and post to general ledger as appropriate.
3. Total, rule and crossfoot the journals.
4. Prepare a schedule of accounts receivable and a schedule of accounts payable.

The following is the partial chart of accounts for Abby's Toy House:

Assets
110 Cash
112 Accounts Receivable
114 Prepaid Rent
116 Prepaid GST
121 Delivery Truck

Liabilities
210 Accounts Payable
218 GST Payable

Owner's Equity
310 A. Ellen, Capital

Revenue
410 Toy Sales
412 Sales Returns and Allowances
414 Sales Discounts

Cost of Goods
510 Toy Purchases
512 Purchases Returns and Allowances
514 Purchases Discount

Expenses
610 Salaries Expense
612 Cleaning Expense

19XX
March 1 Abby Ellen invested $8,000 in the toy store.
    1 Paid three months' rent in advance, cheque no. 1, $3,000, plus GST.
    1 Purchased merchandise from Earl Miller Company on account, $4,000, plus GST. Invoice No. 410, dated March 2, terms 2/10, n/30.
    3 Sold merchandise to Bill Burton on account, $1,000, plus GST. Invoice No. 1, terms 2/10, n/30.
    6 Sold merchandise to Jim Rex on account, $700, plus GST. Invoice No. 2, terms 2/10, n/30.
    8 Purchased merchandise from Earl Miller Co. on account, $1,200, plus GST. Invoice No. 415, dated March 9, terms 2/10, n/30.
    9 Sold merchandise to Bill Burton on account, $600, plus GST. Invoice No. 3, terms 2/10, n/30.

9   Paid cleaning service $300, plus GST. Cheque no. 2.

10   Jim Rex returned merchandise that cost $300 (before GST) to Abby's Toy House. Abby issued credit memorandum No. 1 to Jim Rex for $300, plus GST.

10   Purchased merchandise from Minnie Katz on account, $4,000, plus GST. Invoice No. 311, dated March 11, terms 1/15, n/60.

12   Paid Earl Miller Co. invoice No. 410, dated March 2, cheque no. 3.

13   Sold $1,300 (plus GST) of toy merchandise for cash.

13   Paid salaries, $600, cheque no. 4.

14   Returned merchandise to Minnie Katz in the amount of $1,000, plus GST. Abby's Toy House issued debit memorandum No. 1 to Minnie Katz.

15   Sold merchandise for cash $4,000, plus GST.

16   Received payment from Jim Rex, invoice No. 2 (less returned merchandise) less discount.

16   Bill Burton paid invoice No. 1.

16   Sold toy merchandise to Amy Rose on account, $4,000, plus GST. Invoice No. 4, terms 2/10, n/30.

20   Purchased delivery truck on account from Sam Katz Garage, $3,000, plus GST. Invoice No. 111, dated March 21 (no discount).

22   Sold to Bill Burton merchandise on account, $900, plus GST. Invoice No. 5, terms 2/10, n/30.

23   Paid Minnie Katz balance owed, cheque no. 5.

24   Sold toy merchandise on account to Amy Rose, $1,100, plus GST. Invoice No. 6, terms 2/10, n/30.

25   Purchased toy merchandise, $600, plus GST. Cheque no. 6.

26   Purchased toy merchandise from Woody Smith on account, $4,800, plus GST. Invoice No. 211, dated March 27, terms 2/10, n/30.

28   Bill Burton paid invoice No. 5, dated March 22.

28   Amy Rose paid invoice No. 6, dated March 24.

28   Abby invested an additional $5,000 in the business.

28   Purchased merchandise from Earl Miller Co., $1,400, plus GST. Invoice No. 436, dated March 29, terms 2/10, n/30.

30   Paid Earl Miller Co. invoice No. 436, cheque no. 7.

30   Sold merchandise to Bonnie Flow Company on account, $3,000, plus GST. Invoice No. 7, terms 2/10, n/30.

GROUP B PROBLEMS

7B-1. (GST not involved in this problem.) From the following transactions of Judy Clark's sporting goods shop, journalize in the purchases journal and record and post as appropriate:

Journalizing, recording, and posting a purchases journal.

19XX

June   4   Bought merchandise on account from Rolo Co., invoice No. 400, dated June 5, terms 2/10, n/30; $1,800.

5   Bought store equipment from Norton Co., invoice No. 518, dated June 6; $6,000.

8   Bought merchandise on account from Aster Co., invoice No. 411, dated June 5, terms 2/10, n/30; $400.

14   Bought store supplies on account from Aster Co., invoice No. 415, dated June 13; $1,200.

Journalizing, recording, and posting a purchases journal with GST as well as recording the issuing of a debit memorandum and preparing a schedule of accounts payable.

7B-2. As the accountant of Mabel's Natural Food Store (1) journalize the following transactions into the purchases (p. 10) or general journal (p. 2), (2) record and post as appropriate, and (3) prepare a schedule of accounts payable. Beginning balances are in your working papers.

19XX

May 8   Purchased merchandise on account from Broward Co., invoice No. 420, dated May 9, terms 2/10, n/60; $500, plus GST.

10   Purchased merchandise on account from Aton Co., invoice No. 400, dated May 11, terms 2/10, n/60; $900, plus GST.

12   Purchased store supplies on account from Midden Co., invoice No. 510, dated May 13, $700, plus GST.

14   Issued debit memo No. 7 to Aton Co. for merchandise returned, $400, plus GST. (From invoice No. 400.)

17   Purchased office equipment on account from Relar Co., invoice No. 810, dated May 18, $750, plus GST.

24   Purchased additional store supplies on account from Midden Co., invoice No. 516, dated May 25, $850, plus GST.

Journalizing, recording, and posting a cash payments journal with GST. Preparing a schedule of accounts payable.

7B-3. Wendy Jones has hired you as her bookkeeper to record the following transactions in the cash payments journal. She would like you to record and post as appropriate and supply her with a schedule of accounts payable. (Beginning balances are in your workbook or Problem 7A-3, p. 259 in the text.)

19XX

May 1   Bought a delivery truck for $8,000 cash, plus GST. Cheque no. 21, payable to Randy Rosse Co.

3   Paid half the amount owed Henry Co. from previous purchases of computer merchandise on account, less a 5% purchases discount, cheque no. 22.

6   Bought computer merchandise from Jane Co. for $900 cash, plus GST. Cheque no. 23.

18   Bought additional computer merchandise from Jane Co., cheque no. 24, $1,000, plus GST.

24   Paid Xon Co. the amount owed less a 5% purchases discount, cheque no. 25.

28   Paid rent expense to Regan Realty Trust, cheque no. 26, $3,000, plus GST.

29   Paid half the amount owed Soy Co., no discount, cheque no. 27.

30   Paid utilities expense to County Utility, cheque no. 28, $425, plus GST.

Comprehensive Review Problem with GST. All special journals and the general journal. Schedule of accounts payable and accounts receivable.

7B-4. As the new accountant for Abby's Toy House, your task is to

1. Journalize the transactions for the month of March.
2. Record to subsidiary ledgers and post to the general ledger as appropriate.
3. Total, rule and crossfoot the journals.
4. Prepare a schedule of accounts receivable and a schedule of accounts payable.

(Use the same chart of accounts as in Problem 7A-4, p. 260. Your workbook has all the forms you need to complete this problem.)

19XX

March 1   Abby invested $4,000 in the new toy store.

1   Paid two months' rent in advance, cheque no. 1, $1,000, plus GST.

1   Purchased merchandise from Earl Miller Company, invoice No. 410, dated March 2, terms 2/10, n/30; $6,000, plus GST.

3 Sold merchandise to Bill Burton on account, $1,600, plus GST. Invoice No. 1, terms 2/10, n/30.

6 Sold merchandise to Jim Rex on account, $800, plus GST. Invoice No. 2, terms 2/10, n/30.

8 Purchased merchandise from Earl Miller Company, $800, plus GST. Invoice No. 415, dated March 9, terms 2/10, n/30.

9 Sold merchandise to Bill Burton on account, $700, plus GST. Invoice No. 3, terms 2/10, n/30.

9 Paid cleaning service, $400, plus GST. Cheque no. 2.

10 Jim Rex returned merchandise that cost $200 (plus GST) to Abby. Abby issued credit memorandum No. 1 to Jim Rex for $200, plus GST.

10 Purchased merchandise from Minnie Katz, $7,000, plus GST. Invoice No. 311, dated March 11, terms 1/15, n/60.

12 Paid Earl Miller Co. invoice No. 410, dated March 2, cheque no. 3.

13 Sold $1,500, (plus GST) of toy merchandise for cash.

13 Paid salaries, $700, cheque no. 4.

14 Returned merchandise to Minnie Katz in the amount of $500, plus GST. Abby issued debit memorandum No. 1 to Minnie Katz.

15 Sold merchandise for cash, $4,800, plus GST.

16 Received payment from Jim Rex for invoice No. 2 (less returned merchandise) less discount.

16 Bill Burton paid invoice No. 1.

16 Sold toy merchandise to Amy Rose on account, $6,000, plus GST. Invoice No. 4, terms 2/10, n/30.

20 Purchased delivery truck on account from Sam Katz Garage, $2,500, plus GST. Invoice No. 111, dated March 21 (no discount).

22 Sold to Bill Burton merchandise on account, $2,000, plus GST. Invoice No. 5, terms 2/10, n/30.

23 Paid Minnie Katz balance owed, cheque no. 5.

24 Sold toy merchandise on account to Amy Rose, $2,000, plus GST. Invoice No. 6, terms 2/10, n/30.

25 Purchased toy merchandise, $800, plus GST. Cheque no. 6.

26 Purchased toy merchandise from Woody Smith on account, $5,900, plus GST. Invoice No. 211, dated March 27, terms 2/10, n/30.

28 Bill Burton paid invoice No. 5, dated March 22.

28 Amy Rose paid invoice No. 6, dated March 24.

28 Abby invested an additional $3,000 in the business.

28 Purchased merchandise from Earl Miller Co., $4,200, plus GST. Invoice No. 436, dated March 29, terms 2/10, n/30.

30 Paid Earl Miller Co. invoice No. 436, cheque no. 7.

30 Sold merchandise to Bonnie Flow Company on account, $3,200, plus GST. Invoice No. 7, terms 2/10, n/30.

GROUP C PROBLEMS

7C-1. (GST not involved in this problem.) Brent Walker recently opened an imported foods store. As the bookkeeper of his store, please journalize, record, and post when appropriate the following transactions (account numbers are: Store Supplies, 115; Store Equipment, 141; Accounts Payable, 210; Purchases, 510):

Journalizing, recording, and posting a purchases journal.

19XX
May 4 Bought merchandise on account from Convey Co., invoice No. 751, dated May 5, terms 2/10, n/30; $640.

5   Bought store equipment from Reliable Co., invoice No. 1202, dated May 6; $4,620.

8   Bought merchandise on account from Brendan Co., invoice No. 401, dated May 9; terms 1/10, n/30; $1,640.

14 Bought store supplies on account from Convey Co., invoice No. 823 dated May 14; $810.

Journalizing, recording, and posting a purchases journal with GST as well as recording the issuing of a debit memorandum and preparing a schedule of accounts payable.

7C-2. Felicity's Fabric Co. uses a purchases journal (p. 21) and a general journal (p. 32) to record the following transactions (continued from July):

19XX

August 3   Purchased fabric for resale from European Import Fabrics Co., invoice No. 653, dated August 2, terms net 15 days; $1,234, plus GST.

8   Purchased merchandise on account from Eddyn Co., invoice No. 250, dated August 9, terms 2/10, n/60; $830, plus GST.

10 Purchased merchandise on account from Forward Co., invoice No. 1124, dated August 11, terms 1/10, n/60; $1,584, plus GST

12 Purchased store supplies on account from Lavoy Co., invoice No. 712, dated August 13, $2,540, plus GST

14 Issued debit memo No. 8 to Eddyn Co. for merchandise returned, $130, (plus GST) from invoice No. 250.

17 Purchased office equipment on account from Reliant Co., invoice No. 873, dated August 18, $1,440, plus GST.

24 Purchased additional store supplies on account from Lavoy Co., invoice No. 816, dated August 25, terms 2/10, n/30; $650, plus GST.

29 Purchased fabric for resale from European Import Fabrics Co., invoice No. 713, dated August 27, terms net 15 days; $2,455, plus GST.

The fabric store has decided to keep a separate column for the purchases of supplies in the purchases journal and also has a separate column for GST. Your task is to:

1. Journalize the transactions.
2. Post and record as appropriate.
3. Prepare a schedule of accounts payable.

ACCOUNTS PAYABLE LEDGER

NAME	BALANCE
Eddyn Co.	$ 856
European Import	3,267
Forward Co.	1,672
Reliant Co.	2,773
Lavoy	535

PARTIAL GENERAL LEDGER

ACCOUNT	NUMBER	BALANCE
Store Supplies	130	$ —
Prepaid GST	142	2,873
Office Equipment	180	—
Accounts Payable	220	9,103
Purchases	500	86,340
Purchases Returns and Allowances	510	1,374

7C-3. Wendal Boisvert operates a wholesale welding supplies company. All transactions requiring the payment of cash are recorded in the cash payments journal (p. 45). The account balances as of May 1, 19XX, are as follows:

Journalizing, record-
ing, and posting a
cash payments journal
with GST. Preparing a
schedule of accounts
payable.

ACCOUNTS PAYABLE LEDGER

NAME	BALANCE	GST INCLUDED
Dominion Gases Co.	$1,591.40	$ 99.40
Vertal Rod Co.	2,398.94	156.94
Marker Gloves Co.	1,936.70	126.70
Glover Gauges Co.	952.30	62.30
Prism Accessories Co.	3,862.70	252.70

PARTIAL GENERAL LEDGER

ACCOUNT	NUMBER	BALANCE
Cash	100	$ 7,720.00
Prepaid GST	145	2,463.20*
Delivery Truck	170	—
Accounts Payable	200	10,742.04
Welding Purchases	500	43,566.23
Welding Purchases Discount	510	459.41
Rent Expense	670	3,400.00
Utilities Expense	690	934.28

* Will not agree with the amounts included in the accounts payable balances.

Your task is to:

1. Journalize the following transactions.
2. Record to the accounts payable ledger and post to general ledger as appropriate.
3. Prepare a schedule of accounts payable.

19XX

May 1 Paid half the amount owed Dominion Gases Co. from previous purchases on account, less a 2% purchases discount, cheque no. 464.

3 Bought a delivery truck for $18,000 cash plus GST of $1,260, cheque no. 465, payable to City Truck Sales Co.

5 Paid the amount owing to Glover Gauges Co, cheque no. 466.

6 Bought welding merchandise (cash sale) from Vericon Canada Co., cheque no. 467, $1,760, plus GST.

14 Paid the balance due to Prism Accessories Co. after deducting a 5% discount as per usual terms for this company, cheque no. 468.

18 Bought additional welding merchandise (cash sale) from Pulse Co., cheque no. 469, $460, plus GST.

24 Paid Marker Gloves Co. the amount owed less a 2% purchases discount, cheque no. 470.

28 Paid rent expense to Abbott Properties Co., cheque no. 471, $1,560, plus GST.

29 Paid utilities expense to Stoney Plain Utility Co., cheque no. 472, $332, plus GST.

30 Paid $1,000.00 to Vertal Rod Co., no discount, cheque no. 473.

Comprehensive
Review Problem with
GST. All special jour-
nals and the general
journal. Schedule of
accounts payable and
accounts receivable.

7C-4. Janice Roy opened Janice's Book Shop. As her newly hired accountant, your task is to

1. Journalize the transactions for the month of October.
2. Record to subsidiary ledgers and post to general ledger as appropriate.
3. Total, rule and crossfoot the journals.
4. Prepare a schedule of accounts receivable and a schedule of accounts payable as of October 31.

The following is the partial chart of accounts for Janice's Book Shop:

Assets
110 Cash
120 Accounts Receivable
135 Prepaid Rent
138 Prepaid GST
180 Delivery Truck

Liabilities
210 Accounts Payable
218 GST Payable

Owner's Equity
310 J. Roy, Capital

Revenue
410 Book Sales
412 Sales Returns and Allowances
414 Sales Discounts

Cost of Goods
510 Book Purchases
512 Purchases Returns and Allowances
514 Purchases Discount

Expenses
615 Cleaning Expense
650 Salaries Expense

19XX
October 1   Janice Roy invested $18,000 in the book store.
       1   Paid three months' rent in advance, cheque no. 121, $2,400, plus GST.
       1   Purchased merchandise from Milligan Book Company on account, $3,650, plus GST. Invoice No. 410, dated October 2, terms 2/10, n/30.
       3   Sold merchandise to First City Library on account, $1,850, plus GST. Invoice No. 781, terms 2/10, n/30.
       6   Sold merchandise to District College on account, $2,700, plus GST. Invoice No. 782, terms 2/10, n/30.
       8   Purchased merchandise from Milligan Book Co. on account, $3,200, plus GST. Invoice No. 415, dated October 9, terms 2/10, n/30.
       9   Sold merchandise to First City Library on account, $1,600, plus GST. Invoice No. 783, terms 2/10, n/30.
       9   Paid cleaning service $450, plus GST. Cheque no. 122.
     10   District College returned merchandise that cost $280 (before GST) to Janice's Book Shop. Janice issued credit memorandum No. 1 to District College for $280, plus GST.
     10   Purchased merchandise from Winnipeg Book Supply on account, $2,600, plus GST. Invoice No. 311, dated October 11, terms 1/15, n/60.
     12   Paid Milligan Book Co. invoice No. 410, dated October 2, cheque no. 123.
     13   Sold $700 (plus GST) of book merchandise for cash.
     13   Paid salaries, $850, cheque no. 124.
     14   Returned merchandise to Winnipeg Book Supply in the amount of $550, plus GST. Janice's Book Shop issued debit memorandum No. 1 to Winnipeg Book Supply.
     15   Sold merchandise for cash $980, plus GST.

16   Received payment from District College, invoice No. 782 (less returned merchandise) less discount.

16   First City Library paid invoice No. 781.

16   Sold book merchandise to Rural Bookmobile Co. on account, $3,100, plus GST. Invoice No. 784, terms 2/10, n/30.

20   Purchased delivery truck on account from Suburban Auto Sales Co., $17,000, plus GST. Invoice No. 111, dated October 21 (no discount).

22   Sold to First City Library merchandise on account, $2,200, plus GST. Invoice No. 785, terms 2/10, n/30.

23   Paid Winnipeg Book Supply balance owed, cheque no. 125.

24   Sold book merchandise on account to Rural Bookmobile Co., $2,700, plus GST. Invoice No. 786, terms 2/10, n/30.

25   Purchased used book merchandise for cash, $3,600, plus GST. Cheque no. 126.

26   Purchased book merchandise from Smithsonian Book Co. on account, $6,400, plus GST. Invoice No. 211, dated October 27, terms 2/10, n/30.

27   Sold merchandise for cash, $680, plus GST.

28   First City Library paid invoice No. 785, dated October 22.

28   Rural Bookmobile Co. paid invoice No. 786, dated October 24.

28   Janice invested an additional $15,000 in the business.

28   Purchased merchandise from Milligan Book Co., $2,560, plus GST. Invoice No. 436, dated October 29, terms 2/10, n/30.

30   Paid Milligan Book Co. invoice No. 436, cheque no. 127.

30   Sold merchandise to Flower & Company on account, $2,800, plus GST. Invoice No. 787, terms 2/10, n/30.

PRACTICAL ACCOUNTING APPLICATION #1

Angie Co. bought merchandise for $1,000 with credit terms of 2/10, n/30. Owing to the bookkeeper's incompetence, the 2% cash discount was missed. The bookkeeper told Pete Angie, the owner, not to get excited. After all, it was a $20 discount that was missed—not hundreds of dollars. Could you please act as Mr. Angie's assistant and show the bookkeeper that his $20 represents a sizeable equivalent interest cost? In your calculation assume a 360-day year.

Hint: $R = \dfrac{I}{PT}$

PRACTICAL ACCOUNTING APPLICATION #2

Jeff Ryan completed an Accounting I course and was recently hired as the bookkeeper of Spring Co. The special journals have not been posted, nor are Dr. and Cr. used on the column headings. Please assist Jeff by marking the Dr. and Cr headings as well as setting up and posting to the general ledger and recording to the subsidiary ledger. (Only post or record the amounts, since no chart of accounts is provided.)

Sales Journal

Account	PR	Amount
Blue Co.		4 800 00
Jon Co.		5 600 00
Roff Co.		6 400 00
Totals		16 800 00

Purchases Journal

Account	PR	Amount
Ralph Co.		4 000 00
Sos Co.		6 000 00
Jingle Co.		8 000 00
Totals		18 000 00

General Journal

Sales Returns and Allowances	1 600 00	
Accounts Receivable, Jon Co.		1 600 00
Customer returned merchandise		
Accounts Payable, Jingle Co.	800 00	
Purchases, Returns, and Allowances		800 00
Returned defective merchandise		

Cash Receipts Journal*

Cash	Sales Discounts	Accounts Receivable	Sales	Sundry Account Name	PR	Amount
4 704 00	96 00	4 800 00		Blue Co.		
1 960 00	40 00	2 000 00		Jon Co.		
5 000 00			5 000 00	Sales		
20 000 00				Notes Payable		20 000 00
3 136 00	64 00	3 200 00		Roff Co.		
4 600 00			4 600 00	Sales		
39 400 00	200 00	10 000 00	9 600 00	Total		20 000 00

* This company's set of columns differs from that shown in the chapter.

Cash Payments Journal

Account	PR	Sundry	Accounts Payable	Purchases Discounts	Cash
Sos Co.			3 000 00	60 00	2 940 00
Salaries Expense		2 600 00			2 600 00
Jingle Co.			4 000 00	80 00	3 920 00
Salaries Expense		2 600 00			2 600 00
Totals		5 200 00	7 000 00	140 00	12 060 00

ACCOUNTING RECALL
A Cumulative Approach

THIS EXAM REVIEWS CHAPTERS 1 THROUGH 7.

Your *Study Guide and Working Papers* have forms to complete this exam, as well as worked-out solutions. The page references next to each question identify what page to turn back to if you answer the question incorrectly.

PART I Vocabulary Review

Match the terms to the appropriate definition or phrase.

Page Ref.

(241)	1. Trade discount	A. A contra cost-of-goods sold account
(228)	2. F.O.B. destination	B. Issued by a buyer to the seller
(232)	3. Purchases journal	C. Special journal that records buying on account
(184)	4. Sales journal	D. Sales on account
(228)	5. Purchases discount	E. Seller pays cost of freight
(186)	6. Credit memorandum	F. A controlling account
(238)	7. Accounts payable	G. Merchandise for resale
(232)	8. Debit memorandum	H. Payment of cash
(237)	9. Cash payments journal	I. Issued by seller
(227)	10. Purchases	J. Not a cash discount

PART II True or False (Accounting Theory)

(186) 11. Issuing a credit memo results in seller increasing its purchases returns and allowances.

(228) 12. Purchases discounts have a normal balance of a debit.

(232) 13. Buying equipment on account would be recorded in a Purchases Journal.

(239) 14. Each creditor in the Accounts Payable Ledger usually has a debit balance.

(232) 15. Issuing a debit memo will reduce accounts payable for the buyer.

PART III Applications Problem (242)

Journalize, record, and post as appropriate the following transactions. All purchases discounts are 2/10, n/30.

July 1 Issued cheque no. 12 to Sue Willige in payment of June 25 Invoice No. 415 less purchases discount.

　　 8 Issued cheque no. 13 to Roland Co. to pay selling expense due $90 no discount.

　　 9 Issued cheque no. 14 to Ralph Smol in payment of June 30 Invoice No. 417 less purchases discount.

ACCOUNTS PAYABLE LEDGER

NAME	BALANCE	INVOICE NO.
Ralph Smol	$428 ($28 GST)	417
Sue Willige	321 ($21 GST)	415

PARTIAL GENERAL LEDGER

ACCOUNT	NO.	BALANCE
Cash	110	$1,600
Accounts payable	210	749
Purchases discount	511	
Selling expense	610	

CHAPTER EIGHT

BANKING PROCEDURES AND CONTROL OF CASH

IN THIS CHAPTER WE WILL COVER THE FOLLOWING TOPICS:

The internal control policies of a company will depend on things such as number of employees, company size, sources of cash, and so on.

In Chapters 6 and 7 we have developed the special journals of Art's Wholesale Clothing Company. As Art finds his business increasing, he is becoming quite concerned about developing a system of procedures and records for close control over the cash receipts and cash payments of the business. This is called **internal control** and includes control over the store's assets as well as a way of monitoring the company's operations.

Art, his accountant, and a consultant studied the situation and developed the following company policies:

1. Responsibilities and duties of employees will be divided. For example, the person receiving the cash, whether at the register or by opening the mail, will not record this information into the accounting records. The accountant, on the other hand, will not be handling the cash receipts.
2. All cash receipts of Art's Wholesale will be deposited into the bank the same day they arrive.
3. All cash payments will be made by cheque (except petty cash, which will be discussed later in this chapter).
4. Employees will be rotated between jobs. This allows workers to become acquainted with the work of others as well as to prepare for a possible changeover of jobs.
5. Art Newner will sign all cheques after receiving authorization to pay from the departments concerned.
6. At time of payment, all supporting invoices or documents will be stamped paid. That will show when the invoice or document is paid as well as the number of the cheque used.
7. All cheques will be prenumbered. This will control the use of cheques and make it difficult to use a cheque fraudulently without its being revealed at some point.

Let's now look at the chequing account of Art's Wholesale along with specific bank procedures.

LEARNING UNIT 8-1

Bank Procedures, Chequing Accounts, and Bank Reconciliations

Before Art's Wholesale opened on April 1, Art had a meeting at Royal Bank to discuss the steps in opening up and using a chequing account for the company.

OPENING A CHEQUING ACCOUNT

Purpose of a signature card.

The manager of the bank gave Art a signature card to fill out. The signature card includes space for signature(s), business and home addresses, references, type of account, and so on. The manager explained that this was for Art to sign (since he would be signing cheques for the company) so that the bank could check and validate his signature when cheques were presented for payment. The signature card would be kept in the bank's files so that possible forgeries could be spotted.

Art also received preprinted **deposit slips** and a set of cheques. The deposit slips were to be used when Art's Wholesale received cash or cheques from any source and deposited them into the chequing account. One copy of the deposit slip stays with the bank and a duplicate copy remains with the company, so that they can verify that items in the cash receipts journal that make up the deposit have actually been deposited correctly.

Notice on the deposit slip in Figure 8-1 (p. 274) that much of the information is preprinted. This saves time as well as labour in processing the deposit. Many times when the bank is closed Art will place a locked bag (provided by the bank) in a night depository. Overnight the deposit bag is in a safe place, and the bank will credit (increase) his account balance when the deposit is processed.

> When a bank credits your account, it is increasing the balance.

TYPES OF CHEQUE ENDORSEMENT

Before any cheque can be deposited or cashed, the bank requires that it be *endorsed*. Endorsement is the signing of one's name on the *back left-hand side* of the cheque. This process transfers ownership to the bank, which can collect the money from the person or company that issued the cheque. Figure 8-2 (p. 275) shows several common types of **endorsement** that Art's Wholesale could use.

Now let's look at Art's chequebook to see how payments will be recorded.

> Endorsements can be made by using a rubber stamp instead of a handwritten signature.

THE CHEQUEBOOK

Figure 8-3 (p. 276) is an example of the type of cheque used by Art's Wholesale. This **cheque** is a written order signed by Art Newner (the **drawer** or one who writes the cheque) instructing Royal Bank (**drawee**) to pay a specific sum of money to Joe Francis Company, the **payee**, the one to whom the cheque is payable. Note some of the following key points:

> *Drawer*—one who writes the cheque.
> *Drawee*—one who pays money to payee.
> *Payee*—one to whom cheque is payable.

1. The number of the cheque is preprinted, along with the company's address.
2. The cheque stub is filled out first. The stub will be used in recording transactions as well as for future reference. Note here that the beginning balance is $7,100; a deposit of $784 brought a balance of $7,884 before the cheque for $4,000 was written, leaving an ending balance of $3,884.
3. The line drawn before XX/100 is meant to fill space up in the cheque so that changes cannot easily be made in the amount.
4. The amount written in words should start on the far left and should use only one "and" to signify the decimal position.

If the written amount on the cheque doesn't match the amount expressed in figures, Royal Bank will pay the amount written in words, will return the cheque unpaid, or will check with the drawer to see what was meant.

Many companies use chequewriting machines, which type out the amount of the cheque in figures and words on the cheque itself. This prevents anyone from making fraudulent changes on the cheque by hand.

Now let's turn our attention to look at the transactions of Art's Wholesale that affect the chequing account.

FIGURE 8-1   **A Deposit Slip**

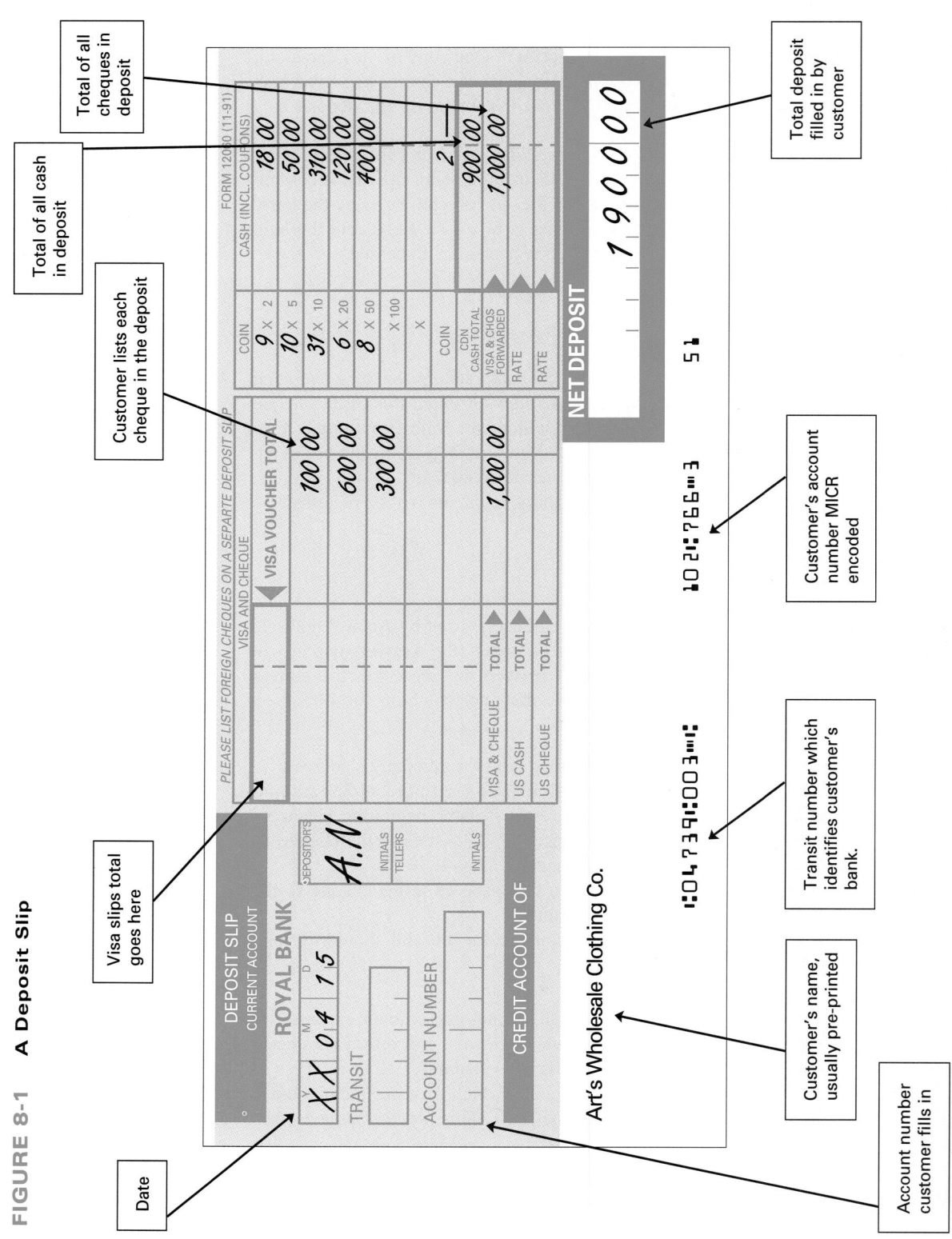

FIGURE 8-2   **Types of Cheque Endorsement**

Types of Cheque Endorsement

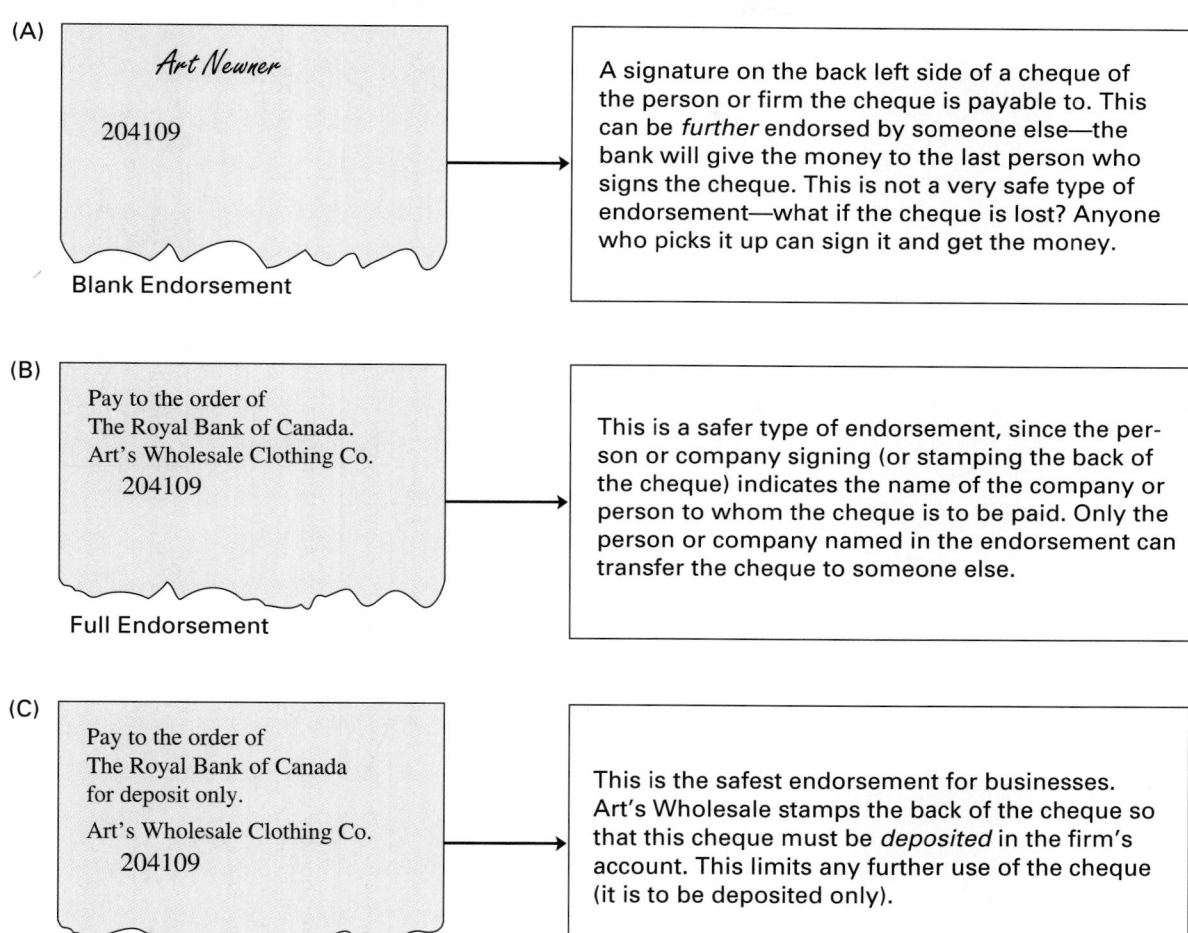

(A)

Art Newner

204109

Blank Endorsement

A signature on the back left side of a cheque of the person or firm the cheque is payable to. This can be *further* endorsed by someone else—the bank will give the money to the last person who signs the cheque. This is not a very safe type of endorsement—what if the cheque is lost? Anyone who picks it up can sign it and get the money.

(B)

Pay to the order of
The Royal Bank of Canada.
Art's Wholesale Clothing Co.
204109

Full Endorsement

This is a safer type of endorsement, since the person or company signing (or stamping the back of the cheque) indicates the name of the company or person to whom the cheque is to be paid. Only the person or company named in the endorsement can transfer the cheque to someone else.

(C)

Pay to the order of
The Royal Bank of Canada
for deposit only.
Art's Wholesale Clothing Co.
204109

Restrictive Endorsement

This is the safest endorsement for businesses. Art's Wholesale stamps the back of the cheque so that this cheque must be *deposited* in the firm's account. This limits any further use of the cheque (it is to be deposited only).

FIGURE 8-3

A Typical Cheque and Cheque Stub

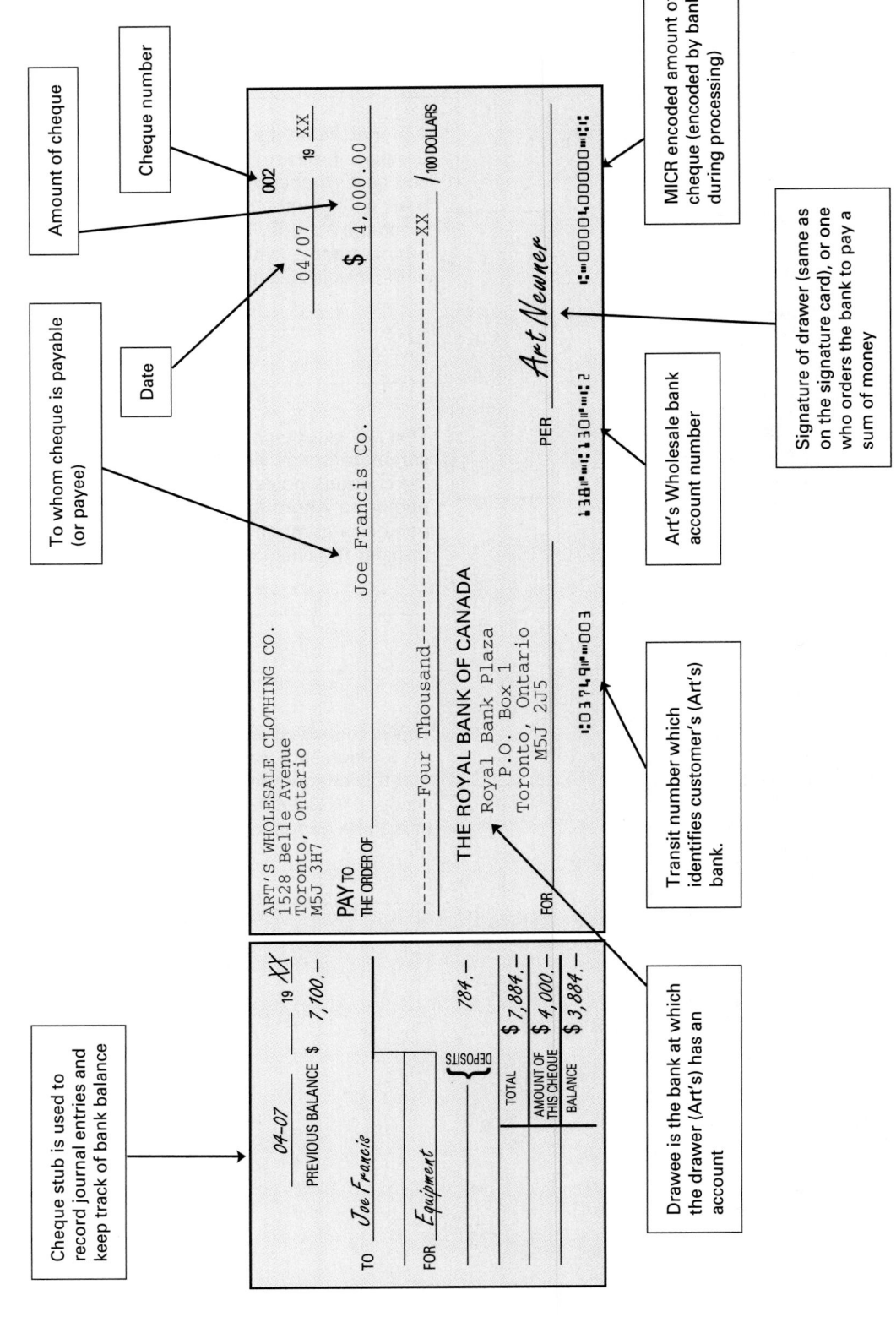

TRANSACTIONS AFFECTING THE CHEQUEBOOK

The transactions of Art's Wholesale for the month of April that affect the chequing account (p. 278) are the same transactions that were shown in Chapters 6 and 7 in the cash receipts and cash payments journal. Remember, all payments of money are by written cheque (except petty cash), and all money (cheques) received is deposited in the bank account.

Today some chequing accounts earn interest. The type of chequing account used by Art's Wholesale has a monthly service charge, but we assume that there is no individual charge for each cheque written, and the account does not pay interest.

YVONNE JAMES: OFFICE MANAGER, BOOKKEEPER

Yvonne James was working as a secretary at a bank when her supervisor suggested that she try bookkeeping. "I learned everything on the job," she says, "and within two months I was a section head. I used to take the manuals home to try to figure out the theory behind what I was doing."

Because she had little experience, Yvonne decided to take some accounting courses at her local community college. "The College Accounting course was helpful because it gave me the fundamental background I needed," she says. "I found that the things I was feeling intuitively were correct. I learned the theory to back up my real life experience."

Yvonne feels that in each of her jobs she has built up her knowledge, and she has reinforced her experience with the courses she needed. For example, a job as a bookkeeper at Nardi Pontiac led her to a course in automotive bookkeeping given by General Motors. "The courses provided a framework, but I also put in a good deal of hard labour. I taught myself," she says. "I was not afraid to make mistakes. I was not afraid to take work home and figure out how to do a task. I also asked a lot of questions."

Yvonne is now Office Manager, Bookkeeper at R. J. Performance Company. As an additional tip for people who want to work in bookkeeping and accounting, she advises, "Learn how to use a computer. It is vital in this field especially if you work for a small company. Knowledge of computers is essential to employers and will make you invaluable."

Note in Figure 8-4 (p. 278) that the bank deposits ($14,324) minus the cheques written ($6,994) give an ending chequebook balance of $7,330.

At the end of April the bank sends Art a statement that the balance of the cash account is $6,919. How can this be? The following section discusses how this occurs and how it should be handled. Let's now look at the process to reconcile the difference between the bank and chequebook balances.

Differences may result because of timing considerations.

THE BANK RECONCILIATION PROCESS

The **bank statement** or report shows the beginning balance of the cash at the start of the month, along with the cheques the bank has paid and any deposits received (see Figure 8-5) (p. 279). Any other charges or additions to the bank balance are indicated by codes found on the statement. All cheques that have been paid by the bank are sent back to Art's Wholesale. These are called **cancelled cheques** because they have been processed by the bank and are no longer negotiable.

FIGURE 8-4
Transactions Affecting Chequebook Balance

BANK DEPOSITS MADE FOR APRIL

DATE OF DEPOSIT	AMOUNT	RECEIVED FROM
April 1	$8,000	Art Newner, Capital
4	784	Cheque–Hal's Clothing
15	900	Cash sales
16	980	Cheque–Bevans Company
22	1,960	Cheque–Roe Company
27	500	Sale of equipment
30	1,200	Cash sales

Total deposits for month: $14,324

CHEQUES WRITTEN FOR MONTH OF APRIL

DATE	CHEQUE NO.	PAYMENT TO:	AMOUNT	DESCRIPTION
April 2	1	Peter Blum	$ 900	Insurance paid in advance
7	2	Joe Francis Co.	4,000	Paid equipment
9	3	Rick Flo Co.	800	Cash purchases
12	4	Thorpe Co.	594	Paid purchases
28	5	Payroll	700	Salaries

Total amount of cheques written: $ 6,994

Cash/cheque	$14,324
Cheques paid	– 6,994
Balance in company chequebook	$ 7,330

The problem is that this ending bank balance of $6,919 does not agree with the amount in Art's chequebook, $7,330, or the balance in the cash account in the ledger, $7,330.

Art's accountant has to find out why there is a difference between the balances and how the records can be brought into balance. This process of reconciling the bank balance on the bank statement vs. the company's chequebook balance is called a **bank reconciliation**, which must be done monthly. To prepare the bank reconciliation Art's accountant takes a number of steps.

Deposits in Transit

Relationship of cash receipts journal to bank reconciliation.

Note below how the $500 and $1,200 are not checked off, since they did not appear on the bank statement.

In comparing the list of deposits received by the bank with the cash receipts journal (Figure 8-6, p. 280), the accountant notices that the two deposits made on April 27 and 30 for $500 and $1,200 were not on the bank's statement. The accountant realizes that in order to prepare this statement, the bank only included information about Art's Clothing up to April 25. These two deposits made by Art were not shown on the monthly bank statement, since they arrived at the bank after the statement was printed. This timing becomes a consideration in the reconciliation process. The deposits not yet added onto the bank balance are called **deposits in transit**. These two deposits need to be added to the bank balance shown on the bank statement.

FIGURE 8-5   **Bank Statement**

ROYAL BANK PLAZA BRANCH
P.O. BOX 1
TORONTO, ONTARIO
M5J 3H7

03749

ART'S WHOLESALE CLOTHING CO.
1528 BELLE AVENUE
TORONTO, ONTARIO
M5J 3H7

Account Statement

Account No.
138 180 2

Period	
From	**To**
Apr 01/XX	Apr 25/XX

Enclosures	**Page**
3	**1**

Date	Transaction Description		Cheques & Debits	Deposits & Credits	Balance
Apr 01	Balance Forward				.00
Apr 01	Deposit			8,000.00	8,000.00
Apr 02	Cheque -	001	900.00		7,100.00
Apr 04	Deposit			784.00	7,884.00
Apr 07	Cheque -	002	4,000.00		3,884.00
Apr 09	Cheque -	003	800.00		3,084.00
Apr 15	Deposit			900.00	3,984.00
Apr 16	Deposit			980.00	4,964.00
Apr 22	Deposit			1,960.00	6,924.00
Apr 25	SERVICE CHARGE		5.00		6,919.00

No. of Debits	Total Amount	No. of Credits	Total Amount
4	5,705.00	5	12,624.00

**Deposits in transit:
These unrecorded
deposits could result
if a deposit were
placed in a night
depository on the last
day of the month.**

Art's chequebook is not affected, since the two deposits have already been added to its balance. The bank has no way of knowing that the deposits are coming until they are received.

Outstanding Cheques

**Relationship of cash
payments journal to
bank reconciliation.**

The accountant places the cheques returned by the bank in numerical order (1, 2, 3, etc.). He opens the cash payments journal (Figure 8-7) and places a checkmark (√) next to each payment cheque that was returned by the bank. This indicates that the amount shown in the cash payments journal has been paid and the bank has returned the cheques processed (or cancelled after payment). The accountant notices in the cash payments journal that two payments were not made by the bank and these cheques, #4 and #5, were not returned by the bank. On Art's books these

**Cheque nos. 4 and 5
are outstanding.**

two cheques had been deducted from the chequebook balance; therefore, these **outstanding cheques**, or cheques that have not been presented to the bank for payment, are deducted from the bank balance. At some point these cheques will reach the bank. Keep in mind that *Art's* chequebook balance has already sub-

**Cheques outstanding:
Drawn by depositor
but have not reached
bank for payment.**

tracted the amount of these two cheques; it is the *bank* that has no idea these cheques have been written. When they are presented for payment, then the bank will reduce the amount of the balance.

**Art's Wholesale Clothing Company
Cash Receipts Journal**

Page 1

Date		Cash Dr.	Sales Discounts Dr.	Accounts Receivable Cr.	Sales Cr.	Account Name	Post. Ref.	Amount Cr.
19XX April	1	✔ 8 0 0 0 00				Art Newner, Capital	311	8 0 0 0 00
	4	✔ 7 8 4 00	1 6 00	8 0 0 00		Hal's Clothing	✔	
	15	✔ 9 0 0 00			9 0 0 00	Cash Sales	✗	
	16	✔ 9 8 0 00	2 0 00	1 0 0 0 00		Bevans Company	✔	
	22	✔ 1 9 6 0 00	4 0 00	2 0 0 0 00		Roe Company	✔	
	27	5 0 0 00				Store Equipment	121	5 0 0 00
	30	1 2 0 0 00			1 2 0 0 00	Cash Sales	✗	
	30	14 3 2 4 00	7 6 00	3 8 0 0 00	2 1 0 0 00			8 5 0 0 00
		(111)	(413)	(113)	(411)			(X)

FIGURE 8-6

**Cash Receipts
Journal**

The accountant also notices a bank service charge of $5. This means that Art's chequebook balance should be lowered by $5.

The accountant is continually on the lookout for **NSF (Nonsufficient Funds)** cheques. This means that when the company deposits a cheque, occasionally it will be returned due to the customer's lack of sufficient funds. If this happens, it will result in Art's Wholesale having less money than was thought and thus having to (1) lower the chequebook balance and (2) try to collect the amount from the customer. The bank would notify Art's Wholesale of an NSF (or other deductions) cheque by a **debit memorandum**. Think of a <u>de</u>bit memorandum as a <u>de</u>duction from the depositor's balance. Since to a bank, a customer's account represents a liability

De bit memorandum:

<u>De</u>ducted from
balance

Art's Wholesale Clothing Company
Cash Payments Journal

Page 1

Date	Chq. No.	Account Debited	Post. Ref.	Sundry Payable Dr.	Accounts Payable Dr.	Purchases Discount Cr.	Cash Cr.	
19XX								
April 2	1	Prepaid Insurance	116	9 00 00			9 00 00	✔
7	2	Joe Francis Company	✔		4 00 0 00		4 00 0 00	✔
9	3	Purchases	511	8 00 00			8 00 00	✔
12	4	Thorpe Company	✔		6 00 00	6 00	5 94 00	
28	5	Salaries Expense	611	7 00 00			7 00 00	
30				2 4 00 00	4 6 00 00	6 00	6 9 94 00	
				(X)	(211)	(512)	(111)	

FIGURE 8-7

Cash Payments Journal

(the bank must pay out funds if the customer so directs), any reduction in the fund balance requiures a debit – hence the term debit memorandum. Of course, a debit memorandum is recorded by a credit (to cash) on the books of the customer.

If the bank acts as a collecting agent for Art's Wholesale, say in collecting notes, it will charge Art a small fee, and the net amount collected will be added to Art's bank balance. The bank will send to Art a **credit memorandum** verifying the increase in the depositor's balance. This would be recorded by a debit in the company's books as the bank account (an asset) is increasing.

Credit memorandum: Addition to balance

A bank reconciliation can be done on the back of the bank statement (see Figure 8-8, below). Note that the chequebook balance of $7,330 less the $5 service charge will in fact equal the adjusted balance in Box 5.

HOW TO BALANCE THIS STATEMENT WITH YOUR RECORD OF DEPOSITS AND WITHDRAWALS

1. Mark off on your account record all deposits and withdrawals appearing on the front of this account statement.
2. Enter any deposits and withdrawals not recorded in your account record (i.e., bank interest or fees).
3. Complete the worksheet below. If we can be of assistance to you, please contact us.

ACCOUNT RECONCILIATION WORKSHEET

ENTER the closing balance shown on the front of this account statement: 6,919.00

ADD all deposits/credits which do not
appear on this account statement: 500.00
                                                                                      1,200.00

TOTAL additions: > +   1,700.00

SUB-TOTAL: 8,619.00

SUBTRACT all withdrawals/debits which do not
appear on this account statement: 4   594.00
                                                         5   700.00

TOTAL subtractions: > −   1,294.00

This balance should agree with your record of deposits and withdrawals: 7,325.00

FIGURE 8-8

Bank Reconciliation Using Back of Bank Statement

A journal entry is also needed to bring the ledger accounts of cash and service charge expense up to date. Any adjustment to the chequebook balance results in a journal entry. The following entry was made to accomplish this:

Adjustments to the chequebook balance must be journalized and posted. This keeps the depositor's ledger accounts (especially cash) up to date.

April	30	Service Charge Expense*			5 00	
		Cash				5 00

* Could be recorded as miscellaneous expense.

Example of a More Comprehensive Bank Reconciliation

The bank reconciliation of Art's Wholesale, which we just did, was not as complicated as it might have been for many other companies. Let's take a moment to look at the bank reconciliation for Monroe Company, which is based on the following:

Keep in mind that both the bank and the depositor can make mistakes that will not be discovered until the reconciliation process.

1. Chequebook balance: $3,978.
2. Balance reported by bank: $5,230.
3. Recorded in journal cheque no. 108 for $54 *more* than should have been when store equipment was purchased.
4. Bank collected a note ($2,000) for Monroe, charging a collection fee of $10.
5. A bounced cheque for $252 (NSF) has to be covered by Monroe. The bank has lowered Monroe's balance by $252 (see Figure 8-9).
6. Bank service charge of $10.
7. Deposits in transit, $1,084.
8. Cheques not yet processed by the bank:

DM: Remember, a debit memorandum is sent by the bank indicating a reduction in depositor's balance. Examples: NSF, cheque printing.

CHEQUE	AMOUNT
191	$204
198	250
201	100

Monroe Company
Bank Reconciliation as of June 30, 19XX

Chequebook Balance			Balance per Bank		
Ending Chequebook Balance		$3,978	Ending Bank Statement Balance		$5,230
Add:			Add:		
Error in recording			Deposits in Transit		1,084
Cheque no. 108	$54				$6,314
Proceeds of a note*					
less collection					
charge by bank	1,990	2,044	Deduct:		
		$6,022	Cheque no. 191........ $204		
			198........ 250		
Deduct:			201........ 100		554
NSF Cheque	$252				
Bank Service Charge	10	262			
Reconciled Balance		$5,760	Reconciled Balance		$5,760

* We will discuss Notes Receivable in a later chapter—for now, think of it as a kind of written Accounts Receivable.

Note the following journal entries needed to update Monroe Company's books. *Every time an adjustment is made in the reconciliation process to the chequebook balance, a journal entry will be needed.*

19XX								
June	30	Cash		1990 00				
		Collection Expense		10 00				
		Notes Receivable*				2000 00		
	30	Cash		54 00				
		Store Equipment				54 00		
	30	Acct. Rec., Alvin Sooth		252 00				
		Cash				252 00		
	30	Miscellaneous Expense		10 00				
		Cash				10 00		

CM: A credit memo-randum is sent by a bank indicating an increase in depositor's balance. Example: collecting a note.

Remember: If Monroe Company's chequing account was the type that earned interest, it would have increased the chequebook balance.

* We will discuss Notes Receivable in a later chapter—for now, think of it as a kind of written Accounts Receivable.

Before summing up this unit, let's look at two interesting trends in the banking field.

NEW TRENDS IN BANKING
Electronic Funds Transfer

Many financial institutions have developed or are developing a way to transfer funds among parties electronically, without the use of paper cheques. The system that does this is called **electronic funds transfer (EFT)**. Let's look at an example.

Grant MacEwan Community College, with appropriate authorization from its employees, deposits their payroll cheques directly into each employee's bank account, rather than issuing paper cheques. The bank, on receiving computer-coded payroll data, adds each employee's payroll amount to his or her account. This saves time and the possible loss or theft of payroll cheques.

Another good example is the automatic teller machine (ATM). Expect to see these machines used for more transactions than simple banking chores. Sale of stamps, bus passes, and similar items is a real possibility. In the future we will see bank cards used in fast food chains and other retail establishments (the term **Debit Card** is used in connection with these transactions).

Cheque Truncation (Safekeeping)

Some banks do not return cancelled cheques to the depositor but use a procedure called **cheque truncation** or **safekeeping**. What this means is that the bank holds a cancelled cheque for a specific period of time (usually 90 days) and then keeps a microfilm copy handy. What happens if a copy of a cheque is needed? For a small fee the bank provides the depositor with the cheque or a photocopy. (Photocopies will be accepted as evidence by the Tax Department for tax returns and audits.)

Truncation cuts down on the amount of "paper" that is returned to customers and thus provides substantial cost savings. It is estimated that over 5 million cheques are written each day in Canada.

At this point, you should be able to

1. Define and explain the need for deposit slips. (p. 273)
2. Explain where the Bankers' Association transit number is located on the cheque and what its purpose is. (p. 274)
3. List as well as compare and contrast the three common types of cheque endorsement. (p. 275)
4. Explain the structure of a cheque. (p. 276)
5. Define and state the purpose of a bank statement. (pp. 277-278)
6. Explain the relationship of special journals to the bank reconciliation process. (pp. 278-279)
7. Explain deposits in transit, cheques outstanding, service charge, and NSF. (pp. 278-279)
8. Explain the difference between a debit memorandum and a credit memorandum. (pp. 280-281)
9. Explain how to do a bank reconciliation. (p. 282)
10. Explain electronic funds transfer and cheque truncation. (p. 283)

□ SELF-REVIEW QUIZ 8-1

Indicate, by placing an X under it, the heading that describes the appropriate action for each of the following situations:

SITUATION	ADD TO BANK BALANCE	DEDUCT FROM BANK BALANCE	ADD TO CHEQUEBOOK BALANCE	DEDUCT FROM CHEQUEBOOK BALANCE
1. Bank service charge				
2. Deposits in transit				
3. NSF cheque				
4. A $50 cheque was written and recorded by the company as $60				
5. Proceeds of a note collected by the bank				
6. Cheque outstanding				

■ *SOLUTION TO SELF-REVIEW QUIZ 8-1*

SITUATION	ADD TO BANK BALANCE	DEDUCT FROM BANK BALANCE	ADD TO CHEQUEBOOK BALANCE	DEDUCT FROM CHEQUEBOOK BALANCE
1				X
2	X			
3				X
4			X	
5			X	
6		X		

The Establishment of a Petty Cash Fund

Art realized how time-consuming and expensive it would be to write cheques for small amounts to pay for postage, small supplies, delivery charges, and so on. What was needed was a **petty cash fund**. It was estimated that for any given month, Art's Wholesale would need a fund of $60 to cover small expenditures. A cheque payable to the order of the custodian was drawn and cashed to establish the fund. The cash was placed in a small metal box with a simple lock which gave control of the fund to the custodian. Payments out of the fund were only made when a receipt or other supporting documentation was presented by the person requesting the money.

Petty Cash is an asset on the balance sheet.

SETTING UP THE FUND

Shown here is the transaction analysis chart for the establishment of a $60 petty cash fund, which would be entered in the cash payments journal on May 1, 19XX.

1 Accounts Affected	2 Category	3 ↑ ↓	4 Rules
Petty Cash	Asset	↑	Dr.
Cash (cheques)	Asset	↓	Cr.

Petty Cash is an asset, which is established by writing a new cheque. The Petty Cash account is debited only once unless a greater or lesser amount of petty cash is needed on a regular basis.

			Cash Payments Journal						
									Page 2
Date	Chq. No.	Account Debited	PR	Sundry Dr.	Accounts Payable Dr.	Purchases Discount Cr.	Cash Cr.		
19XX May 1	6	Petty Cash	112	60 00			60 00		

Note the new asset called *Petty Cash*; this new asset was created by writing cheque no. 6, thereby reducing the asset Cash. In reality, the total assets stay the same; what has occurred is a shift from the asset Cash (cheque no. 6) to a new asset account called Petty Cash.

The Petty Cash account is not debited or credited again if the size of the fund is not changed. If the $60 fund is used up very quickly, the fund should be increased. If the fund is too large, the Petty Cash account should be reduced.

But who is responsible for controlling the petty cash fund? Art gives his office manager, John Sullivan, the responsibility and the authority to make payments from the petty cash fund. In other companies the cashier or secretary may be in charge of petty cash.

The cheque for $60 is drawn to the order of the custodian, cashed, and the proceeds turned over to John Sullivan, the custodian.

MAKING PAYMENTS FROM THE PETTY CASH FUND

John Sullivan has the responsibility for filling out a **petty cash voucher** for each cash payment made from the petty cash fund.

Note that the voucher (shown in Figure 8-10) when completed will include

1. The voucher number (which will be in sequence): 1.
2. The date: May 2.
3. The person or organization to whom the payment was made: Al's Cleaners.
4. The amount of payment: $3.00.
5. The reason for payment: cleaning.
6. The signature of the person who approved the payment: John Sullivan.
7. The signature of the person who received the payment from petty cash: Art Newner.
8. The account to which the expense will be charged.

Vouchers in box
+ Cash in box
_____
= Original amount placed in petty cash

The completed vouchers are placed in the petty cash box. No matter how many vouchers John Sullivan fills out, *the total of (1) the vouchers in the box and (2) the cash on hand should equal the original amount of petty cash with which the fund was established ($60).*

FIGURE 8-10   **Petty Cash Voucher**

Petty Cash Voucher No. 1	
Date: May 2, 19XX	*Amount:* _$3.00_
Paid To: Al's Cleaners	
For: Cleaning Package	
	Approved By: John Sullivan
	Payment Received By: Art Newner
Debit Account No.: 619	

Assume that at the end of May the following items are documented by petty cash vouchers in the petty cash box as having been paid by John Sullivan:

19XX
May 2 Cleaning package, $3.00.
     5 Postage stamps, $9.00.
     8 First aid supplies, $15.00.
     9 Delivery expense, $6.00.
    14 Delivery expense, $15.00.
    27 Postage stamps, $6.00.

Think of the auxiliary petty cash record as a work sheet that gathers information for the journal entry.

John records this information in the **auxiliary petty cash record** shown in Figure 8-11. It is not a special journal, but an aid to John—an auxiliary record that is not essential but is quite helpful as part of the petty cash system. You may want to think of the auxiliary petty cash as an optional work sheet. Let's look at how to replenish the petty cash fund.

FIGURE 8-11   **Auxiliary Petty Cash Record**

Date	Voucher No.	Description	Receipts	Payments	Postage Expense	Delivery Expense	Sundry Account	Amount
							Category of Payments	
19XX May 1		Establishment	60 00					
2	1	Cleaning		3 00			Cleaning	3 00
5	2	Postage		9 00	9 00			
8	3	First Aid		15 00			Misc.	15 00
9	4	Delivery		6 00		6 00		
14	5	Delivery		15 00		15 00		
27	6	Postage		6 00	6 00			
		Total	60 00	54 00	15 00	21 00		18 00

HOW TO REPLENISH THE PETTY CASH FUND

No postings will be done from the auxiliary book; it is not a journal. At some point the summarized information found in the auxiliary petty cash record will be used as a basis for a journal entry in the cash payments journal and eventually posted to appropriate ledger accounts to reflect up-to-date balances.

This $54 of expenses (see Figure 8-11) is recorded in the cash payments journal (Figure 8-12) and a new cheque, no. 17, for $54 is cashed and returned to John Sullivan. The petty cash box now once again reflects $60 cash. The old vouchers that were used are stamped to indicate that they have been processed and the fund replenished.

FIGURE 8-12

Establishment and Replenishment of Petty Cash Fund

Cash Payments Journal

Establishment   Page 2

Date	Chq. No.	Accounts Debited	PR	Sundry Cr.	Accounts Payable Dr.	Purchases Discount Cr.	Cash Cr.
19XX May 1	6	Petty Cash	112	60 00			60 00

Replenishment

	31	Postage Expense	616	15 00			
		Delivery Expense	620	21 00			
		Cleaning Expense	619	3 00			
	17	Misc. Expense	617	15 00			54 00

Note that in the replenishment process the debits in the cash payments journal (above) are a summary of the totals (except sundry) of expenses or other items from the auxiliary petty cash record. Posting of these specific expenses will assure

In replenishment, old expenses are updated in journal and ledger to show where money has gone.

Auxiliary before replenishment.

A new cheque is written in the replenishment process, which is payable to the custodian, cashed by Sullivan, and the cash placed in the petty cash box.

that the expenses will not be understated on the income statement. *The end result is that our petty cash box is filled, and we have justified which accounts the petty cash money was spent for. Think of replenishment as a single, summarizing entry.*

Remember, if at some point the petty cash fund is to be greater than $60, a cheque can be written that will increase Petty Cash and decrease Cash. If the Petty Cash account balance is to be reduced, we can credit or reduce Petty Cash. But for our present purpose Petty Cash will remain at $60.

The auxiliary petty cash record after replenishment would look as follows (keep in mind no postings are made from the auxiliary):

Auxiliary Petty Cash Record

Date	Voucher No.	Description	Receipts	Payments	Postage Expense	Delivery Expense	Sundry Account	Sundry Amount
19XX May 1		Establishment	60 00					
2	1	Cleaning		3 00			Cleaning	3 00
5	2	Postage		9 00	9 00			
8	3	First Aid		15 00			Misc.	15 00
9	4	Delivery		6 00		6 00		
14	5	Delivery		15 00		15 00		
27	6	Postage		6 00	6 00			
		Totals	60 00	54 00	15 00	21 00		18 00
		Ending Balance		6 00				
			60 00	60 00				
		Ending Balance	6 00					
31		Replenishment	54 00					
31		Balance (New)	60 00					

The diagram in Figure 8-13 (p. 289) may help you put the sequence together.

Before concluding this unit, let's look at how Art will handle a change fund and problems with cash shortages and overages.

Change Fund is an asset on the balance sheet.

THE CHANGE FUND AND CASH SHORT AND OVER

If a company like Art's Wholesale expects to have many cash transactions occurring, it may be a good idea to establish a **change fund**. This is a fund that is placed in the cash register drawer and used to make change for customers who pay cash. Art decides to put $120 in the change fund, made up of various denominations of bills and coins. Let's look at a transaction analysis chart for this sort of procedure.

FIGURE 8-13

Steps Involving Petty Cash

Has nothing to do with petty cash.

In this step the old expenses are listed in cash payments journal and a new cheque is written to replenish.

Date		Description	New Cheque Written	Recorded in Cash Payments Journal	Petty Cash Voucher Prepared	Recorded in Auxiliary Petty Cash Record
19XX Jan.	1	Establishment of				
		petty cash for $60	X	X		X
	2	Paid salaries,				
		$2,000	X	X		
	13	Paid $10 from petty				
		cash for Band-Aids			X	X
	19	Paid $8 from petty				
		cash for postage			X	X
	24	Paid light bill,				
		$200	X	X		
	29	Replenishment of				
		petty cash to $60	X	X		X

1 Accounts Affected	2 Category	3 ↑ ↓	4 Dr./Cr.
Change Fund	Asset	↑	Dr.
Cash	Asset	↓	Cr.

At the close of the business day Art will deposit in the bank the cash taken in for the day but will place the amount of the change fund back in the safe in the office. He will set up the change fund (the same $120) in the appropriate denominations for the next business day.

Now let's look at how to record errors that are made in making change, called cash short and over.

Cash Short and Over

Errors often occur in making change, and so the amount of cash will often be higher or lower than it should be. An account called **Cash Short and Over** will accumulate these shortages or overages. Shortages are debited to the account; overages are credited. At the end of the accounting period, if there are more shortages than overages (debit balance), the net shortage is shown on the income statement as a miscellaneous expense. If the ending balance is an overage (credit balance), it is reported on the income statement as miscellaneous income.

Beg. change fund
+ Cash register total
= Cash should have on hand
− Counted cash
= Shortage or overage of cash

Example 1:   Cash register tapes don't agree with cash receipts.

Cash Short & Over

Shortages	Overages
↑	↑
Misc. Expense	Misc. Income

Situation 1: Overage

		Dec.	5	Cash		550			
				Cash short					
				and over			1		
				Sales			549		

Situation 2: Shortage

		Dec.	15	Cash		600			
				Cash short					
				and over			5		
				Sales			605		

Example 2:   Petty Cash has a shortage of $8. The facts are:

$200   Petty Cash account
160   in receipts for expenses
32   in coin and currency

A general journal entry would look as follows:

Using Cash Short and Over with Petty Cash.

Individual Expenses	160	
Cash Short and Over	8	
Cash		168

Keep in mind that in actuality we would use a cash payments journal as well as debit *each* individual expense.

If an auxiliary petty cash record is used to record the cash short and over, it would be recorded as a payment of $8 under the category of payments in the sundry column.

At this time you should be able to

1. State the purpose of a petty cash fund. (p. 285)
2. Prepare a journal entry to establish a petty cash fund. (p. 285)
3. Prepare a petty cash voucher. (p. 286)
4. Explain the relationship of the auxiliary petty cash record to the petty cash process. (p. 286)
5. Prepare a journal entry to replenish Petty Cash to its original amount. (p. 287)
6. Explain why individual expenses are debited in the replenishment process. (pp. 287-288)
7. Explain how a change fund is established. (p. 288)
8. Explain how Cash Short and Over could be a miscellaneous expense. (p. 288)

☐   **SELF-REVIEW QUIZ 8-2**

As the custodian of the petty cash fund it is your task to prepare entries to establish the fund on October 1, as well as to replenish the fund on October 31. Please keep an auxiliary petty cash record.

19XX
Oct.   1   Establish petty cash fund for $90, cheque no. 8.
       5   Voucher 11, delivery expense, $21.
       9   Voucher 12, delivery expense, $15.
       10   Voucher 13, office repair expense, $24.

17   Voucher 14, general expense, $12.
25   Voucher 15, general expense, $6.
30   Replenishment of petty cash fund, $78, cheque no. 108. (Cheque would be payable to the custodian.)

Cheques to establish and replenish Petty Cash would be made out to the custodian.

■ SOLUTION TO SELF-REVIEW QUIZ 8-2

Cash Payments Journal

Page 4

Date	Chq. No.	Accounts Debited	PR	Sundry Dr.	Accounts Payable Dr.	Purchases Discount Cr.	Cash Cr.
19XX Oct. 1	8	Petty Cash	*	90 00			90 00
31		Delivery Expense		36 00			
		General Expense		18 00			
	108	Office Repair Expense		24 00			78 00

* The PR would show posting. Deleted for simplicity at this point.

Auxiliary Petty Cash Record

Date	Voucher No.	Description	Receipts	Payments	Delivery Expense	General Expense	Sundry Account	Amount
19XX Oct. 1		Establishment	90 00					
5	11	Delivery		21 00	21 00			
9	12	Delivery		15 00	15 00			
10	13	Repairs		24 00			Office Repair	24 00
17	14	General		12 00		12 00		
25	15	General		6 00		6 00		
		Totals	90 00	78 00	36 00	18 00		24 00
		Ending Balance		12 00				
			90 00	90 00				
30		Ending Balance	12 00					
31		Replenishment	78 00					
Nov. 1		New Balance	90 00					

SUMMARY OF KEY POINTS AND KEY TERMS

LEARNING UNIT 8-1

1. Restrictive endorsement limits any further negotiation of a cheque.
2. Cheque stubs are filled out first before a cheque is written.
3. The payee is the person the cheque is payable to. The drawer is the one who orders the bank to pay a sum of money. The drawee is the bank that the drawer has an account with.
4. The process of reconciling the bank balance with the company's balance is called the bank reconciliation. The timing of deposits, when the bank statement was issued, etc., often results in differences between the bank balance and the chequebook balance.
5. Deposits in transit are added to the bank balance.
6. Cheques outstanding are subtracted from the bank balance.
7. NSF means that a cheque has insufficient funds to be credited to a chequing account; therefore the amount is not included in the bank balance and thus the chequing account balance is lowered.
8. When a bank debits your account they are deducting an amount from your balance. A credit to the account is an increase to your balance.
9. All adjustments to the chequebook balance require journal entries.

ATM: Automatic teller machine.

Bank reconciliation: This is the process of reconciling the chequebook balance with the bank balance given on the bank statement.

Bank statement: A report sent by a bank to a customer indicating the previous balance, individual cheques processed, individual deposits received, service charges, and ending bank balance.

Cancelled cheque: A cheque that has been processed by a bank and is no longer negotiable.

Cheque: A form used to indicate a specific amount of money that is to be paid by the bank to a named person or company.

Cheque truncation (safekeeping): Procedure whereby cheques are not returned to drawer with the bank statement but are instead kept at the bank for a certain amount of time before being first transferred to microfilm and then destroyed.

Credit memorandum: Increase in depositor's balance.

Debit memorandum: Decrease in depositor's balance.

Deposits in transit: Deposits that were made by customers of a bank but did not reach, or were not processed by, the bank before the preparation of the bank statement.

Deposit slip: A form provided by a bank for use in depositing money or cheques into a chequing account.

Drawee: Bank that drawer has an account with.

Drawer: Person who writes a cheque.

Endorsement: *Blank*—could be further endorsed. *Full*—restricts further endorsement to only the person or company named. *Restrictive*—restricts any further endorsement.

EFT (electronic funds transfer): An electronic system that transfers funds without use of paper cheques.

Internal control: A system of procedures and methods to control a firm's assets as well as monitor its operations.

NSF (Nonsufficient Funds): Notation indicating that a cheque has been written on an account that lacks sufficient funds to back it up.

Outstanding cheques: Cheques written by a company or person that were not received or not processed by the bank before the preparation of the bank statement.

Payee: The person or company the cheque is payable to.

LEARNING UNIT 8-2

1. Petty Cash is an asset found on the balance sheet.

2. The auxiliary petty cash record is an auxiliary book; thus no postings are done from this book. Think of it as an optional work sheet.

3. When a petty cash fund is established, the amount is entered as a debit to Petty Cash and a credit to Cash in the cash payments journal.

4. At time of replenishment of the petty cash fund, all expenses are debited (by category) and a credit to Cash (a new cheque) results. This replenishment, when journalized and posted, updates the ledger from the journal.

5. The only time the Petty Cash account is used is to establish the fund to begin with or bring the fund to a higher or lower level. If the petty cash level is deemed sufficient, all replenishments will debit specific expenses and new cheques written. The asset Petty Cash will remain the same.

6. A change fund is an asset that is used to make change for customers.

7. Cash Short and Over is an account that is either a miscellaneous expense or miscellaneous income, depending on whether the ending balance is shortage or overage.

Auxiliary petty cash record: A supplementary record for summarizing petty cash information.

Cash Short and Over: The account that records cash shortages and overages. If ending balance is a debit, it is recorded on the income statement as a miscellaneous expense; if it is a credit, it is recorded as miscellaneous income.

Change fund: Fund made up of various denominations that is used to make change to customers.

Petty cash fund: A fund (source) that allows payment of small amounts without the writing of cheques.

Petty cash voucher: A petty cash form to be completed when money is taken out of petty cash.

BLUEPRINT OF A BANK RECONCILIATION

CHEQUEBOOK BALANCE			BALANCE PER BANK		
Ending Balance per Books		$XXX	Ending Bank Statement Balance (last figure on bank statement)		$XXX
Add:			Add:		
Recording of errors that understate balance	XXX		Deposits in transit (amount not yet credited by bank)	XXX	
Proceeds of notes collected by bank or other items credited (added) by bank but not yet updated in chequebook	XXX	XXX	Bank errors	XXX	XXX
Deduct:			Deduct:		
Recording of errors that overstate balance	XXX		List of outstanding cheques (amount not yet debited by bank)	XXX	
Service charges	XXX		Bank errors	XXX	
Printing charges	XXX				XXX
NSF, cheque, etc., or other items debited (charged) by bank but not yet updated in chequebook	XXX				
Reconciled Balance (Adusted Balance)		XXX $XXX	Reconciled Balance (Adusted Balance)		$XXX

DISCUSSION QUESTIONS

1. What is the purpose of internal control?
2. What is the advantage of having preprinted deposit tickets?
3. Explain the difference between a blank endorsement and a restrictive endorsement.
4. Explain the difference between payee, drawer, and drawee.
5. Why should cheque stubs be filled out first, before the cheque itself is written?
6. A bank statement is sent twice a month. True or false? Please explain.
7. Explain the end product of a bank reconciliation.
8. Why are cheques outstanding subtracted from the bank balance?
9. An NSF results in a bank issuing the depositor a credit memorandum. Agree or disagree. Please support your response.
10. Why do adjustments to the chequebook balance in the reconciliation process need to be journalized?
11. What is EFT?

12. What is meant by cheque truncation or safekeeping?
13. Petty cash is a liability. Accept or reject.
14. Explain the relationship of the auxiliary petty cash record to the cash payments journal.
15. At time of replenishment, why are the totals of individual expenses debited?
16. Explain the purpose of a change fund.
17. Explain how Cash Short and Over can be a miscellaneous expense.

EXERCISES

1. From the following information, construct a bank reconciliation for Norry Co. as of July 31, 19XX. Then prepare journal entries if needed.

Bank reconciliation.

Ending chequebook balance	$420
Ending bank statement balance	300
Deposits (in transit)	200
Outstanding cheques	95
Bank service charge (debit memo)	15

2. In general journal form (to keep it simple), prepare journal entries to establish a petty cash fund on July 1 and replenish it on July 31.

Establishing and replenishing petty cash.

July   1   A $40 petty cash fund is established.
      31   At end of month $12 cash plus the following paid vouchers exist: donations expense, $10; postage expense, $7; office supplies expense, $7; miscellaneous expense, $4.

3. If in Exercise 2 cash on hand was $11, prepare the entry to replenish the petty cash on July 31.

Cash overage in replenishment.

4. If in Exercise 2 cash on hand was $13, prepare the entry to replenish the petty cash on July 31.

Cash shortage in replenishment.

5. At the end of day the clerk for Pete's Variety Shop noticed an error in the amount of cash he should have. Total cash sales from the sales tape were $1,100 while the total cash in the register was $1,056. Pete keeps a $30 change fund in his shop. Prepare an appropriate general journal entry to record the cash sale as well as reveal the cash shortage.

Calculate cash shortage with Change Fund.

GROUP A PROBLEMS

8A-1. Rose Company received a bank statement from T D Bank indicating a bank balance of $6,950. Based on Rose's cheque stubs, the ending chequebook balance was $5,825. Your task is to prepare a bank reconciliation for Rose Company as of July 31, 19XX, from the following information (please journalize entries as needed):

Preparing a bank reconciliation including collection of a note.

A. Cheques outstanding: no. 124, $600; no. 126, $850.
B. Deposits in transit, $960.
C. Bank service charge, $18.
D. T D Bank collected a note for Rose, $660, less a $7 collection fee.

**Preparing a bank rec-
onciliation with NSF
using back side of a
bank statement.**

8A-2. From the bank statement (opposite), please (1) complete the bank reconciliation for Rick's Deli found on the reverse of the bank statement, and (2) journalize the appropriate entries as needed.

    A. A deposit of $3,000 is in transit.
    B. Rick's Deli has an ending chequebook balance of $6,600.
    C. Cheques outstanding: no. 111, $600; no. 119, $1,200; no. 121, $330.
    D. Jim Rice's cheque for $300 bounced due to lack of sufficient funds.

**Establishment and
replenishment of
petty cash.
Relationship to
special journals
and auxiliary petty
cash record.**

8A-3. The following transactions occurred in April and were related to the cash payments journal and petty cash fund of Merry Co.:

19XX
April 1   Issued cheque no. 14 for $80 to establish a petty cash fund.
      5   Paid $5 from petty cash for postage, voucher no. 1.
      8   Paid $10 from petty cash for office supplies, voucher no. 2.
    15   Issued cheque no. 15 to Reliable Corp. for $200 less a 2% discount for past purchases on account.
    17   Paid $8 from petty cash for office supplies, voucher no. 3.
    20   Issued cheque no. 16 to Roger Corp., $600, less a 5% discount from past purchases on account.
    24   Paid $4 from petty cash for postage, voucher no. 4.
    26   Paid $9 from petty cash for local church donation, voucher no. 5 (this is a miscellaneous payment).
    28   Issued cheque no. 17 to Roy Kloon to pay for office equipment, $700.

From the chart of accounts: Petty Cash, 120; Office Equipment, 130; Postage Expense, 610; Office Supplies Expense, 620; Miscellaneous Expense, 630. The headings of the cash payments and auxiliary petty cash records are as follows:

				Cash Payments Journal			*Page 2*
Date	Cheque No.	Accounts Debited	PR	Sundry Dr.	Accounts Payable Dr.	Purchases Discounts Cr.	Cash Cr.

						Auxiliary Petty Cash Record			Category of Payments		
Date	Voucher No.	Description	Receipt	Payment	Postage Expense	Office Supplies Expense	Sundry Account	Sundry Amount

Your task is to
    1. Record the appropriate entries in the cash payments journal as well as the auxiliary petty cash record as needed.
    2. Be sure to replenish the petty cash fund on April 30 (cheque no. 18).

BANK OF SASKATCHEWAN
10050 - 101 Street
Regina, Saskatchewan
S4J 6E2

03749

RICK'S DELI
8811 - 102 Street
Regina, SA
S3A 3G6

Account Statement

Account No.
241 673 6

Period	
From	**To**
Feb 01/XX	Feb 28/XX

Enclosures	Page
2	**1**

Date	Transaction Description		Cheques & Debits	Deposits & Credits	Balance
Feb 01	Balance Forward				6,000.00
Feb 02	Cheque -	108	90.00		
Feb 03	Cheque -	114	210.00		5,700.00
Feb 10	Deposit			300.00	
Feb 10	Cheque -	116	150.00		5,850.00
Feb 14	Deposit			600.00	6,450.00
Feb 15	Cheque -	113	600.00		5,850.00
Feb 20	Deposit			300.00	
Feb 20	NSF Returned Item		300.00		5,850.00
Feb 22	Deposit			1,200.00	7,050.00
Feb 24	Cheque -	117	1,200.00		5,850.00
Feb 26	Deposit			180.00	6,030.00
Feb 28	Cheque -	120	600.00		
Feb 28	Service Charge		30.00		5,400.00

No. of Debits	Total Amount	No. of Credits	Total Amount
8	3,180.00	5	2,580.00

8A-4. From the following, record the transactions into Logan's auxiliary petty cash record and cash payments journal (p. 33) as needed:

Establishing and replenishing petty cash including a cash shortage.

19XX

Oct. 1 A cheque was drawn (no. 444) payable to Roberta Floss, petty cashier, to establish a $100 petty cash fund.

5 Paid $14 for postage stamps, voucher no. 1.

9 Paid $12 for delivery charges on goods for resale, voucher no. 2.

12 Paid $8 for donation to a church (Miscellaneous Expense), voucher no. 3.

14 Paid $9 for postage stamps, voucher no. 4.

17 Paid $8 for delivery charges on goods for resale, voucher no. 5.

27 Purchased computer supplies from petty cash for $8, voucher no. 6.

28 Paid $4 for postage, voucher no. 7.

29 Drew cheque no. 618 to replenish petty cash and a $3 shortage.

GROUP B PROBLEMS

Preparing a bank reconciliation including collection of a note.

8B-1. As the bookkeeper of Rose Company you received the bank statement from T D Bank indicating a balance of $9,185. The ending chequebook balance was $8,215. Prepare the bank reconciliation for Rose Company as of July 31, 19XX, and prepare journal entries as needed based on the following:

A. Deposits in transit, $3,600.
B. Bank service charges, $29.
C. Cheques outstanding: no. 111, $590; no. 115, $1,255.
D. T D Bank collected a note for Rose, $2,760, less a $6 collection fee.

Preparing a bank reconciliation with NSF using back side of a bank statement.

8B-2. Based on the following, please (1) complete the bank reconciliation for Rick's Deli found on the reverse of the bank statement (opposite), and (2) journalize the appropriate entries as needed.

A. Cheques outstanding: no. 110, $80; no. 116, $160; no. 118, $52.
B. A deposit of $416 is in transit.
C. The chequebook balance of Rick's Deli shows an ending balance of $798.
D. Jim Rice's cheque for $40 bounced due to lack of sufficient funds.

Establishment and replenishment of petty cash. Relationship to special journals and auxiliary petty cash record.

8B-3. From the following transactions, (1) record the entries as needed in the cash payments journal of Merry Co. as well as the auxiliary petty cash record, and (2) replenish the petty cash fund on April 30 (cheque no. 8).

19XX

April 1 Issued cheque no. 4 for $60 to establish a petty cash fund.

5 Paid $9 from petty cash for postage, voucher no. 1.

8 Paid $12 from petty cash for office supplies, voucher no. 2.

15 Issued cheque no. 5 to Reliable Corp. for $400 less a 2% discount.

17 Paid $7 from petty cash for office supplies, voucher no. 3.

20 Issued cheque no. 6 to Roger Corp., $300, less a 5% discount from past purchases on account.

24 Paid $6 from petty cash for postage, voucher no. 4.

26 Paid $12 from petty cash for local church donation, voucher no. 5 (this is a miscellaneous payment).

28 Issued cheque no. 7 to Roy Kloon to pay office equipment, $800.

BANK OF SASKATCHEWAN
10050 - 101 Street
Regina, Saskatchewan
S4J 6E2

03749

RICK'S DELI
8811 - 102 Street
Regina, SA
S3A 3G6

Account Statement

Account No.
241 673 6

Period	
From	To
Apr 01/XX	Apr 30/XX

Enclosures	Page
2	**1**

Date	Transaction Description		Cheques & Debits	Deposits & Credits	Balance
Apr 01	Balance Forward				718.00
Apr 02	Cheque -	108	12.00		
Apr 03	Cheque -	114	36.00		670.00
Apr 10	Deposit			40.00	
Apr 10	Cheque -	115	20.00		690.00
Apr 14	Deposit			80.00	770.00
Apr 15	Cheque -	113	80.00		690.00
Apr 20	Deposit			40.00	
Apr 20	NSF Returned Item		40.00		690.00
Apr 22	Deposit			160.00	850.00
Apr 24	Cheque -	117	160.00		690.00
Apr 26	Deposit			24.00	714.00
Apr 28	Cheque -	109	80.00		
Apr 28	Service Charge		2.00		632.00

No. of Debits	Total Amount	No. of Credits	Total Amount
8	430.00	5	344.00

Chart of accounts includes: Petty Cash 120; Office Equipment, 130; Postage Expense, 610; Office Supplies Expense, 620; Miscellaneous Expense, 630. Use the same headings as in Problem 8A-3 (p. 232).

Establishing and replenishing petty cash including a cash shortage.

8B-4. From the following, record the transactions into Logan's auxiliary petty cash record and cash payments journal (p. 33) as needed:

19XX

Oct.	1	Roberta Floss, the petty cashier, cashed a cheque, no. 444, to establish a $90 petty cash fund.
	5	Paid $16 for postage stamps, voucher no. 1.
	9	Paid $14 for delivery charges on goods for resale, voucher no. 2.
	12	Paid $6 for donation to a church (Miscellaneous Expense), voucher no. 3.
	14	Paid $10 for postage stamps, voucher no. 4.
	17	Paid $7 for delivery charges on goods for resale, voucher no. 5.
	27	Purchased computer supplies from petty cash for $9, voucher no. 6.
	28	Paid $3 for postage, voucher no. 7.
	29	Drew cheque no. 618 to replenish petty cash and a $4 shortage.

GROUP C PROBLEMS

Preparing a bank reconciliation including collection of a note.

8C-1. Regina Company received a bank statement from Royal Bank indicating a bank balance of $4,128. Based on Regina's cheque stubs, the ending chequebook balance was $3,398. Your task is to prepare a bank reconciliation for Regina Company as of May 31, 19XX, from the following information (please journalize entries as needed):

A. Cheques outstanding: no. 354, $267; no. 356, $690; no. 347, $352
B. Deposits in transit, $1,254.
C. Bank service charge, $23.
D. Royal Bank collected a note for Regina, $834, less a $11 collection fee.
E. Notice received that a cheque from Fred Brown, a customer, was returned NSF, $125.

Preparing a bank reconciliation with NSF using back side of a bank statement.

8C-2. From the following June 28, 19XX bank statement, please (1) complete a bank reconciliation for Freda's Flower Shop, and (2) journalize the appropriate entries as needed.

A. A deposit of $2,870 is in transit.
B. Freda's Flower Shop has an ending cash account balance of $4,961.
C. Cheques outstanding: no. 231, $290; no. 245, $895; no. 246, $78; no 247, $455.
D. Joan Brice's cheque for $125 bounced due to non-sufficient funds.
E. Cheque no. 241 for utilities expense was entered in the cash payments journal as $358.
F. The cheque for $672 shown by the bank as paid on July 28 was actually a cheque of the Acme Machine Shop. This error will be corrected by the bank next month. The bank apologized for their error.

BANK OF INDUSTRY AND COMMERCE
48 JAMES STREET
HALIFAX, NOVA SCOTIA
B4T 2L0

08179

FREDA'S FLOWER SHOP
121 SPRING GARDEN ROAD
HALIFAX, NS
B5H 3E6

Account Statement

Account No.	
914 817 2	

Period	
From	**To**
Jun 29/XX	Jul 28/XX

Enclosures	**Page**
2	**1**

Date	Transaction Description		Cheques & Debits	Deposits & Credits	Balance
Jul 01	Balance Forward				2,624.00
Jul 02	Cheque -	241	385.00		2,239.00
Jul 03	Cheque -	240	410.00		1,829.00
Jul 10	Deposit			1,712.00	
Jul 10	Cheque -	243	250.00		3,291.00
Jul 14	Deposit			950.00	4,241.00
Jul 15	Cheque -	242	1,214.00		3,027.00
Jul 16	Deposit			125.00	3,152.00
Jul 20	NSF Returned Item		125.00		3,027.00
Jul 22	Deposit			1,260.00	4,287.00
Jul 24	Cheque -	248	1,410.00		2,877.00
Jul 26	Deposit			780.00	3,657.00
Jul 28	Cheque -	1126	672.00		
Jul 28	Service Charge		16.00		2,969.00

No. of Debits	Total Amount	No. of Credits	Total Amount
8	4,482.00	5	4,827.00

8C-3. The following transactions occurred in March and were related to the cash payments journal and petty cash fund of Jenkins & Co.:

Establishment and replenishment of petty cash. Relationship to special journals and auxiliary petty cash record.

19XX
March 1   Issued cheque no. 314 for $200 to establish a petty cash fund.
        5   Paid $45 from petty cash for postage, voucher no. 1.
        8   Paid $32 from petty cash for office supplies, voucher no. 2.
       15   Issued cheque no. 315 to Schuller Corp. for $1,390 less a 2% discount for past purchases on account.
       17   Paid $28 from petty cash for office supplies, voucher no. 3.
       20   Issued cheque no. 316 to The Norton Group, $940, less a 5% discount for past purchases on account.
       24   Paid $54 from petty cash for postage, voucher no. 4.
       26   Paid $20 from petty cash for local church donation, voucher no. 5 (this is a miscellaneous payment).
       28   Issued cheque no. 317 to Klondike Office Equipment to pay for office equipment, $2,700.

From the chart of accounts: Petty Cash, 105; Office Equipment, 170; Postage Expense, 645; Office Supplies Expense, 640; Miscellaneous Expense, 630. The headings of the cash payments and auxiliary petty cash records are the same as for 8A-3.

Your task is to
  1. Record the appropriate entries in the cash payments journal as well as the auxiliary petty cash record as needed.
  2. Be sure to replenish the petty cash fund on March 31 (cheque no. 318).

8C-4. From the following, record the transactions into Brennan Co.'s auxiliary petty cash record and cash payments journal (p. 24) as needed:

Establishing and replenishing petty cash including a cash shortage.

19XX
Oct. 1   A cheque was drawn (no. 772) payable to Rob Kiriak, petty cashier, to establish a $250 petty cash fund.
       5   Paid $34 for postage stamps, voucher no. 1.
       9   Paid $15 for delivery charges on goods for resale, voucher no. 2.
      12   Paid $25 for donation to a church (Miscellaneous Expense), voucher no. 3.
      14   Paid $49 for postage stamps, voucher no. 4.
      17   Paid $9 for delivery charges on goods for resale, voucher no. 5.
      27   Purchased computer supplies from petty cash for $18, voucher no. 6.
      28   Paid $24 for postage, voucher no. 7.
      29   Drew cheque no. 813 to replenish petty cash (a $3 shortage was apparent when the cash was balanced).

PRACTICAL ACCOUNTING APPLICATION #1

Karen Johnson, the bookkeeper of Hoop Co., has appointed Jim Pool as the petty cash custodian. The following transactions occurred in November:

19XX
Nov. 25   Cheque no. 441 was written and cashed to establish a $50 petty cash fund.
      27   Paid $8.50 delivery charge for goods purchased for resale.

29 Purchased office supplies for $12 from petty cash.
30 Purchased postage stamps for $15 from petty cash.

On December 3 Jim received the following internal memo:

> TO: *Jim Pool*
> FROM: *Karen Johnson*
> RE: *Petty Cash*
>
> *Jim, I'll need $5 for postage stamps. By the way, I noticed that our petty cash account seems to be too low. Let's increase its size to $100.*

Could you help Jim replenish petty cash on December 3 by providing him with a general journal entry? Support your answer and indicate whether Karen was correct.

PRACTICAL ACCOUNTING APPLICATION #2

Ginger Company has a policy of depositing all receipts and making all payments by cheque. On receiving the bank statement, Bill Free, a new bookkeeper, is quite upset that the balance in cash in the ledger is $4,209.50 while the ending bank balance is $4,440.50. Bill is convinced the bank has made an error. Based on the following facts, is Bill's concern warranted? What other suggestions could you offer Bill in the bank reconciliation process?

(a) The Nov. 30 cash receipts, $611, had been placed in the bank's night depository after banking hours and consequently did not appear on the bank statement as a deposit.

(b) Two debit memorandums and a credit memorandum were included with the returned cheque. None of the memorandums had been recorded at the time of the reconciliation. The first debit memorandum had a $130 NSF cheque written by Abby Ellen. The second was a $6.50 debit memorandum for service charges. The credit memorandum was for $494 and represented the proceeds less a $6 collection fee from a $500 non-interest-bearing note collected for Ginger Company by the bank.

(c) It was also found that cheques no. 942 for $71.50 and no. 947 for $206.50, both written and recorded on Nov. 28, were not among the cancelled cheques returned.

(d) Bill found that cheque no. 899 was correctly drawn for $1,094, in payment for a new cash register. However, this cheque had been recorded as though it were for $1,148.

(e) The October bank reconciliation showed two cheques outstanding on September 30, no. 621 for $152.50 and no. 630 for $179.30. Cheque no. 630 was returned with the November bank statement, but cheque no. 621 was not.

PRACTICAL ACCOUNTING APPLICATION #3

On March 2, 19XX the accountant for Mansfield Carpet Co. was injured in a skiing accident and was advised not to return to work for 6 weeks. The owners of the company are anxious to ensure that the company's bank is reconciled and have asked you to perform this task. You are presented with the following information:

(a) Bank Reconciliation prepared by the regular accountant at January 31, 19XX.

MANSFIELD CARPET CO.
BANK RECONCILIATION
JANUARY 31,19XX

Balance Per Bank Statement:		$ 8,364.02
Add, Deposit in Transit:		2,576.03
		10,940.05
Less, Outstanding Cheques:		
No. 417	$ 28.30	
419	1,043.25	
423	1,722.30	2,793.85
Balance per General Ledger:		$ 8,146.20

(b) General ledger listing of Bank Account (#110) for the month of February (see p. 305).

(c) Bank statement from the Royal Bank for the month ending February 26, 19XX (see p. 306).

Required:
Prepare the necessary reconciliation and any journal entries necessary at Feb. 28, 19XX.

Date: 11 Mar. XX   11:06 am   MANSFIELD CARPET CO.   Page: 1
G/L Listing
                                    General Ledger Listing as of 28 Feb XX

G/L listing for account   [110]   to [110]
for department   [   ] to [222],
for fiscal period   [2] 0   [2],
sorted by   [Account   ].

Last posting sequence number: 4

Acct. Dept.

Pd	Srce	Date	Description	Reference	Posting Entry	Batch Entry	Debits	Credits	Net Change/ Balance
	110	Bank							8,146.20
2	GL-GJ	01 Feb XX	KING PROPERTY	CHQ 404	2 - 1	2 - 1		974.15	
2	GL-GJ	01 Feb XX	SANDRA SMYTHE - Deposit	1007	2 - 2	2 - 2	8,145.38		
2	GL-GJ	02 Feb XX	INGRID LUNDREN - Deposit	1008	2 - 3	2 - 3	909.50		
2	GL-GJ	02 Feb XX	CAMPUS COPY SHOPPE	CHQ 424	2 - 4	2 - 4		133.75	
2	GL-GJ	02 Feb XX	BENJAMIN YEE	02 - 05	2 - 5	2 - 5	4,381.65		
2	GL-GJ	05 Feb XX	LITEMORE NEON SIGNS	CHQ 425	2 - 6	2 - 6		80.25	
2	GL-GJ	05 Feb XX	NORM & JANET TAYLOR - Deposit	1009	2 - 7	2 - 7	969.01		
2	GL-GJ	06 Feb XX	NAME - IT!	CHQ 426	2 - 9	2 - 9		240.75	
2	GL-GJ	07 Feb XX	JERRY SIMON - Deposit	1011	2 - 10	2 - 10	2,782.00		
2	GL-GJ	07 Feb XX	SAXONY WOOL MILLS	CHQ 427	2 - 11	2 - 11		4,559.11	
2	GL-GJ	07 Feb XX	QUALITY CARPET COMPANY	CHQ 428	2 - 12	2 - 12		6,829.28	
2	GL-GJ	07 Feb XX	JODY ARCHER	CHQ 429	2 - 13	2 - 13		25.00	
2	GL-GJ	08 Feb XX	CITY PHONE COMPANY	CHQ 430	2 - 14	2 - 14		121.75	
2	GL-GJ	08 Feb XX	CITY UTILITY COMPANY	CHQ 431	2 - 15	2 - 15		111.14	
2	GL-GJ	08 Feb XX	JOE'S GAS BAR	CHQ 432	2 - 16	2 - 16		94.66	
2	GL-GJ	08 Feb XX	WOOD'S STATIONERY	CHQ 433	2 - 17	2 - 17		1,091.40	
2	GL-GJ	02 Feb XX	CASH	CHQ 434	2 - 18	2 - 18		100.00	
2	GL-GJ	09 Feb XX	IVY LEUNG - Deposit	1012	2 - 19	2 - 19	2,169.96		
2	GL-GJ	09 Feb XX	EMILY MANSFIELD - Salary	CHQ 435	2 - 20	2 - 20		697.35	
2	GL-GJ	09 Feb XX	JAMES MANSFIELD - Salary	CHQ 436	2 - 21	2 - 21		697.35	
2	GL-GJ	09 Feb XX	RBC/TERMPLAN LOAN PAYMENT	02 - 22	2 - 22	2 - 22		601.87	
2	GL-GJ	09 Feb XX	RBC/DEMAND LOAN INTEREST	02 - 23	2 - 23	2 - 23		695.20	
2	GL-GJ	13 Feb XX	PAT HARPER - Deposit	1013	2 - 27	2 - 27	404.46		
2	GL-GJ	15 Feb XX	CITY LIGHTING	CHQ 437	2 - 29	2 - 29		112.50	
2	GL-GJ	15 Feb XX	FREDDY DUNCAN	CHQ 438	2 - 30	2 - 30		2,010.40	
2	GL-GJ	15 Feb XX	RECEIVER GENERAL FOR CANADA	CHQ 439	2 - 31	2 - 31		993.04	
2	GL-GJ	15 Feb XX	VOID	CHQ 440	2 - 32	2 - 32	0.00		
2	GL-GJ	16 Feb XX	WILSON INSURANCE AGENCY	CHQ 441	2 - 33	2 - 33		802.50	
2	GL-GJ	16 Feb XX	COMMUNITY CALENDAR	CHQ 442	2 - 34	2 - 34		246.10	
2	GL-GJ	16 Feb XX	STANDARD NEWS	CHQ 443	2 - 35	2 - 35		909.50	
2	GL-GJ	16 Feb XX	T C CHURCHILL - Deposit	1015	2 - 36	2 - 36	3,610.18		
2	GL-GJ	16 Feb XX	RBC/LOAN PROCESSING CHARGE	02 - 37	2 - 37	2 - 37		40.00	
2	GL-GJ	19 Feb XX	BEATRICE DAY - Deposit	1016	2 - 38	2 - 38	4,068.68		
2	GL-GJ	22 Feb XX	JOAN ANDERSON - Deposit	02 - 44	2 - 44	2 - 44	2,569.07		
2	GL-GJ	23 Feb XX	EMILY MANSFIELD - Salary	CHQ 444	2 - 46	2 - 46		697.35	
2	GL-GJ	23 Feb XX	JAMES MANSFIELD - Salary	CHQ 445	2 - 47	2 - 47		697.35	
2	GL-GJ	24 Feb XX	BOB JONES	CHQ 446	2 - 49	2 - 49		240.00	
2	GL-GJ	26 Feb XX	MICHEL ROBICHAUD - Deposit	02 - 53	2 - 53	2 - 53	3,456.10		
2	GL-GJ	26 Feb XX	JUDY CARMICHAEL - Deposit	1022	2 - 54	2 - 54	1,218.20		
2	GL-GJ	28 Feb XX	DMJ CONSTRUCTION - Deposit	02 - 55	2 - 55	2 - 55	1,786.90		
2	GL-GJ	28 Feb XX	FREDDY DUNCAN	CHQ 447	2 - 56	2 - 56		1,950.90	
2	GL-GJ	28 Feb XX	GEORGE BETTS	CHQ 448	2 - 57	2 - 57		1,213.20	
2	GL-GJ	28 Feb XX	GREENBRIAR RESTAURANT	CHQ 449	2 - 58	2 - 58		76.15	9,429.09

                        Acct 110 - Balance, Feb 28, 19XX   17,575.29

ROYAL BANK
MAIN BRANCH
10107 JASPER AVENUE
EDMONTON ALTA
T5J 1W9   03749

MANSFIELD CARPET CO
BAY 215
10620 - 104 AVENUE
EDMONTON AB
T5J 3G2

Account Statement

Account No.
124-629-7

Period	
From	**To**
Jan 27/XX	Feb 26/XX

Enclosures	**Page**
	1

Date	Transaction Description		Cheques & Debits	Deposits & Credits	Balance
	Balance Forward				8,364.02
Jan 27	Deposit			2,576.03	10,940.05
Jan 28	Cheque -	404	974.15		
	Cheque -	419	1,043.25		8,922.65
Jan 29	Cheque -	423	1,722.30		7,200.35
Jan 30	Cheque -	424	133.75		7,066.60
Feb 01	Deposit			8,145.38	15,211.98
Feb 02	Deposit			5,291.15	
	Cheque -	434	100.00		20,403.13
Feb 03	Deposit			969.01	21,372.14
Feb 06	Deposit			2,782.00	
	Cheque -	425	80.25		
	Loan Payment - Principal		601.87		
	Loan Interest		695.20		22,776.82
Feb 07	Cheque -	430	121.75		
	Cheque -	436	697.35		
	Cheque -	435	697.35		21,260.37
Feb 08	Deposit			2,169.96	
	Cheque -	431	111.14		23,319.19
Feb 10	Cheque -	433	1,091.40		
	Cheque -	432	94.66		
	Cheque -	428	6,829.28		
	Cheque -	426	240.75		15,063.10
Feb 13	Deposit			404.46	
	Loan Management Fee		40.00		
	Cheque -	438	2,010.40		
	Cheque -	427	4,559.11		
	Cheque -	437	112.50		8,745.55
Feb 14	Deposit			3,610.18	12,355.73
Feb 15	Deposit			4,068.68	
	Cheque -	429	25.00		16,399.41
Feb 17	Cheque -	441	802.50		15,596.91
Feb 20	Cheque -	422	246.10		
	NSF Returned		404.46		14,946.35
Feb 21	NSF Charge		15.00		14,931.35
Feb 24	Cheque -	444	697.35		
	Cheque -	445	697.35		13,536.65
Feb 25	Deposit			2,569.07	
	Cheque -	439	993.04		15,112.68
Feb 26	Deposit			4,674.30	
	Cheque -	446	240.00		
	Service Charge		18.45		19,528.53

No. of Debits	Total Amount	No. of Credits	Total Amount
30	26,095.71	11	37,260.22

ACCOUNTING RECALL
A Cumulative Approach

THIS EXAM REVIEWS CHAPTERS 1 THROUGH 8.

Your *Study Guide and Working Papers* have forms to complete this exam, as well as worked-out solutions. The page references next to each question identify what page to turn back to if you answer the question incorrectly.

PART I Vocabulary Review

Match the terms to the appropriate definition or phrase.

Page Ref.

(288)	1. Cash short and over	A. A supplementary record
(275)	2. Blank endorsement	B. Person who writes a cheque
(273)	3. Payee	C. A process of reconciling
(273)	4. Drawer	D. Recorded on the income statement
(280)	5. Outstanding cheques	E. Person or company to whom the cheque is payable
(278)	6. Bank reconciliation	F. Lacks sufficient funds
(287)	7. Auxiliary petty cash record	G. Cheque truncation
(283)	8. Safekeeping	H. Add to bank balance
(278)	9. Deposits in transit	I. Cheques written but not processed by bank
(280)	10. NSF	J. Could be further endorsed

PART II True or False (Accounting Theory)

(285) 11. Petty cash is a liability.

(287) 12. The auxiliary petty cash record is a special journal.

(275) 13. Restrictive endorsements limit any further negotiation of a cheque.

(280) 14. NSF result in lowering the bank balance in the reconciliation process.

(287) 15. In replenishment, the old expenses are shown and a new cheque is written.

PART III Applications Problem (283)

From the following calculate the reconciled balance.

Chequebook balance	$755.09
Bank balance	602.05
Interest earned	12.42
Deposits in transit	401.95
Service charge	13.05
Cheques outstanding	249.54

PAYROLL CONCEPTS AND PROCEDURES: EMPLOYEE TAXES

IN THIS CHAPTER WE WILL COVER THE FOLLOWING TOPICS:

Becoming an expert in the subject of payroll and related issues can take a long time. This is because:

1. There are many federal and provincial laws which affect payroll, and they change periodically.
2. Sometimes employers and employees view each other with suspicion in matters concerning payroll. This requires special care to get the figures right.
3. The actual computation and payment of a payroll is quite detailed, leaving room for a number of mistakes to occur.

In Canada today a company has two common alternatives to processing a payroll manually:

- use a microcomputer with appropriate software;
- contract with a payroll service (either an independent service or one connected with a chartered bank).

Either alternative is attractive to medium or large-sized companies. Many smaller companies continue to process their payroll manually, thus avoiding the costs of the more sophisticated alternatives.

In this chapter we will examine the details of a payroll for the ABC Company Ltd. for the first week in March. We will stress those things which affect individual employees. The next chapter examines the same subject from the employer's point of view.

In this chapter and the next, many deductions, maximum amounts and minimum amounts are obtained from recently published figures from Revenue Canada. Students should be aware that these will change at least annually. Your instructor may supply you with the most up-to-date figures, but the supplied Appendices are probably adequate for most purposes.

LEARNING UNIT 9-1

Important Laws and How They Affect Payroll

A number of laws and regulations at the federal and provincial level govern payroll. We will look at several of them here.

MINIMUM WAGE LAWS

Each province has a law which sets the lowest hourly wage that can legally be paid to an employee. The actual **minimum wage** varies somewhat from province to province and has a very small effect on the subject of payroll.

However, such laws also set out the maximum number of hours an employee can be asked to work per day and per week before an *overtime* premium must be paid. A typical requirement (and the one we shall adopt) is that employees who work more than 8 hours per day or 40 hours per week must be paid at time and one half for the overtime hours.

Suppose Janet Johnson worked the following hours during our example week:

Monday	7 hours
Tuesday	8 hours
Wednesday	11 hours
Thursday	8 hours
Friday	7 hours
Saturday	4 hours
Total	45 hours for the week

If Janet's hourly rate were $10.00 per hour, her gross wages for the week would be computed as follows:

Regular time	40 hours @ $10.00/hr	$400.00
Overtime	5 hours @ $15.00/hr	75.00
Total Earnings		$475.00

Sometimes employers arrive at the same total by a slightly different calculation:

Regular rate	45 hours @ $10.00/hr	$450.00
Overtime rate (or premium)	5 hours @ $5.00/hr	25.00
Total Earnings		$475.00

This second approach stresses the cost of overtime. A manager can more easily recognize the added cost of asking employees to work longer hours. We will use the first approach in this chapter, since it reflects the point of view of the employee.

FEDERAL AND PROVINCIAL INCOME TAX

The federal and each provincial government require employees to pay a tax based on the income they earn. The details of our **income tax** system are not covered here, but we need to know a few essentials:

1. Taxes are *calculated* once a year: employees must file a tax return by April 30 for the year ended the previous December 31. However, the tax is *collected* from employees by payroll deductions each pay period.

2. The federal and provincial governments (except Quebec) cooperate by having a single tax deduction which is then divided up according to a legal formula. The amount of income tax an employee must pay is determined by a large number of factors such as number of dependents, level of earnings, other sources of income, permitted deductions, and so on. The amount of income tax deducted from an employee's pay for a week is found by consulting the tables in a booklet called *Payroll Deductions Tables (T4032)*, which is provided by Revenue Canada Taxation. These tables vary somewhat from province to province but the example shown (based on the province of Ontario) is typical (see Appendix 9-1 at the end of this chapter). The ranges of earnings per week are shown on the left and the figures in the 11 columns of deductions shown across the page get smaller as they go from left to right. These figures correspond to increasing levels of exemptions claimed by an employee on a form called a **TD1** (Figure 9-1, pp. 312-313). In our example, Janet Johnson is claiming the normal deduction for a single person, **net claim code 1**. Actually, she may be divorced, separated, or married to a husband who is also earning income, thus making him ineligible as a dependent.

Payroll Periods can be: Weekly: 52 pay periods/year Bi-Weekly: 26 pay periods/year Semi-Monthly: 24 pay periods/year Monthly: 12 pay periods/year.

The employer is not responsible for verifying the claims made by employees on their TD1 forms.

Notice that the procedure for deducting income tax is not very precise. The actual tax that Janet will have to pay for the year will depend on dozens of factors, some of them quite personal (such as whether she has paid any deductible tuition fees during the taxation year, or whether she has charitable donations to claim). The purpose of the deduction tables is to ensure that wage earners pay about as much tax as they would owe on their earnings for the week. Sometimes employees have to pay extra tax when they file their annual tax returns, but usually they get a refund. This is because the tables tend to ignore many allowable tax deductions.

In our example, Janet Johnson will have $88.15 in tax deducted from her pay this week. Refer to Appendix 9-1 and be sure you see where this figure is obtained.

CANADA OR QUEBEC PENSION PLAN

About 25 years ago the **Canada and Quebec Pension Plans** were introduced. Their purpose was to provide a pension benefit (as well as certain other benefits) for Canadians at retirement. The law requires a deduction of $2\frac{1}{2}$% from the earnings of each taxpayer in Canada who is at least 18 years of age but not 70 years or older. (Earnings of less than $63.46 per week are not subject to this deduction. Likewise, earnings in excess of $33,400 per year are not subject to the $2\frac{1}{2}$% levy.) The rate is in the process of being gradually increased, to top out at just over 4% around the turn of the century. This increase is necessary to ensure that funds are available to meet the requirements of Canadians who will be claiming benefits early in the next century.

It is possible to compute the necessary deduction for CPP for each employee, but the federal government has provided detailed tables in the booklet *Payroll Deductions Tables (T4032)* to make this unnecessary (see Appendix 9-2 and Learning Unit 9-2). As you can see, Janet Johnson will have a CPP deduction of $10.29—($475.00 – 63.46) × .025—made from her wages this pay period. The federal government maintains a precise record of the CPP payments made by each Canadian because the benefits we will receive are related to the contributions we make.

Recently, the government has been sending a summary of CPP contributions they have made to each worker in Canada.

UNEMPLOYMENT INSURANCE PLAN

It is a requirement for virtually all employees, regardless of age, to participate in Canada's **Unemployment Insurance Plan**. (Employees working less than 15 hours in a week and earning less than 20% of the maximum weekly insurable earnings are not required to pay UI premiums. There are a number of other exceptions as well.) This plan entitles workers to a certain level of income if they become unemployed. The details of the UI plan are very complex and a full discussion of the plan is beyond the scope of this text.

In each pay period an amount of 3% is deducted from employees' wages. This deduction applies only to the first $38,740 per year (or $745 per week) according to the tables we are using. Fortunately, the deductions are rather straightforward for most employees and can be found in the same booklet as the CPP deductions (see Appendix 9-3 at the end of this chapter). In Janet Johnson's case, she will have a UI deduction of $14.25 ($475 × .03) made from her wages for this week.

Revenue Canada   Revenu Canada
Taxation   Impôt

page 1

TD1(E)
Rev. 93

1993 Personal Tax Credit Return

Family name (Please print)	Usual first name and initials	Employee number
JOHNSON	JANET	N/A

Address
123 Main Street

Any City, Province   Postal code X1X 1X1

For non-residents only
Country of permanent residence

Social insurance number
1 2 3 4 5 6 7 8 9

Date of birth
Day 0 3   Month 1 2   Year 1 9 6 6

You have to complete this form if:
• you have a new employer (or payer);
• your status changed since the last time you filled out this form; or
• you claimed three or more dependent children when you filled out this form for the 1992 taxation year.

Income includes: salary, wages, commissions, and any other remuneration; superannuation or pension benefits including an annuity payment made under a superannuation or pension fund or plan; Unemployment Insurance benefits, including training allowances; and payments under registered retirement income funds or registered retirement savings plans.

Instructions
Please fill out this form so your employer (or payer) will know how much tax to deduct regularly from your pay. Regular deductions will help you avoid having a balance to pay when you file your income tax return. If you do not fill out this form, tax will be deducted from your pay using only the basic personal amount of $6,456 (item 2 below) as the amount of your personal tax credit claim.

Give the completed form to your employer or payer. If you are a pensioner who receives Canada Pension Plan benefits, or Old Age Security or Guaranteed Income Supplement payments, please send the completed form to your Health and Welfare Canada regional office.

Need help?
If you need help to complete this form, see the additional information on page 2 under "Notes to employees and payees." If you still need help, ask your employer (or payer), or call the Source Deductions section of your local taxation office.

1. **Are you a non-resident of Canada?** (See note 1 on page 2.)
   • If Yes – answer the next question.
   • If No – go to item 2.
   Yes ☐   No ☒

   If you are a non-resident, will you be including less than 90% of your 1993 total world income when figuring out the taxable income you earned in Canada?
   • If Yes – enter claim code 0 in the box at line 16, then sign and date the form at item 19.
   • If No – go to item 2.
   Yes ☐   No ☒

2. **Basic personal amount.** Everyone may claim this amount, then go to item 3.   ► $ 6,456   2.

3. **Are you supporting your spouse with whom you live?** (See note 2 on page 2. Common-law relationships could qualify.)   Yes ☐   No ☒
   • If Yes – figure out your claim amount below.
   • If No – go to item 4.

   Claim amount calculation:
   Identify whether the amount in A, B, or C will be your spouse's net income for 1993. Enter the claim amount at line 3, then go to item 4. (See notes 2, 3, and 4 on page 2.)
   Note: A spouse claimed here cannot be claimed again at item 6.

   A) spouse's net income under $538 – enter $5,380 at line 3.
   B) spouse's net income between $538 and $5,918 – figure out your claim amount in the box to the right. →→→
   C) spouse's net income over $5,918 – enter $0 at line 3.

   $ 5,918
   Minus: Spouse's net income (   )
   Enter this amount at line 3 $

   ► 3.

4. **Do you have any dependants who will be under 19 at the end of 1993?**   Yes ☐   No ☒
   • If Yes – indicate how many in the box at line 4, then go to item 5.
   • If No – go to item 5.
   ☐ 4.

5. **Are you single, divorced, separated, or widowed and supporting a dependent relative who lives with you?** (See note 5 on page 2.)   Yes ☐   No ☒
   • If Yes – answer the next question.
   • If No – go to item 6.

   Is that dependent relative either your parent or grandparent?   Yes ☐   No ☒
   • If Yes – figure out the amount of that dependant's net income for 1993, then go to the claim amount calculation for line 5.
   • If No – answer the next question.

   Was that dependent relative under 19 at the end of 1993?   Yes ☐   No ☒
   • If Yes – figure out the amount of that dependant's net income for 1993, then go to the claim amount calculation for line 5.
   • If No – answer the next question.

   Is that dependent relative 19 or older and infirm?   Yes ☐   No ☒
   • If Yes – figure out the amount of that dependant's net income for 1993, then go to the claim amount calculation for line 5.
   • If No – answer the next question.

   Claim amount calculation:
   Identify whether the amount in A, B, or C will be your dependant's net income for 1993. Calculate the claim amount for each dependant separately, and enter the total claim amount at line 5, then go to item 6. (See note 4 on page 2 to figure out net income.)
   Note: A dependant claimed here cannot be claimed again at item 6.

   A) net income under $538 – enter $5,380 at line 5.
   B) net income between $538 and $5,918 – figure out your claim amount in the box to the right. →→→
   C) net income over $5,918 – enter $0 at line 5.

   $ 5,918
   Minus: Dependant's net income (   )
   Enter this amount at line 5 $

   ► 5.

6. **If you are supporting a dependent relative who is 18 or older and infirm, identify whether the amount in A, B, or C will be that dependant's net income for 1993 and enter the claim amount at line 6,** then go to item 7. (See note 3 on page 2 to figure out net income.)
   Note: A dependant claimed at line 3 or 5 cannot be claimed again at line 6.

   A) dependant's net income under $2,690 – enter $1,583 at line 6.
   B) dependant's net income between $2,690 and $4,273 – figure out your claim amount in the box to the right. →→→
   C) dependant's net income over $4,273 – enter $0 at line 6.

   $ 4,273
   Minus: Dependant's net income (   )
   Enter this amount at line 6 $

   ► 6.

7. **Do you receive eligible pension income?** (See note 6 on page 2.)   Yes ☐   No ☒
   • If Yes – enter your eligible pension income OR $1,000 (whichever is less) at line 7, then go to item 8.
   • If No – go to item 8.
   ► 7.

8.   Total (Add lines 2, 3, and 5 to 7, then enter the amount at line 8.) Please enter this amount at line 9 on page 2.   ► $ 6,456   8.

FIGURE 9-1   TD1

9.   Total (from line 8 on page 1.) ► $ **6,456** 9.   page 2

10. Will you be 65 or older at the end of 1993?
- If Yes – enter $3,482 at line 10, then go to item 11.
- If No – go to item 11.   Yes No ☐ ☒ ► _____ 10.

11. Are you a person with a disability? (See note 7 below.)
- If Yes – enter $4,233 at line 11, then go to item 12.
- If No – go to item 12.   Yes No ☐ ☒ ► _____ 11.

12. Are you a student?
- If Yes – figure out your claim amount below, then go to item 13.
- If No – go to item 13.   Yes No ☐ ☒

  – Claim **tuition fees** paid for courses you take in 1993 at a university, college, or certified education institution. $ _____

  – Claim an **education amount** of $80 for each month or part month in 1993 that you will be enrolled full-time in a qualifying educational program at a university, college, or a school offering job retraining courses or correspondence courses. (Part-time students who are eligible for the disability tax credit, or who have written certification from a medical doctor that they are disabled, can also claim this credit.) $ _____

  – If you expect to receive scholarships, fellowships, or bursaries in 1993, subtract the amount by which they exceed $500 from your tuition fees and education amount. $ (_____)

                                                            Total (Enter the amount at line 12.) $ _____ ► _____ 12.

13. Are you claiming unused pension income, age, disability, tuition fees, or education amounts transferred from your spouse or dependants? (See notes 2 and 8 below.)
- If Yes – figure out your claim amounts below.
- If No – go to item 14.   Yes No ☐ ☒

  – If your **spouse receives eligible pension income**, you can claim any unused balance of your spouse's eligible pension amount to a maximum of $1,000. (See note 6 below.)   ► $ _____

  – If your spouse **will be 65 or older** in 1993, you can claim any unused balance of your spouse's age amount to a maximum of $3,482.   ► $ _____

  – If your **spouse or dependant is disabled**, you can claim any unused balance of that person's disability amount to a maximum of $4,233. (See note 7 below.)   ► $ _____

  – If you are supporting a **spouse or dependant who is attending a university, college, or a certified educational institution,** you can claim the unused balance of that person's tuition fees and education amount to a maximum of $4,000. (See note 8 below.)   ► $ _____

                                                            Total (Enter the amount at line 13.) $ _____ ► _____ 13.

14. Total claim amount – Add lines 9 to 13, then enter the amount at line 14.   ► $ **6456** 14.

15. Is your estimated total income for 1993 less than your total claim amount at line 14?
- If Yes – enter E in the box at line 16, and tax will **not** be deducted from your pay, then go to item 17.
- If No – go to item 16.   Yes No ☐ ☒

16. Claim code – Match your total claim amount at line 14 with the table below to determine your claim code, and enter this code in the box to the right. If you already have a code in the box, go to item 17.   [1] 16.

17. Do you want to increase the amount of tax to be deducted from your salary or from other amounts paid to you such as pensions, commissions, etc.? (See note 9 below.)
- If Yes – enter the amount of additional tax you wish to have deducted from each payment at line 17.
- If No – go to item 18.   Yes No ☐ ☒ ► $ _____ 17.

18. Will you be living in the Yukon Territory, Northwest Territories, or another designated area for more than six months in a row beginning or ending in 1993?
- If Yes – claim $7.50 **basic residency amount** for each day you live in a designated area; and an **additional residency amount** of $7.50 for each day you live in and maintain a "dwelling" in that designated area, if you are the only person within that dwelling during that period claiming the **basic residency amount**. The maximum amount you can claim depends on the category of your designated area. (See note 10 below.) Enter the amount at line 18.
- If No – go to item 19.   Yes No ☐ ☒ ► $ _____ 18.

19. I certify that the information given in this return is correct and complete.

Signature _*Janett Johnson*_   Date _Jan 7, 19XX_

If your status changes, complete a new return within seven days. It is an offence to make a false return.

Notes to employees and payees

1.   If you are in doubt about your **non-resident** status, contact the Source Deductions section of your local taxation office. If you are a non-resident, and you will be including 90% or more of your 1993 total world income when determining the taxable income you earned in Canada, you can claim personal amounts. For more information, contact your local taxation office.

2.   A **spouse** includes a common-law spouse (that is a person of the opposite sex with whom you cohabit in a conjugal relationship.) To be considered common-law spouses, the two individuals have to have had such a relationship for at least 12 months, or be the natural or adoptive parents of the same child.

3.   If you **marry** during the year, or enter into a common-law relationship as described in note 2, your spouse's net income includes the income earned before and during marriage.

4.   **Net income**, for tax withholding purposes, is the total annual income from all sources including salary, pensions, Old Age Security, Unemployment Insurance, Workers' Compensation, and social assistance payments, minus annual deductions for registered pension plan and registered retirement savings plan contributions.

5.   A **dependant** is an individual who is dependent on you for support and is either under 19 at the end of 1993, or 19 or older and physically or mentally infirm. This includes a child, grandchild, parent, grandparent, brother, sister, aunt, uncle, niece, or nephew (including in-laws). Except in the case of a child or grandchild, this individual must also be living in Canada.

6.   **Eligible pension income** includes pension payments received from a pension plan or fund as a life annuity, and foreign pension payments. It does not include payments from the Canada or Quebec Pension Plan, Old Age Security, Guaranteed Income Supplement, or lump-sum withdrawals from a pension fund.

7.   To claim a **disability amount**, an individual has to be severely impaired (mentally or physically) in 1993, and have a Disability Tax Credit Certificate. Such an impairment has to markedly restrict the individual's daily living activities. The impairment has to have lasted, or be expected to last for a continuous period of at least 12 months.

8.   Your spouse or dependants have to first use any applicable pension income, age, disability, tuition fee, and education amounts to reduce their federal tax to zero before you are entitled to use any balance of these amounts.

9.   You may find it convenient to deduct additional tax at line 17 for other income you receive that has little or no tax deducted from it. (e.g. Unemployment Insurance benefits, Old Age Security payments, or investment or rental income. If you want to change this extra deduction later, you have to fill out a new Form TD1.

10.   **"Dwelling"** means a self-contained domestic establishment and includes a house, apartment, or similar place where you sleep and eat. It does **not** include a bunkhouse, dormitory, hotel room, or a boarding house room. For more information, including a list and the categories of designated areas, and instructions for figuring out the amount of tax that should be deducted, see the Northern Residents Deductions Tax Guide, available at any taxation office.

1993 claim codes	
Total claim amount Over – Not over	Claim code
No claim amount	0
$ 0 – $6,456	1
6,456 – 8,037	2
8,037 – 9,619	3
9,619 – 11,202	4
11,202 – 12,783	5
12,783 – 14,364	6
14,364 – 15,946	7
15,946 – 17,527	8
17,527 – 19,109	9
19,109 – 20,693	10
20,693 – and over	X
No tax withholding required	E

Cette formule existe aussi en français.

FIGURE 9-1   **TD1 (continued)**

CPP AND UI: SOME ADDITIONAL INFORMATION

Students should be aware that unique CPP deduction tables are supplied for weekly, bi-weekly, semi-monthly, and monthly pay periods. In calculating the CPP deduction per pay period there is no maximum contribution per period—just an annual upper limit ($752.50 for 1993).

The UI deduction, however, is different. A single table is used for all pay periods. As can be seen from the bottom of the UI table (see Appendix 9-3), there are maximum deductions which vary according to pay period. This takes some getting used to, but is probably not as complex as it seems, since each company usually has a single pay period (ABC Company Ltd.'s is weekly, for instance) and there will be a single maximum to remember for each company ($22.35 for ABC Company Ltd., since it has a weekly pay period). Students should be aware that the deductions for UI may be increasing further due to the stated intention of our government to have UI benefits funded entirely by employers and employees. Future tables will include the new maximum deductions, if approved by legislature.

Changes made to the UI law in Canada may require higher premiums from both employers and employees in the future.

WORKERS' COMPENSATION PLANS

In all provinces, workers' incomes are protected in the event of an injury which occurs on the job. Since the cost of this protection is typically paid by the employer, no deductions are made from employees' wages. We will not pursue this matter further in this textbook.

VARIOUS UNION AGREEMENTS

Most unions operate under laws which are enacted provincially or federally. In many businesses, workers have been organized into bargaining units, or unions. Normally, the union and the employer agree that **union dues** be deducted from the employees' wages and forwarded to the union treasurer, usually monthly. In our example, the ABC Company Ltd. does not have unionized employees and therefore no deductions are shown.

OTHER DEDUCTIONS

Other deductions are sometimes made from an employee's earnings. Details will vary from one employer to another but the following deductions are normal in Canada:

1. medical and dental insurance premiums
2. company pension plan—current service
3. company pension plan—past service
4. charitable donations
5. Canada Savings Bonds installments
6. parking charges
7. social fund charges
8. repayment of loans or advances
9. long-term income replacement premiums
10. life insurance premiums.

At this point you should be able to

1. Calculate regular and overtime earnings. (p. 310)
2. Explain the purpose of a TD1 form. (p. 310)
3. Determine income tax deductions given a completed TD1 form and total earnings. (pp. 310-311)
4. Determine a deduction for CPP from tables supplied. (p. 311)
5. Determine a deduction for UI from tables supplied. (p. 311)
6. Explain the operation of maximum deductions for both CPP and UI. (p. 311)
7. Describe in general terms the nature of certain other routine deductions. (p. 314)

□   **SELF-REVIEW QUIZ 9-1**

Using the tables in Appendices 9-1, 9-2, and 9-3, determine the gross pay and deductions for income tax, CPP, and UI for Peter Black, a single taxpayer who worked 42 hours last week at a wage rate of $10.00 per hour.

■   *SOLUTION TO SELF-REVIEW QUIZ 9-1*

Gross Pay

40 hours @ $10.00/hr	$400.00
2 hours @ $15.00/hr	30.00
Gross Pay	$430.00

Deductions

Income tax (from Appendix 9-1)	$76.50	
CPP (from Appendix 9-2)	9.16	
UI (from Appendix 9-3)	12.90	
Total Deductions		$ 98.56
Net Pay (430.00 – 98.56)		$331.44

LEARNING UNIT 9-2

A Typical Payroll

The ABC Company Ltd. has six employees to be paid for the first week of March. They are listed below, together with the number of hours each worked and their rates of pay:

NAME	HOURS	RATE
Janet Johnson	45	$10.00/hr
Peter Black	42	10.00/hr
John Chernochan	44	8.00/hr
Tony Chui	40	11.00/hr
Beth Madora	35	8.00/hr
Elaine Dumont, Manager	40	800.00/wk

To keep things simple, we assume no carry forward balances into the month of March. In reality there would usually be such balances (tax, CPP, and UI payable, for example).

FIGURE 9-2   **Payroll Summary**

Employee Name	Net Claim Code	Rate of Pay	Hours Worked	Earnings		
				Regular	Overtime	Gross Pay
Janet Johnson	1	10/Hr.	45	4 0 0 00	7 5 00	4 7 5 00
Peter Black	1	10/Hr.	42	4 0 0 00	3 0 00	4 3 0 00
John Chernochan	4	8/Hr.	44	3 2 0 00	4 8 00	3 6 8 00
Tony Chui	1	11/Hr.	40	4 4 0 00		4 4 0 00
Beth Madora	1	8/Hr.	35	2 8 0 00		2 8 0 00
Elaine Dumont	3	800/W	40	8 0 0 00		8 0 0 00
				2 6 4 0 00	1 5 3 00	2 7 9 3 00
	(A)	(B)	(C)	(D)	(E)	(F)

ABC Company Ltd.
Payroll summary
Week 1, March, 19XX

Employees are paid weekly at the ABC Company Ltd. The following payroll summary (Figure 9-2) has been prepared based upon tables and calculations covered earlier in this chapter. Don't worry if the summary appears a bit complicated—we will deal with each column in turn.

THE PAYROLL SUMMARY IN DETAIL

A. NET CLAIM CODE   Employers require employees to complete and sign a TD1 exemption form at the beginning of employment and in early January each year thereafter. As can be seen from Figure 9-1, this form allows employees to specify their exemption status so that an appropriate amount of income tax can be deducted. The net claim code for each employee is shown in this column. You can see that four of the employees are claiming a net claim code of 1, resulting in the maximum income tax deduction at their earnings level. The other two employees (John and Elaine) presumably have dependents which allow them to specify a higher net claim code, with a lower income tax deduction at their earnings level.

B. RATE OF PAY   The rates of pay are as set out above. Notice that all employees except Elaine are paid on an hourly basis. Elaine, as manager, receives a weekly salary.

Many medium to large-sized companies use a computer to help prepare their payroll. The data output from a computerized payroll is often remarkably similar to the illustrations in this chapter.

C. HOURS WORKED   Each employee may work a different number of hours in each week. Remember that *overtime* rates will apply to hours in excess of 40 per week or 8 per day. Notice also that Elaine's hours are shown even though she is not paid according to the number of hours she worked. It is typical to record daily the hours worked by each employee. A weekly total is then transferred to this column in the payroll summary.

	Deductions																				
FIT			CPP			UI			Medical			Charitable			Net Pay				Chq. No.
8	8	15	1	0	29	1	4	25					2	00	3	6	0	31	1407
7	6	50		9	16	1	2	90		9	00		2	00	3	2	0	44	1408
3	9	80		7	61	1	1	04	1	7	00		2	00	2	9	0	55	1409
7	8	50		9	41	1	3	20					2	00	3	3	6	89	1410
3	7	90		5	41		8	40		9	00		2	00	2	1	7	29	1411
1	9	1	00	1	8	36	2	2	35	1	7	00		2	00	5	4	9	29	1412
5	1	1	85	6	0	24	8	2	14	5	2	00	1	2	00	2	0	7	4	77
(G)			(H)			(I)			(J)			(K)			(L)				(M)

D. REGULAR EARNINGS   Regular earnings are computed based upon regular hours per week—or, as in Elaine's case, a salary.

E. OVERTIME EARNINGS   The segregation of overtime earnings helps the owners of ABC Company Ltd. to control this expensive use of employees' time. A common practice is to hire an additional employee when this figure becomes too high.

F. GROSS PAY   Each employee earns a total amount per week. It is this figure which governs the legally required deductions.

G. INCOME TAX DEDUCTION   From Appendix 9-1 we have already seen that Janet's income tax deduction is $88.15. Make sure that you can find the amounts deducted from the other employees in Appendix 9-1.

H. CPP DEDUCTION   Appendix 9-2 is the source for these CPP deductions.

I. UI DEDUCTION   See Appendix 9-3 to trace each employee's UI deductions. Remember that UI deductions are not required on earnings over $745 per week. This is why Elaine's deduction for UI is $22.35—the maximum for any one week.

J. MEDICAL DEDUCTION   The law regarding medical deductions varies from one province to another. Some provinces do not require a deduction for provincial health care plans. In our example, a deduction is required from each household. This explains why no deductions are made from Janet's and Tony's wages. We may assume that they are covered by their spouses' deductions.

K. CHARITABLE DEDUCTION   Each employee has agreed to a weekly deduction to support a charitable cause—perhaps world hunger relief.

L. NET PAY   This is each employee's gross pay less all deductions, often known as **take-home pay**.

M. CHEQUE NUMBER   A cheque is issued to each employee for the exact amount due. When the cheques are issued, their numbers are written here.

At this point you should be able to

1. Calculate earnings, deductions and net pay for an employee. (pp. 309-317)
2. Describe the preparation of a payroll summary. (pp. 316-317)
3. Explain the purpose of each column in a payroll summary. (p. 316)

☐ **SELF-REVIEW QUIZ 9-2**

If a new employee, Robert Meade, begins employment next week, calculate his gross and net pay assuming a TD1 net claim code of 3, 40 hours worked, a wage of $8.00/hr, and no medical or charitable deduction.

■ *SOLUTION TO SELF-REVIEW QUIZ 9-2*

Did you calculate a net pay of $268.19? Details are:

Gross Pay	40 hours @ $8.00/hr		$320.00
Deductions			
	Income Tax (from Appendix 9-1)	$35.80	
	CPP (from Appendix 9-2)	6.41	
	UI (from Appendix 9-3)	9.60	
	Medical	0.00	
	Charitable	0.00	
	Total Deductions		51.81
Net Pay (320.00 − 51.81)			$268.19

LEARNING UNIT 9-3
Recording and Payment

The details in Figure 9-2 are used to make the journal entry shown below which records the payroll for the first week in March for the ABC Company Ltd.:

	Salaries and Wages Expense	2 7 9 3 00		
	Income Taxes Payable		5 1 1 85
	CPP Payable		6 0 24
	UI Payable		8 2 14
	Medical Plan Payable		5 2 00
	Charitable Contributions Payable		1 2 00
	Salaries and Wages Payable		2 0 7 4 77
	To record payroll for first week in March		

Some companies keep separate track of different salary or wage expenses. For instance, it is useful to separate Elaine's salary from the wages of the other workers. The owners can then separate the cost of management from the cost of labor. It is also useful to further break down the labor cost into more detail. Consider the additional information available to the owners if we assume that Tony and Beth are sales personnel. The debit to **Sales Wage expense** would be $720.00 ($440.00 + $280.00). Instead of the single debit of $2793.00 to an account called **Salaries and Wages expense**, we would now have three debits:

Management Salaries Expense		800 00
Sales Wage Expense		720 00
Wages Expense		1 273 00

(The credit side of the entry would not change.)

If we assume that the ABC Company Ltd. uses this more detailed method, then the entry would be posted to the ledger accounts as summarized below (opening balances are ignored):

Mgmnt Salaries Expense	**Sales Wages Expense**	**Wages Expense**
800.00	720.00	1273.00
Expense on the Income Statement	Expense on the Income Statement	Expense on the Income Statement

Income Taxes Payable	**CPP Payable**	**UI Payable**
511.85	60.24	82.14
Liability on the Balance Sheet	Liability on the Balance Sheet	Liability on the Balance Sheet

Medical Plan Payable	**Charitable Donations Payable**	**Salaries and Wages Payable**
52.00	12.00	2074.77
Liability on the Balance Sheet	Liability on the Balance Sheet	Liability on the Balance Sheet

Figure 9-3 summarizes the main elements of the payroll process.

FIGURE 9-3   The Payroll Recording and Posting Process

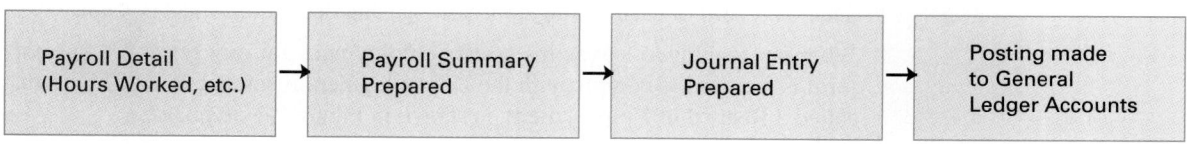

LAST STEP DIRECTLY AFFECTING EMPLOYEES

From the employees' point of view the best part of the payroll process is receiving their net pay each week. The ABC Company Ltd. writes a cheque to each employee in payment of his or her weekly **take-home pay** (see columns L and M, Figure 9-2). As each cheque is written, it is recorded in the *Cash Disbursements Journal*, as shown in Figure 9-4, below.

FIGURE 9-4   Cash Disbursements Journal

			Cash Disbursements Journal							

Date	Chq. No.	Account Payment To	PR	Sundry Dr.	Accounts Payable Dr.	Wages and Salaries Payable Dr.	Purchases Discount Cr.	Cash Cr.
19XX Mar. 9	1407	Janet Johnson				360 31		360 31
9	1408	Peter Black				320 44		320 44
9	1409	John Chernochan				290 55		290 55
9	1410	Tony Chui				336 89		336 89
9	1411	Beth Madora				217 29		217 29
9	1412	Elaine Dumont				549 29		549 29

The total of Salaries and Wages Payable is posted at the end of the month as a debit.

When the **Cash Disbursements Journal** is posted, the balance in the **Salaries and Wages Payable** account will be reduced to zero. This is as it should be, since the amount recorded as payable, $2074.77 has been paid by cheques 1407-1412 and the amount remaining to be paid is nil. Please remember that the **Cash Disbursements Journal** is posted at the end of the month. It is only after the cheques have been issued, recorded, and posted that the balance in the **Salaries and Wages Payable** account will be zero.

Most companies pay their employees by cheque, although in a very few cases, companies pay out actual cash. Many large companies transfer wages directly to their employees' bank accounts. Some companies have a separate bank account on which they issue their payroll cheques. The main reason for this practice is to simplify the payment process and reconciliation of bank accounts, especially when the number of employees is large.

EMPLOYEE'S EARNINGS RECORD

In order to meet legal requirement, the ABC Company Ltd. must keep a separate record of each employee's earnings. This record is essential for the following reasons:

1. Each year (by February 28) ABC Company Ltd. must prepare and deliver to each employee a summary of the previous calendar year's earnings and related deductions. This form is known as a **T4 (or T4A)**. Refer to Figure 9-5 for a sample of this form. Notice that in order to complete this form accurately, a detailed record of each employee's earnings and deductions must be kept.

2. When an employee leaves his or her employment for any reason, a special form is required to comply with the Unemployment Insurance laws. This form, called a **Record of Employment**, is shown in Figure 9-6 on p. 322.

FIGURE 9-5   T4

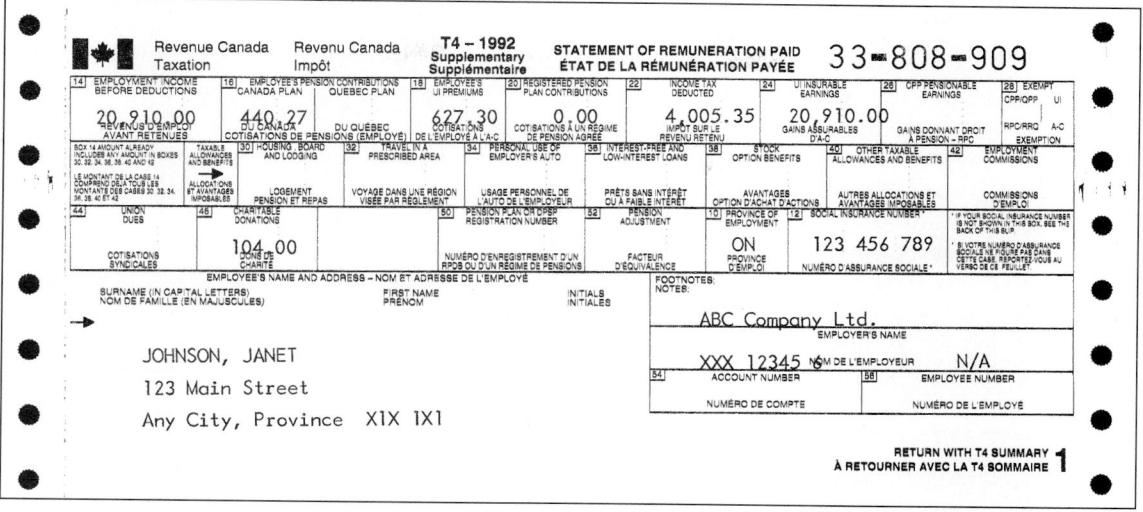

3. In deducting both CPP and UI, it is necessary to keep deducting only as long as an employee's earnings are below a certain level. We have already seen that UI has a maximum deduction of $22.35 per week or $1,162.20 per year. CPP is payable up to a maximum of $752.50 each year. Therefore it is necessary to stop making deductions when these amounts are reached.

Figure 9-7 shows a partial Employee's Earnings Record for Janet Johnson for the latest year. (See p. 323.)

At this point you should be able to

1. Record a payroll from a payroll summary. (p. 316)
2. Break down gross wages into more detail. (p. 316)
3. Post the entry recording the payroll into appropriate ledger accounts. (p. 319)
4. Demonstrate the payment of net pay to employees by cheque. (p. 320)
5. Record the cheques to employees in the Cash Disbursements Journal. (p. 320)
6. Illustrate the employee's earnings record. (pp. 320-321)
7. Describe the Record of Employment form. (pp. 320, 322)
8. State the upper limit of UI and CPP deductions. (p. 311)

☐ SELF-REVIEW QUIZ 9-3

Indicate whether the following statements are true or false:

1. All payroll registers are special journals. This means no payroll entry is ever needed.
2. Income Tax Payable is a liability on the balance sheet.
3. Salaries and Wages Expense has a normal balance of a credit.
4. Employee's Earnings Records are optional for an employer.
5. The Record of Employment form must be completed annually for each employee.
6. All wages must be paid by cheque.
7. Cheques paying wages must be recorded in the Cash Disbursements Journal.

Employment and Immigration Canada **Emploi et Immigration Canada**

EMPLOYER: THE GUIDE – HOW TO COMPLETE THE RECORD OF EMPLOYMENT PROVIDES DETAILED INSTRUCTION
EMPLOYEUR: LE GUIDE – COMMENT REMPLIR LE RELEVÉ D'EMPLOI, FOURNIT DES INSTRUCTIONS PRÉCISES

RECORD OF EMPLOYMENT (ROE) / RELEVÉ D'EMPLOI (RE)
IF COMPLETING THIS FORM BY HAND, USE A PEN AND PRESS FIRMLY / SI VOUS REMPLISSEZ LE FORMULAIRE À LA MAIN, UTILISEZ UN STYLO À BILLE ET APPUYEZ

1 SERIAL NO. / N° DE SÉRIE

2 SERIAL NO. OF RECORD AMENDED OR REPLACED
N° DE SÉRIE DU RELEVÉ MODIFIÉ OU REMPLACÉ

3 EMPLOYER'S PAYROLL REFERENCE NO.
N° DE RÉFÉRENCE DU REGISTRE DE PAYE DE L'EMPLOYEUR

4 EMPLOYER'S NAME AND ADDRESS / NOM ET ADRESSE DE L'EMPLOYEUR

5 REVENUE CANADA, TAXATION ACCT. NO.
N° DE COMPTE À REVENU CANADA, IMPÔT

6 COMMUNICATION PREFERRED IN/COMMUNICATIONS DE PRÉFÉRENCE EN
☐ ENGLISH / ANGLAIS   ☐ FRENCH / FRANÇAIS

7 POSTAL CODE / CODE POSTAL

8 PAY PERIOD TYPE / GENRE DE PÉRIODE DE PAYE

9 EMPLOYEE'S NAME AND ADDRESS / NOM ET ADRESSE DE L'EMPLOYÉ(E)

10 SOCIAL INSURANCE NO. / N° D'ASSURANCE SOCIALE

	D/J	M	Y/A
11 FIRST DAY WORKED / PREMIER JOUR DE TRAVAIL			
12 LAST DAY WORKED / DERNIER JOUR DE TRAVAIL			
13 U.I. PREMIUMS PAYABLE UP TO / COTISATIONS D'ASSURANCE-CHÔMAGE PAYABLES JUSQU'AU			
14 FINAL PAY PERIOD ENDING DATE / DATE DE LA FIN DE LA DERNIÈRE PÉRIODE DE PAYE			

9 A – OCCUPATION / PROFESSION

15 STARTING WITH THE FINAL PAY PERIOD (P.P.), ENTER THE INSURABLE EARNINGS UP TO A MAXIMUM OF 20 WEEKS. FOR MONTHLY, SEMI-MONTHLY AND 13 P.P., RECORD THE FULL P.P. IN WHICH THE 20th WEEK FALLS.
IF THE INSURABLE EARNINGS TO BE REPORTED ARE AT THE MAXIMUM FOR EACH P.P. CHECK HERE ☐ AND ENTER ONLY THE TOTAL IN BLOCK 15A.

EN COMMENÇANT PAR LA DERNIÈRE PÉRIODE DE PAYE (P.P.), INSCRIRE LE MONTANT DE LA RÉMUNÉRATION ASSURABLE JUSQU'À UN MAXIMUM DE 20 SEMAINES. POUR LES REGISTRES DE PAYE MENSUELS, BIMENSUELS ET CEUX COMPTANT 13 P.P., CONSIGNER TOUTE LA P.P. PENDANT LAQUELLE TOMBE LA 20° SEMAINE. SI LA RÉMUNÉRATION ASSURABLE À DÉCLARER CORRESPOND AU MAXIMUM AU COURS DE CHAQUE P.P., COCHER ICI ☐ ET INSCRIRE SEULEMENT LE TOTAL À LA CASE 15A.

P.P.	INSURABLE EARNINGS RÉMUNÉRATION ASSURABLE	PAY PERIOD EXCEPTION DE PÉRIODE DE PAYE	P.P.	INSURABLE EARNINGS RÉMUNÉRATION ASSURABLE	PAY PERIOD EXCEPTION DE PÉRIODE DE PAYE	P.P.	INSURABLE EARNINGS RÉMUNÉRATION ASSURABLE	PAY PERIOD EXCEPTION DE PÉRIODE DE PAYE	P.P.	INSURABLE EARNINGS RÉMUNÉRATION ASSURABLE	PAY PERIOD EXCEPTION DE PÉRIODE DE PAYE
1			2			3			4		
5			6			7			8		
9			10			11			12		
13			14			15			16		
17			18			19			20		

15 A TOTAL (ROUND TO THE NEAREST DOLLAR) TOTAL (ARRONDIR AU DOLLAR PRÈS) $. 0 0

16 INSURABLE WEEKS IN THE LAST 52 WEEKS OR SINCE THE LAST ROE WAS ISSUED, WHICHEVER IS LESS / SEMAINES ASSURABLES AU COURS DES 52 DERNIÈRES SEMAINES OU DEPUIS LE DERNIER RE, LE NOMBRE LE MOINS ÉLEVÉ ÉTANT RETENU

17 PAYMENTS OR BENEFITS (OTHER THAN REGULAR PAY) PAID IN THE FINAL PAY PERIOD OR PAYABLE AT A LATER DATE
PAIEMENTS OU AVANTAGES (AUTRES QUE LE SALAIRE HABITUEL) PAYÉS AU COURS DE LA DERNIÈRE PÉRIODE DE PAYE OU PAYABLES À UNE DATE ULTÉRIEURE

A – VACATION PAY / INDEMNITÉ DE VACANCES   B – STATUTORY HOLIDAY PAY FOR / JOUR(S) FÉRIÉ(S) PAYÉ(S) POUR LE(S)

	D/J	M	Y/A		D/J	M	Y/A		D/J	M	Y/A
$				$				$				$

C – OTHER MONIES (SPECIFY) / AUTRES SOMMES (PRÉCISER)

$ _____ $ _____ $ _____

IMPORTANT
IF THE ABOVE PAYMENTS ARE INSURABLE, HAVE THEY BEEN ALLOCATED TO THE FINAL PAY PERIOD:
SI LES PAIEMENTS SUSMENTIONNÉS SONT ASSURABLES, ONT-ILS ÉTÉ RÉPARTIS SUR LA DERNIÈRE PÉRIODE DE PAYE:
☐ YES OUI   ☐ NO NON   IF NO, EXPLAIN IN COMMENTS SECTION SI NON, PRÉCISER À LA CASE "OBSERVATIONS"

18 PAID SICK / MATERNITY / PATERNITY LEAVE OR GROUP WAGE LOSS INDEMNITY PAYMENTS (AFTER THE LAST DAY WORKED)
CONGÉ DE MALADIE / MATERNITÉ / PATERNITÉ PAYÉ OU INDEMNITÉS PAYABLES EN VERTU D'UN RÉGIME COLLECTIF D'ASSURANCE-SALAIRE (APRÈS LE DERNIER JOUR DE TRAVAIL)

PAYMENT START DATE DATE DE DÉBUT DU PAIEMENT   D/J M Y/A   FOR POUR   WEEKS / DAYS AMOUNT SEM. / JOURS MONTANT $

19 REASON FOR ISSUING THIS ROE RAISON DU PRÉSENT RELEVÉ ▶ ENTER CODE INSCRIRE LE CODE

FOR FURTHER INFORMATION, CONTACT POUR PLUS DE RENSEIGNEMENTS, APPELER   TELEPHONE / TÉLÉPHONE

20 EXPECTED DATE OF RECALL DATE PRÉVUE DE RAPPEL   D/J M Y/A   ☐ NOT RETURNING RETOUR NON PRÉVU   ☐ UNKNOWN DATE NON CONNUE

21 I AM AWARE THAT IT IS AN OFFENCE TO MAKE FALSE ENTRIES AND HEREBY CERTIFY THAT ALL STATEMENTS ON THIS FORM ARE TRUE.
JE RECONNAIS QUE TOUTE FAUSSE DÉCLARATION CONSTITUE UNE INFRACTION ET J'ATTESTE, PAR LES PRÉSENTES, QUE TOUTES LES DÉCLARATIONS FAITES SUR CE FORMULAIRE SONT VÉRIDIQUES.

22 COMMENTS / OBSERVATIONS

SIGNATURE OF ISSUER / SIGNATURE

NAME OF ISSUER (please print) / NOM DU SIGNATAIRE (en lettres moulées)

23 TELEPHONE NUMBER / NUMÉRO DE TÉLÉPHONE   **24** DATE   D/J M Y/A

INS 2106 RE-P (11-89) EF

NOTE TO EMPLOYEE
THIS IS A VALUABLE DOCUMENT. KEEP IT IN A SAFE PLACE. IF YOU INTEND TO FILE A CLAIM FOR UI BENEFITS YOU SHOULD DO SO IMMEDIATELY. THE REVERSE OF PART 2 CONTAINS IMPORTANT INFORMATION.

À L'EMPLOYÉ(E)
IL S'AGIT D'UN DOCUMENT PRÉCIEUX – CONSERVEZ-LE EN LIEU SÛR. SI VOUS COMPTEZ PRÉSENTER UNE DEMANDE DE PRESTATIONS, VEUILLEZ LE FAIRE IMMÉDIATEMENT. D'IMPORTANTS RENSEIGNEMENTS VOUS SONT FOURNIS AU VERSO DE LA PARTIE 2.

EMPLOYEE'S COPY COPIE DE L'EMPLOYÉ(E) PART / PARTIE **1**

Canada

FIGURE 9-6 **Record of Employment**

FIGURE 9-7 Employee Individual Earnings Record

Name of Employee: Janet Johnson
Social Insurance Number: 123 456 789
Date of Birth: 03/12/66

ABC Company Ltd.
Employee Earnings Record
For the Calendar Year 19XX

Employee Address:
123 Main Street
Any City, Province
A1B 1C1

Week	Net Claim Code	Rate of Pay	Hours Worked	Earnings Regular	Earnings Overtime	Gross Pay	FIT	CCP	UI	Medical	Charitable	Net Pay	Chq. No.
1	1	10/Hr.	40	400 00		400 00	69 35	8 41	12 00	0 00	2 00	308 24	1061
2			40	400 00		400 00	69 35	8 41	12 00	0 00	2 00	308 24	1102
3			42	400 00	30 00	430 00	76 50	9 16	12 90	0 00	2 00	329 44	1150
4			40	400 00		400 00	69 35	8 41	12 00	0 00	2 00	308 24	1194
5			40	400 00		400 00	69 35	8 41	12 00	0 00	2 00	308 24	1237
6			36	360 00		360 00	58 20	7 41	10 80	0 00	2 00	281 59	1291
7			40	400 00		400 00	69 35	8 41	12 00	0 00	2 00	308 24	1322
8			41	400 00	15 00	415 00	72 40	8 79	12 45	0 00	2 00	319 36	1368
9			45	400 00	75 00	475 00	86 10	10 29	14 25	0 00	2 00	362 36	1407
10			40	400 00		400 00	69 35	8 41	12 00	0 00	2 00	308 24	1451
11			40	400 00		400 00	69 35	8 41	12 00	0 00	2 00	308 24	1490
49		11/Hr.	46	440 00	99 00	539 00	104 40	11 89	16 17	0 00	2 00	404 54	3021
50			40	440 00		440 00	78 50	9 41	13 20	0 00	2 00	336 89	3101
51			38	418 00		418 00	73 45	8 86	12 54	0 00	2 00	321 15	3154
52			40	440 00		440 00	78 50	9 41	13 20	0 00	2 00	336 89	3214
Totals for the Year				20 280 00	630 00	20 910 00	4 005 35	440 27	627 30	0 00	104 00	15 733 08	

SOLUTION TO SELF-REVIEW QUIZ 9-3

1. False   2. True   3. False   4. False
5. False. The Record of Employment is required only when an employee leaves.
6. False. Cash or automatic bank transfers are also normal.
7. True, in general, although other possibilities exist, such as special payroll journals.

SUMMARY OF KEY POINTS AND KEY TERMS

LEARNING UNIT 9-1

1. The Minimum Wage Law sets the lowest hourly wage that can be paid to an employee and establishes the maximum number of hours per day and per week that an employee may work before an overtime premium must be paid.

2. Employers may calculate overtime pay separately from regular pay in order to highlight the cost of having employees work overtime.

3. Each pay period, employees are required to pay income tax and to contribute to the Canada Pension and Unemployment Insurance Plans according to their level of earnings. The amount to be deducted for each is found in tables published by the federal government.

4. A TD1 form specifies the net claim code for each employee. This in turn governs the income tax deducted each pay period.

5. CPP and UI have a maximum contribution of $752.50 per year and $1,162.20 per year respectively. (These maximums will change annually.)

6. Other deductions (for example, union dues or company-related matters) may also be made from an employee's earnings.

Canada (or Quebec) Pension Plan: Designed to provide a retirement benefit for all Canadians who contribute to the Plan during their employment years. Requires a payroll deduction from each employee until a yearly maximum is reached. (The maximum we are using is $752.50, but a new maximum is used each year.)

Income Tax Deductions: Amounts withheld from employees' wages each period and sent (on behalf of the employees) to the Federal government. The amount of the deduction is determined by tables published by the federal government, customized for each province.

Minimum Wage Laws: Laws which govern the lowest wage legally payable in a province. Also states the province's rules about overtime premiums and maximum weekly working hours.

Other Deductions: Most employees have a variety of items for which a deduction is required. The exact type and amount of these deductions will vary a great deal from one employer to another. Common examples are union dues and provincial health care premiums.

TD1 Form: A form completed by an employee upon commencement of employment and at least annually thereafter which sets out the deductions claimed by each employee. Net claim code determined by this form affects the amount of income tax deducted.

Unemployment Insurance Plan: A plan which all employees must contribute towards and which provides a certain level of income for those workers who are unemployed. Contributions are made up to a maximum per pay period. (The maximum we are using is $22.35 per week or $96.85 per month.)

LEARNING UNIT 9-2

1. Each pay period a Payroll Summary is prepared. This summary includes the following information for each employee: net claim code; rate of pay; hours worked; regular earnings; overtime earnings; gross pay; income tax deduction; CPP deduction; UI deduction; other deductions such as medical and charitable; net pay; and cheque number.

2. Gross pay determines the level of deductions.

3. Gross pay less deductions equals net, or "take-home," pay.

Payroll Summary: Sometimes known as the Payroll Journal or Payroll Register, this document lists in considerable detail the income, deductions, net pay, and other information for each employee for a given pay period. A total for all employees per category is always shown. Forms the basis for posting to appropriate ledger accounts.

LEARNING UNIT 9-3

1. The payroll register is completed each pay period and provides basic data for recording the payroll.

2. The Salaries and Wages Expense entry is made and posted to ledger accounts. In addition to summarizing the deductions payable, the ledger accounts are used to classify wage expenses by type.

3. Each payroll cheque written is recorded in the Cash Disbursements Journal. Journal totals are posted to the General Ledger monthly.

4. Employers must maintain an Employee's Earnings Record for each employee. The source of the information summarized here is the payroll register.

5. Each year employers must prepare and deliver to each employee a T4 or T4A form which summarizes the employee's earnings and deductions for the calendar year.

6. When an employee leaves, is laid off, or terminated, the employer must complete a Record of Employment form.

Employee's Earnings Record: A page or sheet (or a computer file) which records and totals the details concerning an employee's earnings, deductions, net pay, and identification details for a calendar year. Used in preparing T4 slips.

Record of Employment Form: Special form to be completed for each employee at the end of their employment. Used in helping to prevent abuses to the Unemployment Insurance Act.

T4 Slip: A special form issued annually to each employee summarizing their annual earnings and deductions. Used by employees as a basic document in filing their annual income tax return.

DISCUSSION QUESTIONS

1. Explain how to calculate overtime.

2. Define and state the purpose of completing a T4 form.

3. Usually, claiming more allowances on a TD1 results in receiving more money per paycheck. Please comment.

4. All payroll registers must be special journals. True or false?

BLUEPRINT FOR RECORDING, POSTING, AND PAYING THE PAYROLL

Payroll Register (or journal)

	Deductions				Net Pay	Chq. No.	Distribution of Expense Accounts	
	Inc. Tax	CPP	UI	Med. Ins.			Office Salaries	Market Wages
Payroll transactions for the Period →	XX	XX	XX	XX	XX		XXX	XXX

General Journal

Office Salaries Expense	XXX	
Market Wages Expense	XXX	
Income Tax Payable		XXX
CPP Payable		XXX
UI Payable		XXX
Med. Insurance Payable		XXX
Wages and Salaries Payable		XXX

POST TO LEDGER

Cash Disbursements Journal

Wages and Sal. Pay Dr.	—	—	Cash Cr.
XXX			XXX
XXX			XXX
XXX			XXX
XXX			XXX

Totals posted to Ledger at end of Month

W & S Payable			Income Tax Payable			CPP Payable	
	XX			XX			XX

UI Payble			Med. Ins. Payable			Office Salaries Expense	
	XX			XX		XX	

Market Wages Expense	
XX	

5. Define and state the purpose of CPP or QPP.

6. The employer doesn't have to contribute to the Canada Pension Plan. Agree or disagree?

7. Explain how federal and provincial income tax withholdings are determined.

8. What is a calendar year?

9. Define the purpose of an income tax deduction.

10. What purposes does the employee individual earnings record serve?

11. Explain the differences in determining CPP and UI deductions.

12. Draw a diagram showing how the following relate: (a) weekly payroll; (b) payroll register; (c) individual earnings; (d) journal entries; (e) cash disbursements journal.

13. If you earned $80,000 this year, you would pay more CPP than your brother, who earned $60,000. Do you agree or disagree? Explain.

EXERCISES

1. Calculate the total wages earned for each employee (assume an overtime rate of time and a half over 40 hours):

EMPLOYEE	HOURLY RATE	HOURS WORKED
Bill Run	$10.80	38
Al Roe	12.00	42
Jane Avery	15.00	44

Calculating wages with overtime.

2. Compute the net pay for each employee for the first week of February, using the tables in the text.

EMPLOYEE	STATUS	NET CLAIM CODE	THIS WEEK'S PAY
Mel Jones	Married	1	$500
Janet Right	Single	1	360

Calculating net pay.

The only deductions are for Income Tax, CPP, and UI.

3. Complete the table.

	Category	DR/CR	Account Appears On Which Financial Rept.
CPP Payable			
Income Tax Payable			
Medical Insurance Payable			
Wages and Salaries Payable			
Office Salaries Expense			
Market Wages Expense			

Categorizing accounts.

Payroll register and the journal entry.

4. The following weekly payroll journal entry was prepared by Moore Co. Could you explain which columns of the payroll register the data have come from?

Jan	7	Shop Expense		6 000 00	
		Factory Wages Expense		4 000 00	
		CPP Payable			7 15 00
		Income Tax Payable			2 700 00
		Union Dues Payable			2 10 00
		Wages and Salaries Payable			6 375 00

Paying the payroll.

5. From Exercise 4, prepare an entry to pay the payroll from the cash disbursements journal given the following (on January 9):

EMPLOYEE	EMPLOYEE'S NET PAY	CHEQUE NO.
Bill Bloss	$3,000	111
Joe Ring	1,000	112
Sally Field	2,375	113

(Use the same headings for the cash disbursements journal that we have used in the chapter.)

GROUP A PROBLEMS

9A-1. From the following information, please complete the chart for gross earnings for the week. (Assume an overtime rate of time and a half over 40 hours.)

Calculating gross earnings with overtime.

EMPLOYEE	HOURLY RATE	NO. OF HOURS WORKED	GROSS EARNINGS
A. Fred Rice	$ 8.00	44	
B. Jill Ester	10.00	46	
C. Dave Walk	12.00	38	
D. Marsha Retal	14.00	52	

9A-2. March Company has five salaried employees. Your task is to record the following information into a payroll register for the last week of March.

Completing a payroll register.

EMPLOYEE	DEPT.	NET CLAIM CODE	WEEKLY SALARY
Judy Seey	Sales	1	$630
Al Roe	Office	1	310
Nancy Ryan	Office	2	980
John Tobey	Sales	3	510
Peter Reese	Sales	1	380

Assume that each employee contributes $10 per week for union dues.

9A-3. The bookkeeper for Flynn Co. gathered the following data from employees' individual earnings records as well as daily time cards. Your task is (1) to complete a payroll register on November 8 and (2) to journalize the appropriate entry to record the payroll.

EMPLOYEE	NET CLAIM CODE	M	T	W	T	F	HOURLY RATE	DEPT.	CUM. CPP BEFORE THIS PAYROLL
Bill Smith	1	6	3	8	10	8	$14	Sales	$736.10
Margie Run	2	9	9	9	9	4	8	Office	396.00
Alice Angel	3	8	10	10	10	10	16	Sales	752.50
Ray Miller	1	8	8	8	8	8	6	Office	221.00

Completing a payroll register and journalizing the payroll entry.

Assume the following:
1. Income tax, CPP ,and UIC, are from tables in the end of this chapter. (See Appendices 1-3)
2. Each employee contributes $10 per week for health insurance.
3. Overtime is paid at a rate of time and a half over 40 hours per week.

9A-4. John Wood, Accountant, has gathered the following data for you. Your task is to:

1. Prepare a payroll register on December 5.
2. Journalize and post the payroll entry.
3. Record the payment of the payroll on December 7 to each employee.

EMPLOYEE	NET CLAIM CODE	SALARY	CHQ. NO.	CUM. CPP BEFORE THIS PAYROLL	DEPT.
Joe Boyn	6	$520	29	$349.60	Factory
Jane Allen	1	780	30	474.40	Office
Shelley Roe	2	860	31	672.80	Factory
John Sullivan	1	900	32	742.00	Office

Completing a payroll register, journalizing, posting and recording the payment of net pay.

Assume the following:
1. Income tax is calculated from tables in the text.
2. Union dues are $5 per week.
3. Medical coverage is $16 per week (except for John, whose wife pays the family premium).

GROUP B PROBLEMS

9B-1. From the following information, please complete the chart for gross earnings for the week. (Assume an overtime rate of time and a half over 40 hours.)

	HOURLY RATE	NO. OF HOURS WORKED	GROSS EARNINGS
A. Fred Rice	$ 8.00	46	
B. Jill Ester	11.00	43	
C. Dave Walk	12.00	37	
D. Marsha Retal	15.00	50	

Calculating gross earnings with overtime.

9B-2. March Company has five salaried employees. Your task is to record the following information into a payroll register for the last week of March.

Completing the payroll register.

EMPLOYEE	DEPT.	NET CLAIM CODE	WEEKLY SALARY
Judy Seey	Sales	1	$680
Al Roe	Office	4	330
Nancy Ryan	Office	2	960
John Tobey	Sales	5	480
Peter Reese	Sales	1	350

Assume that each employee contributes $15 per week for union dues.

9B-3. The bookkeeper for Flynn Co. gathered the following data from employees' individual earnings records as well as daily time cards. Your task is (1) to complete a payroll register on November 8 and (2) to journalize the appropriate entry to record the payroll.

Completing the payroll register and journalizing the payroll entry.

EMPLOYEE	NET CLAIM CODE	M	T	W	T	F	HOURLY RATE	DEPT.	CUM. CPP BEFORE THIS PAYROLL
Bill Smith	4	7	3	8	12	8	$16	Sales	$734.60
Margie Run	2	9	10	9	9	4	10	Office	390.60
Alice Angel	3	8	10	10	8	10	15	Sales	752.50
Ray Miller	1	8	7	8	8	8	8	Office	246.20

Assume the following:
1. Income tax, CPP, and UI are from tables at the end of this chapter. (See Appendices 1-3.)
2. Each employee contributes $8 per week for health insurance.
3. Overtime is paid at a rate of time and a half over 40 hours per week or over 8 hours in any day.

9B-4. John Wood, Accountant, has gathered the following data for you. Your task is to:

1. Prepare a payroll register on December 5.
2. Journalize and post the payroll entry.
3. Record the payment of the payroll on December 7 to each employee.

Payroll register completed, journalizing posting and paying the payroll.

EMPLOYEE	NET CLAIM CODE	SALARY	CHQ. NO.	CUM. CPP BEFORE THIS PAYROLL	DEPT.
Joe Boyn	5	$550	29	$347.20	Factory
Jane Allen	4	820	30	477.60	Office
Shelley Roe	2	790	31	741.80	Office
John Sullivan	3	980	32	746.00	Factory

Assume the following:
1. Income tax is calculated from tables in the text.
2. Union dues are $6 per week.
3. Medical coverage is $12 per week (except for John, whose wife pays the family premium).

GROUP C PROBLEMS

9C-1. From the following data, please calculate the gross earnings for each of the five employees who are entitled to time and a half for any hours exceeding 40 for the week or 8 in any given day.

EMPLOYEE	M	T	W	T	F	S	TOTAL HOURS	HOURLY RATE
A. Marcia Goldblum	4	8	8	8	8	4	40	$11.00
B. Phillip Rollins	7	7	7	7	7	7	42	12.00
C. David Ho	8	6	8	11	8	–	41	10.00
D. Alma Sawchuk	8	4	8	8	8	8	44	14.00
E. Thomas Kjellin	8	8	–	12	8	6	42	12.00

Calculating gross earnings with overtime.

9C-2. The employees mentioned in problem 9C-1 (above) work for the Waylon Corporation Ltd. Complete a payroll register for the second week of February using the gross earnings you obtained in answering 9C-1. Assume the following additional information:

EMPLOYEE	NET CLAIM CODE	UNION DUES	MEDICAL PLAN
A	3	11	$25.00
B	1	11	12.50
C	1	11	12.50
D	5	11	25.00
E	4	11	25.00

Completing the payroll register.

9C-3. (Alternative to 9C-2) Assume the following gross earnings for the employees of Waylon Corporation Ltd. for the third week of February. Other information remains the same as in 9C-2. Complete the payroll register for the third week of February.

EMPLOYEE	GROSS EARNINGS
A	$429.00
B	498.00
C	436.00
D	687.00
E	545.00

Completing the payroll register (alternate problem).

9C-4. Refer to the payroll register you completed in 9C-2. Prepare the journal entry necessary to record the payroll for the second week of February.

Recording the payroll entry.

9C-5. (Alternative to 9C-4) Refer to the payroll register you completed in 9C-3. Prepare the journal entry necessary to record the payroll for the third week of February.

Recording the payroll entry (alternate problem).

9C-6. The payroll clerk for the Marlin Company Ltd. has assembled the following data for the company's five employees, before suddenly becoming quite ill. You have been approached to complete the payroll register so that the employees can receive their cheques in a timely fashion. You must (1) complete the payroll register for the week ending October 20, and (2) prepare the entry necessary to record the payroll. Hours in excess of 40 in any week are paid at time and one half.

Completing the payroll register and journalizing the payroll entry.

EMPLOYEE	NET CLAIM CODE	DAILY TIME						RATE	DEPT.	CPP TO DATE	UNION DUES	MEDICAL
		M	T	W	T	F	S					
Carl Ziegler	3	–	8	8	12	12	4	16.00	Sales	$746.40	9	32
Anne Baker	1	8	–	6	10	6	8	14.00	Sales	684.10	9	16
Carla Salis	5	8	8	8	7	8	4	12.00	Admin.	486.70	9	32
Hedy Chan	2	8	8	8	8	8	–	15.00	Admin.	127.40	9	16
Dave Gupta	4	8	8	8	12	8	8	1200.00*	Mgr.	752.50	–	32

* Weekly salary

Comprehensive payroll problem— completing payroll registers, journalizing payrolls and recording cheques issued.

9C-7 Elliot Engineering Inc. is a consulting firm which employs 4 professional staff, 2 casual clerks and yourself as office manager (accountant). Everyone except the clerks is paid a weekly salary. The clerks are paid on an hourly rate and receive time and one half for hours worked in excess of 8 per day or 40 per week. Using the information below, complete the payroll register for the week ending August 21, make the necessary entry to record the payroll for that week, and record the issuance of cheques to each employee. Daily hours for the clerks are shown at the end of the information.

EMPLOYEE	NET CLAIM CODE	RATE OR SALARY	LIFE INS.	DISAB.	MED.	DON.	CPP TO DATE	CHQ. NO.
Chris Mah	6	$1,400.00	$11.20	$28.00	$36.00	$25.00	$752.50	481
Brenda Jacick	3	1,350.00	10.85	27.00	36.00	15.00	732.80	482
Pat Ness	1	1,100.00	9.70	24.00	18.00	10.00	701.70	483
Daj Singh	4	1,000.00	8.40	22.00	36.00	10.00	451.60	484
Tony Dzurko	1	12.00	–	–	18.00	–	127.15	485
Amy Blair	5	14.00	–	–	36.00	5.00	315.60	486
Yourself	2	725.00	5.86	16.00	18.00	5.00	527.60	487

Hourly Employees worked:	M	T	W	T	F	S	TOTAL
Tony Dzurko	8	6	8	8	4	8	42
Amy Blair	10	8	12	6	8	–	44

PRACTICAL ACCOUNTING APPLICATION #1

Small Co., a proprietorship, has two employees, Jim Roy and Janice Alter. The owner of Small Co. is Bert Ryan. During the current pay period, Jim has worked 48 hours and Janice 56. The reason for these extra hours is that both Jim and Janice worked their regular 40-hour work week, plus Jim worked 8 extra hours on Sunday while Janice worked 8 extra hours on Saturday as well as Sunday. Their contract with Small Co. is that they are each paid an hourly rate of $8 per hour with all hours over 40 per week to be time and a half and double time on Sunday. Bert the owner feels he is also entitled to a salary, since he works many hours. He plans to pay himself $425 per week.

As the accountant of Small Co., could you calculate the gross pay for Jim and Janice and offer some advice to Bert regarding his salary?

PRACTICAL ACCOUNTING APPLICATION #2

Marcy Moore recently moved to your city from another large Canadian center. She was employed as an engineer by a large oil company and was rather well paid. She now works as a senior engineer for a newly established consulting firm. Since she moved in October, Marcy had contributed the yearly maximum CPP premiums of $752.50 while employed at the oil company, and feels it is unfair of her new employer to continue to deduct CPP from her salary. She has heard that you are taking an accounting course, and has asked you for your opinion.

What advice can you give her?

APPENDICES 9-1 TO 9-3
Employee Payroll Deductions: Income Tax, CPP, UIC

Ontario
Tax Deductions
Weekly (52 pay periods a year)

Ontario
Retenues d'impôt
C-1
Hebdomadaire (52 périodes de paie par année)

Weekly pay Rémunération hebdomadaire		If the employee's claim code from form TD1 is Si le code de demande de l'employé selon la formule TD1 est										
From De	Less than Moins que	0	1	2	3	4	5	6	7	8	9	10
					Deduct from each pay Retenez sur chaque paie							
	129.	*	.00									
129.-	131.	33.40	.05									
131.-	133.	33.95	.40									
133.-	135.	34.45	.70									
135.-	137.	34.95	1.05									
137.-	139.	35.45	1.35									
139.-	141.	35.95	1.70									
141.-	143.	36.45	2.05									
143.-	145.	37.00	2.35									
145.-	147.	37.50	2.70	.05								
147.-	149.	38.00	3.05	.35								
149.-	151.	38.50	3.35	.70								
151.-	153.	39.00	3.70	1.05								
153.-	155.	39.50	4.00	1.35								
155.-	157.	40.00	4.35	1.70								
157.-	159.	40.55	4.70	2.00								
159.-	161.	41.05	5.00	2.35								
161.-	163.	41.55	5.35	2.70								
163.-	165.	42.05	5.70	3.00								
165.-	167.	42.55	6.00	3.35								
167.-	169.	43.05	6.40	3.70								
169.-	171.	43.60	7.25	4.00								
171.-	173.	44.10	8.10	4.35								
173.-	175.	44.60	9.00	4.65								
175.-	177.	45.10	9.85	5.00								
177.-	179.	45.60	10.70	5.35								
179.-	181.	46.10	11.55	5.65	.35							
181.-	183.	46.60	12.40	6.00	.65							
183.-	185.	47.15	13.30	6.35	1.00							
185.-	187.	47.65	14.15	7.20	1.35							
187.-	189.	48.15	14.80	8.10	1.65							
189.-	191.	48.65	15.30	8.95	2.00							
191.-	193.	49.15	15.80	9.80	2.30							
193.-	195.	49.65	16.30	10.65	2.65							
195.-	197.	50.20	16.85	11.50	3.00							
197.-	199.	50.70	17.35	12.40	3.30							
199.-	201.	51.20	17.85	13.25	3.65							
201.-	203.	51.70	18.35	14.10	4.00							
203.-	205.	52.20	18.85	14.80	4.30							
205.-	207.	52.70	19.35	15.30	4.65							
207.-	209.	53.20	19.85	15.80	4.95							
209.-	211.	53.75	20.40	16.30	5.30							
211.-	213.	54.25	20.90	16.80	5.65	.30						
213.-	215.	54.75	21.40	17.30	5.95	.65						
215.-	217.	55.25	21.90	17.80	6.30	.95						
217.-	219.	55.75	22.40	18.35	7.15	1.30						
219.-	221.	56.25	22.90	18.85	8.00	1.65						
221.-	223.	56.80	23.45	19.35	8.85	1.95						
223.-	225.	57.30	23.95	19.85	9.70	2.30						
225.-	227.	57.80	24.45	20.35	10.60	2.60						
227.-	229.	58.30	24.95	20.85	11.45	2.95						
229.-	231.	58.80	25.45	21.40	12.30	3.30						
231.-	233.	59.30	25.95	21.90	13.15	3.60						
233.-	235.	59.80	26.45	22.40	14.05	3.95						
235.-	237.	60.35	27.00	22.90	14.75	4.25						

* You normally only use claim code "0" for non-resident employees. However, if you have non-resident employees who earn less than the minimum amount shown in the pay column, you may not be able to use these tables. Instead, see the "Step-by-step calculation of tax deductions" in Section "A".

* Le code de demande «0» est normalement utilisé seulement pour les non-résidents. Cependant, si la rémunération de votre employé non résidant est inférieure au montant minimum indiqué dans la colonne «Rémunération», vous ne pourrez pas utiliser les tables. Reportez-vous alors au «Calcul des retenues d'impôt, étape par étape» dans la section «A».

APPENDIX 9-1   Income Tax Deductions

C-2

Ontario											
Tax Deductions						Ontario					
Weekly (52 pay periods a year)						**Retenues d'impôt**					
						Hebdomadaire (52 périodes de paie par année)					

Weekly pay Rémunération hebdomadaire		If the employee's claim code from form TD1 is Si le code de demande de l'employé selon la formule TD1 est										
From De	Less than Moins que	0	1	2	3	4	5	6	7	8	9	10
		Deduct from each pay Retenez sur chaque paie										
237.-	241.	61.10	27.75	23.65	15.50	4.75						
241.-	245.	62.10	28.75	24.70	16.50	5.45	.10					
245.-	249.	63.10	29.75	25.70	17.50	6.10	.75					
249.-	253.	64.15	30.80	26.70	18.55	7.50	1.45					
253.-	257.	65.15	31.80	27.70	19.55	9.20	2.10					
257.-	261.	66.15	32.80	28.75	20.55	10.90	2.75					
261.-	265.	67.20	33.85	29.75	21.60	12.65	3.40					
265.-	269.	68.20	34.85	30.75	22.60	14.35	4.10					
269.-	273.	69.20	35.85	31.80	23.60	15.45	4.75					
273.-	277.	70.25	36.90	32.80	24.65	16.45	5.40	.10				
277.-	281.	71.25	37.90	33.80	25.65	17.45	6.05	.75				
281.-	285.	72.25	38.90	34.85	26.65	18.50	7.40	1.40				
285.-	289.	73.25	39.95	35.85	27.65	19.50	9.10	2.05				
289.-	293.	74.30	40.95	36.85	28.70	20.50	10.85	2.70				
293.-	297.	75.30	41.95	37.85	29.70	21.55	12.55	3.40				
297.-	301.	76.30	42.95	38.90	30.70	22.55	14.30	4.05				
301.-	305.	77.35	44.00	39.90	31.75	23.55	15.40	4.70				
305.-	309.	78.35	45.00	40.90	32.75	24.60	16.40	5.35	.05			
309.-	313.	79.35	46.00	41.95	33.75	25.60	17.40	6.05	.70			
313.-	317.	80.40	47.05	42.95	34.80	26.60	18.45	7.30	1.35			
317.-	321.	81.40	48.05	43.95	35.80	27.60	19.45	9.05	2.05			
321.-	325.	82.40	49.05	45.00	36.80	28.65	20.45	10.75	2.70			
325.-	329.	83.45	50.10	46.00	37.85	29.65	21.50	12.50	3.35			
329.-	333.	84.45	51.10	47.00	38.85	30.65	22.50	14.20	4.00			
333.-	337.	85.45	52.10	48.05	39.85	31.70	23.50	15.35	4.70			
337.-	341.	86.45	53.15	49.05	40.85	32.70	24.55	16.35	5.35			
341.-	345.	87.50	54.15	50.05	41.90	33.70	25.55	17.40	6.00	.70		
345.-	349.	88.50	55.15	51.05	42.90	34.75	26.55	18.40	7.25	1.35		
349.-	353.	89.50	56.15	52.10	43.90	35.75	27.55	19.40	8.95	2.00		
353.-	357.	90.55	57.20	53.10	44.95	36.75	28.60	20.40	10.70	2.65		
357.-	361.	91.55	58.20	54.10	45.95	37.80	29.60	21.45	12.40	3.30		
361.-	365.	92.55	59.20	55.15	46.95	38.80	30.60	22.45	14.15	4.00		
365.-	369.	93.60	60.25	56.15	48.00	39.80	31.65	23.45	15.30	4.65		
369.-	373.	94.60	61.25	57.15	49.00	40.80	32.65	24.50	16.30	5.30		
373.-	377.	95.60	62.25	58.20	50.00	41.85	33.65	25.50	17.35	5.95	.65	
377.-	381.	96.65	63.30	59.20	51.05	42.85	34.70	26.50	18.35	7.15	1.30	
381.-	385.	97.65	64.30	60.20	52.05	43.85	35.70	27.55	19.35	8.90	1.95	
385.-	389.	98.65	65.30	61.25	53.05	44.90	36.70	28.55	20.40	10.60	2.65	
389.-	393.	99.65	66.30	62.25	54.05	45.90	37.75	29.55	21.40	12.35	3.30	
393.-	397.	100.70	67.35	63.25	55.10	46.90	38.75	30.60	22.40	14.05	3.95	
397.-	401.	101.70	68.35	64.25	56.10	47.95	39.75	31.60	23.40	15.25	4.60	
401.-	405.	102.70	69.35	65.30	57.10	48.95	40.75	32.60	24.45	16.25	5.30	
405.-	409.	103.75	70.40	66.30	58.15	49.95	41.80	33.60	25.45	17.30	5.95	.60
409.-	413.	104.75	71.40	67.30	59.15	50.95	42.80	34.65	26.45	18.30	7.10	1.25
413.-	417.	105.75	72.40	68.35	60.15	52.00	43.80	35.65	27.50	19.30	8.80	1.95
417.-	421.	106.80	73.45	69.35	61.20	53.00	44.85	36.65	28.50	20.35	10.55	2.60
421.-	425.	107.80	74.45	70.35	62.20	54.00	45.85	37.70	29.50	21.35	12.25	3.25
425.-	429.	108.80	75.45	71.40	63.20	55.05	46.85	38.70	30.55	22.35	13.95	3.90
429.-	433.	109.85	76.50	72.40	64.25	56.05	47.90	39.70	31.55	23.35	15.20	4.60
433.-	437.	110.85	77.50	73.40	65.25	57.05	48.90	40.75	32.55	24.40	16.20	5.25
437.-	441.	111.85	78.50	74.40	66.25	58.10	49.90	41.75	33.55	25.40	17.25	5.90
441.-	445.	112.85	79.50	75.45	67.25	59.10	50.95	42.75	34.60	26.40	18.25	7.00
445.-	449.	113.90	80.55	76.45	68.30	60.10	51.95	43.75	35.60	27.45	19.25	8.70
449.-	453.	114.90	81.55	77.45	69.30	61.15	52.95	44.80	36.60	28.45	20.30	10.45
453.-	457.	115.90	82.55	78.50	70.30	62.15	53.95	45.80	37.65	29.45	21.30	12.15

APPENDIX 9-1　　Income Tax Deductions (continued)

Ontario
Tax Deductions
Weekly (52 pay periods a year)

Ontario
Retenues d'impôt
Hebdomadaire (52 périodes de paie par année)

C-3

Weekly pay Rémunération hebdomadaire		If the employee's claim code from form TD1 is Si le code de demande de l'employé selon la formule TD1 est										
From De	Less than Moins que	0	1	2	3	4	5	6	7	8	9	10
		Deduct from each pay Retenez sur chaque paie										
457.-	465.	117.45	84.10	80.00	71.85	63.65	55.50	47.35	39.15	31.00	22.80	14.65
465.-	473.	119.45	86.10	82.05	73.85	65.70	57.55	49.35	41.20	33.00	24.85	16.65
473.-	481.	121.50	88.15	84.05	75.90	67.75	59.55	51.40	43.20	35.05	26.90	18.70
481.-	489.	123.55	90.20	86.10	77.95	69.75	61.60	53.40	45.25	37.10	28.90	20.75
489.-	497.	125.55	92.20	88.15	79.95	71.80	63.60	55.45	47.30	39.10	30.95	22.75
497.-	505.	127.60	94.25	90.15	82.00	73.80	65.65	57.50	49.30	41.15	32.95	24.80
505.-	513.	129.60	96.30	92.20	84.00	75.85	67.70	59.50	51.35	43.15	35.00	26.85
513.-	521.	131.65	98.30	94.20	86.05	77.90	69.70	61.55	53.35	45.20	37.05	28.85
521.-	529.	133.70	100.35	96.25	88.10	79.90	71.75	63.55	55.40	47.25	39.05	30.90
529.-	537.	135.70	102.35	98.30	90.10	81.95	73.75	65.60	57.45	49.25	41.10	32.90
537.-	545.	137.75	104.40	100.30	92.15	83.95	75.80	67.65	59.45	51.30	43.15	34.95
545.-	553.	139.80	106.45	102.35	94.20	86.00	77.85	69.65	61.50	53.35	45.15	37.00
553.-	561.	141.80	108.45	104.40	96.20	88.05	79.85	71.70	63.55	55.35	47.20	39.00
561.-	569.	143.85	110.50	106.40	98.25	90.05	81.90	73.75	65.55	57.40	49.20	41.05
569.-	577.	146.45	113.10	109.00	100.85	92.65	84.50	76.30	68.15	60.00	51.80	43.65
577.-	585.	149.60	116.25	112.15	104.00	95.85	87.65	79.50	71.30	63.15	55.00	46.80
585.-	593.	152.75	119.40	115.35	107.15	99.00	90.85	82.65	74.50	66.30	58.15	50.00
593.-	601.	155.95	122.60	118.50	110.35	102.15	94.00	85.85	77.65	69.50	61.30	53.15
601.-	609.	159.10	125.75	121.70	113.50	105.35	97.15	89.00	80.85	72.65	64.50	56.30
609.-	617.	162.30	128.95	124.85	116.70	108.50	100.35	92.15	84.00	75.85	67.65	59.50
617.-	625.	165.45	132.10	128.00	119.85	111.65	103.50	95.35	87.15	79.00	70.85	62.65
625.-	633.	168.60	135.25	131.20	123.00	114.85	106.65	98.50	90.35	82.15	74.00	65.80
633.-	641.	171.80	138.45	134.35	126.20	118.00	109.85	101.65	93.50	85.35	77.15	69.00
641.-	649.	174.95	141.60	137.55	129.35	121.20	113.00	104.85	96.70	88.50	80.35	72.15
649.-	657.	178.20	144.85	140.75	132.60	124.40	116.25	108.10	99.90	91.75	83.55	75.40
657.-	665.	181.40	148.05	144.00	135.80	127.65	119.45	111.30	103.15	94.95	86.80	78.60
665.-	673.	184.65	151.30	147.20	139.05	130.85	122.70	114.50	106.35	98.20	90.00	81.85
673.-	681.	187.85	154.50	150.40	142.25	134.10	125.90	117.75	109.55	101.40	93.25	85.05
681.-	689.	191.10	157.75	153.65	145.50	137.30	129.15	120.95	112.80	104.65	96.45	88.30
689.-	697.	194.30	160.95	156.85	148.70	140.50	132.35	124.20	116.00	107.85	99.70	91.50
697.-	705.	197.50	164.15	160.10	151.90	143.75	135.55	127.40	119.25	111.05	102.90	94.70
705.-	713.	200.75	167.40	163.30	155.15	146.95	138.80	130.65	122.45	114.30	106.10	97.95
713.-	721.	203.95	170.60	166.55	158.35	150.20	142.00	133.85	125.70	117.50	109.35	101.15
721.-	729.	207.20	173.85	169.75	161.60	153.40	145.25	137.05	128.90	120.75	112.55	104.40
729.-	737.	210.40	177.05	173.00	164.80	156.65	148.45	140.30	132.15	123.95	115.80	107.60
737.-	745.	213.65	180.30	176.20	168.05	159.85	151.70	143.50	135.35	127.20	119.00	110.85
745.-	753.	216.90	183.55	179.45	171.30	163.10	154.95	146.75	138.60	130.45	122.25	114.10
753.-	761.	220.15	186.80	182.75	174.55	166.40	158.25	150.05	141.90	133.70	125.55	117.35
761.-	769.	223.45	190.10	186.05	177.85	169.70	161.50	153.35	145.20	137.00	128.85	120.65
769.-	777.	226.75	193.40	189.30	181.15	172.95	164.80	156.65	148.45	140.30	132.10	123.95
777.-	785.	230.05	196.70	192.60	184.45	176.25	168.10	159.90	151.75	143.60	135.40	127.25
785.-	793.	233.30	199.95	195.90	187.70	179.55	171.35	163.20	155.05	146.85	138.70	130.50
793.-	801.	236.60	203.25	199.15	191.00	182.85	174.65	166.50	158.30	150.15	142.00	133.80
801.-	809.	239.90	206.55	202.45	194.30	186.10	177.95	169.80	161.60	153.45	145.25	137.10
809.-	817.	243.20	209.85	205.75	197.60	189.40	181.25	173.05	164.90	156.75	148.55	140.40
817.-	825.	246.45	213.10	209.05	200.85	192.70	184.50	176.35	168.20	160.00	151.85	143.65
825.-	833.	249.75	216.40	212.30	204.15	195.95	187.80	179.65	171.45	163.30	155.15	146.95
833.-	841.	253.05	219.70	215.60	207.45	199.25	191.10	182.90	174.75	166.60	158.40	150.25
841.-	849.	256.30	222.95	218.90	210.70	202.55	194.40	186.20	178.05	169.85	161.70	153.55
849.-	857.	259.60	226.25	222.20	214.00	205.85	197.65	189.50	181.35	173.15	165.00	156.80
857.-	865.	262.90	229.55	225.45	217.30	209.10	200.95	192.80	184.60	176.45	168.25	160.10
865.-	873.	266.20	232.85	228.75	220.60	212.40	204.25	196.05	187.90	179.75	171.55	163.40
873.-	881.	269.45	236.10	232.05	223.85	215.70	207.50	199.35	191.20	183.00	174.85	166.65
881.-	889.	272.75	239.40	235.30	227.15	219.00	210.80	202.65	194.45	186.30	178.15	169.95
889.-	897.	276.05	242.70	238.60	230.45	222.25	214.10	205.95	197.75	189.60	181.40	173.25

APPENDIX 9-1 Income Tax Deductions (continued)

C-4	**Ontario** Tax Deductions **Weekly (52 pay periods a year)**										**Ontario** Retenues d'impôt **Hebdomadaire (52 périodes de paie par année)**

Weekly pay Rémunération hebdomadaire		If the employee's claim code from form TD1 is Si le code de demande de l'employé selon la formule TD1 est										
		0	1	2	3	4	5	6	7	8	9	10
From De	Less than Moins que	Deduct from each pay Retenez sur chaque paie										
897.-	909.	280.15	246.80	242.70	234.55	226.35	218.20	210.05	201.85	193.70	185.55	177.35
909.-	921.	285.10	251.75	247.65	239.50	231.30	223.15	214.95	206.80	198.65	190.45	182.30
921.-	933.	290.00	256.65	252.60	244.40	236.25	228.05	219.90	211.75	203.55	195.40	187.20
933.-	945.	294.95	261.60	257.50	249.35	241.15	233.00	224.80	216.65	208.50	200.30	192.15
945.-	957.	299.85	266.50	262.45	254.25	246.10	237.90	229.75	221.60	213.40	205.25	197.05
957.-	969.	304.85	271.45	267.35	259.20	251.00	242.85	234.70	226.50	218.35	210.20	202.00
969.-	981.	310.00	276.40	272.30	264.15	255.95	247.80	239.60	231.45	223.25	215.10	206.95
981.-	993.	315.20	281.30	277.20	269.05	260.90	252.70	244.55	236.35	228.20	220.05	211.85
993.-	1005.	320.35	286.25	282.15	274.00	265.80	257.65	249.45	241.30	233.15	224.95	216.80
1005.-	1017.	325.50	291.15	287.10	278.90	270.75	262.55	254.40	246.25	238.05	229.90	221.70
1017.-	1029.	330.70	296.10	292.00	283.85	275.65	267.50	259.35	251.15	243.00	234.80	226.65
1029.-	1041.	335.85	301.05	296.95	288.75	280.60	272.45	264.25	256.10	247.90	239.75	231.60
1041.-	1053.	341.05	306.05	301.85	293.70	285.55	277.35	269.20	261.00	252.85	244.70	236.50
1053.-	1065.	346.20	311.25	306.95	298.65	290.45	282.30	274.10	265.95	257.80	249.60	241.45
1065.-	1077.	351.35	316.40	312.10	303.55	295.40	287.20	279.05	270.90	262.70	254.55	246.35
1077.-	1089.	356.55	321.55	317.30	308.70	300.30	292.15	284.00	275.80	267.65	259.45	251.30
1089.-	1101.	361.70	326.75	322.45	313.90	305.30	297.10	288.90	280.75	272.55	264.40	256.25
1101.-	1113.	366.90	331.90	327.65	319.05	310.50	302.00	293.85	285.65	277.50	269.35	261.15
1113.-	1125.	372.05	337.10	332.80	324.25	315.65	307.10	298.75	290.60	282.45	274.25	266.10
1125.-	1137.	377.20	342.25	337.95	329.40	320.80	312.25	303.70	295.55	287.35	279.20	271.00
1137.-	1149.	382.65	347.65	343.40	334.85	326.25	317.70	309.10	300.70	292.55	284.35	276.20
1149.-	1161.	388.55	353.45	349.15	340.65	332.00	323.45	314.90	306.30	298.05	289.85	281.70
1161.-	1173.	394.50	359.20	354.90	346.35	337.80	329.20	320.65	312.10	303.55	295.35	287.20
1173.-	1185.	400.45	364.95	360.70	352.10	343.55	335.00	326.40	317.85	309.30	300.85	292.70
1185.-	1197.	406.40	370.75	366.45	357.90	349.30	340.75	332.20	323.60	315.05	306.50	298.20
1197.-	1209.	412.30	376.50	372.20	363.65	355.10	346.50	337.95	329.40	320.80	312.25	303.70
1209.-	1221.	418.25	382.25	378.00	369.40	360.85	352.30	343.70	335.15	326.60	318.00	309.45
1221.-	1233.	424.20	388.20	383.75	375.20	366.60	358.05	349.50	340.90	332.35	323.80	315.20
1233.-	1245.	430.15	394.10	389.70	380.95	372.40	363.80	355.25	346.70	338.10	329.55	320.95
1245.-	1257.	436.10	400.05	395.65	386.80	378.15	369.60	361.00	352.45	343.90	335.30	326.75
1257.-	1269.	442.00	406.00	401.60	392.75	383.95	375.35	366.80	358.20	349.65	341.10	332.50
1269.-	1281.	447.95	411.95	407.55	398.70	389.85	381.10	372.55	364.00	355.40	346.85	338.25
1281.-	1293.	453.95	417.90	413.45	404.65	395.80	387.00	378.30	369.75	361.20	352.60	344.05
1293.-	1305.	460.00	423.80	419.40	410.60	401.75	392.90	384.10	375.50	366.95	358.40	349.80
1305.-	1317.	466.10	429.75	425.35	416.50	407.70	398.85	390.05	381.30	372.70	364.15	355.55
1317.-	1329.	472.15	435.70	431.30	422.45	413.65	404.80	396.00	387.15	378.50	369.90	361.35
1329.-	1341.	478.20	441.65	437.25	428.40	419.55	410.75	401.90	393.10	384.25	375.70	367.10
1341.-	1353.	484.25	447.60	443.15	434.35	425.50	416.70	407.85	399.05	390.20	381.45	372.85
1353.-	1365.	490.30	453.55	449.10	440.25	431.45	422.60	413.80	404.95	396.15	387.30	378.65
1365.-	1377.	496.35	459.65	455.15	446.20	437.40	428.55	419.75	410.90	402.10	393.25	384.45
1377.-	1389.	502.40	465.70	461.20	452.20	443.35	434.50	425.70	416.85	408.05	399.20	390.35
1389.-	1401.	508.45	471.75	467.25	458.25	449.25	440.45	431.60	422.80	413.95	405.15	396.30
1401.-	1413.	514.50	477.80	473.30	464.30	455.30	446.40	437.55	428.75	419.90	411.10	402.25
1413.-	1425.	520.60	483.85	479.35	470.35	461.35	452.35	443.50	434.70	425.85	417.00	408.20
1425.-	1437.	526.65	489.90	485.40	476.40	467.40	458.40	449.45	440.60	431.80	422.95	414.15
1437.-	1449.	532.70	495.95	491.45	482.45	473.45	464.45	455.45	446.55	437.75	428.90	420.05
1449.-	1461.	538.75	502.00	497.50	488.50	479.50	470.50	461.55	452.55	443.65	434.85	426.00
1461.-	1473.	544.80	508.05	503.55	494.60	485.60	476.60	467.60	458.60	449.60	440.80	431.95
1473.-	1485.	550.85	514.15	509.65	500.65	491.65	482.65	473.65	464.65	455.65	446.75	437.90
1485.-	1497.	556.90	520.20	515.70	506.70	497.70	488.70	479.70	470.70	461.70	452.70	443.85
1497.-	1509.	562.95	526.25	521.75	512.75	503.75	494.75	485.75	476.75	467.75	458.75	449.75
1509.-	1521.	569.00	532.30	527.80	518.80	509.80	500.80	491.80	482.80	473.80	464.80	455.80
1521.-	1533.	575.05	538.35	533.85	524.85	515.85	506.85	497.85	488.85	479.85	470.85	461.85
1533.-	1545.	581.15	544.40	539.90	530.90	521.90	512.90	503.90	494.90	485.90	476.95	467.90
1545.-	1557.	587.20	550.45	545.95	536.95	527.95	518.95	509.95	500.95	492.00	483.00	474.00

APPENDIX 9-1   Income Tax Deductions (continued)

Ontario
Tax Deductions
Weekly (52 pay periods a year)

Ontario   C-5
Retenues d'impôt
Hebdomadaire (52 périodes de paie par année)

Weekly pay Rémunération hebdomadaire		If the employee's claim code from form TD1 is Si le code de demande de l'employé selon la formule TD1 est										
		0	1	2	3	4	5	6	7	8	9	10
From De	Less than Moins que					Deduct from each pay Retenez sur chaque paie						
1557.-	1573.	594.25	557.50	553.05	544.05	535.05	526.05	517.05	508.05	499.05	490.05	481.05
1573.-	1589.	602.30	565.60	561.10	552.10	543.10	534.10	525.10	516.10	507.10	498.10	489.10
1589.-	1605.	610.40	573.65	569.15	560.20	551.15	542.20	533.20	524.20	515.20	506.20	497.20
1605.-	1621.	618.45	581.75	577.25	568.25	559.25	550.25	541.25	532.25	523.25	514.25	505.25
1621.-	1637.	626.55	589.80	585.30	576.30	567.30	558.30	549.35	540.35	531.35	522.35	513.35
1637.-	1653.	634.60	597.90	593.40	584.40	575.40	566.40	557.40	548.40	539.40	530.40	521.40
1653.-	1669.	642.70	605.95	601.45	592.45	583.45	574.45	565.50	556.50	547.50	538.50	529.60
1669.-	1685.	650.75	614.05	609.55	600.55	591.55	582.55	573.55	564.55	555.55	546.55	537.55
1685.-	1701.	658.85	622.10	617.60	608.60	599.60	590.60	581.60	572.65	563.65	554.65	545.65
1701.-	1717.	666.90	630.20	625.70	616.70	607.70	598.70	589.70	580.70	571.70	562.70	553.70
1717.-	1733.	675.00	638.25	633.75	624.75	615.75	606.75	597.75	588.75	579.80	570.80	561.80
1733.-	1749.	683.05	646.35	641.85	632.85	623.85	614.85	605.85	596.85	587.85	578.85	569.85
1749.-	1765.	691.15	654.40	649.90	640.90	631.90	622.90	613.90	604.90	595.95	586.95	577.90
1765.-	1781.	699.20	662.50	658.00	649.00	640.00	631.00	622.00	613.00	604.00	595.00	586.00
1781.-	1797.	707.30	670.55	666.05	657.05	648.05	639.05	630.05	621.05	612.05	603.10	594.05
1797.-	1813.	715.35	678.65	674.15	665.15	656.15	647.15	638.15	629.15	620.15	611.15	602.15
1813.-	1829.	723.40	686.70	682.20	673.20	664.20	655.20	646.20	637.20	628.20	619.20	610.20
1829.-	1845.	731.50	694.75	690.30	681.30	672.30	663.30	654.30	645.30	636.30	627.30	618.30
1845.-	1861.	739.55	702.85	698.35	689.35	680.35	671.35	662.35	653.35	644.35	635.35	626.35
1861.-	1877.	747.65	710.90	706.40	697.45	688.45	679.45	670.45	661.45	652.45	643.45	634.45
1877.-	1893.	755.70	719.00	714.50	705.50	696.50	687.50	678.50	669.50	660.50	651.50	642.50
1893.-	1909.	763.80	727.05	722.55	713.60	704.55	695.55	686.60	677.60	668.60	659.60	650.60
1909.-	1925.	771.85	735.15	730.65	721.65	712.65	703.65	694.65	685.65	676.65	667.65	658.65
1925.-	1941.	779.95	743.20	738.70	729.70	720.70	711.70	702.75	693.75	684.75	675.75	666.75
1941.-	1957.	788.00	751.30	746.80	737.80	728.80	719.80	710.80	701.80	692.80	683.80	674.80
1957.-	1973.	796.10	759.35	754.85	745.85	736.85	727.85	718.85	709.90	700.90	691.90	682.90
1973.-	1989.	804.15	767.45	762.95	753.95	744.95	735.95	726.95	717.95	708.95	699.95	690.95
1989.-	2005.	812.25	775.50	771.00	762.00	753.00	744.00	735.00	726.05	717.05	708.05	699.05
2005.-	2021.	820.30	783.60	779.10	770.10	761.10	752.10	743.10	734.10	725.10	716.10	707.10
2021.-	2037.	828.40	791.65	787.15	778.15	769.15	760.15	751.15	742.15	733.20	724.20	715.20
2037.-	2053.	836.45	799.75	795.25	786.25	777.25	768.25	759.25	750.25	741.25	732.25	723.25
2053.-	2069.	844.55	807.80	803.30	794.30	785.30	776.30	767.30	758.30	749.30	740.35	731.30
2069.-	2085.	852.60	815.90	811.40	802.40	793.40	784.40	775.40	766.40	757.40	748.40	739.40
2085.-	2101.	860.70	823.95	819.45	810.45	801.45	792.45	783.45	774.45	765.45	756.45	747.45
2101.-	2117.	868.75	832.00	827.55	818.55	809.55	800.55	791.55	782.55	773.55	764.55	755.55
2117.-	2133.	876.80	840.10	835.60	826.60	817.60	808.60	799.60	790.60	781.60	772.60	763.60
2133.-	2149.	884.90	848.15	843.70	834.70	825.70	816.70	807.70	798.70	789.70	780.70	771.70
2149.-	2165.	892.95	856.25	851.75	842.75	833.75	824.75	815.75	806.75	797.75	788.75	779.75
2165.-	2181.	901.05	864.30	859.80	850.85	841.80	832.85	823.85	814.85	805.85	796.85	787.85
2181.-	2197.	909.10	872.40	867.90	858.90	849.90	840.90	831.90	822.90	813.90	804.90	795.90
2197.-	2213.	917.20	880.45	875.95	866.95	857.95	848.95	840.00	831.00	822.00	813.00	804.00
2213.-	2229.	925.25	888.55	884.05	875.05	866.05	857.05	848.05	839.05	830.05	821.05	812.05
2229.-	2245.	933.35	896.60	892.10	883.10	874.10	865.10	856.15	847.15	838.15	829.15	820.15
2245.-	2261.	941.40	904.70	900.20	891.20	882.20	873.20	864.20	855.20	846.20	837.20	828.20
2261.-	2277.	949.50	912.75	908.25	899.25	890.25	881.25	872.25	863.30	854.30	845.30	836.30
2277.-	2293.	957.55	920.85	916.35	907.35	898.35	889.35	880.35	871.35	862.35	853.35	844.35
2293.-	2309.	965.65	928.90	924.40	915.40	906.40	897.40	888.40	879.40	870.45	861.45	852.45
2309.-	2325.	973.70	937.00	932.50	923.50	914.50	905.50	896.50	887.50	878.50	869.50	860.50
2325.-	2341.	981.80	945.05	940.55	931.55	922.55	913.55	904.55	895.55	886.55	877.60	868.55
2341.-	2357.	989.85	953.15	948.65	939.65	930.65	921.65	912.65	903.65	894.65	885.65	876.65
2357.-	2373.	997.95	961.20	956.70	947.70	938.70	929.70	920.70	911.70	902.70	893.75	884.70
2373.-	2389.	1006.00	969.30	964.80	955.80	946.80	937.80	928.80	919.80	910.80	901.80	892.80
2389.-	2405.	1014.05	977.35	972.85	963.85	954.85	945.85	936.85	927.85	918.85	909.85	900.85
2405.-	2421.	1022.15	985.40	980.95	971.95	962.95	953.95	944.95	935.95	926.95	917.95	908.95
2421.-	2437.	1030.20	993.50	989.00	980.00	971.00	962.00	953.00	944.00	935.00	926.00	917.00

APPENDIX 9-1   Income Tax Deductions (continued)

Canada Pension Plan Contributions – Cotisations au Régime de pensions du Canada　　B-1

Weekly (52 pay periods) – Hebdomadaire (52 périodes de paie)

0.00 – 178.45

Pay Rémunération From – De	To – À	CPP RPC	Pay Rémunération From – De	To – À	CPP RPC	Pay Rémunération From – De	To – À	CPP RPC	Pay Rémunération From – De	To – À	CPP RPC
.00	63.46	.00	92.06	92.45	.72	120.86	121.25	1.44	149.66	150.05	2.16
63.47	64.05	.01	92.46	92.85	.73	121.26	121.65	1.45	150.06	150.45	2.17
64.06	64.45	.02	92.86	93.25	.74	121.66	122.05	1.46	150.46	150.85	2.18
64.46	64.85	.03	93.26	93.65	.75	122.06	122.45	1.47	150.86	151.25	2.19
64.86	65.25	.04	93.66	94.05	.76	122.46	122.85	1.48	151.26	151.65	2.20
65.26	65.65	.05	94.06	94.45	.77	122.86	123.25	1.49	151.66	152.05	2.21
65.66	66.05	.06	94.46	94.85	.78	123.26	123.65	1.50	152.06	152.45	2.22
66.06	66.45	.07	94.86	95.25	.79	123.66	124.05	1.51	152.46	152.85	2.23
66.46	66.85	.08	95.26	95.65	.80	124.06	124.45	1.52	152.86	153.25	2.24
66.86	67.25	.09	95.66	96.05	.81	124.46	124.85	1.53	153.26	153.65	2.25
67.26	67.65	.10	96.06	96.45	.82	124.86	125.25	1.54	153.66	154.05	2.26
67.66	68.05	.11	96.46	96.85	.83	125.26	125.65	1.55	154.06	154.45	2.27
68.06	68.45	.12	96.86	97.25	.84	125.66	126.05	1.56	154.46	154.85	2.28
68.46	68.85	.13	97.26	97.65	.85	126.06	126.45	1.57	154.86	155.25	2.29
68.86	69.25	.14	97.66	98.05	.86	126.46	126.85	1.58	155.26	155.65	2.30
69.26	69.65	.15	98.06	98.45	.87	126.86	127.25	1.59	155.66	156.05	2.31
69.66	70.05	.16	98.46	98.85	.88	127.26	127.65	1.60	156.06	156.45	2.32
70.06	70.45	.17	98.86	99.25	.89	127.66	128.05	1.61	156.46	156.85	2.33
70.46	70.85	.18	99.26	99.65	.90	128.06	128.45	1.62	156.86	157.25	2.34
70.86	71.25	.19	99.66	100.05	.91	128.46	128.85	1.63	157.26	157.65	2.35
71.26	71.65	.20	100.06	100.45	.92	128.86	129.25	1.64	157.66	158.05	2.36
71.66	72.05	.21	100.46	100.85	.93	129.26	129.65	1.65	158.06	158.45	2.37
72.06	72.45	.22	100.86	101.25	.94	129.66	130.05	1.66	158.46	158.85	2.38
72.46	72.85	.23	101.26	101.65	.95	130.06	130.45	1.67	158.86	159.25	2.39
72.86	73.25	.24	101.66	102.05	.96	130.46	130.85	1.68	159.26	159.65	2.40
73.26	73.65	.25	102.06	102.45	.97	130.86	131.25	1.69	159.66	160.05	2.41
73.66	74.05	.26	102.46	102.85	.98	131.26	131.65	1.70	160.06	160.45	2.42
74.06	74.45	.27	102.86	103.25	.99	131.66	132.05	1.71	160.46	160.85	2.43
74.46	74.85	.28	103.26	103.65	1.00	132.06	132.45	1.72	160.86	161.25	2.44
74.86	75.25	.29	103.66	104.05	1.01	132.46	132.85	1.73	161.26	161.65	2.45
75.26	75.65	.30	104.06	104.45	1.02	132.86	133.25	1.74	161.66	162.05	2.46
75.66	76.05	.31	104.46	104.85	1.03	133.26	133.65	1.75	162.06	162.45	2.47
76.06	76.45	.32	104.86	105.25	1.04	133.66	134.05	1.76	162.46	162.85	2.48
76.46	76.85	.33	105.26	105.65	1.05	134.06	134.45	1.77	162.86	163.25	2.49
76.86	77.25	.34	105.66	106.05	1.06	134.46	134.85	1.78	163.26	163.65	2.50
77.26	77.65	.35	106.06	106.45	1.07	134.86	135.25	1.79	163.66	164.05	2.51
77.66	78.05	.36	106.46	106.85	1.08	135.26	135.65	1.80	164.06	164.45	2.52
78.06	78.45	.37	106.86	107.25	1.09	135.66	136.05	1.81	164.46	164.85	2.53
78.46	78.85	.38	107.26	107.65	1.10	136.06	136.45	1.82	164.86	165.25	2.54
78.86	79.25	.39	107.66	108.05	1.11	136.46	136.85	1.83	165.26	165.65	2.55
79.26	79.65	.40	108.06	108.45	1.12	136.86	137.25	1.84	165.66	166.05	2.56
79.66	80.05	.41	108.46	108.85	1.13	137.26	137.65	1.85	166.06	166.45	2.57
80.06	80.45	.42	108.86	109.25	1.14	137.66	138.05	1.86	166.46	166.85	2.58
80.46	80.85	.43	109.26	109.65	1.15	138.06	138.45	1.87	166.86	167.25	2.59
80.86	81.25	.44	109.66	110.05	1.16	138.46	138.85	1.88	167.26	167.65	2.60
81.26	81.65	.45	110.06	110.45	1.17	138.86	139.25	1.89	167.66	168.05	2.61
81.66	82.05	.46	110.46	110.85	1.18	139.26	139.65	1.90	168.06	168.45	2.62
82.06	82.45	.47	110.86	111.25	1.19	139.66	140.05	1.91	168.46	168.85	2.63
82.46	82.85	.48	111.26	111.65	1.20	140.06	140.45	1.92	168.86	169.25	2.64
82.86	83.25	.49	111.66	112.05	1.21	140.46	140.85	1.93	169.26	169.65	2.65
83.26	83.65	.50	112.06	112.45	1.22	140.86	141.25	1.94	169.66	170.05	2.66
83.66	84.05	.51	112.46	112.85	1.23	141.26	141.65	1.95	170.06	170.45	2.67
84.06	84.45	.52	112.86	113.25	1.24	141.66	142.05	1.96	170.46	170.85	2.68
84.46	84.85	.53	113.26	113.65	1.25	142.06	142.45	1.97	170.86	171.25	2.69
84.86	85.25	.54	113.66	114.05	1.26	142.46	142.85	1.98	171.26	171.65	2.70
85.26	85.65	.55	114.06	114.45	1.27	142.86	143.25	1.99	171.66	172.05	2.71
85.66	86.05	.56	114.46	114.85	1.28	143.26	143.65	2.00	172.06	172.45	2.72
86.06	86.45	.57	114.86	115.25	1.29	143.66	144.05	2.01	172.46	172.85	2.73
86.46	86.85	.58	115.26	115.65	1.30	144.06	144.45	2.02	172.86	173.25	2.74
86.86	87.25	.59	115.66	116.05	1.31	144.46	144.85	2.03	173.26	173.65	2.75
87.26	87.65	.60	116.06	116.45	1.32	144.86	145.25	2.04	173.66	174.05	2.76
87.66	88.05	.61	116.46	116.85	1.33	145.26	145.65	2.05	174.06	174.45	2.77
88.06	88.45	.62	116.86	117.25	1.34	145.66	146.05	2.06	174.46	174.85	2.78
88.46	88.85	.63	117.26	117.65	1.35	146.06	146.45	2.07	174.86	175.25	2.79
88.86	89.25	.64	117.66	118.05	1.36	146.46	146.85	2.08	175.26	175.65	2.80
89.26	89.65	.65	118.06	118.45	1.37	146.86	147.25	2.09	175.66	176.05	2.81
89.66	90.05	.66	118.46	118.85	1.38	147.26	147.65	2.10	176.06	176.45	2.82
90.06	90.45	.67	118.86	119.25	1.39	147.66	148.05	2.11	176.46	176.85	2.83
90.46	90.85	.68	119.26	119.65	1.40	148.06	148.45	2.12	176.86	177.25	2.84
90.86	91.25	.69	119.66	120.05	1.41	148.46	148.85	2.13	177.26	177.65	2.85
91.26	91.65	.70	120.06	120.45	1.42	148.86	149.25	2.14	177.66	178.05	2.86
91.66	92.05	.71	120.46	120.85	1.43	149.26	149.65	2.15	178.06	178.45	2.87

APPENDIX 9-2　　Canada Pension Plan Contributions

B-2 **Canada Pension Plan Contributions – Cotisations au Régime de pensions du Canada**

Weekly (52 pay periods) – Hebdomadaire (52 périodes de paie)

178.46 – 293.65

Pay Rémunération From – De	To – À	CPP RPC	Pay Rémunération From – De	To – À	CPP RPC	Pay Rémunération From – De	To – À	CPP RPC	Pay Rémunération From – De	To – À	CPP RPC
178.46 -	178.85	2.88	207.26 -	207.65	3.60	236.06 -	236.45	4.32	264.86 -	265.25	5.04
178.86 -	179.25	2.89	207.66 -	208.05	3.61	236.46 -	236.85	4.33	265.26 -	265.65	5.05
179.26 -	179.65	2.90	208.06 -	208.45	3.62	236.86 -	237.25	4.34	265.66 -	266.05	5.06
179.66 -	180.05	2.91	208.46 -	208.85	3.63	237.26 -	237.65	4.35	266.06 -	266.45	5.07
180.06 -	180.45	2.92	208.86 -	209.25	3.64	237.66 -	238.05	4.36	266.46 -	266.85	5.08
180.46 -	180.85	2.93	209.26 -	209.65	3.65	238.06 -	238.45	4.37	266.86 -	267.25	5.09
180.86 -	181.25	2.94	209.66 -	210.05	3.66	238.46 -	238.85	4.38	267.26 -	267.65	5.10
181.26 -	181.65	2.95	210.06 -	210.45	3.67	238.86 -	239.25	4.39	267.66 -	268.05	5.11
181.66 -	182.05	2.96	210.46 -	210.85	3.68	239.26 -	239.65	4.40	268.06 -	268.45	5.12
182.06 -	182.45	2.97	210.86 -	211.25	3.69	239.66 -	240.05	4.41	268.46 -	268.85	5.13
182.46 -	182.85	2.98	211.26 -	211.65	3.70	240.06 -	240.45	4.42	268.86 -	269.25	5.14
182.86 -	183.25	2.99	211.66 -	212.05	3.71	240.46 -	240.85	4.43	269.26 -	269.65	5.15
183.26 -	183.65	3.00	212.06 -	212.45	3.72	240.86 -	241.25	4.44	269.66 -	270.05	5.16
183.66 -	184.05	3.01	212.46 -	212.85	3.73	241.26 -	241.65	4.45	270.06 -	270.45	5.17
184.06 -	184.45	3.02	212.86 -	213.25	3.74	241.66 -	242.05	4.46	270.46 -	270.85	5.18
184.46 -	184.85	3.03	213.26 -	213.65	3.75	242.06 -	242.45	4.47	270.86 -	271.25	5.19
184.86 -	185.25	3.04	213.66 -	214.05	3.76	242.46 -	242.85	4.48	271.26 -	271.65	5.20
185.26 -	185.65	3.05	214.06 -	214.45	3.77	242.86 -	243.25	4.49	271.66 -	272.05	5.21
185.66 -	186.05	3.06	214.46 -	214.85	3.78	243.26 -	243.65	4.50	272.06 -	272.45	5.22
186.06 -	186.45	3.07	214.86 -	215.25	3.79	243.66 -	244.05	4.51	272.46 -	272.85	5.23
186.46 -	186.85	3.08	215.26 -	215.65	3.80	244.06 -	244.45	4.52	272.86 -	273.25	5.24
186.86 -	187.25	3.09	215.66 -	216.05	3.81	244.46 -	244.85	4.53	273.26 -	273.65	5.25
187.26 -	187.65	3.10	216.06 -	216.45	3.82	244.86 -	245.25	4.54	273.66 -	274.05	5.26
187.66 -	188.05	3.11	216.46 -	216.85	3.83	245.26 -	245.65	4.55	274.06 -	274.45	5.27
188.06 -	188.45	3.12	216.86 -	217.25	3.84	245.66 -	246.05	4.56	274.46 -	274.85	5.28
188.46 -	188.85	3.13	217.26 -	217.65	3.85	246.06 -	246.45	4.57	274.86 -	275.25	5.29
188.86 -	189.25	3.14	217.66 -	218.05	3.86	246.46 -	246.85	4.58	275.26 -	275.65	5.30
189.26 -	189.65	3.15	218.06 -	218.45	3.87	246.86 -	247.25	4.59	275.66 -	276.05	5.31
189.66 -	190.05	3.16	218.46 -	218.85	3.88	247.26 -	247.65	4.60	276.06 -	276.45	5.32
190.06 -	190.45	3.17	218.86 -	219.25	3.89	247.66 -	248.05	4.61	276.46 -	276.85	5.33
190.46 -	190.85	3.18	219.26 -	219.65	3.90	248.06 -	248.45	4.62	276.86 -	277.25	5.34
190.86 -	191.25	3.19	219.66 -	220.05	3.91	248.46 -	248.85	4.63	277.26 -	277.65	5.35
191.26 -	191.65	3.20	220.06 -	220.45	3.92	248.86 -	249.25	4.64	277.66 -	278.05	5.36
191.66 -	192.05	3.21	220.46 -	220.85	3.93	249.26 -	249.65	4.65	278.06 -	278.45	5.37
192.06 -	192.45	3.22	220.86 -	221.25	3.94	249.66 -	250.05	4.66	278.46 -	278.85	5.38
192.46 -	192.85	3.23	221.26 -	221.65	3.95	250.06 -	250.45	4.67	278.86 -	279.25	5.39
192.86 -	193.25	3.24	221.66 -	222.05	3.96	250.46 -	250.85	4.68	279.26 -	279.65	5.40
193.26 -	193.65	3.25	222.06 -	222.45	3.97	250.86 -	251.25	4.69	279.66 -	280.05	5.41
193.66 -	194.05	3.26	222.46 -	222.85	3.98	251.26 -	251.65	4.70	280.06 -	280.45	5.42
194.06 -	194.45	3.27	222.86 -	223.25	3.99	251.66 -	252.05	4.71	280.46 -	280.85	5.43
194.46 -	194.85	3.28	223.26 -	223.65	4.00	252.06 -	252.45	4.72	280.86 -	281.25	5.44
194.86 -	195.25	3.29	223.66 -	224.05	4.01	252.46 -	252.85	4.73	281.26 -	281.65	5.45
195.26 -	195.65	3.30	224.06 -	224.45	4.02	252.86 -	253.25	4.74	281.66 -	282.05	5.46
195.66 -	196.05	3.31	224.46 -	224.85	4.03	253.26 -	253.65	4.75	282.06 -	282.45	5.47
196.06 -	196.45	3.32	224.86 -	225.25	4.04	253.66 -	254.05	4.76	282.46 -	282.85	5.48
196.46 -	196.85	3.33	225.26 -	225.65	4.05	254.06 -	254.45	4.77	282.86 -	283.25	5.49
196.86 -	197.25	3.34	225.66 -	226.05	4.06	254.46 -	254.85	4.78	283.26 -	283.65	5.50
197.26 -	197.65	3.35	226.06 -	226.45	4.07	254.86 -	255.25	4.79	283.66 -	284.05	5.51
197.66 -	198.05	3.36	226.46 -	226.85	4.08	255.26 -	255.65	4.80	284.06 -	284.45	5.52
198.06 -	198.45	3.37	226.86 -	227.25	4.09	255.66 -	256.05	4.81	284.46 -	284.85	5.53
198.46 -	198.85	3.38	227.26 -	227.65	4.10	256.06 -	256.45	4.82	284.86 -	285.25	5.54
198.86 -	199.25	3.39	227.66 -	228.05	4.11	256.46 -	256.85	4.83	285.26 -	285.65	5.55
199.26 -	199.65	3.40	228.06 -	228.45	4.12	256.86 -	257.25	4.84	285.66 -	286.05	5.56
199.66 -	200.05	3.41	228.46 -	228.85	4.13	257.26 -	257.65	4.85	286.06 -	286.45	5.57
200.06 -	200.45	3.42	228.86 -	229.25	4.14	257.66 -	258.05	4.86	286.46 -	286.85	5.58
200.46 -	200.85	3.43	229.26 -	229.65	4.15	258.06 -	258.45	4.87	286.86 -	287.25	5.59
200.86 -	201.25	3.44	229.66 -	230.05	4.16	258.46 -	258.85	4.88	287.26 -	287.65	5.60
201.26 -	201.65	3.45	230.06 -	230.45	4.17	258.86 -	259.25	4.89	287.66 -	288.05	5.61
201.66 -	202.05	3.46	230.46 -	230.85	4.18	259.26 -	259.65	4.90	288.06 -	288.45	5.62
202.06 -	202.45	3.47	230.86 -	231.25	4.19	259.66 -	260.05	4.91	288.46 -	288.85	5.63
202.46 -	202.85	3.48	231.26 -	231.65	4.20	260.06 -	260.45	4.92	288.86 -	289.25	5.64
202.86 -	203.25	3.49	231.66 -	232.05	4.21	260.46 -	260.85	4.93	289.26 -	289.65	5.65
203.26 -	203.65	3.50	232.06 -	232.45	4.22	260.86 -	261.25	4.94	289.66 -	290.05	5.66
203.66 -	204.05	3.51	232.46 -	232.85	4.23	261.26 -	261.65	4.95	290.06 -	290.45	5.67
204.06 -	204.45	3.52	232.86 -	233.25	4.24	261.66 -	262.05	4.96	290.46 -	290.85	5.68
204.46 -	204.85	3.53	233.26 -	233.65	4.25	262.06 -	262.45	4.97	290.86 -	291.25	5.69
204.86 -	205.25	3.54	233.66 -	234.05	4.26	262.46 -	262.85	4.98	291.26 -	291.65	5.70
205.26 -	205.65	3.55	234.06 -	234.45	4.27	262.86 -	263.25	4.99	291.66 -	292.05	5.71
205.66 -	206.05	3.56	234.46 -	234.85	4.28	263.26 -	263.65	5.00	292.06 -	292.45	5.72
206.06 -	206.45	3.57	234.86 -	235.25	4.29	263.66 -	264.05	5.01	292.46 -	292.85	5.73
206.46 -	206.85	3.58	235.26 -	235.65	4.30	264.06 -	264.45	5.02	292.86 -	293.25	5.74
206.86 -	207.25	3.59	235.66 -	236.05	4.31	264.46 -	264.85	5.03	293.26 -	293.65	5.75

APPENDIX 9-2 **Canada Pension Plan Contributions (continued)**

Canada Pension Plan Contributions – Cotisations au Régime de pensions du Canada   B-3

Weekly (52 pay periods) – Hebdomadaire (52 périodes de paie)

293.66 – 408.85

Pay Rémunération From – De	To – À	CPP RPC	Pay Rémunération From – De	To – À	CPP RPC	Pay Rémunération From – De	To – À	CPP RPC	Pay Rémunération From – De	To – À	CPP RPC
293.66	294.05	5.76	322.46	322.85	6.48	351.26	351.65	7.20	380.06	380.45	7.92
294.06	294.45	5.77	322.86	323.25	6.49	351.66	352.05	7.21	380.46	380.85	7.93
294.46	294.85	5.78	323.26	323.65	6.50	352.06	352.45	7.22	380.86	381.25	7.94
294.86	295.25	5.79	323.66	324.05	6.51	352.46	352.85	7.23	381.26	381.65	7.95
295.26	295.65	5.80	324.06	324.45	6.52	352.86	353.25	7.24	381.66	382.05	7.96
295.66	296.05	5.81	324.46	324.85	6.53	353.26	353.65	7.25	382.06	382.45	7.97
296.06	296.45	5.82	324.86	325.25	6.54	353.66	354.05	7.26	382.46	382.85	7.98
296.46	296.85	5.83	325.26	325.65	6.55	354.06	354.45	7.27	382.86	383.25	7.99
296.86	297.25	5.84	325.66	326.05	6.56	354.46	354.85	7.28	383.26	383.65	8.00
297.26	297.65	5.85	326.06	326.45	6.57	354.86	355.25	7.29	383.66	384.05	8.01
297.66	298.05	5.86	326.46	326.85	6.58	355.26	355.65	7.30	384.06	384.45	8.02
298.06	298.45	5.87	326.86	327.25	6.59	355.66	356.05	7.31	384.46	384.85	8.03
298.46	298.85	5.88	327.26	327.65	6.60	356.06	356.45	7.32	384.86	385.25	8.04
298.86	299.25	5.89	327.66	328.05	6.61	356.46	356.85	7.33	385.26	385.65	8.05
299.26	299.65	5.90	328.06	328.45	6.62	356.86	357.25	7.34	385.66	386.05	8.06
299.66	300.05	5.91	328.46	328.85	6.63	357.26	357.65	7.35	386.06	386.45	8.07
300.06	300.45	5.92	328.86	329.25	6.64	357.66	358.05	7.36	386.46	386.85	8.08
300.46	300.85	5.93	329.26	329.65	6.65	358.06	358.45	7.37	386.86	387.25	8.09
300.86	301.25	5.94	329.66	330.05	6.66	358.46	358.85	7.38	387.26	387.65	8.10
301.26	301.65	5.95	330.06	330.45	6.67	358.86	359.25	7.39	387.66	388.05	8.11
301.66	302.05	5.96	330.46	330.85	6.68	359.26	359.65	7.40	388.06	388.45	8.12
302.06	302.45	5.97	330.86	331.25	6.69	359.66	360.05	7.41	388.46	388.85	8.13
302.46	302.85	5.98	331.26	331.65	6.70	360.06	360.45	7.42	388.86	389.25	8.14
302.86	303.25	5.99	331.66	332.05	6.71	360.46	360.85	7.43	389.26	389.65	8.15
303.26	303.65	6.00	332.06	332.45	6.72	360.86	361.25	7.44	389.66	390.05	8.16
303.66	304.05	6.01	332.46	332.85	6.73	361.26	361.65	7.45	390.06	390.45	8.17
304.06	304.45	6.02	332.86	333.25	6.74	361.66	362.05	7.46	390.46	390.85	8.18
304.46	304.85	6.03	333.26	333.65	6.75	362.06	362.45	7.47	390.86	391.25	8.19
304.86	305.25	6.04	333.66	334.05	6.76	362.46	362.85	7.48	391.26	391.65	8.20
305.26	305.65	6.05	334.06	334.45	6.77	362.86	363.25	7.49	391.66	392.05	8.21
305.66	306.05	6.06	334.46	334.85	6.78	363.26	363.65	7.50	392.06	392.45	8.22
306.06	306.45	6.07	334.86	335.25	6.79	363.66	364.05	7.51	392.46	392.85	8.23
306.46	306.85	6.08	335.26	335.65	6.80	364.06	364.45	7.52	392.86	393.25	8.24
306.86	307.25	6.09	335.66	336.05	6.81	364.46	364.85	7.53	393.26	393.65	8.25
307.26	307.65	6.10	336.06	336.45	6.82	364.86	365.25	7.54	393.66	394.05	8.26
307.66	308.05	6.11	336.46	336.85	6.83	365.26	365.65	7.55	394.06	394.45	8.27
308.06	308.45	6.12	336.86	337.25	6.84	365.66	366.05	7.56	394.46	394.85	8.28
308.46	308.85	6.13	337.26	337.65	6.85	366.06	366.45	7.57	394.86	395.25	8.29
308.86	309.25	6.14	337.66	338.05	6.86	366.46	366.85	7.58	395.26	395.65	8.30
309.26	309.65	6.15	338.06	338.45	6.87	366.86	367.25	7.59	395.66	396.05	8.31
309.66	310.05	6.16	338.46	338.85	6.88	367.26	367.65	7.60	396.06	396.45	8.32
310.06	310.45	6.17	338.86	339.25	6.89	367.66	368.05	7.61	396.46	396.85	8.33
310.46	310.85	6.18	339.26	339.65	6.90	368.06	368.45	7.62	396.86	397.25	8.34
310.86	311.25	6.19	339.66	340.05	6.91	368.46	368.85	7.63	397.26	397.65	8.35
311.26	311.65	6.20	340.06	340.45	6.92	368.86	369.25	7.64	397.66	398.05	8.36
311.66	312.05	6.21	340.46	340.85	6.93	369.26	369.65	7.65	398.06	398.45	8.37
312.06	312.45	6.22	340.86	341.25	6.94	369.66	370.05	7.66	398.46	398.85	8.38
312.46	312.85	6.23	341.26	341.65	6.95	370.06	370.45	7.67	398.86	399.25	8.39
312.86	313.25	6.24	341.66	342.05	6.96	370.46	370.85	7.68	399.26	399.65	8.40
313.26	313.65	6.25	342.06	342.45	6.97	370.86	371.25	7.69	399.66	400.05	8.41
313.66	314.05	6.26	342.46	342.85	6.98	371.26	371.65	7.70	400.06	400.45	8.42
314.06	314.45	6.27	342.86	343.25	6.99	371.66	372.05	7.71	400.46	400.85	8.43
314.46	314.85	6.28	343.26	343.65	7.00	372.06	372.45	7.72	400.86	401.25	8.44
314.86	315.25	6.29	343.66	344.05	7.01	372.46	372.85	7.73	401.26	401.65	8.45
315.26	315.65	6.30	344.06	344.45	7.02	372.86	373.25	7.74	401.66	402.05	8.46
315.66	316.05	6.31	344.46	344.85	7.03	373.26	373.65	7.75	402.06	402.45	8.47
316.06	316.45	6.32	344.86	345.25	7.04	373.66	374.05	7.76	402.46	402.85	8.48
316.46	316.85	6.33	345.26	345.65	7.05	374.06	374.45	7.77	402.86	403.25	8.49
316.86	317.25	6.34	345.66	346.05	7.06	374.46	374.85	7.78	403.26	403.65	8.50
317.26	317.65	6.35	346.06	346.45	7.07	374.86	375.25	7.79	403.66	404.05	8.51
317.66	318.05	6.36	346.46	346.85	7.08	375.26	375.65	7.80	404.06	404.45	8.52
318.06	318.45	6.37	346.86	347.25	7.09	375.66	376.05	7.81	404.46	404.85	8.53
318.46	318.85	6.38	347.26	347.65	7.10	376.06	376.45	7.82	404.86	405.25	8.54
318.86	319.25	6.39	347.66	348.05	7.11	376.46	376.85	7.83	405.26	405.65	8.55
319.26	319.65	6.40	348.06	348.45	7.12	376.86	377.25	7.84	405.66	406.05	8.56
319.66	320.05	6.41	348.46	348.85	7.13	377.26	377.65	7.85	406.06	406.45	8.57
320.06	320.45	6.42	348.86	349.25	7.14	377.66	378.05	7.86	406.46	406.85	8.58
320.46	320.85	6.43	349.26	349.65	7.15	378.06	378.45	7.87	406.86	407.25	8.59
320.86	321.25	6.44	349.66	350.05	7.16	378.46	378.85	7.88	407.26	407.65	8.60
321.26	321.65	6.45	350.06	350.45	7.17	378.86	379.25	7.89	407.66	408.05	8.61
321.66	322.05	6.46	350.46	350.85	7.18	379.26	379.65	7.90	408.06	408.45	8.62
322.06	322.45	6.47	350.86	351.25	7.19	379.66	380.05	7.91	408.46	408.85	8.63

APPENDIX 9-2   Canada Pension Plan Contributions (continued)

B-4   **Canada Pension Plan Contributions – Cotisations au Régime de pensions du Canada**

Weekly (52 pay periods) – Hebdomadaire (52 périodes de paie)

408.86 – 524.05

Pay Rémunération		CPP RPC	Pay Rémunération		CPP RPC	Pay Rémunération		CPP RPC	Pay Rémunération		CPP RPC
From – De	To – À		From – De	To – À		From – De	To – À		From – De	To – À	
408.86 –	409.25	8.64	437.66 –	438.05	9.36	466.46 –	466.85	10.08	495.26 –	495.65	10.80
409.26 –	409.65	8.65	438.06 –	438.45	9.37	466.86 –	467.25	10.09	495.66 –	496.05	10.81
409.66 –	410.05	8.66	438.46 –	438.85	9.38	467.26 –	467.65	10.10	496.06 –	496.45	10.82
410.06 –	410.45	8.67	438.86 –	439.25	9.39	467.66 –	468.05	10.11	496.46 –	496.85	10.83
410.46 –	410.85	8.68	439.26 –	439.65	9.40	468.06 –	468.45	10.12	496.86 –	497.25	10.84
410.86 –	411.25	8.69	439.66 –	440.05	9.41	468.46 –	468.85	10.13	497.26 –	497.65	10.85
411.26 –	411.65	8.70	440.06 –	440.45	9.42	468.86 –	469.25	10.14	497.66 –	498.05	10.86
411.66 –	412.05	8.71	440.46 –	440.85	9.43	469.26 –	469.65	10.15	498.06 –	498.45	10.87
412.06 –	412.45	8.72	440.86 –	441.25	9.44	469.66 –	470.05	10.16	498.46 –	498.85	10.88
412.46 –	412.85	8.73	441.26 –	441.65	9.45	470.06 –	470.45	10.17	498.86 –	499.25	10.89
412.86 –	413.25	8.74	441.66 –	442.05	9.46	470.46 –	470.85	10.18	499.26 –	499.65	10.90
413.26 –	413.65	8.75	442.06 –	442.45	9.47	470.86 –	471.25	10.19	499.66 –	500.05	10.91
413.66 –	414.05	8.76	442.46 –	442.85	9.48	471.26 –	471.65	10.20	500.06 –	500.45	10.92
414.06 –	414.45	8.77	442.86 –	443.25	9.49	471.66 –	472.05	10.21	500.46 –	500.85	10.93
414.46 –	414.85	8.78	443.26 –	443.65	9.50	472.06 –	472.45	10.22	500.86 –	501.25	10.94
414.86 –	415.25	8.79	443.66 –	444.05	9.51	472.46 –	472.85	10.23	501.26 –	501.65	10.95
415.26 –	415.65	8.80	444.06 –	444.45	9.52	472.86 –	473.25	10.24	501.66 –	502.05	10.96
415.66 –	416.05	8.81	444.46 –	444.85	9.53	473.26 –	473.65	10.25	502.06 –	502.45	10.97
416.06 –	416.45	8.82	444.86 –	445.25	9.54	473.66 –	474.05	10.26	502.46 –	502.85	10.98
416.46 –	416.85	8.83	445.26 –	445.65	9.55	474.06 –	474.45	10.27	502.86 –	503.25	10.99
416.86 –	417.25	8.84	445.66 –	446.05	9.56	474.46 –	474.85	10.28	503.26 –	503.65	11.00
417.26 –	417.65	8.85	446.06 –	446.45	9.57	474.86 –	475.25	10.29	503.66 –	504.05	11.01
417.66 –	418.05	8.86	446.46 –	446.85	9.58	475.26 –	475.65	10.30	504.06 –	504.45	11.02
418.06 –	418.45	8.87	446.86 –	447.25	9.59	475.66 –	476.05	10.31	504.46 –	504.85	11.03
418.46 –	418.85	8.88	447.26 –	447.65	9.60	476.06 –	476.45	10.32	504.86 –	505.25	11.04
418.86 –	419.25	8.89	447.66 –	448.05	9.61	476.46 –	476.85	10.33	505.26 –	505.65	11.05
419.26 –	419.65	8.90	448.06 –	448.45	9.62	476.86 –	477.25	10.34	505.66 –	506.05	11.06
419.66 –	420.05	8.91	448.46 –	448.85	9.63	477.26 –	477.65	10.35	506.06 –	506.45	11.07
420.06 –	420.45	8.92	448.86 –	449.25	9.64	477.66 –	478.05	10.36	506.46 –	506.85	11.08
420.46 –	420.85	8.93	449.26 –	449.65	9.65	478.06 –	478.45	10.37	506.86 –	507.25	11.09
420.86 –	421.25	8.94	449.66 –	450.05	9.66	478.46 –	478.85	10.38	507.26 –	507.65	11.10
421.26 –	421.65	8.95	450.06 –	450.45	9.67	478.86 –	479.25	10.39	507.66 –	508.05	11.11
421.66 –	422.05	8.96	450.46 –	450.85	9.68	479.26 –	479.65	10.40	508.06 –	508.45	11.12
422.06 –	422.45	8.97	450.86 –	451.25	9.69	479.66 –	480.05	10.41	508.46 –	508.85	11.13
422.46 –	422.85	8.98	451.26 –	451.65	9.70	480.06 –	480.45	10.42	508.86 –	509.25	11.14
422.86 –	423.25	8.99	451.66 –	452.05	9.71	480.46 –	480.85	10.43	509.26 –	509.65	11.15
423.26 –	423.65	9.00	452.06 –	452.45	9.72	480.86 –	481.25	10.44	509.66 –	510.05	11.16
423.66 –	424.05	9.01	452.46 –	452.85	9.73	481.26 –	481.65	10.45	510.06 –	510.45	11.17
424.06 –	424.45	9.02	452.86 –	453.25	9.74	481.66 –	482.05	10.46	510.46 –	510.85	11.18
424.46 –	424.85	9.03	453.26 –	453.65	9.75	482.06 –	482.45	10.47	510.86 –	511.25	11.19
424.86 –	425.25	9.04	453.66 –	454.05	9.76	482.46 –	482.85	10.48	511.26 –	511.65	11.20
425.26 –	425.65	9.05	454.06 –	454.45	9.77	482.86 –	483.25	10.49	511.66 –	512.05	11.21
425.66 –	426.05	9.06	454.46 –	454.85	9.78	483.26 –	483.65	10.50	512.06 –	512.45	11.22
426.06 –	426.45	9.07	454.86 –	455.25	9.79	483.66 –	484.05	10.51	512.46 –	512.85	11.23
426.46 –	426.85	9.08	455.26 –	455.65	9.80	484.06 –	484.45	10.52	512.86 –	513.25	11.24
426.86 –	427.25	9.09	455.66 –	456.05	9.81	484.46 –	484.85	10.53	513.26 –	513.65	11.25
427.26 –	427.65	9.10	456.06 –	456.45	9.82	484.86 –	485.25	10.54	513.66 –	514.05	11.26
427.66 –	428.05	9.11	456.46 –	456.85	9.83	485.26 –	485.65	10.55	514.06 –	514.45	11.27
428.06 –	428.45	9.12	456.86 –	457.25	9.84	485.66 –	486.05	10.56	514.46 –	514.85	11.28
428.46 –	428.85	9.13	457.26 –	457.65	9.85	486.06 –	486.45	10.57	514.86 –	515.25	11.29
428.86 –	429.25	9.14	457.66 –	458.05	9.86	486.46 –	486.85	10.58	515.26 –	515.65	11.30
429.26 –	429.65	9.15	458.06 –	458.45	9.87	486.86 –	487.25	10.59	515.66 –	516.05	11.31
429.66 –	430.05	9.16	458.46 –	458.85	9.88	487.26 –	487.65	10.60	516.06 –	516.45	11.32
430.06 –	430.45	9.17	458.86 –	459.25	9.89	487.66 –	488.05	10.61	516.46 –	516.85	11.33
430.46 –	430.85	9.18	459.26 –	459.65	9.90	488.06 –	488.45	10.62	516.86 –	517.25	11.34
430.86 –	431.25	9.19	459.66 –	460.05	9.91	488.46 –	488.85	10.63	517.26 –	517.65	11.35
431.26 –	431.65	9.20	460.06 –	460.45	9.92	488.86 –	489.25	10.64	517.66 –	518.05	11.36
431.66 –	432.05	9.21	460.46 –	460.85	9.93	489.26 –	489.65	10.65	518.06 –	518.45	11.37
432.06 –	432.45	9.22	460.86 –	461.25	9.94	489.66 –	490.05	10.66	518.46 –	518.85	11.38
432.46 –	432.85	9.23	461.26 –	461.65	9.95	490.06 –	490.45	10.67	518.86 –	519.25	11.39
432.86 –	433.25	9.24	461.66 –	462.05	9.96	490.46 –	490.85	10.68	519.26 –	519.65	11.40
433.26 –	433.65	9.25	462.06 –	462.45	9.97	490.86 –	491.25	10.69	519.66 –	520.05	11.41
433.66 –	434.05	9.26	462.46 –	462.85	9.98	491.26 –	491.65	10.70	520.06 –	520.45	11.42
434.06 –	434.45	9.27	462.86 –	463.25	9.99	491.66 –	492.05	10.71	520.46 –	520.85	11.43
434.46 –	434.85	9.28	463.26 –	463.65	10.00	492.06 –	492.45	10.72	520.86 –	521.25	11.44
434.86 –	435.25	9.29	463.66 –	464.05	10.01	492.46 –	492.85	10.73	521.26 –	521.65	11.45
435.26 –	435.65	9.30	464.06 –	464.45	10.02	492.86 –	493.25	10.74	521.66 –	522.05	11.46
435.66 –	436.05	9.31	464.46 –	464.85	10.03	493.26 –	493.65	10.75	522.06 –	522.45	11.47
436.06 –	436.45	9.32	464.86 –	465.25	10.04	493.66 –	494.05	10.76	522.46 –	522.85	11.48
436.46 –	436.85	9.33	465.26 –	465.65	10.05	494.06 –	494.45	10.77	522.86 –	523.25	11.49
436.86 –	437.25	9.34	465.66 –	466.05	10.06	494.46 –	494.85	10.78	523.26 –	523.65	11.50
437.26 –	437.65	9.35	466.06 –	466.45	10.07	494.86 –	495.25	10.79	523.66 –	524.05	11.51

APPENDIX 9-2   Canada Pension Plan Contributions (continued)

Canada Pension Plan Contributions – Cotisations au Régime de pensions du Canada   B-5

Weekly (52 pay periods) – Hebdomadaire (52 périodes de paie)

524.06 – 639.25

Pay Rémunération From – De	To – À	CPP RPC	Pay Rémunération From – De	To – À	CPP RPC	Pay Rémunération From – De	To – À	CPP RPC	Pay Rémunération From – De	To – À	CPP RPC
524.06 –	524.45	11.52	552.86 –	553.25	12.24	581.66 –	582.05	12.96	610.46 –	610.85	13.68
524.46 –	524.85	11.53	553.26 –	553.65	12.25	582.06 –	582.45	12.97	610.86 –	611.25	13.69
524.86 –	525.25	11.54	553.66 –	554.05	12.26	582.46 –	582.85	12.98	611.26 –	611.65	13.70
525.26 –	525.65	11.55	554.06 –	554.45	12.27	582.86 –	583.25	12.99	611.66 –	612.05	13.71
525.66 –	526.05	11.56	554.46 –	554.85	12.28	583.26 –	583.65	13.00	612.06 –	612.45	13.72
526.06 –	526.45	11.57	554.86 –	555.25	12.29	583.66 –	584.05	13.01	612.46 –	612.85	13.73
526.46 –	526.85	11.58	555.26 –	555.65	12.30	584.06 –	584.45	13.02	612.86 –	613.25	13.74
526.86 –	527.25	11.59	555.66 –	556.05	12.31	584.46 –	584.85	13.03	613.26 –	613.65	13.75
527.26 –	527.65	11.60	556.06 –	556.45	12.32	584.86 –	585.25	13.04	613.66 –	614.05	13.76
527.66 –	528.05	11.61	556.46 –	556.85	12.33	585.26 –	585.65	13.05	614.06 –	614.45	13.77
528.06 –	528.45	11.62	556.86 –	557.25	12.34	585.66 –	586.05	13.06	614.46 –	614.85	13.78
528.46 –	528.85	11.63	557.26 –	557.65	12.35	586.06 –	586.45	13.07	614.86 –	615.25	13.79
528.86 –	529.25	11.64	557.66 –	558.05	12.36	586.46 –	586.85	13.08	615.26 –	615.65	13.80
529.26 –	529.65	11.65	558.06 –	558.45	12.37	586.86 –	587.25	13.09	615.66 –	616.05	13.81
529.66 –	530.05	11.66	558.46 –	558.85	12.38	587.26 –	587.65	13.10	616.06 –	616.45	13.82
530.06 –	530.45	11.67	558.86 –	559.25	12.39	587.66 –	588.05	13.11	616.46 –	616.85	13.83
530.46 –	530.85	11.68	559.26 –	559.65	12.40	588.06 –	588.45	13.12	616.86 –	617.25	13.84
530.86 –	531.25	11.69	559.66 –	560.05	12.41	588.46 –	588.85	13.13	617.26 –	617.65	13.85
531.26 –	531.65	11.70	560.06 –	560.45	12.42	588.86 –	589.25	13.14	617.66 –	618.05	13.86
531.66 –	532.05	11.71	560.46 –	560.85	12.43	589.26 –	589.65	13.15	618.06 –	618.45	13.87
532.06 –	532.45	11.72	560.86 –	561.25	12.44	589.66 –	590.05	13.16	618.46 –	618.85	13.88
532.46 –	532.85	11.73	561.26 –	561.65	12.45	590.06 –	590.45	13.17	618.86 –	619.25	13.89
532.86 –	533.25	11.74	561.66 –	562.05	12.46	590.46 –	590.85	13.18	619.26 –	619.65	13.90
533.26 –	533.65	11.75	562.06 –	562.45	12.47	590.86 –	591.25	13.19	619.66 –	620.05	13.91
533.66 –	534.05	11.76	562.46 –	562.85	12.48	591.26 –	591.65	13.20	620.06 –	620.45	13.92
534.06 –	534.45	11.77	562.86 –	563.25	12.49	591.66 –	592.05	13.21	620.46 –	620.85	13.93
534.46 –	534.85	11.78	563.26 –	563.65	12.50	592.06 –	592.45	13.22	620.86 –	621.25	13.94
534.86 –	535.25	11.79	563.66 –	564.05	12.51	592.46 –	592.85	13.23	621.26 –	621.65	13.95
535.26 –	535.65	11.80	564.06 –	564.45	12.52	592.86 –	593.25	13.24	621.66 –	622.05	13.96
535.66 –	536.05	11.81	564.46 –	564.85	12.53	593.26 –	593.65	13.25	622.06 –	622.45	13.97
536.06 –	536.45	11.82	564.86 –	565.25	12.54	593.66 –	594.05	13.26	622.46 –	622.85	13.98
536.46 –	536.85	11.83	565.26 –	565.65	12.55	594.06 –	594.45	13.27	622.86 –	623.25	13.99
536.86 –	537.25	11.84	565.66 –	566.05	12.56	594.46 –	594.85	13.28	623.26 –	623.65	14.00
537.26 –	537.65	11.85	566.06 –	566.45	12.57	594.86 –	595.25	13.29	623.66 –	624.05	14.01
537.66 –	538.05	11.86	566.46 –	566.85	12.58	595.26 –	595.65	13.30	624.06 –	624.45	14.02
538.06 –	538.45	11.87	566.86 –	567.25	12.59	595.66 –	596.05	13.31	624.46 –	624.85	14.03
538.46 –	538.85	11.88	567.26 –	567.65	12.60	596.06 –	596.45	13.32	624.86 –	625.25	14.04
538.86 –	539.25	11.89	567.66 –	568.05	12.61	596.46 –	596.85	13.33	625.26 –	625.65	14.05
539.26 –	539.65	11.90	568.06 –	568.45	12.62	596.86 –	597.25	13.34	625.66 –	626.05	14.06
539.66 –	540.05	11.91	568.46 –	568.85	12.63	597.26 –	597.65	13.35	626.06 –	626.45	14.07
540.06 –	540.45	11.92	568.86 –	569.25	12.64	597.66 –	598.05	13.36	626.46 –	626.85	14.08
540.46 –	540.85	11.93	569.26 –	569.65	12.65	598.06 –	598.45	13.37	626.86 –	627.25	14.09
540.86 –	541.25	11.94	569.66 –	570.05	12.66	598.46 –	598.85	13.38	627.26 –	627.65	14.10
541.26 –	541.65	11.95	570.06 –	570.45	12.67	598.86 –	599.25	13.39	627.66 –	628.05	14.11
541.66 –	542.05	11.96	570.46 –	570.85	12.68	599.26 –	599.65	13.40	628.06 –	628.45	14.12
542.06 –	542.45	11.97	570.86 –	571.25	12.69	599.66 –	600.05	13.41	628.46 –	628.85	14.13
542.46 –	542.85	11.98	571.26 –	571.65	12.70	600.06 –	600.45	13.42	628.86 –	629.25	14.14
542.86 –	543.25	11.99	571.66 –	572.05	12.71	600.46 –	600.85	13.43	629.26 –	629.65	14.15
543.26 –	543.65	12.00	572.06 –	572.45	12.72	600.86 –	601.25	13.44	629.66 –	630.05	14.16
543.66 –	544.05	12.01	572.46 –	572.85	12.73	601.26 –	601.65	13.45	630.06 –	630.45	14.17
544.06 –	544.45	12.02	572.86 –	573.25	12.74	601.66 –	602.05	13.46	630.46 –	630.85	14.18
544.46 –	544.85	12.03	573.26 –	573.65	12.75	602.06 –	602.45	13.47	630.86 –	631.25	14.19
544.86 –	545.25	12.04	573.66 –	574.05	12.76	602.46 –	602.85	13.48	631.26 –	631.65	14.20
545.26 –	545.65	12.05	574.06 –	574.45	12.77	602.86 –	603.25	13.49	631.66 –	632.05	14.21
545.66 –	546.05	12.06	574.46 –	574.85	12.78	603.26 –	603.65	13.50	632.06 –	632.45	14.22
546.06 –	546.45	12.07	574.86 –	575.25	12.79	603.66 –	604.05	13.51	632.46 –	632.85	14.23
546.46 –	546.85	12.08	575.26 –	575.65	12.80	604.06 –	604.45	13.52	632.86 –	633.25	14.24
546.86 –	547.25	12.09	575.66 –	576.05	12.81	604.46 –	604.85	13.53	633.26 –	633.65	14.25
547.26 –	547.65	12.10	576.06 –	576.45	12.82	604.86 –	605.25	13.54	633.66 –	634.05	14.26
547.66 –	548.05	12.11	576.46 –	576.85	12.83	605.26 –	605.65	13.55	634.06 –	634.45	14.27
548.06 –	548.45	12.12	576.86 –	577.25	12.84	605.66 –	606.05	13.56	634.46 –	634.85	14.28
548.46 –	548.85	12.13	577.26 –	577.65	12.85	606.06 –	606.45	13.57	634.86 –	635.25	14.29
548.86 –	549.25	12.14	577.66 –	578.05	12.86	606.46 –	606.85	13.58	635.26 –	635.65	14.30
549.26 –	549.65	12.15	578.06 –	578.45	12.87	606.86 –	607.25	13.59	635.66 –	636.05	14.31
549.66 –	550.05	12.16	578.46 –	578.85	12.88	607.26 –	607.65	13.60	636.06 –	636.45	14.32
550.06 –	550.45	12.17	578.86 –	579.25	12.89	607.66 –	608.05	13.61	636.46 –	636.85	14.33
550.46 –	550.85	12.18	579.26 –	579.65	12.90	608.06 –	608.45	13.62	636.86 –	637.25	14.34
550.86 –	551.25	12.19	579.66 –	580.05	12.91	608.46 –	608.85	13.63	637.26 –	637.65	14.35
551.26 –	551.65	12.20	580.06 –	580.45	12.92	608.86 –	609.25	13.64	637.66 –	638.05	14.36
551.66 –	552.05	12.21	580.46 –	580.85	12.93	609.26 –	609.65	13.65	638.06 –	638.45	14.37
552.06 –	552.45	12.22	580.86 –	581.25	12.94	609.66 –	610.05	13.66	638.46 –	638.85	14.38
552.46 –	552.85	12.23	581.26 –	581.65	12.95	610.06 –	610.45	13.67	638.86 –	639.25	14.39

APPENDIX 9-2   Canada Pension Plan Contributions (continued)

B-6

Canada Pension Plan Contributions – Cotisations au Régime de pensions du Canada

Weekly (52 pay periods) – Hebdomadaire (52 périodes de paie)

639.26 – 3342.85

Pay Rémunération From – De	To – À	CPP RPC	Pay Rémunération From – De	To – À	CPP RPC	Pay Rémunération From – De	To – À	CPP RPC	Pay Rémunération From – De	To – À	CPP RPC
639.26	639.65	14.40	1272.86	1282.85	30.36	1992.86	2002.85	48.36	2712.86	2722.85	66.36
639.66	640.05	14.41	1282.86	1292.85	30.61	2002.86	2012.85	48.61	2722.86	2732.85	66.61
640.06	640.45	14.42	1292.86	1302.85	30.86	2012.86	2022.85	48.86	2732.86	2742.85	66.86
640.46	640.85	14.43	1302.86	1312.85	31.11	2022.86	2032.85	49.11	2742.86	2752.85	67.11
640.86	641.25	14.44	1312.86	1322.85	31.36	2032.86	2042.85	49.36	2752.86	2762.85	67.36
641.26	641.65	14.45	1322.86	1332.85	31.61	2042.86	2052.85	49.61	2762.86	2772.85	67.61
641.66	642.05	14.46	1332.86	1342.85	31.86	2052.86	2062.85	49.86	2772.86	2782.85	67.86
642.06	642.45	14.47	1342.86	1352.85	32.11	2062.86	2072.85	50.11	2782.86	2792.85	68.11
642.46	642.85	14.48	1352.86	1362.85	32.36	2072.86	2082.85	50.36	2792.86	2802.85	68.36
642.86	652.85	14.61	1362.86	1372.85	32.61	2082.86	2092.85	50.61	2802.86	2812.85	68.61
652.86	662.85	14.86	1372.86	1382.85	32.86	2092.86	2102.85	50.86	2812.86	2822.85	68.86
662.86	672.85	15.11	1382.86	1392.85	33.11	2102.86	2112.85	51.11	2822.86	2832.85	69.11
672.86	682.85	15.36	1392.86	1402.85	33.36	2112.86	2122.85	51.36	2832.86	2842.85	69.36
682.86	692.85	15.61	1402.86	1412.85	33.61	2122.86	2132.85	51.61	2842.86	2852.85	69.61
692.86	702.85	15.86	1412.86	1422.85	33.86	2132.86	2142.85	51.86	2852.86	2862.85	69.86
702.86	712.85	16.11	1422.86	1432.85	34.11	2142.86	2152.85	52.11	2862.86	2872.85	70.11
712.86	722.85	16.36	1432.86	1442.85	34.36	2152.86	2162.85	52.36	2872.86	2882.85	70.36
722.86	732.85	16.61	1442.86	1452.85	34.61	2162.86	2172.85	52.61	2882.86	2892.85	70.61
732.86	742.85	16.86	1452.86	1462.85	34.86	2172.86	2182.85	52.86	2892.86	2902.85	70.86
742.86	752.85	17.11	1462.86	1472.85	35.11	2182.86	2192.85	53.11	2902.86	2912.85	71.11
752.86	762.85	17.36	1472.86	1482.85	35.36	2192.86	2202.85	53.36	2912.86	2922.85	71.36
762.86	772.85	17.61	1482.86	1492.85	35.61	2202.86	2212.85	53.61	2922.86	2932.85	71.61
772.86	782.85	17.86	1492.86	1502.85	35.86	2212.86	2222.85	53.86	2932.86	2942.85	71.86
782.86	792.85	18.11	1502.86	1512.85	36.11	2222.86	2232.85	54.11	2942.86	2952.85	72.11
792.86	802.85	18.36	1512.86	1522.85	36.36	2232.86	2242.85	54.36	2952.86	2962.85	72.36
802.86	812.85	18.61	1522.86	1532.85	36.61	2242.86	2252.85	54.61	2962.86	2972.85	72.61
812.86	822.85	18.86	1532.86	1542.85	36.86	2252.86	2262.85	54.86	2972.86	2982.85	72.86
822.86	832.85	19.11	1542.86	1552.85	37.11	2262.86	2272.85	55.11	2982.86	2992.85	73.11
832.86	842.85	19.36	1552.86	1562.85	37.36	2272.86	2282.85	55.36	2992.86	3002.85	73.36
842.86	852.85	19.61	1562.86	1572.85	37.61	2282.86	2292.85	55.61	3002.86	3012.85	73.61
852.86	862.85	19.86	1572.86	1582.85	37.86	2292.86	2302.85	55.86	3012.86	3022.85	73.86
862.86	872.85	20.11	1582.86	1592.85	38.11	2302.86	2312.85	56.11	3022.86	3032.85	74.11
872.86	882.85	20.36	1592.86	1602.85	38.36	2312.86	2322.85	56.36	3032.86	3042.85	74.36
882.86	892.85	20.61	1602.86	1612.85	38.61	2322.86	2332.85	56.61	3042.86	3052.85	74.61
892.86	902.85	20.86	1612.86	1622.85	38.86	2332.86	2342.85	56.86	3052.86	3062.85	74.86
902.86	912.85	21.11	1622.86	1632.85	39.11	2342.86	2352.85	57.11	3062.86	3072.85	75.11
912.86	922.85	21.36	1632.86	1642.85	39.36	2352.86	2362.85	57.36	3072.86	3082.85	75.36
922.86	932.85	21.61	1642.86	1652.85	39.61	2362.86	2372.85	57.61	3082.86	3092.85	75.61
932.86	942.85	21.86	1652.86	1662.85	39.86	2372.86	2382.85	57.86	3092.86	3102.85	75.86
942.86	952.85	22.11	1662.86	1672.85	40.11	2382.86	2392.85	58.11	3102.86	3112.85	76.11
952.86	962.85	22.36	1672.86	1682.85	40.36	2392.86	2402.85	58.36	3112.86	3122.85	76.36
962.86	972.85	22.61	1682.86	1692.85	40.61	2402.86	2412.85	58.61	3122.86	3132.85	76.61
972.86	982.85	22.86	1692.86	1702.85	40.86	2412.86	2422.85	58.86	3132.86	3142.85	76.86
982.86	992.85	23.11	1702.86	1712.85	41.11	2422.86	2432.85	59.11	3142.86	3152.85	77.11
992.86	1002.85	23.36	1712.86	1722.85	41.36	2432.86	2442.85	59.36	3152.86	3162.85	77.36
1002.86	1012.85	23.61	1722.86	1732.85	41.61	2442.86	2452.85	59.61	3162.86	3172.85	77.61
1012.86	1022.85	23.86	1732.86	1742.85	41.86	2452.86	2462.85	59.86	3172.86	3182.85	77.86
1022.86	1032.85	24.11	1742.86	1752.85	42.11	2462.86	2472.85	60.11	3182.86	3192.85	78.11
1032.86	1042.85	24.36	1752.86	1762.85	42.36	2472.86	2482.85	60.36	3192.86	3202.85	78.36
1042.86	1052.85	24.61	1762.86	1772.85	42.61	2482.86	2492.85	60.61	3202.86	3212.85	78.61
1052.86	1062.85	24.86	1772.86	1782.85	42.86	2492.86	2502.85	60.86	3212.86	3222.85	78.86
1062.86	1072.85	25.11	1782.86	1792.85	43.11	2502.86	2512.85	61.11	3222.86	3232.85	79.11
1072.86	1082.85	25.36	1792.86	1802.85	43.36	2512.86	2522.85	61.36	3232.86	3242.85	79.36
1082.86	1092.85	25.61	1802.86	1812.85	43.61	2522.86	2532.85	61.61	3242.86	3252.85	79.61
1092.86	1102.85	25.86	1812.86	1822.85	43.86	2532.86	2542.85	61.86	3252.86	3262.85	79.86
1102.86	1112.85	26.11	1822.86	1832.85	44.11	2542.86	2552.85	62.11	3262.86	3272.85	80.11
1112.86	1122.85	26.36	1832.86	1842.85	44.36	2552.86	2562.85	62.36	3272.86	3282.85	80.36
1122.86	1132.85	26.61	1842.86	1852.85	44.61	2562.86	2572.85	62.61	3282.86	3292.85	80.61
1132.86	1142.85	26.86	1852.86	1862.85	44.86	2572.86	2582.85	62.86	3292.86	3302.85	80.86
1142.86	1152.85	27.11	1862.86	1872.85	45.11	2582.86	2592.85	63.11	3302.86	3312.85	81.11
1152.86	1162.85	27.36	1872.86	1882.85	45.36	2592.86	2602.85	63.36	3312.86	3322.85	81.36
1162.86	1172.85	27.61	1882.86	1892.85	45.61	2602.86	2612.85	63.61	3322.86	3332.85	81.61
1172.86	1182.85	27.86	1892.86	1902.85	45.86	2612.86	2622.85	63.86	3332.86	3342.85	81.86
1182.86	1192.85	28.11	1902.86	1912.85	46.11	2622.86	2632.85	64.11			
1192.86	1202.85	28.36	1912.86	1922.85	46.36	2632.86	2642.85	64.36			
1202.86	1212.85	28.61	1922.86	1932.85	46.61	2642.86	2652.85	64.61			
1212.86	1222.85	28.86	1932.86	1942.85	46.86	2652.86	2662.85	64.86			
1222.86	1232.85	29.11	1942.86	1952.85	47.11	2662.86	2672.85	65.11			
1232.86	1242.85	29.36	1952.86	1962.85	47.36	2672.86	2682.85	65.36			
1242.86	1252.85	29.61	1962.86	1972.85	47.61	2682.86	2692.85	65.61			
1252.86	1262.85	29.86	1972.86	1982.85	47.86	2692.86	2702.85	65.86			
1262.86	1272.85	30.11	1982.86	1992.85	48.11	2702.86	2712.85	66.11			

* For earnings above this amount, see the calculation method in the *Employers' Guide to Payroll Deductions*.

* Si la rénumération de votre employé dépasse ce montant, reportez-vous au *Guide de l'employeur – Retenues sur la paie*.

APPENDIX 9-2   Canada Pension Plan Contributions (continued)

B-54 Unemployment Insurance Premiums – Cotisations à l'assurance-chômage

Pay Rémunération From – De	To – À	UI premium Cotisation à l'A-C	Pay Rémunération From – De	To – À	UI premium Cotisation à l'A-C	Pay Rémunération From – De	To – À	UI premium Cotisation à l'A-C	Pay Rémunération From – De	To – À	UI premium Cotisation à l'A-C
.00	.49	.01	24.17	24.49	.73	48.17	48.49	1.45	72.17	72.49	2.17
.50	.83	.02	24.50	24.83	.74	48.50	48.83	1.46	72.50	72.83	2.18
.84	1.16	.03	24.84	25.16	.75	48.84	49.16	1.47	72.84	73.16	2.19
1.17	1.49	.04	25.17	25.49	.76	49.17	49.49	1.48	73.17	73.49	2.20
1.50	1.83	.05	25.50	25.83	.77	49.50	49.83	1.49	73.50	73.83	2.21
1.84	2.16	.06	25.84	26.16	.78	49.84	50.16	1.50	73.84	74.16	2.22
2.17	2.49	.07	26.17	26.49	.79	50.17	50.49	1.51	74.17	74.49	2.23
2.50	2.83	.08	26.50	26.83	.80	50.50	50.83	1.52	74.50	74.83	2.24
2.84	3.16	.09	26.84	27.16	.81	50.84	51.16	1.53	74.84	75.16	2.25
3.17	3.49	.10	27.17	27.49	.82	51.17	51.49	1.54	75.17	75.49	2.26
3.50	3.83	.11	27.50	27.83	.83	51.50	51.83	1.55	75.50	75.83	2.27
3.84	4.16	.12	27.84	28.16	.84	51.84	52.16	1.56	75.84	76.16	2.28
4.17	4.49	.13	28.17	28.49	.85	52.17	52.49	1.57	76.17	76.49	2.29
4.50	4.83	.14	28.50	28.83	.86	52.50	52.83	1.58	76.50	76.83	2.30
4.84	5.16	.15	28.84	29.16	.87	52.84	53.16	1.59	76.84	77.16	2.31
5.17	5.49	.16	29.17	29.49	.88	53.17	53.49	1.60	77.17	77.49	2.32
5.50	5.83	.17	29.50	29.83	.89	53.50	53.83	1.61	77.50	77.83	2.33
5.84	6.16	.18	29.84	30.16	.90	53.84	54.16	1.62	77.84	78.16	2.34
6.17	6.49	.19	30.17	30.49	.91	54.17	54.49	1.63	78.17	78.49	2.35
6.50	6.83	.20	30.50	30.83	.92	54.50	54.83	1.64	78.50	78.83	2.36
6.84	7.16	.21	30.84	31.16	.93	54.84	55.16	1.65	78.84	79.16	2.37
7.17	7.49	.22	31.17	31.49	.94	55.17	55.49	1.66	79.17	79.49	2.38
7.50	7.83	.23	31.50	31.83	.95	55.50	55.83	1.67	79.50	79.83	2.39
7.84	8.16	.24	31.84	32.16	.96	55.84	56.16	1.68	79.84	80.16	2.40
8.17	8.49	.25	32.17	32.49	.97	56.17	56.49	1.69	80.17	80.49	2.41
8.50	8.83	.26	32.50	32.83	.98	56.50	56.83	1.70	80.50	80.83	2.42
8.84	9.16	.27	32.84	33.16	.99	56.84	57.16	1.71	80.84	81.16	2.43
9.17	9.49	.28	33.17	33.49	1.00	57.17	57.49	1.72	81.17	81.49	2.44
9.50	9.83	.29	33.50	33.83	1.01	57.50	57.83	1.73	81.50	81.83	2.45
9.84	10.16	.30	33.84	34.16	1.02	57.84	58.16	1.74	81.84	82.16	2.46
10.17	10.49	.31	34.17	34.49	1.03	58.17	58.49	1.75	82.17	82.49	2.47
10.50	10.83	.32	34.50	34.83	1.04	58.50	58.83	1.76	82.50	82.83	2.48
10.84	11.16	.33	34.84	35.16	1.05	58.84	59.16	1.77	82.84	83.16	2.49
11.17	11.49	.34	35.17	35.49	1.06	59.17	59.49	1.78	83.17	83.49	2.50
11.50	11.83	.35	35.50	35.83	1.07	59.50	59.83	1.79	83.50	83.83	2.51
11.84	12.16	.36	35.84	36.16	1.08	59.84	60.16	1.80	83.84	84.16	2.52
12.17	12.49	.37	36.17	36.49	1.09	60.17	60.49	1.81	84.17	84.49	2.53
12.50	12.83	.38	36.50	36.83	1.10	60.50	60.83	1.82	84.50	84.83	2.54
12.84	13.16	.39	36.84	37.16	1.11	60.84	61.16	1.83	84.84	85.16	2.55
13.17	13.49	.40	37.17	37.49	1.12	61.17	61.49	1.84	85.17	85.49	2.56
13.50	13.83	.41	37.50	37.83	1.13	61.50	61.83	1.85	85.50	85.83	2.57
13.84	14.16	.42	37.84	38.16	1.14	61.84	62.16	1.86	85.84	86.16	2.58
14.17	14.49	.43	38.17	38.49	1.15	62.17	62.49	1.87	86.17	86.49	2.59
14.50	14.83	.44	38.50	38.83	1.16	62.50	62.83	1.88	86.50	86.83	2.60
14.84	15.16	.45	38.84	39.16	1.17	62.84	63.16	1.89	86.84	87.16	2.61
15.17	15.49	.46	39.17	39.49	1.18	63.17	63.49	1.90	87.17	87.49	2.62
15.50	15.83	.47	39.50	39.83	1.19	63.50	63.83	1.91	87.50	87.83	2.63
15.84	16.16	.48	39.84	40.16	1.20	63.84	64.16	1.92	87.84	88.16	2.64
16.17	16.49	.49	40.17	40.49	1.21	64.17	64.49	1.93	88.17	88.49	2.65
16.50	16.83	.50	40.50	40.83	1.22	64.50	64.83	1.94	88.50	88.83	2.66
16.84	17.16	.51	40.84	41.16	1.23	64.84	65.16	1.95	88.84	89.16	2.67
17.17	17.49	.52	41.17	41.49	1.24	65.17	65.49	1.96	89.17	89.49	2.68
17.50	17.83	.53	41.50	41.83	1.25	65.50	65.83	1.97	89.50	89.83	2.69
17.84	18.16	.54	41.84	42.16	1.26	65.84	66.16	1.98	89.84	90.16	2.70
18.17	18.49	.55	42.17	42.49	1.27	66.17	66.49	1.99	90.17	90.49	2.71
18.50	18.83	.56	42.50	42.83	1.28	66.50	66.83	2.00	90.50	90.83	2.72
18.84	19.16	.57	42.84	43.16	1.29	66.84	67.16	2.01	90.84	91.16	2.73
19.17	19.49	.58	43.17	43.49	1.30	67.17	67.49	2.02	91.17	91.49	2.74
19.50	19.83	.59	43.50	43.83	1.31	67.50	67.83	2.03	91.50	91.83	2.75
19.84	20.16	.60	43.84	44.16	1.32	67.84	68.16	2.04	91.84	92.16	2.76
20.17	20.49	.61	44.17	44.49	1.33	68.17	68.49	2.05	92.17	92.49	2.77
20.50	20.83	.62	44.50	44.83	1.34	68.50	68.83	2.06	92.50	92.83	2.78
20.84	21.16	.63	44.84	45.16	1.35	68.84	69.16	2.07	92.84	93.16	2.79
21.17	21.49	.64	45.17	45.49	1.36	69.17	69.49	2.08	93.17	93.49	2.80
21.50	21.83	.65	45.50	45.83	1.37	69.50	69.83	2.09	93.50	93.83	2.81
21.84	22.16	.66	45.84	46.16	1.38	69.84	70.16	2.10	93.84	94.16	2.82
22.17	22.49	.67	46.17	46.49	1.39	70.17	70.49	2.11	94.17	94.49	2.83
22.50	22.83	.68	46.50	46.83	1.40	70.50	70.83	2.12	94.50	94.83	2.84
22.84	23.16	.69	46.84	47.16	1.41	70.84	71.16	2.13	94.84	95.16	2.85
23.17	23.49	.70	47.17	47.49	1.42	71.17	71.49	2.14	95.17	95.49	2.86
23.50	23.83	.71	47.50	47.83	1.43	71.50	71.83	2.15	95.50	95.83	2.87
23.84	24.16	.72	47.84	48.16	1.44	71.84	72.16	2.16	95.84	96.16	2.88

Note: The following are the maximum amounts you can deduct for each pay period.
Remarque : Vous trouverez ci-dessous la cotisation maximale que vous pouvez retenir pour chaque période de paie.

Weekly	Hebdomadaire	22.35	10 pay periods a year	10 périodes de paie par année	116.22
Biweekly	Aux deux semaines	44.70	13 pay periods a year	13 périodes de paie par année	89.40
Semimonthly	Bimensuel	48.42	22 pay periods a year	22 périodes de paie par année	52.83
Monthly	Mensuel	96.85			

Unemployment Insurance Premiums – Cotisations à l'assurance-chômage   B-55

From – De	To – À	UI premium Cotisation à l'A-C	From – De	To – À	UI premium Cotisation à l'A-C	From – De	To – À	UI premium Cotisation à l'A-C	From – De	To – À	UI premium Cotisation à l'A-C
96.17 –	96.49	2.89	120.17 –	120.49	3.61	144.17 –	144.49	4.33	168.17 –	168.49	5.05
96.50 –	96.83	2.90	120.50 –	120.83	3.62	144.50 –	144.83	4.34	168.50 –	168.83	5.06
96.84 –	97.16	2.91	120.84 –	121.16	3.63	144.84 –	145.16	4.35	168.84 –	169.16	5.07
97.17 –	97.49	2.92	121.17 –	121.49	3.64	145.17 –	145.49	4.36	169.17 –	169.49	5.08
97.50 –	97.83	2.93	121.50 –	121.83	3.65	145.50 –	145.83	4.37	169.50 –	169.83	5.09
97.84 –	98.16	2.94	121.84 –	122.16	3.66	145.84 –	146.16	4.38	169.84 –	170.16	5.10
98.17 –	98.49	2.95	122.17 –	122.49	3.67	146.17 –	146.49	4.39	170.17 –	170.49	5.11
98.50 –	98.83	2.96	122.50 –	122.83	3.68	146.50 –	146.83	4.40	170.50 –	170.83	5.12
98.84 –	99.16	2.97	122.84 –	123.16	3.69	146.84 –	147.16	4.41	170.84 –	171.16	5.13
99.17 –	99.49	2.98	123.17 –	123.49	3.70	147.17 –	147.49	4.42	171.17 –	171.49	5.14
99.50 –	99.83	2.99	123.50 –	123.83	3.71	147.50 –	147.83	4.43	171.50 –	171.83	5.15
99.84 –	100.16	3.00	123.84 –	124.16	3.72	147.84 –	148.16	4.44	171.84 –	172.16	5.16
100.17 –	100.49	3.01	124.17 –	124.49	3.73	148.17 –	148.49	4.45	172.17 –	172.49	5.17
100.50 –	100.83	3.02	124.50 –	124.83	3.74	148.50 –	148.83	4.46	172.50 –	172.83	5.18
100.84 –	101.16	3.03	124.84 –	125.16	3.75	148.84 –	149.16	4.47	172.84 –	173.16	5.19
101.17 –	101.49	3.04	125.17 –	125.49	3.76	149.17 –	149.49	4.48	173.17 –	173.49	5.20
101.50 –	101.83	3.05	125.50 –	125.83	3.77	149.50 –	149.83	4.49	173.50 –	173.83	5.21
101.84 –	102.16	3.06	125.84 –	126.16	3.78	149.84 –	150.16	4.50	173.84 –	174.16	5.22
102.17 –	102.49	3.07	126.17 –	126.49	3.79	150.17 –	150.49	4.51	174.17 –	174.49	5.23
102.50 –	102.83	3.08	126.50 –	126.83	3.80	150.50 –	150.83	4.52	174.50 –	174.83	5.24
102.84 –	103.16	3.09	126.84 –	127.16	3.81	150.84 –	151.16	4.53	174.84 –	175.16	5.25
103.17 –	103.49	3.10	127.17 –	127.49	3.82	151.17 –	151.49	4.54	175.17 –	175.49	5.26
103.50 –	103.83	3.11	127.50 –	127.83	3.83	151.50 –	151.83	4.55	175.50 –	175.83	5.27
103.84 –	104.16	3.12	127.84 –	128.16	3.84	151.84 –	152.16	4.56	175.84 –	176.16	5.28
104.17 –	104.49	3.13	128.17 –	128.49	3.85	152.17 –	152.49	4.57	176.17 –	176.49	5.29
104.50 –	104.83	3.14	128.50 –	128.83	3.86	152.50 –	152.83	4.58	176.50 –	176.83	5.30
104.84 –	105.16	3.15	128.84 –	129.16	3.87	152.84 –	153.16	4.59	176.84 –	177.16	5.31
105.17 –	105.49	3.16	129.17 –	129.49	3.88	153.17 –	153.49	4.60	177.17 –	177.49	5.32
105.50 –	105.83	3.17	129.50 –	129.83	3.89	153.50 –	153.83	4.61	177.50 –	177.83	5.33
105.84 –	106.16	3.18	129.84 –	130.16	3.90	153.84 –	154.16	4.62	177.84 –	178.16	5.34
106.17 –	106.49	3.19	130.17 –	130.49	3.91	154.17 –	154.49	4.63	178.17 –	178.49	5.35
106.50 –	106.83	3.20	130.50 –	130.83	3.92	154.50 –	154.83	4.64	178.50 –	178.83	5.36
106.84 –	107.16	3.21	130.84 –	131.16	3.93	154.84 –	155.16	4.65	178.84 –	179.16	5.37
107.17 –	107.49	3.22	131.17 –	131.49	3.94	155.17 –	155.49	4.66	179.17 –	179.49	5.38
107.50 –	107.83	3.23	131.50 –	131.83	3.95	155.50 –	155.83	4.67	179.50 –	179.83	5.39
107.84 –	108.16	3.24	131.84 –	132.16	3.96	155.84 –	156.16	4.68	179.84 –	180.16	5.40
108.17 –	108.49	3.25	132.17 –	132.49	3.97	156.17 –	156.49	4.69	180.17 –	180.49	5.41
108.50 –	108.83	3.26	132.50 –	132.83	3.98	156.50 –	156.83	4.70	180.50 –	180.83	5.42
108.84 –	109.16	3.27	132.84 –	133.16	3.99	156.84 –	157.16	4.71	180.84 –	181.16	5.43
109.17 –	109.49	3.28	133.17 –	133.49	4.00	157.17 –	157.49	4.72	181.17 –	181.49	5.44
109.50 –	109.83	3.29	133.50 –	133.83	4.01	157.50 –	157.83	4.73	181.50 –	181.83	5.45
109.84 –	110.16	3.30	133.84 –	134.16	4.02	157.84 –	158.16	4.74	181.84 –	182.16	5.46
110.17 –	110.49	3.31	134.17 –	134.49	4.03	158.17 –	158.49	4.75	182.17 –	182.49	5.47
110.50 –	110.83	3.32	134.50 –	134.83	4.04	158.50 –	158.83	4.76	182.50 –	182.83	5.48
110.84 –	111.16	3.33	134.84 –	135.16	4.05	158.84 –	159.16	4.77	182.84 –	183.16	5.49
111.17 –	111.49	3.34	135.17 –	135.49	4.06	159.17 –	159.49	4.78	183.17 –	183.49	5.50
111.50 –	111.83	3.35	135.50 –	135.83	4.07	159.50 –	159.83	4.79	183.50 –	183.83	5.51
111.84 –	112.16	3.36	135.84 –	136.16	4.08	159.84 –	160.16	4.80	183.84 –	184.16	5.52
112.17 –	112.49	3.37	136.17 –	136.49	4.09	160.17 –	160.49	4.81	184.17 –	184.49	5.53
112.50 –	112.83	3.38	136.50 –	136.83	4.10	160.50 –	160.83	4.82	184.50 –	184.83	5.54
112.84 –	113.16	3.39	136.84 –	137.16	4.11	160.84 –	161.16	4.83	184.84 –	185.16	5.55
113.17 –	113.49	3.40	137.17 –	137.49	4.12	161.17 –	161.49	4.84	185.17 –	185.49	5.56
113.50 –	113.83	3.41	137.50 –	137.83	4.13	161.50 –	161.83	4.85	185.50 –	185.83	5.57
113.84 –	114.16	3.42	137.84 –	138.16	4.14	161.84 –	162.16	4.86	185.84 –	186.16	5.58
114.17 –	114.49	3.43	138.17 –	138.49	4.15	162.17 –	162.49	4.87	186.17 –	186.49	5.59
114.50 –	114.83	3.44	138.50 –	138.83	4.16	162.50 –	162.83	4.88	186.50 –	186.83	5.60
114.84 –	115.16	3.45	138.84 –	139.16	4.17	162.84 –	163.16	4.89	186.84 –	187.16	5.61
115.17 –	115.49	3.46	139.17 –	139.49	4.18	163.17 –	163.49	4.90	187.17 –	187.49	5.62
115.50 –	115.83	3.47	139.50 –	139.83	4.19	163.50 –	163.83	4.91	187.50 –	187.83	5.63
115.84 –	116.16	3.48	139.84 –	140.16	4.20	163.84 –	164.16	4.92	187.84 –	188.16	5.64
116.17 –	116.49	3.49	140.17 –	140.49	4.21	164.17 –	164.49	4.93	188.17 –	188.49	5.65
116.50 –	116.83	3.50	140.50 –	140.83	4.22	164.50 –	164.83	4.94	188.50 –	188.83	5.66
116.84 –	117.16	3.51	140.84 –	141.16	4.23	164.84 –	165.16	4.95	188.84 –	189.16	5.67
117.17 –	117.49	3.52	141.17 –	141.49	4.24	165.17 –	165.49	4.96	189.17 –	189.49	5.68
117.50 –	117.83	3.53	141.50 –	141.83	4.25	165.50 –	165.83	4.97	189.50 –	189.83	5.69
117.84 –	118.16	3.54	141.84 –	142.16	4.26	165.84 –	166.16	4.98	189.84 –	190.16	5.70
118.17 –	118.49	3.55	142.17 –	142.49	4.27	166.17 –	166.49	4.99	190.17 –	190.49	5.71
118.50 –	118.83	3.56	142.50 –	142.83	4.28	166.50 –	166.83	5.00	190.50 –	190.83	5.72
118.84 –	119.16	3.57	142.84 –	143.16	4.29	166.84 –	167.16	5.01	190.84 –	191.16	5.73
119.17 –	119.49	3.58	143.17 –	143.49	4.30	167.17 –	167.49	5.02	191.17 –	191.49	5.74
119.50 –	119.83	3.59	143.50 –	143.83	4.31	167.50 –	167.83	5.03	191.50 –	191.83	5.75
119.84 –	120.16	3.60	143.84 –	144.16	4.32	167.84 –	168.16	5.04	191.84 –	192.16	5.76

Note: The following are the maximum amounts you can deduct for each pay period.
Remarque : Vous trouverez ci-dessous la cotisation maximale que vous pouvez retenir pour chaque période de paie.

Weekly	Hebdomadaire	22.35	10 pay periods a year	10 périodes de paie par année	116.22
Biweekly	Aux deux semaines	44.70	13 pay periods a year	13 périodes de paie par année	89.40
Semimonthly	Bimensuel	48.42	22 pay periods a year	22 périodes de paie par année	52.83
Monthly	Mensuel	96.85			

APPENDIX 9-3   Unemployment Insurance Premiums (continued)

B-56   **Unemployment Insurance Premiums – Cotisations à l'assurance-chômage**

Pay Rémunération		UI premium Cotisation à l'A-C	Pay Rémunération		UI premium Cotisation à l'A-C	Pay Rémunération		UI premium Cotisation à l'A-C	Pay Rémunération		UI premium Cotisation à l'A-C
From – De	To – À		From – De	To – À		From – De	To – À		From – De	To – À	
192.17 –	192.49	5.77	216.17 –	216.49	6.49	240.17 –	240.49	7.21	264.17 –	264.49	7.93
192.50 –	192.83	5.78	216.50 –	216.83	6.50	240.50 –	240.83	7.22	264.50 –	264.83	7.94
192.84 –	193.16	5.79	216.84 –	217.16	6.51	240.84 –	241.16	7.23	264.84 –	265.16	7.95
193.17 –	193.49	5.80	217.17 –	217.49	6.52	241.17 –	241.49	7.24	265.17 –	265.49	7.96
193.50 –	193.83	5.81	217.50 –	217.83	6.53	241.50 –	241.83	7.25	265.50 –	265.83	7.97
193.84 –	194.16	5.82	217.84 –	218.16	6.54	241.84 –	242.16	7.26	265.84 –	266.16	7.98
194.17 –	194.49	5.83	218.17 –	218.49	6.55	242.17 –	242.49	7.27	266.17 –	266.49	7.99
194.50 –	194.83	5.84	218.50 –	218.83	6.56	242.50 –	242.83	7.28	266.50 –	266.83	8.00
194.84 –	195.16	5.85	218.84 –	219.16	6.57	242.84 –	243.16	7.29	266.84 –	267.16	8.01
195.17 –	195.49	5.86	219.17 –	219.49	6.58	243.17 –	243.49	7.30	267.17 –	267.49	8.02
195.50 –	195.83	5.87	219.50 –	219.83	6.59	243.50 –	243.83	7.31	267.50 –	267.83	8.03
195.84 –	196.16	5.88	219.84 –	220.16	6.60	243.84 –	244.16	7.32	267.84 –	268.16	8.04
196.17 –	196.49	5.89	220.17 –	220.49	6.61	244.17 –	244.49	7.33	268.17 –	268.49	8.05
196.50 –	196.83	5.90	220.50 –	220.83	6.62	244.50 –	244.83	7.34	268.50 –	268.83	8.06
196.84 –	197.16	5.91	220.84 –	221.16	6.63	244.84 –	245.16	7.35	268.84 –	269.16	8.07
197.17 –	197.49	5.92	221.17 –	221.49	6.64	245.17 –	245.49	7.36	269.17 –	269.49	8.08
197.50 –	197.83	5.93	221.50 –	221.83	6.65	245.50 –	245.83	7.37	269.50 –	269.83	8.09
197.84 –	198.16	5.94	221.84 –	222.16	6.66	245.84 –	246.16	7.38	269.84 –	270.16	8.10
198.17 –	198.49	5.95	222.17 –	222.49	6.67	246.17 –	246.49	7.39	270.17 –	270.49	8.11
198.50 –	198.83	5.96	222.50 –	222.83	6.68	246.50 –	246.83	7.40	270.50 –	270.83	8.12
198.84 –	199.16	5.97	222.84 –	223.16	6.69	246.84 –	247.16	7.41	270.84 –	271.16	8.13
199.17 –	199.49	5.98	223.17 –	223.49	6.70	247.17 –	247.49	7.42	271.17 –	271.49	8.14
199.50 –	199.83	5.99	223.50 –	223.83	6.71	247.50 –	247.83	7.43	271.50 –	271.83	8.15
199.84 –	200.16	6.00	223.84 –	224.16	6.72	247.84 –	248.16	7.44	271.84 –	272.16	8.16
200.17 –	200.49	6.01	224.17 –	224.49	6.73	248.17 –	248.49	7.45	272.17 –	272.49	8.17
200.50 –	200.83	6.02	224.50 –	224.83	6.74	248.50 –	248.83	7.46	272.50 –	272.83	8.18
200.84 –	201.16	6.03	224.84 –	225.16	6.75	248.84 –	249.16	7.47	272.84 –	273.16	8.19
201.17 –	201.49	6.04	225.17 –	225.49	6.76	249.17 –	249.49	7.48	273.17 –	273.49	8.20
201.50 –	201.83	6.05	225.50 –	225.83	6.77	249.50 –	249.83	7.49	273.50 –	273.83	8.21
201.84 –	202.16	6.06	225.84 –	226.16	6.78	249.84 –	250.16	7.50	273.84 –	274.16	8.22
202.17 –	202.49	6.07	226.17 –	226.49	6.79	250.17 –	250.49	7.51	274.17 –	274.49	8.23
202.50 –	202.83	6.08	226.50 –	226.83	6.80	250.50 –	250.83	7.52	274.50 –	274.83	8.24
202.84 –	203.16	6.09	226.84 –	227.16	6.81	250.84 –	251.16	7.53	274.84 –	275.16	8.25
203.17 –	203.49	6.10	227.17 –	227.49	6.82	251.17 –	251.49	7.54	275.17 –	275.49	8.26
203.50 –	203.83	6.11	227.50 –	227.83	6.83	251.50 –	251.83	7.55	275.50 –	275.83	8.27
203.84 –	204.16	6.12	227.84 –	228.16	6.84	251.84 –	252.16	7.56	275.84 –	276.16	8.28
204.17 –	204.49	6.13	228.17 –	228.49	6.85	252.17 –	252.49	7.57	276.17 –	276.49	8.29
204.50 –	204.83	6.14	228.50 –	228.83	6.86	252.50 –	252.83	7.58	276.50 –	276.83	8.30
204.84 –	205.16	6.15	228.84 –	229.16	6.87	252.84 –	253.16	7.59	276.84 –	277.16	8.31
205.17 –	205.49	6.16	229.17 –	229.49	6.88	253.17 –	253.49	7.60	277.17 –	277.49	8.32
205.50 –	205.83	6.17	229.50 –	229.83	6.89	253.50 –	253.83	7.61	277.50 –	277.83	8.33
205.84 –	206.16	6.18	229.84 –	230.16	6.90	253.84 –	254.16	7.62	277.84 –	278.16	8.34
206.17 –	206.49	6.19	230.17 –	230.49	6.91	254.17 –	254.49	7.63	278.17 –	278.49	8.35
206.50 –	206.83	6.20	230.50 –	230.83	6.92	254.50 –	254.83	7.64	278.50 –	278.83	8.36
206.84 –	207.16	6.21	230.84 –	231.16	6.93	254.84 –	255.16	7.65	278.84 –	279.16	8.37
207.17 –	207.49	6.22	231.17 –	231.49	6.94	255.17 –	255.49	7.66	279.17 –	279.49	8.38
207.50 –	207.83	6.23	231.50 –	231.83	6.95	255.50 –	255.83	7.67	279.50 –	279.83	8.39
207.84 –	208.16	6.24	231.84 –	232.16	6.96	255.84 –	256.16	7.68	279.84 –	280.16	8.40
208.17 –	208.49	6.25	232.17 –	232.49	6.97	256.17 –	256.49	7.69	280.17 –	280.49	8.41
208.50 –	208.83	6.26	232.50 –	232.83	6.98	256.50 –	256.83	7.70	280.50 –	280.83	8.42
208.84 –	209.16	6.27	232.84 –	233.16	6.99	256.84 –	257.16	7.71	280.84 –	281.16	8.43
209.17 –	209.49	6.28	233.17 –	233.49	7.00	257.17 –	257.49	7.72	281.17 –	281.49	8.44
209.50 –	209.83	6.29	233.50 –	233.83	7.01	257.50 –	257.83	7.73	281.50 –	281.83	8.45
209.84 –	210.16	6.30	233.84 –	234.16	7.02	257.84 –	258.16	7.74	281.84 –	282.16	8.46
210.17 –	210.49	6.31	234.17 –	234.49	7.03	258.17 –	258.49	7.75	282.17 –	282.49	8.47
210.50 –	210.83	6.32	234.50 –	234.83	7.04	258.50 –	258.83	7.76	282.50 –	282.83	8.48
210.84 –	211.16	6.33	234.84 –	235.16	7.05	258.84 –	259.16	7.77	282.84 –	283.16	8.49
211.17 –	211.49	6.34	235.17 –	235.49	7.06	259.17 –	259.49	7.78	283.17 –	283.49	8.50
211.50 –	211.83	6.35	235.50 –	235.83	7.07	259.50 –	259.83	7.79	283.50 –	283.83	8.51
211.84 –	212.16	6.36	235.84 –	236.16	7.08	259.84 –	260.16	7.80	283.84 –	284.16	8.52
212.17 –	212.49	6.37	236.17 –	236.49	7.09	260.17 –	260.49	7.81	284.17 –	284.49	8.53
212.50 –	212.83	6.38	236.50 –	236.83	7.10	260.50 –	260.83	7.82	284.50 –	284.83	8.54
212.84 –	213.16	6.39	236.84 –	237.16	7.11	260.84 –	261.16	7.83	284.84 –	285.16	8.55
213.17 –	213.49	6.40	237.17 –	237.49	7.12	261.17 –	261.49	7.84	285.17 –	285.49	8.56
213.50 –	213.83	6.41	237.50 –	237.83	7.13	261.50 –	261.83	7.85	285.50 –	285.83	8.57
213.84 –	214.16	6.42	237.84 –	238.16	7.14	261.84 –	262.16	7.86	285.84 –	286.16	8.58
214.17 –	214.49	6.43	238.17 –	238.49	7.15	262.17 –	262.49	7.87	286.17 –	286.49	8.59
214.50 –	214.83	6.44	238.50 –	238.83	7.16	262.50 –	262.83	7.88	286.50 –	286.83	8.60
214.84 –	215.16	6.45	238.84 –	239.16	7.17	262.84 –	263.16	7.89	286.84 –	287.16	8.61
215.17 –	215.49	6.46	239.17 –	239.49	7.18	263.17 –	263.49	7.90	287.17 –	287.49	8.62
215.50 –	215.83	6.47	239.50 –	239.83	7.19	263.50 –	263.83	7.91	287.50 –	287.83	8.63
215.84 –	216.16	6.48	239.84 –	240.16	7.20	263.84 –	264.16	7.92	287.84 –	288.16	8.64

Note: The following are the maximum amounts you can deduct for each pay period.
Remarque : Vous trouverez ci-dessous la cotisation maximale que vous pouvez retenir pour chaque période de paie.

Weekly	Hebdomadaire	**22.35**	10 pay periods a year	10 périodes de paie par année	**116.22**
Biweekly	Aux deux semaines	**44.70**	13 pay periods a year	13 périodes de paie par année	**89.40**
Semimonthly	Bimensuel	**48.42**	22 pay periods a year	22 périodes de paie par année	**52.83**
Monthly	Mensuel	**96.85**			

APPENDIX 9-3   **Unemployment Insurance Premiums (continued)**

Unemployment Insurance Premiums — Cotisations à l'assurance-chômage B-57

Pay Rémunération		UI premium Cotisation à l'A-C	Pay Rémunération		UI premium Cotisation à l'A-C	Pay Rémunération		UI premium Cotisation à l'A-C	Pay Rémunération		UI premium Cotisation à l'A-C
From – De	To – À		From – De	To – À		From – De	To – À		From – De	To – À	
288.17 –	288.49	8.65	312.17 –	312.49	9.37	336.17 –	336.49	10.09	360.17 –	360.49	10.81
288.50 –	288.83	8.66	312.50 –	312.83	9.38	336.50 –	336.83	10.10	360.50 –	360.83	10.82
288.84 –	289.16	8.67	312.84 –	313.16	9.39	336.84 –	337.16	10.11	360.84 –	361.16	10.83
289.17 –	289.49	8.68	313.17 –	313.49	9.40	337.17 –	337.49	10.12	361.17 –	361.49	10.84
289.50 –	289.83	8.69	313.50 –	313.83	9.41	337.50 –	337.83	10.13	361.50 –	361.83	10.85
289.84 –	290.16	8.70	313.84 –	314.16	9.42	337.84 –	338.16	10.14	361.84 –	362.16	10.86
290.17 –	290.49	8.71	314.17 –	314.49	9.43	338.17 –	338.49	10.15	362.17 –	362.49	10.87
290.50 –	290.83	8.72	314.50 –	314.83	9.44	338.50 –	338.83	10.16	362.50 –	362.83	10.88
290.84 –	291.16	8.73	314.84 –	315.16	9.45	338.84 –	339.16	10.17	362.84 –	363.16	10.89
291.17 –	291.49	8.74	315.17 –	315.49	9.46	339.17 –	339.49	10.18	363.17 –	363.49	10.90
291.50 –	291.83	8.75	315.50 –	315.83	9.47	339.50 –	339.83	10.19	363.50 –	363.83	10.91
291.84 –	292.16	8.76	315.84 –	316.16	9.48	339.84 –	340.16	10.20	363.84 –	364.16	10.92
292.17 –	292.49	8.77	316.17 –	316.49	9.49	340.17 –	340.49	10.21	364.17 –	364.49	10.93
292.50 –	292.83	8.78	316.50 –	316.83	9.50	340.50 –	340.83	10.22	364.50 –	364.83	10.94
292.84 –	293.16	8.79	316.84 –	317.16	9.51	340.84 –	341.16	10.23	364.84 –	365.16	10.95
293.17 –	293.49	8.80	317.17 –	317.49	9.52	341.17 –	341.49	10.24	365.17 –	365.49	10.96
293.50 –	293.83	8.81	317.50 –	317.83	9.53	341.50 –	341.83	10.25	365.50 –	365.83	10.97
293.84 –	294.16	8.82	317.84 –	318.16	9.54	341.84 –	342.16	10.26	365.84 –	366.16	10.98
294.17 –	294.49	8.83	318.17 –	318.49	9.55	342.17 –	342.49	10.27	366.17 –	366.49	10.99
294.50 –	294.83	8.84	318.50 –	318.83	9.56	342.50 –	342.83	10.28	366.50 –	366.83	11.00
294.84 –	295.16	8.85	318.84 –	319.16	9.57	342.84 –	343.16	10.29	366.84 –	367.16	11.01
295.17 –	295.49	8.86	319.17 –	319.49	9.58	343.17 –	343.49	10.30	367.17 –	367.49	11.02
295.50 –	295.83	8.87	319.50 –	319.83	9.59	343.50 –	343.83	10.31	367.50 –	367.83	11.03
295.84 –	296.16	8.88	319.84 –	320.16	9.60	343.84 –	344.16	10.32	367.84 –	368.16	11.04
296.17 –	296.49	8.89	320.17 –	320.49	9.61	344.17 –	344.49	10.33	368.17 –	368.49	11.05
296.50 –	296.83	8.90	320.50 –	320.83	9.62	344.50 –	344.83	10.34	368.50 –	368.83	11.06
296.84 –	297.16	8.91	320.84 –	321.16	9.63	344.84 –	345.16	10.35	368.84 –	369.16	11.07
297.17 –	297.49	8.92	321.17 –	321.49	9.64	345.17 –	345.49	10.36	369.17 –	369.49	11.08
297.50 –	297.83	8.93	321.50 –	321.83	9.65	345.50 –	345.83	10.37	369.50 –	369.83	11.09
297.84 –	298.16	8.94	321.84 –	322.16	9.66	345.84 –	346.16	10.38	369.84 –	370.16	11.10
298.17 –	298.49	8.95	322.17 –	322.49	9.67	346.17 –	346.49	10.39	370.17 –	370.49	11.11
298.50 –	298.83	8.96	322.50 –	322.83	9.68	346.50 –	346.83	10.40	370.50 –	370.83	11.12
298.84 –	299.16	8.97	322.84 –	323.16	9.69	346.84 –	347.16	10.41	370.84 –	371.16	11.13
299.17 –	299.49	8.98	323.17 –	323.49	9.70	347.17 –	347.49	10.42	371.17 –	371.49	11.14
299.50 –	299.83	8.99	323.50 –	323.83	9.71	347.50 –	347.83	10.43	371.50 –	371.83	11.15
299.84 –	300.16	9.00	323.84 –	324.16	9.72	347.84 –	348.16	10.44	371.84 –	372.16	11.16
300.17 –	300.49	9.01	324.17 –	324.49	9.73	348.17 –	348.49	10.45	372.17 –	372.49	11.17
300.50 –	300.83	9.02	324.50 –	324.83	9.74	348.50 –	348.83	10.46	372.50 –	372.83	11.18
300.84 –	301.16	9.03	324.84 –	325.16	9.75	348.84 –	349.16	10.47	372.84 –	373.16	11.19
301.17 –	301.49	9.04	325.17 –	325.49	9.76	349.17 –	349.49	10.48	373.17 –	373.49	11.20
301.50 –	301.83	9.05	325.50 –	325.83	9.77	349.50 –	349.83	10.49	373.50 –	373.83	11.21
301.84 –	302.16	9.06	325.84 –	326.16	9.78	349.84 –	350.16	10.50	373.84 –	374.16	11.22
302.17 –	302.49	9.07	326.17 –	326.49	9.79	350.17 –	350.49	10.51	374.17 –	374.49	11.23
302.50 –	302.83	9.08	326.50 –	326.83	9.80	350.50 –	350.83	10.52	374.50 –	374.83	11.24
302.84 –	303.16	9.09	326.84 –	327.16	9.81	350.84 –	351.16	10.53	374.84 –	375.16	11.25
303.17 –	303.49	9.10	327.17 –	327.49	9.82	351.17 –	351.49	10.54	375.17 –	375.49	11.26
303.50 –	303.83	9.11	327.50 –	327.83	9.83	351.50 –	351.83	10.55	375.50 –	375.83	11.27
303.84 –	304.16	9.12	327.84 –	328.16	9.84	351.84 –	352.16	10.56	375.84 –	376.16	11.28
304.17 –	304.49	9.13	328.17 –	328.49	9.85	352.17 –	352.49	10.57	376.17 –	376.49	11.29
304.50 –	304.83	9.14	328.50 –	328.83	9.86	352.50 –	352.83	10.58	376.50 –	376.83	11.30
304.84 –	305.16	9.15	328.84 –	329.16	9.87	352.84 –	353.16	10.59	376.84 –	377.16	11.31
305.17 –	305.49	9.16	329.17 –	329.49	9.88	353.17 –	353.49	10.60	377.17 –	377.49	11.32
305.50 –	305.83	9.17	329.50 –	329.83	9.89	353.50 –	353.83	10.61	377.50 –	377.83	11.33
305.84 –	306.16	9.18	329.84 –	330.16	9.90	353.84 –	354.16	10.62	377.84 –	378.16	11.34
306.17 –	306.49	9.19	330.17 –	330.49	9.91	354.17 –	354.49	10.63	378.17 –	378.49	11.35
306.50 –	306.83	9.20	330.50 –	330.83	9.92	354.50 –	354.83	10.64	378.50 –	378.83	11.36
306.84 –	307.16	9.21	330.84 –	331.16	9.93	354.84 –	355.16	10.65	378.84 –	379.16	11.37
307.17 –	307.49	9.22	331.17 –	331.49	9.94	355.17 –	355.49	10.66	379.17 –	379.49	11.38
307.50 –	307.83	9.23	331.50 –	331.83	9.95	355.50 –	355.83	10.67	379.50 –	379.83	11.39
307.84 –	308.16	9.24	331.84 –	332.16	9.96	355.84 –	356.16	10.68	379.84 –	380.16	11.40
308.17 –	308.49	9.25	332.17 –	332.49	9.97	356.17 –	356.49	10.69	380.17 –	380.49	11.41
308.50 –	308.83	9.26	332.50 –	332.83	9.98	356.50 –	356.83	10.70	380.50 –	380.83	11.42
308.84 –	309.16	9.27	332.84 –	333.16	9.99	356.84 –	357.16	10.71	380.84 –	381.16	11.43
309.17 –	309.49	9.28	333.17 –	333.49	10.00	357.17 –	357.49	10.72	381.17 –	381.49	11.44
309.50 –	309.83	9.29	333.50 –	333.83	10.01	357.50 –	357.83	10.73	381.50 –	381.83	11.45
309.84 –	310.16	9.30	333.84 –	334.16	10.02	357.84 –	358.16	10.74	381.84 –	382.16	11.46
310.17 –	310.49	9.31	334.17 –	334.49	10.03	358.17 –	358.49	10.75	382.17 –	382.49	11.47
310.50 –	310.83	9.32	334.50 –	334.83	10.04	358.50 –	358.83	10.76	382.50 –	382.83	11.48
310.84 –	311.16	9.33	334.84 –	335.16	10.05	358.84 –	359.16	10.77	382.84 –	383.16	11.49
311.17 –	311.49	9.34	335.17 –	335.49	10.06	359.17 –	359.49	10.78	383.17 –	383.49	11.50
311.50 –	311.83	9.35	335.50 –	335.83	10.07	359.50 –	359.83	10.79	383.50 –	383.83	11.51
311.84 –	312.16	9.36	335.84 –	336.16	10.08	359.84 –	360.16	10.80	383.84 –	384.16	11.52

Note: The following are the maximum amounts you can deduct for each pay period.
Remarque : Vous trouverez ci-dessous la cotisation maximale que vous pouvez retenir pour chaque période de paie.

Weekly	Hebdomadaire	**22.35**	10 pay periods a year	10 périodes de paie par année	**116.22**
Biweekly	Aux deux semaines	**44.70**	13 pay periods a year	13 périodes de paie par année	**89.40**
Semimonthly	Bimensuel	**48.42**	22 pay periods a year	22 périodes de paie par année	**52.83**
Monthly	Mensuel	**96.85**			

APPENDIX 9-3   Unemployment Insurance Premiums (continued)

B-58   **Unemployment Insurance Premiums – Cotisations à l'assurance-chômage**

Pay Rémunération From – De	To – À	UI premium Cotisation à l'A-C	Pay Rémunération From – De	To – À	UI premium Cotisation à l'A-C	Pay Rémunération From – De	To – À	UI premium Cotisation à l'A-C	Pay Rémunération From – De	To – À	UI premium Cotisation à l'A-C
384.17 -	384.49	11.53	408.17 -	408.49	12.25	432.17 -	432.49	12.97	456.17 -	456.49	13.69
384.50 -	384.83	11.54	408.50 -	408.83	12.26	432.50 -	432.83	12.98	456.50 -	456.83	13.70
384.84 -	385.16	11.55	408.84 -	409.16	12.27	432.84 -	433.16	12.99	456.84 -	457.16	13.71
385.17 -	385.49	11.56	409.17 -	409.49	12.28	433.17 -	433.49	13.00	457.17 -	457.49	13.72
385.50 -	385.83	11.57	409.50 -	409.83	12.29	433.50 -	433.83	13.01	457.50 -	457.83	13.73
385.84 -	386.16	11.58	409.84 -	410.16	12.30	433.84 -	434.16	13.02	457.84 -	458.16	13.74
386.17 -	386.49	11.59	410.17 -	410.49	12.31	434.17 -	434.49	13.03	458.17 -	458.49	13.75
386.50 -	386.83	11.60	410.50 -	410.83	12.32	434.50 -	434.83	13.04	458.50 -	458.83	13.76
386.84 -	387.16	11.61	410.84 -	411.16	12.33	434.84 -	435.16	13.05	458.84 -	459.16	13.77
387.17 -	387.49	11.62	411.17 -	411.49	12.34	435.17 -	435.49	13.06	459.17 -	459.49	13.78
387.50 -	387.83	11.63	411.50 -	411.83	12.35	435.50 -	435.83	13.07	459.50 -	459.83	13.79
387.84 -	388.16	11.64	411.84 -	412.16	12.36	435.84 -	436.16	13.08	459.84 -	460.16	13.80
388.17 -	388.49	11.65	412.17 -	412.49	12.37	436.17 -	436.49	13.09	460.17 -	460.49	13.81
388.50 -	388.83	11.66	412.50 -	412.83	12.38	436.50 -	436.83	13.10	460.50 -	460.83	13.82
388.84 -	389.16	11.67	412.84 -	413.16	12.39	436.84 -	437.16	13.11	460.84 -	461.16	13.83
389.17 -	389.49	11.68	413.17 -	413.49	12.40	437.17 -	437.49	13.12	461.17 -	461.49	13.84
389.50 -	389.83	11.69	413.50 -	413.83	12.41	437.50 -	437.83	13.13	461.50 -	461.83	13.85
389.84 -	390.16	11.70	413.84 -	414.16	12.42	437.84 -	438.16	13.14	461.84 -	462.16	13.86
390.17 -	390.49	11.71	414.17 -	414.49	12.43	438.17 -	438.49	13.15	462.17 -	462.49	13.87
390.50 -	390.83	11.72	414.50 -	414.83	12.44	438.50 -	438.83	13.16	462.50 -	462.83	13.88
390.84 -	391.16	11.73	414.84 -	415.16	12.45	438.84 -	439.16	13.17	462.84 -	463.16	13.89
391.17 -	391.49	11.74	415.17 -	415.49	12.46	439.17 -	439.49	13.18	463.17 -	463.49	13.90
391.50 -	391.83	11.75	415.50 -	415.83	12.47	439.50 -	439.83	13.19	463.50 -	463.83	13.91
391.84 -	392.16	11.76	415.84 -	416.16	12.48	439.84 -	440.16	13.20	463.84 -	464.16	13.92
392.17 -	392.49	11.77	416.17 -	416.49	12.49	440.17 -	440.49	13.21	464.17 -	464.49	13.93
392.50 -	392.83	11.78	416.50 -	416.83	12.50	440.50 -	440.83	13.22	464.50 -	464.83	13.94
392.84 -	393.16	11.79	416.84 -	417.16	12.51	440.84 -	441.16	13.23	464.84 -	465.16	13.95
393.17 -	393.49	11.80	417.17 -	417.49	12.52	441.17 -	441.49	13.24	465.17 -	465.49	13.96
393.50 -	393.83	11.81	417.50 -	417.83	12.53	441.50 -	441.83	13.25	465.50 -	465.83	13.97
393.84 -	394.16	11.82	417.84 -	418.16	12.54	441.84 -	442.16	13.26	465.84 -	466.16	13.98
394.17 -	394.49	11.83	418.17 -	418.49	12.55	442.17 -	442.49	13.27	466.17 -	466.49	13.99
394.50 -	394.83	11.84	418.50 -	418.83	12.56	442.50 -	442.83	13.28	466.50 -	466.83	14.00
394.84 -	395.16	11.85	418.84 -	419.16	12.57	442.84 -	443.16	13.29	466.84 -	467.16	14.01
395.17 -	395.49	11.86	419.17 -	419.49	12.58	443.17 -	443.49	13.30	467.17 -	467.49	14.02
395.50 -	395.83	11.87	419.50 -	419.83	12.59	443.50 -	443.83	13.31	467.50 -	467.83	14.03
395.84 -	396.16	11.88	419.84 -	420.16	12.60	443.84 -	444.16	13.32	467.84 -	468.16	14.04
396.17 -	396.49	11.89	420.17 -	420.49	12.61	444.17 -	444.49	13.33	468.17 -	468.49	14.05
396.50 -	396.83	11.90	420.50 -	420.83	12.62	444.50 -	444.83	13.34	468.50 -	468.83	14.06
396.84 -	397.16	11.91	420.84 -	421.16	12.63	444.84 -	445.16	13.35	468.84 -	469.16	14.07
397.17 -	397.49	11.92	421.17 -	421.49	12.64	445.17 -	445.49	13.36	469.17 -	469.49	14.08
397.50 -	397.83	11.93	421.50 -	421.83	12.65	445.50 -	445.83	13.37	469.50 -	469.83	14.09
397.84 -	398.16	11.94	421.84 -	422.16	12.66	445.84 -	446.16	13.38	469.84 -	470.16	14.10
398.17 -	398.49	11.95	422.17 -	422.49	12.67	446.17 -	446.49	13.39	470.17 -	470.49	14.11
398.50 -	398.83	11.96	422.50 -	422.83	12.68	446.50 -	446.83	13.40	470.50 -	470.83	14.12
398.84 -	399.16	11.97	422.84 -	423.16	12.69	446.84 -	447.16	13.41	470.84 -	471.16	14.13
399.17 -	399.49	11.98	423.17 -	423.49	12.70	447.17 -	447.49	13.42	471.17 -	471.49	14.14
399.50 -	399.83	11.99	423.50 -	423.83	12.71	447.50 -	447.83	13.43	471.50 -	471.83	14.15
399.84 -	400.16	12.00	423.84 -	424.16	12.72	447.84 -	448.16	13.44	471.84 -	472.16	14.16
400.17 -	400.49	12.01	424.17 -	424.49	12.73	448.17 -	448.49	13.45	472.17 -	472.49	14.17
400.50 -	400.83	12.02	424.50 -	424.83	12.74	448.50 -	448.83	13.46	472.50 -	472.83	14.18
400.84 -	401.16	12.03	424.84 -	425.16	12.75	448.84 -	449.16	13.47	472.84 -	473.16	14.19
401.17 -	401.49	12.04	425.17 -	425.49	12.76	449.17 -	449.49	13.48	473.17 -	473.49	14.20
401.50 -	401.83	12.05	425.50 -	425.83	12.77	449.50 -	449.83	13.49	473.50 -	473.83	14.21
401.84 -	402.16	12.06	425.84 -	426.16	12.78	449.84 -	450.16	13.50	473.84 -	474.16	14.22
402.17 -	402.49	12.07	426.17 -	426.49	12.79	450.17 -	450.49	13.51	474.17 -	474.49	14.23
402.50 -	402.83	12.08	426.50 -	426.83	12.80	450.50 -	450.83	13.52	474.50 -	474.83	14.24
402.84 -	403.16	12.09	426.84 -	427.16	12.81	450.84 -	451.16	13.53	474.84 -	475.16	14.25
403.17 -	403.49	12.10	427.17 -	427.49	12.82	451.17 -	451.49	13.54	475.17 -	475.49	14.26
403.50 -	403.83	12.11	427.50 -	427.83	12.83	451.50 -	451.83	13.55	475.50 -	475.83	14.27
403.84 -	404.16	12.12	427.84 -	428.16	12.84	451.84 -	452.16	13.56	475.84 -	476.16	14.28
404.17 -	404.49	12.13	428.17 -	428.49	12.85	452.17 -	452.49	13.57	476.17 -	476.49	14.29
404.50 -	404.83	12.14	428.50 -	428.83	12.86	452.50 -	452.83	13.58	476.50 -	476.83	14.30
404.84 -	405.16	12.15	428.84 -	429.16	12.87	452.84 -	453.16	13.59	476.84 -	477.16	14.31
405.17 -	405.49	12.16	429.17 -	429.49	12.88	453.17 -	453.49	13.60	477.17 -	477.49	14.32
405.50 -	405.83	12.17	429.50 -	429.83	12.89	453.50 -	453.83	13.61	477.50 -	477.83	14.33
405.84 -	406.16	12.18	429.84 -	430.16	12.90	453.84 -	454.16	13.62	477.84 -	478.16	14.34
406.17 -	406.49	12.19	430.17 -	430.49	12.91	454.17 -	454.49	13.63	478.17 -	478.49	14.35
406.50 -	406.83	12.20	430.50 -	430.83	12.92	454.50 -	454.83	13.64	478.50 -	478.83	14.36
406.84 -	407.16	12.21	430.84 -	431.16	12.93	454.84 -	455.16	13.65	478.84 -	479.16	14.37
407.17 -	407.49	12.22	431.17 -	431.49	12.94	455.17 -	455.49	13.66	479.17 -	479.49	14.38
407.50 -	407.83	12.23	431.50 -	431.83	12.95	455.50 -	455.83	13.67	479.50 -	479.83	14.39
407.84 -	408.16	12.24	431.84 -	432.16	12.96	455.84 -	456.16	13.68	479.84 -	480.16	14.40

Note: The following are the maximum amounts you can deduct for each pay period.
Remarque : Vous trouverez ci-dessous la cotisation maximale que vous pouvez retenir pour chaque période de paie.

Weekly	Hebdomadaire	22.35	10 pay periods a year	10 périodes de paie par année	116.22
Biweekly	Aux deux semaines	44.70	13 pay periods a year	13 périodes de paie par année	89.40
Semimonthly	Bimensuel	48.42	22 pay periods a year	22 périodes de paie par année	52.83
Monthly	Mensuel	96.85			

APPENDIX 9-3   **Unemployment Insurance Premiums (continued)**

Unemployment Insurance Premiums — Cotisations à l'assurance-chômage   B-59

Pay Rémunération From – De	To – À	UI premium Cotisation à l'A-C	Pay Rémunération From – De	To – À	UI premium Cotisation à l'A-C	Pay Rémunération From – De	To – À	UI premium Cotisation à l'A-C	Pay Rémunération From – De	To – À	UI premium Cotisation à l'A-C
480.17 –	480.49	14.41	504.17 –	504.49	15.13	528.17 –	528.49	15.85	552.17 –	552.49	16.57
480.50 –	480.83	14.42	504.50 –	504.83	15.14	528.50 –	528.83	15.86	552.50 –	552.83	16.58
480.84 –	481.16	14.43	504.84 –	505.16	15.15	528.84 –	529.16	15.87	552.84 –	553.16	16.59
481.17 –	481.49	14.44	505.17 –	505.49	15.16	529.17 –	529.49	15.88	553.17 –	553.49	16.60
481.50 –	481.83	14.45	505.50 –	505.83	15.17	529.50 –	529.83	15.89	553.50 –	553.83	16.61
481.84 –	482.16	14.46	505.84 –	506.16	15.18	529.84 –	530.16	15.90	553.84 –	554.16	16.62
482.17 –	482.49	14.47	506.17 –	506.49	15.19	530.17 –	530.49	15.91	554.17 –	554.49	16.63
482.50 –	482.83	14.48	506.50 –	506.83	15.20	530.50 –	530.83	15.92	554.50 –	554.83	16.64
482.84 –	483.16	14.49	506.84 –	507.16	15.21	530.84 –	531.16	15.93	554.84 –	555.16	16.65
483.17 –	483.49	14.50	507.17 –	507.49	15.22	531.17 –	531.49	15.94	555.17 –	555.49	16.66
483.50 –	483.83	14.51	507.50 –	507.83	15.23	531.50 –	531.83	15.95	555.50 –	555.83	16.67
483.84 –	484.16	14.52	507.84 –	508.16	15.24	531.84 –	532.16	15.96	555.84 –	556.16	16.68
484.17 –	484.49	14.53	508.17 –	508.49	15.25	532.17 –	532.49	15.97	556.17 –	556.49	16.69
484.50 –	484.83	14.54	508.50 –	508.83	15.26	532.50 –	532.83	15.98	556.50 –	556.83	16.70
484.84 –	485.16	14.55	508.84 –	509.16	15.27	532.84 –	533.16	15.99	556.84 –	557.16	16.71
485.17 –	485.49	14.56	509.17 –	509.49	15.28	533.17 –	533.49	16.00	557.17 –	557.49	16.72
485.50 –	485.83	14.57	509.50 –	509.83	15.29	533.50 –	533.83	16.01	557.50 –	557.83	16.73
485.84 –	486.16	14.58	509.84 –	510.16	15.30	533.84 –	534.16	16.02	557.84 –	558.16	16.74
486.17 –	486.49	14.59	510.17 –	510.49	15.31	534.17 –	534.49	16.03	558.17 –	558.49	16.75
486.50 –	486.83	14.60	510.50 –	510.83	15.32	534.50 –	534.83	16.04	558.50 –	558.83	16.76
486.84 –	487.16	14.61	510.84 –	511.16	15.33	534.84 –	535.16	16.05	558.84 –	559.16	16.77
487.17 –	487.49	14.62	511.17 –	511.49	15.34	535.17 –	535.49	16.06	559.17 –	559.49	16.78
487.50 –	487.83	14.63	511.50 –	511.83	15.35	535.50 –	535.83	16.07	559.50 –	559.83	16.79
487.84 –	488.16	14.64	511.84 –	512.16	15.36	535.84 –	536.16	16.08	559.84 –	560.16	16.80
488.17 –	488.49	14.65	512.17 –	512.49	15.37	536.17 –	536.49	16.09	560.17 –	560.49	16.81
488.50 –	488.83	14.66	512.50 –	512.83	15.38	536.50 –	536.83	16.10	560.50 –	560.83	16.82
488.84 –	489.16	14.67	512.84 –	513.16	15.39	536.84 –	537.16	16.11	560.84 –	561.16	16.83
489.17 –	489.49	14.68	513.17 –	513.49	15.40	537.17 –	537.49	16.12	561.17 –	561.49	16.84
489.50 –	489.83	14.69	513.50 –	513.83	15.41	537.50 –	537.83	16.13	561.50 –	561.83	16.85
489.84 –	490.16	14.70	513.84 –	514.16	15.42	537.84 –	538.16	16.14	561.84 –	562.16	16.86
490.17 –	490.49	14.71	514.17 –	514.49	15.43	538.17 –	538.49	16.15	562.17 –	562.49	16.87
490.50 –	490.83	14.72	514.50 –	514.83	15.44	538.50 –	538.83	16.16	562.50 –	562.83	16.88
490.84 –	491.16	14.73	514.84 –	515.16	15.45	538.84 –	539.16	16.17	562.84 –	563.16	16.89
491.17 –	491.49	14.74	515.17 –	515.49	15.46	539.17 –	539.49	16.18	563.17 –	563.49	16.90
491.50 –	491.83	14.75	515.50 –	515.83	15.47	539.50 –	539.83	16.19	563.50 –	563.83	16.91
491.84 –	492.16	14.76	515.84 –	516.16	15.48	539.84 –	540.16	16.20	563.84 –	564.16	16.92
492.17 –	492.49	14.77	516.17 –	516.49	15.49	540.17 –	540.49	16.21	564.17 –	564.49	16.93
492.50 –	492.83	14.78	516.50 –	516.83	15.50	540.50 –	540.83	16.22	564.50 –	564.83	16.94
492.84 –	493.16	14.79	516.84 –	517.16	15.51	540.84 –	541.16	16.23	564.84 –	565.16	16.95
493.17 –	493.49	14.80	517.17 –	517.49	15.52	541.17 –	541.49	16.24	565.17 –	565.49	16.96
493.50 –	493.83	14.81	517.50 –	517.83	15.53	541.50 –	541.83	16.25	565.50 –	565.83	16.97
493.84 –	494.16	14.82	517.84 –	518.16	15.54	541.84 –	542.16	16.26	565.84 –	566.16	16.98
494.17 –	494.49	14.83	518.17 –	518.49	15.55	542.17 –	542.49	16.27	566.17 –	566.49	16.99
494.50 –	494.83	14.84	518.50 –	518.83	15.56	542.50 –	542.83	16.28	566.50 –	566.83	17.00
494.84 –	495.16	14.85	518.84 –	519.16	15.57	542.84 –	543.16	16.29	566.84 –	567.16	17.01
495.17 –	495.49	14.86	519.17 –	519.49	15.58	543.17 –	543.49	16.30	567.17 –	567.49	17.02
495.50 –	495.83	14.87	519.50 –	519.83	15.59	543.50 –	543.83	16.31	567.50 –	567.83	17.03
495.84 –	496.16	14.88	519.84 –	520.16	15.60	543.84 –	544.16	16.32	567.84 –	568.16	17.04
496.17 –	496.49	14.89	520.17 –	520.49	15.61	544.17 –	544.49	16.33	568.17 –	568.49	17.05
496.50 –	496.83	14.90	520.50 –	520.83	15.62	544.50 –	544.83	16.34	568.50 –	568.83	17.06
496.84 –	497.16	14.91	520.84 –	521.16	15.63	544.84 –	545.16	16.35	568.84 –	569.16	17.07
497.17 –	497.49	14.92	521.17 –	521.49	15.64	545.17 –	545.49	16.36	569.17 –	569.49	17.08
497.50 –	497.83	14.93	521.50 –	521.83	15.65	545.50 –	545.83	16.37	569.50 –	569.83	17.09
497.84 –	498.16	14.94	521.84 –	522.16	15.66	545.84 –	546.16	16.38	569.84 –	570.16	17.10
498.17 –	498.49	14.95	522.17 –	522.49	15.67	546.17 –	546.49	16.39	570.17 –	570.49	17.11
498.50 –	498.83	14.96	522.50 –	522.83	15.68	546.50 –	546.83	16.40	570.50 –	570.83	17.12
498.84 –	499.16	14.97	522.84 –	523.16	15.69	546.84 –	547.16	16.41	570.84 –	571.16	17.13
499.17 –	499.49	14.98	523.17 –	523.49	15.70	547.17 –	547.49	16.42	571.17 –	571.49	17.14
499.50 –	499.83	14.99	523.50 –	523.83	15.71	547.50 –	547.83	16.43	571.50 –	571.83	17.15
499.84 –	500.16	15.00	523.84 –	524.16	15.72	547.84 –	548.16	16.44	571.84 –	572.16	17.16
500.17 –	500.49	15.01	524.17 –	524.49	15.73	548.17 –	548.49	16.45	572.17 –	572.49	17.17
500.50 –	500.83	15.02	524.50 –	524.83	15.74	548.50 –	548.83	16.46	572.50 –	572.83	17.18
500.84 –	501.16	15.03	524.84 –	525.16	15.75	548.84 –	549.16	16.47	572.84 –	573.16	17.19
501.17 –	501.49	15.04	525.17 –	525.49	15.76	549.17 –	549.49	16.48	573.17 –	573.49	17.20
501.50 –	501.83	15.05	525.50 –	525.83	15.77	549.50 –	549.83	16.49	573.50 –	573.83	17.21
501.84 –	502.16	15.06	525.84 –	526.16	15.78	549.84 –	550.16	16.50	573.84 –	574.16	17.22
502.17 –	502.49	15.07	526.17 –	526.49	15.79	550.17 –	550.49	16.51	574.17 –	574.49	17.23
502.50 –	502.83	15.08	526.50 –	526.83	15.80	550.50 –	550.83	16.52	574.50 –	574.83	17.24
502.84 –	503.16	15.09	526.84 –	527.16	15.81	550.84 –	551.16	16.53	574.84 –	575.16	17.25
503.17 –	503.49	15.10	527.17 –	527.49	15.82	551.17 –	551.49	16.54	575.17 –	575.49	17.26
503.50 –	503.83	15.11	527.50 –	527.83	15.83	551.50 –	551.83	16.55	575.50 –	575.83	17.27
503.84 –	504.16	15.12	527.84 –	528.16	15.84	551.84 –	552.16	16.56	575.84 –	576.16	17.28

Note: The following are the maximum amounts you can deduct for each pay period.
Remarque : Vous trouverez ci-dessous la cotisation maximale que vous pouvez retenir pour chaque période de paie.

Weekly	Hebdomadaire	**22.35**	10 pay periods a year	10 périodes de paie par année	**116.22**
Biweekly	Aux deux semaines	**44.70**	13 pay periods a year	13 périodes de paie par année	**89.40**
Semimonthly	Bimensuel	**48.42**	22 pay periods a year	22 périodes de paie par année	**52.83**
Monthly	Mensuel	**96.85**			

APPENDIX 9-3   Unemployment Insurance Premiums (continued)

B-60 Unemployment Insurance Premiums — Cotisations à l'assurance-chômage

Pay Rémunération From – De	To – À	UI premium Cotisation à l'A-C	Pay Rémunération From – De	To – À	UI premium Cotisation à l'A-C	Pay Rémunération From – De	To – À	UI premium Cotisation à l'A-C	Pay Rémunération From – De	To – À	UI premium Cotisation à l'A-C
576.17	576.49	17.29	600.17	600.49	18.01	624.17	624.49	18.73	648.17	648.49	19.45
576.50	576.83	17.30	600.50	600.83	18.02	624.50	624.83	18.74	648.50	648.83	19.46
576.84	577.16	17.31	600.84	601.16	18.03	624.84	625.16	18.75	648.84	649.16	19.47
577.17	577.49	17.32	601.17	601.49	18.04	625.17	625.49	18.76	649.17	649.49	19.48
577.50	577.83	17.33	601.50	601.83	18.05	625.50	625.83	18.77	649.50	649.83	19.49
577.84	578.16	17.34	601.84	602.16	18.06	625.84	626.16	18.78	649.84	650.16	19.50
578.17	578.49	17.35	602.17	602.49	18.07	626.17	626.49	18.79	650.17	650.49	19.51
578.50	578.83	17.36	602.50	602.83	18.08	626.50	626.83	18.80	650.50	650.83	19.52
578.84	579.16	17.37	602.84	603.16	18.09	626.84	627.16	18.81	650.84	651.16	19.53
579.17	579.49	17.38	603.17	603.49	18.10	627.17	627.49	18.82	651.17	651.49	19.54
579.50	579.83	17.39	603.50	603.83	18.11	627.50	627.83	18.83	651.50	651.83	19.55
579.84	580.16	17.40	603.84	604.16	18.12	627.84	628.16	18.84	651.84	652.16	19.56
580.17	580.49	17.41	604.17	604.49	18.13	628.17	628.49	18.85	652.17	652.49	19.57
580.50	580.83	17.42	604.50	604.83	18.14	628.50	628.83	18.86	652.50	652.83	19.58
580.84	581.16	17.43	604.84	605.16	18.15	628.84	629.16	18.87	652.84	653.16	19.59
581.17	581.49	17.44	605.17	605.49	18.16	629.17	629.49	18.88	653.17	653.49	19.60
581.50	581.83	17.45	605.50	605.83	18.17	629.50	629.83	18.89	653.50	653.83	19.61
581.84	582.16	17.46	605.84	606.16	18.18	629.84	630.16	18.90	653.84	654.16	19.62
582.17	582.49	17.47	606.17	606.49	18.19	630.17	630.49	18.91	654.17	654.49	19.63
582.50	582.83	17.48	606.50	606.83	18.20	630.50	630.83	18.92	654.50	654.83	19.64
582.84	583.16	17.49	606.84	607.16	18.21	630.84	631.16	18.93	654.84	655.16	19.65
583.17	583.49	17.50	607.17	607.49	18.22	631.17	631.49	18.94	655.17	655.49	19.66
583.50	583.83	17.51	607.50	607.83	18.23	631.50	631.83	18.95	655.50	655.83	19.67
583.84	584.16	17.52	607.84	608.16	18.24	631.84	632.16	18.96	655.84	656.16	19.68
584.17	584.49	17.53	608.17	608.49	18.25	632.17	632.49	18.97	656.17	656.49	19.69
584.50	584.83	17.54	608.50	608.83	18.26	632.50	632.83	18.98	656.50	656.83	19.70
584.84	585.16	17.55	608.84	609.16	18.27	632.84	633.16	18.99	656.84	657.16	19.71
585.17	585.49	17.56	609.17	609.49	18.28	633.17	633.49	19.00	657.17	657.49	19.72
585.50	585.83	17.57	609.50	609.83	18.29	633.50	633.83	19.01	657.50	657.83	19.73
585.84	586.16	17.58	609.84	610.16	18.30	633.84	634.16	19.02	657.84	658.16	19.74
586.17	586.49	17.59	610.17	610.49	18.31	634.17	634.49	19.03	658.17	658.49	19.75
586.50	586.83	17.60	610.50	610.83	18.32	634.50	634.83	19.04	658.50	658.83	19.76
586.84	587.16	17.61	610.84	611.16	18.33	634.84	635.16	19.05	658.84	659.16	19.77
587.17	587.49	17.62	611.17	611.49	18.34	635.17	635.49	19.06	659.17	659.49	19.78
587.50	587.83	17.63	611.50	611.83	18.35	635.50	635.83	19.07	659.50	659.83	19.79
587.84	588.16	17.64	611.84	612.16	18.36	635.84	636.16	19.08	659.84	660.16	19.80
588.17	588.49	17.65	612.17	612.49	18.37	636.17	636.49	19.09	660.17	660.49	19.81
588.50	588.83	17.66	612.50	612.83	18.38	636.50	636.83	19.10	660.50	660.83	19.82
588.84	589.16	17.67	612.84	613.16	18.39	636.84	637.16	19.11	660.84	661.16	19.83
589.17	589.49	17.68	613.17	613.49	18.40	637.17	637.49	19.12	661.17	661.49	19.84
589.50	589.83	17.69	613.50	613.83	18.41	637.50	637.83	19.13	661.50	661.83	19.85
589.84	590.16	17.70	613.84	614.16	18.42	637.84	638.16	19.14	661.84	662.16	19.86
590.17	590.49	17.71	614.17	614.49	18.43	638.17	638.49	19.15	662.17	662.49	19.87
590.50	590.83	17.72	614.50	614.83	18.44	638.50	638.83	19.16	662.50	662.83	19.88
590.84	591.16	17.73	614.84	615.16	18.45	638.84	639.16	19.17	662.84	663.16	19.89
591.17	591.49	17.74	615.17	615.49	18.46	639.17	639.49	19.18	663.17	663.49	19.90
591.50	591.83	17.75	615.50	615.83	18.47	639.50	639.83	19.19	663.50	663.83	19.91
591.84	592.16	17.76	615.84	616.16	18.48	639.84	640.16	19.20	663.84	664.16	19.92
592.17	592.49	17.77	616.17	616.49	18.49	640.17	640.49	19.21	664.17	664.49	19.93
592.50	592.83	17.78	616.50	616.83	18.50	640.50	640.83	19.22	664.50	664.83	19.94
592.84	593.16	17.79	616.84	617.16	18.51	640.84	641.16	19.23	664.84	665.16	19.95
593.17	593.49	17.80	617.17	617.49	18.52	641.17	641.49	19.24	665.17	665.49	19.96
593.50	593.83	17.81	617.50	617.83	18.53	641.50	641.83	19.25	665.50	665.83	19.97
593.84	594.16	17.82	617.84	618.16	18.54	641.84	642.16	19.26	665.84	666.16	19.98
594.17	594.49	17.83	618.17	618.49	18.55	642.17	642.49	19.27	666.17	666.49	19.99
594.50	594.83	17.84	618.50	618.83	18.56	642.50	642.83	19.28	666.50	666.83	20.00
594.84	595.16	17.85	618.84	619.16	18.57	642.84	643.16	19.29	666.84	667.16	20.01
595.17	595.49	17.86	619.17	619.49	18.58	643.17	643.49	19.30	667.17	667.49	20.02
595.50	595.83	17.87	619.50	619.83	18.59	643.50	643.83	19.31	667.50	667.83	20.03
595.84	596.16	17.88	619.84	620.16	18.60	643.84	644.16	19.32	667.84	668.16	20.04
596.17	596.49	17.89	620.17	620.49	18.61	644.17	644.49	19.33	668.17	668.49	20.05
596.50	596.83	17.90	620.50	620.83	18.62	644.50	644.83	19.34	668.50	668.83	20.06
596.84	597.16	17.91	620.84	621.16	18.63	644.84	645.16	19.35	668.84	669.16	20.07
597.17	597.49	17.92	621.17	621.49	18.64	645.17	645.49	19.36	669.17	669.49	20.08
597.50	597.83	17.93	621.50	621.83	18.65	645.50	645.83	19.37	669.50	669.83	20.09
597.84	598.16	17.94	621.84	622.16	18.66	645.84	646.16	19.38	669.84	670.16	20.10
598.17	598.49	17.95	622.17	622.49	18.67	646.17	646.49	19.39	670.17	670.49	20.11
598.50	598.83	17.96	622.50	622.83	18.68	646.50	646.83	19.40	670.50	670.83	20.12
598.84	599.16	17.97	622.84	623.16	18.69	646.84	647.16	19.41	670.84	671.16	20.13
599.17	599.49	17.98	623.17	623.49	18.70	647.17	647.49	19.42	671.17	671.49	20.14
599.50	599.83	17.99	623.50	623.83	18.71	647.50	647.83	19.43	671.50	671.83	20.15
599.84	600.16	18.00	623.84	624.16	18.72	647.84	648.16	19.44	671.84	672.16	20.16

Note: The following are the maximum amounts you can deduct for each pay period.
Remarque : Vous trouverez ci-dessous la cotisation maximale que vous pouvez retenir pour chaque période de paie.

Weekly	Hebdomadaire	22.35	10 pay periods a year	10 périodes de paie par année	116.22
Biweekly	Aux deux semaines	44.70	13 pay periods a year	13 périodes de paie par année	89.40
Semimonthly	Bimensuel	48.42	22 pay periods a year	22 périodes de paie par année	52.83
Monthly	Mensuel	96.85			

APPENDIX 9-3   Unemployment Insurance Premiums (continued)

Unemployment Insurance Premiums – Cotisations à l'assurance-chômage　B-61

Pay Rémunération From – De	To – À	UI premium Cotisation à l'A-C	Pay Rémunération From – De	To – À	UI premium Cotisation à l'A-C	Pay Rémunération From – De	To – À	UI premium Cotisation à l'A-C	Pay Rémunération From – De	To – À	UI premium Cotisation à l'A-C
672.17	672.49	20.17	696.17	696.49	20.89	720.17	720.49	21.61	744.17	744.49	22.33
672.50	672.83	20.18	696.50	696.83	20.90	720.50	720.83	21.62	744.50	744.83	22.34
672.84	673.16	20.19	696.84	697.16	20.91	720.84	721.16	21.63	744.84	745.16	22.35
673.17	673.49	20.20	697.17	697.49	20.92	721.17	721.49	21.64	745.17	745.49	22.36
673.50	673.83	20.21	697.50	697.83	20.93	721.50	721.83	21.65	745.50	745.83	22.37
673.84	674.16	20.22	697.84	698.16	20.94	721.84	722.16	21.66	745.84	746.16	22.38
674.17	674.49	20.23	698.17	698.49	20.95	722.17	722.49	21.67	746.17	746.49	22.39
674.50	674.83	20.24	698.50	698.83	20.96	722.50	722.83	21.68	746.50	746.83	22.40
674.84	675.16	20.25	698.84	699.16	20.97	722.84	723.16	21.69	746.84	747.16	22.41
675.17	675.49	20.26	699.17	699.49	20.98	723.17	723.49	21.70	747.17	747.49	22.42
675.50	675.83	20.27	699.50	699.83	20.99	723.50	723.83	21.71	747.50	747.83	22.43
675.84	676.16	20.28	699.84	700.16	21.00	723.84	724.16	21.72	747.84	748.16	22.44
676.17	676.49	20.29	700.17	700.49	21.01	724.17	724.49	21.73	748.17	748.49	22.45
676.50	676.83	20.30	700.50	700.83	21.02	724.50	724.83	21.74	748.50	748.83	22.46
676.84	677.16	20.31	700.84	701.16	21.03	724.84	725.16	21.75	748.84	749.16	22.47
677.17	677.49	20.32	701.17	701.49	21.04	725.17	725.49	21.76	749.17	749.49	22.48
677.50	677.83	20.33	701.50	701.83	21.05	725.50	725.83	21.77	749.50	749.83	22.49
677.84	678.16	20.34	701.84	702.16	21.06	725.84	726.16	21.78	749.84	750.16	22.50
678.17	678.49	20.35	702.17	702.49	21.07	726.17	726.49	21.79	750.17	750.49	22.51
678.50	678.83	20.36	702.50	702.83	21.08	726.50	726.83	21.80	750.50	750.83	22.52
678.84	679.16	20.37	702.84	703.16	21.09	726.84	727.16	21.81	750.84	751.16	22.53
679.17	679.49	20.38	703.17	703.49	21.10	727.17	727.49	21.82	751.17	751.49	22.54
679.50	679.83	20.39	703.50	703.83	21.11	727.50	727.83	21.83	751.50	751.83	22.55
679.84	680.16	20.40	703.84	704.16	21.12	727.84	728.16	21.84	751.84	752.16	22.56
680.17	680.49	20.41	704.17	704.49	21.13	728.17	728.49	21.85	752.17	752.49	22.57
680.50	680.83	20.42	704.50	704.83	21.14	728.50	728.83	21.86	752.50	752.83	22.58
680.84	681.16	20.43	704.84	705.16	21.15	728.84	729.16	21.87	752.84	753.16	22.59
681.17	681.49	20.44	705.17	705.49	21.16	729.17	729.49	21.88	753.17	753.49	22.60
681.50	681.83	20.45	705.50	705.83	21.17	729.50	729.83	21.89	753.50	753.83	22.61
681.84	682.16	20.46	705.84	706.16	21.18	729.84	730.16	21.90	753.84	754.16	22.62
682.17	682.49	20.47	706.17	706.49	21.19	730.17	730.49	21.91	754.17	754.49	22.63
682.50	682.83	20.48	706.50	706.83	21.20	730.50	730.83	21.92	754.50	754.83	22.64
682.84	683.16	20.49	706.84	707.16	21.21	730.84	731.16	21.93	754.84	755.16	22.65
683.17	683.49	20.50	707.17	707.49	21.22	731.17	731.49	21.94	755.17	755.49	22.66
683.50	683.83	20.51	707.50	707.83	21.23	731.50	731.83	21.95	755.50	755.83	22.67
683.84	684.16	20.52	707.84	708.16	21.24	731.84	732.16	21.96	755.84	756.16	22.68
684.17	684.49	20.53	708.17	708.49	21.25	732.17	732.49	21.97	756.17	756.49	22.69
684.50	684.83	20.54	708.50	708.83	21.26	732.50	732.83	21.98	756.50	756.83	22.70
684.84	685.16	20.55	708.84	709.16	21.27	732.84	733.16	21.99	756.84	757.16	22.71
685.17	685.49	20.56	709.17	709.49	21.28	733.17	733.49	22.00	757.17	757.49	22.72
685.50	685.83	20.57	709.50	709.83	21.29	733.50	733.83	22.01	757.50	757.83	22.73
685.84	686.16	20.58	709.84	710.16	21.30	733.84	734.16	22.02	757.84	758.16	22.74
686.17	686.49	20.59	710.17	710.49	21.31	734.17	734.49	22.03	758.17	758.49	22.75
686.50	686.83	20.60	710.50	710.83	21.32	734.50	734.83	22.04	758.50	758.83	22.76
686.84	687.16	20.61	710.84	711.16	21.33	734.84	735.16	22.05	758.84	759.16	22.77
687.17	687.49	20.62	711.17	711.49	21.34	735.17	735.49	22.06	759.17	759.49	22.78
687.50	687.83	20.63	711.50	711.83	21.35	735.50	735.83	22.07	759.50	759.83	22.79
687.84	688.16	20.64	711.84	712.16	21.36	735.84	736.16	22.08	759.84	760.16	22.80
688.17	688.49	20.65	712.17	712.49	21.37	736.17	736.49	22.09	760.17	760.49	22.81
688.50	688.83	20.66	712.50	712.83	21.38	736.50	736.83	22.10	760.50	760.83	22.82
688.84	689.16	20.67	712.84	713.16	21.39	736.84	737.16	22.11	760.84	761.16	22.83
689.17	689.49	20.68	713.17	713.49	21.40	737.17	737.49	22.12	761.17	761.49	22.84
689.50	689.83	20.69	713.50	713.83	21.41	737.50	737.83	22.13	761.50	761.83	22.85
689.84	690.16	20.70	713.84	714.16	21.42	737.84	738.16	22.14	761.84	762.16	22.86
690.17	690.49	20.71	714.17	714.49	21.43	738.17	738.49	22.15	762.17	762.49	22.87
690.50	690.83	20.72	714.50	714.83	21.44	738.50	738.83	22.16	762.50	762.83	22.88
690.84	691.16	20.73	714.84	715.16	21.45	738.84	739.16	22.17	762.84	763.16	22.89
691.17	691.49	20.74	715.17	715.49	21.46	739.17	739.49	22.18	763.17	763.49	22.90
691.50	691.83	20.75	715.50	715.83	21.47	739.50	739.83	22.19	763.50	763.83	22.91
691.84	692.16	20.76	715.84	716.16	21.48	739.84	740.16	22.20	763.84	764.16	22.92
692.17	692.49	20.77	716.17	716.49	21.49	740.17	740.49	22.21	764.17	764.49	22.93
692.50	692.83	20.78	716.50	716.83	21.50	740.50	740.83	22.22	764.50	764.83	22.94
692.84	693.16	20.79	716.84	717.16	21.51	740.84	741.16	22.23	764.84	765.16	22.95
693.17	693.49	20.80	717.17	717.49	21.52	741.17	741.49	22.24	765.17	765.49	22.96
693.50	693.83	20.81	717.50	717.83	21.53	741.50	741.83	22.25	765.50	765.83	22.97
693.84	694.16	20.82	717.84	718.16	21.54	741.84	742.16	22.26	765.84	766.16	22.98
694.17	694.49	20.83	718.17	718.49	21.55	742.17	742.49	22.27	766.17	766.49	22.99
694.50	694.83	20.84	718.50	718.83	21.56	742.50	742.83	22.28	766.50	766.83	23.00
694.84	695.16	20.85	718.84	719.16	21.57	742.84	743.16	22.29	766.84	767.16	23.01
695.17	695.49	20.86	719.17	719.49	21.58	743.17	743.49	22.30	767.17	767.49	23.02
695.50	695.83	20.87	719.50	719.83	21.59	743.50	743.83	22.31	767.50	767.83	23.03
695.84	696.16	20.88	719.84	720.16	21.60	743.84	744.16	22.32	767.84	768.16	23.04

Note: The following are the maximum amounts you can deduct for each pay period.
Remarque : Vous trouverez ci-dessous la cotisation maximale que vous pouvez retenir pour chaque période de paie.

Weekly	Hebdomadaire	22.35	10 pay periods a year	10 périodes de paie par année	116.22
Biweekly	Aux deux semaines	44.70	13 pay periods a year	13 périodes de paie par année	89.40
Semimonthly	Bimensuel	48.42	22 pay periods a year	22 périodes de paie par année	52.83
Monthly	Mensuel	96.85			

APPENDIX 9-3　Unemployment Insurance Premiums (continued)

B-62   Unemployment Insurance Premiums — Cotisations à l'assurance-chômage

Pay Rémunération From – De	To – À	UI premium Cotisation à l'A-C	Pay Rémunération From – De	To – À	UI premium Cotisation à l'A-C	Pay Rémunération From – De	To – À	UI premium Cotisation à l'A-C	Pay Rémunération From – De	To – À	UI premium Cotisation à l'A-C
768.17	768.49	23.05	792.17	792.49	23.77	816.17	816.49	24.49	840.17	840.49	25.21
768.50	768.83	23.06	792.50	792.83	23.78	816.50	816.83	24.50	840.50	840.83	25.22
768.84	769.16	23.07	792.84	793.16	23.79	816.84	817.16	24.51	840.84	841.16	25.23
769.17	769.49	23.08	793.17	793.49	23.80	817.17	817.49	24.52	841.17	841.49	25.24
769.50	769.83	23.09	793.50	793.83	23.81	817.50	817.83	24.53	841.50	841.83	25.25
769.84	770.16	23.10	793.84	794.16	23.82	817.84	818.16	24.54	841.84	842.16	25.26
770.17	770.49	23.11	794.17	794.49	23.83	818.17	818.49	24.55	842.17	842.49	25.27
770.50	770.83	23.12	794.50	794.83	23.84	818.50	818.83	24.56	842.50	842.83	25.28
770.84	771.16	23.13	794.84	795.16	23.85	818.84	819.16	24.57	842.84	843.16	25.29
771.17	771.49	23.14	795.17	795.49	23.86	819.17	819.49	24.58	843.17	843.49	25.30
771.50	771.83	23.15	795.50	795.83	23.87	819.50	819.83	24.59	843.50	843.83	25.31
771.84	772.16	23.16	795.84	796.16	23.88	819.84	820.16	24.60	843.84	844.16	25.32
772.17	772.49	23.17	796.17	796.49	23.89	820.17	820.49	24.61	844.17	844.49	25.33
772.50	772.83	23.18	796.50	796.83	23.90	820.50	820.83	24.62	844.50	844.83	25.34
772.84	773.16	23.19	796.84	797.16	23.91	820.84	821.16	24.63	844.84	845.16	25.35
773.17	773.49	23.20	797.17	797.49	23.92	821.17	821.49	24.64	845.17	845.49	25.36
773.50	773.83	23.21	797.50	797.83	23.93	821.50	821.83	24.65	845.50	845.83	25.37
773.84	774.16	23.22	797.84	798.16	23.94	821.84	822.16	24.66	845.84	846.16	25.38
774.17	774.49	23.23	798.17	798.49	23.95	822.17	822.49	24.67	846.17	846.49	25.39
774.50	774.83	23.24	798.50	798.83	23.96	822.50	822.83	24.68	846.50	846.83	25.40
774.84	775.16	23.25	798.84	799.16	23.97	822.84	823.16	24.69	846.84	847.16	25.41
775.17	775.49	23.26	799.17	799.49	23.98	823.17	823.49	24.70	847.17	847.49	25.42
775.50	775.83	23.27	799.50	799.83	23.99	823.50	823.83	24.71	847.50	847.83	25.43
775.84	776.16	23.28	799.84	800.16	24.00	823.84	824.16	24.72	847.84	848.16	25.44
776.17	776.49	23.29	800.17	800.49	24.01	824.17	824.49	24.73	848.17	848.49	25.45
776.50	776.83	23.30	800.50	800.83	24.02	824.50	824.83	24.74	848.50	848.83	25.46
776.84	777.16	23.31	800.84	801.16	24.03	824.84	825.16	24.75	848.84	849.16	25.47
777.17	777.49	23.32	801.17	801.49	24.04	825.17	825.49	24.76	849.17	849.49	25.48
777.50	777.83	23.33	801.50	801.83	24.05	825.50	825.83	24.77	849.50	849.83	25.49
777.84	778.16	23.34	801.84	802.16	24.06	825.84	826.16	24.78	849.84	850.16	25.50
778.17	778.49	23.35	802.17	802.49	24.07	826.17	826.49	24.79	850.17	850.49	25.51
778.50	778.83	23.36	802.50	802.83	24.08	826.50	826.83	24.80	850.50	850.83	25.52
778.84	779.16	23.37	802.84	803.16	24.09	826.84	827.16	24.81	850.84	851.16	25.53
779.17	779.49	23.38	803.17	803.49	24.10	827.17	827.49	24.82	851.17	851.49	25.54
779.50	779.83	23.39	803.50	803.83	24.11	827.50	827.83	24.83	851.50	851.83	25.55
779.84	780.16	23.40	803.84	804.16	24.12	827.84	828.16	24.84	851.84	852.16	25.56
780.17	780.49	23.41	804.17	804.49	24.13	828.17	828.49	24.85	852.17	852.49	25.57
780.50	780.83	23.42	804.50	804.83	24.14	828.50	828.83	24.86	852.50	852.83	25.58
780.84	781.16	23.43	804.84	805.16	24.15	828.84	829.16	24.87	852.84	853.16	25.59
781.17	781.49	23.44	805.17	805.49	24.16	829.17	829.49	24.88	853.17	853.49	25.60
781.50	781.83	23.45	805.50	805.83	24.17	829.50	829.83	24.89	853.50	853.83	25.61
781.84	782.16	23.46	805.84	806.16	24.18	829.84	830.16	24.90	853.84	854.16	25.62
782.17	782.49	23.47	806.17	806.49	24.19	830.17	830.49	24.91	854.17	854.49	25.63
782.50	782.83	23.48	806.50	806.83	24.20	830.50	830.83	24.92	854.50	854.83	25.64
782.84	783.16	23.49	806.84	807.16	24.21	830.84	831.16	24.93	854.84	855.16	25.65
783.17	783.49	23.50	807.17	807.49	24.22	831.17	831.49	24.94	855.17	855.49	25.66
783.50	783.83	23.51	807.50	807.83	24.23	831.50	831.83	24.95	855.50	855.83	25.67
783.84	784.16	23.52	807.84	808.16	24.24	831.84	832.16	24.96	855.84	856.16	25.68
784.17	784.49	23.53	808.17	808.49	24.25	832.17	832.49	24.97	856.17	856.49	25.69
784.50	784.83	23.54	808.50	808.83	24.26	832.50	832.83	24.98	856.50	856.83	25.70
784.84	785.16	23.55	808.84	809.16	24.27	832.84	833.16	24.99	856.84	857.16	25.71
785.17	785.49	23.56	809.17	809.49	24.28	833.17	833.49	25.00	857.17	857.49	25.72
785.50	785.83	23.57	809.50	809.83	24.29	833.50	833.83	25.01	857.50	857.83	25.73
785.84	786.16	23.58	809.84	810.16	24.30	833.84	834.16	25.02	857.84	858.16	25.74
786.17	786.49	23.59	810.17	810.49	24.31	834.17	834.49	25.03	858.17	858.49	25.75
786.50	786.83	23.60	810.50	810.83	24.32	834.50	834.83	25.04	858.50	858.83	25.76
786.84	787.16	23.61	810.84	811.16	24.33	834.84	835.16	25.05	858.84	859.16	25.77
787.17	787.49	23.62	811.17	811.49	24.34	835.17	835.49	25.06	859.17	859.49	25.78
787.50	787.83	23.63	811.50	811.83	24.35	835.50	835.83	25.07	859.50	859.83	25.79
787.84	788.16	23.64	811.84	812.16	24.36	835.84	836.16	25.08	859.84	860.16	25.80
788.17	788.49	23.65	812.17	812.49	24.37	836.17	836.49	25.09	860.17	860.49	25.81
788.50	788.83	23.66	812.50	812.83	24.38	836.50	836.83	25.10	860.50	860.83	25.82
788.84	789.16	23.67	812.84	813.16	24.39	836.84	837.16	25.11	860.84	861.16	25.83
789.17	789.49	23.68	813.17	813.49	24.40	837.17	837.49	25.12	861.17	861.49	25.84
789.50	789.83	23.69	813.50	813.83	24.41	837.50	837.83	25.13	861.50	861.83	25.85
789.84	790.16	23.70	813.84	814.16	24.42	837.84	838.16	25.14	861.84	862.16	25.86
790.17	790.49	23.71	814.17	814.49	24.43	838.17	838.49	25.15	862.17	862.49	25.87
790.50	790.83	23.72	814.50	814.83	24.44	838.50	838.83	25.16	862.50	862.83	25.88
790.84	791.16	23.73	814.84	815.16	24.45	838.84	839.16	25.17	862.84	863.16	25.89
791.17	791.49	23.74	815.17	815.49	24.46	839.17	839.49	25.18	863.17	863.49	25.90
791.50	791.83	23.75	815.50	815.83	24.47	839.50	839.83	25.19	863.50	863.83	25.91
791.84	792.16	23.76	815.84	816.16	24.48	839.84	840.16	25.20	863.84	864.16	25.92

Note: The following are the maximum amounts you can deduct for each pay period.
Remarque : Vous trouverez ci-dessous la cotisation maximale que vous pouvez retenir pour chaque période de paie.

Weekly	Hebdomadaire	22.35	10 pay periods a year	10 périodes de paie par année	116.22
Biweekly	Aux deux semaines	44.70	13 pay periods a year	13 périodes de paie par année	89.40
Semimonthly	Bimensuel	48.42	22 pay periods a year	22 périodes de paie par année	52.83
Monthly	Mensuel	96.85			

APPENDIX 9-3   Unemployment Insurance Premiums (continued)

Unemployment Insurance Premiums – Cotisations à l'assurance-chômage   B-63

Pay Rémunération From – De	To – À	UI premium Cotisation à l'A-C	Pay Rémunération From – De	To – À	UI premium Cotisation à l'A-C	Pay Rémunération From – De	To – À	UI premium Cotisation à l'A-C	Pay Rémunération From – De	To – À	UI premium Cotisation à l'A-C
864.17	864.49	25.93	888.17	888.49	26.65	912.17	912.49	27.37	936.17	936.49	28.09
864.50	864.83	25.94	888.50	888.83	26.66	912.50	912.83	27.38	936.50	936.83	28.10
864.84	865.16	25.95	888.84	889.16	26.67	912.84	913.16	27.39	936.84	937.16	28.11
865.17	865.49	25.96	889.17	889.49	26.68	913.17	913.49	27.40	937.17	937.49	28.12
865.50	865.83	25.97	889.50	889.83	26.69	913.50	913.83	27.41	937.50	937.83	28.13
865.84	866.16	25.98	889.84	890.16	26.70	913.84	914.16	27.42	937.84	938.16	28.14
866.17	866.49	25.99	890.17	890.49	26.71	914.17	914.49	27.43	938.17	938.49	28.15
866.50	866.83	26.00	890.50	890.83	26.72	914.50	914.83	27.44	938.50	938.83	28.16
866.84	867.16	26.01	890.84	891.16	26.73	914.84	915.16	27.45	938.84	939.16	28.17
867.17	867.49	26.02	891.17	891.49	26.74	915.17	915.49	27.46	939.17	939.49	28.18
867.50	867.83	26.03	891.50	891.83	26.75	915.50	915.83	27.47	939.50	939.83	28.19
867.84	868.16	26.04	891.84	892.16	26.76	915.84	916.16	27.48	939.84	940.16	28.20
868.17	868.49	26.05	892.17	892.49	26.77	916.17	916.49	27.49	940.17	940.49	28.21
868.50	868.83	26.06	892.50	892.83	26.78	916.50	916.83	27.50	940.50	940.83	28.22
868.84	869.16	26.07	892.84	893.16	26.79	916.84	917.16	27.51	940.84	941.16	28.23
869.17	869.49	26.08	893.17	893.49	26.80	917.17	917.49	27.52	941.17	941.49	28.24
869.50	869.83	26.09	893.50	893.83	26.81	917.50	917.83	27.53	941.50	941.83	28.25
869.84	870.16	26.10	893.84	894.16	26.82	917.84	918.16	27.54	941.84	942.16	28.26
870.17	870.49	26.11	894.17	894.49	26.83	918.17	918.49	27.55	942.17	942.49	28.27
870.50	870.83	26.12	894.50	894.83	26.84	918.50	918.83	27.56	942.50	942.83	28.28
870.84	871.16	26.13	894.84	895.16	26.85	918.84	919.16	27.57	942.84	943.16	28.29
871.17	871.49	26.14	895.17	895.49	26.86	919.17	919.49	27.58	943.17	943.49	28.30
871.50	871.83	26.15	895.50	895.83	26.87	919.50	919.83	27.59	943.50	943.83	28.31
871.84	872.16	26.16	895.84	896.16	26.88	919.84	920.16	27.60	943.84	944.16	28.32
872.17	872.49	26.17	896.17	896.49	26.89	920.17	920.49	27.61	944.17	944.49	28.33
872.50	872.83	26.18	896.50	896.83	26.90	920.50	920.83	27.62	944.50	944.83	28.34
872.84	873.16	26.19	896.84	897.16	26.91	920.84	921.16	27.63	944.84	945.16	28.35
873.17	873.49	26.20	897.17	897.49	26.92	921.17	921.49	27.64	945.17	945.49	28.36
873.50	873.83	26.21	897.50	897.83	26.93	921.50	921.83	27.65	945.50	945.83	28.37
873.84	874.16	26.22	897.84	898.16	26.94	921.84	922.16	27.66	945.84	946.16	28.38
874.17	874.49	26.23	898.17	898.49	26.95	922.17	922.49	27.67	946.17	946.49	28.39
874.50	874.83	26.24	898.50	898.83	26.96	922.50	922.83	27.68	946.50	946.83	28.40
874.84	875.16	26.25	898.84	899.16	26.97	922.84	923.16	27.69	946.84	947.16	28.41
875.17	875.49	26.26	899.17	899.49	26.98	923.17	923.49	27.70	947.17	947.49	28.42
875.50	875.83	26.27	899.50	899.83	26.99	923.50	923.83	27.71	947.50	947.83	28.43
875.84	876.16	26.28	899.84	900.16	27.00	923.84	924.16	27.72	947.84	948.16	28.44
876.17	876.49	26.29	900.17	900.49	27.01	924.17	924.49	27.73	948.17	948.49	28.45
876.50	876.83	26.30	900.50	900.83	27.02	924.50	924.83	27.74	948.50	948.83	28.46
876.84	877.16	26.31	900.84	901.16	27.03	924.84	925.16	27.75	948.84	949.16	28.47
877.17	877.49	26.32	901.17	901.49	27.04	925.17	925.49	27.76	949.17	949.49	28.48
877.50	877.83	26.33	901.50	901.83	27.05	925.50	925.83	27.77	949.50	949.83	28.49
877.84	878.16	26.34	901.84	902.16	27.06	925.84	926.16	27.78	949.84	950.16	28.50
878.17	878.49	26.35	902.17	902.49	27.07	926.17	926.49	27.79	950.17	950.49	28.51
878.50	878.83	26.36	902.50	902.83	27.08	926.50	926.83	27.80	950.50	950.83	28.52
878.84	879.16	26.37	902.84	903.16	27.09	926.84	927.16	27.81	950.84	951.16	28.53
879.17	879.49	26.38	903.17	903.49	27.10	927.17	927.49	27.82	951.17	951.49	28.54
879.50	879.83	26.39	903.50	903.83	27.11	927.50	927.83	27.83	951.50	951.83	28.55
879.84	880.16	26.40	903.84	904.16	27.12	927.84	928.16	27.84	951.84	952.16	28.56
880.17	880.49	26.41	904.17	904.49	27.13	928.17	928.49	27.85	952.17	952.49	28.57
880.50	880.83	26.42	904.50	904.83	27.14	928.50	928.83	27.86	952.50	952.83	28.58
880.84	881.16	26.43	904.84	905.16	27.15	928.84	929.16	27.87	952.84	953.16	28.59
881.17	881.49	26.44	905.17	905.49	27.16	929.17	929.49	27.88	953.17	953.49	28.60
881.50	881.83	26.45	905.50	905.83	27.17	929.50	929.83	27.89	953.50	953.83	28.61
881.84	882.16	26.46	905.84	906.16	27.18	929.84	930.16	27.90	953.84	954.16	28.62
882.17	882.49	26.47	906.17	906.49	27.19	930.17	930.49	27.91	954.17	954.49	28.63
882.50	882.83	26.48	906.50	906.83	27.20	930.50	930.83	27.92	954.50	954.83	28.64
882.84	883.16	26.49	906.84	907.16	27.21	930.84	931.16	27.93	954.84	955.16	28.65
883.17	883.49	26.50	907.17	907.49	27.22	931.17	931.49	27.94	955.17	955.49	28.66
883.50	883.83	26.51	907.50	907.83	27.23	931.50	931.83	27.95	955.50	955.83	28.67
883.84	884.16	26.52	907.84	908.16	27.24	931.84	932.16	27.96	955.84	956.16	28.68
884.17	884.49	26.53	908.17	908.49	27.25	932.17	932.49	27.97	956.17	956.49	28.69
884.50	884.83	26.54	908.50	908.83	27.26	932.50	932.83	27.98	956.50	956.83	28.70
884.84	885.16	26.55	908.84	909.16	27.27	932.84	933.16	27.99	956.84	957.16	28.71
885.17	885.49	26.56	909.17	909.49	27.28	933.17	933.49	28.00	957.17	957.49	28.72
885.50	885.83	26.57	909.50	909.83	27.29	933.50	933.83	28.01	957.50	957.83	28.73
885.84	886.16	26.58	909.84	910.16	27.30	933.84	934.16	28.02	957.84	958.16	28.74
886.17	886.49	26.59	910.17	910.49	27.31	934.17	934.49	28.03	958.17	958.49	28.75
886.50	886.83	26.60	910.50	910.83	27.32	934.50	934.83	28.04	958.50	958.83	28.76
886.84	887.16	26.61	910.84	911.16	27.33	934.84	935.16	28.05	958.84	959.16	28.77
887.17	887.49	26.62	911.17	911.49	27.34	935.17	935.49	28.06	959.17	959.49	28.78
887.50	887.83	26.63	911.50	911.83	27.35	935.50	935.83	28.07	959.50	959.83	28.79
887.84	888.16	26.64	911.84	912.16	27.36	935.84	936.16	28.08	959.84	960.16	28.80

Note: The following are the maximum amounts you can deduct for each pay period.
Remarque : Vous trouverez ci-dessous la cotisation maximale que vous pouvez retenir pour chaque période de paie.

Weekly	Hebdomadaire	22.35	10 pay periods a year	10 périodes de paie par année	116.22
Biweekly	Aux deux semaines	44.70	13 pay periods a year	13 périodes de paie par année	89.40
Semimonthly	Bimensuel	48.42	22 pay periods a year	22 périodes de paie par année	52.83
Monthly	Mensuel	96.85			

APPENDIX 9-3   **Unemployment Insurance Premiums (continued)**

B-64   Unemployment Insurance Premiums – Cotisations à l'assurance-chômage

Pay Rémunération From – De	To – À	UI premium Cotisation à l'A-C	Pay Rémunération From – De	To – À	UI premium Cotisation à l'A-C	Pay Rémunération From – De	To – À	UI premium Cotisation à l'A-C	Pay Rémunération From – De	To – À	UI premium Cotisation à l'A-C
960.17	960.49	28.81	984.17	984.49	29.53	1008.17	1008.49	30.25	1032.17	1032.49	30.97
960.50	960.83	28.82	984.50	984.83	29.54	1008.50	1008.83	30.26	1032.50	1032.83	30.98
960.84	961.16	28.83	984.84	985.16	29.55	1008.84	1009.16	30.27	1032.84	1033.16	30.99
961.17	961.49	28.84	985.17	985.49	29.56	1009.17	1009.49	30.28	1033.17	1033.49	31.00
961.50	961.83	28.85	985.50	985.83	29.57	1009.50	1009.83	30.29	1033.50	1033.83	31.01
961.84	962.16	28.86	985.84	986.16	29.58	1009.84	1010.16	30.30	1033.84	1034.16	31.02
962.17	962.49	28.87	986.17	986.49	29.59	1010.17	1010.49	30.31	1034.17	1034.49	31.03
962.50	962.83	28.88	986.50	986.83	29.60	1010.50	1010.83	30.32	1034.50	1034.83	31.04
962.84	963.16	28.89	986.84	987.16	29.61	1010.84	1011.16	30.33	1034.84	1035.16	31.05
963.17	963.49	28.90	987.17	987.49	29.62	1011.17	1011.49	30.34	1035.17	1035.49	31.06
963.50	963.83	28.91	987.50	987.83	29.63	1011.50	1011.83	30.35	1035.50	1035.83	31.07
963.84	964.16	28.92	987.84	988.16	29.64	1011.84	1012.16	30.36	1035.84	1036.16	31.08
964.17	964.49	28.93	988.17	988.49	29.65	1012.17	1012.49	30.37	1036.17	1036.49	31.09
964.50	964.83	28.94	988.50	988.83	29.66	1012.50	1012.83	30.38	1036.50	1036.83	31.10
964.84	965.16	28.95	988.84	989.16	29.67	1012.84	1013.16	30.39	1036.84	1037.16	31.11
965.17	965.49	28.96	989.17	989.49	29.68	1013.17	1013.49	30.40	1037.17	1037.49	31.12
965.50	965.83	28.97	989.50	989.83	29.69	1013.50	1013.83	30.41	1037.50	1037.83	31.13
965.84	966.16	28.98	989.84	990.16	29.70	1013.84	1014.16	30.42	1037.84	1038.16	31.14
966.17	966.49	28.99	990.17	990.49	29.71	1014.17	1014.49	30.43	1038.17	1038.49	31.15
966.50	966.83	29.00	990.50	990.83	29.72	1014.50	1014.83	30.44	1038.50	1038.83	31.16
966.84	967.16	29.01	990.84	991.16	29.73	1014.84	1015.16	30.45	1038.84	1039.16	31.17
967.17	967.49	29.02	991.17	991.49	29.74	1015.17	1015.49	30.46	1039.17	1039.49	31.18
967.50	967.83	29.03	991.50	991.83	29.75	1015.50	1015.83	30.47	1039.50	1039.83	31.19
967.84	968.16	29.04	991.84	992.16	29.76	1015.84	1016.16	30.48	1039.84	1040.16	31.20
968.17	968.49	29.05	992.17	992.49	29.77	1016.17	1016.49	30.49	1040.17	1040.49	31.21
968.50	968.83	29.06	992.50	992.83	29.78	1016.50	1016.83	30.50	1040.50	1040.83	31.22
968.84	969.16	29.07	992.84	993.16	29.79	1016.84	1017.16	30.51	1040.84	1041.16	31.23
969.17	969.49	29.08	993.17	993.49	29.80	1017.17	1017.49	30.52	1041.17	1041.49	31.24
969.50	969.83	29.09	993.50	993.83	29.81	1017.50	1017.83	30.53	1041.50	1041.83	31.25
969.84	970.16	29.10	993.84	994.16	29.82	1017.84	1018.16	30.54	1041.84	1042.16	31.26
970.17	970.49	29.11	994.17	994.49	29.83	1018.17	1018.49	30.55	1042.17	1042.49	31.27
970.50	970.83	29.12	994.50	994.83	29.84	1018.50	1018.83	30.56	1042.50	1042.83	31.28
970.84	971.16	29.13	994.84	995.16	29.85	1018.84	1019.16	30.57	1042.84	1043.16	31.29
971.17	971.49	29.14	995.17	995.49	29.86	1019.17	1019.49	30.58	1043.17	1043.49	31.30
971.50	971.83	29.15	995.50	995.83	29.87	1019.50	1019.83	30.59	1043.50	1043.83	31.31
971.84	972.16	29.16	995.84	996.16	29.88	1019.84	1020.16	30.60	1043.84	1044.16	31.32
972.17	972.49	29.17	996.17	996.49	29.89	1020.17	1020.49	30.61	1044.17	1044.49	31.33
972.50	972.83	29.18	996.50	996.83	29.90	1020.50	1020.83	30.62	1044.50	1044.83	31.34
972.84	973.16	29.19	996.84	997.16	29.91	1020.84	1021.16	30.63	1044.84	1045.16	31.35
973.17	973.49	29.20	997.17	997.49	29.92	1021.17	1021.49	30.64	1045.17	1045.49	31.36
973.50	973.83	29.21	997.50	997.83	29.93	1021.50	1021.83	30.65	1045.50	1045.83	31.37
973.84	974.16	29.22	997.84	998.16	29.94	1021.84	1022.16	30.66	1045.84	1046.16	31.38
974.17	974.49	29.23	998.17	998.49	29.95	1022.17	1022.49	30.67	1046.17	1046.49	31.39
974.50	974.83	29.24	998.50	998.83	29.96	1022.50	1022.83	30.68	1046.50	1046.83	31.40
974.84	975.16	29.25	998.84	999.16	29.97	1022.84	1023.16	30.69	1046.84	1047.16	31.41
975.17	975.49	29.26	999.17	999.49	29.98	1023.17	1023.49	30.70	1047.17	1047.49	31.42
975.50	975.83	29.27	999.50	999.83	29.99	1023.50	1023.83	30.71	1047.50	1047.83	31.43
975.84	976.16	29.28	999.84	1000.16	30.00	1023.84	1024.16	30.72	1047.84	1048.16	31.44
976.17	976.49	29.29	1000.17	1000.49	30.01	1024.17	1024.49	30.73	1048.17	1048.49	31.45
976.50	976.83	29.30	1000.50	1000.83	30.02	1024.50	1024.83	30.74	1048.50	1048.83	31.46
976.84	977.16	29.31	1000.84	1001.16	30.03	1024.84	1025.16	30.75	1048.84	1049.16	31.47
977.17	977.49	29.32	1001.17	1001.49	30.04	1025.17	1025.49	30.76	1049.17	1049.49	31.48
977.50	977.83	29.33	1001.50	1001.83	30.05	1025.50	1025.83	30.77	1049.50	1049.83	31.49
977.84	978.16	29.34	1001.84	1002.16	30.06	1025.84	1026.16	30.78	1049.84	1050.16	31.50
978.17	978.49	29.35	1002.17	1002.49	30.07	1026.17	1026.49	30.79	1050.17	1050.49	31.51
978.50	978.83	29.36	1002.50	1002.83	30.08	1026.50	1026.83	30.80	1050.50	1050.83	31.52
978.84	979.16	29.37	1002.84	1003.16	30.09	1026.84	1027.16	30.81	1050.84	1051.16	31.53
979.17	979.49	29.38	1003.17	1003.49	30.10	1027.17	1027.49	30.82	1051.17	1051.49	31.54
979.50	979.83	29.39	1003.50	1003.83	30.11	1027.50	1027.83	30.83	1051.50	1051.83	31.55
979.84	980.16	29.40	1003.84	1004.16	30.12	1027.84	1028.16	30.84	1051.84	1052.16	31.56
980.17	980.49	29.41	1004.17	1004.49	30.13	1028.17	1028.49	30.85	1052.17	1052.49	31.57
980.50	980.83	29.42	1004.50	1004.83	30.14	1028.50	1028.83	30.86	1052.50	1052.83	31.58
980.84	981.16	29.43	1004.84	1005.16	30.15	1028.84	1029.16	30.87	1052.84	1053.16	31.59
981.17	981.49	29.44	1005.17	1005.49	30.16	1029.17	1029.49	30.88	1053.17	1053.49	31.60
981.50	981.83	29.45	1005.50	1005.83	30.17	1029.50	1029.83	30.89	1053.50	1053.83	31.61
981.84	982.16	29.46	1005.84	1006.16	30.18	1029.84	1030.16	30.90	1053.84	1054.16	31.62
982.17	982.49	29.47	1006.17	1006.49	30.19	1030.17	1030.49	30.91	1054.17	1054.49	31.63
982.50	982.83	29.48	1006.50	1006.83	30.20	1030.50	1030.83	30.92	1054.50	1054.83	31.64
982.84	983.16	29.49	1006.84	1007.16	30.21	1030.84	1031.16	30.93	1054.84	1055.16	31.65
983.17	983.49	29.50	1007.17	1007.49	30.22	1031.17	1031.49	30.94	1055.17	1055.49	31.66
983.50	983.83	29.51	1007.50	1007.83	30.23	1031.50	1031.83	30.95	1055.50	1055.83	31.67
983.84	984.16	29.52	1007.84	1008.16	30.24	1031.84	1032.16	30.96	1055.84	1056.16	31.68

Note: The following are the maximum amounts you can deduct for each pay period.
Remarque : Vous trouverez ci-dessous la cotisation maximale que vous pouvez retenir pour chaque période de paie.

Weekly	Hebdomadaire	**22.35**	10 pay periods a year	10 périodes de paie par année	**116.22**
Biweekly	Aux deux semaines	**44.70**	13 pay periods a year	13 périodes de paie par année	**89.40**
Semimonthly	Bimensuel	**48.42**	22 pay periods a year	22 périodes de paie par année	**52.83**
Monthly	Mensuel	**96.85**			

APPENDIX 9-3   Unemployment Insurance Premiums (continued)

Unemployment Insurance Premiums — Cotisations à l'assurance-chômage   B-65

Pay Rémunération From – De	To – À	UI premium Cotisation à l'A-C	Pay Rémunération From – De	To – À	UI premium Cotisation à l'A-C	Pay Rémunération From – De	To – À	UI premium Cotisation à l'A-C	Pay Rémunération From – De	To – À	UI premium Cotisation à l'A-C
1056.17	1056.49	31.69	1080.17	1080.49	32.41	1104.17	1104.49	33.13	1128.17	1128.49	33.85
1056.50	1056.83	31.70	1080.50	1080.83	32.42	1104.50	1104.83	33.14	1128.50	1128.83	33.86
1056.84	1057.16	31.71	1080.84	1081.16	32.43	1104.84	1105.16	33.15	1128.84	1129.16	33.87
1057.17	1057.49	31.72	1081.17	1081.49	32.44	1105.17	1105.49	33.16	1129.17	1129.49	33.88
1057.50	1057.83	31.73	1081.50	1081.83	32.45	1105.50	1105.83	33.17	1129.50	1129.83	33.89
1057.84	1058.16	31.74	1081.84	1082.16	32.46	1105.84	1106.16	33.18	1129.84	1130.16	33.90
1058.17	1058.49	31.75	1082.17	1082.49	32.47	1106.17	1106.49	33.19	1130.17	1130.49	33.91
1058.50	1058.83	31.76	1082.50	1082.83	32.48	1106.50	1106.83	33.20	1130.50	1130.83	33.92
1058.84	1059.16	31.77	1082.84	1083.16	32.49	1106.84	1107.16	33.21	1130.84	1131.16	33.93
1059.17	1059.49	31.78	1083.17	1083.49	32.50	1107.17	1107.49	33.22	1131.17	1131.49	33.94
1059.50	1059.83	31.79	1083.50	1083.83	32.51	1107.50	1107.83	33.23	1131.50	1131.83	33.95
1059.84	1060.16	31.80	1083.84	1084.16	32.52	1107.84	1108.16	33.24	1131.84	1132.16	33.96
1060.17	1060.49	31.81	1084.17	1084.49	32.53	1108.17	1108.49	33.25	1132.17	1132.49	33.97
1060.50	1060.83	31.82	1084.50	1084.83	32.54	1108.50	1108.83	33.26	1132.50	1132.83	33.98
1060.84	1061.16	31.83	1084.84	1085.16	32.55	1108.84	1109.16	33.27	1132.84	1133.16	33.99
1061.17	1061.49	31.84	1085.17	1085.49	32.56	1109.17	1109.49	33.28	1133.17	1133.49	34.00
1061.50	1061.83	31.85	1085.50	1085.83	32.57	1109.50	1109.83	33.29	1133.50	1133.83	34.01
1061.84	1062.16	31.86	1085.84	1086.16	32.58	1109.84	1110.16	33.30	1133.84	1134.16	34.02
1062.17	1062.49	31.87	1086.17	1086.49	32.59	1110.17	1110.49	33.31	1134.17	1134.49	34.03
1062.50	1062.83	31.88	1086.50	1086.83	32.60	1110.50	1110.83	33.32	1134.50	1134.83	34.04
1062.84	1063.16	31.89	1086.84	1087.16	32.61	1110.84	1111.16	33.33	1134.84	1135.16	34.05
1063.17	1063.49	31.90	1087.17	1087.49	32.62	1111.17	1111.49	33.34	1135.17	1135.49	34.06
1063.50	1063.83	31.91	1087.50	1087.83	32.63	1111.50	1111.83	33.35	1135.50	1135.83	34.07
1063.84	1064.16	31.92	1087.84	1088.16	32.64	1111.84	1112.16	33.36	1135.84	1136.16	34.08
1064.17	1064.49	31.93	1088.17	1088.49	32.65	1112.17	1112.49	33.37	1136.17	1136.49	34.09
1064.50	1064.83	31.94	1088.50	1088.83	32.66	1112.50	1112.83	33.38	1136.50	1136.83	34.10
1064.84	1065.16	31.95	1088.84	1089.16	32.67	1112.84	1113.16	33.39	1136.84	1137.16	34.11
1065.17	1065.49	31.96	1089.17	1089.49	32.68	1113.17	1113.49	33.40	1137.17	1137.49	34.12
1065.50	1065.83	31.97	1089.50	1089.83	32.69	1113.50	1113.83	33.41	1137.50	1137.83	34.13
1065.84	1066.16	31.98	1089.84	1090.16	32.70	1113.84	1114.16	33.42	1137.84	1138.16	34.14
1066.17	1066.49	31.99	1090.17	1090.49	32.71	1114.17	1114.49	33.43	1138.17	1138.49	34.15
1066.50	1066.83	32.00	1090.50	1090.83	32.72	1114.50	1114.83	33.44	1138.50	1138.83	34.16
1066.84	1067.16	32.01	1090.84	1091.16	32.73	1114.84	1115.16	33.45	1138.84	1139.16	34.17
1067.17	1067.49	32.02	1091.17	1091.49	32.74	1115.17	1115.49	33.46	1139.17	1139.49	34.18
1067.50	1067.83	32.03	1091.50	1091.83	32.75	1115.50	1115.83	33.47	1139.50	1139.83	34.19
1067.84	1068.16	32.04	1091.84	1092.16	32.76	1115.84	1116.16	33.48	1139.84	1140.16	34.20
1068.17	1068.49	32.05	1092.17	1092.49	32.77	1116.17	1116.49	33.49	1140.17	1140.49	34.21
1068.50	1068.83	32.06	1092.50	1092.83	32.78	1116.50	1116.83	33.50	1140.50	1140.83	34.22
1068.84	1069.16	32.07	1092.84	1093.16	32.79	1116.84	1117.16	33.51	1140.84	1141.16	34.23
1069.17	1069.49	32.08	1093.17	1093.49	32.80	1117.17	1117.49	33.52	1141.17	1141.49	34.24
1069.50	1069.83	32.09	1093.50	1093.83	32.81	1117.50	1117.83	33.53	1141.50	1141.83	34.25
1069.84	1070.16	32.10	1093.84	1094.16	32.82	1117.84	1118.16	33.54	1141.84	1142.16	34.26
1070.17	1070.49	32.11	1094.17	1094.49	32.83	1118.17	1118.49	33.55	1142.17	1142.49	34.27
1070.50	1070.83	32.12	1094.50	1094.83	32.84	1118.50	1118.83	33.56	1142.50	1142.83	34.28
1070.84	1071.16	32.13	1094.84	1095.16	32.85	1118.84	1119.16	33.57	1142.84	1143.16	34.29
1071.17	1071.49	32.14	1095.17	1095.49	32.86	1119.17	1119.49	33.58	1143.17	1143.49	34.30
1071.50	1071.83	32.15	1095.50	1095.83	32.87	1119.50	1119.83	33.59	1143.50	1143.83	34.31
1071.84	1072.16	32.16	1095.84	1096.16	32.88	1119.84	1120.16	33.60	1143.84	1144.16	34.32
1072.17	1072.49	32.17	1096.17	1096.49	32.89	1120.17	1120.49	33.61	1144.17	1144.49	34.33
1072.50	1072.83	32.18	1096.50	1096.83	32.90	1120.50	1120.83	33.62	1144.50	1144.83	34.34
1072.84	1073.16	32.19	1096.84	1097.16	32.91	1120.84	1121.16	33.63	1144.84	1145.16	34.35
1073.17	1073.49	32.20	1097.17	1097.49	32.92	1121.17	1121.49	33.64	1145.17	1145.49	34.36
1073.50	1073.83	32.21	1097.50	1097.83	32.93	1121.50	1121.83	33.65	1145.50	1145.83	34.37
1073.84	1074.16	32.22	1097.84	1098.16	32.94	1121.84	1122.16	33.66	1145.84	1146.16	34.38
1074.17	1074.49	32.23	1098.17	1098.49	32.95	1122.17	1122.49	33.67	1146.17	1146.49	34.39
1074.50	1074.83	32.24	1098.50	1098.83	32.96	1122.50	1122.83	33.68	1146.50	1146.83	34.40
1074.84	1075.16	32.25	1098.84	1099.16	32.97	1122.84	1123.16	33.69	1146.84	1147.16	34.41
1075.17	1075.49	32.26	1099.17	1099.49	32.98	1123.17	1123.49	33.70	1147.17	1147.49	34.42
1075.50	1075.83	32.27	1099.50	1099.83	32.99	1123.50	1123.83	33.71	1147.50	1147.83	34.43
1075.84	1076.16	32.28	1099.84	1100.16	33.00	1123.84	1124.16	33.72	1147.84	1148.16	34.44
1076.17	1076.49	32.29	1100.17	1100.49	33.01	1124.17	1124.49	33.73	1148.17	1148.49	34.45
1076.50	1076.83	32.30	1100.50	1100.83	33.02	1124.50	1124.83	33.74	1148.50	1148.83	34.46
1076.84	1077.16	32.31	1100.84	1101.16	33.03	1124.84	1125.16	33.75	1148.84	1149.16	34.47
1077.17	1077.49	32.32	1101.17	1101.49	33.04	1125.17	1125.49	33.76	1149.17	1149.49	34.48
1077.50	1077.83	32.33	1101.50	1101.83	33.05	1125.50	1125.83	33.77	1149.50	1149.83	34.49
1077.84	1078.16	32.34	1101.84	1102.16	33.06	1125.84	1126.16	33.78	1149.84	1150.16	34.50
1078.17	1078.49	32.35	1102.17	1102.49	33.07	1126.17	1126.49	33.79	1150.17	1150.49	34.51
1078.50	1078.83	32.36	1102.50	1102.83	33.08	1126.50	1126.83	33.80	1150.50	1150.83	34.52
1078.84	1079.16	32.37	1102.84	1103.16	33.09	1126.84	1127.16	33.81	1150.84	1151.16	34.53
1079.17	1079.49	32.38	1103.17	1103.49	33.10	1127.17	1127.49	33.82	1151.17	1151.49	34.54
1079.50	1079.83	32.39	1103.50	1103.83	33.11	1127.50	1127.83	33.83	1151.50	1151.83	34.55
1079.84	1080.16	32.40	1103.84	1104.16	33.12	1127.84	1128.16	33.84	1151.84	1152.16	34.56

Note: The following are the maximum amounts you can deduct for each pay period.
Remarque : Vous trouverez ci-dessous la cotisation maximale que vous pouvez retenir pour chaque période de paie.

Weekly	Hebdomadaire	22.35	10 pay periods a year	10 périodes de paie par année	116.22
Biweekly	Aux deux semaines	44.70	13 pay periods a year	13 périodes de paie par année	89.40
Semimonthly	Bimensuel	48.42	22 pay periods a year	22 périodes de paie par année	52.83
Monthly	Mensuel	96.85			

APPENDIX 9-3   Unemployment Insurance Premiums (continued)

B-66   Unemployment Insurance Premiums – Cotisations à l'assurance-chômage

Pay Rémunération From – De To – À	UI premium Cotisation à l'A-C	Pay Rémunération From – De To – À	UI premium Cotisation à l'A-C	Pay Rémunération From – De To – À	UI premium Cotisation à l'A-C	Pay Rémunération From – De To – À	UI premium Cotisation à l'A-C
1152.17 - 1152.49	34.57	1176.17 - 1176.49	35.29	1200.17 - 1200.49	36.01	1224.17 - 1224.49	36.73
1152.50 - 1152.83	34.58	1176.50 - 1176.83	35.30	1200.50 - 1200.83	36.02	1224.50 - 1224.83	36.74
1152.84 - 1153.16	34.59	1176.84 - 1177.16	35.31	1200.84 - 1201.16	36.03	1224.84 - 1225.16	36.75
1153.17 - 1153.49	34.60	1177.17 - 1177.49	35.32	1201.17 - 1201.49	36.04	1225.17 - 1225.49	36.76
1153.50 - 1153.83	34.61	1177.50 - 1177.83	35.33	1201.50 - 1201.83	36.05	1225.50 - 1225.83	36.77
1153.84 - 1154.16	34.62	1177.84 - 1178.16	35.34	1201.84 - 1202.16	36.06	1225.84 - 1226.16	36.78
1154.17 - 1154.49	34.63	1178.17 - 1178.49	35.35	1202.17 - 1202.49	36.07	1226.17 - 1226.49	36.79
1154.50 - 1154.83	34.64	1178.50 - 1178.83	35.36	1202.50 - 1202.83	36.08	1226.50 - 1226.83	36.80
1154.84 - 1155.16	34.65	1178.84 - 1179.16	35.37	1202.84 - 1203.16	36.09	1226.84 - 1227.16	36.81
1155.17 - 1155.49	34.66	1179.17 - 1179.49	35.38	1203.17 - 1203.49	36.10	1227.17 - 1227.49	36.82
1155.50 - 1155.83	34.67	1179.50 - 1179.83	35.39	1203.50 - 1203.83	36.11	1227.50 - 1227.83	36.83
1155.84 - 1156.16	34.68	1179.84 - 1180.16	35.40	1203.84 - 1204.16	36.12	1227.84 - 1228.16	36.84
1156.17 - 1156.49	34.69	1180.17 - 1180.49	35.41	1204.17 - 1204.49	36.13	1228.17 - 1228.49	36.85
1156.50 - 1156.83	34.70	1180.50 - 1180.83	35.42	1204.50 - 1204.83	36.14	1228.50 - 1228.83	36.86
1156.84 - 1157.16	34.71	1180.84 - 1181.16	35.43	1204.84 - 1205.16	36.15	1228.84 - 1229.16	36.87
1157.17 - 1157.49	34.72	1181.17 - 1181.49	35.44	1205.17 - 1205.49	36.16	1229.17 - 1229.49	36.88
1157.50 - 1157.83	34.73	1181.50 - 1181.83	35.45	1205.50 - 1205.83	36.17	1229.50 - 1229.83	36.89
1157.84 - 1158.16	34.74	1181.84 - 1182.16	35.46	1205.84 - 1206.16	36.18	1229.84 - 1230.16	36.90
1158.17 - 1158.49	34.75	1182.17 - 1182.49	35.47	1206.17 - 1206.49	36.19	1230.17 - 1230.49	36.91
1158.50 - 1158.83	34.76	1182.50 - 1182.83	35.48	1206.50 - 1206.83	36.20	1230.50 - 1230.83	36.92
1158.84 - 1159.16	34.77	1182.84 - 1183.16	35.49	1206.84 - 1207.16	36.21	1230.84 - 1231.16	36.93
1159.17 - 1159.49	34.78	1183.17 - 1183.49	35.50	1207.17 - 1207.49	36.22	1231.17 - 1231.49	36.94
1159.50 - 1159.83	34.79	1183.50 - 1183.83	35.51	1207.50 - 1207.83	36.23	1231.50 - 1231.83	36.95
1159.84 - 1160.16	34.80	1183.84 - 1184.16	35.52	1207.84 - 1208.16	36.24	1231.84 - 1232.16	36.96
1160.17 - 1160.49	34.81	1184.17 - 1184.49	35.53	1208.17 - 1208.49	36.25	1232.17 - 1232.49	36.97
1160.50 - 1160.83	34.82	1184.50 - 1184.83	35.54	1208.50 - 1208.83	36.26	1232.50 - 1232.83	36.98
1160.84 - 1161.16	34.83	1184.84 - 1185.16	35.55	1208.84 - 1209.16	36.27	1232.84 - 1233.16	36.99
1161.17 - 1161.49	34.84	1185.17 - 1185.49	35.56	1209.17 - 1209.49	36.28	1233.17 - 1233.49	37.00
1161.50 - 1161.83	34.85	1185.50 - 1185.83	35.57	1209.50 - 1209.83	36.29	1233.50 - 1233.83	37.01
1161.84 - 1162.16	34.86	1185.84 - 1186.16	35.58	1209.84 - 1210.16	36.30	1233.84 - 1234.16	37.02
1162.17 - 1162.49	34.87	1186.17 - 1186.49	35.59	1210.17 - 1210.49	36.31	1234.17 - 1234.49	37.03
1162.50 - 1162.83	34.88	1186.50 - 1186.83	35.60	1210.50 - 1210.83	36.32	1234.50 - 1234.83	37.04
1162.84 - 1163.16	34.89	1186.84 - 1187.16	35.61	1210.84 - 1211.16	36.33	1234.84 - 1235.16	37.05
1163.17 - 1163.49	34.90	1187.17 - 1187.49	35.62	1211.17 - 1211.49	36.34	1235.17 - 1235.49	37.06
1163.50 - 1163.83	34.91	1187.50 - 1187.83	35.63	1211.50 - 1211.83	36.35	1235.50 - 1235.83	37.07
1163.84 - 1164.16	34.92	1187.84 - 1188.16	35.64	1211.84 - 1212.16	36.36	1235.84 - 1236.16	37.08
1164.17 - 1164.49	34.93	1188.17 - 1188.49	35.65	1212.17 - 1212.49	36.37	1236.17 - 1236.49	37.09
1164.50 - 1164.83	34.94	1188.50 - 1188.83	35.66	1212.50 - 1212.83	36.38	1236.50 - 1236.83	37.10
1164.84 - 1165.16	34.95	1188.84 - 1189.16	35.67	1212.84 - 1213.16	36.39	1236.84 - 1237.16	37.11
1165.17 - 1165.49	34.96	1189.17 - 1189.49	35.68	1213.17 - 1213.49	36.40	1237.17 - 1237.49	37.12
1165.50 - 1165.83	34.97	1189.50 - 1189.83	35.69	1213.50 - 1213.83	36.41	1237.50 - 1237.83	37.13
1165.84 - 1166.16	34.98	1189.84 - 1190.16	35.70	1213.84 - 1214.16	36.42	1237.84 - 1238.16	37.14
1166.17 - 1166.49	34.99	1190.17 - 1190.49	35.71	1214.17 - 1214.49	36.43	1238.17 - 1238.49	37.15
1166.50 - 1166.83	35.00	1190.50 - 1190.83	35.72	1214.50 - 1214.83	36.44	1238.50 - 1238.83	37.16
1166.84 - 1167.16	35.01	1190.84 - 1191.16	35.73	1214.84 - 1215.16	36.45	1238.84 - 1239.16	37.17
1167.17 - 1167.49	35.02	1191.17 - 1191.49	35.74	1215.17 - 1215.49	36.46	1239.17 - 1239.49	37.18
1167.50 - 1167.83	35.03	1191.50 - 1191.83	35.75	1215.50 - 1215.83	36.47	1239.50 - 1239.83	37.19
1167.84 - 1168.16	35.04	1191.84 - 1192.16	35.76	1215.84 - 1216.16	36.48	1239.84 - 1240.16	37.20
1168.17 - 1168.49	35.05	1192.17 - 1192.49	35.77	1216.17 - 1216.49	36.49	1240.17 - 1240.49	37.21
1168.50 - 1168.83	35.06	1192.50 - 1192.83	35.78	1216.50 - 1216.83	36.50	1240.50 - 1240.83	37.22
1168.84 - 1169.16	35.07	1192.84 - 1193.16	35.79	1216.84 - 1217.16	36.51	1240.84 - 1241.16	37.23
1169.17 - 1169.49	35.08	1193.17 - 1193.49	35.80	1217.17 - 1217.49	36.52	1241.17 - 1241.49	37.24
1169.50 - 1169.83	35.09	1193.50 - 1193.83	35.81	1217.50 - 1217.83	36.53	1241.50 - 1241.83	37.25
1169.84 - 1170.16	35.10	1193.84 - 1194.16	35.82	1217.84 - 1218.16	36.54	1241.84 - 1242.16	37.26
1170.17 - 1170.49	35.11	1194.17 - 1194.49	35.83	1218.17 - 1218.49	36.55	1242.17 - 1242.49	37.27
1170.50 - 1170.83	35.12	1194.50 - 1194.83	35.84	1218.50 - 1218.83	36.56	1242.50 - 1242.83	37.28
1170.84 - 1171.16	35.13	1194.84 - 1195.16	35.85	1218.84 - 1219.16	36.57	1242.84 - 1243.16	37.29
1171.17 - 1171.49	35.14	1195.17 - 1195.49	35.86	1219.17 - 1219.49	36.58	1243.17 - 1243.49	37.30
1171.50 - 1171.83	35.15	1195.50 - 1195.83	35.87	1219.50 - 1219.83	36.59	1243.50 - 1243.83	37.31
1171.84 - 1172.16	35.16	1195.84 - 1196.16	35.88	1219.84 - 1220.16	36.60	1243.84 - 1244.16	37.32
1172.17 - 1172.49	35.17	1196.17 - 1196.49	35.89	1220.17 - 1220.49	36.61	1244.17 - 1244.49	37.33
1172.50 - 1172.83	35.18	1196.50 - 1196.83	35.90	1220.50 - 1220.83	36.62	1244.50 - 1244.83	37.34
1172.84 - 1173.16	35.19	1196.84 - 1197.16	35.91	1220.84 - 1221.16	36.63	1244.84 - 1245.16	37.35
1173.17 - 1173.49	35.20	1197.17 - 1197.49	35.92	1221.17 - 1221.49	36.64	1245.17 - 1245.49	37.36
1173.50 - 1173.83	35.21	1197.50 - 1197.83	35.93	1221.50 - 1221.83	36.65	1245.50 - 1245.83	37.37
1173.84 - 1174.16	35.22	1197.84 - 1198.16	35.94	1221.84 - 1222.16	36.66	1245.84 - 1246.16	37.38
1174.17 - 1174.49	35.23	1198.17 - 1198.49	35.95	1222.17 - 1222.49	36.67	1246.17 - 1246.49	37.39
1174.50 - 1174.83	35.24	1198.50 - 1198.83	35.96	1222.50 - 1222.83	36.68	1246.50 - 1246.83	37.40
1174.84 - 1175.16	35.25	1198.84 - 1199.16	35.97	1222.84 - 1223.16	36.69	1246.84 - 1247.16	37.41
1175.17 - 1175.49	35.26	1199.17 - 1199.49	35.98	1223.17 - 1223.49	36.70	1247.17 - 1247.49	37.42
1175.50 - 1175.83	35.27	1199.50 - 1199.83	35.99	1223.50 - 1223.83	36.71	1247.50 - 1247.83	37.43
1175.84 - 1176.16	35.28	1199.84 - 1200.16	36.00	1223.84 - 1224.16	36.72	1247.84 - 1248.16	37.44

Note: The following are the maximum amounts you can deduct for each pay period.
Remarque : Vous trouverez ci-dessous la cotisation maximale que vous pouvez retenir pour chaque période de paie.

Weekly	Hebdomadaire	22.35	10 pay periods a year	10 périodes de paie par année	116.22
Biweekly	Aux deux semaines	44.70	13 pay periods a year	13 périodes de paie par année	89.40
Semimonthly	Bimensuel	48.42	22 pay periods a year	22 périodes de paie par année	52.83
Monthly	Mensuel	96.85			

APPENDIX 9-3   Unemployment Insurance Premiums (continued)

ACCOUNTING RECALL
A Cumulative Approach

THIS EXAM REVIEWS CHAPTERS 1 THROUGH 9.

Your *Study Guide and Working Papers* have forms to complete this exam, as well as worked-out solutions. The page references next to each question identify what page to turn back to if you answer the question incorrectly.

PART I Vocabulary Review

Match the terms to the appropriate definition or phrase.

Page Ref.

(316)	1. Total earnings columns	A. Gross pay less deductions
(285)	2. Petty cash	B. Records gross payroll
(320)	3. T-4 Slip	C. A pension plan for most employees
(317)	4. Tax deductions	D. An asset
(320)	5. Calendar year	E. National insurance plan
(312)	6. TD-1 form	F. Found in provincial information booklets
(311)	7. UI	G. Basis for determining tax deductions
(317)	8. Net pay	H. An annual summary of payroll amounts
(320)	9. Employee individual earning record	I. January 1 to December 31
(311)	10. CPP	J. Updated each pay period

PART II True or False (Accounting Theory)

(310) 11. A bi-weekly pay period results in 24 payrolls each year.

(320) 12. A payroll register is considered a special journal.

(316) 13. The total earnings column of a payroll register shows earnings that are subject to income tax.

(320) 14. Wages and salaries payable records gross pay.

(320) 15. The individual earnings record is updated from the payroll register.

PART III Applications Problem (311, 314)

Amy Jacobs earns $76,000.00 per year. Assuming a CPP rate of 2.8%, and an annual exemption of $3,800.00, calculate the amount of CPP Amy will contribute by way of payroll deductions if the maximum contribution limit salary is $38,600.00.

THE EMPLOYER'S TAX RESPONSIBILITIES: PRINCIPLES AND PROCEDURES

IN THIS CHAPTER WE WILL COVER THE FOLLOWING TOPICS:

1. HOW TO CALCULATE AND RECORD EMPLOYER'S EXPENSES ASSOCIATED WITH PAYROLL. (P. 361)

2. HOW EMPLOYERS REMIT AND RECORD THEIR EMPLOYEES' DEDUCTIONS TO REVENUE CANADA. (P. 363)

3. EMPLOYERS' ANNUAL RESPONSIBILITIES FOR FILING THE T4 SUMMARY FORM. (P. 372)

In the previous chapter we examined how the ABC Company Ltd. calculates its weekly payroll and maintains a record of each employee's earnings. In Canada, employers must remit monthly to the government the totals deducted from their employees in the previous month. Certain employers (those who have more than $15,000 to remit monthly) must send in their withholdings more often. In the balance of this chapter we will assume a smaller employer who remits monthly.

An important fact in our country is that employers share the total cost of CPP and UI. Their share of these payments is considered an expense of doing business and is accounted for as such. In this chapter we will examine how this expense is calculated and illustrate the forms that need to be completed (and sent to the government) as part of the payroll process. We will also examine the accounting procedures which must be followed.

LEARNING UNIT 10-1

Employer's Expenses Associated with Payroll

Employers must apply for a remittance number in order to handle their responsibilities for payroll correctly. A special form called an **Employer Registration** must be submitted which asks the employer to answer several questions about the business's operations. An example of this form **PD20** is shown in Figure 10-1. Once this form is processed, the employer is issued with a permanent unique identification number. This number is used to record correctly the amounts of money sent (we often say **remitted**) to the government each month (or more often in the case of larger employers).

If you take over another employer's business, you must still obtain a new identification number (unless the business is a corporation).

The actual amount sent to the government each month (or more often) depends on three deductions taken from employees' wages:

1. Income Tax
2. Canada (or Quebec) Pension Plan
3. Unemployment Insurance.

A simple formula can be used to ensure that the correct figure is remitted each period:

Income Tax Deducted × 1.0	=	xxx.xx
CPP Deducted × 2.0	=	xxx.xx
UI Deducted × 2.4	=	xxx.xx
TOTAL	=	$xxx.xx

Notice that the income tax amount is sent by the employer, but is not an expense, as the employees are paying it.

We will soon see how this formula works in more detail. Before we look at the details, however, a word of caution: each employer should ensure that the required remittance is made by the due date (usually the 15th day of the month following the payroll deductions). Failure to remit on time usually results in a penalty of 10% of the amount due. This penalty is harsh and should be avoided. Not only is the amount high, but it is not deductible as a business expense for tax purposes.

Revenue Canada **Revenu Canada**
Taxation Impôt

EMPLOYER REGISTRATION

PD20(E)
Rev. 88

• Return copies 1, 2 and 3 to the Taxation Office from which you received this form.

Employer Number Assigned

1. Language in which correspondence is desired. English ☐ French ☐

2. Legal name of entity

Telephone No.

3. Operating or trading name

Telephone No.

4. Mailing address (street no. and name)

5. Location address in Canada (if different than mailing)

| City | Province / State | City | Province |

Country (if other than Canada)

Postal Code

Postal code Zip Code or

6. Date business began operating YR M D

7. Duration of business operation(s)
Year round ☐ Seasonal ☐

8. Date first remuneration is expected to be paid YR M D

9. Estimated number of paid employees within next 12 months

10. Computerized payroll
Yes ☐ No ☐

11. Pay period(s)
Daily ☐ Weekly ☐ Bi-weekly ☐ Semi-monthly ☐ Monthly ☐ Other (specify)

12. Fiscal year-end M D

13. Name of external auditor (if applicable) Telephone:

14. Address at which books and records will be maintained
same as 4 above ☐ same as 5 above ☐ or (specify)

15. Name and address of business' bank

16. Does this entity have a registered pension plan or a D.P.S.P. Yes ☐ No ☐

17. If operation is a franchise, state name and address of franchisor

18. Legal status

☐ Sole proprietorship (indicate name of proprietor in "Responsible Individuals" section below)

☐ Partnership (indicate names of partners in "Responsible Individuals" section below)

☐ Corporation (indicate names of president, vice-president and secretary-treasurer in "Responsible Individuals" section)

☐ Other type of legal status (specify)

Responsible individuals

Title	Surname	Given Name	Home Address: no., street, city, province and postal code	S.I.N.

If a corporation, complete this section

Incorporated in — Year Month

Under ☐ Federal statute
☐ Provincial statute in province of:
☐ Other Canadian law (e.g. Bank Act) — specify
☐ Other country — specify

Corporation Account Number

If foreign ownership, state country

19. Revenue Canada Taxation Employer Number(s), if other than above —

20.(A) State the major activity conducted by this business

1. ☐ Agriculture (incl. services incidental to agriculture)
2. ☐ Fishing and Trapping
3. ☐ Logging, Forestry services
4. ☐ Mining, Milling, Quarrying, Oil wells
5. ☐ Manufacturing
6. ☐ Construction
7. ☐ Transportation (incl. storage)
8. ☐ Communication, Other utilities
9. ☐ Trade to farms/government/export markets
10. ☐ Trade to other businesses
11. ☐ Trade to the general public
12. ☐ Financial institutions, Insurance companies
13. ☐ Real estate operators, Insurance agents

14. ☐ Business services
15. ☐ Government services
16. ☐ Education services
17. ☐ Health, Social services
18. ☐ Accommodation, Food, Beverages services
19. ☐ Household services
20. ☐ Other services

21. ☐ Pension account
22. ☐ Government sponsored program
Program name
Project number

20.(B) State major product manufactured, handled or sold or type of services rendered:

21. I HEREBY CERTIFY that the information provided above is true, correct and complete

Date _____ 19 ___

Signature of Employer or Authorized Officer

Position

FOR OFFICE USE ONLY SIC CODE

1 **TAXROLL**

FIGURE 10-1 **Employer Registration**

HOW TO CALCULATE EMPLOYER'S REMITTANCE

Income Tax

Remember that all employees pay income tax based upon their level of earnings. We saw in Chapter 9 that the ABC Company Ltd. deducted income tax from each employee's earnings. This amount must now be sent to the government. Notice that the amount sent is exactly the same as the amount deducted, since the employer does not contribute to the employee's tax. This part of the required remittance is therefore quite simple: each month employers must send in the exact amount of income tax deducted from employees in the previous month. In our simple formula that is why we multiply by 1.0—the result is exactly the amount deducted.

Some provinces levy higher tax rates than others.

Canada (Quebec) Pension Plan

Each employee also contributes an amount each pay period to CPP (at least until the maximum is reached). In Canada, the employer must match the employee's contribution to CPP. This means that the amount of CPP remitted is exactly double the amount deducted. In our simple formula, that is why we multiply by 2.0—the result is double the amount deducted.

If an employee commences a job with a new employer part way through a calendar year, the deduction of CPP continues without regard to the CPP already paid while employed by the former company. If the employee pays more than the yearly maximum, then a refund of CPP contributions can be claimed by the individual when he or she files their income tax return for the year. The employer's share is not refundable and cannot be recovered.

Unemployment Insurance

Recall that employees contribute an amount each pay period for Unemployment Insurance. Employers also contribute to UI by paying an amount which is 140% of the deductions made from employees. The effect is that the employer must remit 2.4 times the amount deducted from the employees. In our simple formula, that is why we multiply by 2.4—1.0 for the employees' deduction, plus 1.4 for the employer's share.

In Chapter 9, the employer made the following entry for the payroll in the first week in March:

	Date	Account Titles and Description	PR	Dr.	Cr.
		General Journal			
		Management Salaries Expense		800 00	
		Sales Wages Expense		720 00	
		Wages Expense		1273 00	
		Income Taxes Payable			511 85
		CPP Payable			60 24
		UI Payable			82 14
		Medical Plan Payable			52 00
		Charitable Contributions Payable			12 00
		Salaries And Wages Payable			2074 77
		To record payroll for the first week in March			

ABC Company Ltd. must now make the following additional entry to record its liability correctly:

General Journal

Date	Account Titles and Description	PR	Dr.	Cr.
	Employee Benefits Expense (see Note)		175 24	
	CPP Payable (1 × 60.24)			60 24
	UI Payable (1.4 × 82.14)			115 00
	To record employer portion of CPP and			
	UI for week 1, March			

NOTE: This expense is known by many different names—payroll taxes expense, for example. Some employers separate this into UI and CPP portions although this is not usually necessary.

After the above entry is posted, the following T-accounts would be changed as follows:

Employee Benefits Expense		CPP Payable		UI Payable	
175.24**			60.24*		82.14*
			60.24**		115.00**
Expense on the Income Statement		Liability on the Balance Sheet		Liability on the Balance Sheet	

* Original entries from Chapter 9   ** New entries made above

As a final note, students should be aware that employers sometimes share, or pay entirely for, the cost of other employee benefits, such as extended health care, long-term disability insurance, and dental plans. These costs would also be recorded by journal entry at the same time CPP and UI are recorded; however, these are some of the more intricate aspects of payroll and we will not deal with them in detail in this text.

At this point you should be able to

1. Explain the purpose of form PD20. (p. 361)
2. Calculate the employer's share of CPP and UI. (p. 363)
3. Explain when employee deductions must be remitted. (p. 363)
4. Journalize the employer's employee benefits expense. (p. 363)
5. Post the entry made in (4) to appropriate ledger accounts. (p. 364)

☐ SELF-REVIEW QUIZ 10-1

Given the following journal entry for the payroll totals for the second week in March, prepare the entry to record ABC Company Ltd.'s portion of CPP and UI:

General Journal

Date	Account Titles and Description	PR	Dr.	Cr.
	Salaries and Wages Expense		2 8 0 5 00	
	Income Taxes Payable			5 2 2 80
	CPP Payable			6 0 98
	UI Payable			8 2 50
	Medical Plan Payable			5 2 00
	Charitable Contributions Payable			1 2 00
	Salaries and Wages Payable			2 0 7 4 72
	To record payroll for week 2, March			

■ SOLUTION TO SELF-REVIEW QUIZ 10-1

General Journal

Date	Account Titles and Description	PR	Dr.	Cr.
	Employee Benefits Expense		1 7 6 48	
	CPP Payable (1 × 60.98)			6 0 98
	UI Payable (1.4 × 82.50)			1 1 5 50
	To record employer portion of CPP and			
	UI for week 2, March			

LEARNING UNIT 10-2

Completing the Monthly Remittance Form

Smaller employers are required to remit the total amounts due in respect of their payrolls each month by the 15th of the following month. Payment may be made at most financial institutions in Canada or a cheque can be mailed if postmarked to reach the government by the 15th of the month.

We have already seen the ABC Company Ltd.'s entries for the first week in March. Let us assume the following payroll data for the second, third, and fourth weeks:

Income tax × 1
+
CPP × 2
+
UI × 2.4 = Amount remitted.

CPP × 1
+
UI × 1.4 = Employer's expense.

General Journal

Date	Account Titles and Description	Post Ref.	Dr.	Cr.
	Salaries and Wages Expense		2 8 0 5 00	
	Income Taxes Payable			5 2 2 80
	CPP Payable			6 0 98
	UI Payable			8 2 50
	Medical Plan Payable			5 2 00
	Charitable Contributions Payable			1 2 00
	Salaries and Wages Payable			2 0 7 4 72
	To record payroll for week 2, March - see S/R			
	Quiz 10-1			

General Journal

Date	Account Titles and Description	Post Ref.	Dr.	Cr.
	Salaries and Wages Expense		2 7 8 1 00	
	Income Taxes Payable			5 0 8 20
	CPP Payable			6 0 02
	UI Payable			8 1 78
	Medical Plan Payable			5 2 00
	Charitable Contributions Payable			1 2 00
	Salaries and Wages Payable			2 0 6 7 00
	To record payroll for week 3, March - New Data			

General Journal

Date	Account Titles and Description	Post Ref.	Dr.	Cr.
	Salaries and Wages Expense		2 8 5 6 00	
	Income Taxes Payable			5 3 2 40
	CPP Payable			6 1 88
	UI Payable			8 4 03
	Medical Plan Payable			5 2 00
	Charitable Contributions Payable			1 2 00
	Salaries and Wages Payable			2 1 1 3 69
	To record payroll for week 4, March - New Data			

General Journal

Date	Account Titles and Description	Post Ref.	Dr.	Cr.
	Employee Benefits Expense		176 48	
	CPP Payable			60 98
	UI Payable			115 50
	To record employer portion of CPP and UI			
	for the second week of March - see S/R			
	Quiz 10-1			

General Journal

Date	Account Titles and Description	Post Ref.	Dr.	Cr.
	Employee Benefits Expense		174 51	
	CPP Payable			60 02
	UI Payable			114 49
	To record employer portion of CPP and UI			
	for the third week of March - New Data			

General Journal

Date	Account Titles and Description	Post Ref.	Dr.	Cr.
	Employee Benefits Expense		179 52	
	CPP Payable			61 88
	UI Payable			117 64
	To record employer portion of CPP and UI			
	for the fourth week of March - New Data			

After posting, the relevant liability T-accounts would appear as shown:

	Income Taxes Payable	CPP Payable	UI Payable
WEEK 1: Employees	511.85*	60.24*	82.14*
Employer		60.24**	115.00**
WEEK 2: Employees	522.80*	60.98*	82.50*
Employer		60.98**	115.50**
WEEK 3: Employees	508.20*	60.02*	81.78*
Employer		60.02**	114.49**
WEEK 4: Employees	532.40*	61.88*	84.03*
Employer		61.88**	117.64**
Balance (March)	2075.25	486.24	793.08

* Original payroll entry   ** Benefits entry

Since these liability accounts contain the total amounts due, the ABC Company Ltd. can complete the required **Remittance Form (PD7AR)** as shown in Figure 10-2.

ABC Company Ltd. will issue a cheque for $3354.57 dated April 15, payable to the **Receiver General for Canada**. This cheque will be entered in the **Cash Disbursements Journal** in April. When this cheque is entered, the following accounts will be affected:

	General Journal			
Date	*Account Titles and Description*	*Post Ref.*	*Dr.*	*Cr.*
	Income Taxes Payable		2 0 7 5 25	
	CPP Payable		4 8 6 24	
	UI Payable		7 9 3 08	
	Cash			3 3 5 4 57
	To record payment of withholdings			

After these amounts are posted, the liability accounts will appear as shown:

	Income Taxes Payable		CPP Payable		UI Payable
	511.85		60.24		82.14
			60.24		115.00
	522.80		60.98		82.50
			60.98		115.00
	508.20		60.02		81.78
			60.02		114.49
	532.40		61.88		84.03
			61.88		117.64
Balance (March)	2075.25		486.24		793.08
April 15 Balance	2075.25		486.24	793.08	
Balance	0.00		0.00		0.00

FIGURE 10-2

Remittance Form – The top section shows the remittance form, which is filled out and sent to the Receiver General. Section 2 shows the statement returned to the employer from the bank which has deposited the remittance.

1 Revenue Canada / Customs, Excise and Taxation / Revenu Canada / Accise, Douanes et Impôt		**STATEMENT OF ACCOUNT**		PD7A Rev.92
Account number XXX 12345 6	Employer name	ABC COMPANY LTD		010945

Statement of account as of 23 Mar 19XX		Amount paid	Amount owing	You can make your payment where you bank or to.
Transactions processed after this date will appear on the next statement		19XX		Taxation Centre
	Present balance	9,547.20CR		WINNIPEG R3C 3P8

• IMPORTANT - SEE REVERSE •   **EXPLANATION OF CHANGES**

Date	Description	Amount
22 Mar Payment Feb 19XX	Date Recd 15 Mar 19XX	3,146.20CR

Indicate remittance information in this area for your records

CPP contributions	UI premiums	Tax deductions	Current payment	Gross monthly payroll	No. of empl. - last period
486.24	793.08	2,075.25	3,354.57	11,235.00	6

2   PD7A Rev.92

Account number   XXX 12345 6   Employer name   ABC COMPANY LTD

Thank you for your payment.
Please use part 3 to make your next remittance or explain on the back of
part 2 why you will not be remitting.

PIERRE GRAVELLE, QC
DEPUTY MINISTER, DEPARTMENT OF NATIONAL REVENUE, TAXATION

3 Revenue Canada / Customs, Excise and Taxation / Revenu Canada / Accise, Douanes et Impôt	**REMITTANCE FORM FOR CURRENT SOURCE DEDUCTIONS**	Account number XXX 12345 6	For Taxation use only PD7A Rev.92

3

Amount of payment ▷   3 3 5 4 5 7

ABC COMPANY LTD
123 PINE ROAD
ANY CITY, PR   C1B 1A1

If your payment is not for the period indicated, please enter the correct period here ▷   Year   Month

Gross monthly payroll ▷   1 1 2 3 5 0 0

Number of employees in last pay period ▷   6

⑈0 2000⑈ 1 1 7⑈   96

Remember that by April 15 there will be two new weekly payrolls to contend with, so the ledger accounts will not appear exactly as shown above. The amount payable at the end of any month, however, should be accurate when all postings have been made.

Students will recall that employers sometimes pay part or all of the cost of other benefits. These costs are not sent to the Receiver General; instead, they are remitted (usually monthly) to the provincial health care plan and/or private insurance companies which provide the benefits. These details of payroll are handled in a manner similar to the remittance to the Receiver General and are not dealt with further in this text.

At this point you should be able to

1. Explain the balances in the following ledger accounts before the monthly remittance to the Receiver General is made. (p. 368)
   a. Income tax payable
   b. CPP payable
   c. UI payable
2. Complete form PD7AR for a typical company. (p. 369)
3. Issue and record the cheque which would accompany form PD7AR. (p. 369)
4. Explain how the balances in the ledger accounts noted in (1) above would change after posting the remittance cheque. (p. 368)

☐ SELF-REVIEW QUIZ 10-2

Given the two semi-monthly payrolls summarized by journal entry below, answer the following:

1. What journal entries would be made to record the employer's share of CPP and UI for the month?
2. Post the original entries and the entries you suggested in question 1 to the T-accounts shown. (Not all T-accounts are shown; please ignore the ones not shown.)
3. What amount would the employer remit to the Receiver General by the 15th of the following month?

Here are the semi-monthly journal entries:

	General Journal			
Date	Account Titles and Description	Post Ref.	Dr.	Cr.
	Sales Salaries		2 8 5 0 00	
	Office Salaries		3 2 4 0 00	
	Income Taxes Payable			1 5 6 0 00
	CPP Payable			1 1 2 40
	UI Payable			1 7 7 30
	Salaries and Wages Payable			4 2 4 0 30
	To record payroll data for the first half			
	of the month			

General Journal

Date	Account Titles and Description	Post Ref.	Dr.	Cr.
	Sales Salaries		2 8 5 0 00	
	Office Salaries		3 1 7 5 00	
	Income Taxes Payable			1 4 4 5 00
	CPP Payable			1 1 1 80
	UI Payable			1 7 6 60
	Salaries and Wages Payable			4 2 9 1 60
	To record payroll data for the second half			
	of the month			

Here are the T-accounts to use in part 2 of the Quiz (opening balances are ignored):

Income Tax Payable   **CPP Payable**   **UI Payable**

SOLUTIONS TO SELF-REVIEW QUIZ 10-2

1.

General Journal

Date	Account Titles and Description	Post Ref.	Dr.	Cr.
	Employee Benefits Expense		3 6 0 62	
	CPP Payable			1 1 2 40
	UI Payable (177.30 × 1.4)			2 4 8 22
	To record benefits expense for the first half			
	of the month			

General Journal

Date	Account Titles and Description	Post Ref.	Dr.	Cr.
	Employee Benefits Expense		3 5 9 04	
	CPP Payable			1 1 1 80
	UI Payable (177.30 × 1.4)			2 4 7 24
	To record benefits expense for the second half			
	of the month			

2. Your T-accounts should appear as follows:

Income Tax Payable	CPP Payable	UI Payable
1,560.00	112.40	177.30
1,445.00	112.40	248.22
3,005.00 Bal	111.80	176.60
	111.80	247.24
	448.40 Bal	849.36 Bal

3. The employer would remit $4,302.76 calculated as follows:

Income Tax Payable (bal)	$3,005.00
CPP Payable (bal)	448.40
UI Payable (bal)	849.36
	$4,302.76

LEARNING UNIT 10-3
Employer's Annual T4-T4A Summary

Each year, employers are required to file an annual return called a **T4-T4A Summary** (see Figure 10-3). This return summarizes the information provided to employees on their **T4** forms (see Chapter 9, Figure 9-5).

It is important to note that this form is completed for a calendar year. Even if the fiscal year ends on September 30, the T4-T4A Summary form must be filed for the calendar year (January 1 to December 31). The deadline for submitting this form to both the government and to employees is February 28 each year for the calendar year ended the previous December 31.

Careful, accurate work helps ensure that the filing of the T4-T4A summary is not an unpleasant task.

The completion of this form can be a difficult task because any errors made during the year in completing the payroll register as well as any errors made in preparing the employees' individual T4 slips will be discovered in this final step. The totals shown for CPP, UI, and Income Tax must also agree with the totals remitted according to the monthly PD7AR form (see Figure 10-2).

It is not unusual to find intelligent, hard-working, successful employers who find this aspect of payroll processing to be very difficult. Some computer firms selling payroll software are successful because they promise employers some relief from the manual balancing procedures each February 28. In actual fact, the task is not too difficult—providing that the payroll register is completed with neatness and accuracy and that all subsequent steps are done with care.

In Figure 10-3, the figures were obtained from the Individual Employee Earnings Records as summarized below:

| Employee Name | Total Wages | Deductions | | |
		Income Tax	CPP	UI
Janet Johnson*	$ 20,910.00	4,005.35	440.27	627.30
Peter Black	20,875.00	4,000.50	439.38	626.25
John Chernochan	19,462.00	2,050.10	404.05	583.86
Tony Chui	22,147.00	4,156.20	471.18	664.41
Beth Madora	18,256.50	2,647.60	373.90	547.70
Elaine Dumont	38,400.00	7,425.00	752.50	1,152.00
Other Casual				
Employees (total)	15,620.00	1,641.70	216.40	367.07
Totals	$155,670.50	25,926.45	3,097.68	4,568.59

* Refer to Chapter 9, Figure 9-5 and Figure 9-7.

Revenue Canada **Revenu Canada** **Taxation** **Impôt**	**SUMMARY OF REMUNERATION PAID** (For the year ending December 31, 1992) **SOMMAIRE DE LA RÉMUNÉRATION PAYÉE** (Pour l'année se terminant le 31 décembre 1992)	**T4** SUMMARY SOMMAIRE

1992

Complete this return using the instructions in the *Employers' Guide to Payroll Deductions* or the *Payroll Deductions for Small Business Employers Guide.*

Cette déclaration doit être remplie selon les instructions du *Guide de l'employeur – Retenues sur la paie* ou du *Guide des employeurs qui exploitent une petite entreprise.*

Copy Copie **1**

If you file your T4 return on tape or diskette, tick (√) inside the circle at left. For shipping instructions, see Box "B" on the back of this form.

Si vous produisez votre déclaration T4 sur disquette ou sur bande, cochez (√) le cercle qui figure à gauche. Faites parvenir le tout selon les instructions fournies à la case B au verso de cette formule.

IMPORTANT
EMPLOYER'S NAME AND NUMBER MUST BE THE SAME AS THAT SHOWN ON YOUR PD7A REMITTANCE FORM. THE T4 SUMMARY MUST BE FILED ON OR BEFORE FEBRUARY 28, 1993.

LE NOM ET LE NUMÉRO DE L'EMPLOYEUR DOIVENT ÊTRE LES MÊMES QUE CEUX QUI FIGURENT SUR LA FORMULE DE VERSEMENT PD7A. LA T4 SOMMAIRE DOIT ÊTRE REMPLIE AU PLUS TARD LE 28 FÉVRIER 1993.

Employer account number
Numéro de compte de l'employeur

XXX123456

Name and address of employer
Nom et adresse de l'employeur

ABC Company Ltd.
123 Pine Road
Any City, Province
C1B 1A1

Taxation centre   DO code

Centre fiscal   Code du BD

T4 SUPPLEMENTARY SLIPS TOTALS
For returns with over 300 T4 slips, please see instructions in the *Employers' Guide to Payroll Deductions* about the breakdown of large returns.

TOTAUX DES FEUILLETS *T4 SUPPLÉMENTAIRE*
Pour les déclarations renfermant plus de 300 feuillets T4, consultez le *Guide de l'employeur – Retenues sur la paie* pour la répartition des déclarations volumineuses.

Total number of T4 slips filed Nombre total de feuillets T4 produits	88	110	Number of T4 slips included in the total at left, if the employee's address is in the U.S.A. Nombre de feuillets T4 inclus dans le «Total» indiqué à gauche si l'adresse de l'employé est aux É.-U.
Employment income before deductions	Revenu d'emploi avant retenues	14	155,670.50
Registered pension plan contributions	Cotisations à un régime de pension agréé	20	
Pension adjustment	Facteur d'équivalence	52	
Unemployment Insurance insurable earnings	Gains assurables d'assurance-chômage	24	
Employees' Canada Pension Plan contributions	Cotisations de l'employé au Régime de pensions du Canada	16	3,097.68
Employer's Canada Pension Plan contributions	Cotisations de l'employeur au Régime de pensions du Canada	17	3,097.68
Employee's Unemployment Insurance premiums	Cotisations de l'employé à l'assurance-chômage	18	4,568.59
Employer's Unemployment Insurance premiums	Cotisations de l'employeur à l'assurance-chômage	19	6,396.03
Income tax deducted	Impôt sur le revenu retenu	22	25,926.45

DEPARTMENTAL USE ONLY

Total deductions reported (16 + 17 + 18 + 19 + 22) Total des retenues déclarées (16 + 17 + 18 + 19 + 22)	80	43,086.43
Remittances for the year – Versements pour l'année	82	43,086.43
Difference – Différence		

We do not charge or refund a difference of less than $2.00.
Une différence inférieure à 2 $ ne sera ni exigée ni remboursée par le Ministère.

Overpayment Paiement en trop 84

Balance due Solde à payer 86

* If you have not paid the total deductions reported, include the balance with this completed return. You may be subject to a penalty for late payment if you have any balance owing.
Si vous n'avez pas payé le montant total des retenues déclarées, veuillez joindre le solde à payer, à la présente déclaration. Tout solde à payer est assujetti à une pénalité pour paiement tardif.

Amount enclosed
Somme jointe

Revenue Canada, Taxation issued registration number(s) for RPP or DPSP – Numéro(s) d'enregistrement émis par Revenu Canada, Impôt pour RPA ou RPDB

71   72   73

Canadian controlled private corporations or unincorporated employers: list the social insurance number of the main shareholder(s) or proprietor(s).
Corporations privées dont le contrôle est canadien ou employeurs non constitués : inscrivez le numéro d'assurance sociale du(des) actionnaire(s) ou du(des) propriétaire(s).

RÉSERVÉ AU MINISTÈRE   74   75

Person to contact about this return – Personne avec qui communiquer au sujet de cette déclaration

76 ELAINE DUMONT
First name – Prénom   Surname – Nom de famille

78 900 123 4567
Area code – Indicatif régional

Telephone number – Numéro de téléphone

CERTIFICATION – ATTESTATION

I HEREBY CERTIFY that the information given in this T4 return (T4 Summary and related T4 Supplementary slips) is true, correct and complete in every way.
J'ATTESTE PAR LA PRÉSENTE que les renseignements fournis dans la déclaration T4 (la *T4 Sommaire* et les feuillets *T4 Supplémentaire* connexes) sont vrais, exacts et complets sous tous les rapports.

Date
February 20, 19XX

Signature of authorized person – Signature de la personne autorisée
Elaine Dumont

Position or office – Titre ou poste
Manager

FOR DEPARTMENTAL USE ONLY: PLEASE DO NOT WRITE IN THIS AREA – RÉSERVÉ AU MINISTÈRE, NE RIEN ÉCRIRE ICI

Transfer Transfert	90	1	Last to current Précédente à courante	91	1	No Non	93	Date	Memo – Note
	2	No action Aucune mesure	Pro Forma	2	Yes Oui	94	A
	3	Other Autre					B	Late filing penalty Pénalité pour production tardive

1	T4 balance Solde T4	1	Override Sauter	3	Delete Supprimer		

Reject number – Numéro de rejet   Prepared by – Établi par   Date

Code 2   Correspond.   Inc.   TPC – CCT   Dressed – MAP   Rev. – Rév.   No Accounts – Aucun n°

Initials – Initiales
Date

* KEEP THE WORKING COPY OF THIS SUMMARY FOR YOUR RECORDS.
* IF YOU DO NOT FILE BY MAGNETIC MEDIA, SEND COPIES 1 AND 2 OF THIS SUMMARY AND COPY 1 OF THE RELATED T4 SUPPLEMENTARY TO THE APPROPRIATE TAXATION CENTRE ADDRESS IN BOX A ON THE BACK OF THIS FORM.

Canadian Human Rights Act Federal Information Bank Number: 15615.

* CONSERVEZ LE BROUILLON DE LA FORMULE SOMMAIRE POUR VOS DOSSIERS.
* SI VOUS NE PRODUISEZ PAS DE DÉCLARATION SUR SUPPORT MAGNÉTIQUE, ENVOYEZ LES COPIES 1 ET 2 DE LA FORMULE SOMMAIRE AINSI QUE LA COPIE 1 DU *T4 SUPPLÉMENTAIRE* CONNEXE AU CENTRE FISCAL APPROPRIÉ, DONT L'ADRESSE FIGURE À LA CASE A AU VERSO DE CETTE FORMULE.

Loi canadienne sur les droits de la personne : Numéro de la banque fédérale de données : 15615.

FIGURE 10-3   Summary of Remuneration Paid

At this point you should be able to

1. Describe the process of filing an annual T4-T4A Summary. (p. 372)
2. Illustrate the completion of the T4-T4A Summary form. (p. 373)

☐ **SELF-REVIEW QUIZ 10-3**

Respond true or false to the following:

1. A T4-T4A Summary form must be filed each year by February 28.
2. A T4-T4A Summary form is sent to each employee by February 28 each year.
3. The completion of the T4-T4A forms can be a difficult task.
4. The total of the individual amounts on all T4-T4A Supplementary forms must equal the totals on the T4-T4A Summary forms.

■ *SOLUTIONS TO SELF-REVIEW QUIZ 10-3*

1. True   2. False   3. True   4. True

SUMMARY OF KEY POINTS AND KEY TERMS

LEARNING UNIT 10-1

1. The employer's remittance to the Receiver General includes (a) Income Tax (employees' share only), (b) CPP (both employees' and employer's share), and (c) UI (again employees' and employer's share).
2. The payroll tax expense is made up of both CPP (same amount as deducted from employees) and UI (1.4 times the amount deducted from employees).
3. Journal entries are made to record the payroll and then to record the employer's share of CPP and UI.
4. Employers sometimes share, or pay entirely for, the cost of other employee benefits (health care, insurance, etc.). These costs would also be recorded by journal entry at the same time as CPP and UI.

Employer identification number: A number given by the federal government which uniquely identifies each employer who is required to forward deductions made from employees. Used to keep track of the exact remittance each employer sends on behalf of their employees.

Remittance formula: A formula which can be used to double check the amount of money being sent in each month on behalf of the employees. Computed as:

FIT deducted $\times$ 1.0	=	xxx.xx
CPP deducted $\times$ 2.0	=	xx.xx
UI deducted $\times$ 2.4	=	xx.xx
Total		xxx.xx

LEARNING UNIT 10-2

1. Employers must complete form PD7AR and submit it with their remittance to the Receiver General by the 15th day of the month following the payroll month. (Larger employers remit more often.)

2. A significant penalty is paid by any employer remitting after the due date.

3. Employers sometimes pay part or all of the cost of health care, insurance plans, etc. on behalf of their employees. These costs are not sent to the Receiver General; instead, they are remitted (usually monthly) to the provincial health care plan and/or private companies which provide the benefits.

Monthly Remittance Form (PD7AR): A form used to calculate and explain the amounts of money sent to the Receiver General periodically on behalf of employees.

LEARNING UNIT 10-3

1. Once each year, by February 28, employers must file an annual T4-T4A Summary form (for the previous calendar year) with the federal government.

2. On or before the same date, each employee must be given a copy of his or her individual earnings summary (T4-T4A Supplementary) form. This form summarizes all relevant payroll information for each employee for the previous calendar year.

3. Unless care is taken in preparing the payroll records throughout the year, the completion of the T4-T4A forms can be a challenging task.

T4-T4A Summary Form: A form sent to the federal government once each year showing the totals of income tax, CPP, and UI deducted from all employees during the last calendar year. The totals on this form must agree exactly with the totals submitted on the various T4-T4A Supplemental forms described below.

T4-T4A Supplemental Forms: A form which is given to each employee by February 28 each year which gives the total of wages earned, FIT, CPP, and UI deducted, and other similar information for the past calendar year. Total of all T4-T4A Supplemental slips must agree with the totals reported on the T4-T4A Summary form. (See above.)

BLUEPRINT OF THE TAX CALENDAR

A Sampling of Dates Involving Employer's Tax Responsibilities

JANUARY 15 (and the 15th of each month)	Form PD7AR	Remit the monthly amount to the Receiver General of Canada. Remember the formula: $1 \times$ Tax deducted + $2 \times$ CPP deducted + $2.4 \times$ UI deducted = Total amount to be remitted
FEBRUARY 28	Forms T-4 and T-4A	Complete these forms and send or deliver them to all persons employed during the year. If an employee leaves or is fired during the year, he or she may require the employer to prepare these forms earlier.

(continued)

FEBRUARY

28	Form T-4 Summary	Send this form, together with copies of the individual T-4 or T-4A forms to the government. The totals on this form must match the match the sum of all individual T-4 and T-4A slips and, as well, must agree with the employer's accounting records.

Certain other forms may be required throughout the year, although they are not subject to an exact timetable:

	Form PD20	Each employer needs to obtain a permanent ID number which permits the government to keep an accurate record of funds remitted. Since this number is permanent, employers will only need to submit this form once.
	ROE (Record of Employment) Form	Whenever an employee ceases his or her employment, this form must be completed and a copy given to the former employee within one week. A copy goes to the government to assist in the fair and efficient administration of the Unemployment Insurance Act.

DISCUSSION QUESTIONS

1. What makes up employee benefits expense?
2. All employers must remit their payroll deductions once a month (by the 15th of the following month). Please comment.
3. The only payroll-related costs borne by employers are CPP and UI. Please comment.
4. A form PD20 must be submitted annually by all employers. True or false?
5. Why could failure to remit employees' deductions on time be costly?
6. Each employer doubles the amount of income tax deducted from employees each month when remitting to the Receiver General of Canada. True or False?
7. Which of the following accurately summarizes the correct formula for determining the monthly remittance to the Receiver General?
   (a) $(2 \times IT) + (2.4 \times CPP) + (2 \times UI)$
   (b) $(1 \times IT) + (2 \times CPP) + (2.4 \times UI)$
   (c) $(1 \times IT) + (2.4 \times CPP) + (2 \times UI)$
   (d) $(2 \times IT) + (2 \times CPP) + (2.4 \times UI)$
8. A remittance form (PD7AR) must be sent to the federal government once each pay period. True or False?
9. Why do some computer firms do a good business selling payroll software to employers?
10. Employers must complete their T4-T4A Summary forms not later than two months after the end of their fiscal year. True or False?

EXERCISES

1. From the following information, prepare a general journal entry to record the employee benefits expense for Jones Company for the weekly payroll of July 9:

		DEDUCTIONS			
EMPLOYEE	TOTAL SALARY	TAX	CPP	UI	NET PAY
Beth Chan	800	175	18	24	583
Bill Williams	800	200	18	24	558
Tom Raymond	700	140	15	21	524

Recording employee benefits expense.

2. From the following information, prepare a general journal entry to record the employee benefits expense for Windsor Company for the monthly payroll for July:

		DEDUCTIONS			
EMPLOYEE	TOTAL SALARY	TAX	CPP	UI	NET PAY
Fred Adams	2,400	600	53	72	1,675
Joanne DeVries	2,200	435	48	66	1,651
Heather Sovereign	1,800	315	38	54	1,393
Gail Stasniuk	1,900	400	40	57	1,403

Recording employee benefits expense.

3. What amount will the Windsor Company send to the Receiver General in the month of August (for July payroll)? See 2 above.

Remittance calculation.

4. For the first two weeks of March, the Star Company had payroll details as shown below:

				DEDUCTIONS			
EMPLOYEE	HOURS	RATE	TOTAL PAY	TAX	CPP	UI	NET PAY
Tony Beaufort	80	15	1,200	275	27	36	862
Isabel Brown	70	16	1,120	270	25	34	791
Jim Francis	80	17	1,360	310	31	41	978

Recording payroll tax expense Stage 1.

Prepare the general journal entry to record the employee benefits expense for the two week period.

5. For the last two weeks in March, the Star Company had payroll details as shown below:

				DEDUCTIONS			
EMPLOYEE	HOURS	RATE	TOTAL PAY	TAX	CPP	UI	NET PAY
Tony Beaufort	75	15	1,125	235	25	34	831
Isabel Brown	85	16	1,360	370	30	41	919
Jim Francis	80	17	1,360	310	30	41	979

Recording employee benefits expense Stage 2.

Prepare the general journal entry to record the employee benefits expense for the last two week period.

6. There are only four payroll weeks in March. Calculate the total remittance that Star Company would make to the Receiver General in the month of April based on its March payroll activities. Refer to 4 and 5 above.

Calculating a remittance—multi-periods.

GROUP A PROBLEMS

10A-1. The Payroll Register for the Rice Company is summarized below for the month of April:

| | | | | | DEDUCTIONS | | | |
| | TOTAL | | | | MED- | UNION | NET | CHQ. |
EMPLOYEE	SALARY	TAX	CPP	UI	ICAL	DUES	PAY	NO.
Jane Mueller	2,400	575	53	72	18	20	1,662	718
Frank O'Day	2,400	510	53	72	36	20	1,709	719
Jeremy Owens	2,000	450	43	60	36	20	1,391	720
Isaac Goldman	2,100	410	46	63	36	20	1,525	721

Recording employee benefits expense and subsequent entries.

The union dues are remitted to the treasurer of the union by the 10th day of the next month. Rice Company matches its employees' contributions to the medical plan. Assume that the information in the above table has been recorded as cheques 718-721 were issued.

Required:
(a) Record the company's benefits expense assuming no such entry was made when cheques 718-721 were recorded.
(b) In May, the Rice Company issued the following three cheques:
   (1) May 10, 19XX to the Employees' Union, cheque no. 751.
   (2) May 15, 19XX to the Receiver General, cheque no. 762.
   (3) May 20, 19XX to the Provincial Health Care Insurance Company, cheque no. 775.
   How much was each cheque for?
(c) What entries would be made to record the three cheques in (b) above?

10A-2. Pebbles, Inc. recorded the following details in its payroll journal for March:

| | | | | | DEDUCTIONS | | | | |
| | | | | | | MED- | UNION | NET | CHQ. |
EMPLOYEE	SALARY	TAX	CPP	UI	LTD	ICAL	DUES	PAY	NO.
Albert King	2,600	670	58	78	24	18	25	1,727	1318
Julio Caravelle	2,100	435	46	63	40	36	25	1,455	1319
Elizabeth Downey	2,500	620	56	75	24	18	25	1,682	1320
Mary Phillips	2,400	530	53	72	24	18	25	1,678	1321
Karen Freeman	1,800	375	38	54	24	18	25	1,266	1322

Recording employee benefits expense and subsequent calculations.

Union dues are remitted by the end of the following month to the Employees Union Treasurer. Employees pay 100% of the Long Term Disability (LTD). Pebbles, Inc. matches its employees' contributions to the medical plan and remits by the 20th of the following month.

Required:
(a) Assume that there was no employees benefit expense recognized as the payroll register was recorded. Give the general journal entry necessary to record this employee benefits expense for March.
(b) List the cheques, together with their amounts and dates, which Pebbles, Inc. would issue in April in respect of the above payroll data.

10A-3. The Candy Co. pays its workers twice each month. Data for the two pay periods in June is shown below:

First half of June:

EMPLOYEE	HOURS	RATE	TOTAL PAY	TAX	CPP	UI	UNION	CHARITABLE	NET PAY	CHQ. NO.
Jean LaRoche	90	12	1,080	250	24	32	12	5	757	472
Kevin Commings	95	14	1,330	320	30	40	12	5	923	473
Alan Blakeney	85	13	1,105	215	24	33	12	5	816	474
Joy Peabody	92	14	1,288	325	29	39	12	5	878	475

Second half of June:

EMPLOYEE	HOURS	RATE	TOTAL PAY	TAX	CPP	UI	UNION	CHARITABLE	NET PAY	CHQ. NO.
Jean LaRoche	94	12	1,128	265	25	34	12	5	787	507
Kevin Commings	95	14	1,330	320	30	40	12	5	923	508
Alan Blakeney	90	13	1,170	230	26	35	12	5	862	509
Joy Peabody	96	15	1,440	386	33	43	12	5	961	510

Union dues must be remitted to the Union Treasurer by the 15th of the following month. Candy Co. matches the employees' charitable contributions on a 2 to 1 basis. Donations are mailed to World Hunger Relief semi-annually. Deductions from all employees to May 31 this year have totalled $225. A cheque will be sent for the first half of the year on July 5, 19XX.

Recording employee benefits expense—a more comprehensive example.

Required:
(a) Assuming that the payroll register has been posted, but no entries have been made for employee benefits expense for June, make the two journal entries that are necessary to record this expense for Candy Co. for June.
(b) Give details of the various cheques which will be issued in July based on Candy Co.'s payroll activities for the year so far.

10A-4. The Ripcord Parachute Club employs three people and pays them on a weekly basis. Payroll data for the four weeks in February is given below:

Week 1—February

EMPLOYEE	SAL.	TAX	CPP	UI	LTD	PEN	MED	NET PAY	CHQ. NO.
Bill Lyons	700	170	16	21	5	35	12	441	814
Jackie McGregor	650	170	15	20	5	33	8	399	815
Anne Chapman	750	200	17	22	5	38	8	460	816

Week 2—February

EMPLOYEE	SAL.	TAX	CPP	UI	LTD	PEN	MED	NET PAY	CHQ. NO.
Bill Lyons	700	170	16	21	5	35	12	441	832
Jackie McGregor	700	190	16	21	5	35	8	425	833
Anne Chapman	750	200	17	22	5	38	8	460	834

Week 3—February

EMPLOYEE	SAL.	DEDUCTIONS						NET PAY	CHQ. NO.
		TAX	CPP	UI	LTD	PEN	MED		
Bill Lyons	700	170	16	21	5	35	12	441	856
Jackie McGregor	700	190	16	21	5	35	8	425	857
Anne Chapman	750	200	17	22	5	38	8	460	858

Week 4—February

EMPLOYEE	SAL.	DEDUCTIONS						NET PAY	CHQ. NO.
		TAX	CPP	UI	LTD	PEN	MED		
Bill Lyons	750	190	17	22	5	38	12	466	871
Jackie McGregor	700	190	16	21	5	35	8	425	872
Anne Chapman	800	220	18	22	5	40	8	487	873

Assume: Employees pay 100% of the cost of Long Term Disability (LTD). Employees contribute 5% of their salary to the pension plan; the employer contributes 6% of the employees' salary to the plan. Medical cost is split 50/50 by employees and employer. All payroll-related deductions are paid on the 15th of March.

Required:

Recording employee benefits expense— multi-periods.

(a) In recording the payroll journal in February the bookkeeper for the Ripcord Parachute Club did not record any expense for employee benefits. Give the four journal entries which should be made for the month to record this expense.

Posting routine entries for a monthly period.

(b) Post the entries from the payroll journal and the entries in (a) above to the T-accounts shown below. (You may ignore the accounts which are not shown.)

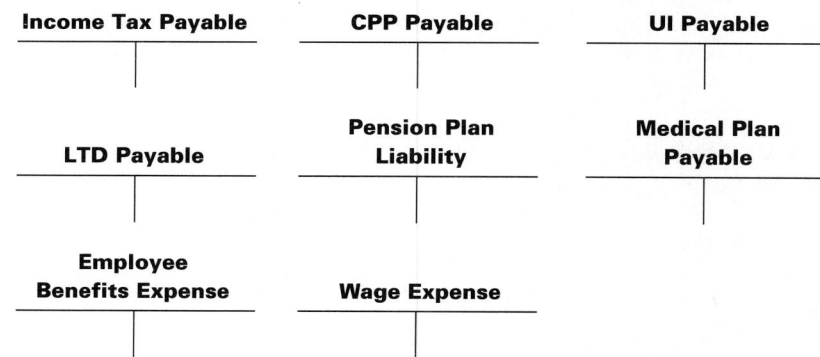

Income Tax Payable   **CPP Payable**   **UI Payable**

LTD Payable   **Pension Plan Liability**   **Medical Plan Payable**

Employee Benefits Expense   **Wage Expense**

Calculating remittances.

(c) List the cheques and the amounts of the cheques which will be issued on March 15 for the February payroll.

GROUP B PROBLEMS

10B-1. The Payroll Register for the Rice Company is summarized below for the month of April:

	TOTAL				MED-	UNION	NET	CHQ.
EMPLOYEE	SALARY	TAX	CPP	UI	ICAL	DUES	PAY	NO.
Jane Mueller	2,500	615	56	75	20	25	1,709	718
Frank O'Day	2,300	470	51	69	40	25	1,645	719
Jeremy Owens	2,200	530	48	66	40	25	1,491	720
Isaac Goldman	2,000	370	43	60	40	25	1,462	721

(DEDUCTIONS span TAX, CPP, UI, MED-ICAL, UNION DUES)

The union dues are remitted to the treasurer of the union by the 10th day of the next month. Rice Company matches its employees' contributions to the medical plan. Assume that the information in the above table has been recorded as cheques 718-721 were issued.

Recording employee benefits expense and subsequent entries.

Required:
(a) Record the company's benefits expense assuming no such entry was made when cheques 718-721 were recorded.
(b) In May, the Rice Company issued the following three cheques:
   1. May 10, 19XX to the Employees' Union, cheque no. 751.
   2. May 15, 19XX to the Receiver General, cheque no. 762.
   3. May 20, 19XX to the Provincial Health Care Insurance Company, cheque no. 775.
   How much was each cheque for?
(c) What entries would be made to record the three cheques in (b) above?

10B-2. Pebbles, Inc. recorded the following details in its payroll journal for March:

						MED-	UNION	NET	CHQ.
EMPLOYEE	SALARY	TAX	CPP	UI	LTD	ICAL	DUES	PAY	NO.
Albert King	2,500	630	56	75	22	15	22	1,680	1318
Julio Caravelle	2,000	400	43	60	38	30	22	1,407	1319
Elizabeth Downey	2,500	620	56	75	22	15	22	1,690	1320
Mary Phillips	2,300	490	51	69	22	15	22	1,671	1321
Karen Freeman	1,800	375	38	54	22	15	22	1,274	1322

(DEDUCTIONS span TAX, CPP, UI, LTD, MED-ICAL, UNION DUES)

Union dues are remitted by the end of the following month to the Employees Union Treasurer. Employees pay 100% of the Long Term Disability (LTD). Pebbles, Inc. matches its employees' contributions to the medical plan and remits by the 20th of the following month.

Recording employee benefits expense and subsequent calculations.

Required:
(a) Assume that there was no employees' benefit expense recognized as the payroll register was recorded. Give the general journal entry necessary to record this employee benefits expense for March.
(b) List the cheques, together with their amounts and dates, which Pebbles, Inc. would issue in April in respect of the above payroll data.

10B-3. The Candy Co. pays its workers twice each month. Data for the two pay periods in June is shown below:

First half of June:

| | | | TOTAL | DEDUCTIONS | | | | | NET | CHQ. |
EMPLOYEE	HOURS	RATE	PAY	TAX	CPP	UI	UNION	CHARI-TABLE	PAY	NO.
Jean LaRoche	85	12	1,020	225	22	31	15	8	719	472
Kevin Commings	100	14	1,400	350	32	42	15	8	953	473
Alan Blakeney	85	13	1,105	215	24	33	15	8	810	474
Joy Peabody	90	14	1,260	315	28	38	15	8	856	475

Second half of June:

| | | | TOTAL | DEDUCTIONS | | | | | NET | CHQ. |
EMPLOYEE	HOURS	RATE	PAY	TAX	CPP	UI	UNION	CHARI-TABLE	PAY	NO.
Jean LaRoche	99	12	1,188	285	26	36	15	8	818	507
Kevin Commings	95	14	1,330	320	30	40	15	8	917	508
Alan Blakeney	96	13	1,248	265	28	37	15	8	894	509
Joy Peabody	95	15	1,425	380	32	43	15	8	947	510

Recording employee benefits expense—a more comprehensive example.

Union dues must be remitted to the Union Treasurer by the 15th of the following month. Candy Co. matches the employees' charitable contributions on a 2 to 1 basis. Donations are mailed to World Hunger Relief semi-annually. Deductions from all employees to May 31 this year have totalled $350. A cheque will be sent for the first half of the year on July 5, 19XX.

Required:
(a) Assuming that the payroll register has been posted, but no entries have been made for employee benefits expense for June, make the two journal entries that are necessary to record this expense for Candy Co. for June.
(b) Give details of the various cheques which will be issued in July based on Candy Co.'s payroll activities for the year so far.

10B-4. The Ripcord Parachute Club employs three people and pays them on a weekly basis. Payroll data for the four weeks in February are given below:

Week 1—February

| | | DEDUCTIONS | | | | | | NET | CHQ. |
EMPLOYEE	SAL.	TAX	CPP	UI	LTD	PEN	MED	PAY	NO.
Bill Lyons	800	200	18	22	8	40	10	502	814
Jackie McGregor	650	160	15	20	8	33	6	408	815
Anne Chapman	750	200	17	22	8	38	6	459	816

Week 2—February

| | | DEDUCTIONS | | | | | | NET | CHQ. |
EMPLOYEE	SAL.	TAX	CPP	UI	LTD	PEN	MED	PAY	NO.
Bill Lyons	800	200	18	22	8	40	10	502	832
Jackie McGregor	700	180	16	21	8	35	6	434	833
Anne Chapman	750	200	17	22	8	38	6	459	834

Week 3—February

EMPLOYEE	SAL.	DEDUCTIONS						NET PAY	CHQ. NO.
		TAX	CPP	UI	LTD	PEN	MED		
Bill Lyons	800	200	18	22	8	40	10	502	856
Jackie McGregor	700	180	16	21	8	35	6	434	857
Anne Chapman	750	200	17	22	8	38	6	459	858

Week 4—February

EMPLOYEE	SAL.	DEDUCTIONS						NET PAY	CHQ. NO.
		TAX	CPP	UI	LTD	PEN	MED		
Bill Lyons	850	225	20	22	8	43	10	522	871
Jackie McGregor	700	180	16	21	8	35	6	434	872
Anne Chapman	800	220	18	22	8	40	6	486	873

Assume: Employees pay 100% of the cost of Long Term Disability (LTD). Employees contribute 5% of their salary to the pension plan; the employer contributes 6% of the employees' salary to the plan. Medical cost is split 50/50 by employees and employer. All payroll related deductions are paid on the 15th of March.

Required:

(a) In recording the payroll journal in February the bookkeeper for the Ripcord Parachute Club did not record any expense for employee benefits. Give the four journal entries which should be made for the month to record this expense.

Recording employee benefits expense— multi-periods.

(b) Post the entries from the payroll journal and the entries in (a) above to the T-accounts shown below. (You may ignore the accounts which are not shown.)

Posting routing entries for a monthly period.

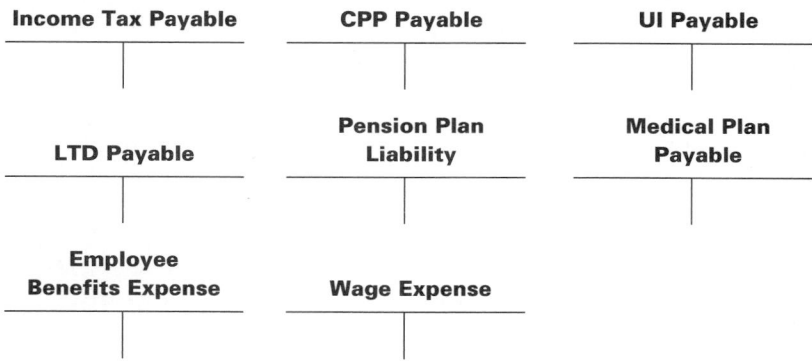

Income Tax Payable   CPP Payable   UI Payable

LTD Payable   Pension Plan Liability   Medical Plan Payable

Employee Benefits Expense   Wage Expense

(c) List the cheques and the amounts of the cheques which will be issued on March 15 for the February payroll.

GROUP C PROBLEMS

10C-1 The payroll register for Mission Hardware Ltd. for the month of May is shown below:

EMPLOYEE	SAL.	FIT	CPP	UI	HEALTH	LTD.	UNION	NET PAY	CHQ. NO.
James Wiler	2,200	490	48	66	24	33	22	1,517	343
Mona Chan	1,850	325	39	56	40	28	22	1,340	344
Ken Haverstock	1,900	340	41	57	24	29	22	1,387	345
Veronica Chan	2,300	538	51	69	24	35	22	1,561	346
Clyde Vortmann	1,700	270	36	51	40	25	22	1,256	347
	9,950	1,963	215	299	152	150	110	7,061	

(DEDUCTIONS covers FIT through UNION)

Recording benefits expense and computing and entering cheques issued re: payroll.

Union dues must be submitted to the treasurer of the union by the 20th day of the next month. Mission matches the employees' contributions to the Long Term Disability plan and the total must be sent to the insurance company by the 10th of each month following the payroll. Assume that all payroll information except for benefits has been recorded as the cheques 343 – 347 were issued.

Required:
(a) Record Missions' benefits expense for the month of May.
(b) In June, Mission issued the following 3 cheques:
   1. Cheque 381 - June 10, to the ABC Insurance Company for the LTD.
   2. Cheque 387 - June 15, to the Receiver General for Canada for employee deductions.
   3. Cheque 396 - June 15, to the Hardware Employees Union, Local 471, for union dues.
   How much was each cheque for?
(c) What entry would be made in the General Journal to record each cheque in (b) above?

10C-2 Counterpoint Counselling Inc. recorded the following details in its Professional Payroll Journal for July:

EMPLOYEE	SAL.	FIT	CPP	UI	CHAR.	LIFE INS.	ASSN. DUES	HEALTH	NET PAY	CHQ. NO.
Pamela Stark	3,800	1,140	88	97	80	38	35	72	2,250	828
Paul Dupris	4,100	1,276	96	97	90	41	35	72	2,393	829
Jan Amos	3,450	948	79	97	70	35	35	44	2,142	830
Dora Tokarsky	4,700	1,621	111	97	100	47	35	72	2,617	831
Bill March	4,600	1,580	108	97	100	46	35	44	2,590	832
Kendall Ng	3,900	1,180	91	97	80	39	35	72	2,306	833
	24,550	7,745	573	582	520	246	210	376	14,298	

Recording benefits expense and liabilities; calculating dates and amounts of cheques to be issued.

Counterpoint matches the charitable donation of each employee and forwards the total on the 25th of each month to the Canadian Centre for Counselling Research. Association dues are sent to the Provincial Counsellors Society on the 20th of each month. Life insurance premiums are remitted to ABCD Insurance Company Ltd. by the 20th day of the following month. Health insurance premiums are remitted to the Provincial Health Care Organization by the 15th of the next month, at the same time as the employee deductions are sent to the Receiver General for Canada.

Required:

(a) Give the general journal entry necessary to complete the recording of this payroll assuming no entry was made for benefits or related expenses when the payroll was recorded.

(b) List the cheques along with their amounts and dates which Counterpoint would issue in the month of August, in respect of this payroll.

10C-3 Refer to Problem 9C-2 at the end of the last chapter.

Required:

(a) Give the general journal entry necessary to recognize all payroll benefits expense arising from that payroll, given the entry you made in Chapter 9.

Recording benefits expense and liabilities.

10C-4 Refer to Problem 9C-3 at the end of the last chapter.

Required:

(a) Give the general journal entry necessary to recognize all payroll benefits expenses arising from that payroll, given the entry you made in Chapter 9.

Recording benefits expense and liabilities.

10C-5 Munchkin Bakery Ltd. pays its employees every two weeks (26 pay periods per year). There are two pay periods in the month of March and details of each pay period follow:

March 12 Payroll

EMPLOYEE	WAGES OR SALARY	FIT	CPP	UI	HEALTH	UNION	NET PAY	CHQ. NO.
Claire Patin	1,600 (s)	368	37	48	18	6	1,123	477
Roy Rocque	965 (w)	232	21	29	18	6	659	478
Adam Chan	1,114 (w)	286	25	33	32	6	732	479
Judy Dell	945 (w)	244	20	28	32	6	615	480
Moira Saunders	1,086 (w)	248	24	32	18	6	758	481
Totals	5,710	1,378	127	170	118	30	3,887	

March 26 Payroll

EMPLOYEE	WAGES OR SALARY	FIT	CPP	UI	HEALTH	UNION	NET PAY	CHQ. NO.
Claire Patin	1,600 (s)	368	37	48	18	6	1,123	524
Roy Rocque	980 (w)	240	21	29	18	6	666	525
Adam Chan	1,092 (w)	270	24	33	32	6	727	526
Judy Dell	980 (w)	256	21	29	32	6	636	527
Moira Saunders	1,124 (w)	262	25	34	18	6	779	528
Totals	5,776	1,396	128	173	118	30	3,931	

Recording benefits expense and related liabilities for two pay periods, plus calculating details of payroll benefits cheques to be issued.

Union dues must be remitted to the Bakery Union treasurer by the 28th of the following month, while Health premiums are matched by Munchkin and remitted to the Provincial Treasurer by the 10th of the month following. A cheque is sent to the Receiver General by the 15th of each following month as well.

Required:

(a) Assuming that the payroll register has been journalized but no other related entries made, prepare the two journal entries necessary to record the benefits expense for March.

(b) Give the details of all cheques which Munchkin will issue in April with respect to payroll.

Recording benefits expense and related liabilities for five pay periods in a month, plus calculating details of payroll benefits cheques to be issued.

10C-6 The Grierson Auto Repair Company pays each of its employees weekly each Friday. During the month of May there were five pay periods which are detailed below:

GRIERSON AUTO REPAIR COMPANY

WEEK 1

EMPLOYEE	WEEKLY EARNINGS	FIT	CPP	UI	UNION DUES	HEALTH PLAN	DENTAL PLAN	NET PAY	CHQ. NO.
Jesus Lopez	690.00	140.50	15.66	20.70	6.00	12.40	8.50	486.24	3314
Marina Viosky	735.00	177.05	16.79	22.05	6.00	8.60	8.50	496.01	3315
Pat Smith	816.00	209.85	18.81	22.35	6.00	8.60	8.50	541.89	3316
Leroy Wynott	850.00	197.65	19.66	22.35	6.00	12.40	8.50	583.44	3317
Pamela Barnes	675.00	150.40	15.29	20.25	6.00	12.40	8.50	462.16	3318
Weekly Totals	3,766.00	875.45	86.22	107.70	30.00	54.40	42.50	2,569.73	

WEEK 2

EMPLOYEE	WEEKLY EARNINGS	FIT	CPP	UI	UNION DUES	HEALTH PLAN	DENTAL PLAN	NET PAY	CHQ. NO.
Jesus Lopez	676.00	134.10	15.31	20.28	6.00	12.40	8.50	479.41	3378
Marina Viosky	755.00	186.80	17.29	22.35	6.00	8.60	8.50	505.46	3379
Pat Smith	834.00	219.70	19.26	22.35	6.00	8.60	8.50	549.59	3380
Leroy Wynott	850.00	197.65	19.66	22.35	6.00	12.40	8.50	583.44	3381
Pamela Barnes	675.00	150.40	15.29	20.25	6.00	12.40	8.50	462.16	3382
Weekly Totals	3,790.00	888.65	86.82	107.58	30.00	54.40	42.50	2,580.05	

WEEK 3

EMPLOYEE	WEEKLY EARNINGS	FIT	CPP	UI	UNION DUES	HEALTH PLAN	DENTAL PLAN	NET PAY	CHQ. NO.
Jesus Lopez	704.00	143.75	16.01	21.12	6.00	12.40	8.50	496.22	3421
Marina Viosky	736.00	177.05	16.81	22.08	6.00	8.60	8.50	496.96	3422
Pat Smith	798.00	203.25	18.36	22.35	6.00	8.60	8.50	530.94	3423
Leroy Wynott	850.00	197.65	19.66	22.35	6.00	12.40	8.50	583.44	3424
Pamela Barnes	675.00	150.40	15.29	20.25	6.00	12.40	8.50	462.16	3425
Weekly Totals	3,763.00	872.10	86.14	108.15	30.00	54.40	42.50	2,569.71	

WEEK 4

EMPLOYEE	WEEKLY EARNINGS	DEDUCTIONS						NET PAY	CHQ. NO.
		FIT	CPP	UI	UNION DUES	HEALTH PLAN	DENTAL PLAN		
Jesus Lopez	688.00	137.30	15.61	20.64	6.00	12.40	9.25	486.80	3488
Marina Viosky	724.00	173.85	16.51	21.72	6.00	8.60	9.25	488.07	3489
Pat Smith	822.00	213.10	18.96	22.35	6.00	8.60	9.25	543.74	3490
Leroy Wynott	850.00	197.65	19.66	22.35	6.00	12.40	9.25	582.69	3491
Pamela Barnes	675.00	150.40	15.29	20.25	6.00	12.40	9.25	461.41	3492
Weekly Totals	3,759.00	872.30	86.04	107.31	30.00	54.40	46.25	2,562.70	

WEEK 5

EMPLOYEE	WEEKLY EARNINGS	DEDUCTIONS						NET PAY	CHQ. NO.
		FIT	CPP	UI	UNION DUES	HEALTH PLAN	DENTAL PLAN		
Jesus Lopez	718.00	150.20	16.36	21.54	6.00	12.40	9.25	502.25	3535
Marina Viosky	762.00	190.10	17.46	22.35	6.00	8.60	9.25	508.24	3536
Pat Smith	828.00	216.40	19.11	22.35	6.00	8.60	9.25	546.29	3537
Leroy Wynott	850.00	197.65	19.66	22.35	6.00	12.40	9.25	582.69	3538
Pamela Barnes	675.00	150.40	15.29	20.25	6.00	12.40	9.25	461.41	3539
Weekly Totals	3,833.00	904.75	87.89	108.84	30.00	54.40	46.25	2,600.87	

Required:

(a) Assuming that the payroll register has been journalized but no other related entries made, prepare the five journal entries necessary to record the benefits expense for May, 19xx. The employees pay the entire cost of union dues, the health plan, and the dental plan.

(b) Give the details of all cheques which Grierson will issue in June, 19xx with respect to payroll.

PRACTICAL ACCOUNTING APPLICATION

The Tidy Tax Return Co. employs 50 extra people for the period February 1 through April 30 each year in order to process a large volume of tax returns. Each employee receives $10 per hour and works 40 hours a week (for 14 weeks). Early in May, all 50 additional workers are laid off.

A personnel service has offered to supply the needed 50 workers at a cost of $12 per hour. The managers of Tidy Tax Return Co. are not sure whether to accept the new offer.

Please prepare a memo to the management outlining the advantages of using the personnel service bureau and also the advantage of continuing with the present arrangement. Do not restrict your answer to financial considerations only.

NOTE: For this chapter there is only one Practical Accounting Application.

COMPREHENSIVE REVIEW PROBLEM
Payroll

You have just completed Chapters 9 and 10, which deal with payroll, employee and employer taxes, and employer tax responsibilities. The comprehensive review problem presented here will give you a chance to complete a payroll cycle and put into practice the principles of these two chapters. A complete set of forms is provided in the working papers.

Data
1. Calder Company has four employees; their TD-1 information is shown at the end of this problem.
2. Employees are paid weekly; salaried workers are involved in sales, hourly (nonsalaried) workers do administrative work. An overtime rate of one and one half times their hourly rate is paid to nonsalaried employees.
3. Calder Company deducts income tax, CPP, and UI in accordance with tables published by the federal government for use in each province. Students should use whichever tables are supplied by their course instructor, or may use the tables illustrated in Chapter 9.
4. All workers contribute 3 percent of their pay for union dues, and $15.00 each week for medical insurance.
5. Remember to pay attention to maximums for CPP and UI.

EMPLOYEE	HOURS REGULAR	OVERTIME	PAY RATE	CUMULATIVE PAY BEFORE THIS PERIOD
Sullivan, John	40	4	10.00	4,200
French, Melissa	salary	—	890.00	39,250
Lee, Mark	40	5	12.00	16,100
Swanson, Sue	salary	—	1,000.00	33,000

Instructions:
1. Complete a payroll register for a week ended November 30.
2. Prepare general journal entries to record the payroll as well as the tax responsibilities of Calder Company.
3. Record the paying of the payroll (same date as payroll). Cheques 110, 111, 112, and 113 go to the four employees.
4. The balances in the various liability account prior to this payroll were as follows:

FIT	$2,450.00
CPP	485.00
UI	680.00
Union dues	275.00
Medical	180.00

Calculate the balance that should be in each of these accounts after posting all relevant entries for the November 30 payroll.
5. Prepare general journal entries which would record the payment of these liabilities on December 15. The three cheque numbers are 147, 148, and 149.
6. Note that the employees' TD-1 forms show the following claim codes:

John Sullivan	=	1	Mark Lee	=	2
Melissa French	=	5	Sue Swanson	=	3

ACCOUNTING RECALL
A Cumulative Approach

THIS EXAM REVIEWS CHAPTERS 1 THROUGH 10

Your *Study Guide and Working Papers* have forms to complete this exam, as well as worked-out solutions. The page references next to each question identify what page to turn back to if you answer the question incorrectly.

PART I Vocabulary Review

Match the terms to the appropriate definition or phrase.

Page Ref.

(369)	1. PD7AR	A. A liability account
(364)	2. Payroll tax expense	B. Form used to obtain an employer ID No.
(204)	3. Controlling account	C. Agrees two differing amounts
(314)	4. Union dues	D. Rarely an expense
(69)	5. Fiscal year	E. Form sent with remittance
(373)	6. T4-T4A Summary	F. Employer's share of deductions
(281)	7. Bank reconciliation	G. Any 52-week period
(320)	8. Record of employment	H. Filled out only when an employee leaves or is fired
(314)	9. Medical plan payable	I. Agrees with total of many accounts
(362)	10. PD20	J. Form summarizing calendar year events in the payroll

PART II True or False (Accounting Theory)

(363) 11. Income tax deductions are part of the payroll tax expense.

(365) 12. Remittances are sent to the Receiver General each quarter.

(310) 13. Employees often must pay more income tax than has been deducted from their pay cheques.

(320) 14. Employers are required by law to file a record of employment form for each employee annually.

(362) 15. Each employer must obtain a unique identification number from the federal government to permit employees deductions to be tracked accurately.

PART III Applications Problem (361)

From the following information, calculate the employer's tax expense for the month of March. The employer has agreed to match the employees dollar for dollar for amounts deducted for charitable purposes:

EMPLOYEE	MONTHLY SALARY	NET CLAIM CODE	CHARITABLE	UNION DUES
F. Shields	2,900	4	25	16
B. Chan	1,950	1	14	16
K. Gold	3,500	2	35	–

THE SYNOPTIC JOURNAL
(Sometimes called the
Combined Journal)

IN THIS CHAPTER WE WILL COVER THE FOLLOWING TOPICS:

1. DEFINING METHODS OF ACCOUNTING: ACCRUAL BASIS, CASH BASIS, AND MODIFIED CASH BASIS. (P. 393)

2. RECORDING, JOURNALIZING, AND POSTING TRANSAC-TIONS FOR A SYNOPTIC JOURNAL OF A PROFESSIONAL SERVICE COMPANY USING A MODIFIED CASH BASIS OF ACCOUNTING. (P. 395)

3. RECORDING, JOURNALIZING, AND POSTING TRANSAC-TIONS FOR A SYNOPTIC JOURNAL OF A MERCHANDISE COMPANY USING THE ACCRUAL BASIS OF ACCOUNTING. (P. 402)

In the first ten chapters of this text we have used general journals and special jour-nals in recording business transactions. Over the years many students have asked how to set up journals for starting their own small business. They have felt that the general journals were too simple and the special journals were too detailed. In dealing with this topic, the chapter is broken down into two units:

LEARNING UNIT 11-1   Journal for a dentist, Dr. Gail Walensa—a pro-fessional service company that uses a modified cash system.

LEARNING UNIT 11-2   Synoptic journal for Art's Wholesale Clothing Company—a merchandise company that uses an accrual approach.

From these two presentations, students should be able to take accounting theory and procedures and apply them to their own business record-keeping needs.

Before we start the first unit, however, we need to talk about the difference between the cash basis of accounting and the accrual basis of accounting.

In the chapters so far we have been using the accrual basis of accounting, which is based on the *matching principle*. The matching principle says that you record revenue when it is earned (not when the money actually comes in), and you record expenses when they are incurred in producing revenue (not when they are paid).

In the cash basis of accounting, revenue is recorded when cash is received, and expenses are recorded when they are paid.

Companies choose the accrual basis because they want to show earned revenue along with the expenses that were incurred to earn that revenue. They can do so with the accrual basis but not always with the cash basis. Service companies some-times use the cash basis because it is simpler, more convenient and provides enough information for the decisions they need to make.

Let's look at the difference between accrual and cash bases with the following example: John Mills earned real estate commissions of $100,000, of which he received $60,000 in cash. Expenses were $25,000, of which $10,000 was paid in cash.

Accrual accounting:
* **earned revenue**
* **incurred expenses**

Cash accounting:
* **cash received**
* **cash paid**

Many service compa-nies will use the cash method if they have no inventories.

COMPARISON OF CASH BASIS WITH ACCRUAL BASIS
FOR MONTH OF JULY 19XX

CASH BASIS		ACCRUAL BASIS	
Revenue (received)	$60,000	Revenue (earned)	$100,000
Expenses (paid)	10,000	Expenses (incurred)	25,000
Net income	$50,000	Net income	$ 75,000

Note how net income differs according to which system is used. Keep in mind that all revenue and expenses will show up eventually if the cash basis is used, but not in this accounting period.

Now let's look at the record-keeping needs of a dentist, Dr. Gail Walensa, who wants to use a cash-basis system of accounting because of its simplicity and convenience.

Synoptic Journal:
A Modified Cash System for a Service Company

Dr. Walensa's accountant has informed her that keeping strictly to a cash-basis system is difficult to do. The reason is that because of tax regulations, Dr. Walensa's accountant would be distorting financial reports by using a strictly cash system. She feels that the best system for a dentist will be a combination of the cash and accrual methods. This combination is known as the **modified cash-basis** or **hybrid** method. Under this method Dr. Walensa will record professional fees only when cash is received and record expenses only when paid in cash. To satisfy the tax department, an adjustment for amounts accrued at year-end is required before financial statements are prepared (not illustrated here). The following exceptions, however, are an attempt to clearly reflect income and minimize distortion of the financial reports:

Dentists can't charge entire cost of dental equipment to the year it was purchased for cash.

1. Long-lived assets (equipment, building, etc.) are treated the same under cash and accrual accounting. This means that the amount paid for equipment in one year may not be treated as expense of just that period; Dr. Walensa will be depreciating or allocating the cost of her dental equipment over a period of years.
2. Insurance premiums and purchases of a large amount of supplies are treated the same under cash and accrual accounting. This means that the amount consumed or used up is shown as an expense in the current year and that the amount on hand is carried over into the next accounting period.

Only the supplies *used up* are shown as an expense.

These exceptions require adjusting entries (which we saw before under accrual accounting) when the modified cash basis is used.

Two types of personal services might use a modified cash basis. They are:

1. Professional services—lawyers, doctors, dentists, accountants, and so on.
2. Business services—real estate, insurance, software support, and so on.

The chart of accounts for Dr. Walensa is provided in Figure 11-1. Note that, unlike a chart of accounts on the accrual basis, there are no categories for Accounts Receivable, Accounts Payable, or Salaries Payable (these are added at year-end by the accountant). This chart of accounts does have titles for handling the exceptions (for example, Accumulated Depreciation, Prepaid Insurance, etc.). There is no supplies account under assets, since Dr. Walensa is not buying a large amount of supplies, and thus all can be shown as Dental Supplies Expense without distorting the financial reports.

The transactions that occurred for the month of November are listed on p. 394. We will show you the recording of these transactions in the **synoptic journal**—a special journal that will replace the general journal and save journalizing and posting labour. The synoptic journal has the same basic features as other special journals that we introduced in Chapters 6 and 7. Remember, each business will design the headings of the synoptic journal to fit its individual needs. Often it is not unusual to find such journals with a total of 24 columns, or even more—although we will be keeping things at a more manageable size in this textbook. Accounts that are used most often are the ones that should have a special column. This will save time when journalizing and posting.

Another important point is that GST is not included in the earlier examples in this text, but is covered at the end of Learning Unit 11-2.

FIGURE 11-1
Chart of
Accounts

**DR. WALENSA
CHART OF ACCOUNTS**

Assets
111 Cash
113 Petty Cash Fund
131 Prepaid Insurance
141 Office Furniture
142 Accum. Dep., Office Furniture
151 Dental Equipment
152 Accum. Dep., Dental Equipment
161 Auto
162 Accum. Dep., Auto

Liabilities
211 Due to Receiver General
212 Other Payroll Ded. Payable
213 Notes Payable

Owner's Equity
311 G. Walensa, Capital
312 G. Walensa, Withdrawals
313 Income Summary

Revenue
411 Professional Fees

Expenses
511 Automobile Expense
512 Rent Expense
513 Salaries Expense
514 Telephone Expense
515 Dep. Exp., Office Furniture
516 Dep. Exp., Dental Equipment
517 Dep. Exp., Auto
518 Miscellaneous Expense
519 Insurance Expense
520 Dental Supplies Expense
521 Payroll Tax Expense

TRANSACTIONS FOR DR. WALENSA

19XX
Nov. 1　Paid $200 office rent for November, cheque no. 61.
1　Received cheques for $3,000 from patients for dental work.
4　Paid telephone bill, $80, cheque no. 62.
4　Issued cheque no. 63 to Bill Blan Insurance Agency for premium on insurance for three years, $600.
8　Purchased dental supplies from Roe Suppliers, $150, cheque no. 64.
8　Received cheques from patients, $1,600.
8　Calculated current cash balance.
11　Issued cheque no. 65 to Moe Gas for automobile expenses charged during October, $80.

Example of a modified cash system.

11　Dr. Walensa withdrew $500 for personal use, cheque no. 66.
14　Issued cheque no. 67 to V.P. Suppliers Company for dental supplies charged during October, $250.
15　Paid office salaries for the period Nov. 1 to Nov. 15, $2,000, cheque no. 68.
15　Cash receipts from patients totalled $2,800 for the week.
15　Calculated current cash balance.
19　Collected $800 from insurance companies for patients' accounts.
21　Purchased dental supplies from J. Labs, $200, cheque no. 69.
22　Cash receipts for the week totalled $2,900.
22　Calculated current cash balance.
27　Issued cheque no. 70 for charitable contributions, $300.

27 Purchased dental supplies from J. Labs, $100, cheque no. 71.
28 Received cheques from patients' insurance companies totalling $3,300.
29 Paid office salaries for the period November 15 to November 30, $1,500, cheque no. 72.
30 Calculated current cash balance and crossfooted journal.

RECORDING TRANSACTIONS IN THE SYNOPTIC JOURNAL

The synoptic journal for Dr. Walensa is shown in Figure 11-2, p. 396. Note that the bank balance can be calculated at any time. For example, in the explanation column, note the beginning balance of $9,500. On Nov. 8 the current balance was calculated as follows:

	Beg. Balance	$ 9,500
+	Deposits	4,600
−	Cheques written	1,030
	Ending Balance	$13,070 (recorded in explanation column)

As we saw with special journals before, this synoptic journal is proved in the following way:

	DR.	CR.
Cash	$14,400	$ 5,960
Sundry	5,260	
Professional Fees		14,400
Dental Sup. Exp.	700	
	$20,360	$20,360

Proving the journal.

POSTING THE SYNOPTIC JOURNAL

Since this is a modified cash system, there are no subsidiary ledgers for accounts receivable or accounts payable. Companies using a modified cash basis may keep information about any receivables or payables in an informal memorandum record till cash is received or paid. During the month, items entered into the sundry column can be updated in the general ledger. At the end of the month the totals of Cash, Professional Fees, and Dental Supplies Expense would be posted to the general ledger. The account numbers are shown at the bottom of the columns of the synoptic journal to show that the totals were posted. The (X) means that no posting is necessary. The total of the sundry column is not posted because the various items making up the total are posted individually.

Memorandum records can be used in a modified cash system.

RECORDING PAYROLL DEDUCTIONS AND EMPLOYER'S TAX EXPENSE

Back in Chapters 9 and 10 we studied payroll, with the payroll register recording gross pay, deductions, and net pay. From the payroll register a general journal entry is prepared to record the payroll. We also discussed using a general journal

Dr. Walensa
Synoptic Journal

Month: _November_

Cash Deposits Dr.	Cheques Cr.	Chq. No.	Date	Explanations	PR	Sundry Dr.	Sundry Cr.	Professional Fees Cr.	Dental Supplies Expense Dr.
			19XX	Cash Balance 9,500					
	200 00	61	Nov. 1	Rent Expense	512	200 00			
3000 00			1	Professional Fees	X			3000 00	
	80 00	62	4	Telephone Expense	514	80 00			
	600 00	63	4	Prepaid Insurance	131	600 00			
	150 00	64	7	Roe Supplies	X				150 00
1600 00			8	Professional Fees 13,070	X			1600 00	
	80 00	65	11	Auto Expense	511	80 00			
	500 00	66	11	G. Walensa, Withd.	312	500 00			
	250 00	67	14	V.P. Suppliers	X				250 00
	2000 00	68	15	Salaries Expense	513	2000 00			
2800 00			15	Professional Fees 13,040	X			2800 00	
800 00			19	Professional Fees	X			800 00	
	200 00	69	21	J. Labs	X				200 00
2900 00			22	Professional Fees 16,540	X			2900 00	
	300 00	70	27	Miscellaneous Expense	518	300 00			
	100 00	71	27	J. Labs	X				100 00
3300 00			28	Professional Fees	X			3300 00	
	1500 00	72	29	Salaries Expense 17,940	513	1500 00			
14400 00	5960 00					5260 00		14400 00	700 00
(111)	(111)					(X)		(411)	(520)

$20,360 = $20,360

FIGURE 11-2

The Synoptic Journal

to record the employer's payroll tax expense before it is paid (for CPP and UI). The record keeping involved in paying an employee will be quite similar in a synoptic journal using the cash-basis method, but recording the employer's payroll tax expense will change.

Why? In the cash-basis method of accounting the owner's share of CPP as well as UI will not be recorded until they are paid. Under accrual accounting we recorded them when they were incurred, not when they were paid.

Let's look at the partially completed synoptic journal on p. 398 and explain each entry. For simplicity we are ignoring the remittance requirements and monthly reports that we covered in the payroll chapters.

A. Bill Smith's gross salary of $500 is recorded as a salary expense, and the deductions for FIT, CPP, and UI are listed as liabilities until the employer makes the remittance. Note that the cheque is written for $375 (net pay). The same procedure is followed for Joe Ring.

B. On June 13 the remittance to the Receiver General is assumed made. This means the employer pays the CPP and UI for the employee as well as the matching share along with the FIT deducted from the employees' paycheques.

Key point: The payroll tax expense is now being recorded for the employer's share of CPP and UI, since it is now being *paid*. Note that the cheque amount is for $264.80, which includes the following:

Fed. Inc. Tax Payable	140.00
CPP Payable	24.00
Payroll tax expense – CPP	24.00
UI Payable	32.00
Payroll tax expense – UI ($32.00 × 1.4)	44.80
	264.80

The end result is to reduce the liabilities owed as well as record the employer's share of CPP and UI as payroll tax expense. When the remittance is actually made to the Receiver General for Canada, the following entry is made:

	Dr.	Cr.
Income tax payable	xxx.xx	
CPP payable	xx.xx	
UI payable	xx.xx	
Payroll tax expense	xx.xx	
Cash		xxx.xx

In summary, sometimes companies will record the expense portion of CPP and UI when the *payroll* is paid, instead of when the remittance is made. If this is the case then when the remittance is made they will record this entry:

	Dr.	Cr.
Income tax payable	xxx.xx	
CPP payable	xx.xx	
UI payable	xx.xx	
Cash		xxx.xx

At this point you should be able to

1. Explain the modified cash basis of accounting. (p. 393)
2. Journalize transactions into a synoptic journal. (pp. 395-396)
3. Calculate the current bank balance of a synoptic journal. (p. 396)
4. Prove a synoptic journal. (p. 396)
5. Explain how to record payroll as well as payroll tax expense into a synoptic journal. (pp. 395, 396)

Synoptic Journal

	Royal Bank		Chq. No.	Date	Accounts or Explanations	PR	Sundry		Professional Fees Cr.	Salary Expense Dr.	Payroll Deductions		
	Deposits Dr.	Cheques Cr.					Dr.	Cr.			Income Tax Payable Cr.	CPP Payable Cr.	UI Payable Cr.
(A)		375 00	33	May 5	Bill Smith	X				500 00	90 00	15 00	20 00
		229 00	34	5	Joe Ring	X				300 00	50 00	9 00	12 00
(B)		264 80	50	June 9	Receiver General								
					Tax Payable	211	140 00						
					CPP Payable	212	24 00						
					UI Payable	213	32 00						
					Payroll Tax Exp	521	68 80 *						

* Calculated as $[(\$24.00 \times 1) + 32.00 \times 1.4]$

□ SELF-REVIEW QUIZ 11-1

Answer true or false to the following:

1. A modified cash system will only have one exception, long-lived assets, in the adjustment process.
2. A cash-basis system in a chart of accounts usually has titles for Due to Receiver General and Payroll Deductions Payable.
3. Headings of synoptic journals can be modified to meet the needs of the user.
4. The cash balance can easily be updated in a synoptic journal.
5. Payroll tax expense will be recorded when the remittance is made to the Receiver General.

■ *SOLUTIONS TO SELF-REVIEW QUIZ 11-1*

1. F   2. F   3. T   4. T   5. T

LEARNING UNIT 11-2

Synoptic Journal for
Art's Wholesale Clothing Company

Back in Chapters 6 and 7 we developed the sales journal, cash receipts journal, purchases journal, cash payments journal, and general journal for Art's Wholesale Clothing Company. Many small businesses that are concerned with saving journalizing, recording, and posting labor, however, are not concerned about division of labor (having a bookkeeper working on each special journal), since they have only one bookkeeper. Such businesses may want the advantages provided by special journals but would like to reduce the number of journals needed. This unit will develop a synoptic journal, a book of original entry, that dispenses with the special journals, yet gains their advantages in journalizing, recording, and posting for a company that uses an accrual accounting approach. (In order to focus on the basics of the synoptic journal, payroll details are not described at this point.)

Our goal in this unit is to place all the special journals for Art's Wholesale into the following synoptic journal:

											Month: April				Page 1

Date	Explanations	Cheque No.	PR	Sundry Dr. Cr.	Cash Dr. Cr.	Acct. Rec. Dr. Cr.	Acct. Pay. Dr. Cr.	Sales Cr.	Sales Dis. Dr.	Pur. Dr.	Pur. Dis. Cr.

If Art decided to use the synoptic journal, he and the accountant would go over the chart of accounts. They would be concerned with setting up columns in the synoptic journal for accounts in which transactions would occur frequently. Based on their analysis, Art and the accountant agreed to set up the following special columns in a synoptic journal.

Note that since Art's business uses *accrual* accounting, we now have columns for Accounts Receivable and Accounts Payable.

Cash Dr. This column records increases in cash.

Cash Cr. This column records decreases in cash.

Accounts Receivable Dr. This column records amounts owed from sales on account.

Accounts Receivable Cr. This column records amounts paid by customers from past sales on account.

Accounts Payable Dr. This column reflects amounts paid to creditors.

Accounts Payable Cr. This column reflects amounts owed to creditors.

Sales Cr. This column records all sales made for cash or on account.

Sales Discount Dr. This column records the amounts of discounts taken by customers.

Art's Wholesale Clothing Company
Synoptic Journal

Date		Explanation	Chq. No.	PR	Sundry Dr.	Sundry Cr.	Cash Dr.	Cash Cr.
19XX								
Apr.	1	Art Newner, Cap		311		8 000 00	8 000 00	
	2	Prepaid Ins.	1	116	9 00 00			9 00 00
	3	Hal's Clothing		✔				
	3	Freight-In, Abby Blake		512 ✔	5 0 00			
	4	Equip., Joe Francis		121 ✔	4 000 00			
	4	Hal's Clothing		✔			7 84 00	
	6	Thorpe Co.		✔				
	6	Bevans Co.		✔				
	7	J. Francis Co.	2	✔				4 000 00
	7	J. Sullivan Co.		✔				
	9	Purchases	3	✘				8 00 00
	9	Pur. R&A, Thorpe Co.		514 ✔		2 00 00		
	12	Thorpe Co.	4	✔				5 94 00
	12	Sales R&A, Bevans Co.		412 ✔	6 00 00			
	12	Abby Blake Co.		✔				
	15	Cash Sales		✘			9 00 00	
	16	Bevans Co.		✔			9 80 00	
	18	Roe Co.		✔				
	22	Roe Co.		✔			1 96 0 00	
	24	Roe Co.		✔				
	25	Sup., J. Sullivan		115 ✔	5 00 00			
	27	Store Equip.		121		5 00 00	5 00 00	
	28	Salaries Expense	5	611	7 00 00			7 00 00
	28	Mel's Dept. St.		✔				
	29	Mel's Dept. St.		✔				
	30	Cash Sales		✘			1 200 00	
		Totals			6 750 00	8 700 00	14 324 00	6 994 00
					(X)	(X)	(111)	(111)

Purchases Dr. All purchases of merchandise for resale are recorded in this column.

Purchases Discount Cr. This column records the amounts of discounts Art receives by paying for purchases before the discount period expires.

Sundry Dr., Cr. These two columns record transactions that do not occur very frequently. If a transaction occurs and no special columns are set up to record part or all of it, it can be recorded in the sundry columns.

Figure 11-3 (pp. 400-401) shows the completed synoptic journal for the month of April for Art's Wholesale Clothing Company (we will go over the recordings and postings in a moment).

Month: April

Accounts Receivable Dr.	Accounts Receivable Cr.	Accounts Payable Dr.	Accounts Payable Cr.	Sales Cr.	Sales Disc. Dr.	Purch. Dr.	Purch. Disc. Cr.
800.00				800.00			
			5050.00			5000.00	
			4000.00				
	800.00				16.00		
			800.00			800.00	
1600.00				1600.00			
		4000.00					
			980.00			980.00	
						800.00	
		200.00					
		600.00					6.00
	600.00						
			600.00			600.00	
				900.00			
	1000.00				20.00		
2000.00				2000.00			
	2000.00				40.00		
500.00				500.00			
			500.00				
900.00				900.00			
700.00				700.00			
				1200.00			
6500.00	4400.00	4800.00	11930.00	8600.00	76.00	8180.00	6.00
(113)	(113)	(211)	(211)	(411)	(413)	(511)	(513)

FIGURE 11-3

Synoptic Journal Completed

The synoptic journal can be proved as follows:

Account Title	Dr.	Cr.
Sundry	$ 6 7 5 0 00	$ 8 7 0 0 00
Cash	14 3 2 4 00	6 9 9 4 00
Accounts Receivable	6 5 0 0 00	4 4 0 0 00
Accounts Payable	4 8 0 0 00	11 9 3 0 00
Sales		8 6 0 0 00
Sales Discounts	7 6 00	00
Purchases	8 1 8 0 00	00
Purchases Discount		6 00
Totals	$40 6 3 0 00	$40 6 3 0 00

Checking the accuracy of the synoptic journal. *(margin note)*

RECORDING AND POSTING THE SYNOPTIC JOURNAL

The recording and posting rules we learned for Art's special journals will hold true for the synoptic journal. Here are some key points:

1. (√). Record to accounts receivable or accounts payable subsidiary ledgers daily.
2. Sundry. Update the general ledger account on a daily basis. Use the ledger account number as a posting reference.
3. An (X) in the PR column indicates no posting, since the total is posted at the end of the month. An (X) below the total means that the total of the column is not posted.

End of Month

CJ1 (Synoptic Journal, page 1) will be placed in PR of ledger account, where information from journal is updated in ledger. *(margin note)*

Total of each column except sundry will be posted to the general ledger at the end of the month. Note that the account number from the ledger is placed at the bottom of the column in the synoptic journal, indicating that the total was posted to that account.

Note the following when a synoptic journal is used:

1. Charge *and* cash sales are recorded in the sales column.
2. Purchases returns, sales returns, etc., are recorded in sundry, since no general journal is used with a synoptic journal.
3. Adjusting and closing entries will be recorded in the sundry columns.

Adjusting and closing entries would be recorded in the sundry columns of a synoptic journal. *(margin note)*

Whether Art uses a synoptic journal or a set of special journals, the schedule of accounts receivable and accounts payable will be the same, as will the trial balance.

To sum up, the synoptic journal is an option for small businesses that do not have many transactions. Lawyers, doctors, dentists, and other professionals may use a synoptic journal, which may be modified in many ways to suit their individual needs.

As the business grows, the volume of transactions may increase, possibly creating the need for more specialized journals rather than just the synoptic journal. For example, if a company adds bookkeepers to its accounting department, management must be prepared to provide a system of dividing the work to be done. This division of labor may play an important part in determining the types of special journals that are needed.

Before stating the objectives of this unit, let's look at a sample of how a synoptic journal might look if it included Provincial Sales Tax Payable and GST (see

Figure 11-4, p. 404). Notice in Figure 11-4 that at the end of the month we will still post to the general ledger the totals of accounts receivable, sales, sales tax payable, and GST payable. Keep in mind that sales tax payable and GST payable are liabilities shown on the balance sheet. Also bear in mind that the principles of recording PST and GST have not changed at all from Chapters 6 and 7 where we covered them in detail. The main difference is that now we are including both collections and remittances in the same journal.

Another point worth stressing is that in the modern business world there is less need to study the large synoptic journal with a lot of intensity. If a large synoptic journal is necessary due to complex transactions (or a large volume of these) a computer plus some inexpensive software is perhaps a better solution. See the material in Appendix A for additional details and remember that a knowledge of manual bookkeeping and accounting procedures means that a computerized system can be more useful and efficient.

If a retail company has many sales returns and allowances as well as purchases, the following synoptic journal heading could be designed.

				Synoptic Journal						
										Page 1
Cash and sundry would be located here.	Acct. Rec. Dr. Cr.	Sales Cr.	Sales R. & A. Dr.	Acct. Pay Dr. Cr.	Sales Tax Payable Cr.	Purch. Dr.	Sup. Dr.	Office Equip. Dr.		

Now at this point you should be able to

1. Journalize transactions into the synoptic journal for a merchandise company. (pp. 399-402)
2. Explain how to record and post the synoptic journal. (p. 402)
3. Compare special journals (cash payments, receipts, etc.) and the synoptic journal. (pp. 402-403)
4. Explain how sales tax and GST could be recorded in a synoptic journal. (p. 403)

□ SELF-REVIEW QUIZ 11-2

Based on the synoptic journal presented in this unit, classify each statement as true or false.

1. Synoptic journals are less efficient than other types of special journals.
2. The total of the cash column is posted daily.
3. The total of the sundry column is not posted.
4. The total of the sales column is not posted.
5. All synoptic journals have the same headings.
6. Synoptic journals cannot be proved.
7. Subsidiary ledgers are posted from the cash column.
8. The synoptic journals is used for large companies.
9. A dentist could use a synoptic journal.
10. A lawyer will always use a synoptic journal.

FIGURE 11-4   Synoptic Journal with Sales Tax and GST

Synoptic Journal

Date	Explanation	Chq. No.	PR	Sundry Dr.	Sundry Cr.	Cash Dr.	Cash Cr.	Accounts Receivable Dr.	Accounts Receivable Cr.
19XX									
May 1	Bill Jones		✔					1 1 6 00	
May 8	Alice Smith		✔					4 5 4 00	
May 15	Alice Smith - Pmt. = 2%	376	✔			4 4 6 00			4 5 4 00
May 7	Birchmount Co.		✔						
May 9	Cooper & Co.		✔						
May 18	Cooper & Co. - Pmt. = 2%		✔				6 3 0 0 00		

Recorded immediately to the Accounts Receivable or Accounts Payable ledgers

Totals posted at the end of the month to the General Ledger

Month-end Totals: Cash Dr. 4 4 6 00, Cash Cr. 6 3 0 0 00, Accounts Receivable Dr. 5 7 0 00, Accounts Receivable Cr. 4 5 4 00

■ SOLUTION TO SELF-QUIZ 11-2

1. False
2. False
3. True
4. False
5. False
6. False
7. False
8. False
9. True
10. False

Accounts Payable Dr.	Accounts Payable Cr.	GST Dr.	GST Cr.	Sales Cr.	Sales Disc. Dr.	Purch. Dr.	Purch. Disc. Cr.	Sales Tax Cr.
			7 00	1 0 0 00				9 00
			2 8 00	4 0 0 00				3 6 00
					8 00			
	1 1 7 7 00	7 7 00				1 1 0 0 00		
	6 4 2 0 00	4 2 0 00				6 0 0 0 00		
6 4 2 0 00							1 2 0 00	
6 4 2 0 00	7 5 9 7 00	4 9 7 00	3 5 00	5 0 0 00	8 00	7 1 0 0 00	1 2 0 00	4 5 00

SUMMARY OF KEY POINTS AND KEY TERMS

LEARNING UNIT 11-1

1. A company with inventory will not use the cash method.
2. The modified cash system is used because federal and provincial requirements make a strictly cash-basis system difficult to implement without distorting financial reports.
3. The modified cash system will require adjustments for depreciation, insurance premiums, and large amounts of supplies purchased. Adjustments will be recorded in the sundry columns of the synoptic journal and additional adjustments can be made at year end.

4. No accounts for Accounts Payable or Accounts Receivable are used in the chart of accounts for a modified cash system. Companies use memorandums to keep track of receivables or payables until money is received or paid.

5. The bank balance (cash balance) can be determined at any time when a synoptic journal is used.

6. A synoptic journal can be proved by listing debits and credits.

7. The payroll tax expense for the employer using a cash-basis system is recorded when the remittance is made. In the cash-basis system no *liability* accounts exist for Due to Receiver General or other payroll taxes payable; you record them when *paid* as part of Payroll Tax Expense.

RUTH RAMOS: ASSISTANT DIRECTOR FOR FISCAL OPERATIONS, CONTROLLER FOR HEAD START, MAJOR NOT-FOR-PROFIT ORGANIZATION

Ruth Ramos started out as a secretary/bookkeeper and quickly discovered that she preferred working with numbers. When she was hired as a secretary at Head Start, a nonprofit child development program, it was not long before she took on bookkeeping duties, relying on her previous job experience.

As Ruth took on more responsibilities, she felt the need to have a solid academic background in accounting. "I decided to take my job seriously and go back to school," she says. Her employer offered tuition reimbursement for job-related courses so she began taking bookkeeping and accounting courses.

"Getting a background in accounting has been enormously helpful," she says. "The College Accounting course gave me a more thorough understanding of the theory, and helped me to learn the language of accounting."

Ruth is now Assistant Director for Fiscal Operations, Controller for a major Head Start operation. Her responsibilities include preparing budget proposals for million dollar programs. She is also responsible for day to day cost analysis, payroll, general ledger and journal, trial balances, and monthly financial statements. She prepares for outside audits and supervises a staff of seven bookkeepers.

"My courses helped me to understand how to read budgets and how to prepare them," she says. "The first time I had to work with outside auditors, I was scared stiff. But now I feel confident. I know my stuff, and the auditors have been impressed with my knowledge."

"Going back to school was the best decision I ever made," Ruth says. "The courses gave me confidence in my job and gave me the confidence to continue my education."

Modified cash-basis method (hybrid): The accounting method that records revenue when cash is received, and expenses when they are paid. Adjustments to long-lived assets, as well as insurance premiums and amounts of supplies on hand, are required by provincial and federal laws so that financial reports will not be distorted.

LEARNING UNIT 11-2

1. A synoptic journal for Art's Wholesale replaces the individual special journals (SJ, CRJ, PJ, CPJ, GJ).

2. Many small companies use a synoptic journal.

3. A synoptic journal on an accrual basis uses columns for accounts receivable and accounts payable. Subsidiary ledgers will be recorded during the month. The total of the sundry columns is not posted.

4. Adjusting and closing entries will be recorded in the sundry columns.

Accrual accounting synoptic journal: A special journal that combines the features of the sales, cash payments, cash receipts, purchases, and general journals.

BLUEPRINT OF A TYPICAL CHART OF ACCOUNTS
FOR A LAWYER USING A MODIFIED CASH BASIS
(INCLUDING PAYROLL)

Assets

Royal Bank	111
Petty Cash	112
Office Supplies	113
Prepaid Insurance	114
Office Equip.	115
Accum. Dep., Office Equip.	116
Automobiles	117
Accum. Dep., Auto	118

No Accounts Receivable account

Liabilities

Income Tax Payable	211
CPP Payable	212
UI Payable	213
Notes Payable	214

No Accounts Payable account

Owner's Equity

J. Smith, Capital	311
J. Smith, Withdrawals	312
Income Summary	313

Revenue

Only recorded when cash received ← Revenue

Professional Fees	411

Expenses

Dep. Exp., Office Equip.	511
Dep. Exp., Auto	512
Insurance Expense	513
Office Supplies Expense	514
Dues	515
Postage	516
Payroll Tax Expense	517
Rent Expense	518
Salary Expense	519
Telephone Expense	520
Miscellaneous Expense	521

For adjustments so financial reports will not be distorted

Records the tax expense for employer when the CPP, UI, and income tax is remitted

DISCUSSION QUESTIONS

1. All companies with inventory must use the cash basis of accounting. Agree or disagree.
2. Why does the strictly cash basis tend to distort financial reports?
3. List three adjustments that may result in a modified cash system.
4. Explain how a company can change its method of accounting.
5. A modified cash system has an accounts receivable as well as accounts payable ledger. Agree or disagree. Please support your answer.
6. Explain how a cash balance can be calculated during the month when using a synoptic journal.
7. How is a synoptic journal proved?
8. Explain why there are no accounts for Due to Receiver General or other payroll taxes payable in the chart of accounts in the cash basis.
9. What purpose would an informal memorandum serve when dealing with accounts payable and accounts receivable in a modified cash system?
10. Explain when the Payroll Tax Expense account will be updated in a modified cash system.
11. Explain how a synoptic journal for an accrual-based company will aid in reducing the number of special journals needed.
12. If a company is expanding, a synoptic journal could be efficient. Please respond.

EXERCISES

Identifying adjustment titles for a modified cash system.

1. In a modified cash system, which of the following titles may need adjustments?

Cash
Supplies
Prepaid Insurance
Equipment
Notes Payable
A. Swan, Capital
A. Swan, Withdrawals
Commission Sales
Salary Expense

Posting a synoptic journal using the accrual approach.

2. Avon Company uses a synoptic journal with the following headings:

Sundry	Dr.	Cr.
Accounts Receivable	Dr.	Cr.
Accounts Payable	Dr.	Cr.
Commission Sales		Cr.
Salary Expense	Dr.	
Cash	Dr.	Cr.

(a) How can the balance of cash be determined at any point in the month?
(b) Which column total will not be posted?
(c) Do you think Avon Company has subsidiary ledgers? Please explain.
(d) Which columns will be used to record the payment of advertising expense?

3. Listed below are the accounts used by Dr. Jonson, who keeps his records on a strictly cash basis. As his accountant, which titles do you think could be added to use a modified cash system? Assume that a large amount of supplies is bought.

Preparing a chart of accounts for a modified cash system.

Cash; Notes Payable; L. Jonson, Capital; L. Jonson, Withdrawals; Professional Fees; Auto Expense; Rent Expense; Office Furniture Expense; Insurance Expense; Medical Supplies Expense.

4. Using the headings of the synoptic journal for Dr. Walensa (p. 396), indicate when postings would occur.

Explaining postings of a synoptic journal for a modified cash basis.

19XX
May 3   Al Henson invested $4,000 in the dental business.
     8   Paid three months' insurance premiums, $1,200.
    15   Received cheques from patients, $900.
    19   Paid office salaries, $500.

5. Using the headings of the synoptic journal for Art's Wholesale (pp. 400-401), indicate when recordings and postings would occur.

Explaining recordings and postings of a synoptic journal using an accrual approach.

19XX
May 2   Joe Davis invested $12,000 in the business.
     5   Bought $600 of merchandise for cash.
     8   Cash sale, $600.
    19   Received $400 less a 3% discount from Alvie Corp. from past sale on account.

GROUP A PROBLEMS

11A-1. Dr. Lovejoy, M.D., uses the following chart of accounts:

CHART OF ACCOUNTS

Assets
111 Alberta Bank
113 Petty Cash
114 Prepaid Insurance
115 Medical Supplies
121 Medical Equipment
122 Accumulated Depreciation, Medical Equipment
123 Office Furniture
124 Accumulated Depreciation, Office Furniture
125 Auto
126 Accumulated Depreciation, Auto

Liabilities
211 Notes Payable

Owner's Equity
311 Pete Lovejoy, Capital
312 Pete Lovejoy, Withdrawals
313 Income Summary

Revenue
411 Professional Fees

Expenses
511 Rent Expense
512 Donation Expense
513 Salaries Expense
514 Medical Supplies Expense
515 Depreciation Expense, Medical Equipment
516 Depreciation Expense, Office Furniture
517 Depreciation Expense, Automobile
518 Insurance Expense
519 Telephone Expense
610 Cleaning Expense
611 Miscellaneous Expense

Journalizing transactions of a modified cash system in a synoptic journal.

The headings of the synoptic journal are as follows:

									Page 1	
Date	*Explanations*	*PR*	*Sundry Dr. Cr.*	*Medical Supplies Dr.*	*Dr. Lovejoy, Withdrawals Dr.*	*Cleaning Expense Dr.*	*Prof. Fees Cr.*	*Chq. No.*	*Alberta Dr.*	*Bank Cr.*

From the transactions listed below:
1. Journalize them in the synoptic journal.
2. Prove the synoptic journal.

19XX
May 1   Dr. Lovejoy deposited $6,000 in the practice.
    3   Paid rent for the month to Foster Realty, $800, cheque no. 1.
    8   Bought medical equipment from Ace Supply Co., $1,500, cheque no. 2.
   12   Bought medical supplies from Lone Co., $700, cheque no. 3.
   15   Received cash from patients; $2,800.
   18   Bought additional medical supplies from Lone Co., $1,200, cheque no. 4.
   19   Dr. Lovejoy withdrew $600 for personal use; cheque no. 5.
   21   Paid Al's Janitorial Service, $300, cheque no. 6.
   24   Received cash from patients, $1,900.
   25   Paid for postage stamps, $40 (miscellaneous expense); cheque no. 7.
   27   Paid salaries for month, $1,400; cheque no. 8.
   28   Paid Al's Janitorial Service, $400; cheque no. 9.
   29   Dr. Lovejoy withdrew $400 for personal use; cheque no. 10.

11A-2. The following is the chart of accounts of Al Fox, M.D.:

Journalizing transactions of a modified cash system into a synoptic journal with headings for payroll deductions as well as recording payroll tax expense.

CHART OF ACCOUNTS

Assets
111 Bank of Regina
112 Prepaid Insurance
113 Medical Supplies
122 Accumulated Depreciation, Office Equipment

Liabilities
211 Due to Receiver General
212 Other Payroll Taxes Payable

Owner's Equity
311 Al Fox, Capital
312 Al Fox, Withdrawals
313 Income Summary

Revenue
411 Professional Fees

Expenses
511 Rent Expense
512 Medical Supplies Expense
513 Salaries Expense
514 Payroll Tax Expense
515 Telephone Expense
516 Depreciation Expense, Office Equipment
517 Insurance Expense
518 Cleaning Expense
519 Miscellaneous Expense

The headings of Dr. Fox's synoptic journal are follows:

	Date	Explan.	PR	Bank of Regina Dr. Cr.	Chq. No.	Prof. Fees Cr.	Sal. Exp. Dr.	Payroll Deductions			Med. Supp. Dr.	Sundry Dr. Cr.
								Income Tax Payable Cr.	CPP Payable Cr.	UI Payable Cr.		

Page 1

From the transactions listed below:
1. Journalize them in the synoptic journal (beginning balances are provided in the working papers).
2. Prove the synoptic journal.

19XX
May 1 Received $3,000 from patients.
    3 Issued cheque no. 480 to Lane Drug for medical supplies, $600.
    5 Issued cheque no. 481 to A. Realty to pay three months' insurance premiums, $1,200.
    9 Received cheques from patients, $2,000.
    12 Issued the following payroll cheques to his staff:

EMPLOYEE	CHQ. NO.	GROSS PAY	FIT	CPP	UI	NET PAY
Abby Slat	482	$ 700	$140	$18	$21	$ 521
Jane Reeves	483	600	120	16	18	446
Bob Swan	484	500	100	14	15	371
		$1,800	$360	$48	$54	$1,338

    18 Issued cheque no. 485 to Lane Drug for medical supplies, $400.
    25 Dr. Fox withdrew $700 for personal use, cheque no. 486.
    28 Dr. Fox made the necessary remittance to the Receiver General from payroll of May 12, cheque no. 487. (Don't forget Dr. Fox's share of CPP and UI.)

11A-3. Debra Clark, a recent graduate of a medical school, has decided to open her own office. Based on the advice of her accountant, she will use a synoptic journal. The following is the chart of accounts for Dr. Clark's office:

CHART OF ACCOUNTS

Assets
111 Cash
112 Accounts Receivable
113 Prepaid Insurance
121 Office Equipment

Liabilities
211 Accounts Payable

Owner's Equity
311 D. Clark, Capital
312 Income Summary

Revenue
411 Medical Fees

Expenses
511 Telephone Expense
512 Cleaning Expense
513 Utilities Expense

Journalizing and proving synoptic journal, recording transactions using an accrual basis of accounting.

The headings of Dr. Clark's synoptic journal are:

Synoptic Journal														
											Month		*Page 1*	
Date	Expl.	Chq. No.	PR	Sundry Dr. Cr.	Cash Dr.	Cash Cr.	Acct. Rec. Dr.	Acct. Rec. Cr.	Acct. Pay Dr.	Acct. Pay Cr.	Office Equip. Dr.	Medical Fees Cr.		

Your task is to

1. Record the following transactions in the synoptic journal. Complete the PR column as if you were recording and posting.
2. Prove the synoptic journal.

19XX

July   1   Debra Clark invested $7,000 cash and $4,000 of office equipment in the practice.

        1   Paid insurance on the office for one year in advance, $1,700, cheque no. 1.

        9   Purchased office equipment on account from Smith Stationery Co., $400.

      12   Purchased office equipment on account from Vole Stationery Co., $700.

      18   Completed vaccination of each schoolchild at Salem Elementary School, $3,000 on account.

      18   Received $900 cash for medical fees earned.

      19   Performed a complete examination for Alvin Ray's son, $75 on account.

      20   Paid Smith Stationery one-half the amount owed from July 9 transaction, cheque no. 2.

      26   Paid telephone bill, $90, cheque no. 3.

      27   Paid utilities, $170, cheque no. 4.

      28   Paid Toby Cleaning Co. for cleaning service performed, $100, cheque no. 5.

      29   Paid one-half the amount owed Vole Stationery Company from July 12 transaction, cheque no. 6.

11A-4. (GST (7%) and PST (9% – not cumulative) involved in this problem.) Buzzy Sullivan opened a dry-cleaning store that also sold accessories. The following is the chart of accounts for Buzzy's Cleaning Company.

CHART OF ACCOUNTS

Assets
111 Cash
112 Accounts Receivable
113 Prepaid Insurance
115 Prepaid GST
121 Cleaning Equipment

Liabilities
211 Accounts Payable
212 Note Payable
215 GST Collected
217 PST Payable

Owner's Equity
311 B. Sullivan, Capital
312 Income Summary

Revenue
411 Cleaning Sales
412 Sales Discount
413 Accessory Sales

Cost of Goods Sold
511 Purchases
512 Purchases Returns and Allowances
513 Purchases Discounts

Expenses
611 Utilities Expense
612 Advertising Expense
613 Cleaning Supplies Expense

Journalizing, recording, and posting synoptic journal for a company using the accrual basis of accounting.

Here are the transactions for the month of January:

19XX
Jan. 1   Buzzy Sullivan invested $8,000 cash in the business.
       8   Paid a five-year insurance policy in advance, $1,500 (no taxes), cheque no. 1.
      10   Purchased merchandise on account from Role Company, $900, plus GST.
      12   Cleaned shirts for cash, $650, plus PST and GST.
      15   Cleaned suits on account for Pete Daley, $200, plus PST and GST.
      17   Purchased cleaning equipment on account from Ral Co., $900, plus GST.
      20   Borrowed $6,000 from National Bank.
      21   Cleaned shirts for Pete Daley for $50, plus PST and GST on account.
      24   Received entire payment from Pete Daley for January 15 transaction less a 2% discount.
      25   Purchased merchandise on account from Bomb Co., $250, plus GST
      26   Cleaned slacks on account for Alice Small, $15, plus PST and GST.
      27   Paid amount due to Role Company less a 2% discount for January 10 transaction, cheque no. 2.
      28   Returned $100 of cleaning equipment to Ral Company for faulty workmanship. (Remember the GST.)
      29   Paid Bomb Company the amount due re: January 25 purchase less a 10% discount, cheque no. 3.
      30   Cash sales, $800, plus PST and GST.
      30   Received amount due from Alice Small re: January 26 transaction, less a 20% sales discount.

Your task is to
   1. Set up accounts in the general ledger (some accounts may not be used in January).
   2. Set up accounts in the accounts payable and accounts receivable ledgers as needed.
   3. Journalize the above transactions.
   4. Record to the accounts payable and accounts receivable ledger as appropriate.

5. Post to the general ledger as appropriate.
6. Prove the sum of the subsidiary ledgers equal to the controlling accounts.
7. Prove the synoptic journal.

The headings of the synoptic journal of Buzzy's Cleaning Company will be as follows:

Buzzy's Cleaning Company
Synoptic Journal

Date	Explanation	Chq. No.	PR	Sundry		Cash		Accounts Receivable		Accounts Payable		G.S.T.		Clean. Revenue	Sales Disc.	Purch.	Purch. Disc.	9% Sales Tax
				Dr.	Cr.	Dr.	Cr.	Dr.	Cr.	Dr.	Cr.	Dr.	Cr.	Cr.	Dr.	Dr.	Cr.	Cr.

GROUP B PROBLEMS

Journalizing transactions of a modified cash system into a synoptic journal.

11B-1. Using the chart of accounts of Dr. Lovejoy from Problem 11A-1 (p. 325), record the following transactions in the synoptic journal and then prove the journal:

19XX
May 1   Dr. Lovejoy deposited $9,000 in the practice.
     3   Paid rent for the month to Jane Jones Realty, $700, cheque no. 1.
     8   Bought medical supplies from Able Co., $750, cheque no. 2.
    12   Bought medical equipment from Jane's Supply, $4,000, cheque no. 3.
    15   Received cash from patients, $3,000.
    18   Bought additional medical supplies from Able Co., $910, cheque no. 4.
    19   Dr. Lovejoy withdrew $790 for personal use, cheque no. 5.
    21   Paid Ron's Janitorial Service, $500, cheque no. 6.
    24   Received cash from patients, $3,400.
    25   Paid for postage stamps, $30 (miscellaneous expense), cheque no. 7.
    27   Paid salaries for month, $1,600, cheque no. 8.
    28   Paid Ron's Janitorial Service, $300, cheque no. 9.
    29   Dr. Lovejoy withdrew $300 for personal use, cheque no. 10.

Journalizing transactions of a modified cash system into a synoptic journal with headings for payroll deductions, and recording payroll tax expenses.

11B-2. Using the chart of accounts for Dr. Fox from Problem 11A-2 (p. 410), record the following transactions in the synoptic journal and then prove the journal. (Beginning balances are in your working papers.)

19XX
May 1   Received $4,000 from patients.
     3   Issued cheque no. 563 to Lane Drug for medical supplies, $700.
     5   Issued cheque no. 564 to J. Realty to pay three months' insurance premiums, $900.
     9   Received cheques from patients, $3,000.
    12   Issued the following payroll cheques:

EMPLOYEE	CHQ. NO.	GROSS PAY	FIT	CPP	UI	NET PAY
Abby Slat	565	$ 900	$210	$25	$27	$ 638
Jane Reeves	566	800	190	22	24	564
Bob Swan	567	600	130	15	18	437
		$2,300	$530	$62	$69	$1,639

18   Issued cheque no. 568 to Lane Drug for medical supplies, $900.
25   Dr. Fox withdrew $400 for personal use, cheque no. 569.
28   Dr. Fox sent cheque to Receiver General re: payroll of May 12, cheque no. 570. (Don't forget Dr. Fox's share of CPP and UI.)

11B-3. Using the chart of accounts of Debra Clark from Problem 11A-3 (p. 327) journalize the following transactions and prove the synoptic journal. Fill in the PR column as if you were actually recording and posting to the ledger.

Journalizing, recording, and posting synoptic journal used to record transactions utilizing accrual basis of accounting.

19XX
July   1   Debra Clark invested $6,000 cash and $4,000 of office equipment in the practice.
      1   Paid insurance on the office for one year in advance, $1,200, cheque no. 1.
      9   Purchased office equipment on account from Smith Stationery Co., $1,400.
    12   Completed physical examinations on each schoolchild at Simcoe Elementary School, $2,000 on account.
    18   Received $700 cash for medical fees earned.
    19   Performed a complete examination for Alvin Ray's son, $200 on account.
    20   Paid Smith Stationery one-half the amount owed from July 9 transaction, cheque no. 2.
    26   Paid telephone bill, $95, cheque no. 3.
    27   Paid utilities, $60, cheque no. 4.
    28   Paid Toby Cleaning Co. for cleaning service performed, $75, cheque no. 5.

11B-4. (GST (7%) and PST (8% – not cumulative) are involved in this problem.) Buzzy Sullivan opened a dry-cleaning store that also sold accessories. The chart of accounts and synoptic journal headings for Buzzy's Cleaning Company are given in Problem 11A-4 (p. 412). Here are the transactions for the month of January:

19XX
Jan.   1   Buzzy Sullivan invested $6,000 cash in the business.
      8   Paid for a five-year company insurance policy in advance, $1,200, cheque no. 101 (no GST or PST).
    10   Purchased merchandise on account from Role Company, $700, plus GST.
    12   Cleaned shirts for cash, $950, plus GST and PST.
    15   Cleaned suits on account for Pete Daley, $500, plus GST and PST.
    17   Purchased cleaning equipment on account from Ral Co., $600, plus GST.
    20   Borrowed $4,000 from National Bank.
    21   Cleaned shirts on account for P. Daley, $50, plus GST and PST.
    24   Received entire payment from P. Daley less a 2% discount from January 15 transaction.

25   Purchased merchandise on account from Bomb Company, $90, plus GST.

26   Cleaned silk blouse on account for Alice Small, $20, plus GST and PST.

27   Paid Role Company the amount due (less a 2% discount) for merchandise that was purchased on January 10, cheque no. 102.

28   Returned $200 of cleaning equipment to Ral Company for faulty workmanship. (Remember the GST.)

29   Paid Bomb Company the amount due (less a 10% discount) re: purchases made on account on January 25, cheque no. 103.

30   Cash sales, $700, plus GST and PST.

Your task is to journalize, record, post, and prove the synoptic journal for the cleaning company. See problem 11A-4 for detailed requirements.

GROUP C PROBLEMS

Journalizing transactions of a modified cash system into a synoptic journal.

11C-1. Using a chart of accounts similar to Problem 11A-1 (p. 409), record the following transactions for Carla Walgee, Physiotherapist, in her synoptic journal and then prove the journal:

19XX
May   1   Ms. Walgee deposited $15,000 in the practice.
      3   Paid rent for the month to Abby Glenn Realty, $1,100, cheque no. 341.
      8   Bought supplies from Perkins Co., $750, cheque no. 342.
      12   Bought exercise equipment from Atlas Supply, $7,500, cheque no. 343.
      15   Received cash from patients, $4,200.
      18   Bought additional supplies from Perkins Co., $840, cheque no. 344.
      19   Ms. Walgee withdrew $1,200 for personal use, cheque no. 345.
      21   Paid Rockford Janitorial Service, $350, cheque no. 346.
      24   Received cash from patients, $4,800.
      25   Paid for postage stamps, $70 (miscellaneous expense), cheque no. 347.
      27   Paid salary to Brenda Curtis for month, $1,950, cheque no. 348.
      28   Paid Rockford Janitorial Service, $350, cheque no. 349.
      29   Ms. Walgee withdrew another $1,200 for personal use, cheque no. 350.

Journalizing transactions of a modified system into a synoptic journal with headings for payroll deductions, and recording payroll tax expenses.

11C-2. Using a chart of accounts similar to Problem 11A-2 (p. 410), record the following transactions for Sandy Williams, Dentist, in the synoptic journal and then prove the journal. (Beginning balances are given in your working papers.)

19XX
June 1   Received $6,350 from patients.
      3   Issued cheque no. 230 to Walkins Drug for dental supplies, $765.
      5   Issued cheque no. 231 to Game Agencies to pay six months' insurance premiums, $2,100.
      9   Received cheques from patients, $4,460.
      12   Issued the following payroll cheques:

EMPLOYEE	CHQ. NO.	GROSS PAY	FIT	CPP	UI	NET PAY
Ted Forth	232	$ 800	$165	$21	$ 24	$ 590
Carol Hahn	233	900	183	23	27	667
Ed Birch	234	700	146	17	21	516
Kim Shaw	235	1,100	245	29	33	793
		$3,500	$739	$90	$105	$2,566

18   Issued cheque no. 236 to Walkins Drug for dental supplies, $1,340.
25   Dr. Williams withdrew $2,400 for personal use, cheque no. 237.
26   Issued the following payroll cheques:

EMPLOYEE	CHQ. NO.	GROSS PAY	FIT	CPP	UI	NET PAY
Ted Forth	238	$ 850	$175	$22	$ 25	$ 628
Carol Hahn	239	900	183	23	27	667
Ed Birch	240	700	146	17	21	516
Kim Shaw	241	1,100	245	29	33	793
		$3,550	$749	$91	$106	$2,604

28   Dr. Williams sent the remittance cheque to the Receiver General for the payrolls of June 12 and 26, cheque no. 242. (Don't forget Dr. Williams's share of CPP and UI.)

11C-3. Using a chart of accounts similar to Problem 11A-3 (p. 411) journalize the following transactions for Sammy Wong, Optometrist, and prove the synoptic journal. Fill in the PR column as if you were actually recording and posting to the ledger.

Journalizing, recording, and posting synoptic journal used to record transactions utilizing accrual basis of accounting.

19XX
April   1   Dr. Wong invested $18,000 cash and $38,000 of optical equipment in the practice.
        1   Paid insurance premium for one year in advance, $3,260, cheque no. 761.
        8   Purchased office equipment on account from Adobe Stationery Co., $3,480.
       12   Completed optical examinations on each schoolchild at Eastside Elementary School, $4,700 on account.
       18   Received $2,650 cash for professional fees earned.
       19   Performed a complete optical examination for Ms. Rachel Flemming, a famous film star, $340 on account.
       20   Paid Adobe Stationery one-half the amount owed from April 8 transaction, cheque no. 762.
       26   Paid telephone bill, $65, cheque no. 763.
       27   Paid utilities, $120, cheque no. 764.
       28   Paid Neally Cleaning Co. for services performed, $275, cheque no. 765.
       30   Received first payment from Eastside Elementary School, $1,600.

11C-4. (GST (7%) and PST (6% – not cumulative) are involved in this problem.) Freda Schragge opened a Gun Repair Shop that also sold guns and accessories. The chart of accounts for her shop is shown below. Here are the transactions for the month of October:

19XX

Oct. 1   Freda Schragge invested $21,000 cash in the business.
      8   Paid First City Agency Co. for a three-year insurance policy in advance, $840, cheque no. 101 (no GST or PST).
     10   Purchased merchandise on account from Colt & Co., $2,100, plus GST.
     12   Repaired guns for five customers for cash, $630, plus GST and PST.
     13   Sold gun for cash, $650, plus GST and PST.
     15   Repaired gun collection on account for Vince Lombardi, $1,340, plus GST and PST.
     16   Freda withdrew $400 for personal expenses, cheque no. 102
     17   Purchased repair equipment on account from Sattrap Co., $13,600, plus GST.
     20   Borrowed $15,000 from National Bank.
     21   Repaired guns on account for Vince Lombardi, $130, plus GST and PST.
     22   Sold set of antique pistols for cash, $2,400, plus GST and PST.
     24   Received payment from Vince Lombardi for October 15 transaction less a 2% discount.
     25   Purchased merchandise on account from Apex Company, $960, plus GST.
     26   Cleaned shotgun on account for J. Fresnel, $30, plus GST and PST.
     27   Paid Colt & Co. for merchandise purchased October 10 less a 2% discount, cheque no. 103.
     28   Returned $200 of repair equipment to Sattrap Co. due to faulty workmanship. (Remember the GST.)
     29   Paid Apex Company the amount owed (less a 5% discount) re: purchases made on account on October 25, cheque no. 104.
     30   Repairs made for cash, $900, plus GST and PST.

CHART OF ACCOUNTS

Assets
111 Cash
112 Accounts Receivable
113 Prepaid Insurance
115 Prepaid GST
121 Repair Equipment

Liabilities
211 Accounts Payable
212 Note Payable
215 GST Collected

Owner's Equity
311 F. Schragge, Capital
312 F. Schragge, Withdrawals
315 Income Summary

Revenue
411 Gun Sales
412 Gun Sales Discount
413 Repair Revenue

Cost of Goods Sold
511 Purchases
512 Purchases Returns and Allowances
513 Purchases Discounts

Expenses
611 Utilities Expense
612 Advertising Expense
613 Supplies Expense

The headings for the Synoptic Journal should look like this:

Date	Explanation	Chq. No.	PR	Sundry		Cash		Accounts Receivable		Accounts Payable		GST Paid/Coll	Repairs Revenue	Gun Sales	Sales Disc.	Purch.	Purch. Disc.	Sales Tax Payable
				Dr.	Cr.	Dr.	Cr.	Dr.	Cr.	Dr.	Cr.	(DR.) or Cr.	Cr.	Cr.	Dr.	Dr.	Cr.	Cr.

Your task is to journalize, record, post, and prove the business's synoptic journal for October, 19XX.

PRACTICAL ACCOUNTING APPLICATION #1

Jeff Smith has been running his business on a strictly cash basis. At a party over the weekend he met an accountant who told him that his business should use a modified cash system. Jeff has brought you his chart of accounts so that you may revise it as well as lay out a synoptic journal. Using the following chart of accounts for Jeff Smith, please design a synoptic journal for him. Allow columns for payroll deductions.

CHART OF ACCOUNTS

Assets
111 Cash
113 Petty Cash

Liabilities
211 Notes Payable

Owner's Equity
311 J. Smith, Capital
312 J. Smith, Withdrawals
313 Income Summary

Revenue
411 Professional Fees

Expenses
511 Insurance Expense
512 Furniture Expense
514 Medical Equipment Expense
515 Medical Supplies Expense
516 Salary Expense
517 Telephone Expense
518 Miscellaneous Expense

PRACTICAL ACCOUNTING APPLICATION #2

Margie Heaves is about to open a dry-cleaning shop. She has hired you to design a synoptic journal for her shop. It will definitely be a small business with a limited number of transactions that are not too complicated. After analyzing Margie's company, you develop the following chart of accounts:

1. Cash.
2. Accounts Receivable.
3. Equipment.
4. Accounts Payable.

5. Cleaning Sales.
6. Wage Expense.
7. Supplies Expense.
8. Miscellaneous Expense.

Margie has asked you to provide her, as soon as possible, with a justification for your design of the parts of the synoptic journal. Be prepared to support the synoptic journal you present to her. Please label all headings of the journal in terms of Debits and Credits. What titles are missing from the chart of accounts?

ACCOUNTING RECALL
A Cumulative Approach

THIS EXAM REVIEWS CHAPTERS 1 THROUGH 11

Your *Study Guide and Working Papers* have forms to complete this exam, as well as worked-out solutions. The page references next to each question identify what page to turn back to if you answer the question incorrectly.

PART I Vocabulary Review

Match the terms to the appropriate definition or phrase.

Page Ref.

(393)   1. Hybrid   A. A special journal

(401)   2. Sundry   B. Amounts deducted from employees plus employer's share of CPP and UI

(395)   3. (X)   C. Records revenue when cash is received

(399)   4. Accrual accounting   D. Accounts payable

(402)   5. (√)   E. Verification

(397)   6. Due to Rec. Gen. of Canada   F. No posting

(395)   7. Payroll tax expense   G. Record to subsidiary

(204)   8. Controlling account   H. Records revenue when earned

(395)   9. Crossfoot   I. Miscellaneous

(393)   10. Synoptic journal   J. CPP + UI (employer's share)

PART II True or False (Accounting Theory)

(182)   11. We post to Subsidiary Ledgers and record to General Ledgers.

(393)   12. Small businesses could use synoptic journals.

(402)   13. Adjusting entries would be recorded in the sundry columns of a special journal.

(404)   14. Sales tax payable has a normal balance of a debit.

(183)   15. The total of accounts receivable is posted to the subsidiary ledger.

PART III Applications Problem (402)

Assuming a modified cash basis combined journal, indicate when postings would occur.

May   9   Pete Saley invests $3,000 in business.
       14   Paid two months insurance premiums, $1,400.
       21   Received cheques from customers, $800.
       24   Paid office salaries, $600.

CHAPTER TWELVE

PREPARING A WORK SHEET FOR A MERCHANDISE COMPANY

IN THIS CHAPTER WE WILL COVER THE FOLLOWING TOPICS:

In Chapters 6 and 7 we discussed the special journals and subsidiary ledgers of a merchandise company, and in Chapters 9 and 10 we looked at payroll record-keeping practices and procedures. Now our attention will shift to recording adjustments and completing a work sheet for a merchandise company. Learning Unit 12-1 will introduce two new adjustments that we have not yet discussed, Merchandise Inventory and Unearned Rent. Learning Unit 12-2 will show how to complete the work sheet with these new adjustments.

LEARNING UNIT 12-1

Adjustments for Merchandise Inventory and Unearned Rent

An important item in a merchandise company work sheet and financial records is *Merchandise Inventory*. This means the goods that a company has available to sell to customers. There are several ways of keeping track of the cost of goods sold and quantity of inventory that a company has on hand. In Chapter 16 we will discuss the **perpetual inventory system**, which is used by companies with low volume sales and high unit prices, and in which the record of inventory is continually updated throughout the year. Most such companies use a computer to keep track of their inventory records.

In this chapter we will discuss the **periodic inventory system**, in which the balance in inventory is updated only at the end of the accounting period. This system is used by smaller companies which sell a variety of merchandise with low unit prices. The number of companies using this system of accounting for inventory is still significant but is declining. This is because of the increasing availability of computers and software which together encourage the use of the more useful and informative perpetual system.

Let's take as an example the merchandise inventory of Art's Wholesale Clothing Company. Let's assume Art's Wholesale started the year with $19,000 worth of merchandise; this is called **beginning merchandise inventory** or simply **beginning inventory**. During the period, the cost of beginning inventory does not change; instead, all purchases of merchandise are recorded in the Purchases account. During the period $52,000 worth of merchandise was purchased and recorded in the Purchases account.

At the end of the period, the company takes a physical count of the merchandise in stock; this amount is called **ending merchandise inventory** or simply **ending inventory** and is calculated on an inventory sheet as shown in Figure 12-1 (p. 424).

This $4,000, which is the ending inventory for this period, will be the beginning inventory for the next period.

When the income statement is prepared, the cost of goods sold section will require two distinct numbers for inventory. The beginning inventory adds to the cost of goods sold, while the ending inventory is subtracted from the cost of goods sold. Remember that the two figures for beginning and ending inventory were calculated months apart. Thus they cannot merely be combined to come up with one inventory figure; that would not be accurate.

Cost of goods sold:
Beginning inventory
+ Net purchases
– Ending inventory
_____
= Cost of goods sold

FIGURE 12-1

Ending Inventory Sheet

	Art's Wholesale Clothing Company Ending Inventory Sheet as of December 31, 19X2		
Amount	*Explanation*	*Unit Cost*	*Total*
20	Ladies' Jackets code 14-0	$50	$1,000
10	Men's Hats code 327	10	100
90	Men's Shirts code 423	10	900
100	Ladies' Blouses code 481	20	2,000
			$4,000

Counted by _____   *Checked and priced by* _____

ADJUSTMENT FOR MERCHANDISE INVENTORY

First adjustment transfers amount in beginning inventory from Merchandise Inventory to Income Summary.

Adjusting the Merchandise Inventory account is a two-step process because we want to keep both beginning inventory and ending inventory amounts separate; we cannot simply combine them. So the first step deals with beginning merchandise inventory.

GIVEN: BEGINNING INVENTORY, $19,000:   Our first adjustment removes that amount from the asset account (Merchandise Inventory) and transfers it to Income Summary. We do this by crediting Merchandise Inventory for $19,000 and debiting Income Summary for the same amount. This is shown below in T-account form and on a transaction analysis chart:

Note that Income Summary has no normal balance of debit or credit.

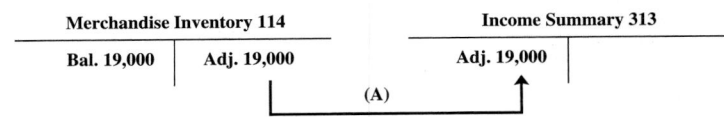

Accounts Affected	Category	↑ ↓	Rules
Income Summary	—	—	Dr.
Merchandise Inventory	Asset	↓	Cr.

Second adjustment updates inventory account with a figure for ending inventory.

(The adjusting entries would be entered first on the work sheet and then formally recorded in the general journal.)

The second step is to enter the amount of ending inventory ($4,000) in the Merchandise Inventory account. This is done to record the amount of goods on hand at the end of the period as an asset, and to subtract this amount from the cost of goods sold (since we have not sold this inventory yet). To do this we debit Merchandise Inventory for $4,000 and credit Income Summary for the same amount. This is shown below in T-account form and on a transaction analysis chart:

Let's look at how this process or method of recording merchandise inventory is reflected in the balance sheet and income statement (see Figure 12-2). Note that

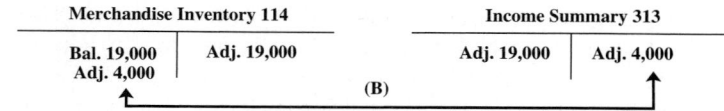

Accounts Affected	Category	↑ ↓	Rules
Merchandise Inventory	Asset	↑	Dr.
Income Summary	—	—	Cr.

the $19,000 of beginning inventory is assumed sold and is shown on the income statement as part of the cost of goods sold. The ending inventory of $4,000 has not been sold and so is subtracted from the cost of goods sold on the income statement. The ending inventory for this period becomes the next period's beginning inventory. When the income statement is prepared, we will need a figure for beginning inventory as well as a figure for ending inventory.

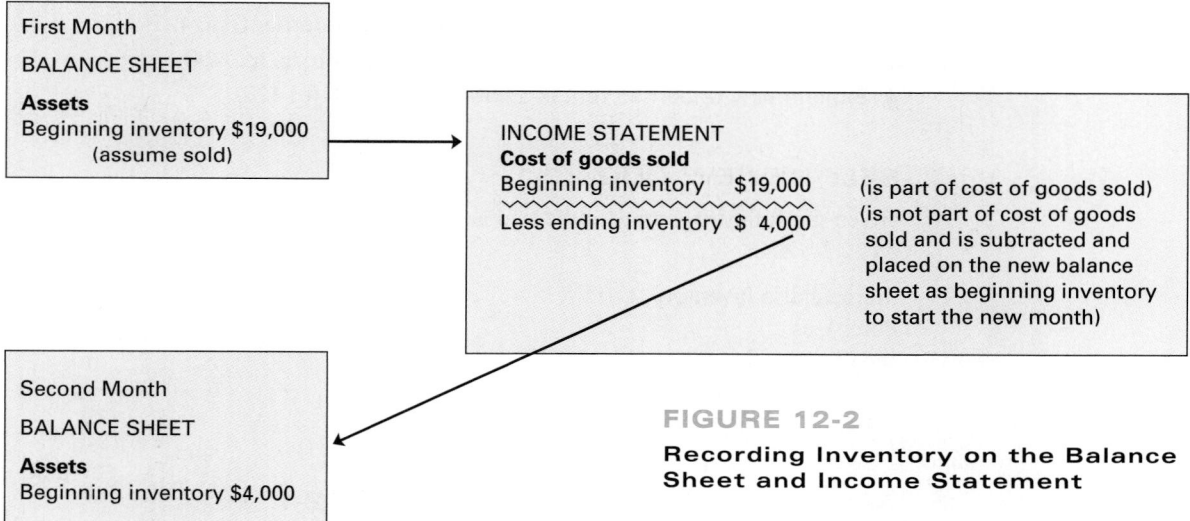

FIGURE 12-2

Recording Inventory on the Balance Sheet and Income Statement

The second adjustment we will discuss in this unit concerns an account that we have never dealt with before, Unearned Rent.

ADJUSTMENT FOR UNEARNED RENT

A new account we have not seen before is a liability called Unearned Rent. This account records the amount collected for rent before the service has been provided (renting the space). For example, Art's Wholesale is subletting some unneeded space to Jesse Company for $200 per month. Jesse Company sends Art a cheque for $600 for three months' rent paid in advance. This unearned rent ($600) is also often called Rent Received in Advance. Regardless of the exact name, it is a liability on the balance sheet because Art's Wholesale owes Jesse Company three months' worth of occupancy.

Received cash for renting space in future.

Cash	A	↑	Dr.
Unearned Rent	Liab.	↑	Cr.

The adjustment When rental income is earned:

Unearned Rent	Liab.	↓	Dr.
Rental Income	Other Rev.	↑	Cr.

When Art's Wholesale fulfils a portion of the rental agreement (when Jesse Company has been in the space for a period of time), this liability account will be reduced and the account called Rental Income will be increased, because Art's Wholesale will have earned the rent. Rental Income is another type of revenue for Art's Wholesale, in addition to its revenue earned from sales of merchandise.

There are other types of unearned revenue besides unearned rent—examples would be subscriptions for magazines, legal fees collected before the work is performed, insurance, and so on. The key point is that revenue, under accrual accounting, is recognized when it is *earned*, whether money is received then or not. Here Art's Wholesale collected cash in advance for a service that it has not performed as yet. Thus a liability called Unearned Rent is the result. Art's Wholesale may have the cash, but no Rental Income is recorded until it is *earned*.

In the next unit we will show how to record the adjustment to Rental Income when the work sheet is completed.

Now at this point you should be able to

1. Define the periodic method of inventory accounting. (p. 423)
2. Explain why beginning and ending inventory are two separate figures in the cost of goods sold section on the income statement. (p. 423)
3. Show how to calculate a figure for ending inventory. (p. 424)
4. Explain why unearned rent is a liability account. (p. 425)

☐ SELF-REVIEW QUIZ 12-1

Given the following, prepare the two adjusting entries for Merchandise Inventory on 12/31/XX:

Merchandise Inventory, 1/1/XX	$ 6,000
Purchases	9,000
Merchandise Inventory, 12/31/XX	5,000
Cost of Goods Sold	10,000
Unearned Magazine Subscriptions	8,000

■ *SOLUTION TO SELF-REVIEW QUIZ 12-1*

Dec.	31	Income Summary	6 0 0 0 00	
		Merchandise Inventory		6 0 0 0 00
	31	Merchandise Inventory	5 0 0 0 00	
		Income Summary		5 0 0 0 00

Completing the Work Sheet

In this unit we will prepare a work sheet for Art's Wholesale Clothing Company. For convenience we reproduce the company's chart of accounts in Figure 12-3.

Figure 12-4 (p. 428) shows the trial balance that was prepared on Dec. 1, 19XX, from the general ledger of Art's Wholesale (note it is placed directly on the first two columns of the work sheet).

In looking at the trial balance (p. 428) we see many new titles that have appeared since we completed a trial balance for a service company back in Chapter 5. Let's look specifically at these new titles in the summary in Table 12-1, p. 429.

CHART OF ACCOUNTS

Assets 100–199
111 Cash
112 Petty Cash
113 Accounts Receivable
114 Merchandise Inventory
115 Supplies
116 Prepaid Insurance
121 Store Equipment
122 Accum. Depreciation,
    Store Equipment

Liabilities 200–299
211 Accounts Payable
212 Salary Payable
213 Income Tax Payable
214 CPP Payable
215 UI Payable
218 Unearned Rent
220 Mortgage Payable

Owner's Equity 300–399
311 Art Newner, Capital
312 Art Newner, Withdrawals
313 Income Summary

Revenue 400–499
411 Sales
412 Sales Returns and Allowances
413 Sales Discount
414 Rental Income

Cost of Goods Sold 500–599
511 Purchases
512 Purchases Discount
513 Purchases Returns and Allowances
514 Freight-In

Expenses 600–699
611 Salary Expense
612 Payroll Tax Expense
613 Depreciation Expense,
    Store Equipment
614 Supplies Expense
615 Insurance Expense
616 Postage Expense
617 Miscellaneous Expense
618 Interest Expense
619 Cleaning Expense
620 Delivery Expense

FIGURE 12-3

Art's Wholesale Clothing Company Chart of Accounts

FIGURE 12-4

Trial Balance Section of the Work Sheet

	Trial Balance	
	Dr.	Cr.
Cash	12 9 2 0 00	
Petty Cash	1 0 0 00	
Accounts Receivable	14 5 0 0 00	
Merchandise Inventory	19 0 0 0 00	
Supplies	8 0 0 00	
Prepaid Insurance	9 0 0 00	
Store Equipment	4 0 0 0 00	
Acc. Dep., Store Equip.		4 0 0 00
Accounts Payable		17 9 0 0 00
Income Tax Payable		1 2 4 0 00
CPP Payable		2 6 0 00
UI Payable		2 0 0 00
Unearned Rent		6 0 0 00
Mortgage Payable		2 3 2 0 00
Art Newner, Capital		7 9 0 5 00
Art Newner, Withdrawals	8 6 0 0 00	
Income Summary		
Sales		95 0 0 0 00
Sales Returns and Allowances	9 5 0 00	
Sales Discount	6 7 0 00	
Purchases	52 0 0 0 00	
Purchases Discount		8 6 0 00
Purchases Returns and Allowances		6 8 0 00
Freight-In	4 5 0 00	
Salary Expense	11 7 0 0 00	
Payroll Tax Expense	4 2 0 00	
Postage Expense	2 5 00	
Miscellaneous Expense	3 0 00	
Interest Expense	3 0 0 00	
	127 3 6 5 00	127 3 6 5 00

TABLE 12-1   Summary of New Account Titles

TITLE	CATEGORY	REPORT (s) FOUND ON	NORMAL BALANCE	TEMPORARY OR PERMANENT
Petty Cash	Asset	Balance Sheet	Dr.	Permanent
Merchandise Inventory* (Beginning)	Asset	Balance Sheet from prior period	Dr.	Permanent
	Cost of Goods Sold	Income Statement of current period		
Income Tax Payable	Liability	Balance Sheet	Cr.	Permanent
CPP Payable	Liability	Balance Sheet	Cr.	Permanent
UI Payable	Liability	Balance Sheet	Cr.	Permanent
Unearned Rent **	Liability	Balance Sheet	Cr.	Permanent
Mortgage Payable	Liability	Balance Sheet	Cr.	Permanent
Sales	Revenue	Income Statement	Cr.	Temporary
Sales Returns and Allowances	Contra Revenue	Income Statement	Dr.	Temporary
Sales Discount	Contra Revenue	Income Statement	Dr.	Temporary
Purchases	Cost of Goods Sold	Income Statement	Dr.	Temporary
Purchases Discount	Contra Cost of Goods Sold	Income Statement	Cr.	Temporary
Purchases Returns and Allowances	Contra Cost of Goods Sold	Income Statement	Cr.	Temporary
Freight-In	Cost of Goods Sold	Income Statement	Dr.	Temporary
Payroll Tax Expense	Expense	Income Statement	Dr.	Temporary
Postage Expense	Expense	Income Statement	Dr.	Temporary
Interest Expense	Other Expense	Income Statement	Dr.	Temporary

* The ending inventory of current period is a contra-cost of goods sold on the income statement and will be an asset on the balance sheet for next period.

** Referred to as Unearned Revenue.

Note the following:

(1) **Mortgage Payable** is a liability account that records the increases and decreases in the amount of debt owed on a mortgage. We will discuss this more in the next chapter, when financial reports are prepared.

(2) **Interest Expense** represents a non-operating expense for Art's Wholesale and thus is categorized as Other Expense. The interest would be a regular expense if it were incurred for business purposes. We will also be looking at this in the next chapter.

(3) **Unearned Revenue** is a liability account that records receipt of payment for goods and services in advance of delivery. Unearned Rent is a particular example of this general type of account.

We have already discussed Adjustments A & B (p. 424), which make up the two-step process involved in adjusting Merchandise Inventory at the end of the accounting period. Now we will go on to show T accounts and transaction analysis charts for some more adjustments that need to be made at this point in a merchandise firm, just as they do in a service company.

ADJUSTMENT (C) RENTAL INCOME EARNED BY ART'S WHOLESALE, $200:

A month ago, Cash was increased by $600, as was a liability, Unearned Rent. Art's Wholesale received payment in advance but had not earned the rental income. Now, since $200 has been earned, the liability is reduced and Rental Income can be recorded for the $200.

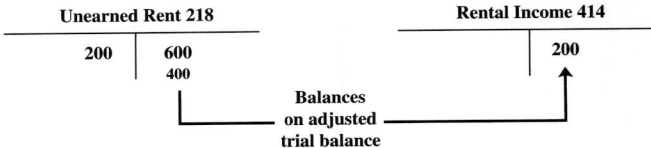

| Unearned Rent | Liability | ↓ | Dr. | $200 |
| Rental Income | Other Revenue | ↑ | Cr. | $200 |

ADJUSTMENT (D) SUPPLIES ON HAND, $300:

$500 worth of supplies has been used up; thus there is a need to increase Supplies Expense and decrease the asset Supplies.

| Supplies Expense | Expense | ↑ | Dr. | $500 |
| Supplies | Asset | ↓ | Cr. | $500 |

ADJUSTMENT (E) INSURANCE EXPIRED, $300:

Since insurance has expired by $300, Insurance Expense is increased by $300 and the asset Prepaid Insurance is decreased by $300.

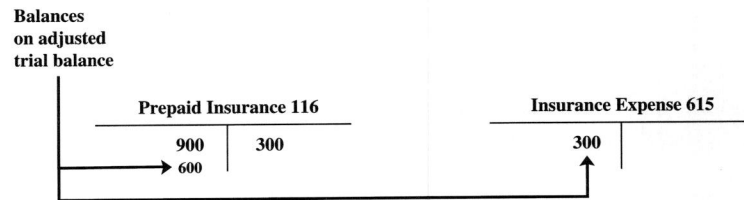

| Insurance Expense | Expense | ↑ | Dr. | $300 |
| Prepaid Insurance | Asset | ↓ | Cr. | $300 |

ADJUSTMENT (F) DEPRECIATION EXPENSE, $50:   When
depreciation is taken, depreciation expense and accumulated depreciation are both
increased by $50. Note that the cost of the store equipment remains the same.

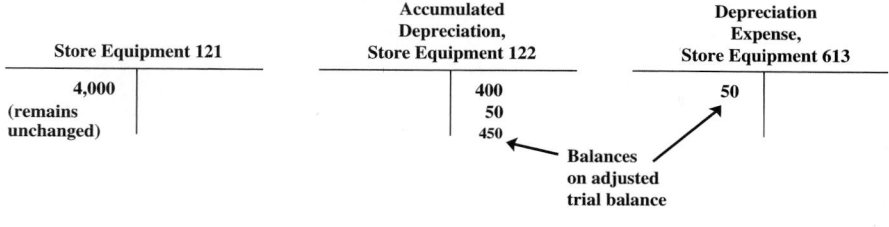

| Dep. Exp., Store Equip. | Expense | ↑ | Dr. | $50 |
| Acc. Dep., Store Equip. | Contra Asset | ↑ | Cr. | $50 |

ADJUSTMENT (G) SALARIES ACCRUED, $600:   The $600
in Salaries Accrued causes an increase in Salaries Expense and Salaries Payable.

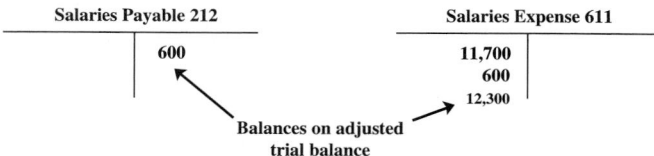

| Salaries Expense | Expense | ↑ | Dr. | $600 |
| Salaries Payable | Liability | ↑ | Cr. | $600 |

Figure 12-5 shows the work sheet with the adjustments and adjusted trial balance column filled out. Note that the adjustment numbers in Income Summary from beginning and ending inventory are also carried over to the adjusted trial balance and are *not* combined.

The next step in completing the work sheet is to fill out the income statement columns from the adjusted trial balance, as shown in Figure 12-6 (p. 433).

The next step in completing the work sheet is to fill out the balance sheet columns (Figure 12-7, p. 434). Note how only ending inventory is carried over to the balance sheet from the adjusted trial balance column. Take time also to look at the placement of the payroll tax liabilities as well as Unearned Rent on the work sheet.

Figure 12-8 is the completed work sheet, on pp. 435-436.

At this point you should be able to
1. Complete adjustments for a merchandise company. (pp. 424, 425)
2. Complete a work sheet. (p. 427)

FIGURE 12-5   **Work Sheet with Three Columns Filled Out**

	Trial Balance Dr.	Trial Balance Cr.	Adjustments Dr.	Adjustments Cr.	Adjusted Trial Bal. Dr.	Adjusted Trial Bal. Cr.
Cash	12 9 2 0 00				12 9 2 0 00	
Petty Cash	1 0 0 00				1 0 0 00	
Accounts Receivable	14 5 0 0 00				14 5 0 0 00	
Merchandise Inventory	19 0 0 0 00		(B)4 0 0 0 00	(A)19 0 0 0 00	4 0 0 0 00	
Supplies	8 0 0 00			(D) 5 0 0 00	3 0 0 00	
Prepaid Insurance	9 0 0 00			(E) 3 0 0 00	6 0 0 00	
Store Equipment	4 0 0 0 00				4 0 0 0 00	
Acc. Dep., Store Equip.		4 0 0 00		(F) 5 0 00		4 5 0 00
Accounts Payable		17 9 0 0 00				17 9 0 0 00
Income Tax Payable		1 2 4 0 00				1 2 4 0 00
CPP Payable		2 6 0 00				2 6 0 00
UI Payable		2 0 0 00				2 0 0 00
Unearned Rent		6 0 0 00	(C) 2 0 0 00			4 0 0 00
Mortgage Payable		2 3 2 0 00				2 3 2 0 00
Art Newner, Capital		7 9 0 5 00				7 9 0 5 00
Art Newner, Withdrawals	8 6 0 0 00				8 6 0 0 00	
Income Summary			(A)19 0 0 0 00	(B)4 0 0 0 00	19 0 0 0 00	4 0 0 0 00
Sales		95 0 0 0 00				95 0 0 0 00
Sales Returns and Allowances	9 5 0 00				9 5 0 00	
Sales Discount	6 7 0 00				6 7 0 00	
Purchases	52 0 0 0 00				52 0 0 0 00	
Purchases Discount		8 6 0 00				8 6 0 00
Purchases Returns and Allowances		6 8 0 00				6 8 0 00
Freight-In	4 5 0 00				4 5 0 00	
Salary Expense	11 7 0 0 00		(G) 6 0 0 00		12 3 0 0 00	
Payroll Tax Expense	4 2 0 00				4 2 0 00	
Postage Expense	2 5 00				2 5 00	
Miscellaneous Expense	3 0 00				3 0 00	
Interest Expense	3 0 0 00				3 0 0 00	
	127 3 6 5 00	127 3 6 5 00				
Rental Income				(C) 2 0 0 00		2 0 0 00
Supplies Expense			(D) 5 0 0 00		5 0 0 00	
Insurance Expense			(E) 3 0 0 00		3 0 0 00	
Depreciation Exp. Store Equip.			(F) 5 0 00		5 0 00	
Salary Payable				(G) 6 0 0 00		6 0 0 00
			24 6 5 0 00	24 6 5 0 00	132 0 1 5 00	132 0 1 5 00

FIGURE 12-6   Income Statement Section of the Work Sheet

$19,000 of beginning inventory is assumed sold during the period and thus is part of the cost of goods sold. By placing it in the debit column of Income Summary we increase the cost of goods sold.

$4,000 is the cost of ending inventory at the end of the period. It is assumed to be unsold and therefore is not part of the cost of goods sold. By placing it in the credit column of Income Summary we reduce the cost of goods sold.

$95,000 is the credit balance of Sales, The Sales Returns and Allowances, $950, and Sales Discount, $670, are placed on the debit side, which represents a reduction to total sales:
(Cr.) Sales
(Dr.) Less: Sales Returns and Allowances
(Dr.) Less: Sales Discount

The purchases account, $52,000, is on the debit side, reflecting an increase in costs due to purchasing additional merchandise. The Purchases Discount, $860, and Purchases Returns and Allowances, $680, are on the credit side, which reduces cost of purchases:
(Dr.) Purchases
(Cr.) Less: Purchases Returns and Allowances
(Cr.) Less: Purchases Discount

Freight-In adds to the cost of goods sold.

Rental Income, which falls under the category "other income" for Art's Wholesale, is increased by $200, because the first month's rental agreement has been fulfilled.

	Income Statement	
	Dr.	Cr.
Income Summary*	19 0 0 0 00	4 0 0 0 00
Sales		95 0 0 0 00
Sales Returns and Allowances	9 5 0 00	
Sales Discount	6 7 0 00	
Purchases	52 0 0 0 00	
Purchases Discount		8 6 0 00
Purchases Returns and Allowances		6 8 0 00
Freight-In	4 5 0 00	
Salaries Expense	12 3 0 0 00	
Payroll Tax Expense	4 2 0 00	
Postage Expense	2 5 00	
Miscellaneous Expense	3 0 00	
Interest Expense	3 0 0 00	
Rental Income		2 0 0 00
Supplies Expense	5 0 0 00	
Insurance Expense	3 0 0 00	
Depreciation Expense, Store Equip.	5 0 00	
Salaries Payable		
	86 9 9 5 00	100 7 4 0 00
Net Income	13 7 4 5 00	
	100 7 4 0 00	100 7 4 0 00

* Remember, we do *not* combine the $19,000 and $4,000 in Income Summary. When we prepare the cost of goods sold section for the formal financial report, we will need both a beginning and an ending figure for inventory.

FIGURE 12-7   **Balance Sheet Section of the Work Sheet**

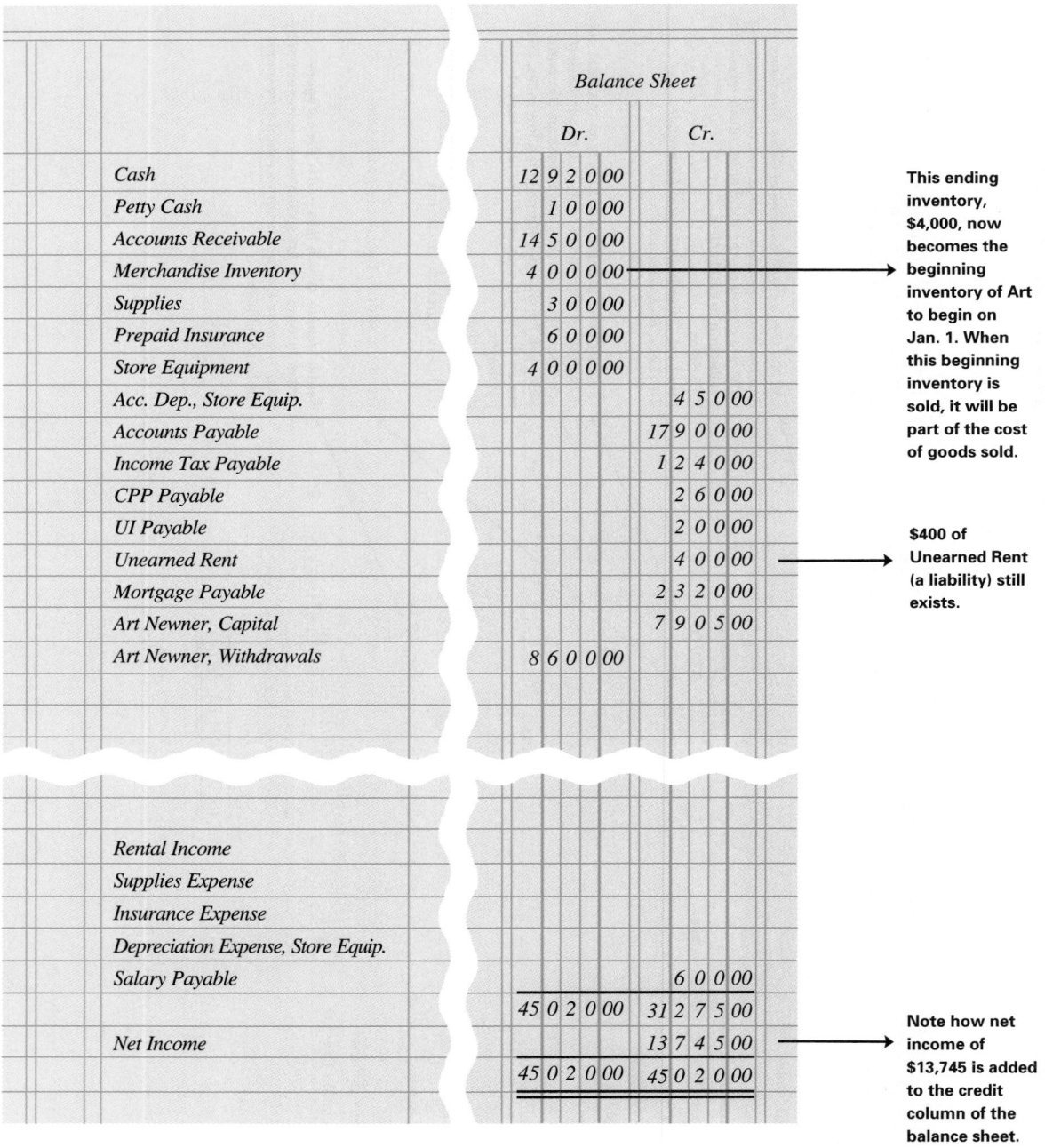

	Balance Sheet	
	Dr.	Cr.
Cash	12 9 2 0 00	
Petty Cash	1 0 0 00	
Accounts Receivable	14 5 0 0 00	
Merchandise Inventory	4 0 0 0 00	
Supplies	3 0 0 00	
Prepaid Insurance	6 0 0 00	
Store Equipment	4 0 0 0 00	
Acc. Dep., Store Equip.		4 5 0 00
Accounts Payable		17 9 0 0 00
Income Tax Payable		1 2 4 0 00
CPP Payable		2 6 0 00
UI Payable		2 0 0 00
Unearned Rent		4 0 0 00
Mortgage Payable		2 3 2 0 00
Art Newner, Capital		7 9 0 5 00
Art Newner, Withdrawals	8 6 0 0 00	
Rental Income		
Supplies Expense		
Insurance Expense		
Depreciation Expense, Store Equip.		
Salary Payable		6 0 0 00
	45 0 2 0 00	31 2 7 5 00
Net Income		13 7 4 5 00
	45 0 2 0 00	45 0 2 0 00

This ending inventory, $4,000, now becomes the beginning inventory of Art to begin on Jan. 1. When this beginning inventory is sold, it will be part of the cost of goods sold.

$400 of Unearned Rent (a liability) still exists.

Note how net income of $13,745 is added to the credit column of the balance sheet.

FIGURE 12-8   Completed Work Sheet

Work Sheet
For year ended December 31, 19X2

	Trial Balance Dr.	Trial Balance Cr.	Adjustments Dr.	Adjustments Cr.	Adjusted Trial Balance Dr.	Adjusted Trial Balance Cr.	Income Statement Dr.	Income Statement Cr.	Balance Sheet Dr.	Balance Sheet Cr.
Cash	1292000				1292000				1292000	
Petty Cash	10000				10000				10000	
Accounts Receivable	1450000				1450000				1450000	
Merchandise Inventory	1900000		(B)400000	(A)1900000	400000				400000	
Supplies	80000			(D)50000	30000				30000	
Prepaid Insurance	90000			(E)30000	60000				60000	
Store Equipment	400000				400000				400000	
Acc. Dep., Store Equip.		40000		(F)5000		45000				45000
Accounts Payable		1790000				1790000				1790000
Income Tax Payable		124000				124000				124000
CPP Payable		26000				26000				26000
UI Payable		20000				20000				20000
Unearned Rent		60000	(C)20000			40000				40000
Mortgage Payable		232000				232000				232000
Art Newner, Capital		790500				790500				790500
Art Newner, Withdrawals	860000				860000				860000	
Income Summary			(A)1900000	(B)400000	1900000	400000	1900000	400000		
Sales		9500000				9500000		9500000		
Sales Returns and Allowances	95000				95000		95000			
Sales Discount	67000				67000		67000			
Purchases	5200000				5200000		5200000			
Purchases Discount		86000				86000		86000		
Purchases Returns and Allowances		68000				68000		68000		
Freight-In	45000				45000		45000			
Salary Expense	1170000		(G)60000		1230000		1230000			
Payroll Tax Expense	42000				42000		42000			
Postage Expense	2500				2500		2500			
Miscellaneous Expense	3000				3000		3000			
Interest Expense	30000				30000		30000			
	12736500	12736500								
Rental Income				(C)20000		20000		20000		
Supplies Expense			(D)50000		50000		50000			
Insurance Expense			(E)30000		30000		30000			
Depreciation, Store Equip.			(F)5000		5000		5000			
Salary Payable				(G)60000		60000				60000
			2465000	2465000	13201500	13201500	8699500	10074000	4502000	3127500
Net Income							1374500			1374500
							10074000	10074000	4502000	4502000

☐ **SELF-REVIEW QUIZ 12-2**

From the trial balance shown here, complete a work sheet for Ray Company. Additional data includes: (A and B) On December 31, 19XX, ending inventory was calculated as $200; (c) Storage Fees Earned, $516; (d) Rent expired, $100; (e) Depreciation Expense, Office Equipment, $60; (F) Salaries Accrued, $200.

Account Titles	Trial Balance Dr.	Trial Balance Cr.
Cash	2 4 8 6 00	
Merchandise Inventory	8 2 4 00	
Prepaid Rent	1 1 5 2 00	
Prepaid Insurance	6 0 00	
Office Equipment	2 1 6 0 00	
Accumulated Depreciation, Office Equipment		5 6 0 00
Unearned Storage Fees		2 5 1 6 00
Accounts Payable		1 0 0 00
B. Ray, Capital		1 9 3 2 00
Income Summary	—	—
Sales		11 0 4 0 00
Sales Returns and Allowances	5 4 6 00	
Sales Discount	2 1 6 00	
Purchases	5 2 5 6 00	
Purchases Returns and Allowances		1 6 8 00
Purchases Discount		1 0 2 00
Salaries Expense	2 0 1 6 00	
Insurance Expense	1 3 9 2 00	
Utilities Expense	9 6 00	
Plumbing Expense	2 1 4 00	
	16 4 1 8 00	16 4 1 8 00

■ **SOLUTION TO SELF-REVIEW QUIZ 12-2**

Solution is shown on p. 437.

Ray Company
Work Sheet
For year ended December 31, 19XX

Account Titles	Trial Balance Dr.	Trial Balance Cr.	Adjustments Dr.	Adjustments Cr.	Adjusted Trial Balance Dr.	Adjusted Trial Balance Cr.	Income Statement Dr.	Income Statement Cr.	Balance Sheet Dr.	Balance Sheet Cr.
Cash	2486 00				2486 00				2486 00	
Merchandise Inventory	824 00		(B) 200 00	(A) 824 00	200 00				200 00	
Prepaid Rent	1152 00			(D) 100 00	1052 00				1052 00	
Prepaid Insurance	60 00				60 00				60 00	
Office Equipment	2160 00				2160 00				2160 00	
Acc. Dep., Office Equipment		560 00		(E) 60 00		620 00				620 00
Unearned Storage Fees		2516 00	(C) 516 00			2000 00				2000 00
Accounts Payable		100 00				100 00				100 00
B. Ray, Capital		1932 00				1932 00				1932 00
Income Summary			(A) 824 00	(B) 200 00	824 00	200 00	824 00	200 00		
Sales		11040 00				11040 00		11040 00		
Sales Returns and Allowances	546 00				546 00		546 00			
Sales Discount	216 00				216 00		216 00			
Purchases	5256 00				5256 00		5256 00			
Purchases Returns and Allowances		168 00				168 00		168 00		
Purchases Discount		102 00				102 00		102 00		
Salaries Expense	2016 00		(F) 200 00		2216 00		2216 00			
Insurance Expense	1392 00				1392 00		1392 00			
Utilities Expense	96 00				96 00		96 00			
Plumbing Expense	214 00				214 00		214 00			
	16418 00	16418 00								
Storage Fees Earned				(C) 516 00		516 00		516 00		
Rent Expense			(D) 100 00		100 00		100 00			
Depreciation Expense, Equipment			(E) 60 00		60 00		60 00			
Salaries Payable				(F) 200 00		200 00				200 00
			1900 00	1900 00	16878 00	16878 00	10920 00	12026 00	5958 00	4852 00
Net Income							1106 00			1106 00
							12026 00	12026 00	5958 00	5958 00

SUMMARY OF KEY POINTS AND KEY TERMS

LEARNING UNIT 12-1

1. The periodic inventory system updates the record of goods on hand only at the *end* of the accounting period. This system is used by companies with a variety of merchandise with low unit prices.

2. In the periodic inventory system, additional purchases of merchandise during the accounting period will be recorded in the Purchases account. The amount in beginning inventory will remain unchanged during the accounting period. At the end of the period a new figure for ending inventory will be calculated.

3. Beginning inventory at the end of the accounting period is added to the cost of goods sold, while ending inventory is deducted from cost of goods sold.

4. The perpetual inventory system keeps a continuous record of inventory. It is used by companies with low volume and high unit prices, and often utilizes a computer system.

5. Unearned Revenue is a liability account that accumulates revenue that has not been earned yet, although the cash has been received. It represents a liability to the seller until the service or product is performed or delivered.

Beginning merchandise inventory (beginning inventory): The cost of goods on hand in a company to *begin* an accounting period.

Ending merchandise inventory (ending inventory): The cost of goods that remain unsold at the end of the accounting period. It is an asset on the balance sheet.

Periodic inventory system: An inventory system that, at the end of each accounting period, calculates the cost of the unsold goods on hand by taking the cost of each unit times the number of units of each product on hand.

Perpetual inventory system: An inventory system that keeps continual track of each type of inventory by recording units on hand at beginning, units sold, and the current balance after each sale or purchase.

LEARNING UNIT 12-2

1. Two important adjustments in the accounting for a merchandise company deal with the Merchandise Inventory account and with the Unearned Revenue account (unearned rent).

2. Figures for beginning and ending inventory on the Income Summary line on the work sheet are never combined; they are also carried over separately to the adjusted trial balance and income statement columns of the work sheet. On the balance sheet column the figure for ending inventory becomes the beginning inventory figure for the new accounting period.

3. When a company delivers goods or services for which it has been paid in advance, an adjustment is made to reduce the liability account Unearned Revenue and to increase an earned revenue account.

Mortgage Payable: A liability account showing the amount owed on a mortgage.

Unearned Revenue: A liability account that records receipt of payment for goods or services in advance of delivery. When the goods or services are delivered, an adjustment is made to reduce Unearned Revenue and increase earned revenue. (The example we used in this chapter is Unearned Rent.)

BLUEPRINT OF A WORK SHEET FOR A MERCHANDISE COMPANY

Account Titles	Adjustments Dr.	Adjustments Cr.	Adjusted Trial Balance Dr.	Adjusted Trial Balance Cr.	Income Statement Dr.	Income Statement Cr.	Balance Sheet Dr.	Balance Sheet Cr.
Cash			X				X	
Petty Cash			X				X	
Accounts Receivable			X				X	
Merchandise Inventory	X-E	X-B	X-E				X-E	
Supplies			X				X	
Equipment			X				X	
Accum. Dep., Equipment				X				X
Accounts Payable				X				X
Income Tax Payable				X				X
CPP Payable				X				X
UI Payable				X				X
Unearned Sales				X				X
Mortgage Payable				X				X
A. Flynn, Capital				X				X
A. Flynn, Withdrawals			X				X	
Income Summary*	X-B	X-E	X-B	X-E	X-B	X-E		
Sales				X		X		
Sales Returns and Allow.			X		X			
Sales Discount			X		X			
Purchases			X		X			
Purchases Ret. and Allow.				X		X		
Purchases Discount				X		X		
Freight-In			X		X			
Salary Expense			X		X			
Payroll Tax Expense			X		X			
Insurance Expense			X		X			
Depreciation Expense			X		X			
Salaries Payable				X				X
Rental Income				X		X		

* Note that the figures for beginning inventory (X-B) and ending inventory (X-E) are never combined on the Income Summary line of work sheet. When the formal income statement is prepared, two distinct figures for inventory will be used to explain and calculate cost of goods sold. Beginning inventory adds to cost of goods sold; ending inventory reduces cost of goods sold.

DISCUSSION QUESTIONS

1. When would a company consider using a periodic inventory system?
2. What is the function of the Purchases account?
3. A low-volume, high-unit-price inventory requires a company to use a periodic inventory system. Accept or reject, and support your answer.
4. Explain why Unearned Revenue is a liability account.
5. In a periodic system of inventory, the balance of beginning inventory will remain unchanged during the period. True or false?
6. What is the purpose of an inventory sheet?
7. Why do many Unearned Revenue accounts have to be adjusted?
8. Explain why figures for beginning and ending inventory are not combined on the Income Summary line of the work sheet.

EXERCISES

Categorizing account titles.

1. Indicate the normal balance and category of each of the following accounts:

   (a) Purchases Returns and Allowances
   (b) Merchandise Inventory (beginning of period)
   (c) Freight-In
   (d) Payroll Tax Expense
   (e) Purchases Discount
   (f) Sales Discount
   (g) CPP Payable
   (h) Unearned Revenue

Calculating net sales, cost of goods sold, gross profit, and net income.

2. From the following, calculate (a) net sales, (b) cost of goods sold, (c) gross profit, and (d) net income:

Sales, $22,000; Sales Discount, $500; Sales Returns and Allowances, $250; Beginning Inventory, $650; Net Purchases, $13,200; Ending Inventory, $510; Operating Expenses, $3,600.

Unearned revenue.

3. Allan Co. had the following balances on December 31, 19XX:

Cash		Unearned Janitorial Service	
2,100			600

Janitorial Service	
	7,200

The accountant for Allan has asked you to make an adjustment, since $400 of janitorial services has just been performed for customers who had paid two months. Construct a transaction analysis chart.

Calculating cost of goods sold.

4. Lesan Co. purchased merchandise costing $400,000. Calculate the cost of goods sold under the following different situations:

   (a) Beginning inventory $40,000 and no ending inventory.
   (b) Beginning inventory $50,000 and a $60,000 ending inventory.
   (c) No beginning inventory and a $30,000 ending inventory.

5. On note paper, prepare a work sheet from the following information:

Preparing a
work sheet.

(a and b) Merchandise Inventory—ending	13
(c) Store Supplies on hand	4
(d) Depreciation on Store Equipment	4
(e) Accrued Salaries	2

Moore Co.
Trial Balance
December 31, 19XX

	Dr.	Cr.
Cash	8 00	
Accounts Receivable	5 00	
Merchandise Inventory	11 00	
Store Supplies	10 00	
Store Equipment	20 00	
Accumulated Depreciation, Store Equipment		6 00
Accounts Payable		5 00
J. Moore, Capital		34 00
Income Summary	—	—
Sales		64 00
Sales Returns and Allowances	9 00	
Purchases	23 00	
Purchases Discount		3 00
Freight-In	3 00	
Salaries Expense	10 00	
Advertising Expense	13 00	
Totals	112 00	112 00

GROUP A PROBLEMS

12A-1. Based on the accounts listed below, calculate:

Calculating net sales,
cost of goods sold,
gross profit and
net income.

(a) Net sales.
(b) Cost of goods sold.
(c) Gross profit.
(d) Net income.

NOTE: *Chapters 6 (p. 179) and 7 (p. 227) review these terms.*

Accounts Payable	$ 2,200
Operating Expenses	1,490
J. Jensen, Capital	8,200
Purchases	4,250
Freight-In	60
Ending Merchandise Inventory, Dec. 31, 19XX	1,240
Sales	9,210
Accounts Receivable	1,389
Cash	656
Purchases Discount	132
Sales Returns and Allowances	185

Beg. Merchandise Inventory, Jan. 1, 19XX	1,560
Purchases Returns and Allowances	247
Sales Discount	352

Comprehensive Problem. Completing a work sheet for a merchandise company.

12A-2. From the following trial balance and additional data, complete a work sheet for Jim's Hardware.

Jim's Hardware
Trial Balance
December 31, 19XX

	Dr.	Cr.
Cash	7 8 6 00	
Accounts Receivable	1 1 5 2 00	
Merchandise Inventory	6 0 0 00	
Prepaid Insurance	6 8 4 00	
Store Equipment	2 1 6 0 00	
Accumulated Depreciation, Store Equipment		6 6 0 00
Accounts Payable		5 1 6 00
Jim Spool, Capital		1 6 3 2 00
Income Summary	—	—
Hardware Sales		11 0 4 0 00
Hardware Sales Returns and Allowances	5 4 6 00	
Hardware Sales Discount	2 1 6 00	
Purchases	5 2 5 6 00	
Purchases Discount		1 6 8 00
Purchases Returns and Allowances		1 0 2 00
Wages Expense	1 7 1 6 00	
Rent Expense	7 9 2 00	
Telephone Expense	1 1 4 00	
Miscellaneous Expense	9 6 00	
	14 1 1 8 00	14 1 1 8 00

Assume the following:
   (a and b) Ending inventory on Dec. 31 is calculated at $310.
   (c) Insurance expired, $150.
   (d) Depreciation on store equipment, $60.
   (e) Accrued wages, $90.

12A-3. The owner of Waltz Company has asked you to prepare a work sheet from the following trial balance and additional data:

Comprehensive Problem. Completing a work sheet.

Waltz Company
Trial Balance
December 31, 19XX

	Dr.	Cr.
Cash	5 4 0 8 00	
Petty Cash	2 4 0 00	
Accounts Receivable	2 5 1 2 00	
Beginning Merchandise Inventory, Jan. 1	5 0 9 2 00	
Prepaid Rent	6 1 6 00	
Office Supplies	9 4 4 00	
Office Equipment	9 2 8 0 00	
Accumulated Depreciation, Office Equipment		7 6 0 0 00
Accounts Payable		5 9 6 4 00
K. Waltz, Capital		5 4 7 6 00
K. Waltz, Withdrawals	4 8 0 0 00	
Income Summary	—	—
Sales		52 4 8 4 00
Sales Returns and Allowances	9 6 00	
Sales Discount	2 4 0 0 00	
Purchases	29 3 1 6 00	
Purchases Discount		1 6 00
Purchases Returns and Allowances		3 4 8 00
Office Salaries Expense	7 4 0 8 00	
Insurance Expense	2 4 0 0 00	
Advertising Expense	8 0 0 00	
Utilities Expense	5 7 6 00	
	71 8 8 8 00	71 8 8 8 00

Additional data:
   (a and b) Ending merchandise inventory on December 31, $1,805.
   (c) Office supplies used up, $210.
   (d) Rent expired $195.
   (e) Depreciation expense on office equipment, $550.
   (f) Office salaries earned but not paid, $310.

Comprehensive Problem. Completing a work sheet with payroll and unearned revenue.

12A-4. From the following trial balance and additional data, complete the work sheet for Ron's Wholesale Clothing Company.

Ron's Wholesale Clothing Company
Trial Balance
December 31, 19XX

	Dr.	Cr.
Cash	4 460 00	
Petty Cash	300 00	
Accounts Receivable	7 500 00	
Beginning Merchandise Inventory, Jan. 1	9 000 00	
Supplies	1 000 00	
Prepaid Insurance	850 00	
Store Equipment	2 500 00	
Accumulated Depreciation, Store Equipment		1 500 00
Accounts Payable		10 635 00
Income Tax Payable		1 060 00
CPP Payable		108 00
UI Payable		150 00
Unearned Storage Fees		357 00
Ron Win, Capital		12 500 00
Ron Win, Withdrawals	4 300 00	
Income Summary	—	—
Sales		45 000 00
Sales Returns and Allowances	1 475 00	
Sales Discounts	1 335 00	
Purchases	26 000 00	
Purchases Discount		550 00
Purchase Returns and Allowances		400 00
Freight-In	225 00	
Salaries Expense	12 000 00	
Payroll Taxes Expense	420 00	
Interest Expense	895 00	
	72 260 00	72 260 00

Additional data:
   (a and b) Ending merchandise inventory on December 31, $6,000.
   (c) Supplies on hand, $400.
   (d) Insurance expired, $600.
   (e) Depreciation on store equipment, $400.
   (f) Storage fees earned, $176.

GROUP B PROBLEMS

12B-1. From the following accounts, calculate (a) net sales, (b) cost of goods sold, (c) gross profit, (d) net income.

Calculating net sales, cost of goods sold, gross profit, and net income.

Sales Discount	$ 452
Purchases Returns and Allowances	64
Beginning Merchandise Inventory, Jan. 1, 19XX	79
Sales Returns and Allowances	191
Purchases Discounts	42
Cash	3,895
Accounts Receivable	441
Sales	3,950
Ending Merchandise Inventory, Dec. 31, 19XX	75
Freight-In	41
Purchases	1,152
R. Roland, Capital	1,950
Operating Expenses	895
Accounts Payable	129

12B-2. As the accountant for Jim's Hardware, you have been asked to complete a work sheet from the following trial balance as well as additional data.

Comprehensive Problem. Completing a work sheet for a merchandise company.

Jim's Hardware
Trial Balance
December 31, 19XX

	Dr.	Cr.
Cash	9 6 0 00	
Accounts Receivable	1 6 0 0 00	
Merchandise Inventory	7 3 6 00	
Prepaid Insurance	1 1 1 2 00	
Store Equipment	3 2 0 0 00	
Accumulated Depreciation, Store Equipment		1 6 8 0 00
Accounts Payable		1 4 0 8 00
J. Spool, Capital		2 5 7 6 00
Income Summary	—	—
Hardware Sales		14 8 0 0 00
Hardware Sales Returns and Allowances	7 2 8 00	
Hardware Sales Discount	6 8 8 00	
Purchases	7 0 8 8 00	
Purchases Discount		2 4 0 00
Purchases Returns and Allowances		2 4 8 00
Wages Expense	2 3 0 4 00	
Rent Expense	1 8 4 0 00	
Telephone Expense	5 5 2 00	
Miscellaneous Expense	1 4 4 00	
	20 9 5 2 00	20 9 5 2 00

Additional data:
- (a and b) Cost of ending inventory on December 31, $480.
- (c) Insurance expired, $112.
- (d) Depreciation on store equipment, $90.
- (e) Accrued wages, $150.

Comprehensive Problem. Completing a work sheet.

12B-3. From the following, complete a work sheet for Waltz Company.

Waltz Company
Trial Balance
December 31, 19XX

	Dr.	Cr.
Cash	3 800 00	
Petty Cash	100 00	
Accounts Receivable	3 400 00	
Merchandise Inventory	5 204 00	
Prepaid Rent	1 200 00	
Office Supplies	1 360 00	
Office Equipment	9 680 00	
Accumulated Depreciation, Office Equipment		4 040 00
Accounts Payable		7 964 00
K. Waltz, Capital		5 476 00
K. Waltz, Withdrawals	5 000 00	
Income Summary	—	—
Sales		52 462 00
Sales Returns and Allowances	116 00	
Sales Discount	2 200 00	
Purchases	29 296 00	
Purchases Discount		1 208 00
Purchases Returns and Allowances		1 350 00
Office Salaries Expense	7 408 00	
Insurance Expense	2 200 00	
Advertising Expense	800 00	
Utilities Expense	736 00	
	72 500 00	72 500 00

Additional data:
- (a and b) Ending merchandise inventory on December 31, $1,600.
- (c) Office supplies on hand, $90.
- (d) Rent expired, $110.
- (e) Depreciation expense on office equipment, $250.
- (f) Salaries accrued, $180.

12B-4. From the following trial balance and additional data, complete the work sheet for Ron's Wholesale Clothing Company.

Comprehensive Problem. Completing a work sheet with payroll and unearned revenue.

Ron's Wholesale Clothing Company
Trial Balance
December 31, 19XX

	Dr.	Cr.
Cash	2 600 00	
Petty Cash	30 00	
Accounts Receivable	3 000 00	
Beginning Merchandise Inventory, Jan. 1	3 600 00	
Supplies	270 00	
Prepaid Insurance	180 00	
Store Equipment	1 000 00	
Accumulated Depreciation, Store Equipment		496 00
Accounts Payable		4 590 00
Income Tax Payable		590 00
CPP Payable		74 00
UI Payable		100 00
Unearned Storage Fees		350 00
Ron Win, Capital		2 734 00
Ron Win, Withdrawals	1 800 00	
Income Summary	——	——
Sales		19 400 00
Sales Returns and Allowances	560 00	
Sales Discounts	480 00	
Purchases	8 600 00	
Purchases Discount		240 00
Purchase Returns and Allowances		160 00
Freight-In	100 00	
Salaries Expense	6 000 00	
Payroll Taxes Expense	194 00	
Interest Expense	320 00	
	28 734 00	28 734 00

Additional data:
(a and b) Ending merchandise inventory on December 31, $2,000.
(c) Supplies on hand, $50.
(d) Insurance expired, $55.
(e) Depreciation on store equipment, $100.
(f) Storage fees earned, $115.

GROUP C PROBLEMS

Calculating net sales, cost of goods sold, gross profit, and net income.

12C-1. Based on the accounts listed below, calculate:

(a) Net sales.
(b) Cost of goods sold.
(c) Gross profit.
(d) Net income.

NOTE: *Chapters 6 and 7 review these terms.*

Accounts Payable	$ 3,800
Operating Expenses	1,150
P. Juarez, Capital	12,460
Purchases	6,785
Freight-In	157
Ending Merchandise Inventory, Dec. 31, 19XX	1,670
Sales	13,730
Accounts Receivable	2,675
Cash	1.456
Purchases Discount	262
Sales Returns and Allowances	315
Beg. Merchandise Inventory, Jan. 1, 19XX	1,940
Purchases Returns and Allowances	466
Sales Discount	376

Comprehensive Problem. Completing a work sheet for a merchandise company.

12C-2. From the following trial balance and additional data, complete a work sheet for Corocan Tile Company.

Additional data:
(a and b) Ending merchandise inventory on October 31, $12,488.00
(c) Supplies on hand, $462.20
(d) Insurance expired, $496.40
(e) Depreciation on equipment, $872.00
(f) Advertising bill received, $450.00 plus GST of $31.50.

Corocan Tile Company
Trial Balance
October 31, 19XX

	Dr.	Cr.
Cash	1 710 40	
Petty Cash	200 00	
Accounts Receivable	4 316 70	
Beginning Merchandise Inventory, Nov. 1	13 467 00	
Supplies	733 00	
Prepaid Insurance	914 00	
GST Prepaid	748 52	
Tile Cutting Equipment	7 820 00	
Accumulated Depreciation, Equipment		1 466 00
Accounts Payable		16 782 40
GST Collected		1 673 58
Income Tax Payable		1 771 00
CPP Payable		246 20
UI Payable		373 80
Winnie Corocan, Capital		6 395 44
Winnie Corocan, Withdrawals	6 338 00	
Income Summary	—	—
Sales		69 356 28
Sales Returns and Allowances	1 388 24	
Sales Discounts	715 42	
Purchases	42 772 64	
Purchases Discount		882 30
Purchase Returns and Allowances		512 86
Freight-In	425 70	
Salaries Expense	15 870 00	
Payroll Taxes Expense	1 426 00	
Interest Expense	614 24	
	99 459 86	99 459 86

12C-3. The owner of Chapel Antique Clock Company has asked you to prepare a work sheet from the following trial balance and additional data:

Chapel Antique Clock Company
Trial Balance
May 31, 19XX

	Dr.	Cr.
Cash	762 40	
Petty Cash	150 00	
Accounts Receivable	2 715 96	
Beginning Clock Inventory, June 1	10 766 42	
Repair Supplies	624 30	
Prepaid Insurance	753 76	
GST Prepaid	696 14	
Clock Repair Equipment	4 300 00	
Accumulated Depreciation, Repair Equipment		1 248 90
Accounts Payable		8 686 92
GST Collected		912 47
Income Tax Payable		1 155 40
CPP Payable		167 70
UI Payable		278 60
Mike Patel, Capital		5 566 09
Mike Patel, Withdrawals	4 380 00	
Income Summary	—	—
Sales		57 245 18
Sales Returns and Allowances	267 10	
Sales Discounts	176 42	
Purchases	31 488 92	
Purchases Discount		277 44
Purchase Returns and Allowances		512 86
Freight-In	96 31	
Salaries Expense	13 475 00	
Payroll Taxes Expense	1 276 40	
Advertising Expense	721 68	
Rent Expense	2 788 00	
Utilities Expense	612 75	
	76 051 56	76 051 56

Additional data:
  (a and b) Ending clock inventory on May 31, $8,476.90
  (c) Supplies used during period, $378.20
  (d) Insurance expired, $514.70
  (e) Depreciation on equipment, $652.40
  (f) Advertising bill received, $235.00 plus GST of $16.45

12C-4. From the following trial balance and additional data, complete the work sheet for Gwendolyn's Archery Sales Company.

Comprehensive Problem. Completing a work sheet with payroll and unearned revenue.

Gwendolyn's Archery Sales Company
Trial Balance
April 30, 19XX

	Dr.	Cr.
Cash	2 467 93	
Petty Cash	75 00	
Accounts Receivable	764 82	
Beginning Merchandise Inventory, May 1	17 368 44	
Supplies on hand	896 26	
Prepaid Insurance	1 158 20	
GST Prepaid	1 458 76	
Equipment	8 975 00	
Accumulated Depreciation, Equipment		5 762 14
Accounts Payable		21 479 50
GST Collected		2 444 70
Income Tax Payable		974 70
CPP Payable		132 50
UI Payable		178 32
Gwen Sterling, Capital		11 373 06
Gwen Sterling, Withdrawals	8 450 00	
Income Summary	—	—
Sales		78 422 76
Sales Returns and Allowances	467 13	
Sales Discounts	472 38	
Purchases	56 381 58	
Purchases Discount		782 40
Purchase Returns and Allowances		1 328 37
Freight-In	376 82	
Salaries Expense	14 762 80	
Payroll Taxes Expense	1 566 23	
Advertising Expense	2 572 84	
Rent Expense	3 720 00	
Utilities Expense	944 26	
	122 878 45	122 878 45

Additional data:
 (a and b) Ending merchandise inventory on April 30, $23,477.10
 (c) Supplies on hand at end of April, $467.30
 (d) Insurance expired, $688.45
 (e) Depreciation on equipment, $882.30
 (f) Utilities bill received, $78.00 plus GST of $5.46

PRACTICAL ACCOUNTING APPLICATION #1

Kim Andrews prepared the following income statement on a cash basis for Ed Sloan, M.D.:

Ed Sloan, M.D.
Income Statement
For year ended December 31, 19X2

Professional Fees Earned	50 000 00
Expenses	18 000 00
Net Income	32 000 00

Ed Sloan has requested information from Kim as to what his professional fees earned would be under the accrual-basis system of accounting. Kim has asked you to provide Dr. Sloan with this information, based on the following facts that Kim ignored in the original preparation of the financial report:

	19X1	19X2
Accrued Professional Fees	$4,200	$5,300
Unearned Professional Fees	6,200	4,250

PRACTICAL ACCOUNTING APPLICATION #2

Abby Jay is having a difficult time understanding the relationship of sales, cost of goods sold, gross profit, and net income for a merchandise company. As the accounting lab tutor, you have been asked to sit down with Abby and explain how to calculate the missing amounts in each situation listed below. Keep in mind that each situation is a distinct and separate business problem.

	SALES	BEG. INV.	PURCHASES	END INV.	COST OF GOODS SOLD	GROSS PROFIT	EXPENSE	NET INCOME OR LOSS
Sit. 1	320,000	200,000	160,000	?	260,000	?	80,000	?
Sit. 2	380,000	140,000	?	180,000	200,000	?	100,000	80,000
Sit. 3	480,000	200,000	?	160,000	?	220,000	140,000	80,000
Sit. 4	?	160,000	280,000	140,000	?	160,000	140,000	?
Sit. 5	440,000	160,000	260,000	?	240,000	?	100,000	?
Sit. 6	280,000	120,000	?	140,000	160,000	?	?	40,000
Sit. 7	?	160,000	200,000	120,000	?	160,000	?	−20,000
Sit. 8	320,000	?	200,000	140,000	?	120,000	?	40,000

ACCOUNTING RECALL
A Cumulative Approach

THIS EXAM REVIEWS CHAPTERS 1 THROUGH 12

Your *Study Guide and Working Papers* have forms to complete this exam, as well as worked-out solutions. The page references next to each question identify what page to turn back to if you answer the question incorrectly.

PART I Vocabulary Review

Match the terms to the appropriate definition or phrase.

Page Ref.

(429)	1. Interest expense	A. A liability
(429)	2. Sales return and allowance	B. Cost of goods sold
(423)	3. Ending merchandise inventory	C. Continual track
(431)	4. Accumulated depreciation	D. Contra asset
(425)	5. Income summary	E. Non-operating expense
(426)	6. Rental income	F. New figure for capital
(429)	7. Unearned revenue	G. Subtracted from cost of goods sold
(429)	8. Purchases	H. Other income
(153)	9. Closing	I. Contra revenue account
(423)	10. Perpetual inventory	J. Used in adjusting merchandise inventory

PART II True or False (Accounting Theory)

(425) 11. Unearned rent is an asset.

(423) 12. Beginning and ending inventory are combined on the worksheet.

(423) 13. Ending inventory is added to cost of goods sold.

(428) 14. Due to Receiver General of Canada is a liability that includes only amounts deducted from employees.

(152) 15. The normal balance of income summary is a debit.

PART III Applications Problem (435)

From the following Trial Balance and Adjustment Data complete a worksheet for Bill's Antique Shop for year ended December 31, 19XX.

Trial Balance	Dr.	Cr.
Cash	4 1 0 0 00	
Accounts Receivable	23 8 0 0 00	
Merchandise Inventory	20 0 0 0 00	
Prepaid Insurance	6 0 0 00	
Equipment	18 0 0 0 00	
Accumulated Depreciation, Equipment		1 0 0 0 00
Unearned Rent		5 0 0 00
Accounts Payable		11 0 0 0 00
B. J. Jensen, Capital		50 0 0 0 00
B. J. Jensen, Withdrawals	15 0 0 0 00	
Income Summary	—	—
Sales		279 0 0 0 00
Sales Returns and Allowances	3 0 0 0 00	
Sales Discounts	4 5 0 0 00	
Purchases	180 0 0 0 00	
Purchases Returns and Allowances		1 5 0 0 00
Purchases Discount		3 5 0 0 00
Freight-In	2 5 0 0 00	
Salaries Expense	45 0 0 0 00	
Advertising Expense	10 0 0 0 00	
Rent Expense	12 0 0 0 00	
Utility Expense	8 0 0 0 00	
	346 5 0 0 00	346 5 0 0 00

Adjustment Data:
- (a + b) Ending merchandise inventory, December 31, 19XX: $24,000
- (c) Insurance expense: $200
- (d) Depreciation: $1,000
- (e) Salaries owed: $500
- (f) Rent earned: $100

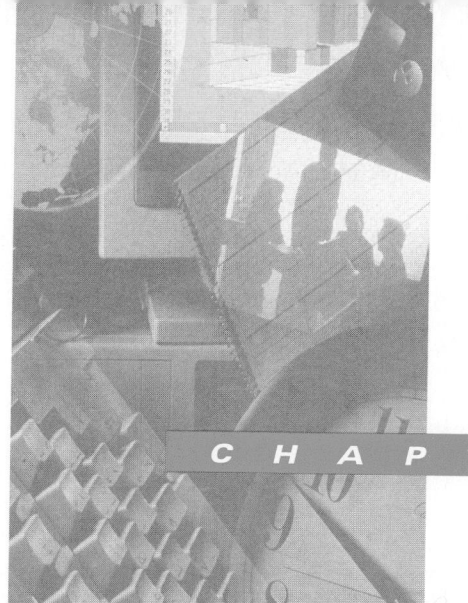

COMPLETION OF THE ACCOUNTING CYCLE FOR A MERCHANDISE COMPANY

IN THIS CHAPTER WE WILL COVER THE FOLLOWING TOPICS:

1. PREPARING FINANCIAL REPORTS FOR A MERCHANDISE COMPANY. (P. 456)

2. RECORDING ADJUSTING AND CLOSING ENTRIES. (P. 467)

3. PREPARING A POST-CLOSING TRIAL BALANCE. (P. 467)

4. DEALING WITH REVERSING ENTRIES. (P. 470)

In Chapter 12 we covered adjustments and completing a work sheet for a merchandise company. In this chapter we will discuss the steps involved in completing the accounting cycle for a merchandise company: preparing financial reports, journalizing and posting adjusting and closing entries, preparing a post-closing trial balance, and reversing entries. First we will deal with preparing financial reports at the close of the accounting cycle.

LEARNING UNIT 13-1

Preparing Financial Reports

As we discussed in Chapter 5, when we were dealing with a service company rather than a merchandise company, the three financial reports can be prepared from the work sheet. Let's begin by looking at how Art's Wholesale Clothing Company prepares the income statement.

THE INCOME STATEMENT

See Chapters 6 and 7 for a review of terms such as net sales, cost of goods sold, and operating expenses.

Art is interested in knowing how well his business performed for the year ended December 31, 19XX. What were its net sales? Were there many returns of goods from dissatisfied customers? What was the cost of the goods brought into the store versus the selling price received? How many goods were returned to suppliers? What is the cost of the goods that have not been sold? What was the cost of the Freight-In account? The income statement in Figure 13-1 (p. 457) is prepared from the income statement columns of the work sheet. (Review it first, and then we will explain each section of the income statement and where on the work sheet the information came from.)

Note that there are no debit or credit columns on the formal income statement — the inside columns on financial reports are used for subtotaling, not for debit and credit.

Note how the income statement is broken down into several sections. Remembering the sections can help you make sense of the statement and set it up correctly on your own. Basically what it presents is this:

	Net Sales
−	Cost of goods Sold
=	Gross Profit
−	Operating Expenses
=	Net Income from Operations
+	Other Income
−	Other Expenses
=	Net Income

Let's take these sections one at a time and see where the figures come from on the work sheet.

Art's Wholesale Clothing Company
Income Statement
For year ended December 31, 19X2

Revenue:			
Gross Sales			$95 0 0 0 00
Less: Sales Ret. and Allow.	$ 9 5 0 00		
Sales Discount	6 7 0 00	1 6 2 0 00	
Net Sales			$93 3 8 0 00
Cost of Goods Sold:			
Merchandise Inventory, 1/1X2		$52 0 0 0 00	
Purchases	$190 0 0 0 00		
Less: Purch. Discount	$ 8 6 0 00		
Purch. Ret. and Allow.	1 5 4 0 00		
Net Purchase	$50 4 6 0 00		
Add: Freight-In	4 5 0 00		
Net Cost of Purchases	$50 9 1 0 00		
Cost of Goods Available for Sale		$69 9 1 0 00	
Less: Merch. Inv., 12/31/X2		4 0 0 0 00	
Cost of Goods Sold		65 9 1 0 00	
Gross Profit			$27 4 7 0 00
Operating Expense:			
Salaries Expense	$12 3 0 0 00		
Payroll Tax Expense	4 2 0 00		
Dep. Exp. Store Equip.	5 00		
Supplies Expense	5 0 0 00		
Insurance Expense	3 0 0 00		
Postage Expense	2 5 00		
Miscellaneous Expense	3 00		
Total Operating Expenses		13 6 2 5 00	
Net Income from Operations		$13 8 4 5 00	
Other Income:			
Rental Income	$ 2 0 0 00		
Other Expenses:			
Interest Expense	3 0 0 00	1 0 0 00	
Net Income			$13 7 4 5 00

Art's Wholesale Clothing Company
Partial Worksheet
For year ended December 31, 19X2

	Income Statement	
	Dr.	Cr.
Income Summary	19 0 0 0 00	4 0 0 0 00
Sales		95 0 0 0 00
Sales Returns and Allowances	9 5 0 00	
Sales Discount	6 7 0 00	
Purchases	52 0 0 0 00	
Purchases Discount		8 6 0 00
Purchases Ret. and Allow.		6 8 0 00
Freight-In	4 5 0 00	
Salaries Expense	12 3 0 0 00	
Payroll Tax Expense	4 2 0 00	
Postage Expense	2 5 00	
Miscellaneous Expense	3 00	
Interest Expense	3 0 0 00	
Rental Income		2 0 0 00
Supplies Expense	5 0 0 00	
Insurance Expense	3 0 0 00	
Depreciation Exp. Store Equip.	5 00	
Salaries Payable		
	86 9 9 5 00	100 7 4 0 00
Net Income	13 7 4 5 00	
	100 7 4 0 00	100 7 4 0 00

FIGURE 13-1

Partial Work Sheet and Income Statement

Revenue Section

NET SALES: The first major category of the income statement shows net sales. The figure here of $93,380 is *not* found on the work sheet—the accountant must take the individual amounts for gross sales, sales returns and allowances, and sales discount found on the work sheet and *combine* them to arrive at a figure for net sales. Thus although the work sheet has the individual components, it is not until the formal income statement that these individual amounts are summarized in one figure for net sales.

Cost of Goods Sold Section

Sales
- Sales Ret. & Allow.
- Sales Discount

= Net Sales

On the work sheet we separate figures for Merchandise Inventory. The $19,000 represents the beginning inventory of the period, while the $4,000, calculated from an inventory sheet, is the ending inventory. Note on the financial report how the cost of goods sold section uses two separate figures for inventory. Remember that in the periodic system goods brought in during the accounting period are added to the Purchases account, not to the Merchandise Inventory account.

Beg. Inventory
+ Net Cost of Purchases
- Ending Inventory

= Cost of Goods Sold

Note that the following numbers are not found on the work sheet but are shown on the formal income statement (they are combined by the accountant in preparing the income statement):

> Net Purchases: $50,460 (Purchases – Purchases Discount – Purchases Returns and Allowances)
> Net Cost of Purchases: $50,910 (Net Purchases + Freight-In)
> Cost of Goods Available for Sale: $69,910 (Beginning Inventory + Net Cost of Purchases)
> Cost of Goods Sold: $65,910 (Cost of Goods Available for Sale – Ending Inventory)

Gross Profit

Net Sales
- Cost of Goods Sold

= Gross Profit

The figure for gross profit ($27,470) is arrived at by subtracting cost of goods sold from net sales ($93,380 – $65,910). The gross profit figure of $27,470 is not found by itself on the work sheet, but, like others we have discussed, is calculated by the accountant from separate figures on the work sheet.

Operating Expenses Section

The total of the operating expenses does not appear on its own on the work sheet; to get this figure of $13,625 the accountant adds up all the expenses on the work sheet that resulted from doing business.

Many companies break expenses down into those directly related to the selling activity of the company (**selling expenses**) and those related to administrative or office activity (**administrative expenses** or **general expenses**). Here's a sample list broken down into these two categories:

Operating Expenses:
    Selling Expenses:
        Sales Salaries Expense
        Delivery Expense
        Advertising Expense
        Depreciation Expense, Store Equipment
        Insurance Expense
           Total Selling Expenses

    Administrative Expenses:
        Rent Expense
        Office Salaries Expense
        Utilities Expense
        Supplies Expense
        Depreciation Expense, Office Equipment
           Total Administrative Expenses
               Total Operating Expenses

Other Income (or Other Revenue) Section

This section will record any revenue other than revenue from sales. For example, Art's Wholesale makes a profit from subletting a portion of a building, earning Rental Income of $200, and that income goes in this section.

Other Expense Section

This section will record nonoperating expenses—those not related to the main operating activities of the business. For example, Art's Wholesale owes $300 interest on money it has borrowed.

STATEMENT OF OWNER'S EQUITY

The information used to complete the statement of owner's equity comes from the balance sheet columns of the work sheet. Keep in mind the capital account in the ledger should be checked to see if any additional investments have occurred during the period. Note in the diagram on p. 457 how the work sheet aids in this. The ending figure of $13,050 for Art Newner, Capital, will be carried over to the balance sheet, which is the final report we will look at in this chapter.

Statement of owner's equity is the same for a merchandise business as for a service firm.

THE BALANCE SHEET

The diagram in Figure 13-2 (p. 461) shows how a work sheet is used to aid in the preparation of the balance sheet. The following is called a **classified balance sheet** because assets and liabilities are broken down into more detail.

    Let's look at each of the categories on the classified balance sheet in turn.

    Current assets are defined as cash and assets that will be converted into cash or used up during the normal operating cycle of the company or one year, whichever is longer. (Think of the **operating cycle** as the time period it takes a company to buy and sell merchandise and then collect accounts receivable.)

Any additional investment by owner would be added to his or her beginning capital amount.

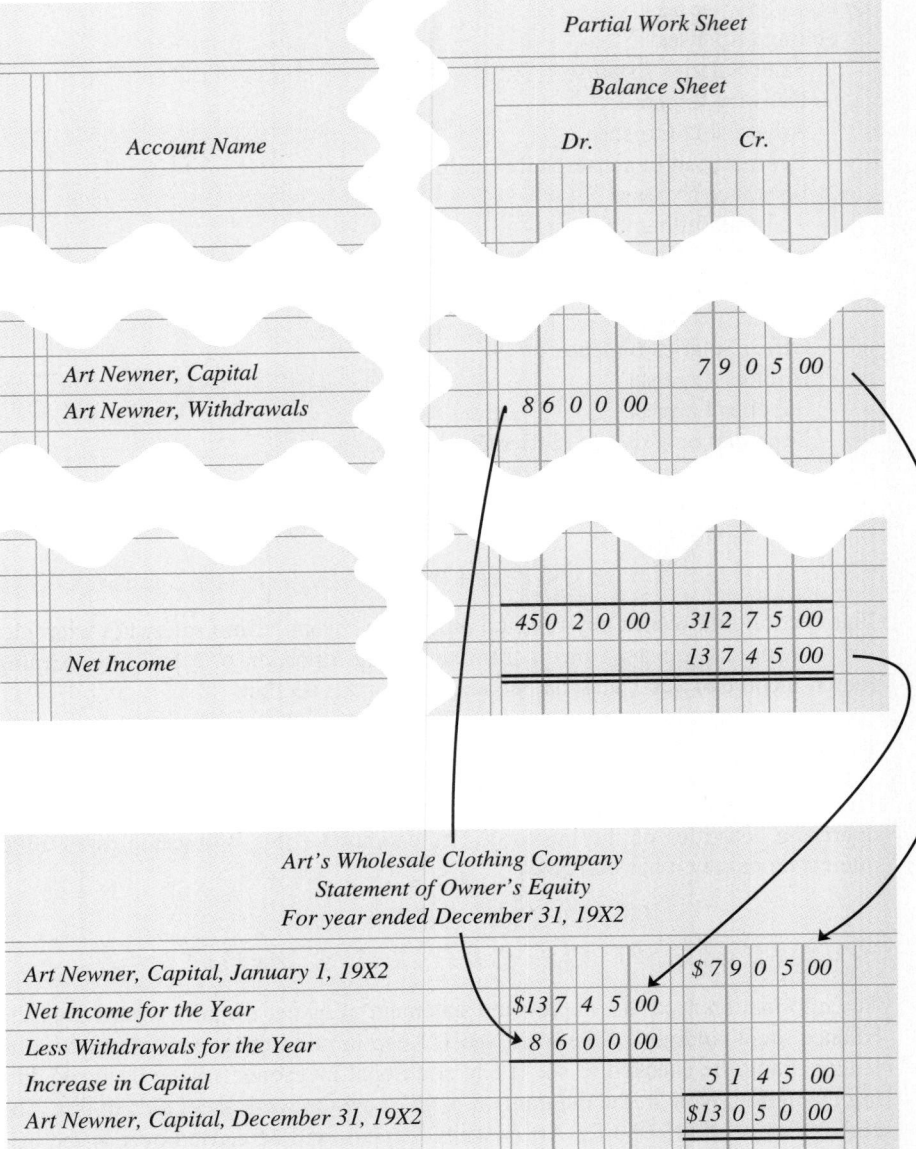

Partial Work Sheet

| | | Balance Sheet | |
Account Name		Dr.	Cr.
Art Newner, Capital			7 9 0 5 00
Art Newner, Withdrawals		8 6 0 0 00	
		45 0 2 0 00	31 2 7 5 00
Net Income			13 7 4 5 00

Art's Wholesale Clothing Company
Statement of Owner's Equity
For year ended December 31, 19X2

Art Newner, Capital, January 1, 19X2			$ 7 9 0 5 00
Net Income for the Year	$13 7 4 5 00		
Less Withdrawals for the Year	8 6 0 0 00		
Increase in Capital			5 1 4 5 00
Art Newner, Capital, December 31, 19X2			$13 0 5 0 00

Accountants list current assets in order of how easily they can be converted into cash (this is called *liquidity*). In some cases Accounts Receivable can be turned into cash more quickly than Merchandise Inventory—for example, it can be quite difficult to sell an outdated computer in a computer store, or to sell last year's model car this year.

Plant and Equipment are long-lived assets that are used in the production or sale of goods or services. Art's Wholesale has only one plant asset, store equipment; other plant assets could include buildings and land. The assets are usually listed in order according to how long they will last; the shortest-lived assets are listed first. Land would always be the last asset listed (and land is never depreciated). Note that we still show the cost of the asset less its accumulated depreciation.

FIGURE 13-2 **Partial Work Sheet and Balance Sheet**

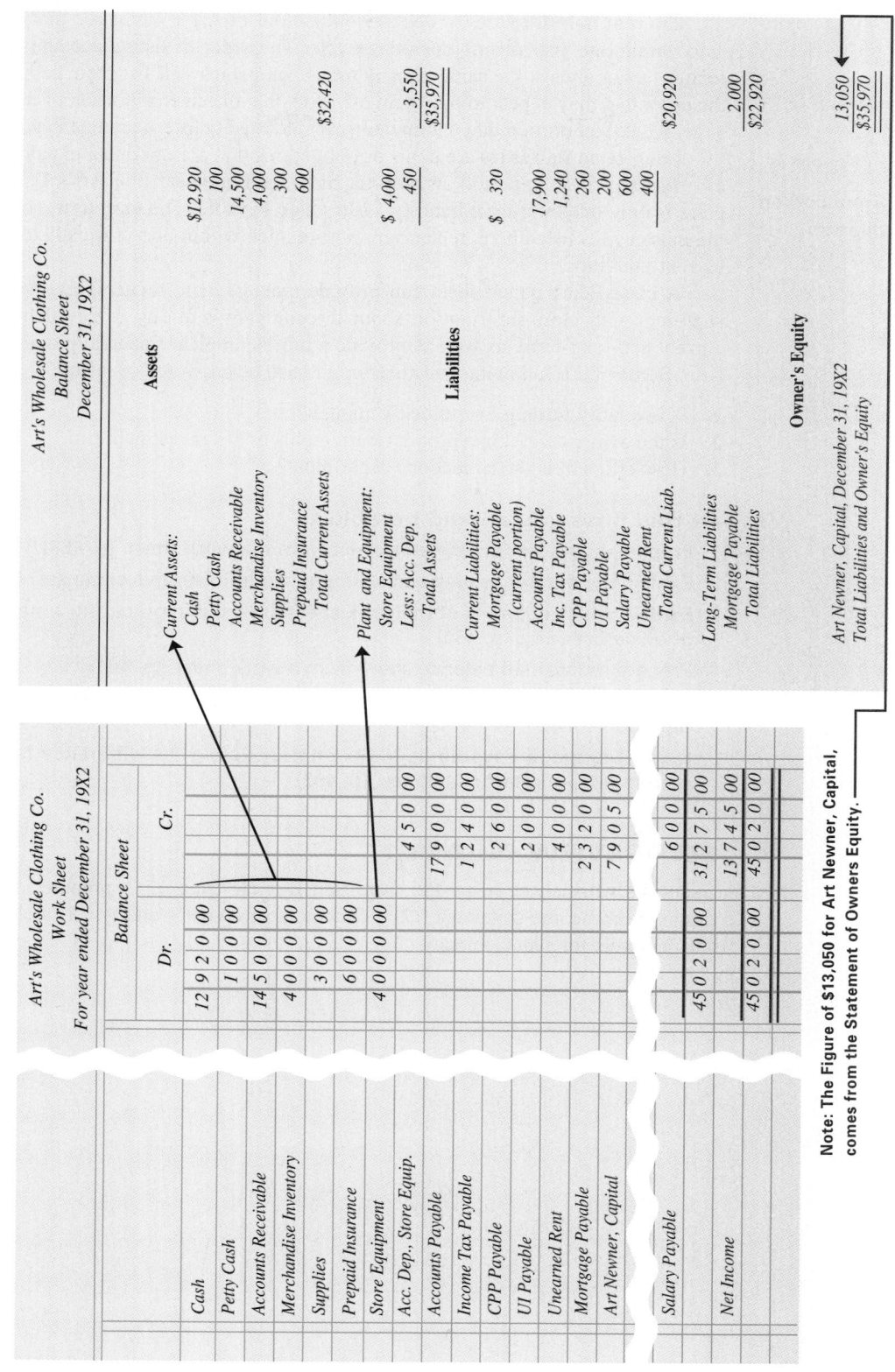

Art's Wholesale Clothing Co.
Work Sheet
For year ended December 31, 19X2

	Balance Sheet	
	Dr.	Cr.
Cash	12 9 2 0 00	
Petty Cash	1 0 0 00	
Accounts Receivable	14 5 0 0 00	
Merchandise Inventory	4 0 0 0 00	
Supplies	3 0 0 00	
Prepaid Insurance	6 0 0 00	
Store Equipment	4 0 0 0 00	
Acc. Dep., Store Equip.		4 5 0 00
Accounts Payable		17 9 0 0 00
Income Tax Payable		1 2 4 0 00
CPP Payable		2 6 0 00
UI Payable		2 0 0 00
Unearned Rent		4 0 0 00
Mortgage Payable		2 3 2 0 00
Art Newner, Capital		7 9 0 5 00
Salary Payable		6 0 0 00
	45 0 2 0 00	31 2 7 5 00
Net Income		13 7 4 5 00
	45 0 2 0 00	45 0 2 0 00

Art's Wholesale Clothing Co.
Balance Sheet
December 31, 19X2

Assets

Current Assets:		
Cash	$12,920	
Petty Cash	100	
Accounts Receivable	14,500	
Merchandise Inventory	4,000	
Supplies	300	
Prepaid Insurance	600	
Total Current Assets		$32,420
Plant and Equipment:		
Store Equipment	$ 4,000	
Less: Acc. Dep.	450	
Total Assets		3,550
		$35,970

Liabilities

Current Liabilities:		
Mortgage Payable		
(current portion)	$ 320	
Accounts Payable	17,900	
Inc. Tax Payable	1,240	
CPP Payable	260	
UI Payable	200	
Salary Payable	600	
Unearned Rent	400	
Total Current Liab.		$20,920
Long-Term Liabilities		
Mortgage Payable		2,000
Total Liabilities		$22,920

Owner's Equity

Art Newner, Capital, December 31, 19X2		13,050
Total Liabilities and Owner's Equity		$35,970

Note: The Figure of $13,050 for Art Newner, Capital, comes from the Statement of Owners Equity.

Current liabilities are the debts or obligations of Art's Wholesale that must be paid within one year or one operating cycle. The order of listing accounts in this section is not always the same—many times companies will list their liabilities in the order that they expect to pay them off. Note that the current portion of the mortgage, $320 (that portion due within one year), is listed before Accounts Payable.

Mortgage Payable:
$2,320
– 320 current portion
$2,000 long-term

Long-term liabilities are debts or obligations that are not due and payable for a comparatively long period, usually for more than one year. For Art's Wholesale there is only one long-term liability—Mortgage Payable. The long-term portion of the mortgage is listed here; the current portion, due within one year, is listed under current liabilities.

A classified balance sheet can provide management, owners, creditors, and suppliers with more information about the company's ability to pay debts, both current and long-term, as well as provide a more complete financial picture of the firm. Some of the following questions might also be answered or raised:

1. Is inventory turning over quickly enough?
2. Is the owner receiving a proper return on his or her investment?
3. How efficient is the collections department?

At this time you should be able to

1. Prepare a detailed income statement from the work sheet. (p. 458)
2. Explain the difference between selling and administrative expenses. (p. 458)
3. Explain which columns of the work sheet are used in preparing a statement of owner's equity. (p. 460)
4. Prepare a classified balance sheet from a work sheet. (p. 461)
5. Explain as well as compare current assets with plant and equipment. (pp. 459-460)
6. Using Mortgage Payable as an example, explain the difference between current and long-term liabilities. (p. 462)

☐ ### SELF-REVIEW QUIZ 13-1

Using the work sheet on p. 436 from Self-Review Quiz 12-2, prepare in proper form (1) an income statement, (2) a statement of owner's equity, (3) a classified balance sheet for Ray Company.

SOLUTION TO SELF-REVIEW QUIZ 13-1

1.

	Ray Company								

Ray Company
Income Statement
For year ended December 31, 19XX

Revenue:				
Sales			$11 0 4 0 00	
Less: Sales Ret. and Allow.	$ 5 4 6 00			
Sales Discount	2 1 6 00		7 6 2 00	
Net Sales			$10 2 7 8 00	
Cost of Goods Sold:				
Merchandise Inventory, 1/1/XX		$ 8 2 4 00		
Purchases	$ 5 2 5 6 00			
Less: Pur. Ret. and Allow.	$ 1 6 8 00			
Purchases Discount	1 0 2 00	2 7 0 00		
Net Purchases		$ 4 9 8 6 00		
Cost of Goods Available for Sale		$ 5 8 1 0 00		
Less: Merchandise Inv., 12/31/XX		2 0 0 00		
Cost of Goods Sold			5 6 1 0 00	
Gross Profit			$ 4 6 6 8 00	
Operating Expenses				
Salaries Expense	$ 2 2 1 6 00			
Insurance Expense	1 3 9 2 00			
Utilities Expense	9 6 00			
Plumbing Expense	2 1 4 00			
Rent Expense	1 0 0 00			
Depreciation Exp., Equip.	6 0 00			
Total Operating Expenses			4 0 7 8 00	
Net Income from Operations			$ 5 9 0 00	
Other Income:				
Storage Fees			5 1 6 00	
Net Income			$ 1 1 0 6 00	

2.

Ray Company
Statement of Owner's Equity
For year ended December 31, 19XX

B. Ray, Capital, 1/1/XX	$ 1 9 3 2 00
Net Income for the Year	1 1 0 6 00
B. Ray, Capital, 12/31/XX	$ 3 0 3 8 00

3.

Ray Company
Balance Sheet
December 31, 19XX

Assets

Current Assets:

Cash	$2 4 8 6 00		
Merchandise Inventory	2 0 0 00		
Prepaid Rent	1 0 5 2 00		
Prepaid Insurance	6 0 00		
Total Current Assets		$3 7 9 8 00	

Plant and Equipment

Office Equipment	$2 1 6 0 00		
Less: Accumulated Depreciation	6 2 0 00	1 5 4 0 00	
Total Assets		$5 3 3 8 00	

Liabilities

Current Liabilities

Accounts Payable	$ 1 0 0 00		
Salaries Payable	2 0 0 00		
Unearned Storage Fees	2 0 0 0 00		
Total Liabilities		$2 3 0 0 00	

Owner's Equity

B. Ray, Capital, December 31, 19XX		3 0 3 8 00	
Total Liabilities and Owner's Equity		$5 3 3 8 00	

LEARNING UNIT 13-2

Journalizing and Posting Adjusting and Closing Entries; Preparing the Post-Closing Trial Balance

JOURNALIZING AND POSTING ADJUSTING ENTRIES

From the work sheet of Art's Wholesale, repeated here in Figure 13-3 (p. 465) for your convenience, the adjusting entries can be journalized from the adjustments column and posted to the ledger. Keep in mind that the adjustments have been placed only on the work sheet, not on the ledger—at this point the ledger still contains only unadjusted amounts.

FIGURE 13-3   **Completed Work Sheet**

Art's Wholesale Clothing Co.
Work Sheet
For year ended December 31, 19X2

Account	TB Dr	TB Cr	Adj. Dr	Adj. Cr	ATB Dr	ATB Cr	I/S Dr	I/S Cr	B/S Dr	B/S Cr
Cash	12,920.00				12,920.00				12,920.00	
Petty Cash	100.00				100.00				100.00	
Accounts Receivable	14,500.00				14,500.00				14,500.00	
Merchandise Inventory	19,000.00		(B)4,000.00	(A)19,000.00	4,000.00				4,000.00	
Supplies	800.00			(D)500.00	300.00				300.00	
Prepaid Insurance	900.00			(E)300.00	600.00				600.00	
Store Equipment	4,000.00				4,000.00				4,000.00	
Acc. Dep., Store Equip.		400.00		(F)50.00		450.00				450.00
Accounts Payable		17,900.00				17,900.00				17,900.00
Income Tax Payable		1,240.00				1,240.00				1,240.00
CPP Payable		260.00				260.00				260.00
UI Payable		200.00				200.00				200.00
Unearned Rent		600.00	(C)200.00			400.00				400.00
Mortgage Payable		2,320.00				2,320.00				2,320.00
Art Newner, Capital		7,905.00				7,905.00				7,905.00
Art Newner, Withdrawals	8,600.00				8,600.00				8,600.00	
Income Summary			(A)19,000.00	(B)4,000.00	19,000.00	4,000.00	19,000.00	4,000.00		
Sales		95,000.00				95,000.00		95,000.00		
Sales Returns and Allowances	950.00				950.00		950.00			
Sales Discount	670.00				670.00		670.00			
Purchases	52,000.00				52,000.00		52,000.00			
Purchases Discount		860.00				860.00		860.00		
Purchases Returns and Allowances		680.00				680.00		680.00		
Freight-In	450.00				450.00		450.00			
Salary Expense	11,700.00		(G)600.00		12,300.00		12,300.00			
Payroll Tax Expense	420.00				420.00		420.00			
Postage Expense	25.00				25.00		25.00			
Miscellaneous Expense	30.00				30.00		30.00			
Interest Expense	300.00				300.00		300.00			
	127,365.00	127,365.00								
Rental Income				(C)200.00		200.00		200.00		
Supplies Expense			(D)500.00		500.00		500.00			
Insurance Expense			(E)300.00		300.00		300.00			
Depreciation Exp. Store Equip.			(F)50.00		50.00		50.00			
Salary Payable				(G)600.00		600.00				600.00
			24,650.00	24,650.00	132,015.00	132,015.00	86,995.00	100,740.00	45,020.00	31,275.00
Net Income							13,745.00			13,745.00
							100,740.00	100,740.00	45,020.00	45,020.00

The journalized and posted adjusting entries are shown on p. 466. Note that the liability Unearned Rent is reduced by $200 and Rental Income has increased by $200.

Art's Wholesale Clothing Co.
General Journal

Page 2

Date	Account Titles and Description	PR	Dr.	Cr.
	Adjusting Entries			
31	Income Summary	313	19 000 00	
	Merchandise Inventory	114		19 000 00
	Transferred beginning inventory			
	to Income Summary			
31	Merchandise Inventory	114	4 000 00	
	Income Summary	313		4 000 00
	Records cost of ending inventory			
31	Unearned Rent	218	2 00 00	
	Rental Income	414		2 00 00
	Rental Income earned			
31	Supplies Expense	614	5 00 00	
	Supplies	115		5 00 00
	Supplies consumed			
31	Insurance Expense	615	3 00 00	
	Prepaid Insurance	116		3 00 00
	Insurance expired			
31	Dep. Exp., Store Equipment	613	5 0 00	
	Acc. Dep., Store Equipment	122		5 0 00
	Depreciation on equipment			
31	Salary Expense	611	6 00 00	
	Salary Payable	212		6 00 00
	Accrued salary			

PARTIAL LEDGER

Merchandise Inventory 114	
19,000	19,000
4,000	

Accum. Dep., Store Equipment 122	
	400
	50

Income Summary 313	
19,000	4,000

Dep. Expense, Store Equip. 613	
50	

Supplies 115	
800	500

Salary Payment 212	
	600

Supplies Expense 614	
500	

Salary Exp. 611	
12,000	
600	

Prepaid Insurance 116	
900	300

Unearned Rent 218	
200	600

Insurance Expense 615	
300	

Rental Income 414	
	200

JOURNALIZING AND POSTING CLOSING ENTRIES

Back in Chapter 5 we discussed the closing process for a service company. The goals of closing have not changed. They are to clear all temporary accounts in the ledger to zero and update capital in the ledger to its latest balance. A merchandise company will also use the work sheet and the following steps to complete the closing process:

1. Close all balances on the income statement credit column of the work sheet except Income Summary by Debits and credit the total to the Income Summary account.
2. Close all balances on the income statement debit column of the work sheet *except Income Summary* by Credits and debit the total to the Income Summary account.
3. Transfer the balance of the Income Summary account to the Capital account.
4. Transfer the balance of the owner's Withdrawal account to the Capital account.

Let's look now at the journalized closing entries in Figure 13-4 (p. 468).

When these entries are posted, all the temporary accounts will have zero balances in the ledger, and the Capital account will be updated with a new balance.

Let's take a moment to look at the Income Summary account in T-account form:

Income Summary 313

Adj.	19,000	4,000	Adj.
Clos.	67,995	96,740	Clos.
	86,995	100,740	
Net income ⟶ Clos.	13,745		

Note that Income Summary before the closing process contains the adjustments for Merchandise Inventory. The end result is that the net income of $13,745 is closed to the Capital account.

THE POST-CLOSING TRIAL BALANCE

The post-closing trial balance shown on p. 469 (top) is prepared from the general ledger. Note first that all temporary accounts have been closed and thus are not shown on this post-closing trial balance. Note also that the ending inventory figure of the last accounting period, $4,000, becomes the beginning inventory figure on Jan. 1, 19X3.

At this point you should be able to

1. Journalize and post adjusting entries for a merchandise company. (p. 464)
2. Explain the relationship of the work sheet to the adjusting and closing process (pp. 464-466)
3. Complete the closing process for a merchandise company. (pp. 465-466)
4. Prepare a post-closing trial balance and explain why ending merchandise inventory is not a temporary account. (p. 467)

FIGURE 13-4
General Journal

Art's Wholesale Clothing Co.
General Journal

Page 2

Date		Account Titles and Description	PR	Dr.	Cr.
19XX		*Closing Entries*			
Dec.	31	Sales	411	95 000 00	
		Rental Income	414	2 00 00	
		Purchases Income	512	8 60 00	
		Purchases Ret. and Allow.	513	6 80 00	
		Income Summary	313		96 740 00
		Transfers credit account balances			
		on income statement column of work sheet			
		to Income Summary.			
	31	Income Summary	313	67 995 00	
		Sales Returns and Allowances	412		9 50 00
		Sales Discount	413		6 70 00
		Purchases	511		52 000 00
		Freight-In	514		4 50 00
		Salaries Expense	611		12 300 00
		Payroll Tax Expense	612		4 20 00
		Postage Expense	616		2 5 00
		Miscellaneous Expense	617		3 0 00
		Interest Expense	618		3 00 00
		Supplies Expense	614		5 00 00
		Insurance Expense	615		3 00 00
		Depreciation Expense, Store Equip.	613		5 0 00
		Transfers all expenses, and reductions to Sales			
		are Closed to Income Summary.			
	31	Income Summary	313	13 745 00	
		A. Newner, Capital	311		13 745 00
		Tranfer of net income to			
		Capital from Income Summary.			
	31	A. Newner, Capital	311	8 600 00	
		A. Newner, Capital, Withdrawals	312		8 600 00
		Closes withdrawals to Capital Accounts.			

□ **SELF-REVIEW QUIZ 13-2**

Using the work sheet from Self-Review Quiz 12-2 (p. 436), journalize the closing entries. (Solution is found at bottom of p. 469.)

Art's Wholesale Clothing Co.
Post-Closing Trial Balance
December 31, 19X2

	Dr.	Cr.
Cash	1 2 9 2 0 00	
Petty Cash	1 0 0 00	
Accounts Receivable	1 4 5 0 0 00	
Merchandise Inventory	4 0 0 0 00	
Supplies	3 0 0 00	
Prepaid Insurance	6 0 0 00	
Store Equipment	4 0 0 0 00	
Accum. Dep., Store Equipment		4 5 0 00
Accounts Payable		1 7 9 0 0 00
Income Tax Payable		1 2 4 0 00
CPP Payable		2 6 0 00
UI Payable		2 0 0 00
Salary Payable		6 0 0 00
Unearned Rent		4 0 0 00
Mortgage Payable		2 3 2 0 00
Art Newner, Capital		1 3 0 5 0 00
	3 6 4 2 0 00	3 6 4 2 0 00

SOLUTION TO SELF-REVIEW QUIZ 13-2

Page 2

Date	Account Titles and Description	PR	Dr.	Cr.
	Closing			
Dec. 31	Sales		11 0 4 0 00	
	Storage Fees Earned		5 1 6 00	
	Purchases Return and Allowances		1 6 8 00	
	Purchases Discount		1 0 2 00	
	Income Summary			11 8 2 6 00
31	Income Summary		10 0 9 6 00	
	Sales Returns and Allowances			5 4 6 00
	Sales Discount			2 1 6 00
	Purchases			5 2 5 6 00
	Salaries Expense			2 2 1 6 00
	Insuranse Expense			1 3 9 2 00
	Utilities Expense			9 6 00
	Plumbing Expense			2 1 4 00
	Rent Expense			1 0 0 00
	Depreciation Exp., Equipment			6 0 00
31	Income Summary		1 1 0 6 00	
	B. Ray, Capital			1 1 0 6 00

LEARNING UNIT 13-3

Reversing Entries

Reversing entries are an option; they are not mandatory.

Now that we have completed the accounting cycle for Art's Wholesale Clothing Company, let's look at an optional way of handling some adjusting entries—it is called reversing entries. **Reversing entries** are general journal entries that are the opposite of adjusting entries. Reversing entries help reduce potential errors and simplify the record-keeping process. Let's look at how Art's bookkeeper handles a reversing entry for salaries at the end of the year (see Figure 13-5).

Note that the permanent account, Salaries Payable, carries over to the new accounting period a $600 balance. *REMEMBER: The $600 was an expense of the prior year.*

On January 8 of the new year the payroll to be paid is $2,000. If the optional reversing entry is *not* used, the bookkeeper makes the following journal entry:

Salaries Payable	600 00		
Salaries Expense	1 400 00		
Cash		2 000 00	

Sal. Exp.	Sal. Pay.	Cash
1,400	600 | 600	| 2,000

To do this the bookkeeper has to refer back to the adjustment on December 31 to determine how much of the salary of $2,000 is indeed a new salary expense and what portion was shown in the old year although not paid. It is easy to see how potential errors can result if the bookkeeper pays the payroll but forgets about the adjustment in the previous year. In this way reversing entries can help avoid potential errors.

Figure 13-6 (p. 471) shows the steps the bookkeeper would take if reversing entries were used: Note that steps (1) and (2) are the same whether the accountant uses reversing entries or not.

FIGURE 13-5

Reversing Entries

(1)
On December 31 after adjusting entry was journalized and posted for $600 of salaries incurred but not paid.

(2)
On January 1 after closing entries have been journalized and posted.

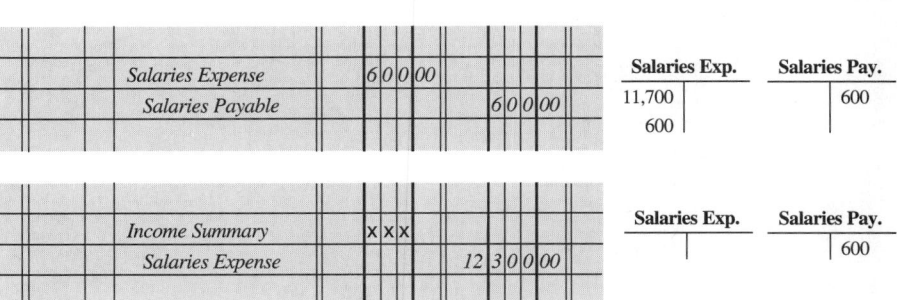

Note that the balance of Salaries Expense is indeed only $1,400, the *true* expense in the new year. Reversing results in switching the adjustment the first day of the new period. Also note that each of the accounts ends up with the same balance no matter which method is chosen. However, using reversing entry for salaries allows the accountant to make the normal entry when it is time to pay salaries.

FIGURE 13-6   **Reversing Entries**

(1)
On December 31 adjustment for salary was recorded.

Salaries Exp.		Salaries Pay.	
11,700			600
600			

(2)
Closing entry on December 31.

Salaries Exp.		Salaries Pay.	
11,700	12,300		600
600			

(3)
On January 1 (first day of the following fiscal period) reverse adjusting entry was made for salary on December 31. (This means "flipping" adjustment.)

Salaries Payable	600 00		
Salaries Expense		600 00	

Salaries Exp.		Salaries Pay.	
	600	600	600

By doing this the liability is reduced to 0. We know it will be paid in this new period but the salaries expense has a credit balance of $600 until the payroll is paid. When the payroll of $2,000 is paid, the following results.

(4)
Paid Payroll $2,000.

Salaries Expense	2 000 00		
Cash		2 000 00	

Salaries Exp.		Cash	
2,000	600		2,000

One should be careful with reversing entries, since not all adjustments can be reversed. Here is a list of the types of adjustments that can be reversed:

1. When there is an increase in an asset account (no previous balance).

    Example: Interest Receivable
    Interest Income

    (Interest earned but not collected; we will cover this in later chapters)

2. When there is an increase in a liability account (no previous balance).

    Example: Wages Expense
    Wages Payable

With the exception of businesses in their first year of operation, accounts such as Accumulated Depreciation or Inventory will have previous balances and thus will *not* be reversed. As we progress in the course, we will take time to review whether reversing takes place or not.

At this point you should be able to

1. Explain the purpose of reversing entries. (p. 470)
2. Complete a reversing entry. (p. 470)
3. Explain when reversing entries can be used. (p. 471)

☐ **SELF-REVIEW QUIZ 13-3**

Explain which of the following situations could be reversed:

1.

Supplies Exp.		Supplies	
200		800	200

2.

Wages Exp.		Wages Payable	
3,000			200
200			

3.

Sales		Unearned Sales	
	4,000	50	200
	50		

■ *SOLUTION TO SELF-REVIEW QUIZ 13-3*

1. Not reversed—asset Supplies is decreasing, not increasing.
2. Reversed—liability is increasing and no previous balance exists.
3. Not reversed—liability is decreasing and a previous balance exists.

SUMMARY OF KEY POINTS AND KEY TERMS

LEARNING UNIT 13-1

1. The formal income statement can be prepared from the income statement columns of the work sheet.
2. There are no debit or credit columns on the formal income statement.
3. The cost of goods sold section has a figure for beginning inventory and a separate figure for ending inventory.
4. Operating expenses could be broken down into selling and administrative expenses.
5. The ending figure for capital is not found on the work sheet. It comes from the statement of owner's equity.
6. A classified balance sheet breaks assets into current and plant and equipment. Liabilities are broken down into current and long-term.

Administrative expenses (general expenses): Expenses such as general office expenses that are incurred indirectly in the selling of goods.

Classified balance sheet: A balance sheet that categorizes assets as current or plant and equipment and groups liabilities as current or long-term.

Current assets: Assets that can be converted into cash or used within one year or the normal operating cycle of the business, whichever is longer.

Current liabilities: Obligations that will come due within one year or within the operating cycle, whichever is longer.

Long-term liabilities: Obligations that are not due or payable for a long time, usually for more than a year.

Operating cycle: Average time it takes to buy and sell merchandise and then collect accounts receivable.

Other expenses: These are non-operating expenses that do not relate to the main operating activities of the business; they appear in a separate section on the income statement. One example given in the text is Interest Expense—interest owed on money borrowed by the company.

Other income: This includes any revenue other than revenue from sales and appears in a separate section on the income statement. Examples would be Rental Income and Storage Fees.

BLUEPRINT OF FINANCIAL REPORTS

(1) Income Statement

Revenue:				
Sales				$ XXX
Less: Sales Ret. and Allow.			$ XXX	
Sales Discount			XXX	XXX
Net Sales				$XXXX
Cost of Goods Sold:				
Merchandise Inventory, 1/1/XX			$ XXX	
Purchases		$XXX		
Less: Purchases Discount	$XXX			
Purch, Ret. and Allow.	XXX	XXX		
Net Purchases		XXX		
Add: Freight-In		XXX		
Net Cost of Purchases			XXX	
Cost of Goods Avail. for Sale			$XXXX	
Less: Merch. Inv., 12/31/XX			XXX	
Cost of Goods Sold				XXXX
Gross Profit				$XXXX
Operating Expenses:				
~~			$ XXX	
~~			XXX	
~~			XXX	
Total Operating Expenses				XXX
Net Income from Operations				$ XXX
Other Income:				
Rental Income			$ XXX	
Storage Fees Income			XXX	
Total Other Income				$ XXX
Other Expenses:				
Interest Expenses			XXX	XXX
Net Income				$ XXX

(continued)

(2) Statement of Owner's Equity

		$XXX
Beginning Capital		XXX
Additional Investments		$XXX
Total Investments		
Net Income*	$XXX	
Less: Withdrawals	XXX	
Increase in Capital		XXX
Ending Capital		$XXX

* From the Income Statement

(3) Balance Sheet

Assets

Current Assets			
Cash		$XXXX	
Accounts Receivable		XXXX	
Merchandise Inventory		XXXX	
Prepaid Insurance		XXXX	
Total Current Assets			$XXXX
Plant and Equipment			
Store Equipment	$XXXX		
Less: Accumulated Depreciation	XXX	$XXXX	
Office Equipment	$XXXX		
Less: Accumulated Depreciation	XXX	XXXX	
Total Plant Equipment			XXXX
Total Assets			$XXXX

Liabilities

Current Liabilities			
Unearned Revenue		$XXX	
Mortgage Payable (current portion)		XXX	
Accounts Payable		XXX	
Salaries Payable		XX	
Income Taxes Payable		XX	
Total Current Liabilities			$XXX
Long Term Liabilities			
Mortgage Payable			$XXX
Total Liabilities			$XXXX

Owner's Equity

Capital*			XXXX
Total Liabilities and Owner's Equity			$XXXX

* From statement of owner's equity

Plant and equipment: Long-lived assets such as buildings or land that are used in the production or sale of goods or services.

Selling expenses: Expenses directly related to the sale of goods.

LEARNING UNIT 13-2

1. The information for journalizing, adjusting, and closing entries can be obtained from the work sheet.

2. In the closing process all temporary accounts will be zero and the capital account is brought up to its new balance.

3. Inventory is not a temporary account. The ending inventory, along with other permanent accounts, will be listed in the post-closing trial balance.

LEARNING UNIT 13-3

1. Reversing entries are optional and could aid in reducing potential errors and simplify the record-keeping process.

2. The reversing entry "flips" the adjustment on the first day of new fiscal period. Thus the bookkeeper need not look back at what happened in the old year when recording the current year's transactions.

3. Reversing entries are only used if (a) assets are increasing and have no previous balance, (b) liabilities are increasing and have no previous balance.

Reversing entries: Year-end optional bookkeeping technique in which certain adjusting entries are reversed or switched on the first day of the new accounting period so that transactions in the new period can be recorded without referring back to prior adjusting entries.

DISCUSSION QUESTIONS

1. Which columns of the work sheet aid in the preparation of the income statement?

2. Explain the components of cost of goods sold.

3. Explain how operating expenses can be broken down into different categories.

4. What is the difference between current assets and plant and equipment?

5. What is an operating cycle?

6. Why journalize adjusting entries after the formal reports have been prepared?

7. Explain the steps of closing for a merchandise company.

8. Temporary accounts could appear on a post-closing trial balance. Agree or disagree.

9. What is the purpose of using reversing entries? Are they mandatory? When should they be used?

EXERCISES

1. From the following accounts, prepare a cost of goods sold section in proper form: Freight-In, $300; Merchandise Inventory, 12/31/X1, $5,000; Purchases Discount, $900; Merchandise Inventory, 12/1/X1, $4,000; Purchases, $58,000; Purchases Returns and Allowances, $1,100.

Preparing cost of goods sold section.

Categorizing and clas-
sifying account titles.

2. Give the category, the classification, and the report(s) on which each of the following appears (for example: **Cash**—asset, current asset, balance sheet):

    (a) Salaries Payable.
    (b) Accounts Payable.
    (c) Mortgage Payable.
    (d) Unearned Legal Fees.
    (e) FIT Payable.
    (f) Office Equipment.
    (g) Land.

Journalizing closing
entries.

3. From the following partial work sheet, journalize the closing entries of December 31 for A. Slow Co.

A. Slow Co.
Work Sheet
For year ended December 31, 19XX

Account Titles	Income Statement Dr.	Income Statement Cr.	Balance Sheet Dr.	Balance Sheet Cr.
Cash			1 9 3 00	
Merch. Inventory			4 5 0 00	
Prepaid Advertising			5 6 1 00	
Prepaid Insurance			3 0 00	
Office Equipment			1 0 8 0 00	
Acc. Dep., Office Equip.				2 1 0 00
Accounts Payable				2 5 8 00
A. Slow, Capital				9 6 6 00
Income Summary	3 6 2 00	4 5 0 00		
Sales		5 5 2 0 00		
Sales Returns And Allow.	2 2 3 00			
Sales Discount	1 0 8 00			
Purchases	2 6 2 8 00			
Purchases Returns and Allow.		3 4 00		
Purchass Discount		5 1 00		
Salaries Expense	1 0 8 3 00			
Insurance Expense	6 9 6 00			
Utilities Expense	4 8 00			
Plumbing Expense	5 7 00			
Advertising Expense	1 5 00			
Dep. Expenses, Office Equip.	3 0 00			
Salaries Payable				7 5 00
	5 2 5 0 00	6 0 5 5 00	2 3 1 4 00	1 5 0 9 00
Net Income	8 0 5 00			8 0 5 00
	6 0 5 5 00	6 0 5 5 00	2 3 1 4 00	2 3 1 4 00

Preparing partially
completed balance
sheet.

4. From the work sheet in Exercise 3, prepare the assets section of a classified balance sheet.

Reversing entry.

5. On December 31, 19X1, $300 of salaries has been accrued. (Salaries before accrued amount totalled $26,000.) The next payroll to be paid will be on February 3, 19X2, for $6,000. Please do the following:

    (a) Journalize and post the adjusting entry (use T accounts).
    (b) Journalize and post the reversing entry on January 1.
    (c) Journalize and post the payment of the payroll. Cash has a balance of $15,000 before the payment of payroll on February 3.

GROUP A PROBLEMS

13A-1. Prepare a formal income statement from the partial work sheet for Babe's Pants Co, below.

Preparing an income statement from a work sheet.

Babe's Pants Co.
Partial Work Sheet
For the year ended December 31, 19XX

Account Titles	Income Statement	
	Dr.	Cr.
Income Summary	3 7 0 00	2 6 0 00
Sales		2 8 0 0 00
Sales Returns and Allow.	1 1 9 00	
Sales Discount	6 4 00	
Purchases	8 7 0 00	
Purchases Returns and Allow.		1 6 7 00
Purchases Discount		1 2 9 00
Freight-In	1 0 2 00	
Salaries Expense	3 0 0 00	
Insurance Expense	2 0 0 00	
Advertising Expense	1 5 5 00	
Rental Income		2 0 0 00
Rent Expense	2 1 5 00	
Dep. Exp., Store Equip.	2 0 0 00	
Salaries Payable		
	2 5 9 5 00	3 5 5 6 00
Net Income	9 6 1 00	
	3 5 5 6 00	3 5 5 6 00

13A-2. Prepare a statement of owner's equity and a classified balance sheet from the work sheet for James Company (p. 478, top). NOTE: Of the Mortgage Payable, $200 is due within one year.

13A-3. (a) Complete the work sheet for Jay's Supplies (p. 479, top).
(b) Prepare an income statement, a statement of owner's equity, and a classified balance sheet. (NOTE: The amount of the mortgage due the first year is $800.)
(c) Journalize the adjusting and closing entries.

Completion of work sheet: preparation of financial reports; journalizing adjusting and closing entries.

13A-4. Using the ledger balances and additional data shown below, do the following for Callahan Lumber for the year ended December 31, 19XX:

1. Prepare the work sheet.
2. Prepare the income statement, statement of owner's equity, and balance sheet.
3. Journalize and post adjusting and closing entries. (Be sure to put beginning balances in the ledger first.)
4. Prepare a post-closing trial balance.
5. Journalize the reversing entry for wages.

Comprehensive Problem. Work sheet preparation: preparing financial reports; journalizing and posting adjusting and closing entries; preparing a post-closing trial balance; journalizing reversing entry.

Preparing statement of owner's equity and a classified balance sheet from a work sheet.

James Company
Work Sheet
For the year ended December 31, 19XX

Account Titles	Balance Sheet Dr.	Balance Sheet Cr.
Cash	23 5 0 0 00	
Petty Cash	9 0 00	
Accounts Receivable	1 3 5 0 00	
Merchandise Inv.	4 0 0 0 00	
Supplies	3 2 5 00	
Prepaid Insurance	5 0 0 00	
Store Equipment	2 8 0 0 00	
Acc. Dep., Store Eq.		7 0 0 00
Automobile	1 7 0 0 00	
Acc. Dep., Auto.		2 2 5 00
Accounts Payable		2 8 0 0 00
Taxes Payable		2 4 0 0 00
Unearned Rent		18 5 0 0 00
Mortgage Payable		4 5 0 00
H. James, Capital		12 4 0 0 00
H. James, With.	1 0 0 00	
Salaries Payable		6 0 0 00
	34 3 6 5 00	38 0 7 5 00
Net Loss	3 7 1 0 00	
	38 0 7 5 00	38 0 7 5 00

Qu. 13A-4 (continued)

ACCT. NO.

No.	Account	Amount
110	Cash	$1,340
111	Accounts Receivable	1,300
112	Merchandise Inventory	4,550
113	Lumber Supplies	269
114	Prepaid Insurance	218
121	Lumber Equipment	3,000
122	Acc. Dep., Lumber Equipment	490
220	Accounts Payable	1,160
221	Wages Payable	
330	J. Callahan, Capital	7,352
331	J. Callahan, Withdrawals	3,000
332	Income Summary	—
440	Sales	22,800
441	Sales Returns and Allowances	200
550	Purchases	14,800
551	Purchases Discount	285
552	Purchases Returns and Allowances	300

Jay's Supplies
Work Sheet
For year ended December 31, 19XX

Account Titles	Trial Balance Dr.	Trial Balance Cr.	Adjustments Dr.	Adjustments Cr.
Cash	2 000 00			
Accounts Receivable	3 000 00			
Merchandise Inventory, 1/1/XX	11 000 00		(B)104 00 00	110 00 00 (A)
Prepaid Insurance	1 880 00			5 00 00 (E)
Equipment	3 400 00			
Acc. Dep., Equipment		1 080 00		4 00 00 (D)
Accounts Payable		5 080 00		
Unearned Training Fees		2 120 00	(C)3 20 00	
Mortgage Payable		1 200 00		
P. Jay, Capital		10 560 00		
P. Jay, Withdrawals	4 280 00			
Income Summary			(A)11 000 00	10 400 00 (B)
Sales		95 800 00		
Sales Returns and Allow.	3 200 00			
Sales Discount	2 600 00			
Purchases	63 600 00			
Purchases Retuns and Allow.		1 360 00		
Purchases Discount		3 20 00		
Freight-In	2 680 00			
Advertising Expense	11 400 00			
Rent Expense	10 000 00			
Salaries Expense	13 600 00			
	132 640 00	132 640 00		
Training Fees Earned				3 20 00 (C)
Dep. Expenses, Equipment			(D)4 00 00	
Insurance Expense			(E)5 00 00	
			22 620 00	22 620 00

Qu. 13A-4 (continued)

660	Wages Expense	2,480
661	Advertising Expense	400
662	Rent Expense	830
663	Dep. Expense, Lumber Equipment	
664	Lumber Supplies Expense	
665	Insurance Expense	

Additional data:

(a, b)	Merchandise inventory, December 31	$4,900
(c)	Lumber supplies on hand, December 31	75
(d)	Insurance expired	150
(e)	Depreciation for the year	250
(f)	Accrued wages on December 31	95

GROUP B PROBLEMS

Preparing an income statement from a work sheet.

13B-1. From the partial work sheet shown below, prepare a formal income statement.

Babe's Pants Co.
Partial Work Sheet
For year ended December 31, 19XX

Account Titles	Income Statement	
	Dr.	Cr.
Income Summary	3 0 0 00	2 9 5 00
Sales		4 1 0 0 00
Sales R & A	1 4 5 00	
Sales Dis.	1 7 5 00	
Purchases	2 0 0 0 00	
Purchases R & A		1 7 5 00
Purchases Dis.		8 5 00
Freight-In	5 0 00	
Salaries Expense	3 6 0 00	
Insurance Expense	2 7 5 00	
Advertising Expense	1 6 5 00	
Rental Income		2 3 0 00
Rent Expense	2 2 5 00	
Dep. Exp., Store Eq.	1 1 5 00	
Salaries Payable		
	3 8 1 0 00	4 8 8 5 00
Net Income	1 0 7 5 00	
	4 8 8 5 00	4 8 8 5 00

Preparing a statement of owner's equity and a classified balance sheet from a work sheet.

13B-2. From the work sheet shown on page 481, top, complete

(a) Statement of owner's equity.
(b) Classified balance sheet.

NOTE: Of the Mortgage Payable, $3,000 is due within one year.

Completing the work sheet; preparing financial reports; journalizing adjusting and closing entries.

13B-3. From the partial work sheet shown on page 482, top, your task is to

1. Complete the work sheet.
2. Prepare the income statement, statement of owner's equity, and classified balance sheet. The amount of the mortgage due the first year is $800.
3. Journalize the adjusting and closing entries.

James Company
Work Sheet
For the year ended December 31, 19XX

Account Titles	Balance Sheet	
	Dr.	Cr.
Cash	2 5 0 0 00	
Petty Cash	5 0 00	
Acc. Rec.	1 3 0 0 00	
Merch. Inv.	4 2 5 0 00	
Supplies	3 4 4 00	
Prepaid Ins.	6 0 0 00	
Store Equip.	18 0 0 0 00	
Acc. Dep., Store Eq.		7 5 0 00
Automobile	2 5 0 0 00	
Acc. Dep., Auto.		5 0 0 00
Acc. Pay.		3 4 5 0 00
Taxes Pay.		2 1 0 0 00
Unearned Rent		11 0 0 0 00
Mortgage Pay.		8 0 0 0 00
H. James, Capital		10 5 0 0 00
H. James, Withdrawals	4 0 0 0 00	
Salaries Payable		1 0 0 00
	33 5 4 4 00	36 4 0 0 00
Net Loss	2 8 5 6 00	
	36 4 0 0 00	36 4 0 0 00

13B-4. From the following ledger balances and additional data on p. 482, do the following:

1. Prepare the work sheet.
2. Prepare the income statement, statement of owner's equity, and balance sheet.
3. Journalize and post adjusting and closing entries. (Be sure to put beginning balances in the ledger first.)
4. Prepare a post-closing trial balance.
5. Journalize the reversing entry for wages.

Comprehensive Problem. Work sheet preparation; preparing financial reports, journalizing and posting adjusting and closing entries; preparing a post-closing trial balance; journalizing reversing entry.

ACCT. NO.

110	Cash	$ 940
111	Accounts Receivable	1,470
112	Merchandise Inventory	5,600
113	Lumber Supplies	260
114	Prepaid Insurance	117
121	Lumber Equipment	2,600
122	Acc. Dep., Lumber Equipment	340
220	Accounts Payable	1,330
221	Wages Payable	

Jay's Supplies
Work Sheet
For year ended December 31, 19XX

Account Titles	Trial Balance Dr.	Trial Balance Cr.	Adjustments Dr.	Adjustments Cr.
Cash	3 0 0 0 00			
Accounts Receivable	3 0 0 0 00			
Merchandise Inventory, 1/1/XX	11 7 0 0 00		(B)8 0 0 0 00	11 7 0 0 00 (A)
Prepaid Insurance	1 0 0 0 00			3 5 0 00 (E)
Equipment	5 0 0 0 00			
Acc. Dep., Equipment		1 9 0 0 00		5 0 0 00 (D)
Accounts Payable		2 1 0 0 00		
Unearned Training Fees		1 4 5 0 00	(C)4 0 0 00	
Mortgage Payable		2 4 0 0 00		
P. Jay, Capital		27 7 5 0 00		
P. Jay, Withdrawals	4 0 0 0 00			
Income Summary			(A)11 7 0 0 00	8 0 0 0 00 (B)
Sales		100 8 0 0 00		
Sales Returns and Allow.	4 1 0 0 00			
Sales Discount	2 8 0 0 00			
Purchases	70 0 0 0 00			
Purchases Returns and Allow.		2 0 0 0 00		
Purchases Discount		1 4 0 0 00		
Freight-In	2 7 0 0 00			
Advertising Expense	8 0 0 0 00			
Rent Expense	8 5 0 0 00			
Salaries Expense	16 0 0 0 00			
	139 8 0 0 00	139 8 0 0 00		
Training Fees Earned				4 0 0 00 (C)
Dep. Expenses, Equipment			(D)5 0 0 00	
Insurance Expense			(E) 3 5 0 00	
			20 9 5 0 00	20 9 5 0 00

330	J. Callahan, Capital	7,562
331	J. Callahan, Withdrawals	3,500
332	Income Summary	—
440	Sales	23,000
441	Sales Returns and Allowances	400
550	Purchases	14,700
551	Purchases Discount	440
552	Purchases Returns and Allowances	545
660	Wages Expense	2,390
661	Advertising Expense	400
662	Rent Expense	840
663	Dep. Exp., Lumber Equipment	
664	Lumber Supplies Expense	
665	Insurance Expense	

Additional data:

(a, b)	Merchandise inventory, December 31	$3,900
(c)	Lumber supplies on hand, December 31	60
(d)	Insurance expired	50
(e)	Depreciation for the year	400
(f)	Accrued wages on December 31	175

GROUP C PROBLEMS

13C-1. From the partial work sheet shown below, prepare a formal income statement for Kate's Pie and Kite Shop.

Kate's Pie and Kite Shop
Partial Work Sheet
For the year ended September 30, 19XX

Account Titles	Income Statement Dr.	Income Statement Cr.
Income Summary	4 2 5 7 82	5 4 7 7 26
Sales		53 5 6 8 25
Sales Returns and Allowances	8 3 4 50	
Sales Discount	3 4 4 75	
Purchases	21 4 5 8 34	
Purchase Returns and Allowances		5 5 8 30
Purchase Discounts		2 3 8 76
Freight-In	4 7 1 58	
Advertising Expense	1 3 5 2 50	
Cleaning Expense	2 4 0 0 00	
Depreciation Expense – Equipment	8 7 5 00	
Insurance Expenses	3 6 8 75	
Rental Income		1 8 0 0 00
Rent Expense	7 2 0 0 00	
Salaries Expense	11 4 5 8 60	
Utilities Expense	2 5 4 2 60	
Salaries Payable		
	53 5 6 4 44	61 6 4 2 57
Net Income	8 0 7 8 13	
	61 6 4 2 57	61 6 4 2 57

13C-2. From the partial work sheet of Castell Ceramics Co. shown on p. 484, complete

(a) Statement of owner's equity.
(b) Classified balance sheet.

NOTE: Of the Mortgage Payable, $1,800 is due within one year.

13C-3. From the partial work sheet of Mikolaski Modern Design Company, shown on page 485, your task is to

1. Complete the work sheet.
2. Prepare the income statement, statement of owner's equity, and classified balance sheet. The amount of the mortgage due the first year is $3,600.
3. Journalize the adjusting and closing entries.

Castell Ceramics Co.
Partial Work Sheet
For the year ended August 31, 19XX

Account Titles	Balance Sheet			
	Dr.		Cr.	
Petty Cash		7 5 00		
Cash	11 5 3 8 62			
Accounts Receivable	18 9 7 6 30			
Merchandise Inventory	22 7 6 6 28			
Supplies on Hand	1 2 6 8 75			
Prepaid Insurance	8 7 5 40			
Prepaid GST	2 1 3 7 64			
Cutting Equipment	18 7 6 0 00			
Accum. Depn. – Cutting Equip.			7 2 5 0 00	
Delivery Van	21 8 7 5 00			
Accum. Depn. – Delivery Van			4 7 8 0 00	
Accounts Payable			27 6 4 8 36	
GST Collected			2 8 7 4 62	
Unearned Rent			1 7 5 0 00	
Chattel Mortgage Payable – Van			15 7 4 2 37	
B. Castell, Capital			42 6 7 5 98	
B. Castell, Withdrawals	14 6 7 0 00			
Salaries Payable			8 6 0 00	
Net Income			9 3 6 1 66	
	112 9 4 2 99		112 9 4 2 99	

13C-4. From the following ledger balances of Brennan Sales Co. as of December 31, 19XX and additional data, do the following:

1. Prepare the work sheet.
2. Prepare the income statement, statement of owner's equity, and balance sheet.
3. Journalize and post adjusting and closing entries. (Be sure to put beginning balances in the ledger first.)
4. Prepare a post-closing trial balance.
5. Journalize the reversing entry for wages.

ACCT. NO.

1100	Cash	$ 720
1110	Accounts Receivable	1,620
1120	Merchandise Inventory	5,910
1130	Supplies on hand	430
1140	Prepaid Insurance	238
1150	Prepaid GST	647
1210	Equipment	8,500
1220	Acc. Dep., Equipment	1,640

Mikolaski Modern Design Company
Work Sheet
For year ended Novemeber 30, 19XX

Account Titles	Trial Balance Dr.	Trial Balance Cr.	Adjustments Dr.	Adjustments Cr.	
Cash in Bank	3 465 78				
Petty Cash	50 00				
Accounts Receivable	11 575 20				
Merchandise Inventory, Dec. 1, 19X4	16 479 22		(B) 25 672 44	16 479 22	(A)
Prepaid Insurance	765 85			2 577 75	(E)
Prepaid GST	1 653 45				
Equipment	21 575 00				
Accumulated Depreciation, Equip.		14 762 40		1 357 60	(D)
Building	28 700 00				
Accumulated Depreciation, Building		21 653 70		647 82	(D)
Mortgage Payable		19 846 52			
Unearned Rent		2 400 00	(C) 800 00		
GST Collected		2 167 85			
L. Mikolaski, Capital		32 420 22			
L. Mikolaski, Withdrawals	16 450 00				
Income Summary			(A) 16 479 22	25 672 44	(B)
Sales		77 327 56			
Sales Discounts and Returns	358 92				
Purchases	42 649 04				
Purchases Returns and Allowances		455 72			
Purchase Discounts		576 22			
Freight-In	632 88				
Advertising Expense	1 245 00				
Cleaning Expense	2 605 60				
Repair Expense	876 20				
Salaries Expense	21 575 60				
Utilities Expense	952 45				
	171 610 19	171 610 19			
Rental Income Earned				800 00	(C)
Depreciation Exp. on Eq. & Building			(D) 2 005 42		
Insurance Expense			(E) 257 75		
			45 214 83	45 214 83	

Qu. 13C-4 (continued)

ACCT. NO.

2200	Accounts Payable	1,660
2210	Wages Payable	
2220	GST Collected	897
3300	W. Brennan, Capital	12,012
3310	W. Brennan, Withdrawals	4,700
3320	Income Summary	—
4400	Sales	31,000
4410	Sales Returns and Allowances	630
5500	Purchases	18,400
5510	Purchases Discount	730
5520	Purchases Returns and Allowances	276
6600	Wages Expense	4,530
6610	Advertising Expense	690

Qu. 13C-4 (continued)

ACCT. NO.

6620	Rent Expense	1,200
6630	Dep. Exp., Equipment	
6640	Supplies Expense	
6650	Insurance Expense	

Additional data:

(a, b) Merchandise inventory, December 31	$4,610
(c) Supplies on hand, December 31	175
(d) Insurance expired	83
(e) Depreciation for the year	875
(f) Accrued wages on December 31	375
(g) Advertising bill received - due next year (add Prepaid GST of $11.20)	160

PRACTICAL ACCOUNTING APPLICATION #1

Chan Company recently had most of its records destroyed in a fire. The information for 19X1 was discovered by the bookkeeper.

Beg. Inv. $1,400
End Inv. 3,000

Chan Corp.
General Journal

Page 2

Date		Description	PR	Debit	Credit
Dec.	31	Income Summary	312	3 6 3 0 00	
		Sales Returns and Allowances	420		1 4 0 00
		Sales Discount	430		3 0 00
		Purchases	500		2 4 0 0 00
		Delivery Expense	600		9 0 00
		Salaries Expense	610		8 4 0 00
		Rent Expense	620		3 0 00
		Office Supplies Expense	630		5 0 00
		Advertising Expense	640		1 0 00
		Dep. Exp., Store Equipment	650		4 0 00
	31	Sales	410	5 5 4 2 00	
		Purchases Discount	510	1 2 0 00	
		Purchases Returns and Allowances	520	1 0 0 00	
		Income Summary	312		5 7 6 2 00
		Income Summary	312	3 7 3 2 00	
		J. Chan, Capital	310		3 7 3 2 00

Please assist the bookkeeper in reconstructing an income statement for 19X1.

PRACTICAL ACCOUNTING APPLICATION #2

Hope Lang, a junior accountant, has the December 31, 19XX, trial balance of Gregot Company sitting on her desk. Attached is a memo from her supervisor requesting that a classified balance sheet be prepared. Hope gathers the following data:

1. A physical inventory at December 31 showed $80,000 on hand.
2. Office supplies on hand was $600.
3. Insurance unexpired was $750.
4. Depreciation (straight-line) is based on a 25-year life.

Using the following trial balance of Gregot Co., please assist Hope with this project. *Hint:* Ending figure for capital is $115,850.

Gregot Company
Trial Balance
December 31, 19XX

	Dr.	Cr.
Cash	11 0 0 0 00	
Accounts Receivable	38 0 0 0 00	
Inventory, Jan. 1	80 0 0 0 00	
Prepaid Insurance	2 0 0 0 00	
Office Supplies	1 0 0 0 00	
Land	17 5 0 0 00	
Building	50 0 0 0 00	
Accumulated Depreciation, Building		10 0 0 0 00
Notes Payable		40 0 0 0 00
Accounts Payable		30 0 0 0 00
G. Gregot, Capital		98 4 0 0 00
G. Gregot, Withdrawals	13 0 0 0 00	
Income Summary	——	——
Retail Sales		329 0 0 0 00
Sales Returns and Allowances	21 0 0 0 00	
Sales Discount	8 0 0 0 00	
Purchases	215 5 0 0 00	
Purchases Returns and Allowances		11 6 0 0 00
Purchases Discounts		4 0 0 0 00
Transportation-in	5 0 0 0 00	
Advertising Expense	2 5 0 0 00	
Wage Expense	55 0 0 0 00	
Utilities Expense	3 5 0 0 00	
	523 0 0 0 00	523 0 0 0 00

COMPREHENSIVE REVIEW PROBLEM
The Corner Dress Shop

Reviewing the Accounting Cycle for a Merchandise Company

(This practice set will help you review all the key concepts of a merchandise company along with the integration of payroll.)

Since you are the bookkeeper of The Corner Dress Shop, we have gathered the following information for you. It will be your task to complete the accounting cycle for March.

The Corner Dress Shop
Post Closing Trial Balance
February 28, 19XX

Cash	1,933.90	
Petty Cash	50.00	
Accounts Receivable	3,011.00	
Merchandise Inventory	5,600.00	
Supplies on hand	624.30	
Prepaid Rent	1,800.00	
GST Prepaid	703.42	
Delivery Truck	16,000.00	
Accumulated Depreciation, Truck		3,450.00
Accounts Payable		2,354.00
GST Collected		1,187.60
Income Tax Payable		2,047.05
CPP Payable		408.62
UI Payable		570.84
Medical Plan Premiums Payable		112.00
Unearned Rent		800.00
B. Loeb, Capital		18,792.51
Totals	29,722.66	29,722.66

Balances in subsidiary ledgers as of March 1:

ACCOUNTS RECEIVABLE		ACCOUNTS PAYABLE	
Bing Co.	$2,241.00	Blew Co.	$1,926.00
Gray Co.	—	Jones Co.	428.00
Ronald Co.	770.00	Moe's Garage	—
(includes 7% GST)		Morris Co.	—

Payroll is paid monthly and employee claim codes are unchanged.

The payroll register for January and February is provided. In March, salaries are as follows (all deductions the same unless indicated):

Mel Case	$1,860	New FIT = $242.45. CPP and UI – use same approach as in Chapter 9.
Jane Holl	2,900	
Jackie Moore	4,300	

Your task is to
1. Set up a general ledger, accounts receivable ledger and accounts payable ledger, auxiliary petty cash record and payroll register. (Be sure to update ledger accounts based on given information in the post-closing trial balance for Feb. 28 before beginning.)
2. Journalize all transactions during March.
3. Prepare the payroll register for March.
4. Update the accounts payable and accounts receivable subsidiary ledgers for March.
5. Post to the general ledger.
6. Prepare a trial balance on a work sheet and complete the work sheet as of March 31, 19XX.
7. Prepare an income statement, statement of owner's equity, and classified balance sheet.
8. Journalize the adjusting and closing entries.
9. Post the adjusting and closing entries to the ledger.
10. Prepare a post-closing trial balance.

The Chart of Accounts for The Corner Dress Shop is as follows:

CHART OF ACCOUNTS

Assets
110 Cash
111 Accounts Receivable
112 Petty Cash
114 Merchandise Inventory
116 Prepaid Rent
117 Supplies on Hand
118 GST Prepaid
120 Delivery Truck
121 Accumulated Depreciation, Truck

Owner's Equity
310 B. Loeb, Capital
320 B. Loeb, Withdrawals
330 Income Summary

Cost of Goods Sold
510 Purchases
512 Purchases Returns and Allowances
514 Purchase Discount

Liabilities
210 Accounts Payable
212 Salaries Payable
214 Income Tax Payable
216 CPP Payable
218 UI Payable
220 Medical Plan Premium Payable
222 Unearned Rent
228 GST Collected

Revenue
410 Sales
412 Sales Returns and Allowances
414 Sales Discount
416 Rental Income

Expenses
610 Sales Salaries Expense
611 Office Salaries Expense
612 Payroll Tax Expense
614 Cleaning Expense
616 Depreciation Expense, Truck
618 Rent Expense
620 Postage Expense
622 Supplies Expense
624 Delivery Expense
626 Miscellaneous Expense

Payroll Register - January

Employee	Net Claim Code	Monthly Salary	Cumulative CPP	FIT
Mel Case	4	1 800 00	—	2 24 20
Jane Holl	1	2 900 00	—	6 49 55
Jackie Moore	3	4 300 00	—	1 1 73 30
Totals		9 000 00		2 0 47 05

Deductions				Net Pay	Chq. No.	Expense Accounts	
CPP	UI	Health	Charitable			Office	Sales
38 13	54 00	28 00	20 00	1 435 67		1 800 00	
65 59	87 00	42 00	30 00	2 025 86			2 900 00
100 59	96 85	42 00	40 00	2 847 26			4 300 00
204 31	237 85	112 00	90 00	6 308 79		1 800 00	7 200 00

Payroll Register - February

Employee	Net Claim Code	Monthly Salary	Cumulative CPP	FIT
Mel Case	4	1 800 00	38 13	2 24 20
Jane Holl	1	2 900 00	65 59	6 49 55
Jackie Moore	3	4 300 00	100 59	1 1 73 30
Totals		9 000 00		2 0 47 05

Deductions				Net Pay	Chq. No.	Expense Accounts	
CPP	UI	Health	Charitable			Office	Sales
38 13	54 00	28 00	20 00	1 435 67		1 800 00	
65 59	87 00	42 00	30 00	2 025 86			2 900 00
100 59	96 85	42 00	40 00	2 847 26			4 300 00
204 31	237 85	112 00	90 00	6 308 79		1 800 00	7 200 00

19XX

March 1 Received amount due from Bing, no discount.

2 Purchased merchandise from Morris Company on account, $10,000, plus GST, terms 2/10, n/30.

2 Paid $6 from the petty cash fund for cleaning package, voucher no. 18 (consider this a cleaning expense – no GST).

3 Sold merchandise to Ronald Company on account, $7,000, plus GST, invoice No. 51, terms 2/10, n/30.

5 Paid $12.84 (includes $0.84 GST) from the petty cash fund for postage, voucher no. 19.

6 Sold merchandise to Ronald Company on account, $5,000, plus GST, invoice No. 52, terms 2/10, n/30.

8 Paid $10 from the petty cash fund for First Aid emergency, voucher no. 20 (no GST).

9 Purchased merchandise from Morris Company on account, $5,000, plus GST, terms 2/10, n/30.

9 Received amount due from Ronald Co. at Feb. 28 less 2% discount.

9 Paid $5 for delivery expense (no GST)from petty cash fund, voucher no. 21.

9 Sold more merchandise to Ronald Company on account, $3,000, plus GST, invoice No. 53, terms 2/10, n/30.

9 Paid cleaning service, $300, plus GST, cheque no. 110.

10 Ronald Company returned merchandise costing $1,000 from invoice No. 52; The Corner Dress Shop issued credit memo No. 10 to Ronald Company for $1,000, plus GST.

11 Purchased merchandise from Jones Company on account, $10,000, plus GST, terms 1/15, n/60.

12 Paid Morris Company invoice dated March 2, cheque no. 111.

13 Sold merchandise for cash, $700, plus GST.

14 Returned merchandise to Jones Company in amount of $2,000; The Corner Dress Shop issued debit memo No. 4 to Jones Company, $2,000, plus GST.

14 Paid $5 from the petty cash fund for delivery expense, voucher no. 22 (no GST).

15 Paid amount due to Receiver General for Canada re February Withholdings – cheque no. 112.

15 Sold merchandise for cash, $29,000, plus GST.

15 B. Loeb withdrew $1,000 for her personal account, cheque no. 113.

15 Paid net amount of GST due at February 28 $484.18, cheque no. 114.

16 Paid amount due to Blew Co. at the end of February, cheque no. 115.

16 Received payment from Ronald Company for invoice No. 52, less discount and less returned merchandise.

16 Ronald Company paid invoice No. 51, $7,490.

16 Sold merchandise to Bing Company on account, $3,200, plus GST, invoice No. 54. terms 2/10, n/30.

21 Purchased another delivery truck on account from Moe's Garage, $17,200, plus GST.

22 Sold merchandise to Ronald Company on account, $4,000, plus GST, invoice No. 55, terms 2/10, n/30.

23 Paid Jones Company the balance owed, cheque no. 116.

24 Sold merchandise to Bing Company, $2,000, plus GST, invoice No. 56, terms 1/10, n/30.

25 Purchased merchandise for cash, $1,000, plus GST, cheque no. 117.

27 Purchased merchandise from Blew Company on account, $6,000, plus GST, terms 2/10, n/30.

27   Paid amount due to Provincial Health Care re: February Payroll, cheque no 118.
28   Ronald Company paid invoice No. 55 dated March 22, less discount.
28   Bing Company paid invoice No. 54 dated March 16.
29   Purchased merchandise from Morris Company on account, $9,000, plus GST, terms 2/10, n/30.
30   Sold merchandise to Gray Company on account, $10,000, plus GST, invoice No. 57, terms 2/10, n/30.
30   Issued cheque no. 119 to replenish the petty cash fund.
30   Recorded March payroll in payroll register.
30   Journalized payroll entry (to be paid on 31st).
30   Journalized employer's payroll tax expense.
31   Paid payroll cheques no. 120, 121, and 122.
31   Remitted total March charitable deductions to World Preventable Disease Foundation. Cheque no. 123.

Additional data:
   (a and b) Ending merchandise inventory, $3,700.
   (c) During March, rent expired, $600.
   (d) Truck depreciated, $150.
   (e) Rental income earned, $200 (one month's rent from subletting).

ACCOUNTING RECALL
A Cumulative Approach

THIS EXAM REVIEWS CHAPTERS 1 THROUGH 13

Your *Study Guide and Working Papers* have forms to complete this exam, as well as worked-out solutions. The page references next to each question identify what page to turn back to if you answer the question incorrectly.

PART I Vocabulary Review

Match the terms to the appropriate definition or phrase.

Page Ref.

(459)	1. Current asset	A. General expenses
(462)	2. Current liabilities	B. Contra asset
(429)	3. Purchases discount	C. Converted into cash or used within one year
(425)	4. Income summary	D. Contra cost of goods sold
(458)	5. Administrative expenses	E. Land
(431)	6. Accumulated depreciation	F. Mortgage payable
(458)	7. Net sales	G. Optional bookkeeping
(460)	8. Plant and equipment	H. A temporary account used only at period end.
(462)	9. Long-term liability	I. Sales-SRA-SD
(470)	10. Reversing entries	J. Due within one year

PART II True or False (Accounting Theory)

(50)   11. There are debit and credit columns on the formal reports.

(470) 12. Reversing entries are the same as adjusting entries.

(470) 13. All adjustments should be reversed.

(460) 14. Equipment is a current asset.

(458) 15. Administrative expenses are directly incurred in the selling of goods.

PART III Applications Problem (467)

From the following worksheet of Bill's Antique Shop for year ended December 31, 19XX complete the Financial Reports and journalize the adjusting and closing entries.

Bill's Antique Shop
Work Sheet

Account Titles	Trial Balance Dr.	Trial Balance Cr.	Adjustments Dr.	Adjustments Cr.	Adjusted Trial Balance Dr.	Adjusted Trial Balance Cr.	Income Statement Dr.	Income Statement Cr.	Balance Sheet Dr.	Balance Sheet Cr.
Cash	4,100.00				4,100.00				4,100.00	
Accounts Receivable	23,800.00				23,800.00				23,800.00	
Merchandise Inventory	20,000.00		(B) 24,000.00	(A) 20,000.00	24,000.00				24,000.00	
Prepaid Insurance	600.00			(C) 200.00	400.00				400.00	
Equipment	18,000.00				18,000.00				18,000.00	
Acc. Dep., Equipment		1,000.00		(D) 1,000.00		2,000.00				2,000.00
Unearned Rent		500.00	(F) 100.00			400.00				400.00
Accounts Payable		11,000.00				11,000.00				11,000.00
B. J. Jensen, Capital		50,000.00				50,000.00				50,000.00
B. J. Jensen, Withdrawals	15,000.00				15,000.00				15,000.00	
Income Summary			(A) 20,000.00	(B) 24,000.00	20,000.00	24,000.00	20,000.00	24,000.00		
Sales		279,000.00				279,000.00		279,000.00		
Sales Returns and Allowances	3,000.00				3,000.00		3,000.00			
Sales Discount	4,500.00				4,500.00		4,500.00			
Purchases	180,000.00				180,000.00		180,000.00			
Purchases Returns and Allowances		1,500.00				1,500.00		1,500.00		
Purchases Discount		3,500.00				3,500.00		3,500.00		
Freight-In	2,500.00				2,500.00		2,500.00			
Salaries Expense	45,000.00		(E) 500.00		45,500.00		45,500.00			
Advertisement Expense	10,000.00				10,000.00		10,000.00			
Rent Expense	12,000.00				12,000.00		12,000.00			
Utility Expense	8,000.00				8,000.00		8,000.00			
	346,500.00	346,500.00								
Insurance Expense			(C) 200.00		200.00		200.00			
Depreciation Expense			(D) 1,000.00		1,000.00		1,000.00			
Salaries Payable				(E) 500.00		500.00				500.00
Rent Earned				(F) 100.00		100.00		100.00		
			45,800.00	45,800.00	372,000.00	372,000.00	286,700.00	308,100.00	85,300.00	63,900.00
Net Income							21,400.00			21,400.00
							308,100.00	308,100.00	85,300.00	85,300.00

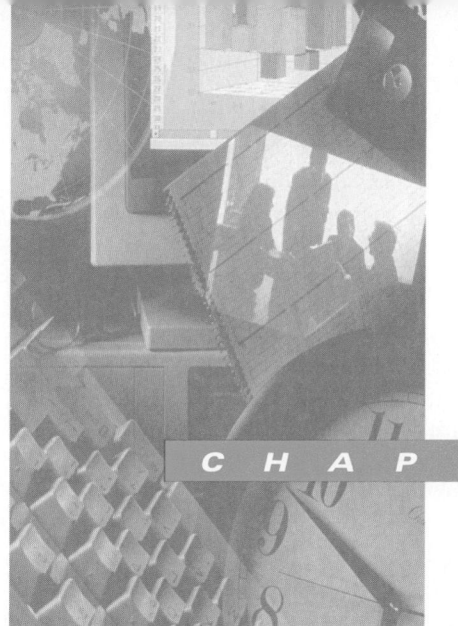

ACCOUNTING FOR BAD DEBTS

IN THIS CHAPTER WE WILL COVER THE FOLLOWING TOPICS:

1. USING THE BAD DEBTS EXPENSE ACCOUNT AND THE ALLOWANCE FOR DOUBTFUL ACCOUNTS ACCOUNT TO RECORD BAD DEBTS. (P. 496)

2. USING THE INCOME STATEMENT APPROACH AND THE BALANCE SHEET APPROACH TO ESTIMATE THE AMOUNT OF BAD DEBTS EXPENSE. (P. 499)

3. PREPARING AN AGING OF ACCOUNTS RECEIVABLE. (P. 501)

4. WRITING OFF AN ACCOUNT USING THE ALLOWANCE FOR DOUBTFUL ACCOUNTS ACCOUNT. (P. 503)

5. USING THE DIRECT WRITE-OFF METHOD. (P. 505)

All companies that sell goods or services on account will eventually have to face the problem of not being able to collect the money owed them. At what point accounts receivable turn into bad debts (or uncollectible accounts), how and what to charge them to, and how to write them off are some of the questions that we will be dealing with in this chapter.

The question of bad debts is important to a company because it affects its credit policy. If a company extends credit too easily, it may end up with too many uncollectible accounts. On the other hand, if the credit policy is too strict, the company will end up losing customers to other firms with easier credit policies—and that could mean a loss in profit just as uncollectible debts do.

In the first learning unit we will look at how bad debts are recorded in the accrual system of accounting.

LEARNING UNIT 14-1

Accrual Accounting and Recording Bad Debts

As we discussed in an earlier chapter, in the accrual system of accounting it is important to match earned revenue with expenses that have been incurred in producing revenue during an accounting period. In other words, in a merchandising firm, for example, it is important to match cost of goods sold with revenue earned by the sale of those goods. And one expense that is incurred as a result of sales on credit or on account is a bad debts expense. The problem is that at the time the sale occurs, one doesn't know whether or not it is going to be uncollectible—one may not know this until much later, possibly a year or so. So how on the books can one match sales with expenses (in this case bad debts expense)?

One way to do this is to estimate at the end of the year what percentage of sales made during that year will turn out to be bad debts. There are several ways of arriving at the percentage, which we will discuss in a later unit, but at the moment let's say that Abby Ellen Company estimates that 1.6 percent of their sales of $100,000 for the year 19X1 will not be collectible; that means that the company expects not to collect $1,600 of the $100,000 owed them from sales.

To handle this situation we need to introduce two accounts that we haven't dealt with before, Bad Debts Expense and Allowance for Doubtful Accounts. **Bad Debts Expense** is an expense account whose normal balance is a debit; it is a temporary account that is closed to Income Summary at year's end. **Allowance for Doubtful Accounts** is a contra asset account that accumulates the expected amount of bad debts as of a given date; its normal balance is a credit. It is a permanent account that is *not* closed to Income Summary at the end of the year.

In the case of Abby Ellen Company, which expects to be unable to collect $1,600 of the $100,000 owed them from sales, at the end of the year (19X1) an adjustment is made debiting Bad Debts Expense and crediting Allowance for Doubtful Accounts for $1,600. This transaction is shown below, along with a transaction analysis chart:

Accounts Receivable
– Allowance for
Doubtful Accounts

= Net Realizable Value

Think of the Allowance for Doubtful Accounts as a reservoir that is filled before bad debts occur. When the customers' bills are declared uncollectible, this reservoir will be drained. Abby Ellen Company estimates that out of its $100,000 of credit sales, $1,600 will prove to be uncollectible, but it does not know at this

Dec.	31	Bad Debts Expense		1 6 0 0 00		
		Allowance For Doubtful Accounts			1 6 0 0 00	
		Record estimate of bad debts.				

	1 Accounts Affected	2 Category	3 ↑ ↓	4 Rules
Will go on income statement as an operating expense and eventually be closed to Income Summary. →	Bad Debts Expense	Expense	↑	Dr.
	Allowance for Doubtful Accounts	Contra Asset	↑	Cr.

Will go on balance sheet as a reduction of Accounts Receivable. The normal balance of the allowance account is a credit. It will not be closed at the end of the period.

time which accounts will be uncollectible. The allowance account is subtracted from Accounts Receivable, leaving a **net realizable value** of $98,400. Net realizable value is the amount Abby Ellen Company expects to collect. When an account is written off, the net realizable value doesn't change, because both the Accounts Receivable and the Allowance for Doubtful Accounts are reduced.

We will do write-offs in Learning Unit 14-3. This is only an introductory example.

Figure 14-1 shows a partial balance sheet to see how the Allowance for Doubtful Accounts relates to Accounts Receivable.

At some point a customer's bill must be written off as uncollectible. Let's look at how Abby Ellen Company would write off the account of Jones Moore on June 5, 19X2. (The sale was made to him in 19X1.)

WRITING OFF AN ACCOUNT DEEMED UNCOLLECTIBLE

Remember, at end of year 19X1 Abby made an adjusting entry increasing Bad Debts Expense (debit) and filling the Allowance for Doubtful Accounts (credit) with the estimate of accounts receivable that would not be collectible.

Writing off an account. *Note:* Bad Debts Expense is not involved.

	Abby Ellen Company Partial Balance Sheet December 31, 19X1		
Assets			
Current Assets:			
Cash		$ 51 4 0 0 00	
Accounts Receivable	$100 0 0 0 00		
Less: Allowance for Doubtful Accounts	1 6 0 0 00	98 4 0 0 00	
Merchandise Inventory		200 0 0 0 00	
Total Current Assets		$349 8 0 0 00	

FIGURE 14-1

Partial Balance Sheet

Now, on June 5, 19X2, Jones Moore's account is deemed to be uncollectible for $200, and the following journal entry is recorded to write off this account:

	19X2					
	June	5	*Allowance for Doubtful Accounts*	2 0 0 00	
			Accounts Receivable, J. Moore		2 0 0 00
			Writing off J. Moore account.		

The bad debts expense was recorded in old year when credit sales were earned.

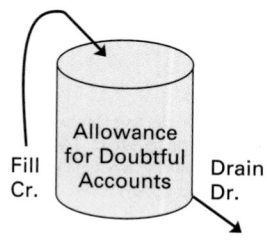

Fill Cr. / Allowance for Doubtful Accounts / Drain Dr.

Note that we did *not* debit the account Bad Debts Expense, since the estimate for this account was made on December 31, 19X1 (and applies to that year, not to 19X2). When that estimate was made, we did not know which customers would turn out to be uncollectible and thus we recorded the estimate in the Allowance for Doubtful Accounts. Now that the debt is identified as uncollectible, we *reduce* or *drain* the Allowance account and reduce the controlling account Accounts Receivable as well as update the accounts receivable ledger. Note that the subsidiary ledger will be credited just as the controlling account is.

At this point you should be able to

1. Define and explain the purpose of Bad Debts Expense and Allowance for Doubtful Accounts. (p. 496)
2. Explain why the subsidiary ledger account cannot be updated at the time the Bad Debts Expense is estimated. (p. 496)
3. Prepare an adjusting entry for Bad Debts Expense. (p. 496)
4. Prepare a partial balance sheet showing the relationship between the Allowance for Doubtful Accounts and Accounts Receivable. (p. 497)
5. Explain net realizable value. (p. 497)
6. Prepare a journal entry to write off a customer's debt in a year following the sale. (p. 498)

☐ **SELF-REVIEW QUIZ 14-1**

Respond true or false to the following:

1. The Bad Debts Expense account should be updated only when the customer's debt is declared to be uncollectible.
2. The Allowance for Doubtful Accounts is a contra asset account on the balance sheet.
3. Bad Debts Expense is part of cost of goods sold.
4. Net realizable value equals Accounts Receivable less Allowance for Doubtful Accounts.
5. When a customer's debt is written off as uncollectible, the account Allowance for Doubtful Accounts is credited.

■ *SOLUTIONS TO SELF-REVIEW QUIZ 14-1*

1. F   2. T   3. F   4. T   5. F

LEARNING UNIT 14-2

The Allowance Method: Two Approaches to Estimating the Amount of Bad Debts Expense

As we said earlier, at the end of the year a company estimates what percentage of the sales that occurred that year will turn out to be uncollectible accounts, or bad debts. How is this estimate arrived at? In this unit we will look at two approaches to making an annual estimate of Bad Debts Expense. The diagram in Figure 14-2 is an overview. Don't memorize it; we will be covering it step by step.

THE INCOME STATEMENT APPROACH

Abby Ellen Company uses the **income statement approach** at the end of the year to calculate how much Bad Debts Expense will be associated with this year's sales. Based on the past several years, the company has averaged Bad Debts Expense of 1 percent of net credit sales. From the following facts, let's prepare an adjusting entry to record the Bad Debts Expense that is based on a percentage of net credit sales.

Bad Debts Expense is based on a percentage of the dollar volume of net credit sales on the income statement.

19X4	DR.	CR.
Sales (all credit)		$95,000
Sales Returns and Allowances	$10,000	
Sales Discount	5,000	
Allowance for Doubtful Accounts		100
Accounts Receivable	7,000	

1 Accounts Affected	2 Category	3 ↑ ↓	4 Rules
Bad Debts Expense	Operating Exp.	↑	Dr.
Allowance for Doubtful Accounts	Contra Asset	↑	Cr.

Analysis:

Sales	$95,000
– SRA	10,000
– SD	5,000
Net Credit Sales	$80,000

Dec. 31	Bad Debts Expense	8 0 0 00	
	Allowance For Doubtful Accounts		8 0 0 00
	Record estimate of bad debts.		
	(.01 × $80,000)		

Note in this income statement approach that the existing credit balance of $100 in the Allowance account is ignored and, when posted, the Allowance account is as follows:

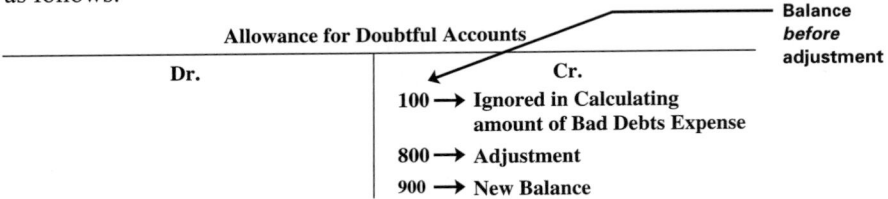

Allowance for Doubtful Accounts

Dr. | Cr.

Balance *before* adjustment

100 → Ignored in Calculating amount of Bad Debts Expense

800 → Adjustment

900 → New Balance

FIGURE 14-2

Two Approaches to Estimating Amount of Bad Debts Expense.

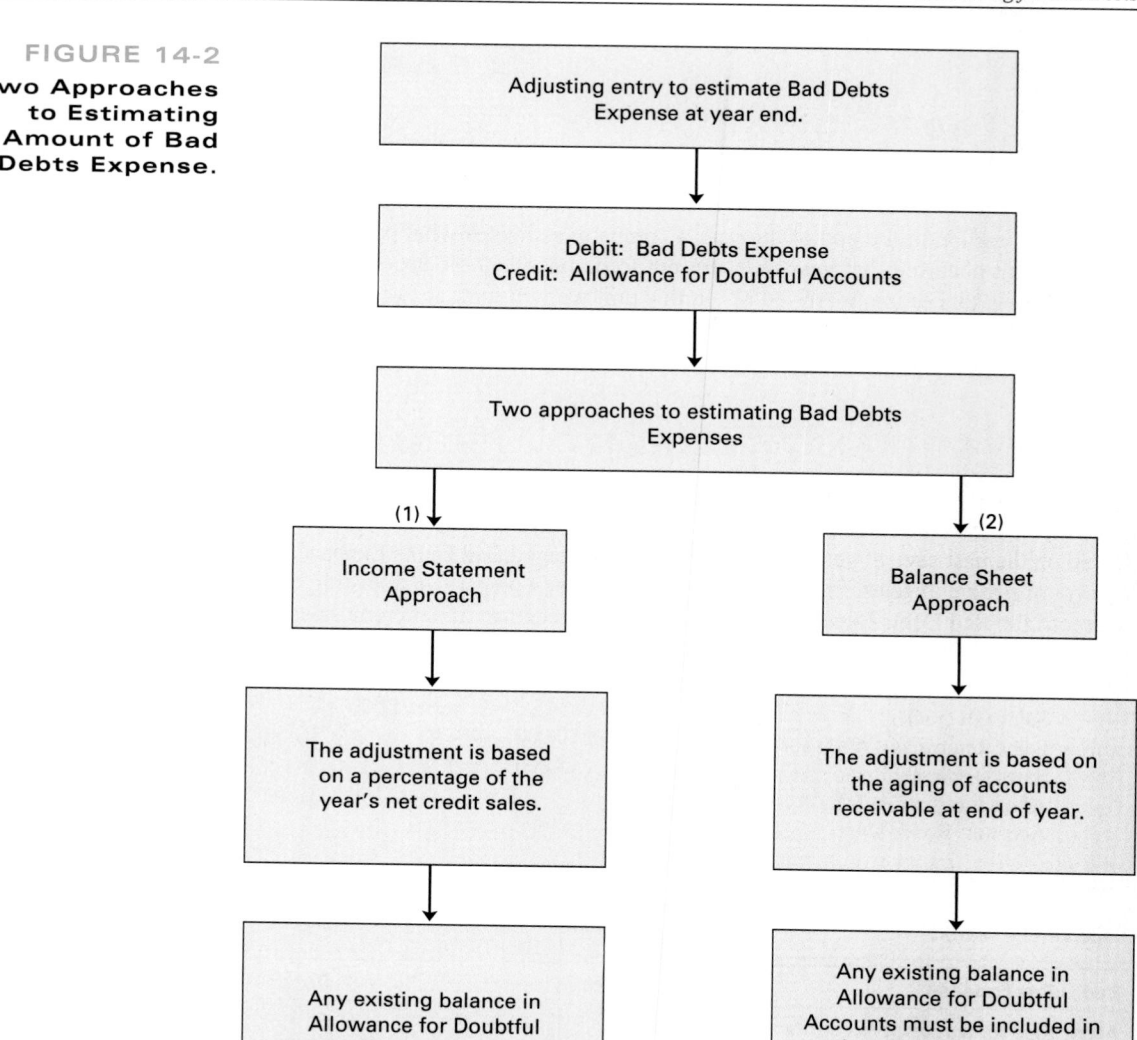

Why? The balance in the Allowance for Doubtful Accounts is ignored, since this approach calculates the amount of bad debts expense *for the year* based on a percent of net credit sales. This approach emphasizes the matching requirements of the income statement. The $100 in the Allowance account represents a carryover of potential bad debts from prior years. Thus the total of $900 represents total potential uncollectible accounts of several periods of sales. If, over the years, the estimate for Bad Debts Expense has been inaccurate, an adjusting entry can be made in the current year's Bad Debts Expense. If this happens, the company may reevaluate its percentage, and use $1\frac{1}{2}$ percent instead of 1 percent.

THE BALANCE SHEET APPROACH

In the income statement approach, the estimate for the Bad Debts Expense used a percent of sales from the income statement as the basis for the adjusting entry. The **balance sheet approach**, on the other hand, uses accounts receivable on the balance sheet as its basis in preparing the adjusting entry to estimate bad debts expense. *Keep in mind that the adjusting entry will take into consideration the existing balance in the Allowance for Doubtful Accounts.* (In the income statement approach the balance in the Allowance account was ignored.)

Let's look now at one balance sheet approach—the aging of Accounts Receivable.

Aging the Accounts Receivable

The longer a bill has been due and not paid, the more likely it is that it is not going to be paid. Therefore, one way of estimating the amount of bad debts for the year just past is to look at Accounts Receivable and analyze it according to how many days past due the accounts are. This is called **aging the Accounts Receivable**. Table 14-1 shows an analysis that the Abby Ellen Company did on December 31, 19X4.

Aging classifies uncollected amounts of individual customers according to days past due.

TABLE 14-1   Aging of Accounts Receivable

NAME OF CUSTOMER	TOTAL BALANCE	NOT YET DUE	DAYS PAST DUE			
			1 – 30	31 – 60	61 – 90	OVER 90
Sarah Elliot	$ 100	$ 100				
Joshua Karras	30			$ 30		
Alan Ledbury	160	160				
John Sullivan	180				$160	$ 20
Sheri Missan	80	80				
Others	6,450	3,260	$2,000	840	40	310
Totals	$7,000	$3,600	$2,000	$870	$200	$330
Percent of total (rounded to nearest whole percent)	100%	51% $\left(\dfrac{\$3,600}{\$7,000}\right)$	29% $\left(\dfrac{\$2,000}{\$7,000}\right)$	12% $\left(\dfrac{\$870}{\$7,000}\right)$	3% $\left(\dfrac{\$200}{\$7,000}\right)$	5% $\left(\dfrac{\$330}{\$7,000}\right)$

Note that 29% of the total receivables for Abby Ellen are past due from 1 to 30 days. (This analysis will also provide feedback to the credit department as to how well the current credit policy is working.) Now let's look at how the company will estimate what balance in the Allowance for Doubtful Accounts is required to meet probable bad debts. The schedule shown in Table 14-2 is prepared to assist the company in calculating the needed balance.

Today, with the computer, an analysis of Accounts Receivable can be completed quickly.

In this schedule Abby Ellen Company has applied a sliding scale of percents (3, 4, 10, 20, 50), based on *previous experience*, to the total amount of receivables due in each time period. For example, of the $200 overdue by 61-90 days, 20 percent or $40 will probably never be paid. Looking at this schedule reveals that Abby Ellen Company needs $480 to cover estimated bad debts. *Presently* the balance in the allowance account is $100. Thus to reach a balance of $480, we must adjust the balance of the account by the following adjusting journal entry:

TABLE 14-2   **Balance Required to Meet Probable Bad Debts**

	AMOUNT	ESTIMATED PERCENT CONSIDERED TO BE BAD DEBTS EXPENSE	AMOUNT NEEDED IN ALLOWANCE FOR DOUBTFUL ACCOUNTS TO COVER ESTIMATED BAD DEBITS EXPENSE
Not Yet Due	$3,600	3	$108 ($3,600 x .03)
Days Past Due			
1–30	2,000	4	80
31–60	870	10	87
61–90	200	20	40
Over 90	330	50	165
Total Accounts Receivable	$7,000	Total Balance Required in Allowance for Doubtful Accounts	$480

The balance in the Allowance for Doubtful Accounts is not ignored.

19X4					
Dec.	31	Bad Debts Expense		3 8 0 00	
		Allowance For Doubtful Accounts			3 8 0 00
		Record estimate of bad debts.			

Bad Debts Expense

Dr.	Cr.
380	

Allowance for Doubtful Accounts

Dr.	Cr.	
	100	Beg. Balance
	380	Adj.
	480	New balance in Allowance

Some companies that feel aging is too time-consuming may estimate bad debts based on a percentage of total Accounts Receivable.

The desired balance of $480 is now reached. If the Allowance had a *debit* balance of $100 before the adjustment, the amount of the adjusting entry would be $580 credit to the Allowance to arrive at the $480 balance. Once again, the adjustment *must* consider the *existing balance* in the Allowance account before the adjusting entry is prepared.

At this point you should be able to

1. Explain the two approaches to estimating Bad Debts Expense. (p. 499)
2. Explain why the balance in the Allowance for Doubtful Accounts is ignored when an adjusting entry for bad debts is prepared in the income statement approach. (p. 499)
3. Show how to prepare an aging of Accounts Receivable. (p. 501)
4. Explain how the aging of Accounts Receivable is used to arrive at the balance required in the Allowance for Doubtful Accounts. (p. 502)

☐ SELF-REVIEW QUIZ 14-2

From the following, prepare an adjusting journal entry for Bad Debts Expense for (1) the income statement approach and (2) the balance sheet approach.

Allowance for Doubtful Accounts

Dr.	Cr.
	400

INCOME STATEMENT APPROACH

Net Sales $160,000
1%   of Net Sales

BALANCE SHEET APPROACH

		PERCENT CONSIDERED BAD DEBTS
Not yet due:	$4,000	4
Days past due:		
1-30	3,000	5
31-60	400	10
Over 60	5,000	30

■ SOLUTION TO SELF-REVIEW QUIZ 14-2

(1)	Dec.	31	Bad Debts Expense	1600 00	
			Allowance For Doubtful Accounts		1600 00
			(.01 × $160,000)		
(2)		31	Bad Debts Expense	1450 00	
			Allowance For Doubtful Accounts		1450 00
			$4,000 × .04 = $ 160		
			3,000 × .05 = 150		
			400 × .10 = 40		
			5,000 × .30 = 1,500		
			$1,850		
			Note allowance adjusted:		
			$1,850 – $400 = $1,450		

LEARNING UNIT 14-3

Writing Off Uncollectible Accounts

This unit will look at two ways to write off uncollectible accounts, one using the Allowance for Doubtful Accounts, the other using the direct write-off method.

WRITING OFF AN ACCOUNT USING THE ALLOWANCE FOR DOUBTFUL ACCOUNTS

Let's assume that on March 18, 19X7, the Abby Ellen Company determines that the account of Jill Sullivan for $900 is uncollectible. (The sale to Jill Sullivan was back

JOYCE THOMAS:
SENIOR TAX ANALYST
MUTUAL BENEFIT LIFE INSURANCE COMPANY

Joyce Thomas came to Mutual Benefit Life Insurance Company immediately after high school. She had a bookkeeping background from high school and got a job in the actuarial department. "I found that I enjoyed the work," she says, "but I knew that I would not get very far with just a high school diploma."

Joyce decided to go back to school to get a diploma in accounting. "It was hard work," she says, "but I received a lot of support from my supervisors." Joyce received promotions as she took more courses and demonstrated her abilities in the office. "In some cases," Joyce says, "the accounting courses I took helped me to understand the reasons behind a job I was already doing. In other cases, the courses helped me to get a better job." Since Joyce was allowed to move to different areas within a large accounting department, she was able to see which jobs she preferred.

Joyce is now a Senior Tax Analyst and is working toward a degree in Accounting. "Combining work with college courses in accounting was a good decision for me," she says. "I am able to earn money in a field I love while getting a degree to help me further my career."

in 19X6.) This means that this Accounts Receivable amount should no longer be considered an asset and should be written off. The following journal entry reduces the Allowance for Doubtful Accounts and reduces the Accounts Receivable controlling account as well as the accounts receivable subsidiary ledger.

19X7					
March	18	Allowance for Doubtful Accounts		9 0 0 00	
		Accounts Receivable, Jill Sullivan			9 0 0 00
		Wrote off Sullivan account.			

Key Points:

1. This journal entry does *not* affect any expenses. Remember, Bad Debts Expense is *not* affected when an account is finally written off. The estimate for Bad Debts Expense was recorded in the previous year before the bad debt actually occurred.
2. If more than one customer is written off, a compound entry can be used, debiting Allowance for the total and crediting each individual account.
3. The net realizable value of Accounts Receivable is unchanged. Let's prove this:

	BALANCES BEFORE THE WRITE-OFF		BALANCES AFTER THE WRITE-OFF
Accounts Receivable	$12,000	$900 write-off →	$11,100
Less: Allowance for Doubtful Accounts	2,000	$900 drain →	1,100
Estimated realizable value	$10,000	no change →	$10,000
	(what to expect to collect)		

Let's look now at what would happen on the books of Abby Ellen Company if Jill Sullivan in the future could pay part or all of the debt.

Let's assume that Jill Sullivan is able to pay off half of her debt and send a cheque to Abby Ellen Company on February 1, 19X8. (Keep in mind the fact that her account was written off on March 18, 19X7, and the original sale was made in 19X6.) To record this, Abby Ellen Company reverses in part the entry that was made to write off the account in the amount expected to be recovered and records the amount received from Jill. The following are the journal entries to record the recovery of $450 out of the original amount of $900:

19X8						
Feb.	1	Accounts Receivable, Jill Sullivan		450 00		
		Allowance for Doubtful Accounts			450 00	
		Restores collectable portion				
	1	Cash		450 00		
		Accounts Receivable, Jill Sullivan			450 00	
		Records payment received				

Reinstates the account.

Records the amount received.

The reason we record both a debit and a credit to Accounts Receivable is that it provides a clear picture of the transactions involving Jill Sullivan. If the company is considering giving credit again to Jill Sullivan, these previous records could be of assistance in determining how much if any credit could be extended. Note how the first entry reinstates the account and the second entry records the cash received.

Let's look now at another method of handling Bad Debts Expense, the direct write-off method.

THE DIRECT WRITE-OFF METHOD

When a company cannot reasonably estimate its Bad Debts Expense, it may use the **direct write-off method**. Using this method, an account that is determined to be uncollectible would be directly written off to this year's Bad Debts Expense account without regard to when the original sale was made. In this method, the Allowance for Doubtful Accounts is not used, since no adjustment is needed at the end of the year to estimate Bad Debts Expense. Let's replay the Jill Sullivan write-off as well as the recovery so that we can make comparisons between the Allowance for Doubtful Accounts method and the direct write-off method. In the recovery we will see a new account title, *Bad Debts Recovered*. Think of it as a revenue account found in the Other Income section of an income statement.

The direct write-off method does not fulfil the matching principle and is not accepted for income tax purposes in Canada.

19X7						
March	18	Bad Debts Expense		900 00		
		Acct. Rec., Jill Sullivan			900 00	
		Wrote off account				

Writing off Jill Sullivan on March 18, 19X7. Note that Allowance account is not used. See p. 504.

Recovery of half the amount owed by Jill Sullivan on Feb. 1, 19X8. Note that Bad Debts Recovered replaces Allowance for Doubtful Accounts. See p. 505.

On the balance sheet, Accounts Receivable is recorded at gross. No Allowance account or realizable amount is used.

19X8					
Feb.	*1*	Acct. Rec., Jill Sullivan		4 5 0 00	
		Bad Debts Recovered			4 5 0 00
		Restores collectable portion			
	1	Cash		4 5 0 00	
		Acct. Rec., Jill Sullivan			4 5 0 00
		Records payment received			

Bad Debts Recov.	Other Revenue	↑	Cr.

In the direct write-off method, when the amount is written off, no Allowance for Doubtful Accounts is used. Rather, the debit is to Bad Debts Expense. On the recovery in years following the sale, instead of crediting the Allowance, the direct method credits **Bad Debts Recovered** (an account in the "Other Revenue" category). This in effect increases the revenue and puts the Accounts Receivable back on the books. If recovery is made in the *same* year, you just reverse the entry you made to write off the account:

19X7					
May	*1*	Acounts Receivable, Jill Sullivan		4 5 0 00	
		Bad Debts Expense			4 5 0 00

INSIGHT INTO INCOME TAX REGULATIONS

For tax purposes the law permits the bad debt reserve method of deducting bad debts. Since the direct charge-off method does vary from generally accepted financial accounting principles, the law follows the CICA Handbook and allows the deduction of an annual reserve.

At this point you should be able to

1. Write off an account using the Allowance for Doubtful Accounts method. (p. 503)

2. Explain why net realizable value is unchanged after a write-off is complete. (p. 504)

3. Prepare journal entries to recover entire or partial amounts that were once declared uncollectible. (p. 505)

4. Explain the direct write-off method and prepare appropriate journal entries for write-off and recovery. (p. 505)

☐ **SELF-REVIEW QUIZ 14-3**

Respond true or false to the following:

1. When an account using the Allowance for Doubtful Accounts method is written off in a period following the sale, the result is a debit to Bad Debts Expense and a credit to Accounts Receivable.
2. The direct write-off method will sometimes use the Allowance for Doubtful Accounts.
3. When an account is written off (using the Allowance for Doubtful Accounts method), net realizable value is unchanged.
4. Bad Debts Recovered is an asset.
5. A debit balance in the Allowance for Doubtful Accounts indicates that the estimate for Bad Debts Expense was too low.

■ *SOLUTIONS TO SELF-REVIEW QUIZ 14-3*

1. F   2. F   3. T   4. F   5. T

SUMMARY OF KEY POINTS AND KEY TERMS

LEARNING UNIT 14-1

1. If accrual accounting is used, Bad Debts Expense should be recognized in the year the sale was earned, even though the actual write-off may not yet have taken place.
2. Bad Debts Expense is an expense found on the income statement.
3. The Allowance for Doubtful Accounts is a contra asset account found on the balance sheet that accumulates the amount of estimated uncollectibles before they are actually written off.
4. Net realizable value equals Accounts Receivable minus Allowance for Doubtful Accounts.
5. When an account is written off, the Allowance for Doubtful Accounts is debited and Accounts Receivable is credited (along with the subsidiary ledger account).

Allowance for Doubtful Accounts: A contra asset account that is subtracted from the Accounts Receivable. This account accumulates the *expected* amount of uncollectibles as of a given date.

Bad Debts Expense: The operating expense account that estimates the amount of credit sales that will probably not be collectible in a given accounting period when the Allowance method is used. For the direct write-off method, this account would be the actual amount written off.

Net realizable value: The amount (Accounts Receivable—Allowance for Doubtful Accounts) that is expected to be collected.

LEARNING UNIT 14-2

1. The two approaches to estimating Bad Debts Expense are the income statement approach and the balance sheet approach.
2. The income statement approach estimates Bad Debts Expense based on a percentage of net sales. (Some companies use credit sales, some use total

sales.) The balance is ignored in the Allowance for Doubtful Accounts when the Bad Debts Expense is estimated from sales of the period.

3. The balance sheet approach estimates the balance required in the Allowance for Doubtful Accounts by aging the Accounts Receivable. The balance in the Allowance account will have to be adjusted based on the aging of the receivables.

Aging of Accounts Receivable: The procedure of classifying accounts of individual customers by age group, where age is the number of days elapsed from due date.

Balance sheet approach: A method used to calculate the amount *required* in the Allowance for Doubtful Accounts to cover expected uncollectibles. This method is based on the Accounts Receivable account and the aging process. The balance in the Allowance account will have to be adjusted.

Income statement approach: A method that estimates the amount of Bad Debts Expense that will result based on a percentage of net credit sales for the period. The balance in the Allowance account will be ignored.

LEARNING UNIT 14-3

After the write-off, net realizable value is unchanged.

1. When an account is written off (using the Allowance account) in years following the sale, the result is to debit the Allowance for Doubtful Accounts and credit Accounts Receivable. Do not debit Bad Debts Expense, as it has already been recorded in the year the sale was earned.

2. When an uncollectible account has been written off and is now recovered, the entry reverses the original write-off by debiting Accounts Receivable and crediting the Allowance for Doubtful Accounts. Then the cash received is debited and the Accounts Receivable is credited.

3. The direct write-off method will recognize the Bad Debts Expense when the customer account is declared uncollectible. The direct method does *not* use the Allowance for Doubtful Accounts, since no estimate is made for bad debts. This method does not follow the matching principle in the accrual basis of accounting.

4. Bad Debts Recovered is classified as "other revenue" when a customer account is reinstated after being written off in the direct method.

Bad Debts Recovered: When an Account Receivable has been written off and is recovered, this account, which is in the "Other Revenue" category, is credited in the direct write-off method if the recovery is in a year *following* the write-off.

Direct write-off method: The method of writing off uncollectibles when they occur and thus not using the Allowance for Doubtful Accounts. This method does not fulfil the matching principle of accrual accounting.

BLUEPRINT SUMMARY OF RECORDING BAD DEBTS EXPENSE, WRITE-OFFS, AND RECOVERY

Situation	ALLOWANCE FOR DOUBTFUL ACCOUNTS METHOD		DIRECT WRITE-OFF METHOD
	A. Income Statement Approach	B. Balance Sheet Approach	

Adjusting entry to record estimated uncollectible accounts	Bad Debts Expense XX
	  Allowance for Doubtful Accounts XX
	Based on percent of net sales.
	Balance in Allowance account
	  is ignored.
		Bad Debts Expense XX
		  Allowance for Doubtful Accounts XX
		Aging of Accounts Receivable
		determines amount needed
		  in Allowance account.
		Balance in Allowance account
		  is adjusted.
			None

Accounts Receivable is determined to be uncollectible	Allowance for Doubtful Accounts XX
	  Accounts Receivable, XX
		Allowance for Doubtful Accounts XX
		  Accounts Receivable, XX
			Bad debts Expense XX
			  Accounts Receivable, XX

Bad Debts are recovered	Accounts Receivable, XX XX
	  Allowance for Doubtful Accounts XX
	Cash XX
	  Accounts Receivable, XX XX
		Accounts Receivable, XX
		  Allowance for Doubtful Accounts XX
		Cash XX
		  Accounts Receivable, XX XX
			Accounts Receivable, XX XX
			  Bad Debts Recovered* XX
			Cash XX
			  Accounts Receivable, XX XX

Balance sheet update	Shows net realizable value	Shows net realizable value	Does not show net realizable value

* Used if recovery is not in the same year as the sale.

DISCUSSION QUESTIONS

1. Explain the matching principle in relationship to recording Bad Debts Expense.
2. What is the purpose of the Allowance for Doubtful Accounts?
3. What is net realizable value?
4. When an Account Receivable is written off, Bad Debts Expense must be debited. True or false? Please discuss.
5. Explain why the Allowance for Doubtful Accounts is a contra asset account.
6. Recording Bad Debts Expense is a closing entry. True or false? Defend your position.
7. The income statement approach used to estimate bad debts is based on Accounts Receivable on the balance sheet. Accept or reject. Why?
8. In which approach is the balance of the Allowance for Doubtful Accounts considered when the estimate of Bad Debts Expense is made? Please explain.
9. Why would a company age its Accounts Receivable?
10. Using the Allowance for Doubtful Accounts method, what journal entries would be made to write off an account as well as later record the recovery of the Accounts Receivable?
11. Why doesn't net realizable value change when an account is written off in the use of the Allowance account?
12. What is the purpose of using a direct write-off method?
13. Explain the purpose of the Bad Debts Recovered account.

EXERCISES

Preparing a partial balance sheet with Allowance for Doubtful Accounts.

1. Jetson Co. has requested that you prepare a partial balance sheet on December 31, 19XX, from the following: Cash, $105,000; Petty Cash, $60; Accounts Receivable, $60,000; Bad Debts Expense, $40,000; Allowance for Doubtful Accounts, $12,000; Merchandise Inventory, $18,000.

Calculating Bad Debts Expense by income statement approach.

2. Given the following information:

Accounts Receivable		Sales		Sales Returns and Allowances	
30,000			110,000	500	

Allowance for Sales Discount		Doubtful Accounts	
9,500			5,000

journalize the adjusting entry on December 31, 19XX, for Bad Debts Expense, which is estimated to be 4 percent of net sales. The income statement approach is used.

Calculating Bad Debts Expense by balance sheet approach.

3. Assuming that in Exercise 2 the balance sheet approach is used, prepare a journalized adjusting entry for Bad Debts Expense. Based on an aging of Accounts Receivable, an $8,000 balance in the Allowance account will be needed to cover bad debts.

4. The Austin Co., which uses an Allowance for Doubtful Accounts, had the following transactions in 19X5 and 19X6. (Use the income statement approach.)

19X5
Dec. 31   Recorded Bad Debts Expense of $12,000.

19X6
Apr. 3   Wrote off Angie Ring account of $4,000 as uncollectible.
June 4   Wrote off Mike Catuc account of $3,000 as uncollectible.

19X7
Aug. 5   Recovered $500 from Mike Catuc.

(a) Journalize the transactions. (They use the income statement approach in estimating bad debts.)
(b) Journalize how Austin Co. would record the Mike Catuc bad debt situation if the direct write-off method were used.

Journalizing adjustment for Bad Debts as well as reinstatement by Allowance method; comparison with direct write-off method.

5. Rowe Company had credit sales of $200,000 during 19X7. The balance in the Allowance for Doubtful Accounts is a $1,000 debit balance. Journalize the Bad Debts Expense for December 31 using each of the following methods:

(a) Bad Debts Expense is estimated at 1/2 percent of credit sales.
(b) The aging of Accounts Receivable indicates that $2,200 will be required in the Allowance account to cover Bad Debts Expense.

Journalizing adjustments for Bad Debts Expense (1) based on percent of sales, (2) based on aging of Accounts Receivable with balance of Allowance for Doubtful Accounts, a debit balance.

GROUP A PROBLEMS

14A-1. The Palter Co. has requested that you prepare journal entries from the following (this company uses the Allowance for Doubtful Accounts method based on the income statement approach).

19X7
Dec. 31   Recorded Bad Debts Expense of $11,000.

19X8
Jan. 7   Wrote off Gene Smore's account of $800 as uncollectible.
Mar. 5   Wrote off Paul Jane's account of $600 as uncollectible.
July 8   Recovered $300 from Paul Jane.
Aug. 19   Wrote off Bob Seager's account of $1,300 as uncollectible.
Aug. 24   Wrote off Jill Neuman's account of $750 as uncollectible.
Nov. 19   Recovered $400 from Bob Seager.

The income statement approach: journalizing Bad Debts Expense and writing accounts off.

14A-2. Given the information presented at the top of p. 512:

(a) Prepare on December 31, 19X8, the adjusting journal entry for Bad Debts Expense.
(b) Prepare a partial balance sheet on December 31, 19X8, showing how net realizable value is calculated.
(c) If the balance in the Allowance for Doubtful Accounts was a $300 debit balance, journalize the adjusting entry for Bad Debts Expense on December 31, 19X8.

Balances: Cash, $30,000; Accounts Receivable, $152,000; Allowance for Doubtful Accounts, $300; Inventory, $12,000.

The balance sheet approach: aging analysis and journalizing of Bad Debts Expense.

		Alvie Co. December 31, 19X8	
	Amount	Estimated Percent Considered to be Bad Debts Expense	Estimated Amount Needed in Allowance for Doubtful Accounts
Not yet due	$130,000	.01	
0 – 60	9,000	.05	
61 – 180	8,000	.20	
Over six months	5,000	.40	
	$152,000		

The direct write-off method.

14A-3. T.J. Rack Company uses the direct write-off method for recording Bad Debts Expense. At the beginning of 19X8, Accounts Receivable has a $119,000 balance. Journalize the following transactions for T.J. Rack:

19X8
Mar. 13   Wrote off S. Rose's account for $1,800.
Apr. 14   Wrote off P. Soy's account for $750.

19X9
Nov. 8   P. Soy paid bad debt of $750 that was written off April 14, 19X8.
Dec. 7   Wrote off J. Miller's account as uncollectible, $285.
Dec. 12   Wrote off D. Lovejoy's account for $375 due from sales made on account in 19X7.

Journalizing and posting adjustments for Bad Debts Expense and write-offs and recovery based on balance sheet approach. Preparation of partial balance sheet.

14A-4. Simon Company completed the following transactions:

19X8
Jan. 9   Sold merchandise on account to Ray's Supply, $1,500.
Jan. 15   Wrote off the account of Pete Runnels as uncollectible because of his death, $600.
Mar. 17   Received $400 from Roland Co., whose account had been written off in 19X7. The account was reinstated and the collection recorded.
Apr. 9   Received 10 percent of the $4,000 owed by Lane Drug. The remainder was written off as uncollectible.
June 15   The account of Mel's Garage was reinstated for $1,200. The account was written off three years ago.
Oct. 18   Prepared a compound entry to write the following accounts off as uncollectible: Jane's Diner, $200; Keen Auto, $400; Ralph's Hardware, $600.
Nov. 12   Sold merchandise on account to J.B. Rug, $1,900.
Dec. 31   Based on an aging of Accounts Receivable it was estimated that $7,000 will be uncollectible out of a total of $160,000 in Accounts Receivable.
Dec. 31   Closed Bad Debts Expense to Income Summary.

From the above as well as the following additional data:

	ACCT. NO.	BALANCE
Allowance for Doubtful Accounts	114	$4,100
Income Summary	312	—
Bad Debts Expense	612	—

1. Journalize the transactions.
2. Post to Allowance for Doubtful Accounts, Income Summary, or Bad Debts Expense as needed. (Be sure to record beginning balance in the Allowance account in your workbook.)
3. Prepare a current assets section of the balance sheet. Ending balances needed: Cash, $13,000; Accounts Receivable, $160,000; Office Supplies, $2,110; Merchandise Inventory, $103,000; Prepaid Rent, $1,250.

GROUP B PROBLEMS

14B-1. The Palter Co. has requested that you prepare journal entries from the following (this company uses the Allowance for Doubtful Accounts method based on the income statement approach).

The income statement approach: journalizing Bad Debts Expense and writing accounts off.

19X7
Dec. 31   Recorded Bad Debts Expense of $14,800.

19X8
Jan.   7   Wrote off Woody Tree's account of $1,200 as uncollectible.
Mar.   5   Wrote off Jim Lantz's account of $600 as uncollectible.
July   8   Recovered $600 from Jim Lantz.
Aug. 19   Wrote off Mabel Hest's account of $750 as uncollectible.
Aug. 24   Wrote off Jim O'Reilly's account of $950 as uncollectible.
Nov. 19   Recovered $500 from Mabel Hest.

14B-2. Given the information below, and assuming the following balances: Cash, $42,000; Accounts Receivable, $173,000; Allowance for Doubtful Accounts, $400; Inventory, $12,000:

The balance sheet approach: aging analysis and journalizing of Bad Debts Expense.

(a) Prepare on December 31, 19X8, the adjusting journal entry for Bad Debts Expense.
(b) Prepare a partial balance sheet on December 31, 19X8, showing how net realizable value is calculated.
(c) If the balance in the Allowance for Doubtful Accounts was a $400 debit balance, journalize the adjusting entry for Bad Debts Expense on December 31, 19X8.

| | | *Alvie Co.* | |
		December 31, 19X8	
	Amount	*Estimated Percent Considered to be Bad Debts Expense*	*Estimated Amount Needed in Allowance for Doubtful Accounts*
Not yet due	$150,000	.02	
0 – 60	10,000	.06	
61 – 180	9,000	.20	
Over six months	4,000	.40	
	$173,000		

The direct write-off method.

14B-3. T.J. Rack Company uses the direct write-off method for recording Bad Debts Expense. At the beginning of 19X8, Accounts Receivable has a $88,000 balance. Journalize the following transactions for T.J. Rack:

19X8
Mar. 13   Wrote off Jill Diamond's account for $1,950.
Apr. 14   Wrote off Buffy Hall's account for $900.

19X9
Nov. 8   Buffy Hall paid debt of $900 that was written off April 14, 19X8.
Dec. 7   Wrote off Joe Francis's account as uncollectible, $880.
Dec. 12   Wrote off Joe Martin's account for $410 from sales made on account in 19X7.

Journalizing and posting adjustments for Bad Debts Expense and write-offs and recovery based on balance sheet approach. Partial balance sheet prepared.

14B-4. Simon Company completed the following transactions:

19X8
Jan. 9   Sold merchandise on account to Lowe's Supply, $1,900.
Jan. 15   Wrote off the account of Kevin Reese as uncollectible because of his death, $700.
Mar. 17   Received $300 from J. James, whose account had been written off in 19X7. The account was reinstated and the collection recorded.
Apr. 9   Received 20 percent of the $5,000 owed by Long Drug. The remainder was written off as uncollectible.
June 15   The account of Morse's Garage was reinstated for $3,100. The account was written off three years ago.
Oct. 18   Prepared a compound entry to write the following accounts off as uncollectible: Sal's Diner, $800; Ring Auto, $1,300; Neel's Hardware, $800.
Nov. 12   Sold merchandise on account to Able Roy, $1,950.
Dec. 31   Based on an aging of Accounts Receivable, it was estimated that $8,000 will be uncollectible out of a total of $170,000 in Accounts Receivable.
Dec. 31   Closed Bad Debts Expense to Income Summary.

From the above as well as the following additional data:

	ACCT. NO.	BALANCE
Allowance for Doubtful Accounts	114	$3,300
Income Summary	312	—
Bad Debts Expense	612	—

1. Journalize the transactions.
2. Post to Allowance for Doubtful Accounts, Income Summary, or Bad Debts Expense as needed.
3. Prepare a current assets section of the balance sheet. Ending balances needed: Cash, $24,000; Accounts Receivable, $170,000; Office Supplies, $3,000; Merchandise Inventory, $94,000; Prepaid Rent, $1,200.

GROUP C PROBLEMS

14C-1. The Samsom Co. has requested that you prepare journal entries from the following (this company uses the Allowance for Doubtful Accounts method based on the income statement approach).

The income statement approach: journalizing Bad Debts Expense and writing accounts off.

19X7
Dec. 31   Recorded Bad Debts Expense of $8,500.

19X8
Jan. 7   Wrote off Helen Jamison's account of $650 as uncollectible.
Mar. 5   Wrote off Rob Hart's account of $300 as uncollectible.
July 8   Recovered $200 from Rob Hart.
Aug. 19   Wrote off Brian Brisk's account of $1,450 as uncollectible.
Aug. 24   Wrote off Ellen Watt's account of $475 as uncollectible.
Nov. 19   Recovered $800 from Brian Brisk.

14C-2. Given the information presented below:

(a) Prepare on December 31, 19X4, the adjusting journal entry for Bad Debts Expense.
(b) Prepare a partial balance sheet on December 31, 19X4, showing how net realizable value is calculated.
(c) If the balance in the Allowance for Doubtful Accounts was a $300 debit balance, journalize the adjusting entry for Bad Debts Expense on December 31, 19X4.

The balance sheet approach: aging analysis and journalizing of Bad Debts Expense.

	Amount	Estimated Percentage Considered to be Bad Debts Expense	Estimated Amount Needed in Allowance for Doubtful Accounts
	Dominion Company December 31, 19X4		
Not yet due	$96 0 0 0 00	.01	
0 – 30	12 0 0 0 00	.05	
31 – 60	8 0 0 0 00	.15	
61 – 180	4 0 0 0 00	.25	
Over six months	6 0 0 0 00	.45	
	$126 0 0 0 00		

Balances: Cash, $16,400; Accounts Receivable, $126,000; Allowance for Doubtful Accounts, $500; Inventory, $53,700.

14C-3. Camping Equipment Company uses the direct write-off method for recording Bad Debts Expense. At the beginning of 19X5, Accounts Receivable has a $86,700 balance. Journalize the following transactions for the company:

The direct write-off method.

19X5
Mar. 23   Wrote off F. Robichaud's account for $1,760.
Jun. 9   Wrote off K. Cheung's account for $835.

19X6
Aug. 15   K. Cheung paid bad debt of $835 that was written off June 9, 19X5.
Dec. 5   Wrote off S. Lowe's account as uncollectible, $360.
Dec. 18   Wrote off R. Patel's account for $412 due from sales made on account in 19X4.

Journalizing and posting adjustments for Bad Debts Expense and write-offs and recovery based on balance sheet approach. Partial balance sheet prepared.

14C-4. Prospecting Supply Company completed the following transactions:

19X6
Jan.   8   Sold merchandise on account to May Expeditions, $3,580.
Feb. 19   Wrote off the account of Avery Fischer as uncollectible because of his death, $872.
Mar. 14   Received $600 from Maximum Co., whose account had been written off in 19X5. The account was reinstated and the collection recorded.
Apr.   5   Received 25 percent of the $7,500 owed by Airborne Surveys. The remainder was written off as uncollectible.
July 18   The account of Hallicrafter Explorations was reinstated for $3,200. The account was written off three years ago.
Oct. 28   Prepared a compound entry to write the following accounts off as uncollectible: Corbett Co., $300; Quark Co., $750; Lonely Expeditions, $458.
Nov. 17   Sold merchandise on account to Partridge Surveys, $2,600.
Dec. 31   Based on an aging of Accounts Receivable it was estimated that $6,500 will be uncollectible out of a total of $142,000 in Accounts Receivable.
Dec. 31   Closed Bad Debts Expense to Income Summary.

From the above as well as the following additional data:

	ACCT.NO.	BALANCE
Allowance for Doubtful Accounts	1124	$7,250
Income Summary	3100	—
Bad Debts Expense	6125	—

1. Journalize the transactions.
2. Post to Allowance for Doubtful Accounts, Income Summary, or Bad Debts Expense as needed. (Be sure to record beginning balance in the Allowance account in your workbook.)
3. Prepare a current assets section of the balance sheet. Ending balances needed: Cash, $16,742; Accounts Receivable, $142,000; Office Supplies, $2,630; Merchandise Inventory, $107,000; Prepaid Rent, $3,500.

PRACTICAL ACCOUNTING APPLICATION #1

Joan Rivers, the newly hired bookkeeper of Lyon Company, has until 5:00 P.M. today to prepare an analysis on December 31 of Accounts Receivable by age as well as record the entry for Bad Debts Expense. Please assist Joan, who has found the following invoices and balances scattered on her desk. Terms of all sales are n/30.

| Jones Co. |
| May 12 $1,500 |

| Ron Co. |
| Aug. 18 $700 |

| Roger Co. |
| Dec. 18 $1,400 |

| Bill Co. |
| Oct. 5 $125 |

| Doe Co. |
| Nov. 1 $ 900 |
| Dec. 18   1,200 |

| Joe Co. |
| Sept. 5 $1,200 |

| Francis Co. |
| July 8 $200 |
| July 15 $400 |

| Balance in Allowance |
| for Doubtful Accounts $350 |

Not yet due	1%
1-30	3%
31-60	8%
61-90	12%
Over 90	30%

PRACTICAL ACCOUNTING APPLICATION #2

TO: Al Jones   Sept. 30, 19XX
FROM: Peter Flynn, Pres.
RE: Bad Debts

At a party last night a friend of mine told me that we should not be using the direct write-off method. He told me that it doesn't fulfil the matching principle of accounting. Give me your arguments to support or reject this information.

ACCOUNTING RECALL
A Cumulative Approach

THIS EXAM REVIEWS CHAPTERS 1 THROUGH 14

Your *Study Guide and Working Papers* have forms to complete this exam, as well as worked-out solutions. The page references next to each question identify what page to turn back to if you answer the question incorrectly.

PART I Vocabulary Review

Match the terms to the appropriate definition or phrase.

Page Ref.

(501)	1. Aging of accounts receivable	A. In alphabetical order
(506)	2. Bad debts recovered	B. Balance in allowance account will have to be adjusted
(181)	3. Ending merchandise inventory	C. Operating expense
(496)	4. Allowance for doubtful accounts	D. Does not use allowance for doubtful accounts
(460)	5. Plant and equipment	E. Classifying of accounts
(182)	6. Subsidiary ledgers	F. Land
(496)	7. Net realizable value	G. Contra asset account
(505)	8. Direct write-off method	H. Other revenue
(501)	9. Balance sheet approach	I. Subtracted from cost of goods sold
(496)	10. Bad debt expense	J. Accounts receivable less allowance for doubtful accounts

PART II True or False (Accounting Theory)

(497) 11. In the income statement approach any existing balance in the allowance for doubtful account is ignored.

(500) 12. The income statement approach is based on aging of accounts receivable.

(505) 13. Allowance for doubtful accounts is used in the direct write-off method.

(496) 14. The allowance for doubtful accounts is listed on the income statement.

(497) 15. A debit to the allowance account will increase it.

PART III Applications Problem (499)

From the following transactions prepare journal entries. (The Company uses the allowance for doubtful accounts method based on the income statement approach)

19X7

Dec. 31:   Recorded bad Debts Expense of $16,000

19X8

Jan.   8:   Wrote off Al Smith's account of $14,000 as uncollectible
Mar.   9:   Wrote off Billie French's account of $700 as uncollectible
July 15:   Recovered $700 from Billie French
Aug.   6:   Wrote off Alice Fall's account of $650 as uncollectible
Sept. 9:   Wrote off Pete Reston's account of $900 as uncollectible
Nov. 18:   Recovered $400 from Alice Fall

NOTES RECEIVABLE
AND NOTES PAYABLE

IN THIS CHAPTER WE WILL COVER THE FOLLOWING TOPICS:

1. DETERMINING INTEREST CALCULATIONS AND MATURITY DATES ON NOTES. (P. 521)

2. JOURNALIZING ENTRIES TO RECORD RENEWAL OF A NOTE, DISHONORING OF A NOTE, EVENTUAL RECEIPT OF PAYMENT, AND NOTE GIVEN IN EXCHANGE FOR EQUIPMENT PURCHASED. (P. 526)

3. DISCOUNTING AN INTEREST-BEARING NOTE RECEIVABLE AND RECORDING A DISCOUNTED NOTE THAT HAS BEEN DISHONORED. (P. 531)

4. HANDLING ADJUSTMENTS FOR INTEREST EXPENSE AND INTEREST INCOME. (P. 536)

Notes receivable—asset. Notes payable—liability.

So far the accounts receivable and accounts payable transactions we have been discussing have not involved formal written promises (a purchase order or a sales receipt is not a formal written promise). In this chapter we will turn to transactions by buyers and sellers that do require formal written promises, also called promissory notes or notes. The notes record amounts owed to a company by others (notes receivable) and amounts the company itself owes (notes payable).

There are a number of reasons why a company uses notes instead of informal promises:

1. To record sales of high-cost items such as farm machinery or construction equipment that have long-term credit periods (usually over 60 days).
2. To give additional time to settle past due accounts.
3. To borrow money from a bank.
4. To collect a fee for the use of one's money over a period of time. This is called **interest**. If one lends money, one gets interest; if one borrows money, one pays interest.
5. To have a stronger legal claim for collecting a past due account. In this case the note acts as formal proof of the transaction.

Before looking at recording notes receivable and notes payable, let's first discuss the structure of a note and how to determine interest calculations and *maturity dates* (when the note comes due).

LEARNING UNIT 15-1

Promissory Notes, Calculations, and Determining Maturity Dates

A **promissory note** (often called simply a *note*) is a written promise by a borrower to pay a certain sum of money to the lender at a fixed future date. The following is a promissory note that Able Company issued to Green Company. Take a moment to look at the structure of the note, shown in Figure 15-1 below. The following explanation is keyed to the figure:

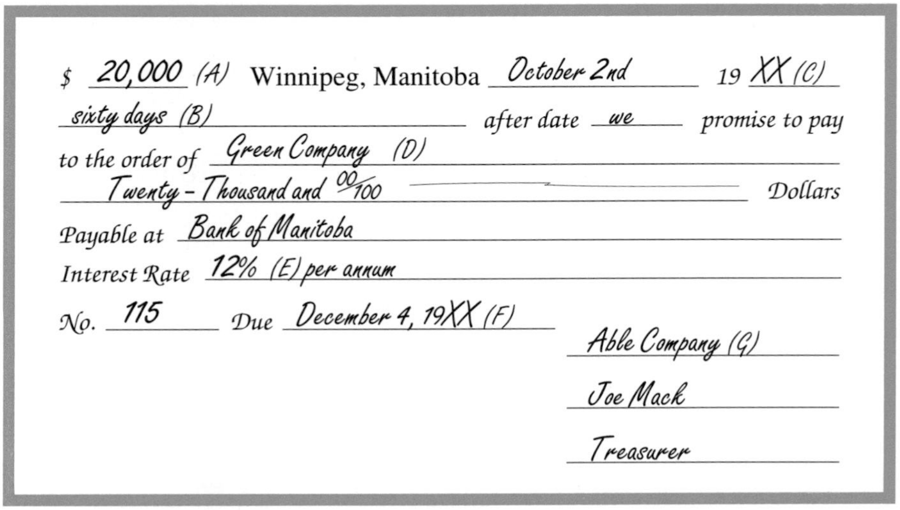

$ 20,000 (A) Winnipeg, Manitoba October 2nd 19 XX (C)
sixty days (B) after date we promise to pay
to the order of Green Company (D)
Twenty-Thousand and 00/100 Dollars
Payable at Bank of Manitoba
Interest Rate 12% (E) per annum
No. 115 Due December 4, 19XX (F)
Able Company (G)
Joe Mack
Treasurer

FIGURE 15-1

A Promissory Note

(A) Able Company is borrowing $20,000; this amount is called the **principal**.

(B) Money is being borrowed for 60 days.

(C) The note is issued on October 2, 19XX.

Think of the payee as the lender.

(D) The Green Company is the **payee** to whom the note is payable.

(E) The note carries a 12 percent annual interest rate. (Even though the note is for 60 days, interest is stated as a yearly rate.)

(F) The date the note will come due, December 4, 19XX, is called the **maturity date** and includes 3 days grace—a common practice in Canada.

The maker is often also called the payor or debtor.

(G) Able Company is the **maker**, or the one promising to pay the note plus interest when it comes due.

Most interest on notes will be paid on maturity date. We will cover exceptions later in chapter.

Think of the maker (Able Company) as the borrower, who thus calls this obligation a **note payable**. On the other side of the coin the payee (Green Company) views this note as an asset called a **note receivable**. What will be interest expense for Able Company will be interest income for Green Company. Remember, interest expense is classified on the income statement as "other expenses," and interest income is "other income."

HOW TO CALCULATE INTEREST

The formula for calculating the interest on a note is:

Interest = Principal × Rate × Time

| The face value or amount stated on note indicating amount borrowed | Percent per year | Years or fraction of year |

Let's look at some illustrative situations to show specific interest calculation:

Interest calculated for one year on a $6,000 12 percent note:

$12\% = .12$ or $\frac{12}{100}$

$$I = P \times R \times T$$
$$I = \$6,000 \times .12 \times 1$$
$$I = \$720$$

Interest calculated for five months on an $8,000 10 percent note:

Time is expressed in twelfths of a year; thus 5 months is $\frac{5}{12}$.

$$I = P \times R \times T$$
$$= \$8,000 \times .10 \times \frac{5}{12}$$
$$= \$333.33$$

Interest calculated for exact number of days based on a 365-day year, 60 days at 6 percent on a $4,000 note: When the note is given in days, the fraction for time is

$$\frac{\text{exact number of days} + 3 \text{ days grace}}{365}$$

So we have

$$I = P \times R \times T$$
$$= \$4,000 \times .06 \times \frac{63}{365}$$
$$= \$41.42$$

Interest calculated for specific three-month period. $5,000, 8% note dated June 1, 19XX.

Time is expressed in terms of three specific months:

June	30 days
July	31 days
Aug.	31 days
Grace period	3 days
total	95 days

So we have

$$I = P \times R \times T$$
$$= 5000 \times .08 \times \frac{95}{365}$$
$$= \$104.11$$

> Common business practice in Canada is to use 365 days, but occasionally 360 days is used as a quick approximation.

Optional:
    Shortcut to Figuring Interest on Notes: The 6 percent, 60-Day Method and Its Variations: Sometimes to ease calculations it is assumed that a year has 360 days. When that assumption is made, the interest on any note that is 6 percent for 60 days is always equal to 1 percent of the principal of the note:

$$.06 \times \frac{60}{360} = .01$$

Thus when the rate times the number of days equals 360, it is equal to 1 percent, and the interest is calculated by moving the decimal two places to the left. For example:

> Note: Each rate multiplied times the number of days equals 360.

$4,000 at 6 percent for 60 days = $40

$481.40 at 6 percent for 60 days = $4.81

$6,000 at 10 percent for 36 days = $60

HOW TO DETERMINE MATURITY DATE

Maturity Date Determined by Exact Days

To determine the maturity date of a 90-day note* dated June 21, the following could be set up (or you could count on a calendar):

> 30 Days have September, April, June, and November, all the rest have 31, except February which has 28 (29 during a leap year).

* Remember to add 3 days grace.

Number of days remaining in June (30 − 21)	9
Days in July	31
Days in August	31
Number of days at end of August	71
Days in September to reach 90	22
Term of note	93

Thus the maturity date of the note is September 22.

Another way to calculate the maturity date is to use a table of days in a year (see Table 15-1).

The original note is dated June 21. Look at the top of the table for June and down the left column to day 21. The point of intersection reveals that June 21 is the 172 day of the year. If we add 172 and 93 (length of note) we get 265. By searching in the table for 265, we see the date of maturity is September 22.

TABLE 15-1   **Days in a Year**

DAY OF MONTH	JAN.	FEB*	MAR.	APR.	MAY	JUNE	JULY	AUG.	SEPT.	OCT.	NOV.	DEC.	DAY OF MONTH
1	1	32	60	91	121	152	182	213	244	274	305	335	1
2	2	33	61	92	122	153	183	214	245	275	306	336	2
3	3	34	62	93	123	154	184	215	246	276	307	337	3
4	4	35	63	94	124	155	185	216	247	277	308	338	4
5	5	36	64	95	125	156	186	217	248	278	309	339	5
6	6	37	65	96	126	157	187	218	249	279	310	340	6
7	7	38	66	97	127	158	188	219	250	280	311	341	7
8	8	39	67	98	128	159	189	220	251	281	312	342	8
9	9	40	68	99	129	160	190	221	252	282	313	343	9
10	10	41	69	100	130	161	191	222	253	283	314	344	10
11	11	42	70	101	131	162	192	223	254	284	315	345	11
12	12	43	71	102	132	163	193	224	255	285	316	346	12
13	13	44	72	103	133	164	194	225	256	286	317	347	13
14	14	45	73	104	134	165	195	226	257	287	318	348	14
15	15	46	74	105	135	166	196	227	258	288	319	349	15
16	16	47	75	106	136	167	197	228	259	289	320	350	16
17	17	48	76	107	137	168	198	229	260	290	321	351	17
18	18	49	77	108	138	169	199	230	261	291	322	352	18
19	19	50	78	109	139	170	200	231	262	292	323	353	19
20	20	51	79	110	140	171	201	232	263	293	324	354	20
21	21	52	80	111	141	(172)	202	233	264	294	325	355	21
22	22	53	81	112	142	173	203	234	(265)	295	326	356	22
23	23	54	82	113	143	174	204	235	266	296	327	357	23
24	24	55	83	114	144	175	205	236	267	297	328	358	24
25	25	56	84	115	145	176	206	237	268	298	329	359	25
26	26	57	85	116	146	177	207	238	269	299	330	360	26
27	27	58	86	117	147	178	208	239	270	300	331	361	27
28	28	59	87	118	148	179	209	240	271	301	332	362	28
29	29		88	119	149	180	210	241	272	302	333	363	29
30	30		89	120	150	181	211	242	273	303	334	364	30
31	31		90		151		212	243		304		365	31

* For leap years, February has 29 days, and the number of each day after February 28 is one greater than the number given in the table.

Maturity Date Determined by Number of Months

If the note were expressed in months rather than days, the table or calendar would not be needed. The maturity date could be found by counting the months from the date the note was issued, regardless of number of days in each month. Let's look at several examples:

DATE OF NOTE	LENGTH OF NOTE	MATURITY DATE
March 31	2 months + 3 days	June 3
April 30	3 months + 3 days	Aug. 3
July 31	2 months + 3 days	Oct. 3

At this point you should be able to

1. Explain the advantages of using notes instead of informal promises. (p. 521)
2. Define and explain the structure of a promissory note. (p. 521)
3. Calculate interest on notes in days, monthly, or yearly. (pp. 522-523)
4. Calculate maturity date by days in the month, by special chart, or by months. (pp. 523-524)

☐ SELF-REVIEW QUIZ 15-1

1. Calculate the interest for the following:
   (a) $10,000   12%   1 year   (ignore days of grace)
   (b) $ 9,000   13%   7 months   (ignore days of grace)
   (c) $ 7,000   10%   80 days   (with 3 days of grace)

2. Find the maturity date of an 80-day note dated March 3 by (a) days in each month, (b) using a days-in-a-year chart.

3. Find the maturity date of a note dated March 31, due in 5 months.

■ *SOLUTIONS TO SELF-REVIEW QUIZ 15-1*

1. (a) $10,000 \times .12 \times 1 = \$1,200$.
   (b) $\$9,000 \times .13 \times 7/12 = \$682.50$.
   (c) $\$7,000 \times .10 \times 83/365 = \$159.18$.

2. (a)

Number of days remaining in March (31 − 3)	28
Days in April	30
Number of days at end of April	58
Days in May to reach 83	25
Maturity date—May 25	

   (b) March 3   62 days
                    + 83
                    ―――
                    142 May 22

3. March 31, April, May, June, July, August 31 + 3 days = Sept. 3.

LEARNING UNIT 15-2

Recording Notes

We will use general journal entries to keep things simple instead of using special journals.

To understand how notes may be used to extend credit periods as well as to see how a note is paid off, let's look at some illustrative transactions involving Mace Company and Jane Company.

SALE OF MERCHANDISE ON ACCOUNT.
On August 1, 19XX, Mace Company sold $6,000 of merchandise on account to Jane Company.

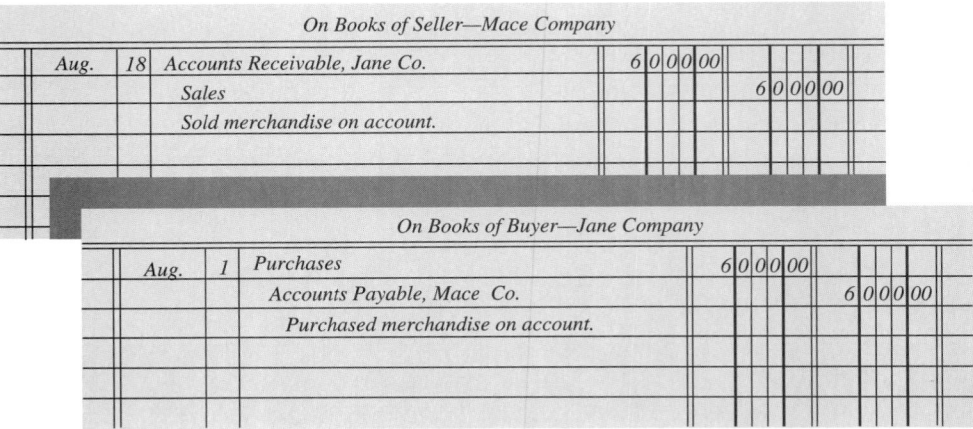

			On Books of Seller—Mace Company		
Aug.	18	Accounts Receivable, Jane Co.		6 0 0 0 00	
		Sales			6 0 0 0 00
		Sold merchandise on account.			

			On Books of Buyer—Jane Company		
Aug.	1	Purchases		6 0 0 0 00	
		Accounts Payable, Mace Co.			6 0 0 0 00
		Purchased merchandise on account.			

On September 1, the end of the credit period, Jane Company gave a $6,000, 60-day, 13 percent note to Mace Company to gain additional time to settle the past due account. The following entries would be made on the books of the buyer and seller.

TIME EXTENSION WITH A NOTE

Notes Receivable is a current asset on the balance sheet.

			Seller — Mace Company		
Sept.	1	Notes Receivable		6 0 0 0 00	
		Accounts Receivable, Jane Co.			6 0 0 0 00
		Received 60-day, 13% note for extension			
		of past due account.			

			Buyer—Jane Company		
Sept.	1	Accounts Payable, Mace Co.		6 0 0 0 00	
		Notes Payable			6 0 0 0 00
		Issued 60-day, 13% note for extension			
		of past due account.			

When this transaction is journalized, both Accounts Receivable and Accounts Payable are reduced. With notes a subsidiary ledger is usually *not* needed, since the file of the notes provides all the information.

Notes Payable is a current liability on the balance sheet.

Have you thought why Mace would accept this note as an extension? Because

1. If Jane Company doesn't pay, a formal written promise is in hand and is easier to enforce, legally speaking.
2. Interest accumulates on the note.

Seller ➝

> The end result of this transaction is a shifting of assets of Mace Company from Accounts Receivable to Notes Receivable.

Buyer ➝

> For Jane Company the result is a shift in liabilities from Accounts Payable to Notes Payable.

NOTE DUE AND PAID AT MATURITY

Now let's look at the journal entries that will be made if Jane Company pays off the note on November 3.

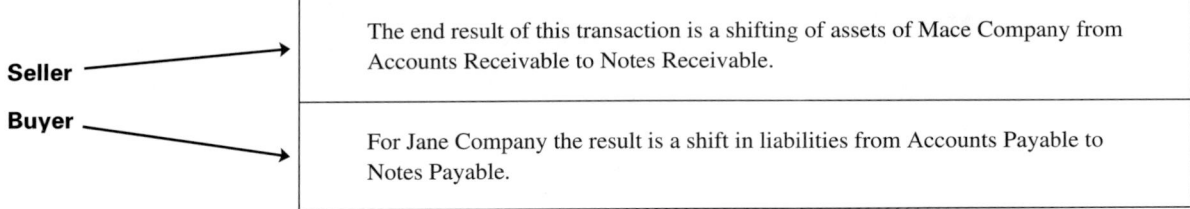

		Seller—Mace Company		
Nov.	3	Cash	6 1 3 4 63	
		Notes Receivable		6 0 0 0 00
		Interest Income		1 3 4 63
		Collected Jane Company note.		

($6,000 × .13 × $\frac{63}{365}$ = $134.63 Interest Income)

		Buyer—Jane Company		
Nov.	3	Notes Payable	6 0 0 0 00	
		Interest Expense	1 3 4 63	
		Cash		6 1 3 4 63
		Paid note to Mace Company.		

($6,000 × .13 × $\frac{63}{365}$ = $134.63 Interest Income)

It is important to emphasize that the interest is calculated on the maturity date of the note, plus 3 days grace, or November 3.

NOTE RENEWED AT MATURITY

If Jane Company is unable to pay the $6,134.63 at maturity, it is possible for the company to renew all or part of the note. Let's assume that the company can pay the interest of $134.63 and give another note for 90 days at 13 percent.

The transaction could be recorded as follows on the books of the buyer and seller:

			Seller—Mace Company										
Nov.	3	Cash				1	3	4	63				
		Notes Receivable (new)			6	0	0	0	00				
		Notes Receivable (old)								6	0	0	00
		Interest Income									1	3	4	63
		Interest of old note collected											
		and renewal of note for 90 days.											

			Buyer—Jane Company										
Nov.	3	Notes Payable			6	0	0	0	00				
		Interest Expense				1	3	4	63				
		Notes Payable (new)								6	0	0	00
		Cash									1	3	4	63
		Interest of old note paid											
		and renewal of note recorded.											

Notice on the seller's books how the interest is received, the old note is cancelled, and the new note is put on the books.

Now let's look at another alternative, the case in which Jane Company fails to pay the original note at maturity, but the note will *not* be renewed.

DISHONORED NOTE

If Jane Company fails to pay the **maturity value** (the $6,000 principal plus interest of $134.63) on October 31, the note is said to be **dishonored**. Another way of saying this is to say that Jane Company has **defaulted** on its note. On Jane's and Mace's books the amounts in Notes Receivable and Notes Payable will then be removed and transferred back to Accounts Receivable and Accounts Payable, because the note has reached the maturity date. At the same time, whether the note is paid or not, the interest expense is due and payable and should be recorded (for Mace Company this is Interest Income and for Jane Company it is Interest Expense).

Let's see what entries will look like if Jane Company first defaults and then finally pays the amount owed on December 1. To keep it simple, no additional charges will be calculated for the extra month Jane Company has taken to pay off the amount owed to Mace Company.

Before we conclude this unit, let's discuss how a note may be given in exchange for an asset purchased.

Seller—Mace Company

	(A) Nov.	3	Accounts Receivable, Jane Co.	6 1 3 4 63		
			Interest Income		1 3 4 63	
			Note Receivable		6 0 0 0 00	
			Recorded note receivable dishonored.			

Buyer—Jane Company

	(A) Nov.	3	Notes Payable	6 0 0 0 00		
			Interest Expense	1 3 4 63		
			Accounts Payable, Mace Co.		6 1 3 4 63	
			Recorded note payable dishonored.			

Seller—Mace Company

	(B) Dec.	1	Cash	6 1 3 4 63		
			Accounts Receivable, Jane Co.		6 1 3 4 63	
			Recorded payment of note receivable			
			dishonored.			

Only unmatured
notes are in the
Notes Receivable
account.

Buyer—Jane Company

	(B) Dec.	1	Accounts Payable, Mace Co.	6 1 3 4 63		
			Cash		6 1 3 4 63	
			Payment of note payable dishonored.			

NOTE GIVEN IN EXCHANGE FOR EQUIPMENT PURCHASED

Jane Company decided to buy from Ronald Company some display racks for $7,000. Because the price was high, Jane Company gave a note instead of buying the racks on account. The note issued by Jane Company was a 60-day, 9 percent interest-bearing note for $7,000. This transaction is recorded on the books of the buyer and seller as follows:

When the note is paid at maturity, the same transactions we previously discussed would result.

			Seller—Ronald Company				
May	9	Notes Receivable		7 0 0 0 00		
		Sales			7 0 0 0 00	
		Sold display racks with a 60-day, 9% note.				

			Buyer—Jane Company				
May	9	Store Equipment		7 0 0 0 00		
		Notes Payable			7 0 0 0 00	
		Purchased display racks with a 60-day,				
		9% note.				

At this point you should be able to

1. Journalize entries for buyer and seller to record the extension of a past due account by issuing a note. (p. 526)
2. Explain why a subsidiary ledger may not be needed with Notes Payable and Notes Receivable. (p. 527)
3. Journalize entries for the buyer and seller to record renewal of a note, dishonoring of a note, eventual receipt of payment, and a note given in exchange for equipment purchased. (pp. 527-529)

☐ **SELF-REVIEW QUIZ 15-2**

Journalize the following transactions for Action Company:

(A) Action Company sold $8,000 of merchandise on account to Brian Company.
(B) Action Company received a 60-day, $8,000, 12 percent note for a time extension of past due account of Brian Company.
(C) Collected the Brian Company note on the maturity date.
(D) Brian Company renewed the note for 90 days and paid interest on the old note. (Alternative to C.)
(E) Assuming that Brian Company defaulted in (C), record the note receivable dishonored.
(F) Brian Company paid note receivable dishonored.

■ *SOLUTION TO SELF-REVIEW QUIZ 15-2*

(A)	Accounts Receivable, Brian Co.		8 0 0 0 00		
	Sales			8 0 0 0 00	
(B)	Notes Receivable		8 0 0 0 00		
	Accounts Receivable, Brian Co.			8 0 0 0 00	
(C)	Cash		8 1 6 6 00		
	Interest Income			1 6 6 00	
	Notes Receivable			8 0 0 0 00	
	($8,000 × .12 × $\frac{63}{365}$ = $166)*				
(D)	Cash		1 6 6 00		
	Notes Receivable		8 0 0 0 00		
	Notes Receivable			8 0 0 0 00	
	Interest Income			1 6 6 00	
(E)	Accounts Receivable, Brian Company		8 1 6 6 00		
	Notes Receivable			8 0 0 0 00	
	Interest Income			1 6 6 00	
(F)	Cash		8 1 6 6 00		
	Accounts Receivable, Brian Company			8 1 6 6 00	

LEARNING UNIT 15-3
How to Discount Customers' Notes

Many times a company that accepts notes from customers will not (or cannot) wait to receive its cash until the maturity date. Instead, it goes to a bank and exchanges the note for cash; this is called **discounting**. The company will endorse the note and receive the *maturity value* of the note (principal plus interest) less what the bank charges for holding the note from the date of discounting until the maturity date. The time period during which the bank holds the note (until maturity) is called the **discount period**.

Think of the bank discount as the cost of cashing in a note before maturity.

The amount that the bank charges the company is called the **bank discount**. It is the difference between what the company receives from the bank and the maturity value of the note. The actual amount of money the company receives when a note is discounted is called the **proceeds** (maturity value less the bank discount).

Now let's take a look at Marvin Company and how it discounts an interest-bearing note receivable. The best way to understand the process is to take it step by step.

HOW TO DISCOUNT AN INTEREST-BEARING NOTE RECEIVABLE

Marvin Company received an $8,000, 90-day, 12 percent note from Jee Company dated Oct. 1. On October 31 Marvin Company needed cash to finance its inven-

What Marvin Company will receive from bank is called the proceeds.

tory, so it discounted the note to Royal Bank, which charges a bank discount rate of 14 percent. An overview of the process is shown in Figure 15-2.

FIGURE 15-2   **Discounting an Interest-Bearing Note Receivable**

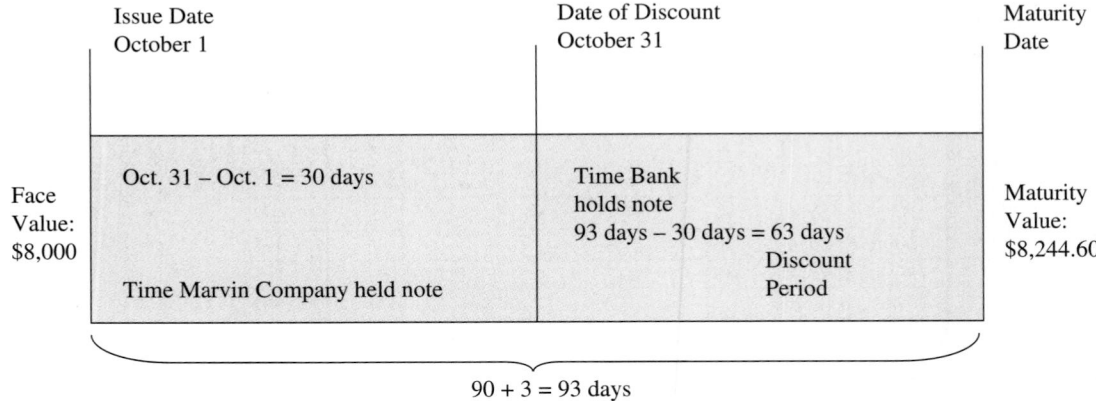

$$90 + 3 = 93 \text{ days}$$

Step 1. Find the *maturity value* of the note:

(a) $\$8,000 \times .12 \times 93/365 = \$244.60$ interest

Find maturity value.

(b) Maturity value = principal + interest
                   = $\$8,000 + \$244.60$
                   = $\underline{\underline{\$8,244.60}}$

Calculate discount period.

Step 2. Calculate the *discount period* (number of days from the date of discounting until the maturity date):

93 days	note + grace period
− 30 days	expired before discounting (Oct. 31 − Oct. 1)
= 63 days	that bank holds note until it comes due

Calculate bank discount.

Step 3. Calculate the *bank discount* (what the bank charges Marvin Company for holding the note until maturity): To do this we use the following formula:

Bank discount = maturity value × bank discount rate × no. of days bank holds note until maturity/365 days

= $\$8,244.60 \times .14 \times 63/365$
= $\$199.23$

Note that the bank discount is based on the maturity value, because we are borrowing the maturity value for the number of days in the discount period.

Calculate proceeds.

Step 4. Calculate the *proceeds* (what Marvin Company receives from the bank in the discounting process):

Proceeds = maturity value − bank discount
         = $\$8,244.60 − \$199.23$
         = $\$8,045.37$

If Marvin Company could have waited until the maturity date, it would have received $8,244.60. By discounting the note the company lost interest of $199.23, or the cost charged by the bank to hold the note until maturity. Let's look at how Marvin Company would record this on its books (again for simplicity we use general journal entries rather than special journals).

Oct.	31	Cash		8 0 4 5 37		
		Notes Receivable			8 0 0 0 00	
		Interest Income			4 5 37	
		Discounted Jee's Company				
		90-day, 12% note at 14%				

Journalizing the discounted note receivable:

$ 8,045.37
– 8,000.00
$ 45.37
(Interest Income)

Now we see Interest Income, since the proceeds Marvin Company received were more than the face value of the note ($8,000). In actuality, if the proceeds had been *less* than the $8,000, Marvin Company would have incurred an interest expense. How could this happen? If Marvin Company held the note for only a short period of time and Royal Bank had a bank discount rate much higher than the original note, it is very possible that the proceeds to Marvin Company might have been less than the $8,000. For example, suppose this same note of Marvin Company was discounted after being held only 2 days, and the bank's discount rate was 18 percent. The bank discount, or amount the bank charges, would be calculated as follows:

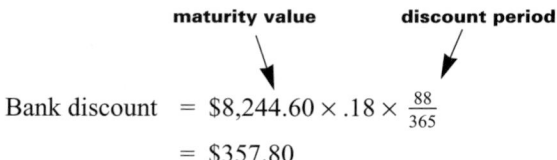

maturity value   **discount period**

$$\text{Bank discount} = \$8,244.60 \times .18 \times \tfrac{88}{365}$$
$$= \$357.80$$

Thus the proceeds to Marvin Company would be:

$$\text{Proceeds} = \$8,244.60 - \$357.80$$
$$= \$7,886.80$$

Note that here Marvin Company is receiving *less* than the $8,000 face value of the note. The general journal entry of Marvin Company would thus look as follows:

Oct.	31	Cash	7 8 8 6 80		
		Interest Expense	1 1 3 20		
		Notes Receivable		8 0 0 0 00	

Now the question arises as to who is liable for the note if Jee Company fails to pay the note at maturity.

PROCEDURE WHEN A DISCOUNTED NOTE IS DISHONORED

When Marvin Company endorsed the note to Royal Bank, the company agreed to pay the note at maturity if Jee Company failed to pay. The potential liability that may result (or not) is called a **contingent liability**. Until the note is paid, Marvin Company will state this contingent liability as a footnote on its balance sheet. If the note had been endorsed *without recourse*, then Marvin Company would have no liability.

At some point before maturity, Jee Company is notified that Royal Bank is holding the note. Let's assume that the maturity date is reached and Jee Company defaults. Royal Bank notifies Marvin Company and charges Marvin Company the full amount of the note, including interest and a $5 protest fee, which is the charge made by Royal Bank for notifying Marvin Company that the note was presented to the maker for payment and was not received. Thus the bank charges Marvin Company (and Marvin will in turn charge Jee Company) the following:

Note	$8,000.00
Interest	244.60
Protest Fee	5.00
	$8,249.60

The following entry is recorded on Marvin Company's book:

Dec.	30	Accounts Receivable, Jee Co.	8 2 4 9 60	
		Cash		8 2 4 9 60
		To record default		

You can be sure that Marvin Company will try to collect this $8,249.60 from Jee Company. Marvin Company may charge additional interest for this delay in paying the $8,249.60. For simplicity we have left this step out. If the $8,249.60 becomes uncollectible, the account could be written off as a bad debt using the Allowance for Doubtful Accounts method discussed in Chapter 14.

At this point you should be able to

1. Define and explain discounting, maturity value, discount period, bank discount, proceeds. (p. 531)

2. Explain the four steps required in discounting an interest-bearing note receivable. (p. 532)

3. Prepare a journal entry to record the proceeds of a note. (p. 533)

4. Define contingent liability and compare it with an endorsement without recourse. (p. 534)

5. Journalize the entry to record a discounted note that has been dishonored. (p. 534)

☐ SELF-REVIEW QUIZ 15-3

Al Gene Company received a $10,000, 60-day, 12 percent note from Broom Company dated July 5. On August 3 Al Gene Company discounted the note to their Bank, which charged a bank discount rate of 15 percent.

(a) Complete the four steps (p. 532) to discount the note.
(b) Journalize the entry to record the proceeds.
(c) Journalize the entry if a default occurs, assuming a $5 protest fee.

■ *SOLUTIONS TO SELF-REVIEW QUIZ 15-3*

(a) *Step 1.*   Maturity value (principal + interest):

$$I = \$10,000 \times .12 \times \tfrac{63}{365}$$

$$= \$207.12$$

$$MV = \$10,000 + \$207.12$$

$$= \$10,207.12$$

Step 2.   Discount period:

July 31
−5
<u>   </u>
26   days Al Gene held note in July
<u> 3 </u>   days Al Gene held note in August
29   days Al Gene held note

63   days
<u>−29 </u> days
34   days bank holds note

Step 3.   Bank discount:

$$\text{Bank discount} = \text{maturity value} \times \text{bank discount rate} \times \frac{\text{no. of days bank holds note until maturity}}{365}$$

$$= \underset{\text{(step 1)}}{\$10,207.12} \times \underset{\text{(given in facts)}}{.15} \times \tfrac{34}{365}$$

$$= \$142.62$$

Step 4.   Proceeds:

Proceeds = maturity value − bank discount
$$= \$10,207.12 - \$142.62$$
$$= \$10,064.50$$

(b)

Aug.	3	Cash	10 0 6 4 50		
		Notes Receivable		10 0 0 0 00	
		Interest Income		6 4 50	
		Discounted Broom Company			
		12% note at 15%			

(c)

Sept.	3	Accounts Receivable, Broom Co.	10 2 1 2 12		
		Cash		10 2 1 2 12	

LEARNING UNIT 15-4

Discounting One's Own Note: Handling Adjustments for Interest Expense and Interest Income

DISCOUNTING ONE'S OWN NOTE

In the last unit we looked at how a note of a customer was discounted. Now our attention shifts to Jones Company, which is borrowing $10,000 by giving Alberta Bank its own 12 percent, 60-day note on December 16, 19XX. In this case Alberta Bank deducts the interest *in advance*. The following is the formula to calculate the bank discount (cost of borrowing) and the proceeds (what Jones Company gets):

Note that maturity value here is the same as the original principal, since interest is deducted in advance.

$$\text{Bank discount} = \left(\begin{array}{c}\text{maturity}\\\text{value}\end{array}\right) \times \left(\begin{array}{c}\text{interest}\\\text{rate}\end{array}\right) \times \left(\begin{array}{c}\text{discount}\\\text{period}\\\hline 365\end{array}\right)$$

$$= \quad \$10,000 \quad \times \quad .12 \quad \times \quad \frac{60}{365}$$

$$= \quad \$200$$

$$\text{Proceeds} = \text{maturity value} - \text{discount}$$
$$= \$10,000 - \$200$$
$$= \$9,800$$

Discount on Notes Payable is a contra liability.

Thus Jones Company receives $9,800 and at the time of maturity will pay back $10,000. The $200 of interest is recorded in a new account called **Discount on Notes Payable**. This is a contra liability account that is subtracted from Notes Payable on the balance sheet, where it looks like this:

Current Liabilities:
Notes Payable   *$10,000*
Less: Discount on Notes Payable   *200*
                                                                     $9,800

Later in this unit, when we talk about adjustments, you will see that as the note matures, the discount will be reduced and then charged to Interest Expense. But for now let's record the journal entry for Jones Company as it discounts its own note with interest deducted in advance:

Dec.	16	Cash		9 8 0 0 00		
		Discount on Notes Payable		2 0 0 00		
		Notes Payable			10 0 0 0 00	
		Discounted own note at 12%				

Accounts Affected	Category	↑ ↓	Rules	
Cash	Asset	↑	Dr.	$9,800
Discount on Notes Payable	Contra Liability	↑	Dr.	$200
Notes Payable	Liability	↑	Cr.	$10,000

When the note is paid, the accountant will debit Notes Payable for $10,000 and credit Cash for $10,000.

NOTE: Although the bank interest rate is stated at 12 percent, the truth is that Jones Company really has the use of only $9,800. To calculate the true interest rate, which is called the effective interest rate, the following formula applies:

Effective interest rate: The cost of borrowing the $10,000 is not 12% but really almost $12\frac{1}{4}$%.

$$\text{Effective interest rate} = \frac{(\text{Maturity value of note}) \times (\text{bank interest rate})}{\text{amount of cash proceeds received from note}}$$

$$= \frac{\$10,000 \times .12}{\$9,800}$$

$$= 12.24 \text{ percent}$$

Now let's look at how adjustments will be handled for some of the transactions presented in this chapter.

INTEREST: THE NEED FOR ADJUSTMENTS

Because interest-bearing notes are often taken out and then paid off in different accounting periods, it is necessary to adjust or bring up-to-date Interest Income and Interest Expense. The following diagram shows why we need to adjust, as well as who does the adjusting:

Let's look at how to record adjustments for Interest Income and Interest Expense from the following: Bog Company receives a $24,000, 60-day, 10 percent note on December 16 from Jan Company.

ACCRUED INTEREST INCOME

> Must adjust for income that has been earned during the period but has not been received or recorded because payment is not yet due.

Note Receivable *(seller)*

ACCRUED INTEREST EXPENSE

> Must adjust for interest that has been incurred during the period but has not been paid or recorded because payment is not yet due.

(A) Note Payable *(buyer)*
(B) Company's own discounted note

Step 1.   Calculate interest on the note:

$$\text{Interest} = \$24,000 \times .10 \times \frac{63}{365}$$

$$= \$414.25$$

Step 2.   Calculate the number of days the note has already run before the end of the current period (see Figure 15-3 below):

Dec. 31   (end of period)
– Dec. 16   (starting date of note)
15   days

FIGURE 15-3   Adjusting for Interest Accrued

Issue Date | Financial Statement Prepared | Due Date
December 16 | December 31 | Feb. 14

(15 days of interest accured)

Step 3.   Calculate interest incurred for this period:

$$\$24,000 \times .10 \times \frac{15}{365} = \$98.63$$

Step 4.   Prepare the adjusting journal entries:

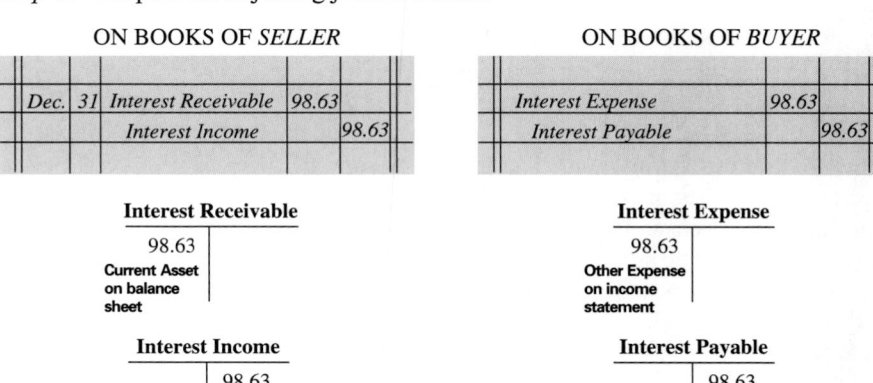

ON BOOKS OF *SELLER*

| Dec. | 31 | Interest Receivable | 98.63 | |
| | | Interest Income | | 98.63 |

Interest Receivable
98.63
Current Asset on balance sheet

Interest Income
98.63
Other Income on income statement

ON BOOKS OF *BUYER*

| | | Interest Expense | 98.63 | |
| | | Interest Payable | | 98.63 |

Interest Expense
98.63
Other Expense on income statement

Interest Payable
98.63
Current Liability on balance sheet

When the note is paid off on February 14, the following entries are made, assuming that no reversing entry is used.*

			Seller		
Feb.	14	Cash		24 4 1 4 25	
		Interest Receivable			9 8 63
		Notes Receivable			24 0 0 0 00
		Interest Income			3 1 5 62

			Buyer		
Feb.	14	Notes Payable		24 0 0 0 00	
		Interest Expense		3 1 5 62	
		Interest Payable		9 8 63	
		Cash			24 4 1 4 25

Note that by *not* using reversing entries the bookkeeper of the buyer and seller had to recall the amount of accrued interest that was recorded in the *old* year so that this year's interest expense or income would not be overstated.

The last adjustment deals with a firm discounting its own note. Back on p. 536, at the beginning of this unit, we saw Jones Company discounting its own note on December 16 for $10,000 for 60 days at 12 percent interest. Jones Company actually received $9,800 and recorded the $200 interest deducted in advance by the bank in a contra liability account called *Discount on Notes Payable*.

Discount on Notes Payable		**Interest Expense**	
200			

---

* If a reversing entry is used, the following entries are made:

			Seller		
Feb.	14	Cash		24 4 1 4 25	
		Notes Receivable			24 0 0 0 00
		Interest Income			4 1 4 25

			Buyer		
Feb.	14	Notes Payable		24 0 0 0 00	
		Interest Expense		4 1 4 25	
		Cash			24 4 1 4 25

At the end of December, 15 days out of the 60 days have passed. Thus one-fourth of the interest on this note should be recorded in the old year. To record this interest we reduce the amount in the Discount on Notes Payable by $50 ($\frac{1}{4}$ × $200). The following journal entry is made:

Dec.	31	Interest Expense		50 00	
		Discount on Notes Payable			50 00
		Recognition of expense incurred.			

Accounts Affected	Category	↑ ↓	Rules	
Interest Expense	**Other Expense**	↑	**Dr.**	**$50**
Discount on Notes Payable	**Contra Liability**	↓	**Cr.**	**$50**

The current liability on the balance sheet will look as follows:

See p. 536 for comparison of this section before discount on note is reduced.

CURRENT LIABILITIES:
Notes Payable $10,000
Less: Discount on Notes Payable   150
                                                              $9,850

When the note is paid the following journal entry will result:

$\frac{45 \text{ days}}{60 \text{ days}} \times \text{\$200}$

Feb.	14	Notes Payable		10 0 00 00	
		Interest Expense		1 50 00	
		Discount on Notes Payable			1 50 00
		Cash			10 0 00 00

At this point you should be able to

1. Explain the purpose of the Discount on Notes Payable account. (p. 536)
2. Calculate the effective interest rate. (p. 537)
3. Make adjustments for interest income and interest expense at end of period. (p. 538)
4. Adjust the Discount on Notes Payable account. (p. 539)

☐ **SELF-REVIEW QUIZ 15-4**

Answer true or false to the following:

1. No bank deducts interest in advance.
2. Discount on Notes Payable is a contra liability account.
3. When Discount on Notes Payable is reduced, Interest Expense results.
4. Effective rate of interest is lower than the stated rate.
5. Reversing entries are never used to adjust interest at the end of a period of time.

■ *SOLUTIONS TO SELF-REVIEW QUIZ 15-4*

1. F   2. T   3. T   4. F   5. F

SUMMARY OF KEY POINTS AND KEY TERMS

LEARNING UNIT 15-1

1. A promissory note is a written promise by a borrower to pay a certain sum of money to a lender at a fixed future date. The note may be interest-bearing or non-interest-bearing.
2. The payee is the party to whom the note is payable.
3. The maker is the one who will pay the promissory note.
4. Maturity date is the time when note comes due.
5. Interest = principal × rate × $\dfrac{\text{number of days}}{365}$

Interest: The cost of using money for a period of time.

Maker: One promising to pay a note.

Maturity date: Due date of the promissory note.

Note payable: A promissory note from the maker's point of view.

Note receivable: A promissory note from the payee's point of view.

Payee: One to whom note is payable.

Principal: The face amount of the note.

Promissory note: A formal written promise by a borrower to pay a certain sum at a fixed future date.

LEARNING UNIT 15-2

1. Notes Payable is a current liability on the balance sheet.
2. Notes do not need subsidiary ledgers.
3. Interest Income for the payee is Interest Expense for the maker.
4. A note that is not paid at maturity is said to be dishonored.
5. Notes may be renewed as well as issued to buy assets.

Default: Failure of maker to pay the maturity value of a note when due.

Dishonored note: A note that was not paid at maturity by the maker.

Maturity value: The value of the note that is due on the date of maturity (principal + interest).

LEARNING UNIT 15-3

1. Maturity value = principal + interest.
2. Discount period = number of days from date of discounting until maturity date.
3. Bank discount = what the bank charges for holding a note until the maturity date, as shown in the formula:

$$\text{Bank discount} = \text{maturity value} \times \text{bank discount rate} \times \frac{\text{no. of days bank holds note (till maturity + 3 days)}}{365 \text{ days}}$$

4. Proceeds = what one receives from bank in the discounting process (the maturity value minus the bank discount).
5. If a discounted note is dishonored, the original holder of the note may be liable for payment unless the note was endorsed without recourse. This is called contingent liability.

Bank discount: What the bank charges to hold a note until maturity (maturity value — proceeds).

Contingent liability: Liability on the part of one who discounts a note to pay if the maker of the note defaults at maturity date.

Discounting a note: The process or act of transferring the note to a bank before the maturity date.

Discount period: The amount of time the bank holds a note that was discounted until the maturity date.

Proceeds: Maturity value less bank discount.

LEARNING UNIT 15-4

1. In discounting one's own note, the interest is usually deducted in advance.
2. The interest that is deducted in advance is recorded in a contra-liability account called Discount on Notes Payable.
3. The effective interest rate is higher than the stated rate.
4. At the end of the period, adjustments are made for Interest Income and Interest Expense that have accrued or built up. These entries can be reversed on the first day starting the next period to simplify recording when interest is paid or received in the new period.
5. The interest in the Discount on Notes Payable account is adjusted by reducing the Discount on Notes Payable and recording it as interest expense.

Discount on Notes Payable: The amount of interest deducted in advance by the lender. This account reduces Notes Payable to actual cash value.

Effective interest rate: The true rate of simple interest.

BLUEPRINT FOR NOTES PAYABLE AND NOTES RECEIVABLE

SELLER

Sales of merchandise on account

Accounts Receivable, XXX		
Sales		

Time extension with a note

Notes Receivable		
Accounts Receivable, XXX		

Note due and paid

Cash		
Interest Income		
Notes Receivable		

Note renewed at maturity

Cash		
Notes Receivable (new)		
Notes Receivable (old)		
Interest Income		

Note given in exchange for equipment purchased

Notes Receivable		
Sales		

BUYER

Sales of merchandise on account

Purchases		
Accounts Payable, XXX		

Time extension with a note

Accounts Payable, XXX		
Notes Payable		

Note due and paid

Notes Payable		
Interest Expense		
Cash		

Note renewed at maturity

Notes Payable (old)		
Interest Expense		
Notes Payable (new)		
Cash		

Note given in exchange for equipment purchased

Store Equipment		
Notes Payable		

(continued)

BLUEPRINT FOR NOTES PAYABLE AND NOTES RECEIVABLE (CONT'D)

SITUATIONS AFFECTING SELLER ONLY

Disounting a note— receiving nore than face value

Cash		
Interest Income		
Notes Receivable		

Discounting a note— receiving less than face value

Cash		
Interest Expense		
Notes Receivable		

Discounted note dishonored

Accounts Receivable, XXX		
Cash		

Discounting one's own note

Cash		
Discount on Notes Payable		
Notes Payable		

(continued)

BLUEPRINT FOR NOTES PAYABLE AND NOTES RECEIVABLE (CONT'D)

ADJUSTMENTS	SELLER	BUYER
Adjust interest	19X1 Dec. 31 — Interest Receivable / Interest Income	19X1 Dec. 31 — Interest Expense / Interest Payable
Note paid (no reversing entry was made)	19X2 Feb. 1 — Cash / Interest Receivable / Interest Income / Notes Receivable	19X2 Feb. 1 — Interest Expense / Interest Payable / Notes Payable / Cash
Note paid (reversing entry was made)	Feb. 1 — Cash / Interest Income / Notes Receivable	Feb. 1 — Interest Expense / Notes Payable / Cash
Recognizing interest from discount on Notes Payable	Dec. 1 — Interest Expense / Discount on Notes Payable	

DISCUSSION QUESTIONS

1. List three reasons why a company may use Notes Payable instead of Accounts Payable.
2. Explain the parts of a promissory note.
3. What is the difference between finding a maturity date by (a) days or (b) months?
4. Notes Receivable is a current liability on the balance sheet. Accept or reject. Why?
5. Why is a subsidiary ledger not needed for notes?
6. Only matured notes are listed in the Notes Receivable account. Please discuss.
7. Explain what will happen if a maker defaults on a note. (Assume the note has not been discounted.)
8. List the four steps to arrive at proceeds in the process of discounting a note.
9. What is meant by contingent liability?
10. When could interest be deducted in advance by a lender?
11. What is the normal balance of the Discount on Notes Payable account?
12. How is the effective interest rate calculated?
13. How could Discount on Notes Payable be adjusted?

EXERCISES

Calculating interest. **1.** Calculate the interest for the following:

(a) $14,000   8%   1 year
(b) $20,000   10%   7 months
(c) $ 9,000   12%   80 days

Determining maturity date without tables. **2.** Determine the maturity date for each of the following without the use of tables:

NOTE ISSUED	LENGTH OF TIME
(a) January 17, 19X4	30 days
(b) July 14, 19X4	90 days
(c) May 31, 19X4	4 months
(d) June 25, 19X4	75 days

Determining maturity date by table. **3.** Using the table in the text (p. 524), prove your answers for Exercise 2.

Discounting a note and journalizing entry for proceeds. **4.** On May 15, 19X4, Ralph Co. gave Blue Co. a 180-day, $9,000, 8 percent note. On July 21 Blue Co. discounted the note at 9 percent.

(a) Journalize the entry for Blue to record the proceeds.
(b) Record the entry for Blue if Ralph fails to pay at maturity.

Discount on Notes Payable. **5.** Howard Slater negotiated a bank loan for $30,000 for 120 days at a bank rate of 10 percent. Assuming the interest is deducted in advance, prepare the entry for Howard to record the bank loan.

GROUP A PROBLEMS

15A-1. Journalize the following entries for (1) the buyer and (2) the seller. Record all entries for the buyer first.

Journalizing Notes Receivable and Notes Payable along with note dishonored.

19X9

June	11	Morgan Company sold $5,000 of merchandise on account to Connors Company (terms, net 30 days).
July	11	Morgan received a 90-day, $5,000, 8 percent note for a time extension of past due account of Connors Company.
Oct.	12	Collected the Connors Company note on the maturity date.
Oct.	12	Assuming Connors Company defaulted on its July 11 note, record the dishonored note.
Oct.	18	Connors Company paid the note receivable that was dishonored on October 12 (no additional interest is charged).

15A-2. On May 1, 19X4, Apples Company received a $30,000, 90-day, 9 percent note from Fletcher Company dated May 1. On June 20, 19X4, Apples discounted the note at their Bank at a discount rate of 10 percent.

Identifying steps in discounting a note along with journal entry.

1. Calculate the following:
   (a) Maturity value of the note.
   (b) Number of days the bank will hold the note till maturity date.
   (c) Bank discount.
   (d) Proceeds.
2. Journalize the entry to record the proceeds.

15A-3. Journalize the following transactions for Joye Company:

Discounting of one's own note.

19X1

June	18	Joye discounted its own $40,000, 90-day note at Ontario Bank at 10 percent.
Sept.	16	Paid the amount due on the note of June 18. (Be sure to record interest expense from Discount on Notes Payable.)
Nov.	2	Joye discounted its own $20,000, 120-day note at Ontario Bank at 11 percent.
Dec.	31	Record the adjusting entry for interest expense.

15A-4. Journalize the following transactions for Rochester Company:

Comprehensive Problem. Integration of Notes Receivable and Notes Payable with Allowance for Doubtful Accounts and discounting.

19XX

Apr.	18	Received $15,000, 80-day, 11 percent note from Mark Castle in payment of account past due.
May	9	Wrote off the Hal Balmer account as uncollectible for $600. (Rochester uses the Allowance method to record bad debts.)
July	10	Mark Castle paid Rochester the note in full.
Nov.	11	Gave Reech Company a $9,000, 30-day, 12 percent note as a time extension of account now past due.
Nov.	15	Hal Balmer paid Rochester amount previously written off on May 9.
Dec.	3	Discounted its own $5,000, 90-day note at their bank at 10 percent.
Dec.	5	Received a $10,000, 60-day, 12 percent note dated December 5 from Beverly Fields in payment of account past due.
Dec.	14	Paid principal and interest due on note issued to Reech Company from November 11 note.
Dec.	16	Received a $20,000, 60-day, 11 percent note from Larry Company in payment of account past due.
Dec.	28	Discounted the Beverly Fields note to their bank at 13 percent.
Dec.	31	Recorded adjusting entries as appropriate.

GROUP B PROBLEMS

Journalizing Notes Receivable and Notes Payable along with note dishonored.

15B-1. Journalize the following entries for (1) the buyer and (2) the seller.

19X9

July 10   Morgan Company sold $6,000 of merchandise on account to Connors Company (terms, net 30 days).

Aug. 10   Morgan received a 90-day, $6,000, 9 percent note for a time extension of past due account of Connors Company.

Nov. 11   Collected the Connors Company note on the maturity date.

Nov. 11   Assuming Connors Company defaulted on November 8, record the dishonored note.

Nov. 19   Connors Company paid the note receivable that was dishonored on November 11 (no additional interest is charged).

Identifying steps in discounting a note along with journal entry.

15B-2. On June 2, 19X4, Apples Company received a $40,000, 90-day, 11 percent note from Fletcher Company dated June 2. On July 16, 19X4, Apples discounted the note at their Bank at a discount rate of 12 percent.

1. Calculate the following:
   (a) Maturity value of the note.
   (b) Number of days the bank will hold the note till maturity date.
   (c) Bank discount.
   (d) Proceeds.
2. Journalize the entry to record the proceeds.

Discounting of one's own note.

15B-3. As the bookkeeper of Joye Company, record in the general journal the following transactions:

19X2

May   9   Joye discounted its own $25,000, 90-day note at Ontario Bank at 10 percent.

Aug.   7   Paid the amount due on the note of May 9. (Be sure to record interest expense from Discount on Note Payable.)

Oct.   7   Joye discounted its own $18,000, 120-day note at Ontario Bank at 11 percent.

Dec. 31   Record the adjusting entry for interest expense.

Comprehensive Problem. Integration of Notes Receivable and Notes Payable with Allowance for Doubtful Accounts and discounting.

15B-4. Record the following entries into the general journal of Rochester Company:

19XX

May   12   Received $13,000, 90-day, 9 percent note from Mark Castle in payment of account past due.

June 15   Wrote off the Hal Balmer account as uncollectible for $900 using the Allowance method.

Aug. 13   Mark Castle paid Rochester the note in full.

Nov.   2   Gave Reech Company a $20,000, 30-day, 8 percent note as a time extension of account now past due.

Nov. 18   Hal Balmer paid Rochester amount previously written off on June 15.

Dec.   2   Discounted its own $10,000, 90-day note at their bank at 9 percent.

Dec.   2   Received a $6,000, 60-day, 11 percent note dated December 3 from Beverly Fields in payment of account past due.

Dec.   5   Paid principal and interest due on note issued to Reech Company from November 2 note.

Dec. 16   Received a $2,000, 60-day, 11 percent note from Larry Company in payment of account past due.

Dec. 28   Discounted the Beverly Fields note to their bank at 12 percent.

Dec. 31   Recorded adjusting entries as appropriate.

GROUP C PROBLEMS

15C-1. Journalize the following entries for (1) the buyer and (2) the seller. Record all entries for the buyer first.

19X9

June 11 Campbell Company sold $8,000 of merchandise on account to Alexis Company (terms, net 30 days).

July 11 Campbell received a 90-day, $8,000, 9 percent note for a time extension of past due account of Alexis Company.

Oct. 12 Collected the Alexis Company note on the maturity date.

Oct. 12 Assuming Alexis Company defaulted on its July 11 note, record the dishonored note.

Oct. 18 Alexis Company paid the note receivable that was dishonored on October 12 (no additional interest is charged).

Journalizing Notes Receivable and Notes Payable along with note dishonored.

15C-2. On May 1, 19X4, Wynott Company received a $50,000, 120-day, 7 percent note from Flemming Company dated May 1. On June 20, 19X4, Wynott discounted the note at their Bank at a discount rate of 9 percent.

1. Calculate the following:
   (a) Maturity value of the note.
   (b) Number of days the bank will hold the note till maturity date.
   (c) Bank discount.
   (d) Proceeds.
2. Journalize the entry to record the proceeds.

Identifying steps in discounting a note along with journal entry.

15C-3. Journalize the following transactions for Ballis Company:

19X1

June 18 Ballis discounted its own $70,000, 60-day note at Ontario Bank at 12 percent.

Aug. 20 Paid the amount due on the note of June 18. (Be sure to record interest expense from Discount on Notes Payable.)

Nov. 2 Ballis discounted its own $40,000, 180-day note at Ontario Bank at 10 percent.

Dec. 31 Record the adjusting entry for interest expense.

Discounting of one's own note.

15C-4. Journalize the following transactions for Dynamic Company:

19XX

Apr. 18 Received $25,000, 90-day, 10 percent note from Else Ellford in payment of account past due.

May 9 Wrote off the Vic Hallfor account as uncollectible for $800. (Dynamic uses the Allowance method to record bad debts.)

July 20 Else Ellford paid Dynamic the note in full.

Nov. 11 Gave Quincy Company a $12,000, 30-day, 11 percent note as a time extension of account now past due.

Nov. 15 Vic Hallfor paid Dynamic half of the amount previously written off on May 9.

Dec. 3 Discounted its own $15,000, 120-day note at their bank at 12 percent.

Dec. 5 Received a $24,000, 90-day, 14 percent note dated December 5 from Angela Brown in payment of account past due.

Dec. 14 Paid principal and interest due on note issued to Quincy Company from November 11 note.

Comprehensive Problem. Integration of Notes Receivable and Notes Payable with Allowance for Doubtful Accounts and discounting.

Dec. 16 Received a $27,500, 60-day, 12 percent note from Copper Company in payment of account past due.

Dec. 28 Discounted the Angela Brown note to their bank at 15 percent.

Dec. 31 Recorded adjusting entries as appropriate.

PRACTICAL ACCOUNTING APPLICATION #1

Abby Scale, the bookkeeper of Roland Company, is having difficulty calculating the amount that is due Agent Company on March 19. Based on the following information, prepare a detailed calculation of the amount due Agent.

Roland issued Agent a $2,000, 60-day, 12 percent note dated December 19, 19X1. Roland was notified by Agent's Bank that the note had been discounted by Agent and the note would be payable to them. On February 18 the bookkeeper of Roland became ill and the note wasn't paid. Agent's Bank notified Agent and charged them an additional $9 protest fee. On March 19 Abby decided to pay Agent the amount owed. Agent indicated they were charging the maturity value of the note, the protest fee, and interest on both for 30 days beyond maturity at 14 percent.

PRACTICAL ACCOUNTING APPLICATION #2

Moe Ring has left the following notes on your desk. As the new bookkeeper of Ryan Company you realize that no adjusting entries were made in 19X1.

Notes Receivable	
11/25/X1	$20,000
12%	150 days

Notes Payable	
12/16/X1	$33,600
15%	30 days

(a) Please prepare the appropriate adjusting entries.

(b) Moe would like to know whether reversing entries are needed. Prepare a set of T accounts to show what would result on the books in the year 19X2 when the notes are paid (1) if there are no reversing entries, and (2) if reversing entries are made.

ACCOUNTING RECALL
A Cumulative Approach

THIS EXAM REVIEWS CHAPTERS 1 THROUGH 15

Your *Study Guide and Working Papers* have forms to complete this exam, as well as worked-out solutions. The page references next to each question identify what page to turn back to if you answer the question incorrectly.

PART I Vocabulary Review

Match the terms to the appropriate definition or phrase.

Page Ref.

(533)	1. Proceeds	A. Face amount of note
(496)	2. Allowance for doubtful accounts	B. Principal and interest
(522)	3. Notes payable	C. Cost of goods sold account
(528)	4. Maturity value	D. Bank charge
(522)	5. Maker	E. Contra revenue account
(536)	6. Discount on notes payable	F. A liability
(227)	7. Purchases	G. Maturity value less bank discount
(531)	8. Bank discount	H. Reduces notes payable to actual cash value
(179)	9. Sales returns and allowances	I. Contra asset
(522)	10. Principal	J. One promising to pay a note

PART II True or False (Accounting Theory)

(536) 11. Discount on notes payable is a Contra asset account.

(533) 12. Maturity value less bank discount equals proceeds.

(538) 13. When a note is discounted and you receive more than face value it is interest expense.

(522) 14. The payee is the one who will pay the promissory note.

(359) 15. The three tax responsibilities of an employee, include FIT, CPP, and UI.

PART III Applications Problem (531-532)

From the following complete the four steps to discounting a note and provide the general journal entry.

On November 18, Broome Company discounted an $18,000, 12%, 120-day note dated September 8. Use ordinary interest in your calculation.

ACCOUNTING FOR MERCHANDISE INVENTORY

IN THIS CHAPTER WE WILL COVER THE FOLLOWING TOPICS:

1. CALCULATING THE COST OF ENDING INVENTORY AND COST OF GOODS SOLD USING FOUR DIFFERENT METHODS: SPECIFIC INVOICE, WEIGHTED-AVERAGE, FIRST-IN-FIRST-OUT, AND LAST-IN-FIRST-OUT. (P. 553)

2. CALCULATING ENDING INVENTORY BY THE RETAIL METHOD AND THE GROSS PROFIT METHOD. (P. 560)

3. JOURNALIZING TRANSACTIONS IN A PERPETUAL INVENTORY SYSTEM. (P. 564)

Have you ever had the experience at Christmas time of thinking up the perfect present for someone, only to find that everyone else in the world had the same idea, and the stores were out of stock? In recent years we have seen this happen with home computers, video games, and so on. Having the right quantities of inventory is crucial to a retail business: It's bad to run out of stock and miss out on sales revenue, especially at Christmas, but it's also harmful to have too much of an item. A store must consider the cost of carrying inventory, and it must also worry about product obsolescence or the possibility of a fad running out before all the products are sold.

In Chapter 12 we discussed the periodic inventory system, in which inventory is checked and counted only at the beginning and end of the accounting period. In this chapter we will look again at this inventory system, but we will look closer at how to assign a cost to ending inventory and the effect of this cost assignment on the financial reports.

In the last part of the chapter we will discuss how to assign costs to inventory using a *perpetual inventory system*—a system in which the inventory account is updated constantly by each sale or purchase of inventory made during the period.

LEARNING UNIT 16-1

How to Assign Costs to Ending Inventory Items

The method one uses to assign costs to ending inventory will have a direct effect on the company's cost of goods sold and profit. Look at the accompanying diagram and note that in each column ending inventory has a different value assigned to it. Note also how this affects gross profit in each of the four columns.

	A		B		C		D	
Net sales		$50,000		$50,000		$50,000		$50,000
Beginning Inventory	$ 4,000		$ 4,000		$ 4,000		$ 4,000	
Net Purchases	20,000		20,000		20,000		20,000	
Cost of Goods								
Available for Sale	24,000		24,000		24,000		24,000	
Ending Inventory	5,000		6,000		7,000		8,000	
Cost of Goods Sold		19,000		18,000		17,000		16,000
Gross Profit		$31,000		$32,000		$33,000		$34,000

If all inventory brought into a store had the same cost, it would be simple to calculate ending inventory, and we would not have to have this chapter in the book. Unfortunately, things are not that easy; often the very same products are purchased and brought into the store at different costs during the same accounting period. Over the years there have been developed four generally accepted methods to assign a cost to ending inventory. They are: (1) specific invoice, (2) weighted-average, (3) first-in, first-out, and (4) last-in, first-out. Each is based on the flow of costs, not the flow of goods (the actual physical movement of goods sold in a store).

SPECIFIC INVOICE METHOD

Jones Hardware sells rakes. At the end of the period 12 rakes remain unsold. Notice in the accompanying diagram that on January 1, at the start of the accounting period, 10 rakes were on hand, but during the period additional purchases of rakes were made. The price given in the diagram is the purchase price paid by the store—it is not the same as the selling price, which is what the store charges its customers for the rakes. The selling price is not involved here. At the bottom of the diagram you can see that 44 rakes cost Jones Hardware $543.

	GOODS AVAILABLE FOR SALE			CALCULATING COST OF ENDING INVENTORY		
	UNITS	COST	TOTAL	UNITS	COST	TOTAL
January 1 Beg. Inventory	10	@ $10 =	$100			
March 15 Purchased	9	@ 12 =	108	6	@ $12	$72
August 18 Purchased	20	@ 13 =	260	6	@ 13	78
November 15 Purchased	5	@ 15 =	75			
	44		$543	12		$150

Cost of Goods Available for Sale $543
Less: Cost of Ending Inventory   150
= Cost of Goods Sold $393

In the **specific invoice method**, one assigns the cost of ending inventory by identifying each item in that inventory by a specific purchase price and invoice number. Items can be identified by serial number, physical description, or location. Using this method, Jones Hardware knew that 6 of the rakes not sold were from the March 15 invoice and the other 6 were from the August 18 purchase. Thus $150 was assigned as the actual cost of ending inventory. If the total cost of goods available for sale is $543 and we subtract the actual cost of ending inventory ($150), this method provides a figure of $393 for cost of goods sold.

Let's look at pros and cons of this method:

SPECIFIC INVOICE METHOD

PROS

1. Simple to use if company has small amount of high-cost goods—for example, autos, jewels, boats, antiques, and so on.
2. Flow of goods and flow of cost are the same.
3. Costs are matched with the sales they helped to produce.

CONS

1. Difficult to use for goods with large unit volume and small unit prices—for example, nails at a hardware store, packages of toothpaste at a drug store.
2. Difficult to use for decision-making purposes—ordinarily an impractical approach.

WEIGHTED-AVERAGE METHOD

The **weighted-average method** calculates an average unit cost by dividing the *total cost* of goods available for sale by the *total units* of goods available for sale. Since we don't know exactly *which* items are left in ending inventory, we will calculate the average of all the goods we have available in order to come up with a fair approximation of the cost of the ending inventory.

	GOODS AVAILABLE FOR SALE		
	UNITS	COST	TOTAL
January 1 Beg. Inventory	10 @	$10 =	$100
March 15 Purchased	9 @	12 =	108
August 18 Purchased	20 @	13 =	260
November 15 Purchased	5 @	15 =	75
	44		$543

$\frac{\$543}{44}$ = $12.34 weighted-average cost per unit

12 rakes x $12.34 = $148.08

Cost of Goods Available for Sale	$543.00
Less: Cost of Ending Inventory	148.08
= Cost of Goods Sold	$394.92

Here are pros and cons of this method:

WEIGHTED-AVERAGE METHOD

PROS
1. Weighted-average takes into account the number of units purchased at each amount, not a simple average cost. Good for products sold in large volume, such as grains and fuels.
2. Accountant assigns an equal unit cost to each unit of inventory; thus, when the income statement is prepared, net income will not fluctuate as much as with other methods.

CONS
1. Current prices have no more significance than prices of goods bought months earlier.
2. Compared with other methods, the most recent costs are *not* matched with current sales.
3. Cost of ending inventory is not as up to date as it could be using another method.

FIRST-IN, FIRST-OUT METHOD (FIFO)

In the **FIFO method**, one assumes that the oldest goods (rakes, in this case) are sold first. In other words, the first merchandise brought into the store tends to be sold first. Indeed, it is often the sale of these items that prompts the store to buy more of them—as they start to run out, the store purchases more. When costs are assigned in the FIFO method, the cost of the last items brought into the store is assigned to ending inventory and the inventory sold is assigned to cost of goods sold. For example, using our Jones Hardware situation, the ending inventory of 12 rakes on hand is assigned a cost from the last two purchases of rakes (purchases made on November 15 and some purchases made on August 18), $166. Using the FIFO method, it is always assumed that it is the most recently purchased merchandise that has not been sold. Look at how this works out in the following diagram.

	GOODS AVAILABLE FOR SALE			CALCULATING COST OF ENDING INVENTORY		
	UNITS	COST	TOTAL	UNITS	COST	TOTAL
January 1 Beg. Inventory	10	@ $10	= $100			
March 15 Purchased	9	@ 12	= 108			
August 18 Purchased	20	@ 13	= 260	7	@ $13	$ 91
November 15 Purchased	5	@ 15	= 75	5	@ 15	75
	44		$543	12		$166

Cost of Goods Available for Sale $543
Less: Cost of Ending Inventory   166
= Cost of Goods Sold $377

If you are having difficulty with this, think of the inventory as being taken from the bottom layer first, then the next one up, and the next one up, and so on.

The following are the pros and cons of this method:

FIFO METHOD

PROS
1. The cost flow tends to follow the physical flow (most businesses try to sell the old goods first—for example, perishables such as fruit or vegetables).
2. The figure for ending inventory is made up of current costs on the balance sheet (since inventory left over is assumed to be from goods last brought into the store).

CONS
1. During inflation this method will produce higher income on the income statement—thus more taxes to be paid. (We will discuss this later in the chapter.)
2. Recent costs are not matched with recent sales, since we assume *old* goods are sold first.

LAST-IN, FIRST-OUT METHOD (LIFO)

Cost of ending inventory is made up of the *old* inventory.

Under the **LIFO method**, it is assumed that the rakes *most recently acquired* by Jones are sold first. In other words, the last merchandise brought into the store is the first to be sold. As an example of this method, think of a barrel of nails. It is the most recently purchased nails, which are at the top of the barrel, that are sold first—the nails at the bottom of the barrel are sold last. Note in the table at the top of p. 557 that the 12 rakes not sold were assigned costs based on the old inventory of January and March that totaled $124, giving Jones a cost of goods sold of $419.

LIFO assumes *opposite* flow of FIFO.

	GOODS AVAILABLE FOR SALE			CALCULATING COST OF ENDING INVENTORY		
	UNITS	COST	TOTAL	UNITS	COST	TOTAL
January 1 Beg. Inventory	10	@ $10 =	$100	10	@ $10 =	$100
March 15 Purchased	9	@ 12 =	108	2	@ 12 =	24
August 18 Purchased	20	@ 13 =	260			
November 15 Purchased	5	@ 15 =	75			
	44		$543	12		$124

Cost of Goods Available for Sale $543
Less: Cost of Ending Inventory   124
= Cost of Goods Sold $419

These are the pros and cons of this method:

LIFO METHOD

PROS

1. Cost of goods sold is stated at or near current costs, since costs of *latest* goods acquired are used.
2. Matches current costs with current selling prices.
3. During inflation this method produces the lowest net income, which is a tax advantage. (The lower cost of ending inventory means a higher cost of goods sold; with a higher cost of goods sold, gross profit and ultimately net income are smaller, and thus taxes are lower.)

CONS

1. Ending inventory is valued at very old prices.
2. Doesn't match physical flow of goods (but can still be used to calculate flow of costs).

Now we will compare the methods that could be used by Jones Hardware to see the cost of ending inventory and the assigned cost of goods sold.

COMPARISON OF METHODS FOR JONES HARDWARE

	COST OF ENDING INVENTORY	COST OF GOODS SOLD
Specific Invoice	$150.00	$393.00
Weighted-Average	148.08	394.92
FIFO	166.00	377.00
LIFO	124.00	419.00

All four methods are acceptable accounting procedures, and each has its own virtues:

1. This specific invoice method matches exactly costs with revenue—as we have noted before, this is very important in the accrual basis of accounting.
2. The weighted-average method tends to smooth out the fluctuations between FIFO and LIFO.
3. FIFO provides an up-to-date picture of inventory on the balance sheet, since it uses the latest purchases to calculate ending inventory.
4. When prices are rising, LIFO shows the highest costs of goods sold and thus provides some tax advantages.

In accounting there is a **principle of consistency**, which means that once a business selects a particular accounting method, it should follow it consistently from year to year without switching to another method. In the first part of this unit we saw four methods of inventory valuations causing four different results for a business in terms of cost of goods sold and ultimately net income. Therefore, if a company kept switching from LIFO to FIFO each year, significant changes would result in the profit it reported. The financial reports would become undependable. Keeping to the same method lets readers of the financial reports make meaningful comparisons of cost of ending inventory, cost of goods sold, etc., from one year to the next.

The principle of consistency doesn't mean that a company can *never* change from one method of inventory valuation to another. If a change is decided upon, however, the company should fully disclose the change, the effects of the change on profit and inventory valuation, and the justification for change in a footnote on the financial report. This is called the **full disclosure principle** in accounting.

Let's look now at some situations in which a decision must be made about including certain items in the cost of inventory stated on the financial reports.

WHICH ITEMS SHOULD BE INCLUDED IN THE COST OF INVENTORY

Situation 1: Goods in Transit

Goods in transit with terms F.O.B. shipping point are added to cost of inventory.

On the date that inventory is taken, goods in transit should be added to inventory if the firm has ownership of it. For example, goods that Alden Co. buys F.O.B. shipping point would be included in the firm's inventory, since title passes to Alden at shipping point, even though Alden has not yet received the goods.

Situation 2: Goods on Consignment

Goods should be added to the consignor's inventory and not the agent's.

Consignment means that a company (the **consignor**) is selling its goods through an agent (the **consignee**) who doesn't own the goods but has possession of them. Consigned goods belong to the consignor and thus will be added to the consignor's inventory and not to the consignee's.

Situation 3: Damaged or Obsolete Goods

Unsaleable goods are not added to the cost of inventory.

If the goods are not saleable, they should *not* be added to cost of inventory. For those goods that are saleable at a lower price, a conservative estimate should be made of their value and added to the cost of inventory.

At this point you should be able to

1. Calculate cost of ending inventory and cost of goods sold by specific invoice, weighted-average, first-in, first-out, and last-in, first-out method. (pp. 553-557)
2. Explain the pros and cons of each method used to calculate cost of ending inventory and cost of goods sold. (pp. 553-557)
3. Explain the principles of consistency and full disclosure. (p. 558)
4. Explain how goods in transit, goods on consignment, and damaged or obsolete goods are counted in calculating inventory. (p. 558)

☐ SELF-REVIEW QUIZ 16-1

1. From the information given below, calculate the cost of ending inventory as well as the cost of goods sold, using the (a) specific invoice, (b) weighted-average, (c) first-in, first-out, and (d) last-in, first-out methods.

	GOODS AVAILABLE FOR SALE			ADDITIONAL FACT:
	UNITS	COST	TOTAL	INVENTORY NOT SOLD
January 1 Beg. Inventory	40	@ $8 =	$320	
April 1 Purchased	20	@ 9 =	180	40 from January 1
May 1 Purchased	20	@ 10 =	200	4 from May 1
October 1 Purchased	20	@ 12 =	240	4 from October 1
December 1 Purchased	20	@ 13 =	260	
	120		$1,200	

2. Respond True or False to the following:
   (a) It is possible for a company to change from LIFO to FIFO if it follows specific guidelines.
   (b) Goods in transit (shipped F.O.B. shipping point) will not be included as part of the inventory for the purchaser.
   (c) Damaged goods are always added to the cost of inventory.

■ *SOLUTIONS TO SELF-REVIEW QUIZ 16-1*

1. (a) Total cost of goods available for sale $1,200
       Less ending inventory based on specific invoices:
          40 units from Jan. 1 purchased at $8 $320
           4 units from May 1 purchased at $10   40
           4 units from Oct. 1 purchased at $12   48
          48 units in ending inventory   408
       Cost of goods sold $ 792

    (b) $1,200 ÷ 120 units = $10 weighted-average cost per unit.
       Total cost of goods available for sale $1,200
       Less ending inventory priced at weighted-
       average basis: 48 units at $10.00   480
       Cost of goods sold $ 720

    (c) Total cost of goods available for sale $1,200
       Less ending inventory priced on FIFO:
          20 units from Dec. 1 at $13 $260
          20 units from Oct. 1 at $12   240
           8 units from May 1 at $10   80
          48 units in ending inventory   580
       Cost of goods sold $ 620

(d) Total cost of goods available for sale $1,200
      Less ending inventory priced on LIFO:
          40 units from Jan. 1 at $8 $320
           8 units from April 1 purchased at $9   72
          48 units in ending inventory   392
      Cost of goods sold $ 808

2. (a) true;   (b) false;   (c) false.

LEARNING UNIT 16-2

Lower-of-Cost-or-Market Principle; Retail Method; Gross Profit Method

Market **doesn't mean what goods will sell for. It stands for replacement cost.**

So far we have estimated the value of ending inventory by looking at the cost that was paid to bring it into the store. Over the years a traditional conservative principle in accounting has been to price inventory at the **lower of cost or market**. The objective is to place all items on the balance sheet at a conservative figure. *Market* means what it *would have* cost to purchase or replace the goods on that inventory date. By choosing the lower of the two figures, we place a conservative figure for inventory on the balance sheet. In the USA, the procedure for determining the lower of cost and market can be quite complex. Here in Canada, the rule is actually fairly simple: use cost (LIFO, FIFO or whatever) or market—whichever is the lower. Sometimes companies must make a decision as to whether to apply the rule to the whole of inventory, classes of inventory, or to each item in inventory. As long as this decision is made carefully and the results applied in the same way from year to year, the financial results are not materially distorted.

HOW TO ESTIMATE ENDING INVENTORY

Inventory is recorded below cost or replacement cost, since selling price less selling expense is less than current replacement cost.

Retail stores often will prepare interim financial reports (monthly or quarterly) to give managers a basis for decision making. Continually taking a physical inventory of their goods would be time-consuming and expensive. Thus many merchandising businesses estimate their inventory on hand by the **retail method**, a technique for estimating inventory for retail businesses. To use this method, a business must have the following information available:

If there were freight-in charges, they would be added to cost of net purchases.

1. Beginning inventory at cost and at retail (selling price).
2. Cost of net purchases at both cost and at retail.
3. The net sales at retail.

Let's look at the following diagram to see how French Company estimates ending inventory at cost by the retail method.

THE RETAIL INVENTORY METHOD		COST	RETAIL
	Goods Available for Sale:		
	Beginning Inventory	$4,100	$6,900
	Net Purchases	7,900	13,100
Step 1 →	Cost of Goods Available for Sale	$12,000	$20,000
Step 2 →	Cost Ratio (relationship between cost and retail)	$\frac{\$12,000}{\$20,000} = 60\%$	
Step 3 ⇄	Net Sales at Retail		14,100
	Inventory at Retail		$ 6,000
Step 4 →	Ending Inventory at Cost, $6,000 x 0.6	$ 3,600	

French completed the following steps to arrive at the ending inventory cost of $3,600.

Step 1   Calculate cost of goods available for sale at cost and retail.

Step 2   Calculate the cost ratio (cost of goods available for sale at cost divided by cost of goods available for sale at retail). It cost French Company 60 cents for each $1 of sales for these goods.

Step 3   Deduct net sales from retail value of goods available for sale to arrive at an estimated ending inventory at retail.

Step 4   Multiply cost ratio (.60) times ending inventory at retail to arrive at ending inventory at cost. In this case, since 60 cents for each $1 of retail represents cost and we have $6,000 at retail, the end result is $3,600 in cost.

Keep in mind that at year-end French will take a physical inventory.

GROSS PROFIT METHOD

Another method of estimating ending inventory without taking a physical count is the **gross profit method**. This method develops a relationship among sales, cost of goods sold, and gross profit in estimating the cost of ending inventory.

To use this method a company would have to keep track of the following:

1. Average gross profit rate.
2. Net sales, beginning inventory, net purchases.

Freight, if any, would be added to cost of net purchases.

The steps Moose Company takes to estimate its ending inventory are shown in the accompanying diagram. We assume a normal gross profit rate of 30 percent of net sales. If 30 cents on a dollar is profit, 70 cents on a dollar is cost.

THE GROSS PROFIT METHOD			
	Goods Available for Sale:		
	Inventory, January 1, 19XX		$10,000
	Net Purchases		4,000
Step 1 →	Cost of Goods Available for Sale		$14,000
	Less: Estimated Cost of Goods Sold:		
	Net Sales at Retail	$6,000	
Step 2 →	Cost percentage (100% – 30%)	.70	
	Estimated Cost of Goods Sold		4,200
Step 3 →	Estimated Inventory, January 31, 19XX		$ 9,800

Step 1   Moose determines cost of goods available for sale (beginning inventory plus net purchases).

Step 2   Moose estimates cost of goods sold by multiplying cost percentage (70%) times net sales.

Step 3   Moose subtracts cost of goods sold from cost of goods available for sale to arrive at an estimated inventory of $9,800.

This method, besides helping prepare financial reports, can help determine the amount of inventory on hand due to a fire or can verify at end of year the accuracy of the physical inventory.

Before concluding this unit, let's look at how an error made in calculating ending inventory will affect financial reports.

HOW INCORRECT CALCULATION OF ENDING INVENTORY AFFECTS FINANCIAL REPORTS

As we have stated before, an incorrect figure in ending inventory can have an effect on cost of goods sold, gross profit, net income, and current assets as well as owner's capital. Let's look at the diagram below to see—if a mistake is in fact made—what items on the income statement will be affected and what the mistake's impact will be over time.

	CORRECT		INCORRECT	
	19X1	19X2	19X1	19X2
Sales	$200	$300	$200	$300
Cost of Goods Sold:				
Beginning Inventory	$30	$70	$30	$60
Purchases	95	85	95	85
Goods Available for Sale	125	155	125	145
Ending Inventory	−70 55	−100 55	−60 65	−100 45
Gross Profit	$145	$245	$135	$255

SUMMARY

	CORRECT	INCORRECT	DIFFERENCE
Year X1, Gross Profit	$145	$135	−$10
Year X2, Gross Profit	245	255	+ 10
Total effect of mistake after 2 periods			0

Note in the diagram that when the *incorrect* figure of $60 is used for ending inventory in 19X1, it causes cost of goods sold to be $65 instead of $55 and profit to be $135 instead of $145. In other words, when ending inventory is understated ($60 instead of $70), cost of goods sold is overstated and profit is understated.

19X1

When Ending Inventory is Understated $60 instead of $70	Cost of Goods Sold is Overstated $65 instead of $55	Profit is Understated $135 instead of $145

As we look next at 19X2, we see that the ending incorrect inventory of 19X1 is carried as the beginning inventory of 19X2. Thus the understatement of beginning inventory in 19X2 of $60 (instead of $70) causes cost of goods sold to be understated and net income to be overstated.

19X2

| When Beginning Inventory is Understated $60 instead of $70 | Cost of Goods Sold is Understated $45 instead of $55 | Profit is Overstated $255 instead of $245 |

Thus, at the end of 19X2, the error will be self-correcting.

To review, look at the table that follows and prove it to yourself by going back over the previous explanation.

IF THE ITEM IS	OVERSTATED	UNDERSTATED
Beginning Inventory	Profit is Understated	Profit is Overstated
Ending Inventory	Profit is Overstated	Profit is Understated

Ending Inventory works in same direction as Profit. Beginning Inventory is inversely related.

Keep in mind that since ending inventory is recorded as a current asset on the balance sheet, any mistake will cause the assets to be under- or overstated. The statement of owner's equity would also be affected, since we have seen that the net income will be over- or understated.

At this point you should be able to

1. Explain the lower-of-cost-or-market principle. (p. 560)
2. Calculate ending inventory by the retail method. (p. 560)
3. Calculate ending inventory by the gross profit method. (p. 561)
4. Explain how understating or overstating ending inventory will affect financial reports. (pp. 562-563)

☐ SELF-REVIEW QUIZ 16-2

1. Alon Company needs to estimate its month-end inventory. From the following, estimate the cost of ending inventory on September 30 by the retail method:

	COST	RETAIL
Beginning Inventory	$ 8,000	$10,000
Net Purchases	40,000	60,000
Net Sales		30,000

(Carry out the cost ratio to nearest hundredth percent.)

2. Respond True or False to the following:
    (a) Selling price does not necessarily follow cost decreases of goods.
    (b) The lower-of-cost-or-market is not modified to monitor the movement of the selling price.
    (c) Market cost means replacement cost, not selling price.
    (d) If ending inventory is overstated, net income will be overstated.
    (e) If beginning inventory is overstated, net income will be overstated.

■ SOLUTIONS TO SELF-REVIEW QUIZ 16-2

		COST	RETAIL
1.	Beginning Inventory	$ 8,000	$10,000
	Net Purchases	40,000	60,000
	Cost of Goods Available for Sale	$48,000	70,000
	Cost Ratio, $48,000/$70,000 = 68.57%		
	Net Sales at Retail		30,000
	Inventory at Retail		$40,000
	Ending Inventory at Cost,		
	$40,000 × .6857	$27,428	

2. (a) true;   (b) false;   (c) true;   (d) true;   (e) false.

LEARNING UNIT 16-3

Perpetual Inventory System

Up to this point we have presented only periodic inventory systems. Many companies use instead a perpetual inventory system. A **perpetual inventory system** is an accounting system that keeps a continual running balance of the inventory account. Every time a company buys inventory, the Merchandise Inventory account is increased, and every time a company sells inventory, the Merchandise Inventory account is decreased, so that at any time the company will know how much inventory is on hand. Years ago this system was good only for companies that handled high-priced products in limited numbers. Companies with products such as autos, boats, heavy machinery, etc., would use a perpetual inventory system. However, with the use of the computer, many more businesses are able to continually monitor their inventory and thus provide better internal control.

To get a better idea of what makes up the perpetual system, let's look at the comparison chart on p. 565.

Cost of Goods Sold

XXX	
Normal balance	

Will be closed at year's end.

This account records the cost of units sold.

Note in transaction (A) that in the periodic system the Merchandise Inventory account is not updated, while in the perpetual system the sale is recorded along with Merchandise Inventory reduced (sold), and Cost of Goods Sold is immediately recognized (when inventory is sold, the asset is reduced and shown as a cost). In transaction (B), when more inventory is purchased, the perpetual system records additional purchases in the Inventory account, while in the periodic system there is a separate Purchases account. Note in transaction (C) that the freight in the perpetual system is added directly to Inventory. In transaction (D), when goods are returned by the purchaser, the perpetual system reduces Inventory directly, while in the periodic system there is a separate account called Purchases Returns and Allowances. In other words, in a perpetual system, Purchases, Freight, and Purchases Returns and Allowances accounts *do not* exist; Inventory is updated immediately.

Transaction	Periodic System		Perpetual System	
(A) Sold merchandise on account for $20,000 that cost $8,000.	Acc. Rec.	20 000 00	Acc. Rec.	20 000 00
	Sales	20 000 00	Sales	20 000 00
			Cost of Goods Sold	8 000 00
			Merch. Inv.	8 000 00
B) Purchased $900 of merchandise on account.	Purchases	9 00 00	Merch. Inv.	9 00 00
	Acc. Pay.	9 00 00	Acc. Payable	9 00 00
C) Paid freight charge, $50.	Freight-in	5 0 00	Merch. Inv.	5 0 00
	Cash	5 0 00	Cash	5 0 00
D) Returned $400 of merchandise previously bought on account due to defects.	Acc. Pay.	4 00 00	Acc. Payable	4 00 00
	Pur. Ret. and Allow.	4 00 00	Merch. Inv.	4 00 00

When a perpetual system is used, a detailed inventory record is kept manually or by computer. For some retail firms, the cash register is actually a point-of-sale computer, which records merchandise sold as well as updating the inventory records. Figure 16-1 shows an example of an inventory record.

A perpetual system aids in preparing interim reports, because there is an up-to-date balance in Inventory and Cost of Goods Sold.

Inventory Control

Item <u>VX113</u>
Description <u>Digital Clock</u>
Location <u>Storeroom 1</u>

Maximum <u>22</u>
Reorder Level <u>12</u>
Recorder Quantity <u>10</u>

	Received			Sold			Balance		
Date	Units	Cost per Unit	Total	Units	Cost per Unit	Total	Units	Cost per Unit	Total
19XX Jan 1	Balance		FWD				14	50	$ 700
12				2	50	100	12	50	600
19	10	60	600				12	50	
							10	60	1,200
25				8	50	400	4	50	
							10	60	800

FIGURE 16-1

An Inventory Record

Other companies could use LIFO, weighted-average, etc., in a perpetual system.

In this inventory control sheet the company is using the FIFO method to evaluate its inventory. Note on January 25, when 8 items were sold, they were assumed to be sold from the old inventory of 12 units, thus leaving a balance of 4 old units along with 10 of the new units. At end of year all the inventory cards' year-end balances are added, with the total equaling the Inventory account (the controlling account) in the general ledger. There may be need for adjustments due to theft, spoilage, and so on. Please remember that the perpetual inventory system does not eliminate the need for an annual physical count of inventory.

At this point you should be able to

1. Compare and contrast a perpetual inventory system to a periodic inventory system. (p. 564)
2. Journalize entries for a perpetual inventory system. (pp. 564-565)
3. Calculate cost of ending inventory using an inventory control sheet. (p. 565)

□ **SELF-REVIEW QUIZ 16-3**

Journalize the following transactions for a firm that uses a perpetual inventory system.

(A) Sold $200 of merchandise on account that cost $50.
(B) Purchased $250 of merchandise on account.
(C) Paid freight of $30.
(D) Returned $300 of merchandise previously bought on account.

■ *SOLUTIONS TO SELF-REVIEW QUIZ 16-3*

(A) Accounts Receivable	200	
Sales		200
Cost of Goods Sold	50	
Merchandise Inventory		50
(B) Merchandise Inventory	250	
Accounts Payable		250
(C) Merchandise Inventory	30	
Cash		30
(D) Accounts Payable	300	
Merchandise Inventory		300

SUMMARY OF KEY POINTS

LEARNING UNIT 16-1

1. In assigning a cost to ending inventory, the flow of goods may not follow the actual flow of costs.
2. The specific invoice method identifies each item in inventory with a specific invoice in assigning a cost of ending inventory. It matches costs exactly with revenues.
3. The weighted-average method provides an average unit cost of all inventory. It is a compromise between LIFO and FIFO.
4. FIFO assumes the old goods are sold first. Since ending inventory is valued at most recent costs, FIFO provides the most realistic figure for ending merchandise inventory.

5. LIFO assumes the newest goods are sold first. It provides the most realistic figure for cost of goods sold.

6. During inflation LIFO offers the best tax break.

Consignee: Company or person to whom goods are shipped but who doesn't have ownership.

Consignment: Sales of goods through an agent who has possession but not ownership.

Consignor: The one shipping goods to consignee.

Consistency: The accounting principle that requires companies to follow the same accounting methods or procedures from period to period.

FIFO method: Valuing of inventory assuming that the company sells the first goods received in the store.

Full disclosure principle: The accounting principle that requires companies to fully disclose on their financial reports changes in accounting procedures and methods along with effects of the change, as well as justification for change.

LIFO method: Valuing of inventory with the assumption the last goods received in the store are the first to be sold.

Specific invoice method: Valuing of inventory where each item is identified with a specific invoice.

Weighted-average method: Valuing of inventory where each item is assigned the same unit cost. This unit cost is found by dividing cost of goods available for sale by the total number of units for sale.

LEARNING UNIT 16-2

1. In using the lower-of-cost-or-market principle, choose the lower of cost (FIFO, LIFO, or whatever) or replacement cost. While not as complex as the method used in the USA, it serves to place a conservative value on the asset—inventory.

2. The retail inventory method estimates inventory (rather than continually taking a physical count) by multiplying the cost ratio times ending inventory at retail.

3. The retail method can also reduce a physical inventory to cost.

4. The gross profit method is another way of estimating ending inventory without taking a physical count. This method requires calculating an estimated cost of goods sold, which is then subtracted from the cost of goods available for sale.

5. If ending inventory is overstated, net income will be overstated.

6. If beginning inventory is overstated, net income will be understated.

7. A mistake in calculating ending inventory will take two accounting periods to be self-correcting.

Gross profit method: A method for estimating the value of ending inventory. It is based on the assumption that the gross profit of a company remains approximately the same from period to period.

Lower-of-cost-or-market: Valuing of inventory at the lower of cost or replacement cost. This valuing depends on how selling price moves as well as on normal expected profit.

BLUEPRINT: METHODS OF ESTIMATING ENDING INVENTORY

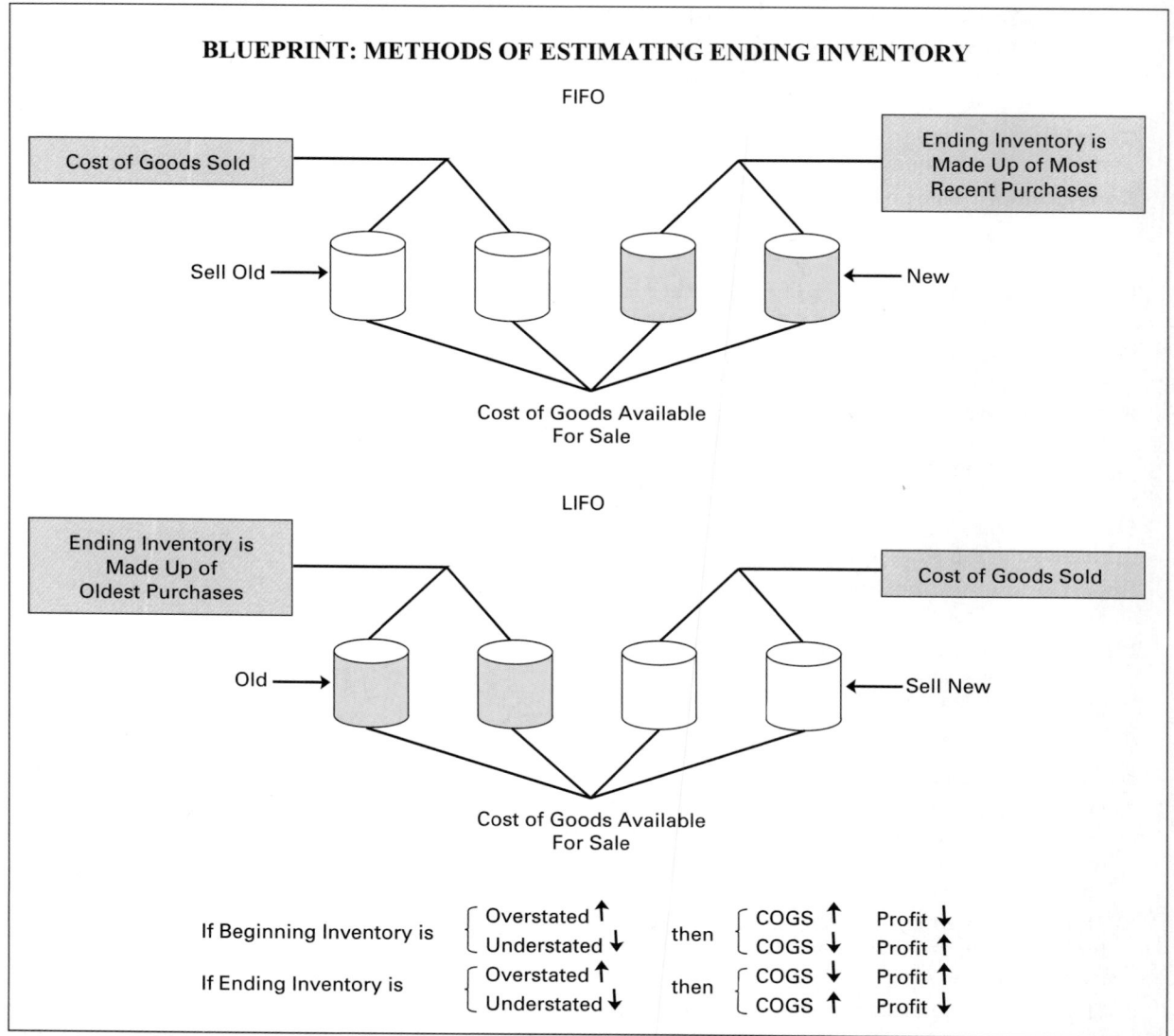

Retail method: A method for estimating the value of ending inventory based on a cost ratio times the ending inventory at retail.

LEARNING UNIT 16-3

1. In a perpetual inventory system the Inventory and Cost of Goods Sold accounts are continually updated.

2. Purchases, Purchases Discounts, and Purchases Returns and Allowances as well as Freight-In are not used in the perpetual inventory system.

3. The perpetual system has a subsidiary ledger of inventory control sheets to update each inventory item that is purchased or sold.

Perpetual inventory system: The inventory system of a company that keeps a continuous inventory of merchandise on hand.

DISCUSSION QUESTIONS

1. How does flow of cost relate to the specific invoice method?
2. What are the four methods of inventory valuation? Explain each.
3. During inflation, which inventory method will provide the lowest income on the income statement?
4. Which inventory method provides the most current valuation of inventory on the balance sheet? Please explain.
5. Explain why goods in transit (F.O.B. shipping point) to buyer and goods issued on consignment are added to inventory valuations.
6. Explain why lower-of-cost-or-market valuation has been modified in recent years.
7. A mistake in ending inventory is self-correcting in the same period. Agree or disagree. Defend your position.
8. When Ending Inventory is understated, what effect will this have on cost of goods sold and net income?
9. What is the cost ratio in the retail inventory method?
10. Why must the average gross profit rate be used in the gross profit method?
11. What are the differences between the periodic and perpetual systems?

EXERCISES

1. From the Loyola Company data given below, assuming a periodic inventory system, calculate the cost of ending inventory and cost of goods sold using the (a) first-in, first-out, (b) last-in, first-out, and (c) weighted-average methods. Loyola sells only one type of product.

FIFO, LIFO, weighted average.

			UNITS	COST PER UNIT
Jan.	1	Beginning inventory	50	$ 9
Mar.	18	Purchased	12	10
Aug.	19	Purchased	40	12
Nov.	8	Purchased	48	13

Ending inventory is 52 units.

2. From the following facts, calculate the correct cost of inventory for Ray Company.

Consignment and freight in calculating cost of inventory.

Cost of inventory on shelf, $4,000, which includes $300 of goods received on consignment.
Goods in transit en route to Ray Company shipped F.O.B. shipping point, $22,000.
Goods in transit en route to Ray shipped F.O.B. destination, $300. Ray has $600 worth of goods on consignment in Alice's Dress Shop.

3. Lyle Company uses the lower-of-cost-or-market principle in valuing inventory. From the following facts, record the cost of the inventory:

Lower-of-cost-or-market.

Original selling price, $550.
Cost, $400.
Replacement cost dropped to $300, but selling price remains at $550.

Retail inventory method.

4. Angel Company's May 1 inventory had a cost of $58,000 and a retail value of $72,000. During May, net purchases cost $255,000 with a retail value of $405,000. Net sales at retail for Angel for May were $225,000. Calculate the ending inventory at cost using the retail inventory method. (Round the cost ratio to the nearest hundredth percent.)

Gross profit method.

5. Amy Company on January 1 had inventory costing $30,000 and during January had net purchases of $67,000. Over recent years Amy's gross profit has averaged 40 percent on sales. Given that the company has net sales of $106,000, calculate an estimated cost of ending inventory using the gross profit method.

GROUP A PROBLEMS

FIFO, LIFO, weighted-average.

16A-1. Ashley Company began the year with 250 units of product B in inventory with a unit cost of $35. The following additional purchases of the product were made:

Apr.	1	300 units @ $40 each
Jul.	5	400 units @ 50 each
Aug.	15	500 units @ 60 each
Nov.	20	150 units @ 70 each

At end of year Ashley Company had 500 units of its product unsold. Your task is to calculate cost of ending inventory as well as cost of goods sold by (a) FIFO, (b) LIFO, (c) weighted-average. (Round weighted-average to nearest cent.)

Retail inventory method.

16A-2. Marge Company uses the retail method to estimate cost of ending inventory for its monthly interim reports. From the following facts, estimate Marge's ending inventory at cost for the end of January. (Round the cost ratio to the nearest tenth percent.)

January 1 inventory at cost	$ 16,500
January 1 inventory at retail	32,000
Net purchases at cost	110,800
Net purchases at retail	195,000
Net sales at retail	191,000

Gross profit method.

16A-3. Over the past 4 years the gross profit rate for Hall Company was 30 percent. Last week a fire destroyed all of Hall's inventory. Luckily all the records for Hall were in a fireproof safe and indicated the following facts:

Inventory (January 1, 19XX)	$ 39,000
Sales	128,500
Sales Returns	3,200
Purchases	78,000
Purchases Returns and Allowances	3,000

Please estimate the cost of inventory that was destroyed in the fire.

Perpetual inventory.

16A-4. Agree Company uses a perpetual inventory system on the FIFO basis. From the information given below, prepare an inventory control sheet. Assume on January 1, 19XX, a beginning inventory of 800 units at a cost of $8 each.

	RECEIVED			SOLD
DATE	QUANTITY	COST PER UNIT	DATE	QUANTITY
Apr. 15	220	$ 5	Mar. 8	500
Nov. 12	1,900	9	Oct. 5	200
Dec. 31	700	12	Nov. 30	400

GROUP B PROBLEMS

16B-1. On January 1, 19XX, Ashley Company began with 150 units of product B in inventory with a unit cost of $20. The following additional purchases of the product were made:

FIFO, LIFO, weighted-average.

Apr.	1	210 units @ $30 each
Jul.	5	500 units @ 40 each
Aug.	15	450 units @ 50 each
Nov.	20	200 units @ 60 each

At end of year Ashley Company had 400 units of its product unsold. Your task is to calculate cost of ending inventory as well as cost of goods sold by (a) FIFO, (b) LIFO, (c) weighted-average. (Round weighted-average to nearest cent.)

16B-2. Marge Company uses the retail method to estimate cost of ending inventory for its monthly interim reports. From the facts given below, estimate Marge's ending inventory at cost for end of January. (Round the cost ratio to the nearest hundredth percent.)

Retail inventory method.

January 1 inventory at cost	$ 17,000
January 1 inventory at retail	35,000
Net purchases at cost	119,000
Net purchases at retail	204,000
Net sales at retail	189,000

16B-3. Over the past 4 years the gross profit rate for Hall Company was 35 percent. Last week a fire destroyed all of Hall's inventory. Luckily all the records for Hall were in a fireproof safe and indicated the following facts:

Gross profit method.

Inventory (January 1, 19XX)	$ 5,400
Sales	127,000
Sales Returns	3,250
Purchases	94,900
Purchases Returns and Allowances	4,100

Using the gross profit method, estimate the cost of inventory that was destroyed in the fire.

16B-4. Agree Company uses a perpetual inventory system on the FIFO basis. From the following information, prepare an inventory control sheet. Assume a beginning inventory of 700 units at a cost of $9 each.

Perpetual inventory.

	RECEIVED			SOLD
DATE	QUANTITY	COST PER UNIT	DATE	QUANTITY
Apr. 15	200	$ 6	Mar. 8	400
Nov. 12	3,000	10	Nov. 30	900
Dec. 31	800	11		

GROUP C PROBLEMS

FIFO, LIFO, weighted-average.

16C-1. Robbins Company began the year with 360 units of product B in inventory with a unit cost of $35. The following additional purchases of the product were made:

Apr. 15   340 units @ $62 each
Jul.   25   425 units @   73 each
Aug.   5   550 units @   85 each
Nov. 26   275 units @   93 each

At end of year Robbins Company had 600 units of its product unsold. Your task is to calculate cost of ending inventory as well as cost of goods sold by (a) FIFO, (b) LIFO, (c) weighted-average. (Round weighted-average to nearest cent.)

Retail inventory method.

16C-2. Pound Company uses the retail method to estimate cost of ending inventory for its monthly interim reports. From the following facts, estimate Pound's ending inventory at cost for the end of March. (Round the cost ratio to the nearest tenth percent.)

March 1 inventory at cost	$ 41,500
March 1 inventory at retail	76,000
Net purchases at cost	180,700
Net purchases at retail	332,400
Net sales at retail	351,800

Gross profit method.

16C-3. Over the past 5 years the gross profit rate for Genesis Company was 35 percent. Last week a fire destroyed all of their inventory. Luckily all the accounting records were in a fireproof safe and indicated the following facts:

Inventory (January 1, 19XX)	$ 81,000
Sales	264,000
Sales Returns	4,200
Purchases	157,500
Purchases Returns and Allowances	2,200

Please estimate the cost of inventory that was destroyed in the fire.

Perpetual inventory.

16C-4. Sawyer Company uses a perpetual inventory system on the FIFO basis. From the information given below, prepare an inventory control sheet. Assume on January 1, 19XX, a beginning inventory of 500 units at a cost of $11 each.

RECEIVED			SOLD	
DATE	QUANTITY	COST PER UNIT	DATE	QUANTITY
Apr. 15	220	$ 8	Mar. 8	300
Nov. 12	1,900	12	Oct. 5	350
Dec. 31	700	14	Nov. 30	800

PRACTICAL ACCOUNTING APPLICATION #1

TO: Tom Hoover
FROM: Jennifer Ring
RE: Inventory Mistakes

The following mistakes have been found on our financial reports:

A   Beginning inventory was reported as $300 when it should have been $100.
B   The figure for ending inventory of $800 was understated by $200.
C   Purchases account of $18,000 was understated by $1,100.
D   Sales were overstated by $2,000.

Indicate what effect these mistakes (treat each one separately) will have on (1) cost of goods sold, (2) gross profit, and (3) owner's equity. Please explain your answers.

PRACTICAL ACCOUNTING APPLICATION #2

Mike Sloy has completed his accounting course at Y College and was recently hired as the office manager of Reel Co. The firm estimates its inventory by the retail method. It has been brought to Mike's attention that Reel has additional markups as well as markdowns. In college Mike's instructor said, "In the retail method you don't have to worry about markups and markdowns—just get the concept." Now Mike is upset, since his job is to compute ending inventory at cost by the retail method that includes markups and markdowns. Could you take the following data and assist Mike? (Round the cost ratio to the nearest hundredth percent.)

Hints: Additional markups add to cost of goods available for sale at retail. Markdowns add to total sales.

Beginning inventory at cost (Jan. 1)	$20,000
Beginning inventory at retail (Jan. 1)	30,000
Additional markups	2,000
Net Sales at retail	57,000
Net purchases at cost	36,000
Net purchases at retail	52,000
Markdowns	1,000

ACCOUNTING RECALL
A Cumulative Approach

THIS EXAM REVIEWS CHAPTERS 1 THROUGH 16

Your *Study Guide and Working Papers* have forms to complete this exam, as well as worked-out solutions. The page references next to each question identify what page to turn back to if you answer the question incorrectly.

PART I Vocabulary Review

Match the terms to the appropriate definition or phrase.

Page Ref.

(553)	1. Perpetual inventory system	A. Contra cost of goods sold
(536)	2. Discount on notes payable	B. Subtracted from cost of goods sold
(496)	3. Allow for Doubtful Accts	C. Uses a cost ratio
(556)	4. LIFO	D. Related to how selling price moves
(560)	5. Retail method	E. Last goods sold first
(560)	6. Lower of cost or market	F. Contra asset
(228)	7. Purchases discount	G. Contra liability
(183)	8. Controlling account	H. Accounts payable
(558)	9. Consignee	I. Continuous inventory of merchandise
(423)	10. Ending inventory	J. Doesn't have ownership

PART II True or False (Accounting Theory)

(563) 11. If ending inventory is overstated then COGS is overstated.

(555) 12. FIFO assumes the old goods are sold first.

(179) 13. Sales Returns and Allowances is a contra cost of goods sold account.

(179) 14. Net sales less cost of goods sold equals gross profit.

(565) 15. In the periodic system the purchases account is not used.

PART III Applications Problem (555-556)

From the following calculate the cost of ending inventory as well as cost of goods sold assuming a FIFO Method. Assume an ending Inventory of 75 units.

	NUMBER PURCHASED	COST PER UNIT	TOTAL
January 1 Inventory	40	$4	$160
April 1 Inventory	60	7	420
July 1 Inventory	50	8	400
December 1 Inventory	55	9	495

ACCOUNTING FORMS SAMPLER

Chapter 1
INCOME STATEMENT FOR A SERVICE COMPANY

<table>
<tr><td colspan="4" align="center">*Assure Realty*
Income Statement
For month ended Novemeber 30, 19XX</td></tr>
<tr><td>*Revenue:*</td><td></td><td></td><td></td></tr>
<tr><td> *Commissions Earned*</td><td></td><td></td><td>*$ 1 3 6 0 00*</td></tr>
<tr><td>*Operating Expenses:*</td><td></td><td></td><td></td></tr>
<tr><td> *Rent Expense*</td><td>*$ 2 00 00*</td><td></td><td></td></tr>
<tr><td> *Advertising Expense*</td><td>*1 5 0 00*</td><td></td><td></td></tr>
<tr><td> *Salaries Expense*</td><td>*9 0 00*</td><td></td><td></td></tr>
<tr><td>   *Total Operating Expenses*</td><td></td><td>*4 4 0 00*</td><td></td></tr>
<tr><td>*Net Income*</td><td></td><td>*$ 9 2 0 00*</td><td></td></tr>
</table>

The income statement is a report written for a specific period of time that lists earned revenue and expenses incurred to produce the earned revenue. The net income or net loss will be used in the statement of owner's equity. There are no debits or credits on financial reports. The inside column is for subtotalling.

Chapter 1
STATEMENT OF OWNER'S EQUITY

<table>
<tr><td colspan="4" align="center">*Assure Realty*
Statement of Owner's Equity
For month ended Novemeber 30, 19XX</td></tr>
<tr><td>*Bill Ryan, Capital, November 1, 19XX*</td><td></td><td></td><td>*$ 5 0 00 00*</td></tr>
<tr><td>*Net Income for November*</td><td>*$ 9 2 0 00*</td><td></td><td></td></tr>
<tr><td>*Less Withdrawals for November*</td><td>*1 0 0 00*</td><td></td><td></td></tr>
<tr><td>*Increase in Capital*</td><td></td><td>*8 2 0 00*</td><td></td></tr>
<tr><td>*Bill Ryan, Capital, November 30, 19XX*</td><td></td><td>*$ 5 8 2 0 00*</td><td></td></tr>
</table>

The statement of owner's equity reveals the causes of a change in capital. This report lists any investments, net income (or net loss), and withdrawals. The ending figure for capital will be used on the balance sheet. Any additional investments would go on this report.

Chapter 1
BALANCE SHEET FOR A SERVICE COMPANY

			Assure Realty Balance Sheet November 30, 19XX			
Assets			Liabilities and Owner's Equity			
Cash	$4 730 00		Liabilities			
Accounts Receivable	640 00		Accounts Payable	$	900 00	
Store Furniture	1 350 00					
			Owner's Equity			
			Bill Ryan, Capital		5 820 00	
			Total Liabilities and			
Total Assets	$ 6 720 00		Owner's Equity	$ 6 720 00		

The balance sheet uses the ending balances of assets and liabilities from the ledger and the capital from the statement of owner's equity. Keep in mind that there are no debits or credits on financial reports.

Chapter 2
TRIAL BALANCE

		Janet Foss Barrister and Solicitor Trial Balance May 31, 19XX	
		Dr.	Cr.
Cash		1 800 00	
Accounts Receivable		750 00	
Office Equipment		750 00	
Accounts Payable			1 200 00
Salaries Payable			675 00
Janet Foss, Capital			1 275 00
Janet Foss, Withdrawals		300 00	
Revenue from Legal Fees			1 350 00
Utilities Expense		300 00	
Rent Expense		450 00	
Salaries Expense		150 00	
Totals		4 500 00	4 500 00

A trial balance is a list of the ending balances of all general ledger accounts, listed in the same order as on the chart of accounts. Note how Withdrawals is listed immediately below Capital.

Chapter 3
GENERAL LEDGER (PARTIAL)

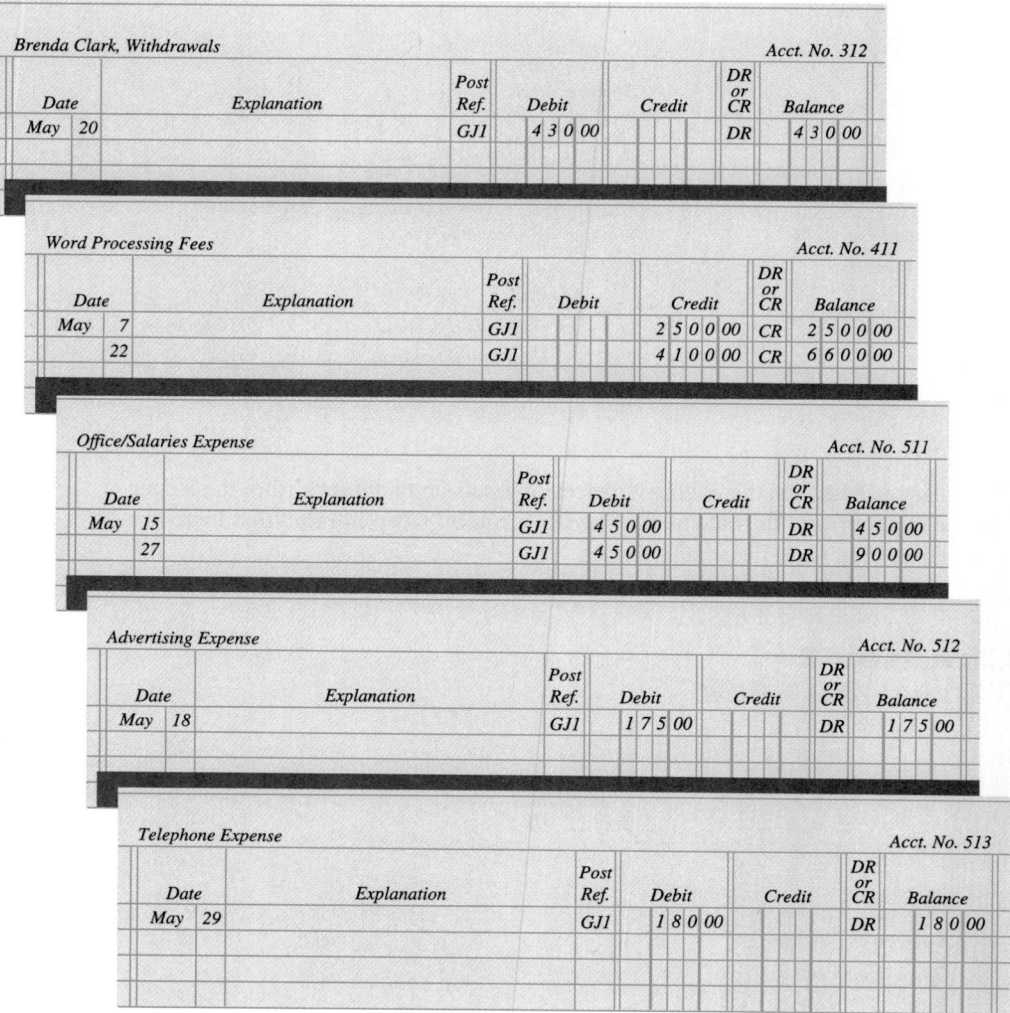

Brenda Clark, Withdrawals   Acct. No. 312

Date	Explanation	Post Ref.	Debit	Credit	DR or CR	Balance
May 20		GJ1	4 3 0 00		DR	4 3 0 00

Word Processing Fees   Acct. No. 411

Date	Explanation	Post Ref.	Debit	Credit	DR or CR	Balance
May 7		GJ1		2 5 0 0 00	CR	2 5 0 0 00
22		GJ1		4 1 0 0 00	CR	6 6 0 0 00

Office/Salaries Expense   Acct. No. 511

Date	Explanation	Post Ref.	Debit	Credit	DR or CR	Balance
May 15		GJ1	4 5 0 00		DR	4 5 0 00
27		GJ1	4 5 0 00		DR	9 0 0 00

Advertising Expense   Acct. No. 512

Date	Explanation	Post Ref.	Debit	Credit	DR or CR	Balance
May 18		GJ1	1 7 5 00		DR	1 7 5 00

Telephone Expense   Acct. No. 513

Date	Explanation	Post Ref.	Debit	Credit	DR or CR	Balance
May 29		GJ1	1 8 0 00		DR	1 8 0 00

The ledger is a collection of accounts where information is accumulated from the postings of the journal. The ledger is the book of final entry. Note each Ledger Account has an Account Number.

Chapter 3
GENERAL JOURNAL

A general journal is a book where transactions are recorded in chronological order. Here debits and credits are shown together on one page. This is the book of original entry. Note that the PR column is left blank in the journalizing process.

Clark's Word Processing Services
General Journal

Page 1

Date		Account Titles and Description	PR*	Dr.	Cr.
19XX					
May	1	Cash		7 0 0 0 00	
		Brenda Clark, Capital			7 0 0 0 00
		Initial investment of cash by owner			
	1	Word Processing Equipment		8 0 0 0 00	
		Cash			2 0 0 0 00
		Accounts Payable			6 0 0 0 00
		Purchase of equip. from Ben Co.			
	1	Prepaid Rent		9 0 0 00	
		Cash			9 0 0 00
		Rent paid in advance (3 months)			
	3	Office Supplies		4 0 0 00	
		Accounts Payable			4 0 0 00
		Purchase of supplies on acct. from Norris			
	7	Cash		2 5 0 0 00	
		Word Processing Fees			2 5 0 0 00
		Cash received from services rendered			
	15	Office Salaries Expense		4 5 0 00	
		Cash			4 5 0 00
		Payment of office salaries			
	18	Advertising Expense		1 7 5 00	
		Accounts Payable			1 7 5 00
		Bill received but not paid from Al's News			
	20	Brenda Clark, Withdrawals		4 3 0 00	
		Cash			4 3 0 00
		Personal withdrawal of cash			
	22	Accounts Receivable		4 1 0 0 00	
		Word Processing Fees			4 1 0 0 00
		Billed Morris Co. for fees earned			
	27	Office Salaries Expense		4 5 0 00	
		Cash			4 5 0 00
		Payment of office salaries			
	28	Accounts Payable		3 0 0 0 00	
		Cash			3 0 0 0 00
		Paid half the amount owed Ben Co.			

Chapter 4
WORK SHEET FOR A SERVICE COMPANY

Clark's Word Processing Services
Work Sheet
For month ended May 31, 19XX

Account Titles	Trial Balance Dr.	Trial Balance Cr.	Adjustments Dr.	Adjustments Cr.	Adjusted Trial Balance Dr.	Adjusted Trial Balance Cr.	Income Statement Dr.	Income Statement Cr.	Balance Sheet Dr.	Balance Sheet Cr.
Cash	2 0 9 0 00				2 0 9 0 00				2 0 9 0 00	
Accounts Receivable	4 1 0 0 00				4 1 0 0 00				4 1 0 0 00	
Office Supplies	4 0 0 00			(A) 3 2 0 00	8 0 00				8 0 00	
Prepaid Rent	9 0 0 00			(B) 3 0 0 00	6 0 0 00				6 0 0 00	
Word Processing Equipment	8 0 0 0 00				8 0 0 0 00				8 0 0 0 00	
Acct. Payable		3 5 7 5 00				3 5 7 5 00				3 5 7 5 00
B. Clark, Capital		7 0 0 0 00				7 0 0 0 00				7 0 0 0 00
B. Clark, Withdrawals	4 3 0 00				4 3 0 00				4 3 0 00	
Word Processing Fees		6 6 0 0 00				6 6 0 0 00		6 6 0 0 00		
Office Salaries Expense	9 0 0 00		(D) 2 5 0 00		1 1 5 0 00		1 1 5 0 00			
Advertising Expense	1 7 5 00				1 7 5 00		1 7 5 00			
Telephone Expense	1 8 0 00				1 8 0 00		1 8 0 00			
	17 1 7 5 00	17 1 7 5 00								
Office Supplies Expense			(A) 3 2 0 00		3 2 0 00		3 2 0 00			
Rent Expense			(B) 3 0 0 00		3 0 0 00		3 0 0 00			
Depreciation Expense W.P. Equip.			(C) 1 0 0 00		1 0 0 00		1 0 0 00			
Accum. Depreciation, W.P. Equip.				(C) 1 0 0 00		1 0 0 00				1 0 0 00
Salaries Payable				(D) 2 5 0 00		2 5 0 00				2 5 0 00
			9 7 0 00	9 7 0 00	17 5 2 5 00	17 5 2 5 00	2 2 2 5 00	6 6 0 0 00	15 3 0 0 00	10 9 2 5 00
Net Income							4 3 7 5 00			4 3 7 5 00
							6 6 0 0 00	6 6 0 0 00	15 3 0 0 00	15 3 0 0 00

The work sheet is a columnar device used by accountants to aid them in completing the accounting cycle. Not a formal report, it assists in completing all the remaining steps of the accounting cycle. In a computerized accounting environment a work sheet is rarely needed.

Chapter 6
SALES JOURNAL

Date 19XX	Customer	Terms	Invoice Number	PR	Accounts Receivable Dr.	Prov. Sales Tax Payable Cr.	GST Payable Cr.	Sales Cr.
April 3	Hal's Clothing	2/10, n30	1602	✓	9 3 6 00	8 0 00	5 6 00	8 0 0 00
6	Bevans Company	net 30 days	1603	✓	1 8 7 2 00	1 6 0 00	1 1 2 00	1 6 0 0 00
18	Roe Company	2/10, n30	1604	✓	2 3 4 0 00	2 0 0 00	1 4 0 00	2 0 0 0 00
24	Mel's Department Store	2/10, n30	1605	✓	5 8 5 00	5 0 00	3 5 00	5 0 0 00
28	Hal's Clothing	2/10, n30	1606	✓	1 0 5 3 00	9 0 00	6 3 00	9 0 0 00
29	Mel's Department Store	2/10, n30	1607	✓	8 1 9 00	7 0 00	4 9 00	7 0 0 00
30	Totals				7 6 0 5 00	6 5 0 00	4 5 5 00	6 5 0 0 00
					(113)	(226)	(238)	(400)

Art's Wholesale Clothing Company
Sales Journal   *Page 1*

A sales journal records sales on account. Note: Check marks show recordings to the Accounts Receivable Subsidiary Ledger have been completed. Totals will be posted at end of month. May be enlarged to show various categories of sales and must include a column for GST.

Chapter 6
ACCOUNTS RECEIVABLE (SUBSIDIARY) LEDGER (PARTIAL)

NAME Bevans Company
ADDRESS 110 Aster Rd., Amherst, NS B4H 3A5

Date	Explanation	Post Ref.	Debit	Credit	Dr. Balance
19XX April 6		SJ1	1 6 0 0 00		1 6 0 0 00
12		GJ1		6 0 0 00	1 0 0 0 00
16		CRJ1		1 0 0 0 00	- 0 -

NAME Hal's Clothing
ADDRESS 91 Century Ave., Winnipeg, MN R2C 4X7

Date	Explanation	Post Ref.	Debit	Credit	Dr. Balance
19XX April 3		SJ1	8 0 0 00		8 0 0 00
4		CRJ1		8 0 0 00	- 0 -

The accounts receivable ledger, organized in alphabetical order, is not in the same book as Accounts Receivable, the controlling account in the general ledger. Subsidiary ledgers have names while general ledgers have account numbers.

Chapter 6
CASH RECEIPTS JOURNAL

Art's Wholesale Clothing Company
Cash Receipts Journal

Date	Description of Receipt	PR	Sundry Cr.	Accounts Receivable Cr.	Sales Cr.	GST Payable Cr.	Sales Discount Dr.	Cash Dr.
April 1	A. Newner, Capital	311	8000 00					8000 00
4	Hal's Clothing	✓		800 00			16 00	784 00
15	Cash Sales	✗			900 00	63 00		963 00
16	Bevans Company	✓		1000 00			20 00	980 00
22	Roe Company	✓		2000 00			40 00	1960 00
27	Store Equipment	121	500 00					500 00
30	Cash Sales	✗			1200 00	84 00		1284 00
30	Totals		8500 00	3800 00	2100 00	147 00	76 00	14471 00

The cash receipts journal records receipt of cash from any source. The total of sundry is not posted. Totals of columns are posted at end of month. The checks indicate that recordings to the subsidiary ledger are up-to-date. Note the column for GST (usually on cash sales only).

Chapter 6
SCHEDULE OF ACCOUNTS RECEIVABLE

Art's Wholesale Clothing Company
Schedule of Accounts Receivable
April 30, 19XX

Mel's Dept. Store	$ 1600 00
Roe Company	500 00
Total Accounts Receivable	$ 2100 00

A schedule of accounts receivable is a listing of the ending balances of customers in the accounts receivable ledger. This total should be the same balance as found in the controlling account, Accounts Receivable, in the general ledger.

Chapter 7
PURCHASES JOURNAL

The purchases journal records the buying of merchandise or other items on account. The purchases (Debit) column records merchandise bought for resale. The sundry column records items not for resale. Note the column for GST payable on purchases.

Art's Wholesale Clothing Company
Purchases Journal

Date		Account Credited	Date of Invoice	Inv. No.	Terms	PR	Accounts Payable Cr.
April	3	Abby Blake Co.	April 3	238	2/10, n/60		5 4 0 3 50
	4	Joe Francis Co.	April 5	388			4 2 8 0 00
	6	Thorpe Company	April 6	415	1/10, n/30		8 5 6 00
	7	John Sullivan Co.	April 6	516	n/10, EOM		1 0 4 6 60
	12	Abby Blake Co.	April 13	272	1/10, n/30		6 4 2 00
	25	John Sullivan Co.	April 26	612			5 3 5 00
	30	Totals					12 7 6 3 00

Page 1

Purchases Dr.	G.S.T. Payable Dr.	Sundry Dr. Account	PR	Amount
5 0 0 0 00	3 5 3 50	Freight-In		5 0 00
	2 8 0 00	Equipment		4 0 0 0 00
8 0 0 00	5 6 00			
9 8 0 00	6 8 60			
6 0 0 00	4 2 00			
	3 5 00	Supplies		5 0 0 00
7 3 8 0 00	8 3 5 10			4 5 5 0 00

Chapter 7
ACCOUNTS PAYABLE (SUBSIDIARY) LEDGER

John Butler Company
18 Reed Rd.
Winnipeg, MN R2B 8G6

Date		Explanation	Post Ref.	Debit	Credit	Cr. Balance
19XX May	7		PJ2		1 0 0 0 00	1 0 0 0 00
	17		PJ2		4 0 0 00	1 4 0 0 00

Flynn Company
15 Foss Ave.
Quebec City, PQ G1L 2W4

Date		Explanation	Post Ref.	Debit	Credit	Cr. Balance
19XX May	5		PJ2		9 0 0 00	9 0 0 00
	13		GJ1	3 0 0 00		6 0 0 00

The accounts payable ledger, organized in alphabetical order, is not in the same book as Accounts Payable, the controlling account in the general ledger. Note: There are no account numbers next to each name.

Chapter 7
CASH PAYMENTS JOURNAL

Wendal's Welding Supplies Co.
Cash Payments Journal

Page 5

Date 199X		Chq. No.	Account Debited	PR	Sundry Dr.	Accounts Payable Dr.	GST Prepaid Dr.	Purchases Discount Cr.	Cash Cr.
April	2	13	Prepaid Insurance (No GST)	116	9 0 0 00				9 0 0 00
	7	14	Joe Francis Co.	✓		4 2 8 0 00			4 2 8 0 00
	9	15	Purchases	511	8 0 0 00		5 6 00		8 5 6 00
	12	16	Thorpe Company	✓		6 0 0 00		6 00	5 9 4 00
	28	17	Salaries	611	7 0 0 00				7 0 0 00
	30		Totals		2 4 0 0 00	4 8 8 0 00	5 6 00	6 00	6 6 3 0 00
					(X)	(211)	(135)	(512)	(111)

All payments of cash (cheque) are recorded in the cash payments journal. Totals posted at end of month (except Sundry). Update subsidiary Ledger during the month (√). Note the column for GST on most things purchased for cash (even if an expensive asset is purchased — a new vehicle for instance).

Chapter 8
BANK RECONCILIATION WITH
JOURNAL ENTRIES

Monroe Company
Bank Reconciliation as of June 30, 19XX

Chequebook Balance			Balance per Bank	
Ending Chequebook Balance		$3,978	Ending Bank Statement Balance	$5,230
Add:			Add:	
Error in recording			Deposits in Transit	1,084
Cheque no. 108	$54			$6,314
Proceeds of a note*				
less collection				
charge by bank	1,990	2,044	Deduct:	
		$6,022	Cheque no. 191..$204	
			198.. 250	
Deduct:			201.. 100	554
NSF Cheque	$252			
Bank Service				
Charge	10	262		
Reconciled Balance		$5,760	Reconciled Balance	$5,760

19XX								
June	30	Cash		1 9 9 0 00				
		Collection Expense		1 0 00				
		Notes Receivable*				2 0 0 0 00		
	30	Cash		5 4 00				
		Store Equipment				5 4 00		
	30	Acct. Rec., Alvin Sooth		2 5 2 00				
		Cash				2 5 2 00		
	30	Miscellaneous Expense		1 0 00				
		Cash				1 0 00		

The process of reconciling the bank statement balance with the company's general ledger balance is called the bank reconciliation. The timing of deposits, when the bank statement was issued, etc., often results in differences between the bank balance and the chequebook balance. Whenever the chequebook is adjusted a journal entry is required.

Chapter 9
PAYROLL REGISTER

Fred's Market
Payroll Register
November 23, 19XX

Employee	Net Claim Code	Weekly Salary	Cumulative CPP	FIT
Flynn, Bob	6	520 00	349 60	61 55
Frost, Abby	1	780 00	474 40	196 70
O'Reilly, Susan	2	860 00	672 80	225 45
Rase, Paula	1	900 00	742 00	246 80
Reagan, Al	3	820 00	142 60	206 15
Weekly Totals		3880 00		936 65

Deductions				Net Pay	Chq. No.	Expense Accounts	
CPP	UI	Health	Union Dues			Factory	Office
11 41	15 60	16 00	5 00	410 44	2314	520 00	
17 86	22 35	16 00	5 00	522 09	2315		780 00
19 86	22 35	16 00	5 00	571 34	2316	860 00	
10 50	22 35		5 00	615 35	2317		900 00
18 84	22 35	16 00	5 00	551 66	2318	820 00	
78 47	105 00	64 00	25 00	2670 88		2200 00	1680 00

1. A payroll register provides the data for journalizing the payroll entry.
2. Deductions from the gross payroll represent liabilities of the employer until paid.
3. The account distribution columns of the payroll register indicate which accounts will be debited to record the total payroll when a journal entry is prepared.
   NOTE: These distribution columns represent gross pay, not net pay.

Chapter 11
SYNOPTIC JOURNAL

No accounts for Accounts Payable or Accounts Receivable are used in the chart of accounts for a modified cash system. Companies use memorandums to keep track of receivables or payables until money is received or paid. This journal is used for many small businesses. A more comprehensive synoptic journal can use columns for accounts receivable and payable if need be.

Dr. Wheeler
Synoptic Journal

Month: *November*

Cash Deposits Dr.	Cheques Cr.	Chq. No.	Date	Explanations	PR	Sundry Dr.	Sundry Cr.	Prof. Fees Cr.	Dental Supplies Expense Dr.
			19XX Nov. 1	Cash Balance 9,500					
	200	61		Rent Expense	512	200 00			
3000 00			1	Professional Fees	✗			3000 00	
	80 00	62	4	Telephone Expense	514	80 00			
	600 00	63	4	Prepaid Insurance	131	600 00			
	150 00	64	7	Roe Supplies	✗				150 00
1600 00			8	Professional Fees	✗			1600 00	
	80 00	65	11	Auto Expense	511	80 00			
	500 00	66	11	G. Wheeler, Withdrawals	312	500 00			
	250 00	67	14	V.P. Suppliers	✗				250 00
	2000 00	68	15	Salaries Expense	513	2000 00			
2800 00			15	Professional Fees 13,040	✗			2800 00	
800 00			19	Professional Fees	✗			800 00	
	200 00	69	21	J. Labs	✗				200 00
2900 00			22	Professional Fees 16,540	✗			2900 00	
	300 00	70	27	Miscellaneous Expense	518	300 00			
	100 00	71	27	J. Labs	✗				100 00
3300 00			28	Professional Fees	✗			3300 00	
	1500 00	72	29	Salaries Expense 17,940	513	1500 00			
14400 00	5960 00					5260 00		14400 00	700 00
(111)	(111)					(X)		(411)	(520)

$20,360 = $20,360

Chapter 13
INCOME STATEMENT FOR A MERCHANDISE COMPANY

Art's Wholesale Clothing Co.
Income Statement
For year ended December 31, 19X2

Revenue:				
Gross Sales				$95 000 00
Less: Sales Ret. and Allow.		$ 950 00		
Sales Discount		670 00	1 620 00	
Net Sales				$93 380 00
Cost of Goods Sold:				
Merchandise Inventory, 1/1X2			$19 000 00	
Purchases		$52 000 00		
Less: Purch. Discount	$ 860 00			
Purch. Ret. and Allow.	680 00	1 540 00		
Net Purchases		$50 460 00		
Add: Freight-In		450 00		
Net Cost of Purchases			50 910 00	
Cost of Goods Available for Sale			$69 910 00	
Less: Merch. Inv., 12/31X2			4 000 00	
Cost of Goods Sold				65 910 00
Gross Profit				$27 470 00
Operating Expenses:				
Salaries Expense			$12 300 00	
Payroll Tax Expense			420 00	
Dep. Exp., Store Equip.			50 00	
Supplies Expense			500 00	
Insurance Expense			300 00	
Postage Expense			25 00	
Miscellaneous Expense			30 00	
Total Operating Expenses				13 625 00
Net Income from Operations				$13 845 00
Other Income:				
Rental Income			$ 200 00	
Other Expense:				
Interest Expense			300 00	100 00
Net Income				$13 745 00

There are no debit or credit columns on the formal income statement. The cost of goods sold section has a figure for beginning inventory and a separate figure for ending inventory.

Chapter 13
BALANCE SHEET FOR A MERCHANDISE COMPANY

Art's Wholesale Clothing Company
Balance Sheet
December 31, 19X2

Assets		
Current Assets:		
Cash	$12 9 2 0 00	
Petty Cash	1 0 0 00	
Accounts Receivable	14 5 0 0 00	
Merchandise Inventory	4 0 0 0 00	
Supplies	3 0 0 00	
Prepaid Insurance	6 0 0 00	
Total Current Assets		$32 4 2 0 00
Plant and Equipment:		
Store Equipment	$ 4 0 0 0 00	
Less: Acc. Dep.	4 5 0 00	3 5 5 0 00
Total Assets		$35 9 7 0 00
Liabilities		
Current Liabilities:		
Mortgage Payable (current portion)	$ 3 2 0 00	
Accounts Payable	17 9 0 0 00	
Income Tax Payable	7 6 0 00	
C.P.P. Payable	1 0 8 00	
U.I. Payable	1 3 2 00	
Salary Payable	1 3 0 0 00	
Unearned Rent	4 0 0 00	
Total Current Liabilities		$20 9 2 0 00
Long-Term Liabilities		
Mortgage Payable		2 0 0 0 00
Total Liabilities		$22 9 2 0 00
Owner's Equity		
Art Newner, Capital, December 31, 19X2		13 0 5 0 00
Total Liabilities and Owner's Equity		$35 9 7 0 00

A classified balance sheet categorizes assets as current or non-current; plant and equipment, and liabilities not to be paid in the next year are classified as long-term.

HOW COMPANIES RECORD CREDIT CARD SALES IN THEIR SPECIAL JOURNALS

RECORDING BANK CREDIT CARDS

EXAMPLE: CREDIT CARD SALES OF $100 MASTER CARD.
It is interesting to note that for bank credit cards (Master Card, Visa) the sales are recorded in the seller's Cash Receipts Journal, since the slips are converted into cash immediately. Bank credit cards are not treated as accounts receivable. The fee the bank charges (about 2% to 5%) is deducted, and the bank credits the depositor's account immediately for the net. The end result for the seller is:

Accounts Affected	Category	↑ ↓	Rule
Cash	Asset	↑	Dr. $97
Credit Card Expense	Expense	↑	Dr. 3
Sales	Revenue	↑	Cr. 100

Cash Receipts Journal

Date	Cash Dr.	Credit Card Expense Dr.	Accounts Receivable Cr.	Sales Credited	Sales Tax Payable Cr.	Sundry Account Name	Amount Cr.
	97 00	3 00		1 0 0 00			

It is the responsibility of the credit card company to sustain any losses (bad debts) from customers' nonpayment. If the bank waits to take the discount till the end of the month, the seller makes a nonpayment entry in the cash payment journal to record the credit card expense; the end result would be credit card expense up and cash balance down. Usually, the bank would send the charge on the monthly bank statement. *Remember: bank credit cards are not treated as accounts receivable.*

RECORDING PRIVATE COMPANY CREDIT CARDS

Private companies such as American Express and Diners Club are considered by most sellers as accounts receivable. The seller periodically summarizes the sales slips and submits them to the private credit card company for payment (these are usually paid within two weeks). Let's look at two situations to show how a company would handle its accounting procedures for these credit sales transactions.

SITUATION 1. On May 4, Morris Company sold merchandise on account $53.50 to Bill Blank. Bill used American Express. Assume Morris Company has low dollar volume and few transactions.

FIGURE B-1

	Date	Invoice	Description of Accounts Receivable	PR	Accounts Receivalbe Dr.	GST Payable Cr.	Sales Cr.
			Sales Journal				
	May 4	692	American Express		53 50	3 50	50 00
			(Bill Blank)				

FIGURE B-2

	Date	Cash Dr.	Sales Discount Dr.	Credit Card Expense Dr.	Accounts Receivable Cr.	Sales Tax Payable Cr.	Account Name	PR	Amount Cr.
					Cash Receipts Journal		Sundry		
	June 8	50 82		2 68	53 50		American Express		
							(Bill Blank)		

• Assume credit card expense of 5%. Note the $2.68 is 5% x $53.50

Note in Figure B-1 how the sale of $50 + GST is recorded in the sales journal. Keep in mind that Morris is treating American Express, not Bill Blank, as the accounts receivable. In Figure B-2 we see on June 8 payment is received from American Express and results in

1. Cash increasing by $50.82.
2. Credit card expense rising by $2.68.
3. Accounts receivable being reduced by the $53.50 originally owed by American Express.

SITUATION 2:   On March 31, Blue Company summarized its credit card sales for American Express. Payment was received on April 13 from American Express. Assume Blue Company has high dollar volume and many transactions.

Note in Figure B-3 how each credit company has its own column set up. In the ledger there is an account set up for each as well; the posting to the ledger would be done at the end of the month. With high volume and the need to record many transactions, the use of these additional columns (versus Figure B-1) will result in increased efficiency. Figure B-4 shows the receipt of money from American Express less the credit card expense charge.

These new titles are found in the general ledger. Subsidiary ledgers are not needed, since a file is kept of all copies submitted for payment.

FIGURE B-3

Blue Company Sales Journal

Date	Invoice Number	Description of Accounts Receivable	PR	Accounts Receivable Dr.	Credit Cards — American Express Dr.	Credit Cards — Diners Club Dr.	G.S.T. Payable Cr.	Credit Card Sales Cr.	Sales Cr.
March 31		Summary of American Express			121 9 80 00		79 80 00	114 0 00 00	
					(112)	(113)		(401)	

Acc. Receivable American Express   112

Total of column posted from sales journal at end of month

Acc. Receivable Diners Club   113

Total of column posted from sales journal at end of month

Credit Card Sales   401

Total of column posted from sales journal at end of month

These new titles are found in the general ledger. Subsidiary ledgers would not be needed, since a file is kept of all copies submitted for payment.

FIGURE B-4

Blue Company Cash Receipts Journal

Date	Cash Dr.	Sales Discount Dr.	Credit Card Expense Dr.	Accounts Receivable Cr.	Credit Card Accounts Rec. — American Express Cr.	Credit Card Accounts Rec. — Diners Club Cr.	Sales Cr.	G.S.T. Payable Cr.	Sundry — Account Name	PR	Sundry — Amount Cr.
April 13	114 6 61 20		7 3 18 80		121 9 80 00				Summary of American Express payments		

Credit Card Expense   510

Total of column posted from cash receipts journal at end of month

COMPUTERS AND ACCOUNTING

**IN THIS APPENDIX WE WILL COVER
THE FOLLOWING TOPICS:**

Throughout this text we have developed a practical set of procedures to provide accounting information about a business. Increasingly over the last two decades many business owners have found that the same accounting reports can be created more quickly and accurately using a computer. In this appendix we will discuss computers and how they, together with appropriate software, are used to maintain bookkeeping records and produce accounting reports.

LEARNING UNIT C-1
Introduction to Computers in Accounting

The first computerized accounting systems were developed in the 1950s. Only the largest organizations could afford the very expensive computer equipment that was available at that time. Since then the price of computer equipment has dropped dramatically. Today even the smallest business can afford a computer capable of keeping its accounting records.

Computerized systems offer many advantages over manual systems:

SPEED.   A computerized system provides information much more quickly than a manual system, because the computer almost instantaneously performs many tasks that are time-consuming when performed manually, such as posting journal entries and calculating payroll.

CREATION OF AN AUDIT TRAIL.   With a good computerized accounting system the accounting records will be well organized with reports documenting each transaction. This provides a clear **audit trail** by which each change in an account's balance can be traced back to the transaction that caused it.

ERROR PROTECTION.   Using a computer greatly reduces the number of errors, because the computer performs mathematical functions much more quickly and accurately than a person can. Also, computerized accounting systems have many built-in error protection features. For instance, in most systems the computer will not accept an entry that does not balance. Automatic posting by the computer helps to prevent such errors as double posting, posting to the wrong account, or posting the wrong amount.

AUTOMATIC REPORT PREPARATION.   The purpose of the accounting process is to provide accurate information about the business to those who need it. We do this through reports. All computerized accounting systems provide printouts of journals and ledgers as well as prepare the Balance Sheet and Income Statement. Most also greatly expand our ability to provide management with information that can improve decision-making. A myriad of management reports that inform management when inventory is low, when customer accounts are overdue, what percentage of profit is being made on each item the business sells, and much other important information, can be generated at the touch of a few buttons. It is generally too time-consuming to frequently prepare these types of reports manually for a small business.

AUTOMATIC DOCUMENT PRINTING. In addition to printing reports, a computerized system can also provide many of the documents used in a business. Using pre-printed forms sold in supply stores or available by mail-order, the computer can print documents such as monthly statements for accounts receivable customers and payroll cheques with year-to-date information on the stubs.

As you can see, computers can greatly aid the accounting process. You might think that such a powerful tool would require a great deal of expertise to use. On the contrary, it takes very little computer knowledge to use a computerized accounting system. As long as you understand the manual accounting process, computerized methods are not difficult to learn. As we said in Chapter 1, the computer is only a tool to aid you in performing the same bookkeeping operations you have learned to do manually. Basically, the computer is used to do the "drudge" or mechanical work of accounting, such as posting. You must still do all of the analysis work, such as deciding which accounts should be debited and credited.

Accounting procedures are basically the same whether they are performed manually or on the computer. In Figure C-1 we review the steps of the accounting cycle as presented in Chapter 5 and compare them with the steps of the accounting cycle in a computerized system.

Computer Basics

A **program** is a set of instructions that tells the computer what to do. Without a program it cannot perform even the simplest of tasks. This does not mean that you must become a **programmer** in order to use a computer for accounting. Since accounting functions are one of the most frequently used computer applications, there are many programs already written to handle accounting data. In order to use the computer for accounting, then, you can simply purchase a program that suits the needs of your business and is compatible with your computer. In Learning Unit C-2 we will discuss the types of packages available, and in Learning Unit C-3 we will give guidelines for purchasing a program and converting your records from a manual system to a computerized system.

FIGURE C-1

Comparing Manual and Computerized Accounting Systems

Accounting Cycle in a Manual System

1. Business transactions occur and generate source documents.
2. Business transactions are analyzed and recorded in a journal.
3. Information is posted from the journal to the ledger.
4. A trial balance is prepared.
5. A work sheet is completed.
6. Financial statements are prepared and typed.
7. Adjusting entries are journalized and posted.
8. Closing entries are journalized and posted.
9. A post-closing trial balance is prepared.

Accounting Cycle in a Computerized System

1. Business transactions occur and generate source documents.
2. Business transactions are analyzed and entered in the computer. The computer prints a journal.
3. The computer posts from the journal to the ledger.
4. The computer prepares a trial balance.

5. Adjusting entries are made and the computer posts them. (No work sheet is usually necessary.)
6. The computer generates and prints financial statements.
7. The computer records and posts closing entries.
8. The computer prepares and prints a post-closing trial balance.

Although you don't need to be a computer expert, you do need to be familiar with some of the computer equipment you will use on a day-to-day basis. Let's look at the various hardware available. Generally, computer equipment is referred to as **hardware** and computer programs are called **software**.

Types of computers are classified according to their speed and the amount of data they can store. Computers can be grouped into three basic classes: mainframes, minicomputers, and microcomputers. In the 1950s the only type of computer available for accounting applications was the mainframe. A **mainframe** computer can handle a large volume of transactions very quickly, but its cost is prohibitive for all but very large businesses. (Today, mainframe computers sell at prices ranging from a quarter million to four million dollars.) In the late 1960s the **minicomputer** was developed. It was less powerful than the mainframe — however, it also was about one-fourth the cost. As technology progressed, a new type of computer was developed — the **microcomputer**. When first developed, microcomputers were not very powerful and were used in large part for playing computer games. However, new ones were soon developed with more memory and speed. Some microcomputers today are more powerful than the mainframes of the 1950s. Best of all, this type of computer is very affordable. A microcomputer capable of keeping business records can be bought complete with monitor and printer for less than $1,500.

Because microcomputers are so affordable, programmers have a very large market for their software programs. In the past few years thousands of software packages have been produced for the microcomputer, making it a very valuable business tool. Since the beginning of the 1980s many comprehensive accounting programs have been written for microcomputers. Due to the volume of data they process, and the number of operators who must gain access to the system at the same time, some medium and large businesses still need mainframes and minicomputers, but microcomputer packages now provide virtually all of the features offered by larger computers and can easily meet the needs of small businesses. By using a local area network (LAN) even very large businesses can do all of their accounting using many microcomputers connected together. Many of the accounting software packages available today are capable of being used on a LAN.

Although we will concentrate here on accounting procedures for microcomputers, basically all procedures are the same no matter what type of computer is used. Figure C-2 shows the hardware for a typical microcomputer. This computer system consists of three main types of components:

Input devices
Central processing unit
Output devices

INPUT DEVICES.   We use **input devices** to feed instructions and data into the computer. An input device usually found on a computer system is a **disk drive**, which reads data and instructions from magnetic disks. The most common form of disk is the floppy **diskette**. This thin, $5\frac{1}{4}$-inch diameter round diskette is enclosed in a square plastic envelope and can store between 360,000 and 1,200,000 characters of data, depending upon its density. They can be bought for about $1 each.

When you want to use the instructions (programs) or data stored on a diskette, you place it in the disk drive and the computer can read the information from it. Replacing the $5\frac{1}{4}$-inch diskette is a diskette that measures $3\frac{1}{2}$-inches square. These diskettes, even though they are physically smaller, can store more data than the larger $5\frac{1}{4}$-inch diskettes, have a sturdier plastic case for better protection, and cost less than $2 each. There is even a newer version of the smaller disk which can store 2.88 Mb of data. These diskettes are still very expensive (about $10 each) but can be expected to decline in price over time.

FIGURE C-2

Photo courtesy of IPC Computers (Canada) Ltd.

In order to use these diskettes, however, your computer must have a disk drive that is designed for a $3\frac{1}{2}$-inch diskette.

Another type of disk drive is the **hard disk**. This disk can store as much information as hundreds of diskettes. Hard drives are permanently mounted in the computer and cost between $300 and $2,000 depending on their storage capacity. As computerized accounting programs for small businesses become more powerful they require more storage space; therefore, most computerized accounting packages can now be run only from a hard disk.

The other input device usually found in a microcomputer system is the keyboard. Much like a typewriter keyboard, this device lets us enter data and instructions.

CENTRAL PROCESSING UNIT.   The **central processing unit (CPU)** is the "brain" of the microcomputer. The CPU does the "thinking" for the computer — it performs mathematical and logical operations and it controls all the other components of the system.

OUTPUT DEVICES.   **Output devices** give us the information we want to receive from the computer. There are several ways the computer can present us with this output. The first device we might use is the **cathode ray tube (CRT)** or **monitor**. The monitor looks like a television set. It allows the user to view data as it is being processed and to receive messages or prompts from the program as it is being run.

The printer can provide printed copies of the information after it has been processed. Examples of the printed copies (also called **hard copies** or **printouts**) we might expect to see in an accounting system include the business's Balance Sheet and Income Statement or payroll cheques.

A third common output device is the diskette drive (which we also listed as an input device). We can save our records as they have been updated during the day's processing by placing them on a diskette. When the computer is turned off at the end of a work session, the internal memory in the CPU "forgets" the data you have put into it. However, the diskette provides us with extra storage. Here your data can be safely stored until you need it again.

Many computers are also equipped with a fourth output device — the tape backup unit. This device allows backups to be made very quickly and has the additional advantage of operating unattended (such as during a coffee break or in the evening) A reliable tape drive can be purchased for under $300 making it virtually a necessity for many accounting computer systems.

These are the basic hardware components of a microcomputer system. Learning to work with them is not difficult if you have a good program to give instructions to the computer. The types of programs that allow this hardware to be used as a computerized accounting system will be explained in the next unit.

At this point you should be able to:

1. State the advantages of using a computerized system. (p. 595)
2. Define the terms "hardware" and "software." (p. 597)
3. Differentiate between mainframe computers, minicomputers, and micro-computers. (p. 597)
4. List the main components of a microcomputer system. (p. 597-599)

☐ SELF-REVIEW QUIZ C-1

Respond true or false to the following:

1. Computerized accounting systems are very expensive and are used only by large businesses.
2. Software is the set of instructions that tell the computer how to complete a task.
3. A keyboard is both an input and output device.
4. Hard copy is information from the computer printed on paper.
5. A bookkeeper or accountant who does not know programming can still use a computer effectively to keep accounting records.
6. Backups of accounting data are only made on floppy diskettes.

■ *SOLUTION TO SELF-REVIEW QUIZ C-1*

1. False   2. True   3. False   4. True   5. True   6. False

LEARNING UNIT C-2

Accounting Software Programs

As we said earlier, accounting procedures cannot be performed on a computer unless there is software to tell the computer what to do. Software programs are sold on diskettes. You insert the diskette into the disk drive, and the computer can read the program instructions written on the diskette. Many types of accounting software are available to meet the differing needs of various businesses.

Accounting packages are usually sold in **modules**. Each module handles a particular area of the accounting records. The most common examples of modules would be packages designed to handle the general ledger, accounts receivable, accounts payable, and payroll work of a business. In addition to these modules, many others are available to help with specific functions such as billing, inventory, forecasting, fixed asset management, and job costing. Generally each module is written on a separate diskette, so that one module can be bought to be used alone or several modules can be bought to be used together.

Many small businesses start out using only one module on a **stand-alone** basis. For instance, payroll procedures are often the first accounting function to be converted from a manual system to a computerized system. This area is ideally suited to computerization because of the repetitive nature of payroll activities and the concentration on mathematical calculation. The accountant for a business could therefore save a great deal of time by putting a large payroll on the computer but still maintaining the rest of the business's records manually.

Other businesses find that they can produce accounting records more efficiently if they computerize *several* accounting functions. When several modules are bought to be used together, this is called **integrated software**. In an integrated system each module handles a different function but also communicates with all the other modules. For instance, in order to record a receipt of payment on accounts receivable, you would make an entry using the accounts receivable module. The journal entry would be recorded in the cash receipts journal in this module, and the customer's account would be automatically updated. In an integrated system this information would also be posted to the general ledger accounts in the general ledger module.

Because accounting packages vary, it is not possible to list the exact procedures involved in recording transactions. However, most computerized systems have many features in common. For instance, virtually all accounting programs are **menu-driven**. This means that when you turn the computer on and start the program, a list of options will be displayed for you to choose from. In order to choose a particular function for the computer to perform, you simply enter the number or letter identifying the option or use the arrow keys on the keyboard to highlight your choice and hit the enter key. Menus make the task of learning to use an accounting program much simpler. The first menu you will see when you enter a program is called a start menu. It will guide you to the section of the program that you wish to use.

Once you choose an option, the computer will either perform the function or display a new set of menu choices to receive more instructions. A typical start menu is shown in Figure C-3.

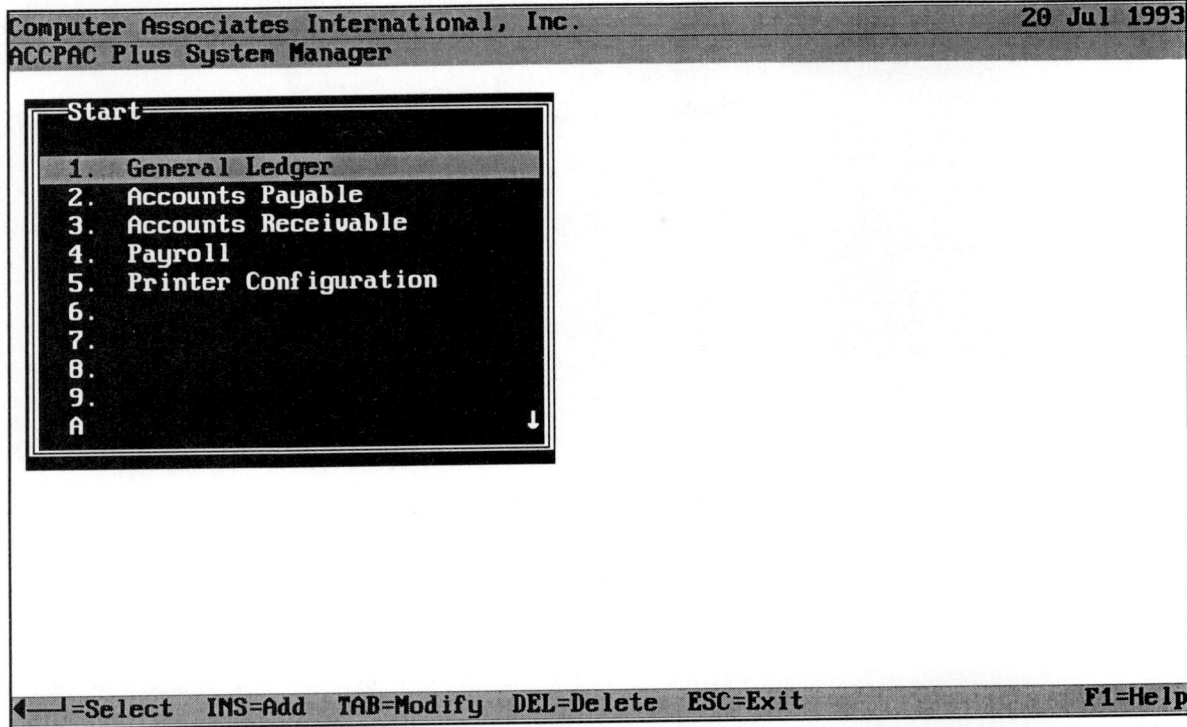

Used with permission of Computer Associates.

FIGURE C-3

**A Typical Start
Menu Screen**

To choose to work with a particular module of this program you would simply choose the appropriate menu option. For instance, to enter the general ledger section of the program you would type a "1."

Generally, in a computerized system (as in a manual system with a large number of transactions) transactions are recorded in batches. Transactions are not recorded the instant they occur. Instead, similar transactions are grouped together and recorded one group at a time. This is called **batch processing** For instance, instead of recording each sale or purchase immediately, we would wait until the end of the day and record all of the sales at one time and then all of the purchases at one time. In the remainder of this unit we will look at four different modules and explain how batches of transactions might be handled by a typical accounting software package.

GENERAL LEDGER MODULE

The general ledger module is the center of an integrated system. All of the general ledger accounts are maintained in this module. Figure C-4 is a typical master menu that might be found in a general ledger module.

One option included in this module is the Reports feature. Through this section of the program we can view the chart of accounts for our business which tells us such information as each account's name, number, normal balance, and type (current asset, plant asset, and so on). Since the program will remember this information, we need enter it only once, using the Housekeeping option.

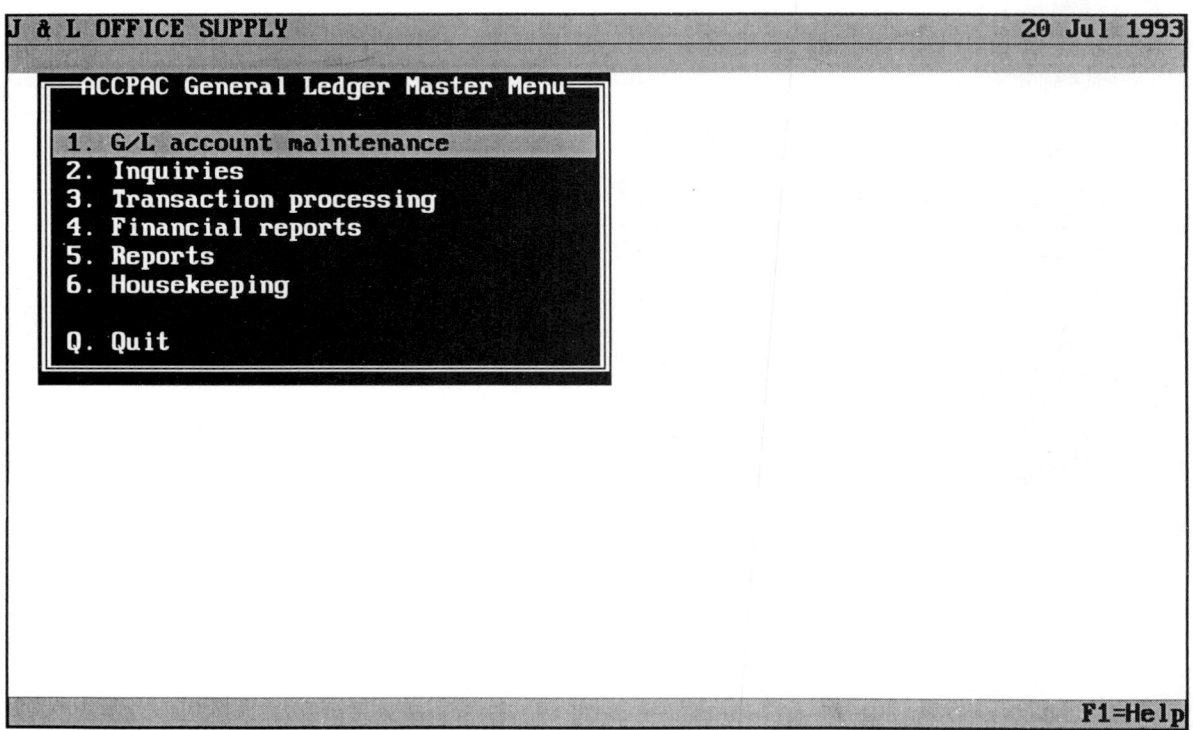

Used with permission of Computer Associates.

FIGURE C-4

A Typical Master Menu Found in a General Ledger Module

This chart can be modified whenever necessary. Once the chart has been set up, you can refer to an account simply by listing its account number — given the account number, the program can supply the name and other information by referring to the chart of accounts.

Journal entries can also be entered through this module using the transaction processing option. Just as shown in a manual system in Chapters 1-5 of this text, some businesses choose to use the general journal as their only book of original entry. In Chapters 6 and 7 we saw the advantages of a multi-journal system for merchandising businesses. The same option exists in a computerized system — the general ledger module can be used on a stand-alone basis, with the general journal as the only book of original entry, or other modules with their special journals can be used in an integrated system.

To enter a journal entry we list the number of each account affected (the computer will supply the account name), the amount of the transaction, and the choice of either debit or credit for the account. Once the transaction has been listed, the program will ask if the entry is correct before recording it. The computer will then check to see if the journal entry balances (if debits equal credits). As an error-protection feature, most programs will not accept the entry if it does not balance. Also, while some programs post the entry immediately, others allow the operator to post all or selected entries at a time of their choosing.

Once the entries have all been made it is a good idea to print the general journal (often called an "edit-listing"). This printout, commonly called a "hard copy," provides a permanent record of the journal entries. It is important that in a computerized system hard copies of all work be kept to document the accounting records. An example of a page of general journal entries is shown in Figure C-5.

FIGURE C-5

**General Journal
Entries**

J&L OFFICE SUPPLY
GENERAL JOUNAL
PAGE 03

TRANS	DATE	ACCT. NO.	ACCT. NAME	DR.	CR.
32	4/20	1360	STORE EQUIP	1800.00	
		2200	ACCOUNTS PAY		1800.00
33	4/20	5400	SALARIES EXP	1900.00	
		2710	INC TAX PAY		399.00
		2711	CPP PAYABLE		135.85
		2712	UI PAYABLE		148.00
		2713	UNION DUES PAY		35.00
		2720	SALARIES PAY		1182.15
34	4/20	5410	PAYROLL TAX EXP	343.05	
		2711	CPP PAYABLE		135.85
		2712	UI PAYABLE		207.20
35	4/21	4130	SALES RET & ALL	86.40	
		2370	SALES TAX PAY	6.05	
		1200	ACCOUNTS REC		92.45
36	4/22	2200	ACCOUNTS PAY	651.00	
		5130	PURCH RET & ALL		651.00
37	4/23	1370	OFFICE EQUIP	243.20	
		2200	ACCOUNTS PAY		243.20
38	4/23	4130	SALES RET & ALL	100.00	
		2370	SALES TAX PAY	7.00	
		1200	ACCOUNTS REC		107.00
39	4/26	1360	STORE EQUIP	400.00	
		2200	ACCOUNTS PAY		400.00
			PAGE TOTALS	5536.70	5536.70

After the general journal has been printed, it should be examined for mistakes. Once this has been done, and any necessary corrections made, the journal can be posted. Posting in a computerized system is a very simple process. Generally, all that is involved is choosing the menu option "Post Transactions." The program will then post and also enter posting references automatically. Obviously this represents a considerable time saving over the manual method of posting. This method is also much more accurate, because the computer is not likely to make a posting error.

It is also important at times to see (on the screen or printed out) the whole general ledger — in order to check each account, for example. A printout of a few general ledger accounts is shown in Figure C-6. Note that the posting references refer to entries posted from *other* journals besides the general journal. These postings came from the other modules, which will be explained later in this unit.

At the end of the financial period, the program can be asked to produce the trial balance. We can use this trial balance as a guideline for making our adjusting entries. Adjusting entries would be recorded using the "Enter Transactions" option

```
J&L OFFICE SUPPLY
GENERAL LEDGER
AS OF 04-30-XX
```

CASH					ACCOUNT NO. 1100

DATE	EXPLANATION	REF	DEBIT	CREDIT	BALANCE
19XX					
0401	BEG. BAL.	——			35540.00 DR
0430	TOTAL	CR12	23671.00		59211.00 DR
0430	TOTAL	CP08		31437.23	27773.77 DR

CHANGE FUND					ACCOUNT NO. 1110

DATE	EXPLANATION	REF	DEBIT	CREDIT	BALANCE
0401	BEG. BAL.	——			300.00 DR

PETTY CASH					ACCOUNT NO. 1120

DATE	EXPLANATION	REF	DEBIT	CREDIT	BALANCE
0401	BEG. BAL.	——			100.00 DR

ACCOUNTS RECEIVABLE					ACCOUNT NO. 1200 DR

DATE	EXPLANATION	REF	DEBIT	CREDIT	BALANCE
0401	BEG. BAL.	——			8743.00 DR
0421		J03		92.45	8650.55 DR
0423		J03		107.00	8543.55 DR
0430	TOTAL	S06	19872.00		28415.55 DR
0430	TOTAL	CR12		25112.00	3303.55 DR

FIGURE C-6

Sample Printout of General Ledger Details

like any other general journal entry. These entries would then be posted using the posting option on the menu. Once this is done, the account balances will be updated and ready to be used on the financial statements.

An important benefit to using a computerized system is that you do *not* have to prepare a work sheet. The reason that we use a work sheet in a manual system is to organize and check data before preparing the financial statements. (By showing the adjustments on the same sheet as the trial balance, we are less likely to make errors in posting and calculating balances.) Since in a computer system we can post very quickly and the computer does the math, the potential for error is reduced and there is a reduced need for a work sheet.

In order to print the financial statements, it may only be necessary to select the option from the menu and the statement will be created automatically. Many accounting programs allow users to customize the financial statements to fit their needs. In this case, users must enter their design for the financial statements before they can be printed for the first time. A flexible package will allow you to print Income Statements that compare the current period to other periods or budget figures. Often, statements that include percentage calculations or figures broken down by departments can be printed.

As we stated in Chapter 5, the closing process is a purely mechanical one. Therefore, most accounting packages include an option allowing you to request that the temporary accounts be automatically cleared to the proper account at the end of each fiscal period. Once this is done, a post-closing trial balance can be prepared by choosing the "View/Print Trial Balance" option in the general ledger menu. Just as in a manual system, this completes the accounting cycle, and our balances are updated and ready to be used in the next accounting period.

Figure C-7 is a chart of the flow of information in a system using a general ledger module. As you can see from this figure, the entire accounting cycle can be completed using the general ledger module of the accounting program. However, many businesses find that they can derive even greater benefit from their computerized system if they use one or more of the other modules in coordination with the general ledger module. Let's examine three common modules.

ACCOUNTS RECEIVABLE MODULE

The accounts receivable module allows us to keep track of our accounts receivable ledger and it provides us with special journals to record transactions that affect accounts receivable. Many A/R programs now also help considerably in tracking and reporting on the GST. In Chapter 6 we discussed the need many businesses had for the sales journal and the cash receipts journal. By using an accounts receivable module a business can also record entries in these special journals using a computerized system. A typical menu for the accounts receivable module is shown in Figure C-8.

When a business first converts its records to a computerized basis, all of the information in the manual accounts receivable ledger must be transferred to this program. Each customer's name and balance will be put on the computer. In addition, it is generally necessary to assign account numbers to the accounts receivable accounts. This makes the task of referring to an account on the computer much easier, since only the account number need be entered and not the entire name. Many businesses assign A/R account numbers that begin with an alphabetic character. In this way they can still keep accounts listed in alphabetic order. For instance, the account number for Ralph's Hardware might be R2020, and the number assigned to Rose's Florist Shoppe would be R2080. As new customers are added, the accountant can use the option to modify the accounts receivable ledger to set up new accounts for them.

As stated earlier, transactions would be recorded in batches. The sales for the day would be recorded at one time using this module. In some programs the sales would be entered in the same format as a manual sales journal. Other programs will allow the accountant to enter each sale in the form of a sales invoice. Not only will the program create a sales journal from these entries but also it can print out actual sales invoices to be sent to customers, thus eliminating the need to prepare these invoices manually. An example of a computer-generated sales invoice is shown in Figure C-9.

FIGURE C-7

**Flow of
Information
Using a General
Ledger Module**

GENERAL LEDGER MODULE

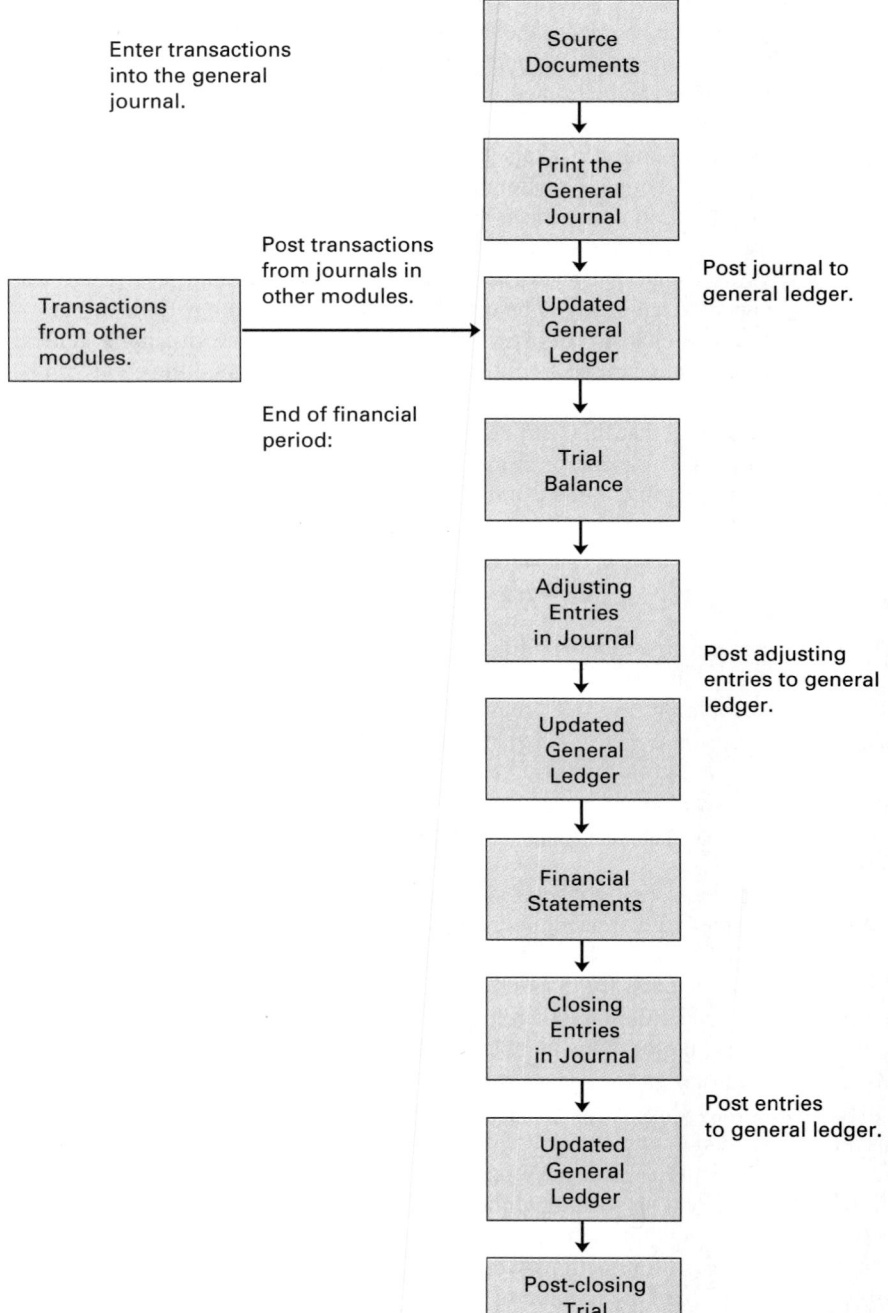

Enter transactions into the general journal.

Post transactions from journals in other modules.

Transactions from other modules.

End of financial period:

Source Documents

Print the General Journal

Updated General Ledger

Post journal to general ledger.

Trial Balance

Adjusting Entries in Journal

Updated General Ledger

Post adjusting entries to general ledger.

Financial Statements

Closing Entries in Journal

Updated General Ledger

Post entries to general ledger.

Post-closing Trial Balance

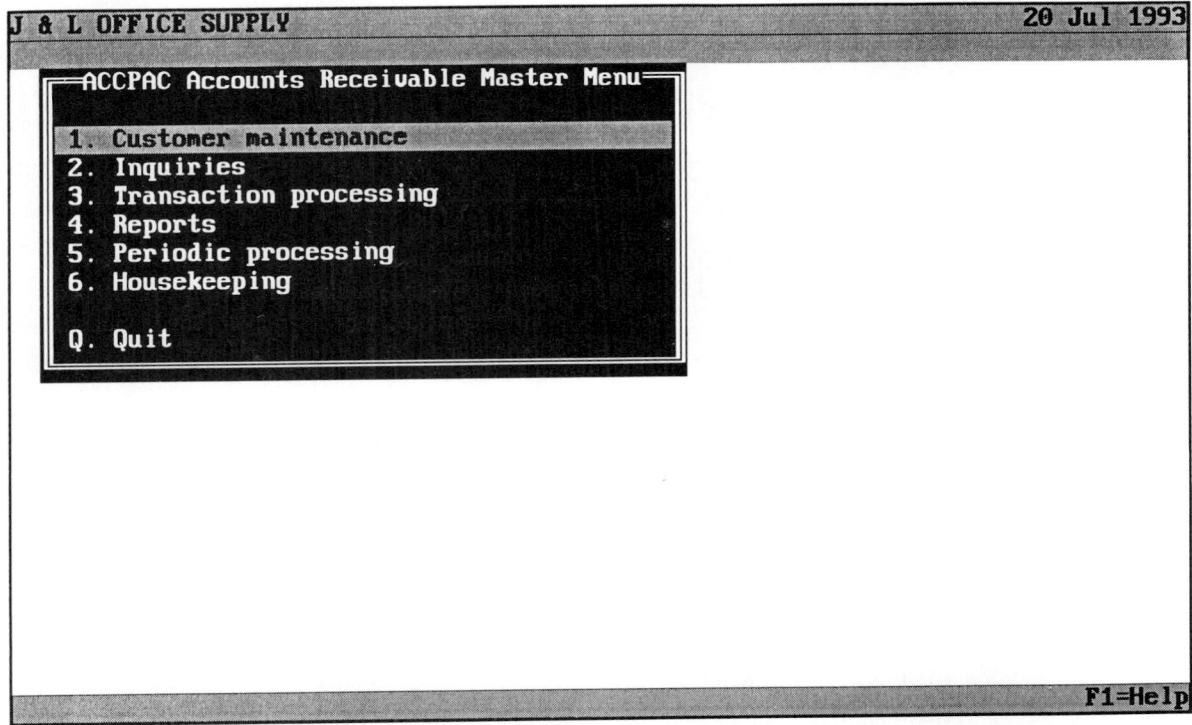

Used with permission of Computer Associates.

Once the sales for the day have been entered, a sales journal can be printed out. A hard copy will be checked for correctness and then saved as a permanent record. This journal can now be posted. Just as in a manual system, the sales journal should be posted to two ledgers — both the accounts receivable ledger in the A/R module and the general ledger in the G/L module. In some software packages this is done automatically when you enter the sales invoice. In others it is done through a separate menu option as shown in Figure C-10 (under Transaction processing).

The other journal found in the A/R module is the cash receipts journal, where all transactions involving a receipt of cash are recorded. A batch of cash receipt transactions will be entered into the computer in the same format in which the entries would be recorded manually. As with the other journals, a hard copy would be printed out and checked for correctness. This journal would also be posted to both the general ledger and the accounts receivable ledger (sometimes in summary form).

In most programs the computer not only will keep a running balance of the A/R ledger accounts but also can print out monthly statements to be sent to customers with details of their present account balance. An example of a monthly statement is shown in Figure C-10.

These programs can also automatically assign finance charges to overdue accounts and prepare an aging of accounts receivable report. If a business is also using an inventory module in its system, each item sold can automatically be subtracted from the inventory. Obviously these functions can save accounting personnel a great deal of time. Figure C-11 on p. 610 shows how information flows in a system that uses an accounts receivable module.

FIGURE C-8

A Typical Menu for the Accounts Receivable Module

FIGURE C-9

J & L Office Supply

1200 Arbor Avenue
New Westminister, BC V6J 3E6
Telephone 604 555 2121

GST Registration # 723454873

Invoice No. 2081

Sold to:

Shaw Engineering Consultants

1400 Veteran's Blvd.

Vancouver, BC V6A 2L3

Ship to:

Same

DATE	ORDER DATE	CUSTOMER NO	SOLD BY	PO NUMBER	SHIP VIA	TERMS
23-04-9X	21-04-9X	SE 9047	KH	0628	Courier	2% 10 days, N30

QUANTITY	QTY SHIPPED	BACK ORDER	DESCRIPTION	PRICE	DISCOUNT	TOTAL
10	10		24X914	7.00		70.00
50	50		87A827	1.25		62.50
20	20		24X820	1.50		30.00
100	100		42B191	.25		25.00

SPECIAL INSTRUCTIONS			SUB TOTAL	187.50
			GST	13.12
			TOTAL	200.62

FIGURE C-10

J & L Office Supply

1200 Arbor Ave.,
New Westminister, BC   V6J 3E6
Telephone 604 555 2121

STATEMENT

DATE
04-30-9X
ACCOUNT NUMBER
SE 9047

SHAW ENGINEERING CONSULTANTS
1400 Veteran's Blvd.
Vancouver, BC   V6A 2L3

$ _____

AMOUNT REMITTED

To ensure proper credit please return this portion of the statement with your payment.

REFERENCE	DATE	CODE	DESCRIPTION	AMOUNT	BALANCE
1974	04-06-9X	I	Invoice	856.00	856.00
1974	04-15-9X	P	Payment - Thanks	840.00	16.00
1974	04-15-9X	A	Discount allowed	16.00	- 0 -
2081	04-23-9X	I	Invoice	200.62	200.62

CODES: I - INVOICE   P - PAYMENT
         C - CR MEMO   A - DISCOUNT ALLOWED

TOTAL AMOUNT DUE $200.62

CURRENT	30 DAYS	60 DAYS	90 DAYS	120 DAYS
$200.62				

Daily transactions
are entered.

Invoices prepared
on printer.

Journals prepared
and printed.

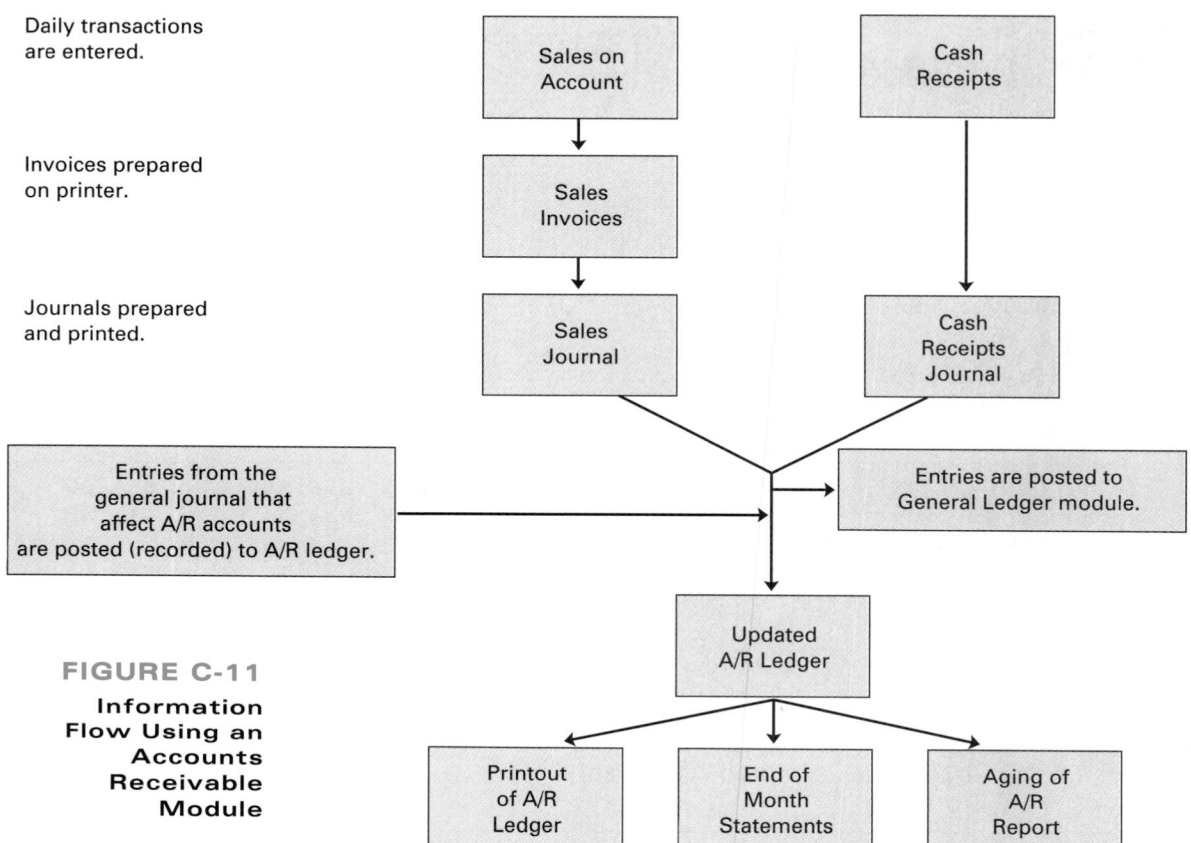

FIGURE C-11

**Information
Flow Using an
Accounts
Receivable
Module**

ACCOUNTS PAYABLE MODULE

Using this module a business can maintain its accounts payable ledger, issue cheques to pay its accounts payable, and generate both the purchases and cash payments journals. A typical accounts payable module menu is shown in Figure C-12.

When we first set up the accounts payable module we will transfer all of the vendor information from the manual A/P ledger. As with accounts receivable, it is usually necessary to assign an account number to each account.

When a purchase invoice is received from a vendor, it is entered into the accounts payable module. From each batch of invoices entered the program will create a purchases journal. From this journal the purchases can be posted to both the accounts payable ledger and the general ledger.

When the time comes to pay invoices, the computerized system can provide a list of each invoice that is due on a particular date. The accountant can list the numbers of each invoice he or she wishes to pay and the amount of the payment. Using pre-printed forms, the computer can actually print out the cheques. Figure C-13 on p. 612 is an example of a computer-generated cheque along with its stub showing information about the invoice paid.

The program will record each cheque as an entry in the cash payments journal. This journal can then be posted to both the accounts payable and general ledgers. The accounts payable module not only keeps an accurate accounts payable ledger but also keeps track of every purchase invoice, when it is due, and the outstanding balance. Even fully paid invoices will be shown, along with the date of payment. Occasionally, we will wish to print a list of all paid invoices for the records and delete them from the computer files. Computerized accounts payable systems are generally very efficient and prevent many errors — such as paying an invoice twice, paying the wrong amount, or mistakenly paying too late to receive the discount. Also, if an inventory module is added to this system, each purchase of merchandise can automatically be added into the inventory list. Figure C-14 on p. 613 shows how information flows in a system using an accounts payable module.

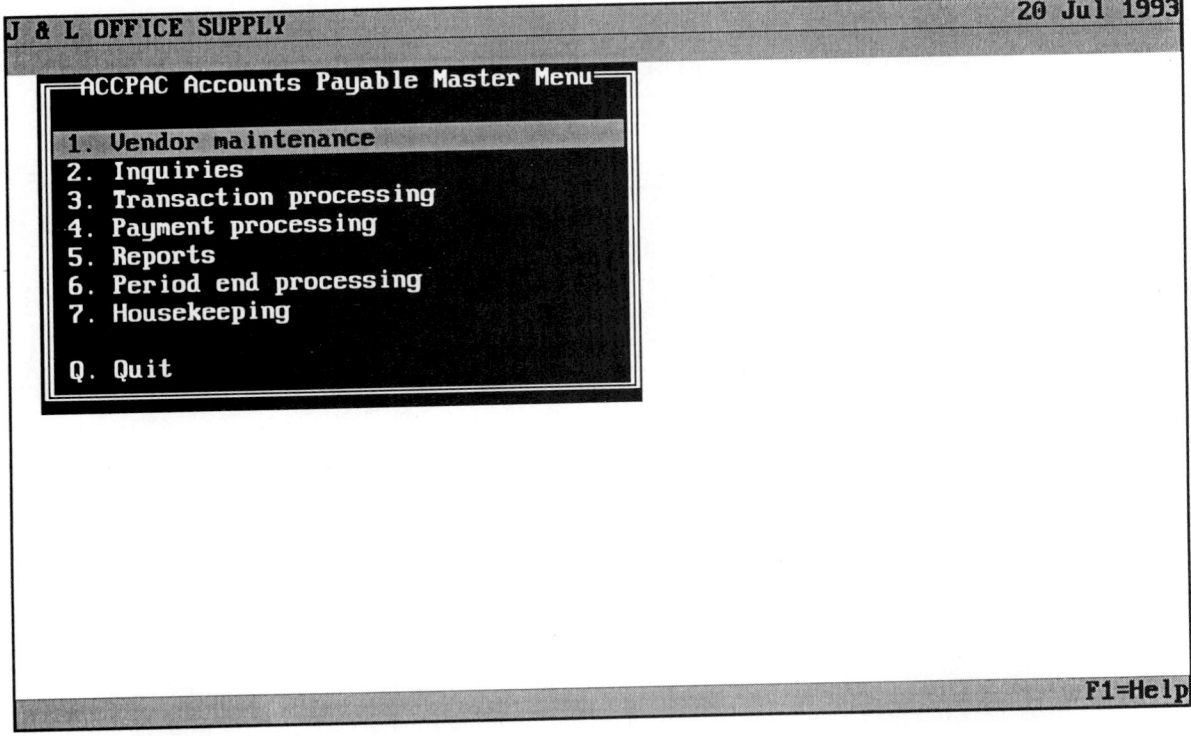

Used with permission of Computer Associates.

PAYROLL MODULE

As stated earlier, payroll activities are ideally suited for a computerized system. A typical payroll module menu is shown in Figure C-15 on p. 614. In order to use the payroll program, we will have to set up a computer file on each employee. These files will contain such information about each employee as name, address, pay rate (if hourly), salary (per pay period), marital status, withholding allowances, and voluntary deductions. This information can be modified at any time (for instance when an employee moves or receives a raise, or when a new employee is hired).

On each payday we will use the Timesheet processing option in the menu to give the computer the information necessary to calculate the payroll. The program will list each employee in order of employee number and show the information that was last entered to calculate the payroll. This information would consist of the

FIGURE C-12

A Typical Accounts Payable Module Menu.

J & L OFFICE SUPPLY   1200 Arbor Ave. New Westminster, B.C. V6J 3E6   CHEQUE   005074

OUR REF NO.	YOUR INV.	INV. DATE	INV. AMOUNT	AMOUNT PAID	DISCOUNT TAKEN	NET CHEQUE AMOUNT
P1028	5673	6-1--XX	3080.00	3080.00		3080.00
P1264	5823	6-17-XX	1420.00	1420.00	28.40	1391.60

TOTAL   4471.60

J & L Office Supply
1200 Arbor Avenue
New Westminister, B.C. V6J 3E6

CHEQUE NO.   DATE
005074   6 - 23 - XX

PAY TO THE   Franklin Paper Co.
ORDER OF   2120 Essen Lane   AMOUNT
               Richmond, B.C. V6T 3A1   4471.60

PAY   Four thousand four hundred seventy one and 60/100 --------
                                                    J & L Office Supply

Royal Bank of Canada (Main Branch)
Royal Bank Plaza, Toronto, Ontario M5J 2J5

                                                    AUTHORIZED SIGNATURE

FIGURE C-13

Computer-Generated Cheque and Stub

number of regular and overtime hours worked, bonuses or commissions to be received, and any special deductions to be taken from this paycheque. For most employees this information does not change from pay period to pay period and will not have to be modified. After the information for the current payroll is entered, the computer will automatically calculate each paycheque. The program will calculate regular pay, overtime pay, gross pay, each deduction (FIT, CPP, UI, etc.), and net pay. The current tax tables should be built into the program so that both federal and provincial taxes can be calculated. Also, the computer knows year-to-date earnings for each employee and can calculate CPP and UI correctly.

Next, we will instruct the program to print the payroll register. After we verify that all information is correct, the payroll cheques can be printed. Using pre-printed cheques, the program can print out cheques and the accompanying stubs. Figure C-16 on p. 615 is an example of a computer-generated paycheque.

Once the payroll cheques have been printed, all that is left to be done for the current payroll is to post the payroll register information to the general ledger and to update all the employees' individual earnings records. Both of these tasks can be performed by simply choosing the appropriate menu option.

Whenever year-to-date payroll information on an employee is needed, a menu option can be chosen to print out the employee's earnings records. At the end of

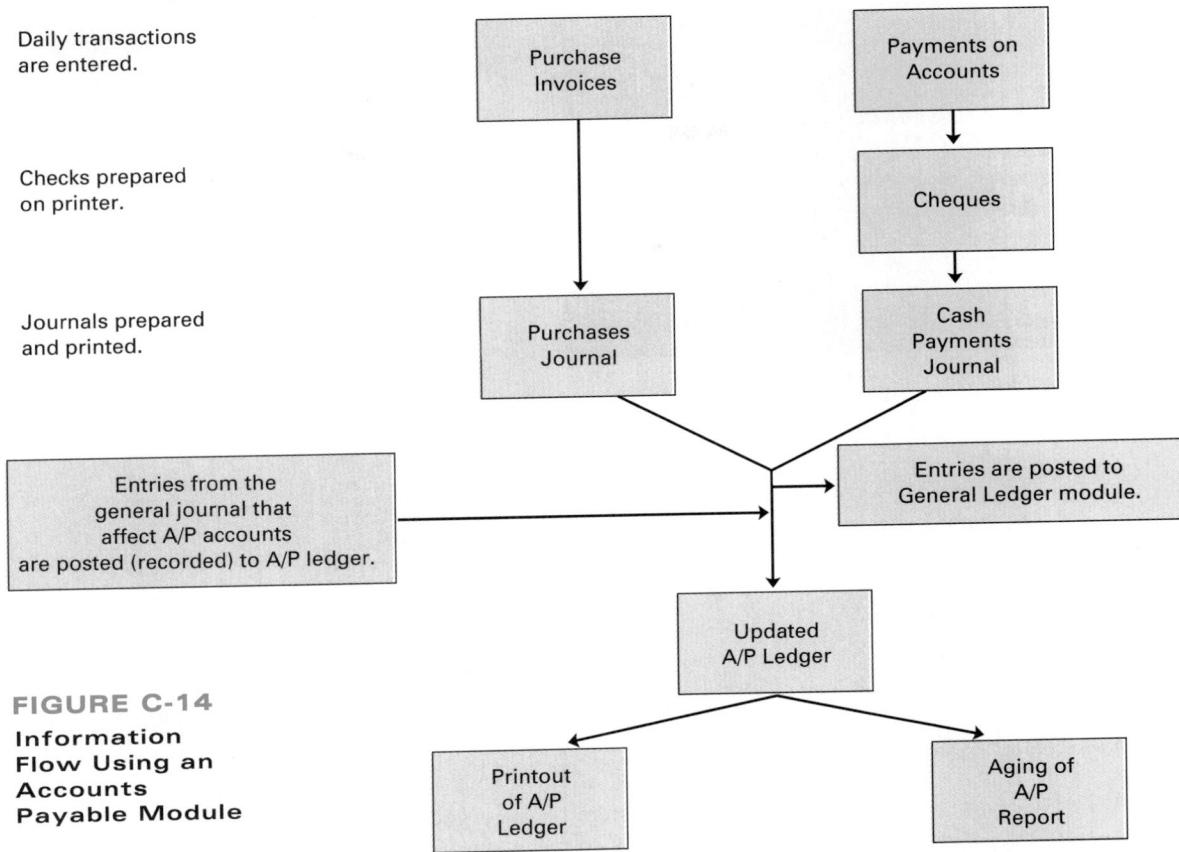

Daily transactions are entered.

Checks prepared on printer.

Journals prepared and printed.

FIGURE C-14

Information Flow Using an Accounts Payable Module

each month the information in the employee's earnings records can be used to prepare TD7-AR forms on appropriate computer paper. Most programs have an option that lets the computer print the forms for you. At the end of the calendar year you must prepare T-4 forms for each employee. You can obtain T-4 forms that will fit into your printer and have the computer fill them out. An example of a computer-generated T-4 is shown in Figure C-17 on p. 616.

Another feature of most payroll software is the ability to quickly and accurately prepare and print Record of Employment forms. These forms are typically quite time-consuming to do manually.

To begin a new year all of the year-to-date totals on the employees' earnings records will be zeroed out. It is always a necessary to make a hard copy of the final employees' earnings records at the end of the year before starting all of the balances over, since the law requires that payroll information be kept a minimum of four years. Figure C-18 on p. 616 shows how information flows in a system using a payroll module.

It is not necessary to memorize the procedures used in this unit. Each software package is slightly different and will not follow these procedures exactly. What is important is that you have enough confidence to pick up the manual for a software package and learn how to use the program in your business. As you can see, the procedures followed in a computerized accounting system are almost identical to those in a manual system. Because of this, it is not difficult for someone who

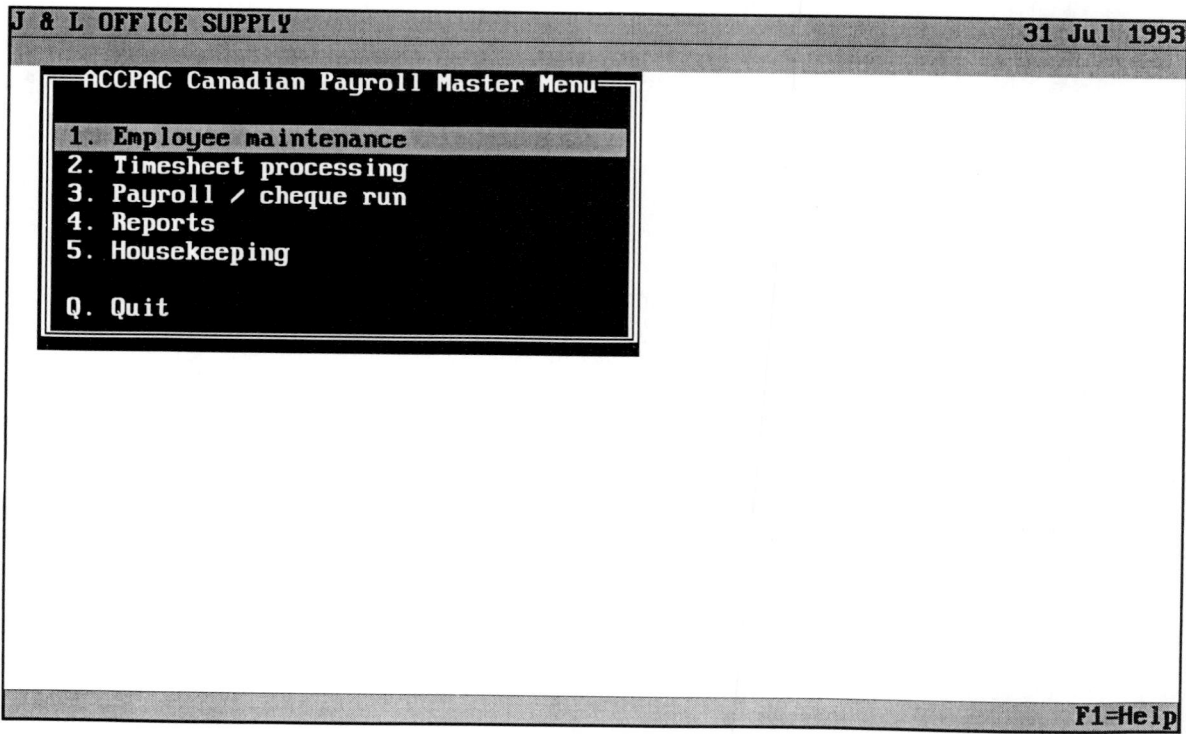

Used with permission of Computer Associates.

FIGURE C-15

A Typical Payroll Module Menu

understands a manual system to use a good computer accounting program. The next unit will explain how to make sure that the accounting package you buy is easy to use, reliable, and suits the needs of your business.

At this point you should be able to:

1. Define and contrast stand-alone modules and integrated software. (p. 600)
2. Explain the term "menu-driven program." (p. 600)
3. Discuss how closely computerized procedures follow manual procedures. (p. 602)
4. List various documents that the computer can generate for the accountant. (pp. 601-613)

☐ **SELF-REVIEW QUIZ C-2**

Respond true or false to the following:

1. It is possible to computerize just one area of the accounting records such as the A/R ledger and not computerize the other areas.
2. No special journals are used in a computerized system.
3. In order to prepare financial statements in a computerized system you must first complete a work sheet.
4. It is necessary to assign account numbers to A/R and A/P accounts in the subsidiary ledgers in a computerized system.
5. Transactions are recorded on the computer in batches of similar transactions rather than in order of occurrence to improve efficiency.

SOLUTION TO SELF-REVIEW QUIZ C-2

1. True   2. False   3. False   4. True   5. True

FIGURE C-16   J & L Office Supply -- 1200 Arbor Avenue -- New Westminister, B.C. V6J 3E6

J & L Office Supply
1200 Arbor Avenue
New Westminister, B.C. V6J 3E6

CHEQUE NO.	DATE
037004	6 - 15 - XX

TO THE
ORDER OF   Roberta R. Lewis

AMOUNT

433.98

PAY   Four hundred thirty-three and 98/100--------------------------------------

Royal Bank of Canada   (Main Branch)
Royal Bank Plaza, Toronto, Ontario M5J 2J5

AUTHORIZED SIGNATURE

Earnings/Gains	Hrs. - Mls.	Rate - Taux	Amount/Montant	Deductions	Amount/Montant
Lewis, Roberta R. 113115					
REGULAR HOURS	16.00	15.87	253.92	FEDERAL TAX	71.83
REGULAR HOURS	16.00	15.87	253.92	CANADA PENSION	10.82
OVERTIME HOURS X 1.5	1.50	23.80	35.71	U.I.C.	16.80
SHIFT DIFFERENTIAL	8.00	.50	4.00	HEALTH CARE	14.50
SHIFT DIFFERENTIAL	8.25	1.50	12.38	UNION DUES	12.00

CHEQUE DATE 6 - 15 -XX	GROSS PAY	559.93	NET PAY	433.98

FIGURE C-17　Computer-Generated T4 Form

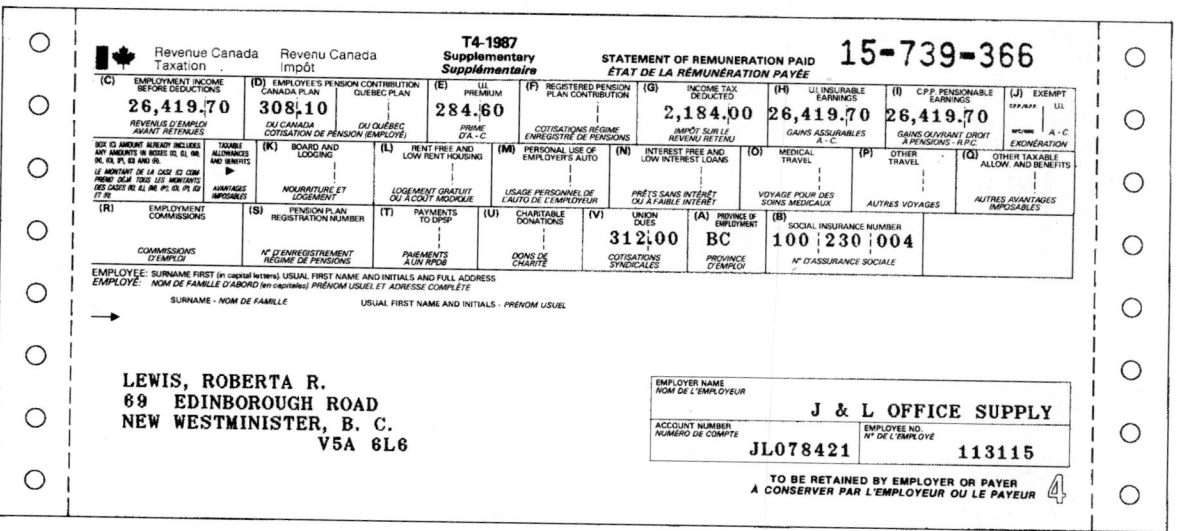

FIGURE C-18

Information Flow Using a Payroll Module

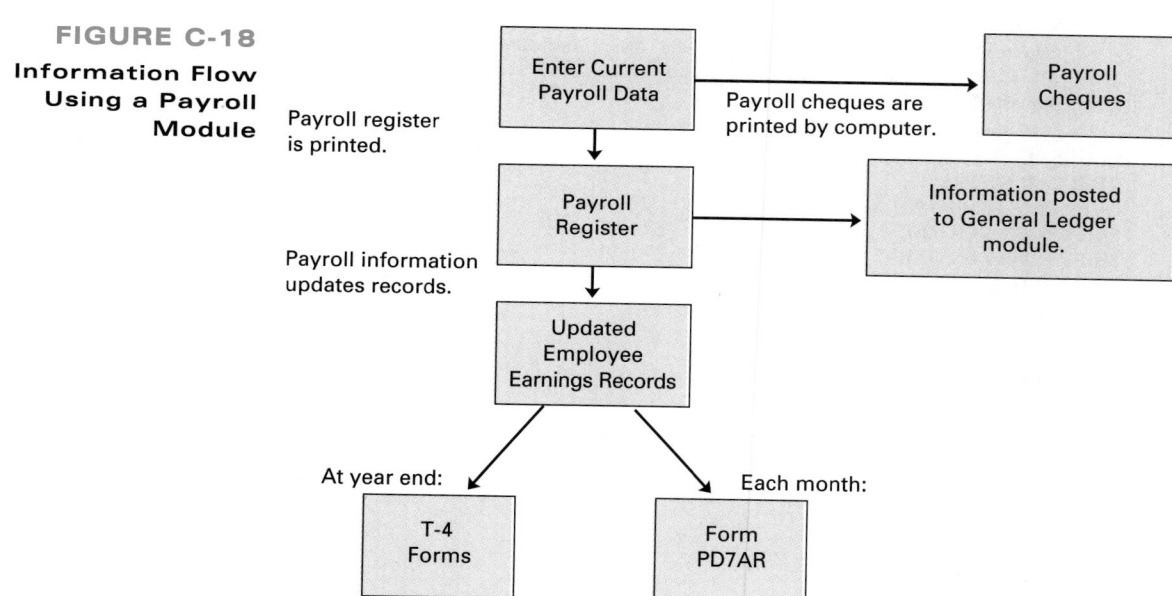

LEARNING UNIT C-3

How to Choose and Use Accounting Software

You have seen in the previous unit that if a business has a good software package, it is not difficult to perform accounting tasks on the computer. The problem most small businesses face when they decide they need to convert to a computerized system is how to buy a good software package. There are over 200 general-use accounting software packages available, many of which are specially created or modified for Canadian businesses.

Some of the considerations important when buying an accounting package are discussed below.

SIMILARITY TO PRESENT PROCEDURES. When you shop for a software package, you should carefully analyze the procedures you are using in your manual accounting system. Although you probably won't find a system that handles every task exactly as you have done in the past, you should be able to find one that will fit your present procedures.

SOFTWARE COMPATIBILITY. Make sure that the software you buy is **compatible** with (will run on) the computer you own. Since different computers have different operating systems, a software package must be written for that computer (or one with which it is compatible) for the software and computer to be able to communicate. If you are not sure whether the program is compatible with your computer ask the software dealer for help. (We assume the dealer is knowledgeable.)

MINIMUM REQUIREMENTS. You should carefully analyze your business to determine whether a particular accounting program is able to meet its needs. For instance, if your business has 300 credit accounts a program that could carry a maximum of 250 accounts would not meet your minimum requirements. Limits in such areas as the number of transactions in a financial period, accounts receivable accounts, accounts payable accounts, general ledger accounts, inventory items, and employees on the payroll should be considered. Consider likely future growth when evaluating the capabilities of each program.

COST. There is a wide range of prices in accounting software today. Prices for good software range from as low as $60 for a fully integrated package with seven modules to as much as a thousand dollars per module. Unlike many other products, price is not necessarily an indicator of quality with software packages. Recently, many software producers have found that by lowering their prices they increase their sales so dramatically that they can still make a good profit. Many of the lower-priced packages are of good quality though they may not offer the reporting flexibility or error controls of more expensive packages.

DOCUMENTATION. A very important factor when setting up a computerized system is how well the program **documentation** is written. Documentation comes in the form of a manual. Unfortunately, many software packages come with complicated or badly organized manuals. Even the best software, if it has a poor instruction manual, can be completely unusable (or at least underutilized). Before purchasing a package you should ask to examine the manual carefully. It is important to make sure that it guides you step by step through each procedure. The manual should be thorough enough to answer questions that will arise when the program is used.

USER SUPPORT.   Another important factor to consider is what kind of **user support** is provided by the company that produced the software. Occasionally you will have questions or problems not covered in the manual. When this happens, you should be able to call or fax a user support line where your questions can be answered. Some software manufacturers provide free support for a limited time after purchase of the program or "sell" support for a stated period of time. You should also be sure that the software producer will provide updates of the program when payroll rates change. (Be careful to enquire about the cost of any update services.)

EMPLOYEE TRAINING.   For some software packages training classes are available through either the makers of the software, the software vendor, or local colleges. For a firm whose employees don't have the time to teach themselves how to use a particular program these classes can be very helpful. Some packages offer tutorials. **Tutorials** are step-by-step instructions that guide the first-time user through hands-on completion of sample tasks on the computer. A few vendors are even offering a video tutorial which can be especially useful if done well.

ERROR PROTECTION.   You should examine the software to determine whether it has adequate **error protection** — built-in controls to prevent errors. Examples would be a feature whereby the program requires the debits to equal the credits before it will accept a journal entry, or a feature that requires you to confirm that a command to delete a file was indeed intentional. This type of protection is virtually essential to a smoothly running accounting system. Another type of error-protection control limits access to programs and data by requiring users to enter a password before being allowed entry to the program — or even better, to certain parts of the program.

DEMONSTRATION.   When considering the purchase of a particular software package you should ask the software dealer to give you a demonstration of the package. A demonstration can reveal much about the ease of use of the program. Choose the dealer with care as not all dealers are equally knowledgeable when it comes to accounting software.

REFERENCES.   One of the most revealing checks that you can make on an accounting package is to ask the software vendor for references. You should request the names of other businesses that have used this software. Just as you would check the references of a new employee, you should ask questions of someone who has used the program. After all, this package will be a significant "member" of your accounting staff. Although it is not always possible, it is particularly helpful if you can find someone who has been using the software for an entire fiscal period. Often problems with software are not evident right away. By speaking to someone who has used the system you can verify its ease of use, reliability, and the quality of the user support. A related issue is the availability of trained operators to replace your own staff as necessary. If a particular software package is well accepted in the marketplace, then it is usually possible to obtain trained operators without too much trouble.

VERTICAL, MODIFIED AND CUSTOM SOFTWARE

Some companies find that as a result of the unusual nature of their accounting procedures, standard accounting packages do not suit their needs very well. In addition to packages that are designed to meet the needs of businesses in general, which are called **horizontal accounting packages**, there are packages that are available for specific types of businesses. For instance, there are programs designed to be used in a dentist's office and packages designed to fit the accounting done in a law firm or a manufacturing plant. These are referred to as **vertical accounting packages**. Since these packages are designed to fit the procedures in a particular type of office, it might be possible to find one that matches a specialized business's needs more closely than a general package would.

If a business can find no ready-made software that is adequate, it still has two options. One option is to have a programmer write a custom program specifically for the company's needs (typically a very costly and lengthy process). The other is to buy a ready-made program and have a programmer modify it. Because of the large variety of software available today, however, these steps are generally not necessary. The vast majority of small businesses are able to buy a ready-made software package that suits their requirements and provides distinct advantages over their manual method. Several of the top-end accounting software packages are now designed to make customization an easy option. Also be aware that many of these same general-purpose packages already have vertical modules written for them.

SETTING UP THE SYSTEM

Once you have purchased an accounting package, the next consideration is setting up the system. This is often the most difficult part of using a computerized system. However, a good program with a well-written manual (and on-line help screens) can make this task relatively easy if the business's books are in good shape before the conversion.

Most software packages require that you perform several tasks in order to set up the system. Though this may be a time-consuming procedure, it is only a one-time job and will be more than worth the trouble in the long run. Many brands of software even make the task of setting up the system much easier by providing a set-up tutorial on disk. This program leads you step by step through normal setup procedures with messages on the monitor. Typical procedures required to be performed before the program can be used are:

- Entering general information about the business, such as name, address, fiscal year, and so on.
- Setting up a chart of accounts. This can be the same list of account numbers and names you used in the manual system.
- Setting up a general ledger file for each account. If the business is not new and manual records have been kept, then it is also necessary to enter present account balances for each account. In many packages this is done by an opening journal entry in the general journal.
- Setting up a customer file. This is equivalent to an accounts receivable ledger. Besides listing the name, address, and balance owed by each customer, it is often

necessary to assign account numbers to each accounts receivable account — even if they were not used in the manual system.

- Setting up a vendor file. This is equivalent to an accounts payable ledger. As with accounts receivable, the vendor's name, address, and the balance we owe each vendor will be transferred from the manual system; in addition, account numbers should be assigned.
- Setting up an employee information file. In order to do payroll calculations the program must have data about each employee. This information would include their name, address, social security number, pay rate, marital status, and details of withholding allowances.
- Formatting of financial statements.
- Defining hardware configuration. This simply means that a program may need to be told what brand of monitor and printer you are using before it can be used. Generally, excellent guidelines for this one-time procedure will be given in the manual.

Although a computerized system will generally run smoothly once it has been set up and you have become accustomed to it, it is always advisable (and expensive!) to continue performing the manual procedures alongside the computerized ones for the first two to three months. By using the two systems in parallel, you can detect problems in the conversion and also confirm the accuracy of the accounting records under the new system. An alternative to the parallel operation is to have the firm's accountant closely monitor the conversion process. Be certain that the accountant is qualified and completely up-to-date on computers before engaging him or her.

CONTROLS IN A COMPUTERIZED ACCOUNTING SYSTEM

When using a computerized system there are some controls that a business must consider. Perhaps the most important new controls are those that prevent the loss of accounting information and ensure the continuance of accounting operations.

In a modern computerized system all records are stored on the hard drive. Care should be taken so that the accounting records will not be lost, damaged, erased or deliberately sabotaged. Sometimes, however, despite careful handling, data will be lost. For this reason it is *essential* that duplicate copies, called *backups*, be made of the accounting data on a routine basis — at least daily. If a backup diskette or tape of the accounting information is made on a daily basis, then at most only one day's worth of transactions would have to be reconstructed if the data should become unusable for any reason.

We have noted several times that hard copies of all journals and ledgers should be kept. Just as in a manual system, it is always a good idea to place an up-to-date copy of the ledgers in a fireproof safe or somewhere off the premises at least once a week to protect against the loss of all accounting records. For the same reason it is necessary to make one extra copy of the accounting data once a week (or month) on floppy diskette or tape and store this copy at an off-site location. This safety copy is called an *archive copy* by most computer accounting professionals.

So that there will not be any disruptions in accounting work, proper care should be taken of all computer equipment. Many businesses buy maintenance contracts from computer repair companies that will make any necessary repairs to hardware during the period it is under contract. Diskettes should be handled carefully and stored properly so that they are not damaged. As valuable as the computer itself may be, it is always true that the cost to reconstruct the accounting data is many times the cost of the hardware. Bear this in mind when devising a security plan for accounting systems.

Other controls in computerized accounting systems are aimed at maintaining the confidentiality of accounting records. In a manual accounting system the chequebooks and payroll information would not be left where unauthorized employees had access to them. The same care must be taken in a computerized office. Unused cheques should be locked safely away. Since these cheques come in a cardboard box like regular printer paper, many offices forget to protect them from theft.

Information in a computerized system can be viewed in several ways. If confidential records (such as payroll) are being entered on the computer, the computer should be located where only the accountant can see the monitor. As in a manual system, confidential information in a printed form should be stored in a place to which only authorized personnel have access. In addition, since backup copies of all accounting information are recorded on diskettes or tapes (discussed in Learning Unit C-1), these diskettes or tapes should also be locked safely away. Many companies also require operators to have their own passwords to allow access to the accounting data, thus helping to ensure confidentiality.

Once the conversion is complete and accounting personnel are comfortable with the new accounting system, efficiency will be greatly increased.

There are some businesses that would not benefit from using a computerized system. However, only the very smallest of businesses with only a few transactions a month would fall into this category. In the past, because of the high cost of computers many businesses sent their accounting work out to computer service centers. These centers keep the accounts of hundreds of businesses. Obviously, though, this type of arrangement involved time lags when information was sent out and had to be processed and then returned. For a small business that does not have an accountant on staff this is still a viable alternative. For the majority of the country's businesses, however, accounting on a microcomputer has become a very affordable and beneficial alternative.

SPREADSHEET PROGRAMS

In addition to the accounting software we have discussed in this chapter there is one other type of software frequently used by accounting personnel. This is the **spreadsheet program**. Spreadsheet programs, such as Excel, Quattro Pro and Lotus 1-2-3, are basically computerized versions of the accountant's calculator, pencil, and columnar paper. A spreadsheet consists of a large number of empty cells (like a blank piece of paper) that the user can fill with numbers or text. Mathematical formulas can be entered to manipulate the numerical data. These programs also contain many commands that allow the user to organize and manipulate data as well as display it in graph form. Spreadsheets can greatly speed the process of preparing reports that include many numbers or calculations. If you need to change one figure in a long totalled column or row on paper, you would have to calculate the totals all over again. In a spreadsheet you need only enter the new figure and the spreadsheet will automatically update any affected totals. This flexibility in manipulating data make spreadsheets particularly useful for creating reports such as cash flow projections, depreciation schedules, and interest tables. A spreadsheet program is a very useful supplement to an accounting package, and many accounting programs permit the accounting data (for example, the trial balance) to be exported in a format which can be read and manipulated by the popular spreadsheets.

THE CHANGING COMPUTERIZED ACCOUNTING FIELD

The field of computerized accounting is still relatively new. The majority of people working in accounting today had little training in computerized accounting in school. It is likely, however, that many of their duties could be performed more efficiently on the computer. For this reason, employers are eager to hire employees with computer skills. This need represents a great opportunity for students who know computer basics and can confidently work with different accounting packages and related programs like spreadsheets.

The computer field is still developing at a rapid pace. Both hardware and software are continuously becoming more powerful and flexible. After you enter the workforce you can continue to enhance your career opportunities by learning new computer skills that will improve your company's accounting system. Magazines and short courses are excellent ways of keeping up with new developments. Be confident that although you may be required to work with many different accounting systems over the years they will all be based on the same accounting principles that you have learned in this textbook.

At this point you should be able to:

1. Discuss what factors are important when purchasing accounting software. (p. 511)
2. Define and contrast horizontal and vertical accounting packages. (p. 513)
3. List several tasks performed during the conversion from a manual system to a computerized system. (p. 513)
4. Explain several of the controls that a business should consider when using a computerized system. (p. 514)
5. Name another type of program, besides General Ledger packages, which is often used by accountants. (p. 515)

□ SELF REVIEW QUIZ C-3

Respond true or false to the following:

1. Low-priced software packages are not as powerful as the higher-priced packages.
2. A user-support line allows you to find out the answer to questions not covered in the manual.
3. Vertical software packages are valuable for businesses such as law offices that have unique accounting procedures.
4. It is important to make backups of all information stored on diskettes to protect against the loss of data.
5. Once the computerized system has been set up, it is no longer necessary to keep any manual records.

■ *SOLUTIONS TO SELF-REVIEW QUIZ C-3*

1. False   2. True   3. True   4. True   5. False

SUMMARY OF KEY POINTS AND KEY TERMS

LEARNING UNIT C-1

1. Many mechanical accounting functions can be performed more quickly and accurately on a computer than manually.

2. Accounting procedures are virtually the same whether they are performed manually or on the computer.

3. Computer equipment is called hardware. The programs or instructions that tell the computer what to do are called software.

4. Until the 1980s the cost of computer equipment was so high that small businesses could not afford to use a computer for their accounting information.

5. Microcomputers are small, inexpensive computer systems powerful enough to keep track of the accounting information of a small business.

6. Input devices allow us to feed information into the computer. Common input devices include the disk drive and the keyboard.

7. The CPU (central processing unit) is the brain of the computer.

8. We get information out of the computer by means of output devices. Common output devices include the monitor, the printer, and the disk drive.

9. Information can be stored on small, thin disks called floppy diskettes.

Audit trail: Notations and references that allow each entry in the accounting records to be traced back to the transaction that generated it.

Central processing unit (CPU): The "brain" of the computer that performs all mathematical and logical functions.

Diskette: A thin magnetic disk in a flexible plastic envelope used to store data.

Disk drive: The input/output device used to read information off a magnetic diskette and to record information onto it.

Hard copy (or printout): A printed version of information on the computer.

Hard disk: A disk made of metal that is mounted permanently in the computer and used to store data.

Hardware: The physical components of the computer equipment.

Input devices: Components of the computer designed to feed information into the CPU.

Mainframe: A large, multi-user computer capable of processing large amounts of data.

Microcomputer: A small, inexpensive computer that serves one user at a time.

Minicomputer: A medium-size computer capable of serving many users but less powerful than a mainframe.

Monitor (or cathode ray tube (CRT)): An output device that resembles a television screen.

Output device: Components of the computer designed to send information from the computer to the user.

Program: A set of instructions that tell the computer what to do.

Programmer: An individual who writes a computer program.

Software: The program, or set of instructions, that tells the computer how to complete a task.

LEARNING UNIT C-2

1. In order to perform accounting on the computer you must have a software program to tell the computer what to do.
2. Accounting packages are sold in modules. Each module handles a different accounting function.
3. A stand-alone system is one in which only one accounting module is being used.
4. An integrated system is one in which two or more modules are used together.
5. Accounting packages are menu-driven.
6. Transactions are generally grouped so that similar transactions are recorded at one time. This is called batch processing.
7. Besides recording journal entries, posting, and providing financial statements, some software packages print many forms such as cheques and invoices.

Batch processing: A method of recording transactions in which similar transactions are grouped together and entered in one session.

Integrated software: A system in which two or more modules are used in conjunction with one another.

Menu-driven: A program that guides the user with a series of choices called menus, which give the user the option of functions he or she wants performed.

Module: A section of a program that performs a certain function or set of functions and can communicate with other modules.

Stand-alone: A system in which only one module is used.

LEARNING UNIT C-3

1. When purchasing an accounting package you should carefully analyze the needs of your business to define what you need from your software.
2. In order for software to work on a computer, the hardware and software must be compatible.
3. A good manual, user support, and employee training programs are beneficial in learning to use a software package.
4. Horizontal accounting packages are software designed to meet the accounting needs of businesses in general.
5. Vertical accounting packages are written to meet the needs of a particular type of business.
6. In order to first set up the accounting software for a business it is necessary to enter information from the manual system into the computer.
7. Controls are needed to protect the privacy of information and to make sure that extra copies of all information (in the form of printouts and backup diskettes) are available if data is lost.

Documentation: Information written about a program to aid the user, often in the form of a manual.

BLUEPRINT OVERVIEW OF INFORMATION FLOW IN AN INTEGRATED SYSTEM

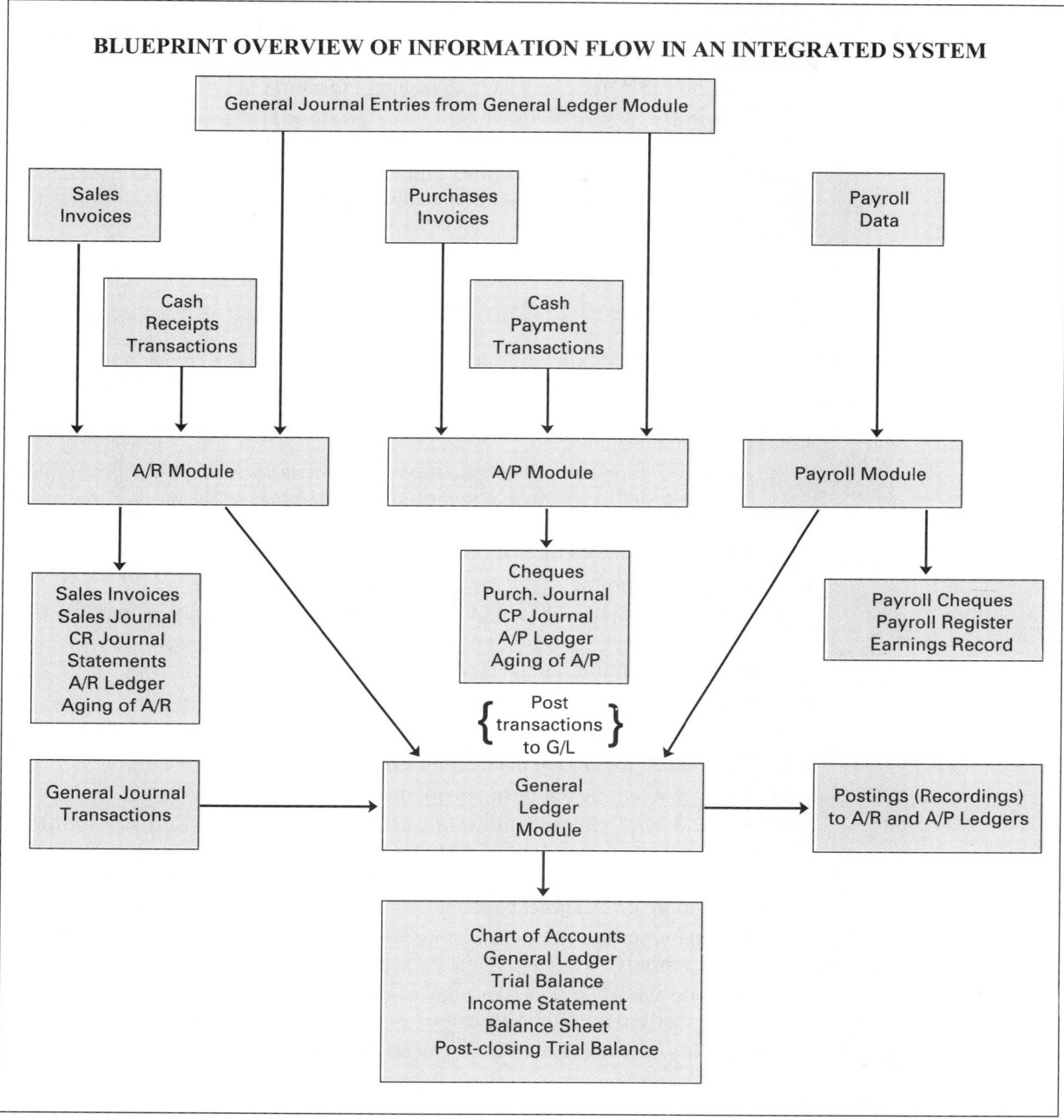

Error protection: A set of controls written into a program and designed to prevent errors such as a transaction where debits do not equal credits.

Horizontal accounting packages: Software packages designed to meet the accounting requirements of a typical business.

Compatible (software): A software package that can communicate with a particular brand of computer.

Spreadsheet program: A type of software that uses commands and mathematical formulae to manipulate text and numerical data.

Tutorial: Instructions on diskette or in written form that guide users through hands-on completion of a sample task on the computer.

User support: A service provided by the producers of a software program designed to answer user questions not covered in the manual.

Vertical accounting packages: Software packages designed to meet the accounting requirements for a specialized business such as a law firm or a construction firm.

DISCUSSION QUESTIONS

1. A business that purchases a good accounting software package does not need a trained accountant or bookkeeper. Agree or disagree. Explain.
2. Name three time-consuming accounting functions that the computer can perform automatically.
3. An accountant or bookkeeper must be knowledgeable about programming in order to use an accounting program. Agree or disagree.
4. Explain the differences in the accounting cycle for a manual system and a computerized system.
5. Define a program.
6. Explain the relationship between mainframes, minicomputers, and microcomputers.
7. Name two common input devices.
8. Name two common output devices.
9. Define a module.
10. Contrast an integrated accounting system and a stand-alone system.
11. What is meant by the term "menu driven" program?
12. Explain why account numbers are assigned to A/R and A/P ledger accounts in a computerized system.
13. Price is probably a significant indication of the quality of a software package. Agree or disagree. Explain.
14. Explain why it is important to ask for references when purchasing software package.
15. Why do we need to make backup diskettes of our work when using a computerized accounting system?
16. How are spreadsheet programs used by accounting personnel?

PRACTICAL ACCOUNTING APPLICATION #1

Michael Tremont, your boss, told you today that although he knows that putting the accounting records on a microcomputer would improve efficiency, he is still reluctant to do so. He is afraid that if a diskette were damaged all of the accounting records would be lost and could not be reconstructed. Since the business you work for has a large volume of transactions and hundreds of credit accounts, you know that a computer would really be beneficial.

Research some methods of protecting accounting information from loss. Write a memo to your boss listing these methods and reassuring him of the safety of a computerized system.

PRACTICAL ACCOUNTING APPLICATION #2

A friend of yours, Lauren LeVaul, runs an alteration business out of her home. She has had some training as a bookkeeper and keeps all of her accounting records herself on a manual basis. She has asked you if she should purchase a computer so that she can keep her accounting records on it. Upon examining her records, you find that she has only about fifteen transactions a week and that they are all recorded in a general journal. Also, since she provides her service on a cash basis only, she sends out no invoices and does not maintain an accounts receivable ledger. She prepares financial statements once a year for tax purposes. Does Lauren need to computerize her records? Please explain to her why or why not.

BARBARA WOODS: ACCOUNTING OPERATIONS SUPERVISOR

After high school training in business and secretarial skills and involvement in a co-op program, Barbara Woods got a job as a secretary for a CA. "I learned many aspects of the business," she says, "and I decided I would like to get more involved in accounting."

Barbara got a job as an account analyst with a major life insurance company and became involved with computerized accounting systems. "At the same time," she says, "I decided I needed to enhance my education. If I wanted to work in accounting I needed some courses in the field."

In accounting courses Barbara found very helpful, she learned the reasons for the things she has been doing. "Still," she says, "the best part for me was working while going to school. A lot of accounting courses are theoretical, but reality is sometimes different. I was able to apply the theory to reality in my everyday job."

Now an accounting operations supervisor, Barbara recommends computer accounting courses for anyone starting out in the field. "I needed the courses to help me move into this field," she says. "I also recommend working in the field while taking classes. The ability to combine theory with practice is invaluable."

INDEX